CONTRACT GOVERNANCE

Contract Governance

Dimensions in Law and Interdisciplinary Research

Edited by

STEFAN GRUNDMANN

Chair of Transnational Private and European Business Law,
European University Institute, Florence, and
Chair of Private Law, Business Law, and Legal Theory,
Humboldt University, Berlin

FLORIAN MÖSLEIN

Chair of Private Law, German, and European Business Law,
Philipps-University, Marburg

KARL RIESENHUBER

Chair of Private Law, German and European Commercial and
Business Law, Ruhr-University, Bochum

OXFORD
UNIVERSITY PRESS

OXFORD
UNIVERSITY PRESS

Great Clarendon Street, Oxford, OX2 6DP,
United Kingdom

Oxford University Press is a department of the University of Oxford.
It furthers the University's objective of excellence in research, scholarship,
and education by publishing worldwide. Oxford is a registered trade mark of
Oxford University Press in the UK and in certain other countries

First Edition published in 2015

Published in the United States of America by Oxford University Press
198 Madison Avenue, New York, NY 10016, United States of America

British Library Cataloguing in Publication Data
Data available

Library of Congress Control Number: 2014958053

ISBN 978–0–19–872320–2

Table of Contents

List of Abbreviations ix
List of Contributors xi

I. THE OVERALL ARCHITECTURE OF CONTRACT GOVERNANCE

1. Contract Governance: Dimensions in Law and Interdisciplinary Research 3
   Stefan Grundmann, Florian Möslein, and Karl Riesenhuber

II. THIRD PARTY IMPACT AND CONTRACT GOVERNANCE PROBLEMS IN HERD BEHAVIOUR

2. The Concept of Herd Behaviour: Its Psychological and Neural Underpinnings 61
   Tatsuya Kameda, Keigo Inukai, Thomas Wisdom, and Wataru Toyokawa

   Law, Economics and More: The Genius of Contract Governance 72
   Peer Zumbansen
3. Moral Hazard and Herd Behaviour in the Financial Crisis 87
   Bruno S. Frey and Reto Cueni

   Whistle-blowing in the Stampede? 100
   Gunther Teubner
4. Herd Behaviour and Third Party Impact as a Legal Concept: On Tulips, Pyramid Games, and Asset-backed Securities 106
   Hans-W. Micklitz

   Summary of the Discussions in Part II 147
   Isabelle Wildhaber

III. GOVERNANCE OF NETWORKS OF CONTRACTS

5. Contract, Uncertainty, and Innovation 155
   Ronald J. Gilson, Charles F. Sabel, and Robert E. Scott

   Getting it Just Right 178
   Gerard Hertig

6. Contractual Networks in Socio-economic Perspective: The Case of the European Financial Crisis (2009–2010) 182
Richard Swedberg

Networks in Socio-economic Perspective: A Proposal for Financial Regulatroy Reform 207
Marc Amstutz

7. Governance Mechanism in Long-term Contracts 218
Michael Klausner

Summary of the Discussions in Part III 234
Florent Thouvenin

IV. GOVERNANCE IN LONG-TERM CONTRACTUAL RELATIONSHIPS

8. Fairness and Reciprocity in Contract Governance 243
Stefan Magen

The Governance of Contractual Relations: A Case for Fairness? 265
Gralf-Peter Calliess

9. Class Actions, Compliance, and Moral Cost 276
Bruno Deffains and Dominique Demougin

Intrinsic and Extrinsic Motivations to Comply with Legal Rules 292
Fernando Gomez and Mireia Artigot i Golobardes

10. Legal Supervision of Commercial Opportunism 301
Clayton P. Gillette

Commercial Opportunism from an Incentive Perspective 327
Urs Schweizer

Summary of the Discussions in Part IV 333
Stefan Wichary

V. CONTRACT GOVERNANCE AND RULE-SETTING

11. Private Regulation and Industrial Organization: Contractual Governance and the Network Approach 343
Fabrizio Cafaggi and Paola Iamiceli

Private Regulations and Networks in Transnational Supply Chains 377
Wolfgang Kerber

12. Flipping Wreck: *Lex Mercatoria* on the Shoals of *Ius Cogens* 383
Hugh Collins

Lex Mercatoria, The ISDA Master Agreement, and *Ius Cogens* 407
Horst Eidenmüller

13. Innovation and the Role of Public-private Collaboration in Contract Governance 413
Katharina Pistor

The Vienna Initiative: A New Mode of Governance? 431
Gunnar Folke Schuppert

Summary of the Discussions in Part V 437
Susanne Augenhofer

VI. CONTRACT GOVERNANCE AND POLITICAL DIMENSIONS

14. Regulating Sovereign Bond Contracts in Europe 451
Kern Alexander

Contract Governance, Disclosure, and Rule-setting between the Market and the Law: A View from Commercial and Company Law 461
Klaus J. Hopt

Index 471

List of Abbreviations

B2B	Business-to-Business
B2C	Business-to-Consumers
B2I	Business-to-Investors
BIS	Bank of International Settlement
BLE	Behavioural Law and Economics
BVB	*Berliner Verkehrsbetriebe*
CAC	Collective Action Clauses
CCP	Central Counterparties
CCE	Central and Eastern Europe
ChFR	Charter of Fundamental Rights of the European Union
CDO	Collaterized Debt Obligation
CDS	Credit Default Swap
CFI	Court of First Instance
CISG	United Nations Convention on Contracts for the International Sale of Goods
CLE	Conventional Law and Economics
DCFR	Draft Common Frame of Reference
EBCI	European Banking Coordinative Initiative
EBRD	European Bank for Reconstruction and Development
ECB	European Central Bank
ECHR	European Convention for the Protection of Human Rights and Fundamental Freedoms
EFSF	European Financial Stability Facility
EIB	European Investment Bank
ELSTAT	Hellenic Statistical Authority
ESRB	European Systemic Risk Board
HACCP	Hazard Critical Control Plan
IASB	International Accounting Standards Board (IASB)
ICANN	Internet Corporation for Assigned Names and Numbers
IFI	International Financial Institutions
IMF	International Monetary Fund
IOSCO	International Organization of Securities Committees
ISDA	International Swaps and Derivatives Association
KWL	*Kommunale Wasserwerke Leipzig*
LBSF	Lehman Brothers Special Financing Inc
LCFI	Large, Complex Financial Institution
MiFID	Markets in Financial Instruments Directive
NGO	Non Governmental Organization
OTC	Over the Counter
PoWD	Posting of Workers Directive
QIA	Qatar Investment Authority
SPV	Special Purpose Vehicle
SWF	Sovereign Wealth Fund

TEN	Techno-Economic Networks
TEU	Treaty on European Union
TFEU	Treaty on the Functioning of the European Union
TPC	Third Party Certification
TPR	Transnational Private Regulation
TUD	Transfer of Undertakings Directive
UCC	Uniform Commercial Code

List of Contributors

Kern Alexander is Professor of Law and Finance at the University of Zurich

Marc Amstutz is Professor of Business Law, Economic Law, and Legal Theory at the University of Fribourg School of Law

Susanne Augenhofer is Professor for Civil Law, European Private Law, Comparative Law, and Market Regulation through Consumer Law and Competition Law at Humboldt University, Berlin

Fabrizio Cafaggi is Director of the Centre for Judicial Cooperation and former Professor of Comparative Law at the European University Institute, Florence

Gralf-Peter Calliess is Professor of Private Law, International, and Comparative Economic Law at the University of Bremen

Hugh Collins is Vinerian Professor of English Law at the University of Oxford and a fellow of All Souls College

Reto Cueni is an affiliated member of the Department of Economics at the University of Zurich

Bruno Deffains is Professor of Economics at Paris 2 Panthéon Assas University and a member of the *Institut Universitaire de France*

Dominique Demougin is Professor and Acting Head of the Economics, Finance, and Accounting Department at the Management School of the University of Liverpool

Horst Eidenmüller is Professor of Private Law, German, European, and International Corporate Law at Ludwig-Maximilians-University, Munich

Bruno S. Frey is Senior Professor of Economics at Zeppelin University, Friedrichshafen

Clayton P. Gillette is Max E. Greenberg Professor of Contract Law at New York University School of Law

Ronald J. Gilson is Charles J. Meyers Professor of Law and Business at Standford Law School, and Marc and Eva Stern Professor of Law and Business at Columbia Law School

Fernando Gomez is Professor of Law and Economics at Pompeu Fabra University School of Law, Barcelona

Mireia Artigot i Golobardes is Professor in the Department of Law at Pompeu Fabra University, Barcelona.

Stefan Grundmann is Professor of Transnational Private Law at the European University Institute, Florence, and Professor of Private Law, German, European, and International Economic Law at Humboldt University Berlin

Gerard Hertig is Professor of Law at the Swiss Federal Institute of Technology, Zurich

Klaus J. Hopt is Professor and Director Emeritus of the Max Planck Institute for Foreign and International Private Law in Hamburg

Paola Iamiceli is Associate Professor at the University of Trento

Keigo Inukai is at the Department of Behavioral Science, Hokkaido University, Sapporo

Tatsuya Kameda is Professor at the Department of Behavioral Science and Director of the Center for Experimental Research in Social Sciences, Hokkaido University, Sapporo

Wolfgang Kerber is Professor of Economic Policy at the University of Marburg

Michael Klausner is Nancy and Charles Munger Professor of Business and Professor of Law at Stanford Law School

Stefan Magen is Professor of Public Law, Legal Philosophy, and Economic Analysis of Law at Ruhr-University Bochum

Hans-W. Micklitz is Professor of Economic Law at the Department of Law, European University Institute, Florence

Florian Möslein is Professor of Private Law, German, and European Business Economic Law at the Philipps-University Marburg, and Schumpeter Fellow at the Munich Centre on Governance, Communication, Public Policy, and Law

Katharina Pistor is Michael I. Sovern Professor of Law at Columbia Law School

Karl Riesenhuber is Professor of Private Law, German, and European Commercial and Economic Law at Ruhr-University Bochum

Charles F. Sabel is Maurice T. Moore Professor of Lawat Columbia Law School

Robert E. Scott is Interim Dean and Alfred McCormack Professor of Law at Columbia Law School

Gunnar Folke Schuppert is Professor Emeritus at the WZB, Social Science Research Center and former Professor of Political and Administrative Sciences, Humboldt University, Berlin

Urs Schweizer is Professor of Economics at Rhenish Friedrich-Wilhelms-University, Bonn

Richard Swedberg is Professor of Sociology at Cornell University

Gunther Teubner is Professor Emeritus of Private Law and Legal Sociology at Goethe-University, Frankfurt am Main

Florent Thouvenin is Assistant Professor (tenure track) for Information and Communication Law at the University of Zurich

Wataru Toyokawa is at the Department of Behavioral Science, Hokkaido University, Sapporo

Stefan Wichary is former Research Assistant at the Department of Private Law, German, and European Commercial and Economic Law at Ruhr-University, Bochum

Isabelle Wildhaber is Assistant Professor of Liablity and Employment Law at the University of St. Gallen

Thomas Wisdom is at the Department of Behavioral Science, Hokkaido University, Sapporo

Peer Zumbansen is Professor at Osgoode Hall Law School, York University, Toronto

PART I

THE OVERALL ARCHITECTURE OF CONTRACT GOVERNANCE

1

Contract Governance: Dimensions in Law and Interdisciplinary Research

Stefan Grundmann, Florian Möslein, and Karl Riesenhuber

I. Introduction and Overview

This book introduces and develops contract governance as a new approach to contract theory. It thereby aims at setting an international and interdisciplinary research agenda for a modern contract law.[1] At its core, contract governance combines insights from governance research and contract theory. As an umbrella term, contract governance therefore covers various and very diverse issues of governance in contract law and contract practice—just as corporate governance does for company law and finance.

In this context, governance is defined as 'the institutional matrix within which transactions are negotiated and executed'.[2] Governance regimes are necessary where risks of opportunism occur or the interests of third parties are involved. In contracts, governance becomes relevant whenever the contractual agreement reaches beyond a mere discrete spot exchange, namely in long-term or network relations and where regulators employ the mechanism of contract to pursue regulatory goals. The latter aim can apply as well to masses of parallel spot contracts, as where, for instance, herd behaviour risks producing adverse effects. When analysing such phenomena, contract governance can obviously draw on a number of existing approaches such as institutional economics, incomplete contracts and relational contracting, networks of contracts theory, regulation theory and private ordering, elements of ordo-liberalism, and the insights of behavioural economics. Governance research may well be seen as the scientific answer to major economic or state crises—which would explain as well why conceptions of corporate and

[1] F. Möslein and K. Riesenhuber, 'Contract Governance – A Draft Research Agenda,' (2009) 5 *European Review of Contract Law* 248–89 (with differentiation of four modes of contract governance, see Section IV of this Chapter); particularly close before, namely in the English literature: J. Brownsword, *Contract Law – Themes for the 21st Century* (Oxford: Clarendon Press, 2nd edn, 2006); H. Collins, *Regulating Contracts* (Oxford: Oxford University Press, 1999).

[2] O. Williamson, 'Transaction-Cost Economics: The Governance of Contractual Relations' (1979) 22 *Journal of Law and Economics* 233–61, 239 (and see also 235: 'by governance structure I refer to the institutional framework within which the integrity of a transaction is decided.')

public governance developed earlier and why the time may now be ripe for contract governance (see Section II of this Chapter). Contract governance proposes a scientific answer that is oriented towards the long-term and is principally aimed at overcoming the isolation of these different existing approaches to contract governance and thus strengthening both their theoretical coverage and their realism.

By bringing these existing approaches together, contract governance opens up new research perspectives. More importantly, contract governance approaches contract law in its entire width. While Williamson and subsequent governance research focussed almost exclusively on long-term contracts and on organizations (corporate governance),[3] markets and exchange contracts require and depend on governance structures as well. After all, the global financial crisis has strikingly shown the third-party impact of contractual arrangements, and it has also shown that in the world of contracts, there is a high risk of mutual contagion because a modern economy is often arranged in networks. In financial markets, contractual transactions like collateralized debt obligations increasingly serve similar purposes to institutions such as credit banks, and the crisis has shown that market- and bank-based financial systems pose similar governance problems.[4] In the Markets in Financial Instruments Directive (2004) (MiFID), a parallel phenomenon, stock exchanges and its contract-based alternatives, which in fact compete with stock exchanges, had been similarly regulated already in 2004. Therefore, Part II of the present work focuses on third party impact of contracting, while Parts III and IV on the network and on the long-term character of the phenomenon of 'organization by contract'. Indeed, at a more fundamental level, exchange contracts on the one hand and long-term contracts on the other hand are not as fundamentally different as governance research hitherto seems to suggest. Both types of contracts do not pose entirely separate issues, but rather comprise part of a continuum.[5] As a consequence, contracts as organization and contracts as exchange need to be seen and analysed within a common framework. Contract governance broadens the perspective accordingly.

Contract governance therefore stands for a holistic, comprehensive approach. It does so also in some other important respects. First, the governance perspective contributes to a genuinely interdisciplinary discussion. As opposed to law and economics, the range of disciplines that 'collaborate' has greatly increased, and

[3] Williamson, n 2; K. Hopt, H. Kanda, M. Roe, E. Wymeersch, and S. Prigge (eds) *Comparative Corporate Governance – the State of the Art and Emerging Research* (Oxford: Oxford University Press, 1998); J. McCahery, P. Moerland, T. Raaijmakers, and L. Renneboog (eds) *Corporate Governance Regimes – Convergence and Diversity*, (Oxford: Oxford University Press, 2002); T. Clarke (ed) *Corporate Governance – Critical Perspectives on Business and Management* (5 vols) (London/New York: Routledge, 2005); K. Hopt, 'Comparative Corporate Governance: The State of the Art and International Regulation' (2011) 59 *American Journal of Comparative Law* 1–73.

[4] As a consequence, the regulation of shadow banking is intensively debated see, inter alia, Financial Stability Board, *Shadow Banking: Scoping the Issues* (2011); European Commission, Green Paper on Shadow Banking, COM(2012) 102 Final. On the variety of financial systems in general see F. Allen and D. Gale, *Comparing Financial Systems* (Cambridge, MA: MIT Press, 2000).

[5] See S. Grundmann, 'The Future of Contract Law' (2011) 7 *European Review of Contract Law* 490–527, esp. 523–5; S. Grundmann, F. Cafaggi, and G. Vettori (eds) *The Organisational Contract – From Exchange to Cooperation in European Contract Law* (Oxford: Hart Publishing, 2013).

these various disciplines contribute on an equal footing, gathering together into one discourse community. With this approach, under the paradigm of regulatory competition and by subjecting rule-setters themselves to a scrutiny of their incentives, questions of rule-making become paramount and turn into a genuinely 'constitutional' question.[6] Beyond institutional economics, governance research includes various different perspectives: law and legal practice, sociology, psychology, and other behavioural sciences. In addition, if mutual consent is an alternative instrument of governance, it is paramount to take insights from contract theory and contract law into account. This broader interdisciplinary approach is what the book aims to illustrate in its overall arrangement. Secondly, contract governance takes a broader range of rule- and decision-makers into account. In addition to hierarchies, mutual and consensual forms of coordination and decision-making come to the fore. Part VI of the present work is devoted to this perspective. One of the central issues in governance theory is the interplay between external and internal impacts on decision-making in institutions (state or corporation)[7] and the analysis of 'weak spots' within a scheme of collaboration, which is where governance arrangements are required.[8] As in corporate governance, we can therefore distinguish external and internal mechanisms of governance, and as in general governance theory, the relevant structures include, but are not limited to, legal mechanisms. As a consequence, the substantive focus of contract governance is inherently broad, taking into account the different levels of rule-making, the different standard-setters, and the different rule-setting schemes and procedures. Finally, and as a consequence of the foregoing, contract governance takes advantage of broader circles of discussion. As in corporate governance, the discussion is not only interdisciplinary, but genuinely international, starting from an analysis of issues and considering solutions in national law or contractual practice as competing models. Moreover, contract governance links the classical contract law debate with modern regulation theory. Summarizing all this, contract governance research is holistic by nature with respect to disciplines, with respect to the discussion of standard setters, with respect to the discussion circles involved—contract law, market regulation, parallels in corporate law—and truly international.

[6] On the limited scope of traditional government (and regulation) in a globalized world, see J. Rosenau and E. -O. Czempiel, *Governance without Government: Order and Change in World Politics* (Cambridge: Cambridge University Press, 1992).

[7] This aspect is broadly taken up in this book in Part II. Ground-breaking in this respect is A. O. Hirshman, *Exit, Voice and Loyalty – Responses to Decline in Firms, Organizations, and States*, (Cambridge, MA: Harvard University Press, 1974); then J. E. Parkinson, *Corporate Power and Responsibility* (Oxford: Clarendon Press, 1995) 178–99; W. Ebke, '*Unternehmenskontrolle durch Gesellschafter und Markt*' in O. Sandrock and W. Jaeger (eds) *Internationale Unternehmenskontrolle und Unternehmenskultur* (Tübingen: Mohr Siebeck, 1994) 7–35, 27; see also n 17.

[8] This aspect is broadly taken up in this book in Part IV. Vulnerability (and a need for governance schemes) is seen if future developments are unforeseeable, but investments specific to this relationship (and not easily to be re-used elsewhere) are made (creating the risk of sunk cost if the relationship is terminated or if the other side devaluates it by behaving opportunistically [moral hazard]), see Williamson, n 2, 233–61; O. Williamson, *Markets and Hierarchies – Analysis and Antitrust Implications* (New York/London: Free Press, 1975) *et passim*; O. Williamson, *The Economic Institutions of Capitalism* (New York: Free Press, 1985) 56–67.

The added value of contract governance, however, is not restricted to broadening the perspective. On the contrary, its broader perspective raises a whole range of new and innovative research questions. Not only are old questions often approached differently, but completely new ones become visible. For example, where the question is whether there is an alternative to mandatory regimes even where mandatory protection is desired, contractual and legal regimes of codetermination and workers representation can be compared and analysed. Such analysis promises to show less intrusive means of regulation.[9] More generally, contract governance challenges the mandatory character of rules by understanding legal and contractual provisions as alternative possibilities of rule-making. Moreover, with its focus on external effects contract governance sheds new light on the market dimension of contracts, for example, with regard to the systemic effects of credit agreements. This approach diverges fundamentally from the very broadly accepted view of contract as producing effects exclusively or at least mostly amongst the parties alone. Conversely, a contract governance perspective proposes to study third party effects of, and on, contracts, positive and negative, in a systematic way, and not only with respect to contractual networks.

The present work approaches issues of contract governance by focusing on particular sets of such real world problems from the perspectives of various disciplines. On this basis, the book proposes to show two advantages of contract governance in more detail: (i) how a governance perspective leads to different and new questions, a good number of which seem to have been neglected in traditional contract law scholarship, and (ii) how these questions are dealt with in a different manner and style. We submit that a governance perspective helps to formulate questions more precisely and to discuss them more thoroughly, with a richer set of tools and possible outcomes.

This book addresses issues of contract governance in four areas:

(1) Contract and third parties: how should the legal framework for the drafting of contracts deal with the problem that different contract solutions have different impacts on third parties and third parties exert their influence on contract solutions? What are the biological, behavioural, and social science models behind this mutual impact (Part II)?

(2) Contracts and networks: how should the regime driving contract practice deal with the problem that contracts are often part of a larger network of relationships, which are both individual contracts and at the same time interdependent? What are the sociological and economic models behind such hybrids (Part III)?

(3) Contracts as organization: how should the regime driving contract practice deal with the problem that contracts, beyond individual exchange (as in the typical sales contract) may also have an 'organizational' function in that they may, and in modern market economies very often do, constitute the

[9] In a similar vein, see I. Ayres, 'Menus Matter', *University of Chicago Law Review* 73 (2006) 3, 4 (with the general goal 'to change the world with less intrusive interventions).

basis of (long-term) collaboration? What are the behavioural, sociological, and economic models behind such schemes of collaboration (Part IV)? All these topics are rather marginal in traditional contract law thinking—but not in current practice.

(4) Part V of this book concentrates on rule-setting as such, namely on (i) contract law and regulation and (ii) on contract law and contract drafting.

Before addressing these specific issues of contract governance, this Chapter addresses three cross-sectional themes, relevant for contract governance more generally and recurrent in the subsequent chapters:

(1) the relationship between the established fields of corporate governance and public governance and the emerging field of contract governance research (Part II);
(2) the issue of levels and of regulation (Part III); and
(3) questions of interdisciplinary discourse (Part IV).

Despite the cross-sectional character of this Chapter, Sections II and III already address the four topics which form the parts of this book: third party impacts, networks, the long-term character of contracts (Part II), and the issue of rule-setting (Part III).

II. Governance of Hierarchies and Governance of Market Relationships

1. Common ground between the governance perspectives

a. From public and corporate governance to contract governance

While governance research has developed richly since the 1970s in the areas of public governance and corporate governance where hierarchies and organizations are concerned, there has not been a similar development in the area of contracts where markets and cooperation are concerned. This is all the more astonishing as governance research is so strongly focused on the search for solutions to which all affected parties could have consented and on arrangements installed by the private actors themselves.

Hierarchies, of course, use state and supranational entities as paradigms. Indeed, the most prominent branch, based on general governance research,[10] can be found in public governance. The term is highly heterogeneous, but in certain parts also closely linked both to contract and to corporate governance. Public governance

[10] M. Bevir (ed) *The SAGE Handbook of Governance* (London: Sage, 2010); R. v. Lüde, D. Moldt and R. Valk (eds) *Selbstorganisation und Governance in Künstlichen und Sozialen Systemen* (Münster: Lit, 2009); G. F. Schuppert, *Alles Governance oder was?* (Baden-Baden: Nomos, 2011).

can be conceived mainly as governance of states.[11] It is then mainly about the allocation and balance of public power. This involves important questions which are also relevant in other hierarchies, including the corporations, and which are therefore less telling for contract governance than corporate governance. Public governance can also be conceived as encompassing all mechanisms by which public law, namely administrative functions, are enhanced by consensus-based mechanisms, thus furthering co-operation between private actors and the public authority or among different public authorities in the search for solutions.[12] This line of governance research has much in common with contract governance, namely the interplay between consensus-based design and the importance of the dimension of public good. In fact, while public governance would seem to be clearly focused on public good(s) in the typical case, it is exactly this interplay between consensus-based design and the dimension of public good that is also important for contract governance (and other branches of governance research in private law areas). As the remainder of this Chapter, and also the following chapters, illustrate one core aspect of governance research involves considering the private law side of contract design and the public regulation side as interdependent. This encompasses, in particular, private contract design *and* market stability; individual *and* institutional functions. The most important remaining difference might be that in contract and corporate governance, the aspect of public good is one of keeping intact a basically market-driven mechanism which is used for finding solutions while in public governance the solution is not seen as one driven mainly by market mechanisms, but rather by (re-)distribution or adjudication, which in turn promotes the public good. The same issue can, of course, be seen as belonging rather to one area in one country and to another in the other one, as the example of the organization of universities illustrates.

On the private law side, one reason for the dominance of the corporation (hierarchy) in governance research may be that the most important economic crises in the G7, G8, and then G20 states centred around issues of the 'firm' and

[11] This strand of research owes a lot to the 'crisis' of globalization and the post Cold War period both leading to an increase in comparison between countries. See on these issues, for instance, K. Dingwerth and P. Pattberg, 'Global Governance as a Perspective on World Politics' (2006) 12 *Global Governance* 185–203; U. Brand, 'Order and Regulation: Global Governance as a Hegemonic Discourse of International Politics?' (2005) 12 *Review of International Political Economy* 155–76; J. Bolton, 'Should We Take Global Governance Seriously?' (2000) 1 *Chicago Journal of International Law* 205–22; M. Shapiro, 'Administrative Law Unbounded: Reflections on Government and Governance' (2001) 8 *Indiana Journal of Global Legal Studies* 369–77; O. J. Sending and I. B. Neumann, 'Governance to Governmentality: Analyzing NGOs, States, and Power' (2006) 50 *International Studies Quarterly* 651–72; ground-breaking in this respect is J. Rosenau and E. -O. Czempiel (eds) *Governance without Government: Order and Change in World Politics* (Cambridge, Mass: Harvard University Press, 1992).

[12] J. Freeman and M. Minow, *Government by Contract: Outsourcing and American Democracy* (Cambridge, Mass: Harvard University Press, 2009); P. Zumbansen, 'The Law of Society: Governance Through Contract' (2007) 14 *Indiana Journal of Global Legal Studies* 191–233 (and further contributions to the symposium 'Governing Contracts: Public and Private Perspectives', published in the same issue); A. Habel, Contract Governance – *eine Verfassungsrechtliche und Rechtsdogmatische Analyse zu Vertraglichen und Vertragsrechtlichen Regelungsstrukturen in Belangen des Gemeinwohls* (Baden-Baden: Nomos Verlagsgesellschaft, 2012).

thus company law. This may not be true of the Japanese and then Asian crises 1991/1992 and 1997/1998,[13] but it was true of the crises in the UK and in the US (and also some other European countries) which have been the focus of much of the scholarly debates. These have concerned issues of control in companies (UK Cadbury Report and Code of Best Practice, now Corporate Governance Code)[14] and in the area of annual accounts, responsibility within the company and their auditing in particular (Enron, Worldcom, Sarbanes Oxley Act).[15] Some of the problems were mainly related to capital markets, but capital market law, despite its strong links to markets and contracts, can be seen as having an equally strong relationship with company law.[16] In other words, company law research and accounting law considerations strongly integrate capital market law problems.

On the private law side, these circumstances may explain why corporate governance research developed so strongly while contract governance did not. The distinction is not, however, justified in substance. This development is largely due to historic coincidence—crises, but also certain features in the scientific

[13] These were genuine bubbles. They were, however, distinct from the financial crisis in 2007/2008/2009 in that while also, then, over-investment in real estate markets was involved, poor contract law design played no role. See for the Japanese and Asian crises: N. Roubini and B. Setser, *Bailouts or Bail-ins? Responding to Financial Crises in Emerging Economies* (Washington DC: Institute for International Economics, 2004); G. Corsetti, P. Pesenti, and N. Roubini, 'Paper Tigers? A Model of the Asian Crisis' (1999) 43 *European Economic Review* 1211–36; G. Corsetti, P. Pesenti, and N. Roubini, 'What Caused the Asian Currency and Financial Crises?' (1999) 11 *Japan and the World Economy* 305–73; G. Kaufman, T. Krueger, and W. Hunter. *The Asian Financial Crisis: Origins, Implications and Solutions* (Boston: Kluwer Academic, 1999); M. Pohlmann, '*Die Entwicklung des Kapitalismus in Ostasien und die Lehren aus der Asiatischen Finanzkrise*' (2004) 32 *Leviathan* 360–81.

[14] Cadbury Committee, *The Financial Aspects of Corporate Governance* (London: Gee Publishing, 1992); Greenbury Committee, *Directors' Remuneration*, (London: Gee Publishing, 1995); Hampel Committee on Corporate Governance, *Final Report* (London: Gee Publishing, 1998) (all available at <http://www.ecgi.org/codes/>). London Stock Exchange Committee on Corporate Governance, *The Combined Code: Principles of Good Governance and Code of Best Practice* (1998 and 2000) (available at <http://www.ecgi.org/codes/documents/combined_code.pdf>). Now Corporate Governance Code (available at <http://frc.org.uk/corporate/ukcgcode.cfm>).

[15] The Sarbanes-Oxley Act of 2002 (available at <http://www.soxlaw.com>); on the Act see: J. Chung, J. Farrar, P. Puri, and L. Thorne, 'Auditor Liability to Third Parties after Sarbanes-Oxley: An International Comparison of Regulatory and Legal Reforms' (2010) 19 *Journal of International Accounting, Auditing and Taxation* 66–78; H.-J. Hellwig, 'The US Concept of Corporate Governance under the Sarbanes-Oxley Act of 2002 and Its Effects in Europe' (2007) 4 *European Company and Financial Law Review* 417–33; also F. Frugier, *Die Einrichtung Moderner Interner Kontrollsysteme in Unternehmen mit US-amerikanischem Listing. Politische und Betriebliche Rahmenbedingungen und Besonderheiten der Umsetzung des Sarbanes Oxley Act in Deutschland* (Hamburg: Diplomica Verlag, 2009).

[16] 'Final Report of the Committee of Wise Men on the Regulation of European Securities Markets of 15 February 2001', Annex 5, 12, 20ff ('Lamfalussy Report'); P. Mülbert, *Aktiengesellschaft, Unternehmensgruppe und Kapitalmarkt – Die Aktionärsrechte bei Bildung und Umbildung einer Unternehmensgruppe zwischen Verbands – und Anlegerschutzrecht* (München: Beck, 1995); F. Möslein, *Grenzen unternehmerischer Leitungsmacht im markoffenen Verband* (Berlin/New York: de Gruyter, 2007); S. Kalss, *Anlegerinteressen – der Anleger im Handlungsdreieck von Vertrag, Verband, und Markt* (Vienna: Springer, 2001); E. Wymeersch, 'Factors and Trends of Change in Company Law' (2001) 2 *International and Comparative Company Law Review* 481–501, 484ff; and also, S. Grundmann, *European Company Law – Organization, Finance and Capital Markets* (Antwerp: Intersentia, 2nd edn, 2012) § 1 paras 5ff, § 30, and § 37 paras 36–41.

communities dealing with the respective areas (see Section II(2) later in this Chapter).

In fact, contract and company ('market and firm') can be viewed as the two basic—and often alternative—instruments of economic planning and arrangements. Contract and corporation are the two elementary areas where economic players are invited to create their own designs via party autonomy, and conversely, they are also the two core areas where business regulation sets limits to (and thereby also additionally empowers) the use of individual autonomy (*privatautonomie*) and freedom of contract:[17] The dominant form of regulation with respect to competition is antitrust law. Antitrust law has two main branches, control of cartels and merger control, i.e. contracts and companies. The dominant form of regulation of information problems and asymmetries are again clearly related to firm and market and have been developed because of this source of market failure. This is, on the one hand, capital market and accounting law in the area of company law (firms) and, on the other hand, consumer law with its information model in the area of contract law (markets).[18] Both waves of regulation—and their imposition worldwide—follow important developments in economic theory with respect to the effects of competitive markets in the 1930s through to the 1950s (highly influential for Europe is the Freiburg School) and with respect to information economics in the 1960s and 1970s (from Stigler through to Akerlof and Spence).[19] It would seem highly plausible that the idea of governance that has been considered in long-term relationships (and often in networks), i.e. in 'organization contracts' or schemes, developed in the 1970s and 1980s,[20] should and will follow the same path. In summary, both corporate and contract governance, are equally about individual, private party-driven design, *and* market regulation or, more generally, stability of organization forms and institutions.

[17] For more detail on the following see S. Grundmann, 'On the Unity of Private Law – From a Formal to a Substance Based Concept of Private Law' (2010) *European Review of Private Law* 1055–78, 1057–9, and 1063–6.

[18] On information problems see, for the law of contracts, H. Fleischer, *Informationsasymmetrie im Vertragsrecht* (Tübingen: Mohr Siebeck, 2001); S. Grundmann, 'Information, Party Autonomy and Economic Agents in European Contract Law' (2002) 39 *CMLR* 269–93; for company law see S. Grundmann, '*Information und ihre Grenzen im Europäischen und Neuen Englischen Gesellschaftsrecht*' in U.H. Schneider, P. Hommelhoff, and K. Schmidt (eds) *Festschrift Lutter* (Köln: Otto Schmidt, 2000) 61–82; U. Grohmann, *Das Informationsmodell im Europäischen Gesellschaftsrecht* (Berlin: de Gruyter, 2006); H. Merkt, *Unternehmenspublizität – Offenlegung von Unternehmensdaten als Korrelat der Marktteilnahme* (Tübingen: Mohr Siebeck, 2001); S. Grundmann, W. Kerber, and S. Weatherill (eds) *Party Autonomy and the Role of Information in the Internal Market* (Berlin: de Gruyter, 2001).

[19] G. Akerlof, 'The Market for 'Lemons': Quality Uncertainty and the Market Mechanism' (1970) 84 *Quarterly Journal of Economics* 488–500; A. M. Spence, *Market Signalling – Information Transfer in Hiring and Related Screening Processes* (Cambridge, Mass: Harvard University Press, 1974); G. Stigler, 'The Economics of Information' (1961) 3 *Journal of Political Economy* 213–25; today, for instance, see W. Magat, 'Information Regulation' in P. Newmann (ed) *The New Palgrave Dictionary of Economics*, vol 2 (London: Macmillan, 2002) 307–10; and also Grundmann, Kerber, and Weatherill, n 18.

[20] See n 2.

b. Three common paradigmatic questions between corporate and contract governance

The parallels between firm and market do, however, not end at this rather abstract level. These are not only the two areas where party autonomy is paramount and perhaps the most developed and where certainly limits to and regulation of party autonomy are the most extensive and prominent. On the contrary, much more specific and nevertheless paradigmatic questions can be asked about both areas in a similar way, though hitherto such questions have been mostly directed toward corporate governance. The three fields of questions focussed in the present book illustrate the point. First, there is the relationship of the firm or the contract to third parties who are not part of the company or a party to the contract, respectively, but who are nevertheless affected by it or who can influence the relationship, be it negatively or positively. Secondly, the question cab be posed of how can the relationships between a multitude of persons concerned be conceived—namely where such a multitude exists also in the setting of contracts—and how does the 'constitution' of these relationships influence the rights and duties and the governance arrangements in the overall design. This is the question of networks of contracts and relationships within (contractual und company) arrangements. A third question is about the duration of the relationship and its effects on the problems to be solved between all parties concerned. Arguably, the issues raised by long-term contractual relations are more similar to those of companies than to those of spot contracts, a proximity that would imply that one large part of contract law is closer to company law in its main problems than to the other, an important dividing line. Let us consider these three questions in more detail.

(1) Internal and external perspectives

The first question is about the *internal and external perspectives*. For corporate governance, it is evident and perhaps also the starting-point that instruments of internal and external governance are distinguished from one another and that their interplay is paramount.[21] Thus, shareholder influence within the organization, namely in the general assembly (voice), is distinguished from shareholder influence outside the company's organization, namely the influence they exercise via purchase and sale (exit; Wall Street Rule). Both dimensions are often intimately linked. Takeover law is paradigmatic for the interplay: the takeover bid to shareholders on capital markets, offering to buy their shares (exit, external governance) typically leads to a restructuring of the board as the core decision-making body within the company (internal governance).

A similar interplay of internal and external forces can be seen with respect to questions of the remuneration of management. From a legal perspective, the position of management has a company law dimension (position on the board) and a contract law dimension (contract for services for remuneration).

[21] On the combination of internal and external governance, see n 7. For all this and the examples given (also takeover law) see also Grundmann, n 16, §§ 14 and 30.

Functionally, however, both dimensions are intimately linked which is already evidenced by the fact that remuneration has increasingly become the object of a complicated decision-making process within the company. Since the financial crisis, the relevance of remuneration for the economy as a whole, in particular, has been intensely discussed—on the grounds of its potential third-party effects (see Section II of this Chapter). This last example also shows how important the third party perspective is in the contract law context. Contract arrangements have just as much potential for negative external effects as remuneration schemes. In fact, the financial crisis is paradigmatic for a whole range of adverse external (third-party) effects that contracts may have. Nevertheless, third-party effects are only a minor research topic in traditional contract law doctrine, typically seen as being unworthy of systematic inquiry. The issue of third party-effects may, for example, shed a new light on the controversial (contractual) duty of responsible lending. The question is whether this aspect matters when the design of contract law is at stake, and whether there has to be a governance framework beyond the two parties. Similarly, securitization and the passing on of risks inherent in credit contracts via special purpose vehicles gives the incentives and the legal instruments to the first lender (creditor) to multiply the risks he can take. Moreover, is the design not such that redress to the first creditor (bank) who is the initiator of the product is interrupted while, in the area of sales of goods, Article 4 of the EC Sales Directive of 1999 had introduced a right to redress which the parties were not allowed to interrupt—not even within the B2B distribution chain? In a third step, it is clear that also a credit rating which is erroneously optimistic or disregards systemic risk can hurt not only the partner who contracted for the rating, but third (or fourth, fifth,...) parties as well—all this in a context where rating firms were subject to (usually undisclosed) massive conflicts of interests. Finally, how can the legal arrangement capture the phenomenon that parallel investment behaviour (herd behaviour) may transform individual risks into systemic risks, i.e. understand the phenomenon and develop a legal concept for it on the basis of (interdisciplinary) strands of theory? When is herding problematic, even though often it is seen as having positive effects?

Thus *negative* effects of contract drafting on third parties would seem to be a major issue of concern. At least four distinct forms can be identified in the chain of causation in the financial crisis—each of them interesting in and of itself but not discussed in depth in contract law scholarship: responsible lending; passing on of risks without retaining at least some responsibility; mixing of risks and thus inherently obscuring information; and credit rating under the influence of conflict of interests. All these have to do with the limits set by contract law, but influence market stability as well. Hence the question: can contract theory be amended so as to take the issue of market stability into consideration? A general reference to tort law has proved to be much less nuanced, insensitive to the problem that, in many cases, there is some kind of 'implied promise' involved between 'tortfeasor' and 'victim'. Conversely, for the corporate governance debate—as previously in company law with its focus on creditor protection—adverse effects on third parties are a major research topic. The corporate governance debate indicates that the full picture is worth discussing, with three more dimensions: *positive* effects of contracts on third parties as well as negative, or positive, influence *from third parties* on contracts. Again, the idea that even positive impact from third parties is worth being analyzed becomes evident when turning to corporate governance: of course, the positive effect which (potential) bidders in takeovers may have for disciplining management (already *ex ante*), is a major issue in the corporate governance debate. Likewise, could it not be that someday third parties—offering, for instance, ratings on fair behaviour—become a major factor in, say, markets characterized by long-term relationships, for instance franchise relationships?[22] Thus four dimensions of effects really have to be distinguished: contracts on third parties and third parties on contracts, both positive and negative. All four dimensions would have to be considered from a traditional private law perspective, from a regulatory perspective (antitrust law being, of course, about negative effects of certain contracts, i.e. cartels), and in the private drafting process as such. In all dimensions, the legal framework can help to improve the outcomes, as evidenced, for instance, in the area of ratings. A contract governance approach would favour analysing the question in all three perspectives jointly—contract law, regulation, and the forces present in the drafting process. It would have to be asked at which level it is best to regulate and by which instrument. The financial crisis amply proved that legal and economic sciences are in crisis as well, namely with respect to seeing contracts too much in isolation from the world around. The disregard of third party relationships has a long-standing tradition—one major example being that fiduciary ('trust') relationships have not been conceived as contractual (having third party effects), but only as quasi-proprietary rights and effects.[23]

In the present work, the external effects of contract—namely in situations of herding, as in the financial crisis—are discussed from various perspectives: from a biological/psychological perspective and from an economic perspective as well as from a legal perspective (in most cases with comments from other disciplines). Particular emphasis is placed on the contractual reconstruction of how potentially to internalize costs of external effects.[24] In his contribution to this book, Micklitz starts out from the traditional teaching that external effects are to be caught by tort law only (which does not pay particular attention to the pre-existing relationships between all affected parties). Micklitz then asks how a liability regime could be reconstructed on a contractual basis, rendering parties to the contract liable to third parties, based on the assumption that there are networks of contractual relationships by which also those causing the external effects and those suffering the

[22] See, for instance, S. Grundmann and M. Renner, '*Vertrag und Dritter*' (2013) *Juristenzeitung* 379–89.

[23] See S. Grundmann, 'Trust and Treuhand at the End of the 20th Century – Key Problems and Shift of Interests' (1999) 47 *American Journal of Comparative Law* 401–28, 403–12; more extensively (mainly on the German development) see S. Grundmann, *Der Treuhandvertrag – Insbesondere die Werbende Treuhand* (München. C. H. Beck, 1997) §§ 7 and 8.

[24] See contributions by T. Kameda and colleagues and P. Zumbansen (Chapter 2 and accompanying comment), by B. Frey and R. Cueni and by G. Teubner (Chapter 3 and accompanying comment), and by H.-W. Micklitz (Chapter 4). See also Section IV(3)(1) of this Chapter.

losses are linked at least indirectly (via a chain). This is the basis for asking how implied contractual arrangements between all parties affected could be conceived and how incomplete contracts could be reconstructed so as to reach commitments across the networks of contracts via presumed consensus.

(2) Networks of contracts

The second issue is that of *networks of contracts* ('nexus of contracts')—a concept found both in contract and in company law. In company law, the concept of a nexus of contracts is primarily employed to illustrate how each shareholder—and potentially also stakeholder—or any other player, for instance a manager, has individual incentives, but also rights and duties towards others. Thus, the concept is a perfect image of methodological as well as normative individualism.[25] Based on this concept, it is easy to explain why the legal personality of the company as such does not prevent the existence of direct duties and rights between the different members.[26] The concept of nexus of contracts, however, does not cogently explain whether all members have contractual relationships with all others individually (multi-facetted network) or rather with the company which administers the rights of all the other members in this respect (star-shaped form of nexus). The basic assumption of most laws would seem to be, however, that each member has the right to keep the 'same' proportional share in the profits (and, as a starting-point, also share in the decision-making power) and that each (other) member has the duty to respect this principle and not to gain hidden additional profits. The nexus of contracts is more heterogeneous and complex if stakeholders are included. Whether this is to be assumed is, of course, one of the core divergences which can be sensed in the corporate governance debate in different parts of the world, namely between Europe and the United States.[27]

[25] Path-breaking for the theory of a '*nexus of contracts*', see A. Alchian and H. Demsetz, 'Production, Information Costs, and Business Organization' (1972) 72 *The American Economic Review* 777–95; R. Coase, 'The Nature of the Firm' (1937) 4 *Economica* 386–405; S. Cheung, 'The Contractual Nature of the Firm' (1963) 26 *The Journal of Law and Economics* 1–21; M. Jensen and W. Meckling, 'Theory of the Firm – Managerial Behaviour, Agency Costs and Ownership Structure' (1976) 3 *Journal of Financial Economics* 305–60; W. A. Klein, 'The Modern Business Organization – Bargaining under Constraints' (1982) 91 *The Yale Law Journal* 1521–64; O. Williamson, 'Corporate Governance' (1984) 93 *The Yale Law Journal* 1196–230.

[26] In this respect, it is an interesting development, for instance, that under the German Law on the Plc, in particular situations a fiduciary duty may even be owed by small shareholders to large shareholders: see mainly *Bundesgerichtsho—Official Reports: BGHZ* 103, 184, 194 (Linotype); case law of long standing tradition today, see for instance *BGHZ* 129, 136, 142–4 (Girmes) (also small investors); *BGHZ* 142, 167, 169ff (Hilgers).

[27] For an increasing trend towards stakeholderism recently, see R. E. Freeman, 'A Stakeholder Theory of the Modern Corporation' in L. Hartman (ed) *Perspectives in Business Ethics* (New York: McGraw-Hill, 3rd edn, 2004) 112–22; A. Keay, 'Moving Towards Stakeholderism? Constituency Statutes, Enlightened Shareholder Value, and More: Much Ado About Little?' (2011) 22 *European Business Law Review* 1–49; A. Keay, 'Shareholder Primacy in Corporate Law: Can it Survive? Should it Survive?' (2010) 7 *European Company and Financial Law Review* 369–413; or, describing more objectively the main stream in the different countries, see *Modern Company Law – For a Competitive Economy – The Strategic Framework – A Consultation Document from the Company Law Review Steering Group* (London, February 1999) 37–51 (available at <http://www.bis.gov.uk/>); K. Hopt, 'Common Principles of Corporate Governance in Europe?' in B. Markesinis (ed)

In contract law, the contractual relationships integrated into a network are manifold as well. Think, for example, of networks of suppliers, distribution chains, or in networks of payment systems or syndicated loans, all these constituting in some sense the backbone of the market economy. While all parties have a 'shared' interest in the existence and success of these networks, the jointly pursued purpose—with a pooling of inputs—and the common legal basis—a charter or articles of association—are less clearly defined. The core question is which modifications to general contract law are required to take account of the intended interrelation or network structure of the various contracts. Different legal instruments may come into play. So, for example, the remedies of the parties to the various contracts in a chain may be aligned, or a direct claim within a chain- or network-relation could be allowed—in modification of the general principle of privity. In both instances, general contract law is modified because of the existence of a network.[28]

Those inquiries dealing specifically with networks of contracts unanimously favour some kind of modification of general contract law. The (fairly recent) right to redress in the distribution chain provided for in Article 4 of the EC Sales Directive seems to indicate that legislatures (both on the Union and Member State level) in principle concur. What is disputed, though, is whether direct claims should be the rule or the exception or, conversely, a mere modification within the single contractual link. While important questions may have to be solved in different ways in contract and company law—for instance sharing of profits as the core principle in company law and split accounts, costs and income in the network of contracts—all core questions have to be asked in a very similar way both in company law and in the (network of) contracts setting: whether an added

The Clifford Chance Millenium Lectures – The Coming Together of the Common Law and the Civil Law (Oxford: Hart Publishing, 2000) 105–32, 118ff; comparative law survey in E. Wymeersch, 'A Status Report on Corporate Governance Rules and Practices in Some Continental European States' in K. Hopt, H. Kanda, M. Roe, E. Wymeersch, and S. Prigge (eds) *Comparative Corporate Governance – the State of the Art and Emerging Research* (Oxford: Oxford University Press, 1998) 1045–199, 1079–87 (recognizing consensus in that there should be scrutiny always only when clearly defined procedures have been violated). Even in the US, in principle, stakeholder interests may at least be taken into account: ground-breaking on this is *Shlensky v. Wrigley* 237 N.E.2d 776, 778–80 (Ill App Ct, 1968).

[28] See also, for the different opinions referred to in the text, M. Amstutz, '*Vertragskollisionen: Fragmente für eine Lehre von der Vertragsverbindung*' in H. Honsel, W. Portmann, R. Zäch, and D. Zobl (eds) *Festschrift für Heinz Rey* (Zürich: Schulthess, 2003) 161–76, 168–70; F. Cafaggi, 'Contractual Networks and the Small Business Act – Towards European Principles?' (2008) 4 *European Review of Contract Law* 493–539; S. Grundmann, 'Contractual Networks in German Private Law' in F. Cafaggi (ed) *Contractual Networks, Inter-Firm Cooperation and Economic Growth* (Cheltenham: Edward Elgar Publishing, 2011) 111–62, 126–42; G. Teubner, *Netzwerk als Vertragsverbund - Virtuelle Unternehmen, Franchising, Just-in-time aus Sozialwissenschaftlicher und Juristischer Sicht* (Baden-Baden: Nomos, 2004) 25–8, 141–3, 161ff, *et passim*; M. Wellenhofer, '*Drittwirkung von Schutzpflichten im Netz*' (2006) *Kritische Vierteljahresschrift* 187–207, 192, 194, 196ff, *et passim*; the discussion started with W. Möschel, '*Dogmatische Strukturen des Bargeldlosen Zahlungsverkehrs*' (1986) 186 *Archiv für die Civilistische Praxis* 187–212; M. Rohe, *Netzverträge – Rechtsprobleme Komplexer Vertragsverbindungen* (Tübingen: Mohr-Siebeck, 1998).

income which the network creates or added costs which it incurs should be shared by all; which decision mechanisms should apply (majority, unanimity/consensus); and which management powers should be delegated to one core decision body (such as the franchisor or the board) and which should be direct claims between the members. One thing is clear though: in each setting, party autonomy permit to a large extent the mimicking of the default rules of the other setting (in the charter or in the contract provisions).

In the present work, networks (of contracts) are also discussed from various perspectives: law, economics, and sociology.[29] Again, many issues are inspired by the financial crisis. Gilson, Sabel, and Scott, for developing legal concepts in this context, focus on network arrangements between entrepreneurial innovation and the finance and other contracts needed for carrying this innovation to an end. They conclude that traditional contract law (namely US case law) is not well suited to cope with the governance of these contracts characterized by (highly unforeseeable, incalculable, yet innovative) situations of uncertainty and propose a more flexible system of networks of contracts ('braided contracts'). Also chapters primarily focusing on third party effects—namely those by Frey and Cueni and by Teubner—cannot disregard network effects.

(3) Long-term relationships

A third set of questions is related to the long-term nature of the relationship—evident in the company law setting, but characteristic as well of many contractual relationships, namely those of organizational character. Two approaches are central—the theory of relational contracts[30] and—in fact—general governance research as initiated by Williamson.[31] Both approaches depart from a common starting point: the uncertainty of future developments and needs raises specific problems which fundamentally diverge from those posed by spot contracts. The

[29] See contributions by R. Gilson, C. Sabel, and R. Scott and by G. Hertig (Chapter 5 and accompanying comment) (the former also published in The Kauffman Task Force on Law, Innovation, and Growth, *Rules for Growth: Promoting Innovation and Growth Through Legal Reform* (Kansas City, Mo.: Kauffman, 2011); by R. Swedberg and by M. Amstutz (Chapter 6 and accompanying comment); and by M. Klausner (Chapter 7). See also Section IV(3)(a).

[30] S. Macaulay, 'Non-Contractual Relations in Business – a Preliminary Study' (1963) 28 *American Sociological Review* 55–67; I. R. MacNeil. 'The Many Futures of Contracts' (1974) 47 *Southern California Law Review* 691–816; O. Williamson, 'Markets and Hierarchies – Some Elementary Considerations' (1973) 63 *American Economic Review, Papers and Proceedings* 316–25; and also n 31; then V. Goldberg, 'Relational Exchange – Economic and Complex Contracts' (1980) 23 *American Behavioural Scientist* 337–52; B. Klein, R. G. Crawford, and A. Alchian, 'Vertical Integration, Appropriable Rents, and the Competitive Contracting Process' (1978) 28 *Journal of Law and Economics* 297–326. In German literature, the parallel discussion has taken place very early under the heading of 'long-term obligation' (*dauerschuldverhältnis*), see summary by M. Martinek in *Staudinger Commentary*, vol II (Berlin: de Gruyter, 14th edn, 2006) 'Introduction to §§ 662 et seq.' paras 68–88.

[31] O. Williamson, 'Transaction-Cost Economics: The Governance of Contractual Relations' (1979) 22 *Journal of Law and Economics* 233–61; Williamson, *The Economic Institutions of Capitalism*, n 8, 43–63, 68–84; for a combination of contract law and company law in this respect see Möslein and Riesenhuber, n 1, 248, 251–60.

parties to spot contracts are mainly confronted with the uncertainty of whether the other party will perform. Consequently, the parties' obligations can be described in a fairly complete way. A so-called complete contract, i.e. a contract regulating all potential developments, is more easily conceivable. For long-term relationships, on the other hand, a precise and exhaustive description of the core obligations is impossible, long-term contracts are inherently incomplete. This is the source of a particular set of risks of opportunism. More often than not, long-term relationships require high investments from one party or both and may thus lead to a hold-up situation where one partner can take advantage of the other partner's sunk costs (or relation-specific investment), for instance, by demanding changes in the arrangement or by asking the other party to accept certain breaches.[32] Conversely, there may also be a danger of holding the other partner too strictly to the agreement—for instance with respect to the conditions of termination of labour contracts or credit contracts or also partnership agreements. A termination regime which is too protective increases this danger.

Given the inherent incompleteness of long-term contracts, adjustment mechanisms are required. Various different instruments are at the parties' disposal, and choice of the right one is a core governance issue. In all cases, procedure becomes paramount. Agency is a core instrument in this context—the basic model of a duty to decide in the interest solely of the principal which also applies in company law. This basic model reveals far-reaching similarities in the treatment of a contractual and corporate long-term relationship. The board's fiduciary duty to further the interests of the company/shareholders is particularly prominent. It has been discussed extensively in the company context but much less in the context of contractual long-term relationships, even though the underlying questions are largely identical. In other words, the principal-agent theory which deals in particular with the question of how actions have to be taken in the interest of another person (or pool)[33] should be seen as a theory of company *and* contract law. With respect to risks (and chances) resulting from the long-term duration of the relationship, the similarities between the contractual and the corporate setting are particularly evident and striking. The examples discussed in this context can equally be formulated as those of contract law. Take, for instance, the 'Alaska Packers Case'[34]—like in Williamson's example, this case involved a workforce hired for a place in Alaska—which raised the issue of how proprietary rights and

[32] On this form of opportunism see references in n 6.

[33] Path-breaking in this regard, see M. Jensen and W. Meckling, 'Theory of the Firm: Managerial Behavior, Agency Costs and Ownership Structure' (1976) 3 *Journal of Financial Economics* 305–60; M. Jensen and W. Meckling, 'Separation of Ownership and Control' (1983) 26 *Journal of Law and Economics* 301–25; today M. Roe, *Strong Managers and Weak Owners – The Political Roots of American Corporate Finance* (Princeton, NJ: Princeton University Press, 1994); A. Shleifer and R.W. Vishny, 'A Survey of Corporate Governance' (1997) 52 *Journal of Finance* 737–83; good description also in M. Ruffner, *Die ökonomischen Grundlagen eines Rechts der Publikumsgesellschaft – ein Beitrag zur Theorie der Corporate Governance* (Zurich: Schulthess, 2000) 131ff. For these questions from a strictly contract related perspective see U. Schweizer, *Vertragstheorie*, (Tübingen: Mohr Siebeck, 1999) 33–85, 230–38.

[34] *Alaska Packers' Association v. Domenico*, 117 F. 99 (9th. Cir., 1902).

investment in housing, as well in the local retail store, should be arranged. The model of low search costs and high agency costs[35] is well adapted both to the company law setting and to long-term contractual relationships—more or less depending on the degree of stabilization, for instance via termination prerequisites. It is always the legal shaping of the relationship—in the company law setting *or* in a contractual setting—which makes it adopt more of one characteristic than another, but the particular mix can be largely identical in contractual long-term relationships and in partnerships/companies with respect to termination prerequisites; the important question of compensation; inspection rights into the other actor's actions; and decision-making rights.

In the present work, the long-term dimensions of contracts—namely fairness, reciprocity, and opportunistic behaviour—are again discussed from various perspectives. In other words, it investigates schemes of behaviour and then looks at these from an economic and from a legal perspective.[36] In two case studies, Klausner develops the parallels between corporate and long-term (contractual) relationships, emphasizing their similarity as well as key distinctions. For long-term contracts, integration (pooling) of efforts and assets does not go as far leading to a situation where some problems are less pronounced (some players' apathy), others more pronounced (hold-up situations), and many are very similar. The chapter focusses on governance mechanisms in long-term contractual relationships which can cope with, or minimize, the problems resulting from hold-up situations and moral hazard. Gillette, in his contribution, concentrates on opportunistic behaviour devaluating firm- or relation-specific investments made by the other side or other parties[37]. Starting out with an analysis of legal rules aimed at preventing opportunism and thereby encouraging relation-specific behaviour, Gillette—very much in line with what Williamson assumed—reaches the conclusion that such legal rules may not always achieve this goal. Judge-made rules, in particular, imposed *ex post,* may prove ill-informed or overprotective and thus provide room for opportunistic manoeuvre. This scepticism about rules is not completely shared by Schweizer who, while agreeing in principle, nevertheless sees a much more prominent role at least for default rules. The core of Gillette's contribution is then about how parties can design their own arrangements to protect relation-specific investment. With regard to US law, Gillette concludes that courts too often adversely interfere with contractual arrangements of the parties. At least in a commercial setting, he argues, (virtually unlimited) deference to contractual governance schemes would be preferable.

[35] Jensen and Meckling, n 33.

[36] See contributions by S. Magen and by G. -P. Calliess (Chapter 8 and accompanying comment) by B. Defains and D. Demougin and by F. Gomez (Chapter 9 and accompanying comment), and by C. Gillette and U. Schweizer (Chapter 10 and accompanying comment). See also Section IV(3)(a).

[37] See n 6.

2. Is contract governance needed in addition to corporate governance?

If governance research seems to be particularly promising where contracts lead to relations which have a structure similar to that of a company, is not contract governance simply a plea for extending corporate governance? Could not corporate governance integrate the aspects of contract law? What is the added value of a genuinely contract- and market transaction-centred governance discussion?[38]

First, the recent discussion of the financial crisis indicates that such an 'inclusive' approach would tend to disregard at least a good part of the important problems if, in a particular setting or crisis, the problems are mainly contract- or contract law-related. Secondly, a governance research agenda is important for contract and market transactions in order to fully profit from all the highly important tools and the changes in approach which a governance discussion brings about. The two-fold answer would then be that without contract governance, the discussion is too focused on the paradigm of the firm (disregarding the market), and without contract governance, all the changes in approach discussed are not fully exploited for contract law and in its market context.

a. Corporate governance not reaching deep enough into markets

Corporate governance covers a lot of material, but it does not reach deep enough into market transactions and contractual questions. Looking at how the financial crisis was dealt with would seem to be a good example. Again, market mechanisms (including contract drafting), default rules, and the mandatory framework have to be seen as different aspects of *one* overall governance scheme, taking into account its legal and interdisciplinary perspectives and paying particular attention to the (transnational) rule-setting scenarios.

For the regulatory framework in particular, it becomes evident that the focus is too narrow. One focus was on prudential supervision—and rightly so.[39] Reforms

[38] On these questions, see K. Riesenhuber, 'A Need for Contract Governance?' in S. Grundmann and Y. Atamer (eds) *Financial Services, Financial Crisis and General European Contract Law – Failure and Challenges of Contracting* (Alphen: Kluwer International, 2011) 61–83.

[39] See, for instance, Directive 2009/111/EC of the European Parliament and of the Council Amending Directives 2006/48/EC, 2006/49/EC and 2007/64/EC as regards banks affiliated to central institutions, certain own funds items, large exposures, supervisory arrangements, and crisis management (OJ 2009 L 302/97); on this regime see, e.g., G. Spindler, '*Finanzkrise und Wirtschaftsrecht*' (2010) *Aktiengesellschaft* 601–17, 606ff; broader surveys, also on the lacunae leading to the crisis in V. Acharya and P. Schnabel, 'How Banks Played the Leverage Game' in V. Acharya and M. Richardson (eds) *Restoring Financial Stability – How to Repair a Failed System* (Hoboken: John Wiley & Sons, 2009) 83–100, 86–98; W. Heun, '*Der Staat und die Finanzkrise*' (2010) *Juristenzeitung* 53–62, 57ff and 61ff; see also Directive 2010/76/EU of the European Parliament and of the Council Amending Directives 2006/48/EC and 2006/49/EC as regards capital requirements for the trading book and for re-securitisations, and the supervisory review of remuneration policies (OJ 2010 L 329/3) and n 41. The largest lacuna would still seem to be that there are important professional players active on credit markets who are not or only scarcely covered by the supervisory scheme.

dealt with (i) an increase in own funds, (ii) the question of how all institutions and tools which provide credit can be integrated into the supervisory regime, with extended supervision on a consolidated basis (also covering risks transferred to SPVs and short term guarantees provided for other group members), and (iii) supervision of market risks which can provoke problems similar to those resulting from the 'traditional' risk of non-diversification ('agglutination risks').

Beyond prudential supervision, however, the reform discussion focused on one 'private law' topic only: remuneration of management.[40] This is certainly important and may even constitute a 'systemic' issue. If one considers the EU level though, binding legislation has been enacted in a sector-specific way only.[41] The question why this particular issue attracted more legislative and academic attention than any other private law issue can probably best answered by referring to the fact that there had been a debate about remuneration before in the corporate governance discussion.[42] In any case, not only could the remuneration issue have been considered *also* as a contractual one—certainly on the level of the brokers, but also on the level of management, as rooted in the contract between management and firm—but moreover this issue by no means exhausts the private law defects which lead up to the crisis. In fact, there are some issues which are clearly firm-related, others which are clearly market-related, and still others relating to both firm and market, such as takeovers and remuneration. Contract governance *and* corporate governance, not one *or* the other, would seem to be the approach needed. And given that corporate governance is already so well developed, a crisis like the financial crisis which is now mainly related to deficits in the drafting of contracts is helpful in highlighting this rather obvious statement.

[40] On this issue and the reform steps see: S. Bhagat and R. Romano, 'Reforming Executive Compensation: Simplicity, Transparency and Committing to the Long-term' (2010) 7 *European Company and Financial Law Review* 273–96; G. Ferrarini, N. Moloney, and M.-C. Ungureanu, 'Executive Remuneration in Crisis: A Critical Assessment of Reforms in Europe' (2010) 10 *Journal of Corporate Law Studies* 73–118; Y. Hausmann and E. Bechtold-Orthi, 'Changing Remuneration Systems in Europe and the United States – A Legal Analysis of Recent Developments in the Wake of the Financial Crisis' (2010) 11 *European Business Organisation Law Review* 19–229. The dimension of the issue is, however, disputed, see, for instance, G. L. Clementi, Th. Cooley, M. Richardson, and I. Walter: 'Rethinking Compensation in Financial Firms' in V. Acharya and M. Richardson (eds) *Restoring Financial Stability – How to Repair a Failed System* (Hoboken: John Wiley & Sons, 2009) 197–214; Heun, n 39, 53, 60.

[41] Directive 2010/76/EU; on this directive see n 39; for all listed companies, only recommendations have been enacted: Commission Recommendation 2009/385/EC complementing Recommendations 2004/913/EC and 2005/162/EC as regards the regime for the remuneration of directors of listed companies (K(2009) 3177, OJ 2009 L 120/28) and Commission Recommendation 2009/384/EC on remuneration policies in the financial sector (K(2009) 3159, OJ 2009 L 120/22); on these recommendations see n 3 (namely Hopt (2011) 1, 40–2).

[42] See, for instance, G. Ferrarini and N. Moloney, 'Executive Remuneration and Corporate Governance in the EU: Convergence, Divergence and Reform Perspectives' (2004) 1 *European Company and Financial Law Review* 251–339; and first, in the UK in 1995, the Greenbury Committee, *Directors' Remuneration*, n 14 (disclosure of remuneration and recommendation of an independent committee); and those named in nn 40 and 41. Quite lucidly in the sense that corporate *and* contract governance should be seen in conjunction in such cases: K. Riesenhuber, n 38, 64–77.

There are many other issues which would have deserved just as much, perhaps even more attention with respect to the repercussions on the overall system. For instance, would not a duty of responsible lending—as discussed in the legislative history of the consolidated EC Consumer Credit Directive—[43] have prevented a consistent practice of issuing loans which were given to debtors who systematically did not even have the funds to afford the repayments out of their own income? Would not a mandatory redress rule or scheme—leading from any purchaser of a defective financial product up to the initiator—have prevented initiators from making such loans and then completely selling them off? Did not the lack of such a scheme of redress dramatically reduce the incentive to care about the creditworthiness of the debtors? This is not an abstract question either, given that such a mandatory redress rule does exist in Article 4 of the EC Sales Directive with respect to goods.[44] It can be argued that such a redress rule is at least as appropriate for financial products. And finally, would not a mandatory disclosure rule—at least for all substantial conflicts of interest (like in Article 18 of MiFID)—have prevented rating agencies from structuring toxic bonds and at the same time rating them very positively (without such disclosure)?

Three main contract law factors constituting the chain which led to the financial crisis—sub-prime lending, a complete passing on of risks in distribution chains, and rating under conflicts of interest—were largely left undiscussed in the corporate governance dialogue—as well as in traditional contract law. A contract governance discussion would have been needed for this purpose. These aspects have, of course, been discussed as issues of regulation and prudential supervision. A governance approach would, however, have added the view that regulation and prudential supervision should not be seen in isolation, but in conjunction with their 'private law' side, i.e. the tools of contract law, on which the schemes were based. Thus, with respect to 'the market', private law and supervision were not seen together, as alternatives and mutually reinforcing each other. Such a holistic approach would, however, be needed also for market phenomena and also in a rule-setting perspective. It would indeed be helpful to ask—taking all alternatives into consideration!—which level(s) and which substantive remedy to choose or whether the cumulation of different remedies or levels would be preferable, considering moreover how parties will probably respond to the alternative legal settings.

[43] Arts 8–9 of the Proposal for a Directive of the European Parliament and of the Council on the Harmonization of the Laws, Regulations and Administrative Provisions of the Member States Concerning Credit for Consumers, COM(2002) 443 final; then Directive 2008/48/EC of the European Parliament and of the Council on Credit Agreements for Consumers and Repealing Council Directive 87/102/EEC (OJ 1987 L 133/66). See, for instance, Y. Atamer, 'Duty of Responsible Lending – Should the European Union Take Action?' in S. Grundmann and Y. Atamer (eds) *Financial Services, Financial Crisis and General European Contract Law – Failure and Challenges of Contracting* (Alphen: Kluwer International, 2011) 179–202 (favouring strong paternalism); C. Sunstein, 'Boundedly Rational Borrowing' (2006) 73 *University of Chicago Law Review* 249–70 (favouring weak paternalism).

[44] See Art 4 of Directive 1999/44/EC of the European Parliament and of the Council of 25 May 1999 on certain aspects of the sale of consumer goods and associated guarantees (OJ 1999 L 171/12); on redress, see, i.e.: M. Bridge, C.M. Bianca, and S. Grundmann (eds) *EU Sales Directive – Commentary* (Antwerp/Oxford: Intersentia, 2002) Art 4, paras 12–36.

For 'the firm', i.e. for company law, such a discussion in mutual isolation—of the law of organization and of regulation—would not have happened to the same extent, and the corporate governance discussion helped in developing this more integrated perspective.

The discussion that has been summarized in the preceding paragraphs would seem to indicate that a corporate governance discussion does not reach deep enough into the market side of the question if the problem is genuinely contractual and that it cannot help contract law to develop the vision that indeed contract law tools and regulatory tools—from prudential supervision or investor protection—are to be seen as alternatives: both are capable of improving market structures and of contributing to their stability. As a matter of fact, it seems even peculiar that governance research did not first start in contract law. This is not only the area that is seen as the paradigm of any consensus-based method of problem solving and the 'first' area in traditional private law doctrine in most countries, but Williamson, when he coined the concept and also the term, took his examples mainly from this area.[45] Theoretically, the development could have been just the other way around.

b. Contract law in need of a governance approach

If the first strand of the answer is mainly about the fact that corporate governance does not reach deep enough into market phenomena, the second strand is more about the status of contract law as such: to develop the potential of governance as a tool may well contribute to the modernity (also) of contract law. Contract governance studies can indeed be seen as a particular way to contribute to the modernization of contract law studies.

To this end, the three more concrete issues can be considered which form the core of the present work—contract and third party, contract and network, contract and long-term duration. This will be done in more detail later, but some comments are helpful here. An important aspect of modernization would be that of developing a more integrated view of regulation and private law in market transactions. This integrated view would seem to be indicated by the characteristics of substantive law *and* to correlate with recent trends, but it is still far from being mainstream in a contract law setting (or at least much less so than in company law). A first consideration would be that regulation can not be seen only as a limit to freedom of contract, but also as restoring the actual foundations—the prerequisites—for a meaningful exercise of party autonomy, thus contributing to rather than restraining it.[46] Antitrust would then mainly be about restoring real freedom of choice and negotiation to the other side of the market, and consumer

[45] See n 2.

[46] Ground-breaking in this regard, see F. Böhm, '*Privatrechtsgesellschaft und Marktwirtschaft*' (1966) 17 *Jahrbuch für die Ordnung von Wirtschaft und Gesellschaft (ORDO)* 75–151, esp. 85, 88, 138; W. Eucken, *Grundsätze der Wirtschaftspolitik* (Tübingen: Mohr Siebeck, 6th edn, 1990; 1st edn, 1952) esp. 241–50 *et passim*; see only D. Kennedy, 'A Transnational Genealogy of Proportionality in Private Law' in R. Brownsword, H. Micklitz, L. Niglia, and S. Weatherill (eds) *The Foundations of European Private Law* (Oxford: Hart Publishing, 2011) 185–220.

law would primarily be about allowing an informed choice and negotiation by those contract partners who typically suffer from information problems and asymmetries, etc.

A second consideration would be that regulation and traditional private—in this context—contract law are furthering one common goal, i.e. free and informed choice in the process of formation of contract, but that they do so by focusing on different ways of cure, raising also different problems of proof, etc. One is looking at the overall market structure, the other at the individual position of (proprietary) rights of the parties but, by doing so, this, indirectly, also furthers overall market functions.[47] Thus, regulation in antitrust law requires consideration of the relevant market and that for a good part of this market competition no longer properly works. On the side of regulation, no actual damage has to be proven. If, however, actual damage can be proven, the more recent trends show that there is no reason not to provide also compensation rights for private parties and even encourage action.[48] On the other hand, in contract law settings, the effect on the whole of the market (structure) is not needed; it is not a core category in contract law, but rather actual loss (and lost gains). Third party behaviour may therefore be prohibited because it caused loss—destroying, for instance, a relation-specific investment—even if it did not reach the level of cartelization of whole markets. However, it may again be an argument to prohibit practices by third parties more easily if, in addition, they affect the market structure. Market regulation and contract law could then be considered to constitute what has been called in the German literature (with respect to public law and private law more generally) 'mutually supplementary orders' (*gegenseitige auffangordnungen*).[49]

The third consideration would be that the first steps to close the gap between private law (contract) remedies and market regulation have already been taken.

[47] Particularly striking is the parallelism in capital market law between the scope of protecting individual investors and the scope of protecting the market: see, for instance, very explicit Recitals 2, 5, 17, 31, 34, and 44 of Directive 2004/39/EC of the European Parliament and of the Council of 21 April 2004 on markets in financial instruments amending Council Directives 85/611/EEC and 93/6/EEC and Directive 2000/12/EC of the European Parliament and of the Council and repealing Council Directive 93/22/EC (OJ 2004 L 145/)—the basic Act on securities' exchange in Europe; or, from literature, N. Moloney, *EC Securities Regulation* (Oxford: Oxford University Press, 2nd edn, 2008) 564–71; Grundmann, n 16, § 19 paras 15–17; ground-breaking for Germany (which was late in its development) is K. Hopt, *Kapitalanlegerschutz im Recht der Banken* (Munich: C.H. Beck, 1975) 51ff, 334–7.

[48] White Paper on Damages for Breach of Competition Law, COM(2008) 165 (considering also remedies such as collective actions); on this development see J. Basedow, 'Incentives and Disincentives for the Private Enforcement of EC Competition Law' in T. Egers, C. Ott, J. Bigus, and G. von Wangenheim (eds) *Internationalisierung des Rechts und seine ökonomische Analyse Festschrift für Hans-Bernd Schäfer zum 65. Geburtstag* (Wiesbaden: Gabler, 2008) 499–508; G. Wagner, 'Should Private Enforcement of Competition Law be Strengthened?' in D. Schmittchen and M. Albert (eds) *The More Economic Approach to European Competition Law* (Tübingen: Mohr Siebeck, 2007) 115–29; for the latest developments see V. Pinotti and D. Stepina, 'Antitrust Class Actions in the European Union: Latest Developments and the Need for a Uniform Regime' (2011) 2 *Journal of European Competition Law and Practice* 24–33.

[49] W. Hoffmann-Riem and E. Schmidt-Aßmann (eds) *Öffentliches Recht und Privatrecht als Wechselseitige Auffangordnungen* (Baden-Baden: Nomos, 1996); Grundmann and Renner, n 22.

With respect to the prime field of regulation, i.e. antitrust law, there is already a discussion and even a legislative procedure leading to a particular private law action for damages. It would be desirable to evaluate this trend and inquire more into the general repercussions such a trend may have. For example, what should be the private law actions for violation of regulation (including punitive damages), and what regulatory dimensions can influence interpretation of private law norms and concepts?

For a fourth consideration, one could refer to the old dispute on the nature of default rules: whether they should (primarily) aim at mimicking the assumed will of (the majority of) typical parties or at finding the equilibrium between the interests which the legislature sees as adequate for overall society, taking into account, of course, the preferences of the parties as well.[50] In fact, the result reached in a concrete contract can be seen not only as the result of a (bipolar) negotiation process between the parties, but also as a (triangular) process between the legislature as the author of the default rule and both parties.[51] Contract law and regulation thus have a common goal but with differing approaches, different rule setters, different ways of imposing the standard, different levels at which the rules can be situated. Considering the interplay described and doing so from manifold perspectives as described—taking it as one mega-theme of contract law—would constitute a core feature in a contract governance debate to come. All this shows again that contract governance—just like corporate governance—is just as much about individual, private party driven design as it is about market regulation and stability or more generally, stability of organization forms and institutions.[52]

The plea for a more integrated view of contract drafting, default rules, and market regulation exemplified by these four considerations is, however, at odds with powerful structural characteristics of contract law legislation and scholarship as they currently exist. A contract governance approach may also have been and may still be particularly difficult—and at the same time particularly needed—because of a marked heterogeneity in the subject matter and in the discussion and decision platforms. This is a consideration about the 'contract law community'. First, the legislature would seem to be less 'homogeneous' in contract law than in company (and capital market) law. In the EU scenario, one Directorate General is responsible for company and capital market law, while for contract law several Directorates General are competent with fundamentally diverging 'philosophies', on the side of B2C contracts DG Sanco (with interests also in general contract law), on the side of B2B contracts DG Internal Market (lately also, for

[50] See n 128 and n 150 on the one hand and n 129 on the other.

[51] F. Möslein, *Dispositives Recht – Zwecke, Strukturen und Methoden* (Tübingen: Mohr Siebeck, 2011) esp. 129–50; F. Möslein, 'Governance by Default' in S. Grundmann, B. Haar, H. Merkt, *et al* (eds) *Festschrift für Klaus J. Hopt zum 70. Geburtstag am 24. August 2010* (Berlin: deGruyter, 2010) 2861–80; in a similar vein, see J.-H. Binder, *Regulierungsinstrumente und Regulierungsstrategien im Kapitalgesellschaftsrecht* (Tübingen: Mohr Siebeck, 2012).

[52] In some more detail (with respect to governance taxation) see F. Möslein, '*Steuerrecht und Marktstabilität*' (2012) *Juristenzeitung* 243.

all contracts, DG Justice). In the US, capital markets are mainly regulated under federal law with a strong supervisory and regulatory commission, the SEC, and company law is dominated by one trend setter (Delaware), whereas in contract law, competences are scattered among the states—with the important exception of the Uniform Commercial Code.

Similarly, the scientific community would seem to be less homogeneous in the contract law area, with a split between the '*Civilisti*' and '*Commercialisti*' (which, despite the Italian terminology, is a split which describes the status quo at least in most of the EU), the former primarily 'responsible' for contract law, but mostly neglecting important parts such as financial services (or other commercial) contracts and even more so regulation of markets, the latter often less integrated into the discourse community in core civil law. Within civil law, contract law is, moreover, typically combined with other civil law areas such as torts (thus forming the paradigm of a law of 'obligations'), property or family law, rather than with other modes of shaping economic transactions via party autonomy, namely with company law. There are few typical common discussion platforms between 'contract/market' and 'firm' and not even between 'contract' and 'market'. The same could be said of the courts. There would seem to be more of a trend to have only one leading court competent in company law, a court which guides and accompanies the discussion, which is certainly the case in the US with the Delaware Supreme Court, but also in some EU Member States like Germany and (at least in Germany) also very meaningful joint platforms between practice and academia. The same is more difficult to find for contract law and market regulation. Whereas company law—with its organizational and capital market aspects—is mostly discussed by the same circles of scholars and practitioners, the same is much less true of contract law—with respect to the contractual basis and the regulation affecting it. This status quo may also be influenced to a certain extent by the high heterogeneity of contract types, a consequence of its high degree of flexibility. While companies, associations, and partnerships all share a common aim, contract can be the basis of highly antagonistic and on-the-spot exchange, but also of very intense and long-term cooperation. Certainly, contract governance would need to aim at bridging gaps where they hinder the discussion needed. Contract governance discussion could act as a catalyst when developing a common methodological framework for this large variety of phenomena, which are currently still viewed as being too heterogeneous for such a joint discourse. Even better, a genuine contract governance discussion would probably not fail to develop the links to corporate governance—because they are twins in problems, party autonomy and its regulation, and they can be twins in their modes of discussion.

In fact, there is a continuum from the company law setting to the long-term contractual setting to the more short-term and spot contract setting, but also from market regulation to mandatory contract law to default rules in contract law. And seeing more of a continuum here would be one core challenge, but would as well be typical for a contract governance approach.

III. Multi-level Regulatory Perspectives

1. Levels of regulation

If, following Williamson, governance is defined as 'the institutional matrix within which transactions are negotiated and executed',[53] the issue of the levels of regulation is at the heart of governance in general and of contract governance in particular.[54] The example of the employment relation is a particularly suitable example to illustrate the issue from a legal perspective.

2. Levels of contract governance: employment as an example

If we look at private governance by the parties, there is, first of all, the employment contract. Yet, it is a characteristic of the employment contract as a long-term relation that not all the details of the mutual obligations can be spelled out at the beginning.[55] Some aspects have to be left to renegotiation, but the central contractual instrument of adaptation is the employer's managerial authority. In addition, there are other mechanisms in the vicinity of the managerial authority. Many aspects of work are determined by practice, custom or usage. An established usage may under certain conditions gain the quality of an enforceable promise. Other aspects are governed by autonomous agreement of a group of employees. Yet other aspects may be determined by standard terms or work rules.

At another level of autonomous governance, collective agreements govern the workplace. They are subdivided into different levels as well: some with nation-wide or industry-wide effect, others with effect for a company or a plant or shop-floor. They may be concluded by unions or by employees' representatives of smaller units on the one hand and individual employers or their associations on the other.

[53] See n 2.

[54] See, e.g. H. Fleischer, 'Corporate Governance in *Europa als Mehrebenensystem*' (2012) *ZGR* 160–96; S. Grundmann and W. Kerber, 'European System of Contract Laws – A Map for Combining the Advantages of Centralised and Decentralised Rule-making' in S. Grundmann and J. Stuyck, *An Academic Greenpaper on European Contract Law* (The Hague: Kluwer International, 2002) 295–342; in S. Grundmann and J. Stuyck, 'An Optional European Contract Law Code – Advantages and Disadvantages' (2005) *European Journal of Law and Economics* 21, 215–36; See also Möslein and Riesenhuber, n 1, 248–89. With some adaptations also G. F. Schuppert, 'Contract Governance – *Vorüberlegungen zur Strukturierung einer Neuen Forschungsperspektive*' in S. Grundmann, M. Kloepfer, C. Paulus, and G. Werle (eds) *Festschrift 200 Jahre Juristische Fakultät der Humboldt-Universität zu Berlin: Geschichte, Gegenwart und Zukunft* (Berlin/New York: de Gruyter, 2010) 1333–59, esp at 1340–7. For a different approach of *levels of social analysis,* see O. Williamson, 'The New Institutional Economics: Taking Stock, Looking Ahead' (2000) 38 *Journal of Economic Literature* 595, 596ff.

[55] See the discussion earlier at Section II(1)(b)(3). See also, e.g., H. Collins, *Employment Law* (Oxford: Oxford University Press, 2nd edn, 2010) 6ff; see also H. Collins, 'Legal Regulation of Dependent Entrepreneurs' (1996) 152 *Journal of Institutional and Theoretical Economics* 263–70; A.-S. Vandenberghe, 'Employment Contracts' in K. G. Dau-Schmidt, S. D. Harris, and O. Lobel (eds) *Labor and Employment Law and Economics* (Cheltenham, Edward Elgar Publishing, 2009) 62ff; Williamson, n 6, 218ff ('The employment relationship is, by design, an incomplete form of contracting.').

Collective agreements can in principle be considered as part of private governance. Yet, they may serve as an instrument of public governance, too. With a view to established practice in some Member States, EU law provides for the possibility that directives in the area of social policy may be implemented by collective agreement (Article 153(3) of the Treaty on the Functioning of the European Union (TFEU)). Anti-discrimination directives encourage the social partners to adopt anti-discrimination programmes complementing public regulation (see, for example, Article 21 of Directive 2006/54/EC).

If we focus on public governance (in the sense of public ordering), again we find a multi-layered system. The regulatory cooperation of the EU and the Member States has already been indicated, as has the regulatory cooperation between public authorities and the social partners (on various levels). Regulation may take the form of substantive or procedural rules for the individual employment contract or relationship. It may also take the form of substantive or procedural rules for collective agreements. The EU's 'social dialogue' procedure of Articles 154 and 155 of the TFEU is an example of an intricate mixture of public and private governance.[56] Management and labour, the social partners, are involved in the legislative process from the beginning. They are being consulted on whether there is a need for EU legislation and on the form it should take; and they may request to be given an opportunity to regulate the issue by way of a collective agreement ('framework agreement') which then may be implemented by a Union legislative act. (This is an instance of 'bargaining in the shadow of the law'—or a 'regulatory threat'—and thus a private-public governance- and ordering-mix.)[57]

At another level, issues of constitutional law, fundamental rights in particular, come into play. There are, of course, many established issues such as the prohibition of slavery and forced work or the protection of collective action as a fundamental right. Recent years have evidenced an increasing sensitivity—or sometimes inventory spirit—for issues of fundamental rights. An (in)famous example is, of course, the invention of a fundamental right against age discrimination in the Court of Justice's *Mangold* decision.[58] The long list of 'fundamental social rights' included in the 'solidarity' chapter of the EU's Charter of Fundamental Rights (ChFR)[59] has raised expectations—although the vague and deferential wording (in itself an example of multi-level governance) of almost all of the 'social rights' confirms their limited reach.[60]

[56] For a survey see K. Riesenhuber, *Europäisches Arbeitsrecht* (Heidelberg: C. F. Müller, 2009) § 4 paras 26ff.

[57] See also K. Riesenhuber, '*Schatten des Rechts*' in S. Grundmann, P.O. Mülbert, and M. Roth (eds) *Festschrift für Klaus J. Hopt* (Berlin: de Gruyter, 2010) 1225–43.

[58] ECJ Case C-144/04 *Mangold* [2005] ECR I-9981. See also K. Riesenhuber, 'Case Note: ECJ of 22 November 2005—Case C-144/04—Mangold' (2007) 3 *European Review of Contract Law* 62–71.

[59] Charter of Fundamental Rights of the European Union, reproduced in OJ 2010 C 83/389.

[60] See, e.g., Case C-323/08 *Rodríguez Mayor* [2009] ECR I-11621 paras 58ff (concerning Art 30 ChFR).

3. Aspects of contract governance

Levels of governance raise a multitude of—often conflicting—issues. The large number and disparity of issues leads to the question of meta-governance: how can conflicting governance issues be resolved? We will briefly address this latter issue in Section IV.

a. Coherence

The multi-faceted and multi-layered governance structures in the area of employment law lead to the problem of maintaining coherence. Means to this end may be a clear demarcation of the various levels, for example by supremacy or conflict rules or—for the overall body of law at transcending levels—a pre-structuring in substance by principles.

In this work, Hugh Collins' contribution gives an illustration of the issues involved from another field. If courts from different jurisdictions decide differently on the recognition of a charge over property by way of security for a loan, this may be considered an issue of horizontal levels. As Collins suggests, the issue may also be discussed as a matter of 'global law', i.e. a level on the vertical scale. Such global law can, in this instance, however only be found in the 'law' that the parties created, a *lex mercatoria*. And while such *lex mercatoria* may claim a higher position in terms of its geographic scope of application, national conflict laws (and thereby also national and supra-national substantive laws) assume a higher position in the hierarchy of norms and—certainly traditionally—refuse recognition of such 'private laws' or, in any case, do not without reservation allow their derogation of mandatory national provisions.[61] The governance response to the issue may be different, depending on how we view the reliability and responsibility of the parties concerned, resulting externalities and other public policy issues that public regulation is intended to accommodate.[62]

b. Fundamental rights

Among the principles for the demarcation of different levels of governance, fundamental rights may be particularly prominent and high up in the hierarchy. There are fundamental rights of various actors to be taken into consideration. At the outset, the individual liberty—freedom of contract—of the contracting parties is concerned.[63] Individual liberty is not only a fundamental right in itself

[61] See Recitals 13ff Rome I-Convention. For the discussion in the EU see C. -W. Canaris, '*Die Stellung der 'UNIDROIT-Principles' und der 'Principles of European Contract Law' im System der Rechtsquellen*' in J. Basedow (ed) *Europäische Vertragsrechtsvereinheitlichung und deutsches Recht* (Tübingen: Mohr Siebeck, 2000) 5–31; S. Grundmann, 'General Principles of Private Law and *Ius Commune Modernum* as Applicable Law?' in T. Baum and K. J. Hopt (eds) *Corporations, Capital Markets and Business in the Law* – Liber Amicorum *Richard M. Buxbaum* (Den Haag/London/Boston: Kluwer Law International, 2000) 213–34.

[62] See the different approaches by H. Collins and H. Eidenmüller (Chapter 12 and accompanying comment).

[63] See, e.g., R. A. Epstein, 'In Defense of the Contract at Will' (1984) 51 *University of Chicago Law Review* 957–82.

but a fundamental right that is reinforced by every individual's right to respect for his dignity. Focused on regulation, governance theory always has to assure that it respects individual liberty instead of only using individual contract to a regulatory end.

Employers and employees enjoy freedom of association. The more recent collections of fundamental rights grant employees as a group (or as a collective) rights such as the right to information and consultation (Article 27 of the ChFR). Workers and employers and their organizations have a fundamental right to negotiate and conclude collective agreements and, in cases of conflict, take collective action (Article 28 of the ChFR).

While the state or other public entities (such as the EU) do not as such enjoy fundamental rights, they may rely on the fundamental rights of, for example, employees to justify intervention. Indeed, they may be under an obligation to intervene in order to protect the fundamental rights of individuals or groups.[64] Thus, for example, the Union or Member States may justify protection against unjustified dismissal under Article 30 of the ChFR (although, of course, the provision does not in a strict sense mandate regulation and does not constitute a competence basis).

c. *Subsidiarity*

Conversely, the principle of subsidiarity may be seen as a conflicts rule, albeit a hidden rule, arranging for interplay between the levels:[65]

> Under the principle of subsidiarity... the Union shall act only if and in so far as the objectives of the proposed action cannot be sufficiently achieved by the Member States, either at central level or at regional and local level, but can rather, by reason of the scale or effects of the proposed action, be better achieved at Union level.[66]

While the principle is here spelled out with regard to the vertical division of powers between the Union and the Member States, it may also apply as between public and private entities and as between (private) organizations and individuals, for example Unions and workers. Closely related to issues of fundamental rights—freedom of contract in particular—it provides for a presumption of competence of the smaller entity. Also fundamental freedoms may be seen as rules prescribing subsidiarity of state action as against action taken by private law subjects, thus prescribing subsidiarity for Member States and subjecting them to an outside scrutiny in this respect (by the European Court of Justice).[67]

64 See the seminal decision in Case C-265/95 *Commission v. France* [1997] ECR I-6959. For the theoretical framework see C. -W. Canaris, *Grundrechte und Privatrecht* (Berlin/New York: de Gruyter, 1999) (with a hint at the 'internationality' of the issue at 10ff); C. -W. Canaris, '*Grundrechte und Privatrecht*' (1984) 184 *Archiv für die ivilistische Praxis* 201–46.

65 In a governance context, see recently Fleischer, n 54, 160, 168ff.

66 Art 5(3) TEU. For a recent (and critical) discussion see Möslein, n 51, 77ff.

67 See in more detail and with references from the ECJ case law: S. Grundmann, 'The Concept of the Private Law Society after 50 Years of European and European Business Law' (2008) *European Review of Private Law* 553–81, esp at 558–67.

d. Public and private levels

The issues of fundamental rights on the one hand and subsidiarity on the other also lead to the public-private divide. Subsidiarity, individual autonomy (*privatautonomie*) and freedom of contract can be construed as value judgments in favour of private governance as opposed to public governance and ordering. And indeed, recent years have evidenced a move to private governance also in the area of employment law.

Employee participation in the European Company (*Societas Europaea*) is a prominent example where mandatory public regulation (public governance and ordering) has been superseded by a system of contract governance. For no less than 30 years, repeated and creative attempts of the Member States to agree on a substantive regulation of employee participation in the European Company failed. The breakthrough came with a shift from the substantive approach to a procedural approach of regulation. Instead of providing a one-size-fits-all solution, the legislator opted for a negotiation model pursuant to which employee participation is to be determined, in principle, by way of agreement between the employer-side and the employee-side. The agreement is being negotiated by the representatives of the participating companies and a 'special negotiating body', formed specifically for the purpose of representing the employees—their number and their distribution over Member States—of the participating companies.[68] (Note, incidentally, how the creation of the special negotiating body as well as the determination of the representation on the employer side again raises issues of governance.)[69] The parties can determine employee participation according to their interests and needs—a custom-tailored solution. If they do not reach agreement within the prescribed period of negotiation, the fall-back solution annexed to the Directive applies. The system is mixed with a few mandatory elements with regard to the substance of regulation, a mandatory procedural framework, and considerable room for freedom of contract. The freedom to determine the employee participation is combined, though, with elements of incentives and 'nudges' as they result from the fall-back solution.

The same structure was subsequently employed for the European Cooperative Company (*Societas Cooperativa Privata*) and cross-border mergers. It is also the model discussed for cross-border transfer of the company seat and for the European Private Company (*Societas Privata Europaea*). Contract governance serves various purposes here. It gives back responsibility to the parties concerned, thus at the same time alleviating the legislature of a burden, re-empowering private parties, and providing for additional legitimacy of the employee involvement regimes

[68] For a survey see, e.g., Riesenhuber, n 56, § 29 paras 31ff.

[69] C. Windbichler, '*Der Gordische Mitbestimmungsknoten und das Vereinbarungsschwert – Regulierung durch Selbstregulierung*?' in U. Jürgens, D. Sadowski, G. F. Schuppert, and M. Weiss (eds) *Perspektiven der Corporate Governance – Bestimmungsfaktoren unternehmerischer Entscheidungsprozesse und Mitwirkung der Arbeitnehmer* (Baden-Baden: Nomos, 2007) 282, 291–3.

ultimately installed. Indeed, the negotiation model takes the idea of employee involvement a consequential step further than mandatory models. Negotiated employee participation promises to be better suited to the needs of management and labour in the individual firm. At the same time, procedural safeguards take account of the specific needs of the parties.

In this work, Pistor discusses how switching from hierarchical and coercive forms of governance in the area of global finance to 'inclusive, horizontal, cooperative' forms of governance—i.e. forms of contract governance—may contribute to improving existing structures. She uses the example of the European Banking Coordinative Initiative (EBCI) as a 'full-fledged contractual governance regime'. Drawing on organizational theory, Pistor suggests that the predominant circumstances of uncertainty make contractual governance regimes superior in the financial markets. She expounds in more detail on the central elements—inclusiveness, horizontality, and cooperation—that characterize this model of governance.[70]

e. *Democracy and representation*

Where collectives make rules, this may raise specific questions of legitimacy: democracy, self-determination, and representation. This issue is of considerable relevance also with regard to contract governance. Private rule-making in particular raises intricate issues of legitimacy.[71]

A good (and still virulent) example is participation of the social partners—management and labour—in EU legislation under the social dialogue-procedures of Articles 153 and 154 of the TFEU discussed earlier.[72] Originally, Parliament was not institutionally involved in this form of rule-making at all. Article 155(2)(1) of the TFEU now provides for a right to be informed. Legislation adopted in the social dialogue-procedure cannot draw democratic legitimacy from the European Parliament. The Court of First Instance (CFI) emphasized the necessity for the organizations involved to be representative for their constituents.[73]

Another example is the posting of workers. Posting of workers raises intricate issues of legitimacy and representation on the horizontal level of the various Member States. For the posted employees who, purportedly, are to be protected by the application of the employee protection laws of the host Member State do not have a voice in the making of these laws or in the determination whether and in how far they should apply to them.[74]

[70] See Chapter 13. The mechanisms as such may, of course, not all be new and can be related back to general governance discussion: see comment accompanying Chapter 13.

[71] See in detail G. Bachmann, *Private Ordnung* (Tübingen: Mohr Siebeck, 2006) 159–226.

[72] See n 56.

[73] Case T-135/96 *UEAPME v. Council* [1998] ECR II-2335, paras 88–90.

[74] A. R. Ganesh, 'Appointing Foxes to Guard Henhouses: The European Posted Workers' Directive' (2008) 15 *Columbia Journal of European Law* 123–42.

f. Competition and cartelization

Uniform rules at one level exclude competition at the lower levels.[75] The cartelization of employees in unions was generally accepted in the latter half of the 19th century.[76] On the EU-level, the Court in its *Albany* decision accepted that agreements concluded in the context of collective negotiations between management and labour in pursuit of social policy objectives are not covered by Article 101(1) of the TFEU.[77] This does not exclude the possibility, however, that under fundamental freedoms, standard-setting that covers activities nationwide or even beyond is or might be scrutinized and struck down if amounting to an impediment.[78]

Harmonization of laws of the Member States eliminates competition. Yet social policy legislation of the EU is (at least in principle) limited to minimum standards (Article 153(4) of the TFEU) and some areas, pay in particular, are exempted from EU legislation. Intra-Member State competition is strong where free movement of goods is concerned. Competition on the basis of employment standards is restricted though where free movement of services is concerned. In *Rush Portuguesa,* the Court accepted that:

> Community law does not preclude Member States from extending their legislation, or collective labour agreements entered into by both sides of industry, to any person who is employed, even temporarily, within their territory, no matter in which country the employer is established.[79]

While subsequent decisions have spelled out certain limits to a duplication of standards of employee protection, these limits are rather broad. They do not even coincide with the Union standards of protection. Thus, while EU law provides that every worker is entitled to four weeks of paid annual leave, the Court has accepted that the host Member States may extend this entitlement—in this case six weeks—for posted workers.[80]

The Posting of Workers Directive (PoWD) responds to this judgment with an attempt to coordinate national posting of workers laws and make their operation transparent.

[75] For a comprehensive discussion of issues of the employment market and competition from a legal perspective, see V. Rieble, *Arbeitsmarkt und Wettbewerb Der Schutz von Vertrags- und Wettbewerbsfreiheit im Arbeitsrecht* (Berlin: Springer, 1996).

[76] See, e.g., S. Deakin and G. Morris, *Labour Law* (Oxford: Hart Publishing, 5th edn, 2009) paras 1.4ff; W. Zöllner, K. -G. Loritz, and C. W. Hergenröder, *Arbeitsrecht* (Munich: C. H. Beck, 6th edn, 2008) 22ff.

[77] Case C-67/96 *Albany* [1999] ECR I-5751 paras 52–9.

[78] Case 36/74 *Walrave* [1974] ECR 1405, 1419ff; Case C-415/93 *Bosman* [1995] ECR I-4921, 5065–7; and similar Case 155/73 *Sacchi* [1974] ECR 409, 431ff; Case 13/76 *Doná* [1976] ECR 1333, 1340ff; and Case 90/76 *van Ameyde* [1977] ECR 1091, 1127ff.

[79] Case C-113/89 *Rush Portuguesa* [1990] ECR I-1417 para. 18; to the same effect already Joined Case 62 and 63/81 *Seco* [1980] ECR 223 para. 14; and subsequently Case C-43/93 Vander Elst [1994] ECR I-3803 para. 23; Case C-272/94 *Guiot* [1996] ECR I-1905.

[80] Joined Cases C-49/98, C-50/98, C-52/98 to C-54/98 and C-6898 to C-71/98 *Finalarte* [2001] ECR I-8731 paras 57ff.0

g. *Functions of workers' representation*

If we look at workers' representatives, they may serve various functions. Much of the debate focuses on 'participation', 'representation', and 'industrial democracy'.[81] Indeed, this relates back to the issues discussed earlier.[82] Representation and voice are all the more important where decisions affect a person directly and where the exit option may be restricted. It is quite another issue, of course, whether the respective rights should be mandated by law or left to individual agreement. Let us briefly consider two other aspects: information and adaptation.

In various instances, workers' representatives mediate information.[83] Take the example of the Transfer of Undertakings Directive (TUD). Article 7 of the TUD requires the employers, both transferor and transferee, to provide the representatives of their workers with detailed information about the transfer. The information is certainly too detailed for the rank and file employee. The workers' representatives serve as information intermediaries. While the information is detailed, channelling it through the workers' representatives alleviates the burden of providing it for the employer. The workers' representatives will usually be especially experienced and often specifically trained in handling such information. They will thus be in a position to ask (the right) questions and make additional suggestions. They thus serve similar functions as information intermediaries do more generally, for instance accountants or rating firms whose roles for corporate governance are currently debated.[84] And again, as there is usually only one workers' representation forum, channelling information thus alleviates the burden that comes along with information for employers.

As a long-term relationship, the employment contract requires adaptation over time.[85] Employee representation and the system of collective bargaining can serve as adaptation mechanisms. This is particularly obvious for collective bargaining over wages. But it also applies with regard to employees' representatives at the plant level and their rights to information, consultation, or co-determination with regard to issues of the workplace. As Windbichler puts it '[c]ollective agreements and codetermination at the shop-floor level serve as tools for the necessary redefinition of rights and obligations over time, i.e., they are part of a sophisticated contract governance system.'[86] Other contracts, long-term contracts in

[81] F. Gamillscheg, *Kollektives Arbeitsrecht vol. II – Betriebsverfassung* (Munich: C. H. Beck, 2008) 22ff, 42ff; Zöllner, Loritz and Hergenröder, n 76, 455ff.

[82] See Section III(2)(d).

[83] K. Riesenhuber, '*Arbeitnehmerschutz durch Information beim Betriebsübergang*' in R. Krause, W. Veelken, and K. Vieweg (eds) *Recht der Wirtschaft und der Arbeit in Europa - Gedächtnisschrift für Wolfgang Blomeyer* (Berlin: Duncker & Humblot, 2004) 195-215; K. Riesenhuber, '*Informationspflichten beim Betriebsübergang*' (2004) *Recht der Arbeit* 340–52.

[84] See survey and references in S. Grundmann, n 12, § 14, paras 43–5, 50–3.

[85] See Section III(2).

[86] C Windbichler, 'Cheers and Boos for Employee Involvement: Co-Determination as Corporate Governance Conundrum' (2005) 6 *European Business Organisation Law Review* 6 507–37; C Windbichler, '*Betriebliche Mitbestimmung als Institutionalisierte Vertragshilfe*' in M. Lieb, U. Noack, and H. P. Westermann (eds) *Festschrift for Wolfgang Zöllner* (Köln/Berlin/Bonn/München: Carl Heymanns, 1999) 999–1009; Rieble, n 75, paras 1418ff.

particular, involve similarly intricate governance arrangements, for example franchise agreements.

h. Principal and agent

Levels of contract governance may also be analysed in terms of principle and agent.[87] If we consider issues of employment law with a view to employee protection, who is the best agent of the employee's interests?

This could initially be the employee himself. The concern here is that he may not be in a position to adequately pursue his interest in the market. Yet, this requires more detailed analysis.[88] Secondly, the employer may function as the employee's agent. While certainly the employer pursues his own interest and while, undeniably, there are numerous examples of the worst forms of exploitation there are, in a working market environment, also elements that induce or even force the employer to take the employees' interests into account. Thus, the employer constantly needs to attract employees and thus has to be interested in establishing a good reputation. Again, as the employer cannot control every aspect of his employees' work (thus being potentially exposed to employee-opportunism), he may use remuneration as an incentive to reduce this risk.

Let us pursue the example of employee remuneration that we have already encountered earlier a little further.[89] Following the financial crisis, remuneration has often been discussed as an issue of corporate governance. Indeed, it undeniably is an issue of corporate governance where (a) the manager's remuneration is concerned or (b) remuneration (*boni*) is used as an incentive mechanism for employees whose work is essential (or whose misbehaviour may be fatal) for the company. Yet, remuneration may also be a pure issue of contract governance. So, for example, Akerlof has advanced the thesis that employers pay more than just market-clearing wages so as to induce their employees to excel in their work (as a 'counter-gift').[90] Indeed, subsequent laboratory studies seem to support this

[87] V. P. Goldberg, 'Regulation and Administered Contracts' (1976) 7 *Bell Journal of Economics* 426, 429ff *et passim;* C. Gillette, 'Rolling Contracts as an Agency Problem' (2004) *Wisconsin Law Review* 679–722.

[88] See R. A. Epstein, 'In Defense of the Contract at Will' (1984) 51 *University of Chicago Law Review* 957–82; E. Picker, '*Das Arbeitsrecht zwischen Marktgesetz und Machtansprüchen – Zur Kritik und Korrektur gesetzlicher, "richterrechtlicher" und korporativer Fehlentwicklungen am Beispiel von Betriebsverfassungs-, Kündigungs- und Tarifvertragsrecht*' (2005) *Zeitschrift für Arbeitsrecht* 353–90 on the one hand; P. C. Weiler, *Governing the Workplace – The Future of Labor and Employment Law* (Cambridge, Mass: Harvard University Press, 1990) on the other.

[89] See also K. Riesenhuber, '*Vergütungssysteme unter dem Blick von Governance und Compliance*' in V. Rieble, A. Junker, and R. Giesen (eds) *Finanzkriseninduzierte Vergütungsregulierung und arbeitsrechtliche Entgeltsysteme* (München: Zentrum für Arbeitsbeziehungen und Arbeitsrecht (ZAAR), 2011) 133ff.

[90] G. A. Akerlof, 'Labor Contracts as Partial Gift Exchange' (1982) 97 *Quarterly Journal of Economics* 543–69. See also C Windbichler, '*Das Arbeitsverhältnis als Austausch und "Geschenkverhältnis"*' in H. Hirte, K. Frey, and R. Wank, *Festschrift for Herbert Wiedemann* (Munich: C. H. Beck, 2002) 673–83.

theory.[91] However, more recent empirical research casts doubt on these findings. It appears that above-market remuneration merely works as a short-term incentive.[92] Governance needs to rely on interdisciplinary research, yet, the issues involved may be complex and difficult to prove or falsify.

Then there are collectives on the employee side. Unions and employees' representatives in the firm recommend themselves as agents with their market power derived from the concentration of individual interests and cartelization. Their deficiencies as agent for the individual employee result from the standardization of solutions they offer—by which, on the other hand, they also may mediate between heterogeneous employees' interests—[93] and from the focus on the interests of those whom they represent. The standardization is likely to be over- or under-inclusive, depending on the individual interests and the individual 'strength' or market power. In any event, (mandatory) collective regulation is by definition heteronomous, thus infringing with the individual's self-determination.[94] A focus on, usually, those who are currently employed will often go at the expense of the unemployed. Or, conversely, taking into account of the labour market at large (including the unemployed) may go beyond the unions' mandate.

Legislators and courts, too, have their deficits as agents of the employees. Again, employment protection is put in place for those who are employed and not for the unemployed. Protection of the employed makes entry into employment more difficult for the unemployed. Where courts view themselves as adjudicators who follow the mandate of the law, they will (inevitably) reinforce the same tendency.

i. Substantive and procedural regulation

While substantive rules provide for regulation on a given level, procedural rules do so to a lesser extent, providing only for a framework within which collectives or individuals may make their own rules.[95] The framework may be more or less

[91] E. Fehr, G Kirchsteiger, and A. Riedl, 'Does Fairness Prevent Market Clearing? An Experimental Investigation' (1993) 108 *Quarterly Journal of Economics* 437–60.

[92] U. Gneezy and J. A. List, 'Putting Behavioral Economics to Work: Testing for Gift Exchange in Labor Markets Using Field Experiments' (2006) 74 *Econometrica* 1365–84.

[93] A parallel function of mediator is attributed to the (supervisory) board: see, for instance, the description by P. Davies, 'Board Structure in the UK and Germany: Convergence or Continuing Divergence?' (2000) 4 *International and Comparative Corporate Law Journal* 435–6, 450–5; E.-J. Mestmäcker, *Verwaltung, Konzerngewalt und Rechte der Aktionäre—eine Rechtsvergleichende Untersuchung nach Deutschem Aktienrecht und dem Recht der Corporations in den Vereinigten Staaten*, (Karlsruhe: C.F. Müller, 1958) 81ff; C. Steinbeck, *Überwachungspflicht und Einwirkungsmöglichkeiten des Aufsichtsrats in der Aktiengesellschaft* (Berlin: Dunker & Humblot, 1992) 45–54; this is common ground in comparative law (even if the board member represents a certain group of shareholders or even employees and has been nominated by that group): Wymeersch, n 27, 1079, 1091, 1132ff.

[94] Picker, n 88, 353, 359ff.

[95] For a discussion of different regulatory approaches, see Collins (2010) n 55, 27ff. On 'proceduralization', also discussing the impact of procedural rules on substance, see J.-H. Binder, '*Prozeduralisierung und* Corporate Governance' (2007) *Zeitschrift für Unternehmens- und Gesellschaftsrecht (ZGR)* 745–88.

rigid, providing for a guardrail, a (perhaps 'threatening') 'shadow of the law'[96], an incentive, or a 'nudge'[97].

We have already discussed employee participation in the European Company in the context of public and private levels of governance.[98] It may also be considered from the angle of substantive and procedural regulation. EU employment legislation more often uses procedural elements. So, for example, the European Works Council Directive[99] leaves prior agreements in place and was, indeed, the first directive to provide for a negotiation model. The Information and Consultation Framework Directive, too, leaves room for agreements of different 'practical arrangements'. The Temporary Agency Work Directive provides for a mechanism to accommodate both employee protection and freedom of contract for collective agreements. Collective agreements may provide for less favourable treatment provided that they respect 'the overall protection of temporary agency workers' installed by the directive. The regulatory mechanism thus combines a broad range of freedom with a 'global' control mechanism. While it thus maintains flexibility, the obvious drawback is that the global standard of control is rather diffuse and difficult to predict, leading to legal uncertainty.

j. Complexity—of life and of regulation

Complex issues may require complex rules—or simple rules.[100] In the EU, rules appear to become increasingly complex, in particular taking into account the levels of regulation. New governance structures have to be evaluated with a view to existing structures, in particular with a view to an increasing complexity.

An increasingly prominent example is fundamental rights. Originally, the EEC (as it then was called) primary law did not provide for a catalogue of written fundamental rights. The situation was thus that the German Federal Constitutional Court, in its famous *Solange I* decision, declared that 'as long as' (*solange*) Community law did not provide for protection of fundamental rights, it would exert its own control under the German Constitution (the Basic Law, *Grundgesetz*, of 1949).[101] After the European Court of Justice in its jurisprudence developed fundamental rights as so-called general principles of EC law, the *Bundesverfassungsgericht*, in 1986, declared that it would not use its fundamental rights control as long as the Community maintained a standard of protection that

[96] R. Mnookin and L. Kornhauser, 'Bargaining in the Shadow of the Law: The Case of Divorce' (1979) 88 *Yale Law Journal* 950–97.

[97] R. H. Thaler and C. R. Sunstein, *Nudge: Improving Decisions About Health, Wealth, and Happiness* (New Haven: Yale University Press, 2008).

[98] See Section III(3)(d).

[99] Directive 2009/38/EC of the European Parliament and of the Council of 6 May 2009 on the establishment of a European Works Council or a procedure in Community-scale undertakings and Community-scale groups of undertakings for the purposes of informing and consulting employees (Recast) (OJ 2009 L 122/28).

[100] R. A. Epstein, *Simple Rules for a Complex World* (Cambridge, Mass: Harvard University Press, 1995).

[101] Federal Constitutional Court ('*Bundesverfassungsgericht*', '*BVerfG*'), *BVerfGE* 37, 271.

was substantially equivalent to that of the Basic Law (*Solange II*).[102] While the 1989 Charter of Fundamental Social Rights was rather a political declaration than a binding legal instrument ('solemn press release'), the Charter of Fundamental Rights of 2000 has, since the 2009 Lisbon Treaty acquired the binding force status of EU primary law (Article 6(1)(1) of the Treaty on European Union (TEU)). Next to the fundamental rights as general principles and the fundamental rights of the Charter, there is further the provision of Article 6(3) of the TEU pursuant to which fundamental rights, as guaranteed by the European Convention for the Protection of Human Rights and Fundamental Freedoms (ECHR) and as they result from the constitutional traditions common to the Member States, constitute general principles of the Union's law. So even on the level of EU law, there is a multitude of three distinct collections of fundamental rights, the (simple) general principles as developed by the Court; the ECHR fundamental rights, applicable as general principles; and the Charter fundamental rights. Next, there remain the fundamental rights of the national constitutions. And all Member States are, of course, also party to the ECHR so that its fundamental rights apply here as well. Finally, the EU has committed itself to acceding to the ECHR under Article 6(2) of the TEU. The multitude of regimes certainly may have its merit. So, for example, there may be good reason for installing an outside control so that the Member States or the Union may be subject to supervision by the ECHR (although, of course, that displays distrust in the constitutional courts). Yet, there are evident limits to control of control. And there is a downside to it, too. A multitude of regimes of fundamental rights and of *fora* for their control opens room for manoeuvring: for cherry picking with a view to the fundamental rights sources or with a view to procedural issues. The multitude of sources may also invalidate the opt-out of Poland and the UK to the solidarity-rights of Title IV of the Charter.[103] Indeed, it has been pointed out that in *Viking* and *Laval*, the Court refers to the Charter of Fundamental Rights—but not exclusively—leaving room for founding the right to strike on, say, general principles of EU law as well which would then be sufficient as a source for this right and thus make it applicable to these countries as well.[104]

Anti-discrimination laws are another example. The irregularity that the principle of equal pay for men and women is provided for in Article 157 of the TFEU and thus in the 'constitution' of the EU has historical reasons. Yet, this has not been changed, irrespective of the fact that the Court has subsequently substituted the original economic rationale (competitive disadvantage of French business) to one of social policy.[105] With the invention of a fundamental right against age

[102] Federal Constitutional Court ('*Bundesverfassungsgericht*', '*BVerfG*'), *BVerfGE* 73, 339.

[103] Cf Protocol on the Application of the Charter of Fundamental Rights of the European Union to Poland and to the UK.

[104] A. C. L. Davies, 'One Step Forward, Two Steps Back? The *Viking* and *Laval* Cases in the ECJ' (2008) 38 *Industrial Law Journal* 126, 138.

[105] Case 43/75 *Defrenne II* [1976] ECR 455 para 12; Case C-17/05 *Cadman* [2006] ECR I-9583 para 28; Joined Cases C-270/97 and C-271/97 *Sievers and Schrage* [2000] ECR] I-929 paras 53–7; Case C-256/01 *Allonby* [2004] ECR I-873 para 65. For a critical discussion, see Riesenhuber, n 56, § 9 para 1.

discrimination as a general principle of EU law in *Mangold*,[106] the Court has cemented this development—and, to a certain degree, insulated it from interference by the legislator.[107] This is particularly noteworthy as the issue of age discrimination often involves difficult decisions of social policy—[108] decisions that are best left to the legislator. The Court has, though, stopped short of recognizing more extravagant prohibitions of discrimination as general principles of EU law when confronted with the issue of discrimination on grounds of 'socio-professional category or place of work'.[109]

In EU contract law, the directive has thus far been the central instrument of contract governance (governance of contract law).[110] As a matter of legislative technique, the instrument of a directive warrants revision as does the cooperation of the Court of Justice and national courts. Article 288(3) of the TFEU states that '[A] directive shall be binding, as to the result to be achieved, upon each Member State to which it is addressed, but shall leave to the national authorities the choice of form and method.' It is thus an instrument of multi-level legislation. The idea seems captivating: let the central authority spell out the principles and the decentralized authorities make the rules. But first of all, that is not how it works in practice. Directives tend not to leave much room at all for interpretation by the Member States. But things get more complicated when it comes to implementation and application. Initially, interpretation and judicial development of directives follow their own rules. The multiplicity of language versions and a lack of common legal culture are two factors that make things complicated. Implementation of the rules is not enough. The principles of equivalence and of effectiveness supplement the specified rules of a directive, together with the *effet utile*, resulting in sometimes far-reaching—though not easy to foresee—consequences. And irrespective of the general concept of legislation in two steps, directives may under certain conditions be directly applicable, though only as against the Member States. The Court has, so far, resisted the temptation of recognizing a direct horizontal effect.[111] But it has developed an obligation to construe the national law of the Member States in conformity with the wording and *telos* of the directive. While the theoretical development is clear enough, practical complication and confusion is unavoidable. This is certainly true for individuals subject to the rights and obligations determined by a directive, but also for national courts. Thus, for example, the limits of the obligation of interpretation

[106] Case C-144/04 *Mangold* [2005] ECR I-9981.

[107] For a critical discussion, see Riesenhuber, n 58, 62–71.

[108] See A. G. Geelhoed, Opinion of 16 March 2006: Case C-13/05 *Chacón Navas,* 2006 ECR I-6467, paras 46–56.

[109] Case C-310/10 *Agafiţei* [2011] ECR I-5989.

[110] See the survey in S. Grundmann, *Europäisches Schuldvertragsrecht* (Berlin: de Gruyter, 1999). Notable exceptions (now) are the meta-rules on the applicable law in the Rome-Regulations and the Group Exemption Regulations in EU competition law.

[111] See recently Case C-227/09 *Accardo* [2010] ECR I-10273, paras 45ff; Joined Cases C-397/01 to C-403/01 *Pfeiffer* [2004] ECR I-8835 paras 108ff; Case C-168/95 *Arcaro* [1996] ECR I-4705 para 36; Case C-192/94 *El Corte Inglés* [1996] ECR I-1281 para 16; Case C-91/92 *Faccini Dori* [1994] ECR I-3325 par. 20.

of national law in conformity with a directive are uncertain both on the EU level and on the national level. But this is not the end of it. Where collective agreements are used to implement a directive, there is yet another level involved. To be sure, the collective agreement then replaces the legislation. But the obligation of the social partners vis-à-vis the Member State does not relieve the latter from its obligations in relation to the Union.[112]

4. Constructivism and evolution

Discussing even a few issues of governance makes us cautious and humble. Governance raises a multiplicity of complex issues and requires an interdisciplinary approach. Yet, in many areas, an *ex ante* full-scale investigation into the issues involved from every angle concerned will arguably not be feasible (or not in this life). The example of Akerlof's remuneration theory[113] which has triggered a decade-long debate is sobering. More often than not, though, governance regimes are not created from a clean slate or at a clerk's desk. Instead, they evolve over years in practice in a procedure of trial and error. The example also illustrates the importance of a factual analysis. It is not by accident that 'empirical legal studies' have gained considerable weight in academic debate in recent years. Indeed, empirical studies have to be considered an important tool in the governance discussion as well.

With Hayek, we should be wary of a constructivist approach to regulation.[114] Regulatory restraint finds its basis also in respect for individual liberty. Moreover, the knowledge of the (state as) regulator is inevitably restricted. Contract governance, however, can help overcome both concerns to some extent. In the first place, contract governance is based on consensus. Rather than restricting individual liberty, it is based on individual decisions. Secondly, contract governance takes advantage of private information. Depending upon the circumstances, such information may well be superior to the knowledge of the legislator, namely with respect to very specific or particularly innovative subjects of regulation.[115] On the other hand, however, private parties are for many reasons not necessarily in the best position to regulate themselves. It is therefore important to find an equilibrium between state-made, mandatory regulation, and private, contractual governance. Hence the real challenge lies at a meta-level and consists in designing a framework that allows for such equilibrium, restricting private autonomy (only) insofar as necessary while enabling private rule-making where adequate. In the

[112] Case 143/83 *Commission v. Germany* [1985] ECR 427; Case 235/84 *Commission v. Italy* [1986] ECR 2291.

[113] See Section III(3)(h)

[114] F. A. v. Hayek, *Law, Legislation and Liberty* (London/Henley: Routledge & Kegan Paul, 1973, 1976, 1979).

[115] See, for instance, W. Hoffmann-Riem, *Die Governance-Perspektive in der rechtswissenschaftlichen Innovationsforschung* (Baden-Baden: Nomos, 2011) 31–3: more specifically with respect to corporate law, see J. -H. Binder, *Regulierungsinstrumente und Regulierungsstrategien im Kapitalgesellschaftsrecht* (Tübingen: Mohr Siebeck, 2012).

long-run, such a framework needs to be open for new, potentially better regulatory solutions. It must allow for evolution and innovation of norms, triggered by a dialogue between public and private rule-setters.[116] Designing such a framework requires not only legal skills, but also insights from many other sciences – economics, sociology, behavioural sciences.[117] Sure enough, there is reason to believe that *Orgel's* second law prevails: 'Evolution is cleverer than you are.'[118]

IV. Multitude of Disciplines—An Equilibrium in Law

Governance—and contract governance in particular—is a quintessentially interdisciplinary endeavour. Governance provides a conceptual bridge that facilitates the dialogue across disciplinary borders.[119] Even more, governance theory draws on insights from various behavioural sciences like sociological, political, and economic theory but also neurological and evolutionary sciences.[120] Governance therefore provides a helpful tool for legal academics to learn from other disciplines. At times, traditional contract law scholarship may have taken other disciplines into account as well, be it as auxiliary tools or as standards of comparison.[121] For contract governance, however, such interdisciplinary exchange and dialogue is no less than a core element—a plea to apply them as systematically as possible. Of course, most institutions that are relevant for governance research are designed by (legal) rules, and therefore legal scholarship plays a central role. Yet, governance theory does not limit itself to analysing the structure of such rules. The perspective on contractual and legal rules widens. In addition to the usual *ex post* perspective on concluded events, it takes an *ex ante* view: contract governance understands rules not only as an instrument of dispute resolution, but

[116] In detail, with respect to default rules, see F. Möslein, n 51, 2861, 2869–73; see also K. Pistor, *et al*, 'Innovation in Corporate Law' (2003) 31 *Journal of Comparative Economics* 676.

[117] Recently, in a similar vein, see S. Deakin, 'Legal Evolution—Integrating Economic and Systemic Approaches', (2011) 7 *Review of Law & Economics* 659–83; see also P. Zumbansen and G. -P. Calliess (eds) *Law, Economics and Evolutionary Theory* (Cheltenham: Edward Elgar Publishing, 2010).

[118] Named after the British chemist Leslie E. Orgel (1927–2007) and attributed to the British physicist and biochemist Francis H. C. Crick (1916–2004).

[119] K. van Kersbergen and F. van Waarden, 'Governance as a bridge between disciplines' (2004) 43 *European Journal of Political Research* 143–71; G. F. Schuppert, '*Governance im Spiegel der Wissenschaftsdisziplinen*' in K. van Kersbergen and F. van Waarden (eds) *Governance-Forschung: V ergewisserung über Stand und Entwicklungslinien* (Baden-Baden: Nomos, 2nd edn, 2006) 373ff; in a similar vein, see O. Williamson, 'The Institutions of Governance' (1998) 88 *American Economic Review* 75 ('interdisciplinary undertaking'). (*Werkstattgespräch aus Anlass des 60. Geburtstags von Eberhard Schmidt-Aßmann*), 103ff.

[120] See, for instance, P. Zumbansen, 'Governance from an Interdisciplinary Perspective' in David Levi-Faur (ed) *Oxford Handbook on Governance* (Oxford: Oxford University Press, 2012) with a view on corporate governance in particular see S. Deakin and A. Hughes, 'Comparative Corporate Governance: An Interdisciplinary Agenda' (1997) 24 *Journal of Law and Society* 11–9.

[121] Generally on 'plurality of methods as a challenge' (translation by the authors) see S. Grundmann, '*Methodenpluralismus als Aufgabe*' (1997) 61 *RabelsZ* 423ff.

also as a mechanism for steering and coordinating human behaviour.[122] Hence the governance perspective focusses on the steering effects of rules, necessarily taking into account the reactions of its addressees.[123] The impact of such reactions depends on the character of the rules in question: the less hierarchical and mandatory, the more consensual and contractual the character of these rules, the more important the reactions of addressees for their very effectiveness. Human behaviour therefore plays a crucial role for the understanding, analysis and design of contract governance structures.

Once this interplay between rules and behaviour has been described in some more detail,[124] the need for a dialogue with different behavioural sciences becomes obvious. Behavioural sciences provide models of human behaviour and therefore allow certain predictions about human reactions to specific rules. Contrary to a widespread assumption in the law and economics literature, behavioural sciences provide not just one, but various models of behaviour, differing in their assumptions and also in their predictions. Namely in view of rule-oriented behaviour, it seems paramount to take these differences into account. Contract governance theory therefore needs to draw on insights from a wide range of different behavioural sciences.[125] More importantly, it needs to build on these lessons, taking them into account when conceptualizing legal and extra-legal rules, when predicting their steering effects, but also when designing the architecture of contract governance. Law, legal scholarship, and rule-setting therefore need to bring insights of various behavioural sciences into a specific equilibrium, considering and weighing their respective impact for every single regulatory context. The challenge is not just the application of these insights, but—ideally—translation and even informed choice between approaches—with a view to the institutional and factual settings encountered. This need becomes particularly obvious whenever governance faces phenomena that transcend the bilateral privity of spot contracts—in herding, networks and long-term contracts, the core features taken up in parts 2–4 later in this Section. Nevertheless, these insights are equally essential for contract law rule-setting in general—with basically the same overall challenge.[126]

1. Governance: regulatory structures and human behaviour

Governance is about regulatory structures and human behaviour. Let us consider both aspects in turn. First, contract governance is about regulatory structures, consisting of legal as well as extra-legal rules. Generally speaking, governance is understood as the entirety of various collective impacts on a

[122] Möslein and Riesenhuber, n 1, 248, 257.

[123] For a survey on the term 'governance' S. Burries, M. Kempa, and C. Shearing, 'Changes in Governance: A Cross-Disciplinary Review of Current Scholarship' (2008) 41 *Akron Law Review* 1, 7–12; A. M. Kjaer, *Governance* (Cambridge: Polity Press, 2004) 3–7, with further references; J. Pierre, 'Introduction: Understanding Governance' in J. Pierre (ed) *Debating Governance* (Oxford: Oxford University Press, 2002) 1, 3ff; O.E. Williamson, 'The Economics of Governance' (2005) 95 *American Economic Review* 1.

[124] See Section IV(1). [125] See Section IV(2). [126] See Section IV(3).

social system.[127] The focus is primarily on institutions that shape and coordinate human behaviour. Such institutions largely consist of rules, be they formal or informal, legal or social, strict or flexible. With respect to contracts, rules at various levels shape the regulatory structure that may ultimately have an impact on individual behaviour.[128] At the very top, the institutional framework for contract law rule-making consists mainly of constitutional rules, providing for procedural and substantive guidelines for designing contract law (governance of contract law). At a second level, contract law rules form an institutional framework that influences private contracting (governance by contract law). Contractual arrangements require this infrastructure of contract law, but to some extent, they are also influenced by this 'shadow of contract law'.[129] Contract law may thirdly pursue regulatory goals, steering individual behaviour (governance by means of contract law). Finally, contracts themselves provide an institutional framework, guiding and coordinating the future behaviour of the contracting parties. Therefore contracts are part of the regulatory structure of contract governance as well, even though they are provided by private parties, not by legislative bodies (governance by contract).

Secondly, contract governance is about human behaviour. One of the key elements of governance theory is its focus on how human actors make decisions, on their incentives as well as their utility functions, and on the feedback mechanisms between institutions and behaviour.[130] While political and economic steering such as the 'dirigisme' of the 1970s—which understood control and regulation of a country's economy and social institutions by the state as far-reaching—has largely proven unsuccessful[131] and led to a veritable steering crisis of law (*steuerungskrise des rechts*),[132] the idea of governance changed the perspective. Rather than systematically distinguishing between the state and private actors as subject and objects of such steering attempts, governance theory takes into account the interplay between the two, and thereby focuses on the interaction between

[127] J. Köndgen, '*Privatisierung des Rechts*' (2006) 206 *Archiv für die ivilistische Praxis* 477, 514, following the approach of M. Hill and P. Hupe, *Implementing Public Policy - Governance in Theory and in Practice* (London: Sage, 2002) 13ff. See also text accompanying n 4.

[128] More extensively on these different levels Möslein and Riesenhuber, n 1, 248–89.

[129] Mnookin and Kornhauser, n 96, 950–97; see also K. Riesenhuber, '*Schatten des Rechts – Contract Governance und Governance der Vertragsverhandlungen bei der SE-Mitbestimmung*' in S. Grundmann, B. Haar, H. Merkt, *et al* (eds) *Festschrift for Klaus Hopt* (Berlin: de Gruyter, 2010), 1225–43.

[130] Similar with respect to corporate governance, R. Gilson, 'Corporate Governance and Economic Efficiency: When Do Institutions Matter' (1996) 74 *Washington University Law Quarterly* 327.

[131] In detail G. -P. Calliess, *Prozedurales Recht* (Baden-Baden: Nomos, 1999) 60–83; G. Teubner, '*Das regulatorische Trilemma – Zur Diskussion um Postinstrumentale Rechtsmodelle*' (1984) 13 *Quaderni Fiorentini per la Storia del Pensiero Giuridico Moderno* 60, 120-132; see also Chr Engel, '*Rationale Rechtspolitik und ihre Grenzen*' (2005) *Juristenzeitung* 581, 583–9.

[132] With respect to private law recently G. -P. Calliess, '*Die Steuerungskrise - jetzt auch im Privatrecht?*' in G. -P. Calliess, A. Fischer-Lescano, D. Wilsch, and P. Zumbansen (eds) *Solziologische Jurisprudenz – Festschrift for Gunther Teubner* (Berlin: de Gruyter, 2009) 465–479; see also E. Schmidt-Aßmann, '*Gefährdungen der Rechts- und Gesetzesbindung der Exekutive*' in J. Burmester (ed) *Festschrift for Klaus Stern* (München: C.H. Beck, 1997) 745, 748–50.

institutions (rules) and individual behaviour.[133] In order to analyse this interaction, and to assess the impact and effectiveness of specific rules and regulatory structures, understanding human behaviour is fundamental.

The impact of human behaviour is even greater where the rules in question are not mandatory, strict and hierarchical in character, but optional, flexible, and driven by mutual consent. In other words, the softer the regulatory structure, the more important the reactions of private actors for understanding the functionality of the governance framework.[134] This is because the impact of rules that allow for (certain) deviations is potentially limited. It depends on private actors following these rules at least to some extent, despite their margin of choice. While non-hierarchical rules are typical for governance in general, contract governance is particularly driven by mutual consent.[135] In this perspective, contract governance is an extreme and very 'pure' form of governance, namely if one follows Williamson's perception of the approach which implicitly and partly also explicitly favours the autonomous arrangements set up by the parties themselves. Such consent-dependency is, of course, obvious with respect to governance through contract, requiring the formation of a contract and therefore being literally built on mutual consent. However, mutual consent is equally important for governance by (means of) contract law. This area of law typically consists of default rules that are open for deviations by the parties.[136] If parties are able to contract around default rules, however, law-makers need to take their expected contracting behaviour into account when drafting them. 'By enacting a default rule to govern a contingency, then, lawmakers implicitly render a determination that the desires of the parties to a transaction will be permitted to take precedence over other policy concerns.'[137] As a consequence, parties' preferences, their (hypothetical) consent and their contracting behaviour in general are widely regarded as a yardstick for default rules in contract law.[138] More generally, the contract governance framework cannot be understood without analysing the behaviour of private parties. If they follow certain contract law rules blindly, without even thinking about contracting around them, but also if they take it only as a reference point, default rules become much more influential and can be designed much more

[133] More extensively, see F. Möslein, n 51, 2861, 2875ff.

[134] For a (purely economical) discussion of the impact of soft law on individual behaviour see, for instance, J. Gersen and E. Posner, 'Soft Law: Lessons from Congressional Practice' (2008) 61 *Stanford Law Review* 573, 586–99.

[135] Möslein and Riesenhuber, n 1, 248, 258, 260; K. Riesenhuber, n 38, 61–83, 64.

[136] See, e.g., I. Ayres and R. Gertner, 'Filling Gaps in Incomplete Contracts: An Economic Theory of Default Rules' (1989) 99 *Yale Law Journal* 87; R. Craswell, 'Contract Law, Default Rules, and the Philosophy of Promising' (1989) 88 *Michigan Law Review* 489; A. Schwartz, 'The Default Rule Paradigm and the Limits of Contract Law' (1993) 3 *Southern California Interdisciplinary Law Journal* 389.

[137] R. Korobkin, 'The Status Quo Bias and Contract Default Rules' (1998) 83 *Cornell Law Review* 608, 611.

[138] Often quoted, for instance, Justice Oliver Wendell Holmes in *Globe Refining Co. v. Landa Cotton Oil Co.*, 190 U.S. 540, 543 (1903): '[A]s people when contracting contemplate performance, not breach, they commonly say little or nothing as to what shall happen in the latter event, and thus the common rules have been worked out by common sense, *which has established what the parties probably would have said if they had spoken about the matter*' (emphasis added).

autonomously by the law-maker.[139] Hence the power of default rules ultimately depends on contracting behaviour.[140] Even at the level of governance of contract law, mutual consent and individual behaviour play a certain role. In times that are often described as an 'era of negotiated law',[141] the institutional framework for contract law rule-making itself becomes subject to private actors' choices and preferences, at least to some extent. Parties can—and increasingly do—choose between different national contract laws, or between national and supranational contract laws (like the Uniform International Sales Law or a potential future Common European Sales Law).[142] If contract law as a whole becomes optional, understanding parties' choices is even more essential. In short, Contract Governance, the institutional matrix in which contractual transactions are negotiated and executed,[143] cannot be understood without taking into account human behaviour.

2. Insights from social and behavioural sciences

Contract governance therefore requires interdisciplinary research. While legal scholarship tells us much about regulatory structures, it lacks a specific model of human behaviour. What is therefore required is a more intensive dialogue with other disciplines—not just economics, but social sciences more generally, in particular sciences of human behaviour, including neurobiology.[144] Governance not only provides for a common language which greatly facilitates this dialogue,[145] but even 'offers a unique opportunity for the social sciences to have a meeting point, if not for reunification, after their separation over a century ago.'[146] While the institutional matrix consists largely of contractual and legal rules, its functioning cannot be understood by legal scholarship alone. Contract governance may provide a tool to take advantage of much-needed insights from other disciplines. Default rules, situated at the meso-level of contract governance, may serve as a preliminary illustration for the potential of such interdisciplinary dialogue.[147] By way of example, we will therefore address default rules several times.

[139] In this sense R. Korobkin, n 137, 608, 675, concluding that the '[l]awmakers' choice of default terms is likely to affect contracting parties' preferences for substantive contract terms.'

[140] See extensively Möslein, n 51.

[141] M. Mekki and M. Kloepfer-Pelèse, 'Good Faith and Fair Dealing in the DCFR' (2008) *European Review of Contract Law* 338, 341; in a similar vein, see S. Chassagnard-Pinet and D. Hiez (eds) *Approche Critique de la Contractrualisation* (Paris: L.G.D.J., 2007); Ph. Gérard, F. Ost, and M. de van Kerchove (eds) *Droit Négocié, Droit Imposé?* (Paris: L.G.D.J., 1996).

[142] For a recent account, see H. Eidenmüller, 'The Transnational Law Market, Regulatory Competition, and Transnational Corporations' (2011) 18 *Indiana Journal of Global Legal Studies* 707.

[143] See n 2.

[144] F. Möslein, 'The Focus of Regulatory Reforms in Europe after the Global Financial Crisis: from Corporate to Contract Governance' in W. Sun, J. Stewart, and D. Pollard (eds) *Corporate Governance and the Global Financial Crisis* (Cambridge: Cambridge University Press, 2011) 284, 294.

[145] See references at n 119.

[146] A. Dixit, 'Governance Institutions and Economic Activity' (2009) 99 *American Economic Review* 5, 6.

[147] In much more detail on this example see Möslein, n 51.

a. Economics

Economics provides for a specific, widely-used model of human behaviour, the so-called *homo oeconomicus*.[148] This model corresponds with the theory of rational choice.[149] It is based on the assumption that actors want to maximize their own utility. However, their ability to make rational decisions is limited by various restrictions, for example with respect to money, time, and knowledge.[150] All possible options are evaluated according to subjective preferences. Conceptually, restrictions and preferences need to be strictly dissociated. Legal and contractual norms, however, cannot always be firmly allocated to one of these two categories. While one could well imagine legal rules and even self-imposed standards as restrictions,[151] norms can also be internalized, thereby potentially modifying individual preferences.[152] According to the traditional concept of rational behaviour, however, preferences need to comply with certain formal requirements. These requirements are designed in order to safeguard falsifiability and testability of the behavioural model.[153] However, insofar as stable preferences are postulated, the possibility of internalizing new norms and social learning in general is severely limited.[154] In any event, to decide rationally means to choose the option that maximizes subjective utility. Given that information about future events is limited, this decision has to be taken under uncertainty, on the basis of expected benefits.[155]

[148] G. Kirchgässner, *Homo Oeconomicus: The Economic Model of Behaviour and Its Applications in Economics and Other Social Sciences* (St. Gallen: Springer, 2008).

[149] For a comprehensive introduction, see I. Gilboa, *Rational Choice* (Cambridge: MIT Press, 2010)

[150] To the point is G. Buchanan, *The Economics and the Ethics of Constitutional Order* (Ann Arbor: University of Michigan Press, 1991) 5: 'Without scarcity, there would be no need to choose'; see also G. Becker, 'Nobel Lecture: The Economic Way of Looking at Good Behavior' (1993) 101 *Journal of Political Economy* 385, 386.

[151] See J. Elster, *Ulysses and the Sirens* (Cambridge: Cambridge University Press, 1984); J. Elster, *Ulysses unbound* (Cambridge: Cambridge University Press, 2000).

[152] J. Cross, *A Theory of Adaptive Economic Behaviour* (Cambridge: Cambridge University Press, 1983); R. Heiner, 'The Origin of Predictable Behavior' (1983) 73 *American Economic Review* 560–95 and already F. Knight, 'The Limitations of Scientific Method in Economics' in R. Tugwell (ed) *The Trend of Economics* (New York: Alfred A. Knopf, 1924) 229, 229: 'Life is at bottom an exploration in the field of values, an attempt to discover values, rather than on the basis of knowledge of them to produce and enjoy them to the greatest possible extent.'

[153] Ground-breaking and in more detail, see J. v. Neumann and O. Morgenstern, *Theory of Games and Economic Behavior* (Princeton, NJ: Princeton University Press, 3rd edn, 1953) 73–6; see also H. Eidenmüller, '*Der Homo Oeconomicus und das Schuldrecht: Herausforderungen durch* Behavioral Law and Economics' (2005) *Juristenzeitung* 216, 217.

[154] Rather sceptical, for instance, L. Kornhauser, 'The New Economic Analysis of Law: Legal Rules as Incentives' in N. Mercuro (ed) *Law and Economics* (Boston: Kluwer Academic Publishing, 1989) 27, 28–32; see also R. Cooter, 'Dezentralized Law for a Complex Economy: The Strutural Approach to Adjudicating the New Law Merchant' (1996) 144 *University of Pennsylvania Law Review* 1643, 1661ff; R. E. Scott, 'The Limits of Behavioral Theories of Law and Social Norms' (2000) 86 *Virginia Law Review* 1603, 1637.

[155] This concept ultimately goes back to D. Bernoulli, '*Specimen Theoriae Novae de Mensura Sortis*' (1738) 5 *Commentarii Academiae Scientiarum Imperialis Petropolitanae* 175, translated by L. Sommer, 'Exposition of a New Theory on the Measurement of Risk' (1954) 22 *Econometrica* 22–36.

Applying this behavioural model to the example of default rules shows that utility-maximizing actors will agree on contracting around the default rule if one single actor can be better off without making anyone else worse off (*pareto optimality*).[156] According to Coase's theorem, rational actors will tend to allocate property rights by contractual agreement in a way that maximizes their subjective utility and provides for an efficient outcome.[157] These actors will therefore contract around default rules whenever deviating arrangements are more efficient. As a consequence, the substance of such default rules proves to be irrelevant.[158] However, this theorem depends on specific assumptions, namely on the escapist proposition that no transaction costs arise.[159] Taking into account such transaction costs, default rules gain importance. Nevertheless, in this perspective default rules can only be legitimated if they facilitate efficient transactions, reducing their cost. According to the behavioural model of economics, default rules should therefore imitate the hypothetical consent of the parties concerned.[160] Generally speaking, *homo oeconomicus* will contract around the default whenever this increases his subjective utility.

b. Sociology

Sociology provides another model of behaviour. Entirely different from the forces which drive the *homo oeconomicus* are those driving the so-called *homo sociologicus*.[161] 'The former is 'pulled' by the prospect of future rewards, whereas the latter is 'pushed' from behind by quasi-inertial forces.'[162] Hence external circumstances

[156] V. Pareto, *Manual of Political Economy* (New York: Augustus M. Kelly, 1971 (originally 1897)); more extensively, for instance H. Gravelle and R. Rees, *Microeconomics* (Harlow: Pearsons Education Limited, 3rd edn, 2004) 290–2; H. Eidenmüller, *Effizienz als Rechtsprinzip* (Tübingen: Mohr Siebeck, 3rd edn, 2005) 48–50. However, the criterion does not decide whether a pareto-optimal state is socially desired or just: A. Sen, 'Markets and Freedom: Achievements and Limitations of the Market Mechanism in Promoting Individual Freedom' (1993) 42 *Oxford Economic Papers* 519, 521ff.

[157] R. Coase, 'The Problem of Social Cost' (1969) 3 *Journal of Law and Economics* 1–44.

[158] More extensively I. Ayres and R. Gertner, 'Strategic Contractual Inefficiency and the Optimal Choice of Legal Rules' (1992) 101 *Yale Law Journal* 729, 732 and 737–46; J. S. Johnston, 'Strategic Bargaining and the Economic Theory of Contract Default Rules' (1990) 100 *Yale Law Journal* 615, 624.

[159] Pointedly already Coase, n 157, 1, 8: 'The ultimate result (which maximises the value of production) is independent of the legal position if the pricing system is assumed to work without cost.'

[160] So-called 'majoritarian' or 'market-mimicking' default rules, see I. Ayres and R. Gertner, 'Majoritarian vs. Minoritarian Defaults' (1999) 51 *Stanford Law Review* 1591ff.; R. Craswell, 'Contract Law: General Theories' in B. Bouckaert and G. deGeest (eds) *Encyclopedia of Law and Economics*, vol 3 (Cheltenham: Edward Elgar Publishing, 2000) 1, 3–5; R. Posner, 'Economic Analysis of Contract Law After Three Decades: Success or Failure?' (2003) 112 *Yale Law Journal* 829, 839; H. Unberath and J. Cziupka, '*Dispositives Recht welchen Inhalts? Antworten der ökonomischen Analyse des Rechts*' (2009) 209 *Archiv der Civilistischen Praxis* 37, 48–63.

[161] This expression was coined by R. Dahrendorf, '*Homo Sociologicus. Ein Versuch zur Geschichte, Bedeutung und Kritik der Kategorie der sozialen Rolle*' (1958) 10 *Kölner Zeitschrift für Soziologie und Sozialpsychologie* 178–208, 345–78.

[162] J. Elster, 'Social Norms and Economic Theory' (1989) 3 *Journal of Economic Perspectives* 99; referring to the title of D. Gambetta, *Were they Pushed or did they Jump?* (Cambridge: Cambridge University Press, 1987).

serve as an aid to orientation. Behaviour therefore depends to a much greater extent on the social, moral, and legal context.

The social setting is regarded as the most important determinant for individual behaviour. It consists of '*faits sociaux*', composed of social values and rules of behaviour.[163] Legal rules can also rank among social facts, as long as deviations are sanctioned by negative social consequences (loss of reputation).[164] However, social facts prevail only in the framework of certain social relationships, sharing common values and moral conceptions. A second important component of the sociological model of behaviour concerns the placement of individual actors in the coordinate system of such social relationships. Social positions can be achieved on purpose, but they can also be ascribed without any effort of one's own.[165] Each social position is tied to specific role expectations to which individual actors see themselves exposed.[166] These actors are socially embedded.[167] However, they do not follow such expectations blindly. In a world full of uncertainty, compliant behaviour can reduce complexity and stabilize expectations.[168]

With respect to the example of default rules, *homo sociologicus* proves rather unresponsive to contracting around the default. According to the so-called normative paradigm, human behaviour is guided by role models and normative requirements.[169] Similar to the Coase theorem, however, this paradigm is also based on certain assumptions. Norms need to be sufficiently institutionalized in

[163] Ground-breaking in this respect is E. Durkheim, *The Rules of Sociological Method* (New York: Free Press, 1982; French language orig., 1895) 105–15.

[164] In this sense already, see E. Durkheim, '*La Science Positive de la Morale en Allemagne*' (1887) 24 *Revue Philosophique de la France et de l'étranger* 33–58, 113–42, 275–84, 278: '*les mœurs, les coutumes, les prescriptions du droit positif, les phénomènes économiques en tant qu'ils deviennent l'objet de dispositions juridiques*.'

[165] See R. Linton, *The Study of Man* (New York: Appleton Century Crofts, Inc, 1936) 115: '*Ascribed* statuses are those which are assigned to individuals without reference to their innate differences or abilities. They can be predicted and trained for from the moment of birth. The *achieved* statuses are, as a minimum, those requiring special qualities, although they are not necessarily limited to theses. They are not assigned to individuals from birth, but are left open to be filled through competition and individual effort.'

[166] On the idea of social positions, see also R. K. Merton, *Social Theory and Social Structure* (New York: The Free Press, 3rd edn, 1968) 390–440; S. F. Nadel, *The Theory of Social Structure* (London: Cohen & West, 1957) 20–44.

[167] The concept of embeddedness goes back to K. Polanyi, *The Great Transformation* (Frankfurt am Maim: Suhrkamp, 1978 (English language orig., 1944)) 75; path-breaking on this is M. Granovetter, 'Economic Action and Social Structure: The Problem of Embeddedness' (1985) 91 *American Journal of Sociology* 481, 506. On its prevalence see, for instance M. Guillén, R. Collins, P. England, and M. Meyer, 'The Revival of Economic Sociology' in M. Guillén, R. Collins, P. England, and M. Meyer (eds) *The New Economic Sociology: Developments in an Emerging Field* (New York: Russell Sage Foundation, 2005) 1, 4 ('economic sociology's most celebrated metaphor').

[168] In much more detail, see J. M. Barbalet, *Emotion, Social Theory, and Social Structure* (Cambridge: Cambridge University Press, 1998) 87ff; J. Beckert, '*Die Abenteuer der Kalkulation: Zur sozialen Einbettung ökonomischer Realität*' (2007) *Leviathan – Berliner Zeitschrift für Sozialwissenschaft* 295; see also N. Fligstein, *The Architecture of Markets* (Princeton, NJ: Princeton University Press, 2001): 'creation of stable worlds'; and N. Luhmann, *Vertrauen: Ein Mechanismus der Reduktion Sozialer Komplexität* (Stuttgart: UTB, 4th edn, 2000): 'mechanism to reduce social complexity'.

[169] On its origin (Talcot Parsons) and specifications, see T. Wilson, 'Normative and Interpretative Paradigms in Sociology' in J. Douglas (ed) *Understanding Everyday Life* (London: Routledge & Kegan Paul, 1971) 57ff.

order to establish identifiable expectations; they must also be sufficiently internalized in order to influence needs, goals, and attitudes of individual actors.[170] External institutions develop by circles of innovation, imitation and the creation of traditions, i.e. by a permanent process of socio-cultural objectification.[171] Internalization is effected by an adaptive process of trial and error.[172] As a consequence, only those rules that do not disappoint subjective expectations are internalized, but stand the test as an instrument for reducing uncertainty. Patterns of behaviour therefore develop in long-term individual and collective learning processes, driven by mechanisms of mutation and selection.[173]

c. *Behavioural sciences*

While these two models of behaviour seem to diverge significantly from each other, and perhaps even to be in diametrical contradiction to one other, both are theoretical models of social sciences, based on specific assumptions, focussing on specific interdependencies and thereby simplifying the complexity of human behaviour.[174] While specific outcomes of these models have been tested experimentally, they largely ignore the cognitive and neurobiological underpinnings of human behaviour. Behaviour, thinking, and choice are, however, outcomes that occur in the human brain.[175] It therefore seems important to take psychological and biological findings into account in order to understand how human decisions are made. Indeed, there is an emerging trend towards a biological science of making choices, integrating insights from cognitive psychology and neurobiology into economic, but also sociological models of behaviour.[176] In a similar vein, Kameda illustrates the relevance of

[170] On both components: S. Appelrouth and L. Edles, *Sociological Theory in the Contemporary Era* (Thousand Oaks: Pine Forge Press, 2010) 27ff; W. Sharrock, J. Hughes, and P. Martin, *Understanding Modern Sociology* (London: Sage Publications Ltd, 2003) 29–32.

[171] Similar P. Berger and T. Luckmann, *The Social Construction of Reality* (New York: First Anchor Book Editions, 1967) 54: 'Institutionalization occurs whenever there is a reciprocal typification of habitualized actions by types of actors. Put differently, any such typification is an institution.'

[172] In this sense Heiner, n 152, 560; V. Vanberg, 'Rational Choice, Rule-Following and Institutions: An Evolutionary Perspective' in U. Mäki, B. Gustafsson, and C. Knudsen (eds) *Rationality, Institutions and Economic Methodology* (Oxon/New York: Routledge, 1993) 171, 173; see also Cross, n 152, and Knight, n 152, 229.

[173] Cf D. Barash, *Sociobiology and Behaviour* (Oxford: Elsevier Science Ltd, 1977).

[174] These models are therefore aptly compare to searchlights, irradiating different and subject-specific aspects of human behaviour: K. Möslein, *Der Markt für Managementwissen* (München: Deutscher Universitäts-Verlag, 2005) 56–86 ('*Rationalitäts – und Fachdisziplin – Scheinwerfer*').

[175] D. Kahneman, 'Remarks on Neuroeconomics' in P. Glimcher, C. Camerer, E. Fehr, and R. Poldrack (eds) *Neuroeconomics – Decision Making and the Brain* (2009) 523.

[176] In economic literature see, for instance, P. Glimcher, *Decisions, Uncertainty, and the Brain* (2004); P. Politser, *Neuroeconomics* (2008) and the contributions in P. Glimcher, C. Camerer, E. Fehr, and R. Poldrack (eds) *Neuroeconomics – Decision Making and the Brain* (London: Elsevier, 2009) and D. Houser and K. McCabe (eds) *Neuroeconomics* (Bingley: Emerald Group Publishing Limited, 2008); in sociological literature, on the other hand, see L. Brothers, *Fridays' Footprint - How Society Shapes the Human Mind* (Oxford: Oxford University Press, 1997); M. Gazzaniga, *The Social Brain* (Jackson: Basic Books, 1985) as well as the contributions in J. Cacioppo, *et al* (eds) *Foundations in Social Neuroscience* (Cambridge: The MIT Press, 2002). The dialogue between

biological findings for understanding human behaviour, and Zumbansen qualifies contract governance as a conceptual bridge to improve our understanding of the relevant neural, psychological, and behavioural mechanisms.[177] Most interestingly, neuro-scientific findings underpin both of these seemingly contradictory models, rather than confirming one and discarding the other. By means of functional magnetic resonance imaging, one can localize brain activities for specific decisions. Decisions tend to be made in two different areas of the human brain, the amygdala and the orbital and medial prefrontal cortex, and they follow different patterns accordingly. For instance, a recent study shows that human choices are remarkably susceptible to the manner in which options are presented when decisions are taken in the amygdala, whereas orbital and medial prefrontal cortex activity predicted a reduced susceptibility to such framing effects.[178] In simple terms, the latter area of the brain would seem to follow the *homo oeconomicus* pattern of behaviour, whereas the former would seem to decide largely in accordance with the model of *homo sociologicus*.[179] With respect to the example of default rules, contracting around them seems much more likely in the first case than in the second. To find out whether one or the other mode of thinking prevails under specific circumstances, however, certainly requires additional research and interdisciplinary exchange. In any event, it is crucial to consider both approaches to decision-making, one fast, intuitive, and emotional, the other slower, more deliberative and more logical. In short, 'thinking, fast and slow' needs to be taken into account.[180]

d. Multidisciplinarity

Contract governance should likewise take both models of behaviour into account—and potentially even other disciplines as well. Rather than contradicting each other, these models are rooted in different research interests and perspectives:

> Sociologists typically accuse economics for inappropriately emphasising *choice* while ignoring the relevance of genuinely *rule- or norm-guided behaviour*, and economists tend to criticise sociology for its preoccupation with norms and rules while ignoring the relevance of *choice*.[181]

psychology and sociology started already much earlier, in the ground-breaking H. Gerth and C. Wright Mills, *Character and Social Structure* (New York: Harcourt Brace, 1953); see also J. Piaget, *Le Jugement Moral chez l'enfant* (Paris: Alcan, 1932); L. Kohlberg, *The Psychology of Moral Development* (New York: Joana Cotler Books, 1984).

[177] Chapter 2 and accompanying comment.

[178] B. de Martino, D. Kumaran, B. Seymour, and R. Dolan, 'Frames, Biases, and Rational Decision-Making in the Human Brain' (2006) 313 *Science* 684–7; likewise: R. J. Dolan, 'The Human Amygdala and Orbital Prefrontal Cortex in Behavioural Regulation' (2007) 362 *Philosophical Transactions of the Royal Society B* 787–99.

[179] In a similar sense J. Hewig, *et al*, 'Why Humans Deviate from Rational Choice' (2011) 48 *Psychophysiology* 507–14.

[180] D. Kahneman, *Thinking, Fast and Slow* (London: Penguin, 2011).

[181] V. Vanberg, 'Rules and Choice in Economics and Sociology' (1988) 7 *Jahrbuch für Neue Polöitische Ökonomie* 146, 147.

Yet both models interlock. While the economic model does not take into consideration how preferences originate, the sociological model does not analyse how humans behave in the absence of norms.[182] Both models therefore explain different aspects of human behaviour, and every human decision can be influenced by both kinds of rationality, but to different degrees. As a matter of course, economic and sociological theorists like von Hayek and Max Weber have taken both patterns of behaviour into account.[183] Today, behavioural and identity economics[184] as well as economic sociology[185] contribute to their integration, partly under the telling designation '*homo socioeconomicus*'.[186] All this speaks in favour of methodological pluralism. Rather than presuming one single model of behaviour, contract governance should therefore consider insights of different social and behavioural disciplines, taking advantage of its capacity as a conceptual bridge and meeting point. 'The recommendation is that, awaiting a unified theory, we should be accepting of pluralism.'[187] It may even be that pluralism will (and should) always remain.

[182] Similar, for instance, P. A. Hall and R.C.R. Taylor in K. Soltan, V. Haufler, and E. Uslaner (eds) *Institutions and Social Order* (Ann Arbor: University of Michigan Press, 1998) 15, 17ff ('calculus approach' and 'cultural approach').

[183] On the one hand, F. A. v. Hayek, *Studies in Philosophy, Politics and Economics* (London: Routledge and Kegan Paul, 1967) 56 ('But the rules of which we are speaking generally control or circumscribe only certain aspects of concrete actions by providing a general schema which is then adapted to the particular circumstances. They will often merely determine or limit the range of possibilities within which the choice is made consciously. By eliminating certain kinds of action altogether and by providing certain routine ways of achieving the object, they merely restrict the alternatives on which a conscious choice is required. The moral rules, for example, which have become part of a man's nature will mean that certain conceivable choices will not appear at all among the possibilities between which he chooses. Thus even decisions which have been carefully considered will in part be determined by rules of which the acting person is not aware'); on the other hand: M. Weber, *Wirtschaft und Gesellschaft* (Tübingen: Mohr Siebeck, 5th edn, 1980); *Economy and Society* (Berkeley: University of California Press, 1968) 26 ('It would be very unusual to find concrete cases of action, especially of social action, which were oriented only in one or another of these ways').

[184] On behavioural economics, at a glance C. F. Camerer, G. Loewenstein, and M. Rabin (eds) *Advances in Behavioral Economics* (Princeton, NJ: Princeton University Press, 2004); D. Kahneman and A. Tversky (eds) *Choices, Values, and Frames* (New York: Russell Sage Foundation, 2000); R. Sunstein (ed) *Behavioral Law & Economics* (Cambridge: Cambridge University Press, 2000); ground-breaking in this respect is H. A. Simon, *Homo Rationalis* (Frankfurt am Maim: Campus, 1983); on identity economics: G. Akerlof and R. Kranton, *Identity Economics* (Princeton, NJ: Princeton University Press, 2010); G. Akerlof and R. Kranton, 'Economics and Identity' (2000) 115 *Quarterly Journal of Economics* 715–53; B. D. Bernheim, 'A Theory of Conformity' (1994) 102 *Journal of Political Economy* 841–77; S. -K. Chai, *Choosing an Identity* (Ann Arbor: University of Michigan Press, 2001); D. Cooter, 'Do Good Laws Make Good Citizens? An Economic Analysis of Internalized Norms' (2000) 86 *Virginia Law Review* 1577; R. Frank, *Choosing the Right Pond* (Oxford: Oxford University Press, 1986) and S. Jones, *The Economics of Conformism* (Oxford: Blackwell Publisher, 1984).

[185] At a glance: J. Beckert and M. Zafirovski (eds) *International Encyclopedia of Economic Sociology* (London: Routledge, 2006); S. Granovetter and R. Swedberg, *The Sociology of Economic Life* (Boulder: Westview Press, 2nd edn, 2001); N. Smelser and R. Swedberg (eds) *The Handbook of Economic Sociology* (Princeton, NJ: Princeton University Press, 2nd edn, 2005).

[186] P. Weise, '*Homo Oeconomicus und Homo Sociologicus: Die Schreckensmänner der Sozialwissenschaften*' (1989) 18 *Zeitschrift für Soziologie* 148, 156; similar Vanberg, n 181, 146, 163–5 ('calculating *homo sociologicus*').

[187] O. Williamson, 'The New Institutional Economics: Taking Stock, Looking Ahead' (2000) 38 *Journal of Economic Literature* 595, 595.

3. Application to contract governance

a. An equilibrium of disciplines

The challenge of such integrated, multidisciplinary approach of contract governance consists in specifying the criteria that prove to be decisive for rule-related behaviour. A contract governance analysis needs to weigh these different criteria with respect to any single situation, in order to balance situation-specific equilibria of different methods, models, and disciplines. Empirical legal studies can help to carve out the relevant criteria.[188] While they are multi-layered and highly complex, three major factors stand out: transaction costs, ignorance, and autonomy of individual preferences.

First, compliance even with 'soft' regulatory structures seems more likely as the transaction costs of contracting around rise.[189] Such costs can arise as search and information costs (arising for figuring out or drafting alternative rules), as bargaining costs (arising for the respective consent with the other party), or as enforcement costs (arising for making sure that the other party sticks to the terms of the contract, and for taking appropriate action if this turns out not to be the case).[190] The amount of these costs depends on a multitude of different factors, for instance on the availability of alternative rules. Whenever standard forms are widely used for certain transactions, switching from public-made contract law to this private-made regime is possible at very low transaction cost and therefore very likely. Different factors with an impact on transaction cost may compensate each other. Certain factors may also be influenced by the legislator.[191] For example, to require potentially burdensome formalities for contracting around the default will increase transaction costs, so that private actors are more likely to stick to the standard regime.[192]

Ignorance of private actors is a second important factor. While neo-classical economic theory assumes that information is easily available and easily processable, information and behavioural economics highlight its limits, for instance information asymmetries or decision-making based on heuristics.[193] In the

[188] Similar Y. Listokin, 'The Meaning of Contractual Silence: A Field Experiment' (2010) 2 *Journal of Legal Analysis* 397, 399–401 (with respect to default rules).

[189] Ground-breaking on transaction cost see R. Coase, 'The Nature of the Firm' (1937) 4 *Econometrica* 386, 390 ('cost of using the price mechanism'); similar K. Arrow, 'The Organization of Economic Activity: Issues Pertinent to the Choice of Market versus Non-market Allocations' in Joint Economic Committee of Congress (ed) *Analysis and Evaluation of Public Expenditures: The PPP System* (Washington DC: Government Printing Office, 1969) 47, 48 and, taking up these references, Williamson, n 6, 18 as well as O. E. Williamson, *The Mechanisms of Governance* (Oxford: Oxford University Press, 1999) 5, 93, 161 ('costs of running the economic system').

[190] C. Dahlmann, 'The Problem of Externality' (1979) 22 *Journal of Law and Economics* 141, 148.

[191] See in more detail and with further references, F. Möslein, n 51, 335–437 (with respect to default rules).

[192] See, also on effects in the opposite direction (acceleration of negotiations): R. Cooter, 'The Cost of Coase' (1982) 11 *Journal of Legal Studies* 1, 23; R. Cooter, S. Marks, and R. Mnookin, 'Bargaining in the Shadow of the Law: A Testable Model of Strategic Behavior' (1982) 11 *Journal of Legal Studies* 225, 238–40.

[193] See n 16 and n 171.

context of contract governance, ignorance plays a particularly important role because legal rules (and consensus about their application or about divergent contractual rules) necessarily point to the future.[194] As a matter of fact, this future is unknown: '[i]f we are candid, *knowledge of the future* is a contradiction in terms.'[195] In such a context, rule-guided behaviour is more likely because it helps to reduce uncertainty. Moreover, respective regulatory structures typically concern transactions' auxiliary conditions. Actors will often tend to leave these auxiliary conditions aside and concentrate on the proper substance of the transaction. In many sales contracts, for example, parties will base their decisions on a comparison of product and consideration rather than taking the conditions of warranties into account.[196] For cognitive reasons, choices are made by using simple heuristics, so that human actors turn out to be 'one-reason-decision-makers'.[197] For this reason, auxiliary regulatory structures are seldom challenged even if contracting around would be possible. Yet the degree of uncertainty might change. Individuals can have ('good' or 'bad') experiences and thereby learn to take certain auxiliary conditions into account.[198] Such new information may well lead to a process of adaption that can ultimately challenge conventional regulatory structures.[199]

[194] One could refer to 'constitutional ignorance', a concept that goes back to F. A. v. Hayek, '*Rechtsordnung und Handelnsordnung* (1967)' in F. A. v. Hayek (ed) *Rechtsordnung und Handelnsordnung* (Tübingen: Mohr Siebeck, 2003) 35, 45ff; in more detail on this concept see E. J. Mestmäcker, *Regelbildung und Rechtsschutz in Marktwirtschaftlichen Ordnungen* (Tübingen: Mohr Siebeck, 1985) 8ff; E. Hoppmann, *Prinzipien Freiheitlicher Wirtschaftspolitik* (Tübingen: Mohr Siebeck, 1993) 30; see also the monograph by H. Kunz, *Marktsystem und Information* (Tübingen: Mohr Siebeck, 1985) with the subtitle '*Konstitutionelle Unwissenheit' als Quelle von "Ordnung"*' ('constitutional ignorance as a source of order').

[195] G. L. S. Shackle, *Epistemics & Economics* (Piscataway: Transaction Publishing, 1992) 47.

[196] By exempting price and goods in exchange from the control procedure, Art 4 (2) Unfair Terms Directive is often explained on similar grounds: C.W. Canaris, '*Wandlungen des Schuldvertragsrechts: Tendenzen zu seiner "Materialisierung"*' (2000) 200 *Acta Psychologica* 273, 327; J. Drexl, *Die Wirtschaftliche Selbstbestimmung des Verbrauchers* (Tübingen: Mohr Siebeck, 1998) 329ff; K. Riesenhuber, '*Die Inhaltskontrolle von Vereinbarungen über Hauptleistung und Preis im Europäischen Vertragsrecht*' in T. Pfeiffer, W. Grunsky, and J. Damman (eds) *Gedächtnisschrift for M. Wolf* (München: C.H. Beck, 2011) 123, 124ff.

[197] For respective empirical studies, see R. Shepard, 'On Subjectively Optimum Selections Among Multi-attribute Alternatives' in W. Edwards and A. Tversky (eds) *Decision Making* (Harmondsworth: Penguin Books, 1967) 257–83; J. Shanteau, 'How Much Information Does An Expert Use? Is It Relevant?' (1992) 81 *Acta Psychologica* 75–86; A. Bröder, 'Decision Making with the "Adaptive Toolbox": Influence of Environmental Structure, Intelligence, and Working Memory Load' (2003) 29 *Journal of Experimental Psychology: Learning, Memory and Decision Making* 611–24; J. Rieskamp and U. Hoffrage, 'When Do People Use Simple Heuristics, and How Can We Tell?' in G. Gigerenzer and P. Todd (eds) *Simple Heuristics that Make us Smart* (Oxford: Oxford University Press, 1999) 141–67.

[198] At a glance, on respective psychological and neurobiological research, see M. Domjan, *The Principles of Learning and Behavior* (Belmont: Wadsworth, 6th edn, 2010); R. Kesner and J. Martinez (ed) *Neurobiology of Learning and Memory* (Oxford: Elsevier, 2nd edn, 2007).

[199] Similarly, see Vanberg, n 181, 93, 107ff (decision-making as a 'process in which our paradigms are constantly extended to new situations and modified in the light of experience'); see also Y. Choi, *Paradigms and Conventions* (Ann Arbor: University of Michigan Press, 1993) 47ff.

The third factor concerns the autonomy of preferences.[200] The likelihood of contracting around the default depends on whether individual preferences depend on and are influenced by regulatory structures.[201] Processes of internalization and institutionalization of specific rules would seem to have a potential impact on individual preferences. Preferences for specific legal or contractual rules might develop due to learning effects.[202] They might also be rooted in psychological phenomena like the endowment effects or the status quo bias.[203] Moreover, such preferences can arise because actors feel bound to these rules due to their social and cultural identity.[204] Finally, the order of preferences, seldom a subject of economic discussion, seems very relevant.[205] The more central a specific purpose, the more likely it is that actors behave purpose-rationally in this respect.[206] In other words, while contracting around the default is quite likely with respect to rules that are relevant for purposes which are very important to the actors, it is much less likely with respect to rules that concern auxiliary purposes. Human behaviour corresponds to the model of *homo oeconomicus* in the first case, but it resembles to the model of the *homo sociologicus* in the second.

b. A contract governance context

With respect to contracts, multidisciplinarity and equilibria of disciplines will be required particularly whenever respective transactions go beyond simple, discrete

200 Often taken for granted in economic theory, see G. Stigler and G. Becker, '*De Gustibus Non Est Disputandum*' in K. Cook and M. Levi (eds) *The Limits of Rationality* (Ann Arbor: University of Michigan Press, 1990) 191 ('*de gustibus non est disputandum*').

201 In a similar vein, long ago, see A. Smith, *The Theory of Moral Sentiments* (London: A. Millar, 1759) 269 ('Those general rules of conduct, when they have been fixed in our mind by habitual reflection, are of great use in correcting misrepresentation of self-love concerning what is fit and proper to be done in a particular situation'); in more detail, A. Sen, *On Ethics and Economics* (Oxford: Basil Blackwell, 1987) 87ff.

202 Similarly, see R. Korobkin, 'Behavioral Economics, Contract Formation, and Contract Law' in C.R. Sunstein (ed) *Behavioral Law & Economics* (Cambridge: Cambridge University Press, 2000) 116, 137 ('If lawmakers' choice of default terms alters parties' preferences for contract terms – causing an increase in the strength of their preferences for the default term and a decrease in the strength of their preference for alternative terms – the choice of default terms has the potential to affect *any* private contract').

203 On these phenomena see, on the one hand, R Thaler, 'Toward a Positive Theory of Consumer Choice' (1980) 1 *Journal of Economic Behavoiur & Organization* 39, particularly at 44; Z. Carmon and D. Ariely, 'Focusing on the Forgone: How Value can Appear so Different to Buyers and Sellers' (2000) 27 *Journal of Consumer Research* 360–70; on the other hand, W. Samuelson and R. J. Zeckhauser, 'Status Quo Bias in Decision Making' (1988) 1 *Journal of Risk & Uncertainty* 7–59; D. Kahneman, J. L. Knetsch, and R. H. Thaler, 'Anomalies: The Endowment Effect, Loss Aversion, and Status Quo Bias' (1991) 5 *Journal of Economic Perspectives* 193, 197–9.

204 Akerlof and Kranton (2000), n 184, 715, 717 ('Identity [...] changes the "payoffs" from different actions').

205 From a philosophical perspective, see R. Jeffrey, 'Preference Among Preferences' (1974) 71 *Journal of Philosophy* 377.

206 Even the price can be downgraded to an auxiliary factor, see H. Leibenstein, 'Bandwagon, Snob, and Veblen Effects in the Theory of Consumer's Demand' (1950) 64 *Quarterly Journal of Economics* 183, 202–05; and a ground-breaking view from T. Veblen, *The Theory of the Leisure Class* (New York: Brookride, 1899).

spot contracts and contain relational elements.[207] On the one hand, contracts for the immediate sale and delivery of spot commodities can still be quite easily explained on the basis of the economic model of behaviour. In principle, they can be decided on the basis of a very few identifiable criteria (price and quality), they constitute purely bilateral exchanges and they carry but short-term effects.[208] On the other hand, whenever contracts are of a relational nature, be it because they are concluded under uncertainty, because they involve or affect third parties or because they have long-term bearings, then important governance questions arise.[209] In the same instances, multidisciplinarity becomes an issue of even higher importance.

First, under conditions of uncertainty, humans tend to be highly socially receptive. To maximize utility on a rational basis proves particularly difficult whenever information is lacking, for instance in financial markets where important price fluctuations arise or where highly complex products are traded.[210] Under such circumstances, collective behaviour gains importance, and this may now also be an issue for spot contracts because of their mass character. Individuals may learn from each other (wisdom of crowds), but they may also be influenced by others' hysteria (herding effects).[211] Kameda develops this idea in some detail. For fear of, say, bank-runs, public regulators may feel the need to prevent defective, maladaptive herding, but concurrently risk suppressing expedient societal learning, for both phenomena are underpinned by similar basic mechanisms.[212] And integrating this idea then into a governance perspective, Zumbansen proposes that, as a conceptual bridge, contract governance can improve our understanding of the relevant neural, psychological, and behavioural mechanisms, and might thereby help to segregate the two contrasting collective phenomena.[213] Such interdisciplinary understanding is no less than a precondition for designing effective rules to prevent herding effects, for example by encouraging countervailing forces like whistle-blowing, as is developed more broadly by Frey and Cueni.[214] Even

[207] On relational contracts, see n 26.

[208] In a similar vein, see R. Prasch, *How Markets Work* (Cheltenham: Edward Elgar Publishing, 2008) 29ff.

[209] O. E. Williams, 'Transaction-Cost Economics: The Governance of Contractual Relations' (1979) 22 *The Journal of Law and Economics* 233–61.

[210] So-called 'noise trading', i.e. trading that is not based on specific information, but oriented towards other investors' behaviour, is therefore a much-debated phenomenon in capital market theory, see Stiglitz, 'Using Tax Policy to Curb Speculative Short-term Trading' (1989) 3 *Journal of Financial Services Research* 101, 105–12; L. H. Summers and V. P. Summers, 'When Financial Markets Work Too Well: A Cautious Case For a Securities Tax' (1989) 3 *Journal of Financial Services Research* 261, 268; J. B. De Long, A. Shleifer, L. Summers, and R. Waldmann, 'Positive Feedback Investment Strategies and Destabilizing Rational Speculation' (1990) 45 *Journal of Finance* 379, 379–81.

[211] Ground-breaking from a sociological perspective is G. Le Bon, *The Crowd: A Study of the Popular Mind* (West Valley City: Walking Lion Press, 1895); for the first contributions in economics, see Veblen and Leibenstein, n 206.

[212] For more detail see Chapter 2.

[213] For a broader discussion see comment accompanying Chapter 2.

[214] See Chapter 3 and accompanying comment.

when courts decide on whistle-blowing, governance effects need to be taken into account. Indeed, the discussion of the *Heinisch* decision of the European Court of Human Rights has much to do with its ignorance of respective governance effects.[215] But also in times where market stability is at the top of the legislative agenda in capital market regulation (to name but another example), understanding herding effects seems of paramount importance.[216]

Secondly, third-party effects and more particularly the connectedness of contracts to a nexus raise similar questions, requiring a multidisciplinary analysis. Does the embeddedness in such networks change the behaviour of private actors? Given that every single contract stipulates self-imposed limits for future action, restrictions for individual future action cumulate and intensify. Additionally, however, preferences may also change, given that every single contract potentially changes the placement of individual actors in the coordinate system of social relationships.[217] Respective contracts may well go beyond legal obligations and create new social relationships, with a potential impact on parties' values and moral conceptions.[218] Additionally, and under conditions of uncertainty, mutual confidence plays an important role in effective contracting which, as Swedberg develops in more detail, is likely to follow different patterns in a network as compared to bilateral relationships.[219] Much depends on whether the aggregates have a simple cumulative structure and represent nothing more than the sum of their parts,[220] or whether they have a more complex structure. In the latter case, discrepancies may emerge 'between the motives of individual behaviour and the macroscopic consequences they provoke.'[221] This observation, if true, would even call into question methodological individualism as the very cornerstone of rational choice theory, with far-reaching consequences for the governance analysis of contractual networks.

For long-term contracts, similar considerations apply.[222] Again, embeddedness in social relations and mutual confidence play a much more significant role than in simple spot contracts. Additionally, uncertainty gains additional importance for long-term contracts pointing much further to the unknown future. The incompleteness of long-term contracts and their relational character have already

[215] European Court of Human Rights, *Heinisch v. Germany*, Chamber Judgment, 27 July 2011, App no 28274/08; more extensively on the relevance of whistle blowing for (corporate) governance see N. Bruun, 'Employee's Participation Rights and Business Restructuring' (2011) 2 *European Labour Law Journal* 27, 33ff.

[216] On market stability as legislative *leitmotiv* in the aftermath of the global financial crisis, see Möslein, '*Steuerrecht und Marktstabilität*' (2012) *Juristenzeitung* 243.

[217] In a similar vein, see J. Cannon, R. Achrol, and G. Grundlach, 'Contracts, Norms, and Plural Form Governance' (2000) 28 *Journal of the Academy of Marketing Science* 180.

[218] See, for instance, the various contributions in D. Campbell, H. Collins, and J. Wightman (eds) *Implicit Dimensions of Contract: Discrete, Relational, and Network Contracts* (Dublin: Irish Academic Press, 2003).

[219] Stressing the importance of confidence, with respect to financial markets, see Chapter 6.

[220] Comment accompanying Chapter 6, Section II.

[221] Comment accompanying Chapter 6, Section II.

[222] For a general account, see A. Arrighetti, R. Bachmann, and S. Deakin, 'Contract Law, Social Norms and Inter-firm Cooperation' (1997) 21 *Cambridge Journal of Economics* 171.

been mentioned.[223] Therefore, as Magen develops in some detail, issues of fairness and reciprocity are much more important than in simple spot contracts, and they seem to require multidisciplinary explanations.[224] Beyond that, parties have to rely on social norms and common traditions in order to fill the contractual and legal gaps.[225] Therefore they are likely to attribute major significance to (or maybe even to try to influence) the social and cultural identity of the other party.[226] In labour relations, for example, such common values and social norms often lead to job performances that are much higher than required by the labour contract ('partial gifts').[227] Last but not least, time patterns may even have an impact on the effectiveness of procedural settings. With respect to class actions, for instance, Defains and Demougin argue that intrinsic motivations based on morality may help to solve the problem of externality in the long-run.[228] Beyond the subject of long-term contracts and inquiring into questions of long-term effects more generally, this observation underscores the importance of studying the long-term interaction of individual motivations and the legal environment. Focussing on the relationship between human behaviour and regulatory structures likewise accentuates the need for contract governance research.

V. Challenges and Perspectives

Contract governance certainly is a substantial challenge. As compared to traditional contract law theory, it requires a much wider perspective. It requires taking into account internal and external perspectives of contracting parties within the contractual relationship, but also on the market. In addition, it requires considering phenomena like herding, contractual networks, and long-term contracts. Moreover, it requires analysing a whole range of various levels of regulation, from the legislative sphere to collective bargaining and the individual contract. Last but not least, it requires a multidisciplinary approach, including not only economic, but also sociological and even neuroscientific knowledge. All this makes contract governance an extremely complex, but even more rewarding endeavour. This book is a first attempt to trigger such interdisciplinary discussion.

In the end, contracts themselves might turn out to be much more complex instruments than hitherto discussed. Yet this complexity makes them an even more interesting subject to study. While the global financial crisis has illustrated considerable risks of contractual relationships for the stability of (financial) markets, phenomena like innovation, privatization, and globalization show the limits

[223] See text accompanying n 26 and n 201.

[224] In a similar vein, Chapter 8.

[225] See generally I. R. Macneil, 'Contract Adjustments of Long-Term Economic Relations Under Classical, Neoclassical and Relational Contract Law' (1978) 72 *Northwestern University Law Review* 854.

[226] In a similar vein, see Akerlof and Kranton (2010), n 184, 41–3 (with respect to labor contracts).

[227] See n 86.

[228] See Chapter 9.

of traditional national law-making.[229] Concurrently, contracts come to the fore, inter alia, as an instrument of transnational regulation. In such an era of negotiated law,[230] understanding contract governance becomes of paramount importance. Hence this venture promises to be worth every single effort. Can there be a better moment for venturing into this direction than now? The present book is, of course, only a first step.

[229] In much more detail, and with respect to facilitative contract law, see Möslein, n 51.
[230] See Mekki and Kloepfer-Pelèse, n 141.

PART II

THIRD PARTY IMPACT AND CONTRACT GOVERNANCE PROBLEMS IN HERD BEHAVIOUR

2

The Concept of Herd Behaviour: Its Psychological and Neural Underpinnings

*Tatsuya Kameda, Keigo Inukai, Thomas Wisdom, and Wataru Toyokawa**

In an increasingly connected world, an event in one place, be it economic, political, or social, can cause large-scale chain reactions across many other places. We have abundant examples of this sort, including the recent global financial crisis, the spread of civil uprisings in the Middle East, the widespread success of technological innovations such as the iPad, and so on. Until recently, such mass phenomena have been studied rather sporadically in various social science disciplines without much mutual communication. Yet with advances in technology and new theoretical frameworks, these mass phenomena are becoming a focus of substantive interdisciplinary interests.[1] An umbrella concept, 'herding', has facilitated such cross-disciplinary communication over the last five years.

I. Herd Behaviour: A Definition and Examples

What is meant by herding? Herding refers to an alignment of thoughts or behaviours of individuals in a group. Most importantly, such convergence often emerges through local interactions among agents rather than some purposeful coordination by a central authority or a leading figure in the group. In other words, the apparent coordination of the herd is an emergent property of local interactions.[2]

Textbook examples of herding in the social science literature include riots, panics, fads, mass hysterias, urban legends, economic bubbles, and so on.[3] However, besides these familiar examples, recent research suggests that herding

* All at Hokkaido University, Department of Behavioural Science.

[1] E.g. G. A. Akerlof and R. J. Shiller, *Animal Spirits: How Human Psychology Drives the Economy, and Why It Matters for Global Capitalism* (Princeton, NJ: Princeton University Press, 2009).

[2] R. M. Raafat, N. Chater, and C. Frith, 'Herding in Humans' (2009) 13 *Trends in Cognitive Sciences* 420–8.

[3] See N. J. Smelser, *Theory of Collective Behaviour* (Glencoe, Illinois: Free Press, 1963); R. H. Turner and L. M. Killian, *Collective Behaviour* (Englewood Cliffs, NJ: Prentice-Hall, 4th edn, 1993).

may encompass a much wider range of our social behaviours than had been previously thought.

1. Crimes

The proliferation of crimes in a city may be seen as an example of herding. One of the most striking aspects of crime is that crime rates vary remarkably across time and space. For example, homicide rates across nations in 1990 ranged from 6.1 cases per million in Japan, to 12.6 in Sweden, to 98.0 in the United States. Within the United States, rates of serious crimes in the year ranged from 0.008 per capita in Ridgewood Village, New Jersey to 0.384 in nearby Atlantic City.[4] Such high variances are observed within cities as well, where one street can have much higher crime rates than streets just a few blocks away.

One obvious explanation for such high variances may be that socio-economic conditions also vary over time and space, creating temporal and geographical clusters of crime. However, an econometric analysis by Edward Glaeser and others showed that less than 30 per cent of the variation in cross-city or cross-district crime rates could be explained by the local socio-economic differences. These researchers developed a model in which agents' decisions about crime were a function of their own attributes (e.g., socio-economic as well as psychological attributes) and of their neighbour's decisions about criminal activities. Glaeser and others then estimated impacts of the second element of the model (i.e., social influence from neighbours) for a variety of crimes in the United States in 1985, in 1970, and across New York City in 1985. The overall results showed that positive interaction among agents' decisions about crime was the only viable explanation for the large residual variance not explainable by the local socio-economic conditions. More specifically, the local social influence was strong for larceny and auto theft; moderate for assault, burglary, and robbery; and weak for arson, murder, and rape. These results suggest that one agent's decision to commit crimes (relatively minor crimes in particular) affects his or her neighbour's decisions, which constitutes a positive feedback loop as a whole. The large variations in crime rates across time and space seem to emerge as aggregated outcomes of such individual local decisions.

2. Obesity

Recent research suggests that obesity may be contagious as well.[5] Using a data set from a longitudinal survey on cardiovascular disease (the Framingham Heart Study),[6] Nicholas Christakis and James Fowler examined how social

[4] E. L. Glaeser, B. Sacerdote, and J. A. Scheinkman, 'Crime and Social Interactions' (1996) 111 *Quarterly Journal of Economics* 507–48.

[5] N. A. Christakis and J. H. Fowler, 'The Spread of Obesity in a Large Social Network over 32 Years' (2007) 357 *New England Journal of Medicine* 370–9.

[6] See <http://www.framinghamheartstudy.org/>.

relations in a community affect obesity. The original survey traced health states of people residing in Framingham, Massachusetts over 32 years. Christakis and Fowler focused on family or friendship relations among the participants, and applied longitudinal statistical models to examine whether weight gain in one person was associated with weight gains in his or her friends, siblings, spouse, and neighbours.

Results of the network analysis revealed that obese people (defined as those with a Body Mass Index greater than 30) and non-obese people formed different clusters and that social influences through the network extended up to three degrees of separation. In other words, the average obese person was more likely to have obese friends, friends of friends, and friends of friends of friends than was the average non-obese person. Moreover, a person's chances of becoming obese increased by 57 per cent if he or she had a friend who became obese in the time period, by 40 per cent if a sibling became obese, and by 37 per cent if a spouse became obese. These patterns suggest that obesity spreads through social network like a pathogen. Another person's overeating behaviour affects one's overeating behaviour through the social network, even if he or she does not know the person directly. Segmentations of obese and non-obese people in a community seem to emerge as aggregated consequences of such local influences.

3. Happiness

Happy people and unhappy people also seem to inhabit different clusters in a community. A reanalysis of the Framingham Heart Study data set suggested that these clusters did not simply reflect a tendency for individuals to associate with similar individuals. Instead, these macro patterns resulted from spread of happiness and unhappiness through the social network, just as in the case of obesity. According to the analysis, the probability that one was happy increased by 25 per cent if a friend who lived within a mile became happy, and these local influences also extended up to three degrees of separation. Thus, like obesity, happiness also seems to be contagious.[7]

II. Why Does Herding Occur? Potential Mechanisms

The examples earlier suggest that herding is a robust phenomenon, characterizing a wide range of social behaviours in our life. If so, what are the neural, psychological, or sociological mechanisms that produce herding? This Section reviews potential mechanisms that are thought to underpin herding behaviour.

[7] J. H. Fowler and N. A. Christakis, 'Dynamic Spread of Happiness in a Large Social Network: Longitudinal Analysis over 20 Years in the Framingham Heart Study' (2008) 337 *British Medical Journal* 2338.

1. Emotional contagion, facial mimicry, and mirror neurons

As implied by the saying that your smile makes others happy, humans often reproduce others' emotions in themselves. This phenomenon, which is called emotional contagion,[8] has long been known among psychotherapists who treat depressed clients. Therapists, especially those who are inexperienced, are sometimes 'caught' by their clients' emotions, expressed during interviews, and feel themselves depressed afterwards. Elaine Hatfield and her colleagues see emotional contagion as a primitive, automatic, and unconscious process, and argue that it occurs through a series of steps: when a receiver is interacting with a sender, he or she first perceives the emotional expressions of the sender. The receiver then automatically transfers the perceived emotional expressions to his or her bodily expressions (e.g., facial expressions, postures). Through the process of afferent feedback, these copied bodily expressions are translated into the receiver feeling the same emotion that the sender experienced, which leads to emotional convergence between the sender and the receiver.

Indeed, it can easily be demonstrated that we have a tendency to mimic the facial expressions of others in everyday social interactions. Research suggests that such facial mimicry is an automatic, reflex-like process, in which the observer's facial expression matches the observed facial expression (e.g., happy, sad, fearful, angry, disgusted faces) rather quickly—typically within less than a second.[9] Such automatic mimicry extends to bodily posture, voice pitch, and so on, and is known to emerge very early in human development. Even 12- to 21-day-old infants can imitate both facial and manual gestures displayed by an adult model.[10]

Furthermore, recent developments in neuroscience suggest that there may be a system in our brains that helps us to mirror others' actions. One of the most important recent findings in brain science is the discovery of 'mirror neurons'. In the late 1980s when Giacomo Rizzolatti and others were recording electrical activity in the brain of a macaque, these researchers found neurons that fired both when the animal acted and when the animal observed the same action performed by another. The same neurons fired when the monkey grasped something with its hand, *and* when the monkey observed the experimenter grasping it; however, these neurons did not discharge in response to simple presentation of food or of other interesting objects. The neuron 'mirrored' the motor behaviour of the other,

[8] E. Hatfield, J. T. Cacioppo, and R. L. Rapson, *Emotional Contagion* (New York: Cambridge University Press, 1994).

[9] U. Hess and S. Blairy, 'Facial Mimicry and Emotional Contagion to Dynamic Emotional Facial Expressions and their Influence on Decoding Accuracy' (2001) 40 *International Journal of Psychophysiology* 129–41.

[10] A. N. Meltzoff and M. K. Moore, 'Imitation of Facial and Manual Gestures by Human Neonates' (1977) 198 *Science* 75. This finding was replicated with neonatal chimpanzees, our closest relatives. At less than seven days of age, the chimpanzees could imitate human facial gestures (tongue protrusion and mouth opening): M. Myowa-Yamakoshi, M. Tomonaga, M. Tanaka, and T. Matsuzawa, 'Imitation in Neonatal Chimpanzees (Pan Troglodytes)' (2004) 7 *Developmental Science* 437–42.

as though the observer were in fact executing the motor act. Although it remains controversial, some recent data suggest that a similar 'mirror neuron system' may exist in human brains as well.[11]

Taken together, these psychological, behavioural, and neural findings strongly suggest that aping others may be a fundamentally human activity.

2. Social norms, mutual expectations, and shared stories

Another mechanism for herding involves more conscious, deliberate, or controlled psychological processes, which are distinguishable from our automatic 'aping' propensities as reviewed earlier. These processes have been studied mainly by social psychologists.

Classic experimental demonstrations of such herd behaviours in social psychology include the famous line-comparison study by Solomon Asch where subjects conformed to an erroneous majority view to avoid potential embarrassment or other social sanctions in a group;[12] the optical illusion study by Muzfer Sherif demonstrating that individual perceptions of the illusion converged on a shared social reality (i.e., everybody in the same group ended up seeing the identical optical illusion) through communication;[13] and so on.

A key element underlying these herd behaviours is a fundamental characteristic of our mind, which may be termed 'docility' or receptivity to social norms.[14] Herbert Simon defined this concept as our tendency to depend on others' suggestions, recommendations, persuasion, and information obtained through social channels as a major basis of choice.

Compared to other gregarious species, humans are unique in developing social norms and mutually shared expectations, which inform us about what action is normal, appropriate, or just in a given social situation. As seen in the Asch experiment, the human mind is built to be highly receptive to social norms, and tends to self-censor actions in advance in order to avoid deviating from norms.[15] The human mind is also built to think in terms of, and be influenced by, narratives or stories (sequences of events with an internal logic and dynamics).[16] Stories, especially stories

[11] G. Rizzolatti and L. Craighero, 'The Mirror-Neuron System' (2004) 27 *Annual Review of Neuroscience* 169–92.

[12] S. E. Asch, 'Studies of Independence and Conformity: A Minority of One against a Unanimous Majority' (1956) 70(9) *Psychological Monographs*.

[13] M. Sherif, *The Psychology of Social Norms* (New York: HarperCollins, 1936).

[14] H. A. Simon, 'A Mechanism for Social Selection and Successful Altruism' (1990) 21 *Science* 1665–8; T. Kameda and R. S. Tindale, 'Groups as Adaptive Devices: Human Docility and Group Aggregation Mechanisms in Evolutionary Context' in M. Schaller, J. A. Simpson, and D. T. Kenrick (eds), *Evolution and Social Psychology* (New York: Psychology Press, 2006) 317.

[15] Notice that the high receptivity to social norms is also fundamental to our ability to learn culturally. Humans are a cultural species that can take full advantage of socially-acquired knowledge. Without 'docility' by learners to their 'cultural parents', however, such cognitive capacities would be highly limited. See M. Tomasello, *The Cultural Origins of Human Cognition* (Cambridge, Mass: Harvard University Press, 1999).

[16] R. C. Shank and R. P. Abelson, *Scripts, Plans, Goals and Understanding* (New York: Wiley, 1977).

shared in a community or across a whole society, lead us to see, interpret, have feelings about, and react to things from the shared viewpoint.[17]

This characteristic receptivity of individual minds can yield effects that are visible at the societal level. In the aforementioned case of contagious obesity, for example, one may decide to eat more because the action seems to be normal given one's spouse's or friend's eating practices, which in turn provides a normative stage for another's overeating. Our actions have spill over effects (which economists often call externalities) on others, which can lead to spiralling proliferations of action across a whole society.[18]

3. Rational conformity and information cascades

Sometimes it is rational to conform to majority behaviour in a group, even if one would otherwise choose differently. Hans Christian Andersen's 'The Emperor's New Clothes' provides a case in point. To recall, an Emperor who cares greatly about his appearance and attire hires two tailors who promise him the finest suit of clothes made from a fabric invisible to anyone who is unfit for his position or 'just hopelessly stupid'. The Emperor cannot see the cloth himself, but pretends as if he can for fear of appearing unfit for his position or stupid, and is joined in this pretence by his ministers, subordinates, and general citizens. Notice that the 'spiral of silence'[19] occurs because it is rational to keep quiet given another's silence. Standing up to tell the truth is risky given a possibility (even if it may be small) that the cloth may be visible to another's eyes. And if such a perception holds for everybody simultaneously,[20] this constitutes an equilibrium where any unilateral deviations (seem to) work against the deviator. A bank run which is initially triggered by some groundless rumour provides a similar example, where the (ungrounded) prophecy of bankruptcy can be self-fulfilling through a positive feedback loop.[21]

Information cascades are another example of rational conformity. An information cascade occurs when it is optimal for an individual who has observed the 'consensus' actions of preceding others to follow the predecessors' actions regardless of the private information that the individual has. Sushil Bikhchandani and others illustrated this process by an example of a paper submission to an academic

[17] See G. A. Akerlof and R. J. Shiller, *Animal Spirits: How Human Psychology Drives the Economy, and Why It Matters for Global Capitalism* (Princeton, NJ: Princeton University Press, 2009) for interesting recent examples of influential political-economic stories.

[18] M. Granovetter, 'Threshold Models of Collective Behaviour' (1978) 83 *American Journal of Sociology* 1420–43.

[19] E. Noelle-Neumann, *The Spiral of Silence: Public Opinion – Our Social Skin* (Chicago: University of Chicago Press, 1993).

[20] This situation is called pluralistic ignorance in social psychology: a majority of group members privately reject a norm, but assume (incorrectly) that most others accept it. In other words, this is a situation where no one believes, but everyone thinks that everyone else believes. See D. Katz and F. H. Allport, *Students' Attitudes: A Report of the Syracuse University Reaction Study* (Syracuse, NY: Craftsman Press, 1931).

[21] R. K. Merton, *Social Theory and Social Structure* (New York: Free Press, 1968).

journal. A referee in a first journal reads the submitted paper, assesses its quality, and makes a decision about whether to accept or reject it. Suppose that a referee at a second journal learns that the paper was rejected by the first journal. Assuming that the referee cannot evaluate the paper's quality perfectly, knowledge of the previous rejection should make the referee lean toward rejection. If the paper is rejected at the second journal, this process can continue at other journals, yielding a chain of rejections. Economists proposed a model which proved that, at some stage in a sequential-choice setting, a rational Bayesian decision-maker should ignore his or her private information and act only on the public information obtained from previous decisions. Once this stage is reached, all decision-makers thereafter in the sequence should do the same, yielding an information cascade.[22] And if the earlier decisions in the sequence happen to be erroneous (e.g., rejecting a high-quality paper), the cascade leads to undesirable outcomes.

Information cascades have been studied mainly by economists,[23] and are often associated with various herd behaviours in financial markets, legal decision-making,[24] and so on.

III. Herding and the Wisdom of Crowds

The mechanisms reviewed earlier, ranging from unconscious, automatic mimicry to more reasoned, deliberate conformity to rational herding, are fundamental building blocks of mass or group phenomena. The robustness of these mechanisms, which underlie a wide range of our social behaviours, raises a central question about the nature of herding: is herding always problematic, as is often implied by some popular images (e.g., mass hysterias, mobs, panics, fads, economic bubbles, groupthink, etc)? This question becomes clear if we consider 'the wisdom of crowds', a totally different notion of group behaviour, popularized by James Surowiecki.[25] While herding in humans often refers to defective social processes that degrade toward suboptimal performance, the wisdom of crowds implies highly intelligent group processes that can lead to collective wisdom. How can we reconcile the two contrasting images of collectivities?

[22] S. Bikhchandani, D. Hirshleifer, and I. Welch, 'A Theory of Fads, Fashion, Custom, and Cultural Change as Informational Cascades' (1992) 100 *Journal of Political Economy* 992–1026; A. V. Banerjee, 'A Simple Model of Herd Behaviour' (1992) 107 *Quarterly Journal of Economics* 797–818.

[23] For reviews of laboratory studies, see L. R. Anderson and C. A. Holt, 'Information Cascade Experiments' in C. R. Plott and V. L. Smith (eds), *The Handbook of Experimental Economics Results* (Amsterdam, New York, Oxford, Tokyo: North Holland, 2008) 335–43.

[24] W. Farnsworth, *The Legal Analyst: A Toolkit for Thinking about the Law*. (Chicago: University of Chicago Press, 2007).

[25] J. Surowiecki, *The Wisdom of Crowds: Why the Many are Smarter than the Few and How Collective Wisdom Shapes Business, Economies, Societies and Nations* (New York: Doubleday, 2004).

1. Group decision-making by honeybees

To consider this question, it seems useful to extend our scope to include herd behaviour by non-human animals that also live collective lives. Although humans are a gregarious species, we are arguably not the most gregarious species of all. Our rivals in this respect are eusocial animals, including bees, ants, termites, naked mole rats, etc. Eusocial species are colonial animal species that live in multigenerational family groups, in which the vast majority of individuals cooperate to aid relatively few reproductive group members. They often exhibit extreme task specialization, which makes colonies potentially very efficient in gathering resources.

The puzzle of these species is how they can achieve such high efficiencies collectively, despite the fact that they have relatively much smaller brains as compared to humans. More specifically, how do they avoid defective social processes leading to problematic herd behaviour? We will examine group decision-making by honeybees to address these questions.

In late spring or early summer, as a large hive outgrows its nest, a colony of honeybees often divides itself. The queen leaves with about two-thirds of the worker bees to create a new colony, and a daughter queen stays in the old nest with the rest of the worker bees. The swarm leaving the colony must find a new home in a short time, which is critical to their survival. The leaving swarm, which is composed of 10,000 or so bees, typically clusters on a tree branch, while several hundred scout bees search the neighbourhood for a new home. These scout bees fly out to inspect potential nest sites, and, upon returning to the colony, perform waggle dances to advertize any good sites they have discovered. The duration of the dance depends on a bee's perception of the site's quality: the better the site, the longer the dance. Other scout bees that have not flown out yet, as well as those that have stopped dancing, observe these dances and decide where to visit. In these decisions, the bees are more likely to visit and inspect the sites which have been advertized strongly by many predecessors. This process constitutes a positive feedback loop. Thomas Seeley and others, who conducted a series of experiments with honeybees in natural settings, found that the bees usually could choose the best nest site. Even though none of the bees visits all the potential nest sites individually, they can aggregate partial individual information to form a collective wisdom that enables high-quality decisions.[26]

Although the bees' performance is highly impressive, the puzzle still remains. How do the bees solve the problem of interdependency? As we have seen earlier, the bees communicate their findings via waggle dances which are performed sequentially by scout bees. This could create statistical dependencies among decision-makers, in which initial errors committed by earlier scouts can carry over and be amplified in the sequence. In this sense, the honeybee group decision-making system may be susceptible to the erroneous information cascade.

[26] T. D. Seeley, *Honeybee Democracy* (Princeton, NJ and Oxford: Princeton University Press, 2010).

A recent article has addressed this question theoretically via a computer simulation model. In line with the previous empirical observations, the model assumes that scout bees are dependent on other bees in that they give more attention to nest sites strongly advertized by their predecessors. The bees essentially conform to a majority view in their decisions about where to visit. But, simultaneously, the model assumes that the bees are independent in assessing the quality of the visited site. The duration of the scout's dance, which indexes the strength of the bee's preference for the site, is *not* affected by others' waggle dances, but determined *solely* by her own perception of the site's quality. The computer simulation results showed that, when a suitable mixture of influence and independence exists, the honeybee group decision-making process works well.[27]

2. Collective wisdom on the Internet?

Honeybee nest search provides an impressive example of how animals that have only limited cognitive capacity as individuals can make 'wise' decisions collectively as a swarm. It is also important to note that the 'swarm intelligence'[28] in honeybees emerges not from some purposeful coordination by a central authority (e.g., the queen), but through local interactions among the bees—a key element in the definition of herding as discussed earlier in this Chapter. Interestingly, the honeybee nest-search situation seems to have similar counterparts in modern human societies, where individuals can use public information as well as private information to make a well-informed decision. Examples include information searching on the Internet when buying books or music, choosing a restaurant for dinner, deciding which hotel to stay at, and so on. Potential options are quite large in number, yet our time budget for private information searches is limited. In these occasions, we often visit relevant websites (e.g., Amazon, Yelp) to see how others have decided. Do these social information pooling systems on the Internet, in which individuals informed by predecessors' experiences report their own new experiences to share with others, yield collective wisdom as in the honeybee case?

A recent experiment on a 'cultural market' by Matthew Salganik and others focuses on this point.[29] In cultural markets, sales volumes of hit songs, books, and movies are many times greater than average. This may imply that 'the best' alternatives are qualitatively different from 'the rest', yet experts routinely fail to predict which cultural products will succeed. Why does this failure occur?

[27] C. List, C. Elsholtz, and T. D. Seeley, 'Independence and Interdependence in Collective Decision Making: an Agent-based Model' (2009) 364 *Philosophical Transactions of the Royal Society B* 755–62.

[28] J. Krause, G. D. Ruxton, and S. Krause, 'Swarm Intelligence in Animals and Humans' (2009) 25 *Trends in Ecology and Evolution* 28–34.

[29] M. J. Salganik, P. Sheridan Dodds, and D. Watts, 'Experimental Study of Inequality and Cultural Market' (2006) 311 *Science* 854–6.

Intrigued by the unpredictability of cultural markets, these researchers created an experimental music market, where a total of 14,341 participants downloaded previously unknown songs under one of two conditions—the 'social influence' condition or the 'independent' condition. In both conditions, participants could listen to any song they were interested in to have a direct experience of the product. On top of the individual learning opportunity, participants in the 'social influence' condition were provided social information about how many times each song had been downloaded by previous participants. Notice that there was a structural similarity between the social influence condition and the honeybee nest search situation. In both situations, agents had to make choices between unfamiliar options that could differ in quality. Also, when making individual decisions, social frequency information (predecessors' behaviours) was available, in addition to the opportunities for individual information search.

The experiment revealed several interesting results. First, inequality in overall download counts among songs was much greater in the social influence condition, as compared to the independent condition in which participants could not access to the social-frequency information. Obviously, participants in the social influence condition copied predecessors' choices, which yielded a 'rich get richer' outcome. Thus, the experiment replicated the robust phenomenon in cultural markets that hit songs are many times more successful than average.

Secondly, the most popular song (with the highest download frequency) in the independent condition did not necessarily correspond to the most popular ones in the social influence condition. Mapping of the songs in terms of popularity ranking between the two conditions was at most moderate—the most popular song in the independent condition never did very badly in the social influence condition, and the least popular song never did extremely well either. However, almost any other result could happen. The success of a song in the social influence condition was path-dependent and susceptible to random fluctuations, which may explain why it is difficult for even experts to predict which products will succeed in cultural markets.

Overall, how did the human performance in the experimental music market compare to the honeybee performance in the nest search? A tentative answer does not seem to be favourable to us. Honeybees mix dependence and independence in the nest search. They conform to predecessors to decide which sites to visit, but assess the quality of the visited sites independently from predecessors' evaluations. This leads to the typical swarm's high performance. On the other hand, human participants in the experimental music market seemed to fail to separate the two aspects and rely too much on others' choices. Of course, the inherent subjectivity of music preferences means that the quality of experimental cultural market outcomes cannot be assessed objectively (as the nest choice decisions can). Yet, the lack of correspondence in song-popularity between the independent and the social influence conditions suggests that such subjective preferences are unstable and fragile. In this sense, the hyper-susceptibility of mass behaviour to social influence is problematic not only for marketers of cultural products, but also in many socio-political domains where no demonstrably correct answer exists.

IV. Conclusion

In this Chapter, we have reviewed various manifestations of herding in humans. As we have seen, humans are a highly socially receptive species, as compared with other gregarious animals. Accumulating evidence in various behavioural science disciplines strongly suggests that we humans are equipped with neural, psychological, and behavioural mechanisms that underpin this receptiveness—our abilities to learn from and be influenced by others. It is no doubt that these built-in mechanisms are evolutionary products that have served our survival and fundamentally contributed to our adaptive success on the earth. Yet, these adaptive tools can cause serious errors in modern environments, in which interconnectivities of individuals are much denser and externalities accruing from individual behaviours are much greater and more far-reaching, as compared to ancient environments in which the human mind evolved.

Interestingly, growing evidence in the behavioural sciences also seems to suggest that the two contrasting collective phenomena in humans—maladaptive herding and the wisdom of crowds—are underpinned by similar basic mechanisms. In this sense, the two apparently opposite macro phenomena may be seen as twins produced and governed by the receptivity of our minds. Given this commonality, understanding the neural, psychological, and behavioural mechanisms that could help distinguish these twins will be one of the most important challenges for behavioural sciences in the next decade.[30]

[30] For further discussion, see T. Kameda, T. Tsukasaki, R. Hastie, and N. Berg, 'Democracy under Uncertainty: The Wisdom of Crowds and the Free-Rider Problem in Group Decision Making' (2011) 118 *Psychological Review* 76–96.

Law, Economics, and More: The Genius of Contract Governance

Comment on T. Kameda, K. Inukai, T. Wisdom, and W. Toyokawa, 'The Concept of Herd Behavior: Its Psychological and Neural Underpinnings'

*Peer Zumbansen**

I. The Lawyer's Mindset and the New Twist in Law and Economics

Oliver Wendell Holmes Jr., at that time still sitting on the bench of the Supreme Judicial Court of Massachusetts, notes towards the end of his landmark essay on 'The Path of the Law', that '[w]e cannot all be Descartes or Kant, but we all want happiness.'[1] As students of this text once knew, he continues to remark:

> And happiness, I am sure from having known many successful men, cannot be won simply by being counsel for great corporations and having an income of fifty thousand dollars. An intellect great enough to win the prize needs other food beside success. The remoter and more general aspects of the law are those which give it universal interest. It is through them that you not only become a great master in your calling, but connect your

* Professor at Osgoode Hall Law School, York University, Toronto. This comment builds on a presentation following Professor Kameda's lecture at the Contract Governance Conference, held in Berlin in 2010, organized by Florian Möslein, Karl Riesenhuber, and Stefan Grundmann. I wish to thank the organizers for the invitation, Professor Kameda and his colleagues for being given the honour of responding to their paper, and Tracey Linstead and Aviv Pichhadze for valuable clarifications.

[1] O. W. Holmes Jr., 'The Path of the Law' (1897) 10 *Harvard Law Review* 457, 478. See also O. W. Holmes Jr., On Receiving the Degree of Doctor of Laws, Yale University Commencement (30 June 1886) reprinted in O. W. Holmes Jr. (ed), *The Collected Legal Papers* (Mineola: Dover Publications. Inc, 2007) 33: 'The power of honor to bind men's lives is not less now than it was in the Middle Ages. Now as then it is the breath of our nostrils; it is that for which we live, for which, if need be, we are willing to die. It is that which makes the man whose gift is the power to gain riches sacrifice health and even life to the pursuit. It is that which makes the scholar feel that he cannot afford to be rich.'

subject with the universe and catch an echo of the infinite, a glimpse of its unfathomable process, a hint of the universal law.[2]

There is much in these lines to ponder, for sure. Holmes' essay, throughout, reads—and was meant—as a wholehearted assault on dearly held beliefs regarding the objective nature of abstract legal principles, the separation of law and morality, and the construction of legal rules in following the command of logic. Heralded—by no-one else than one of the founding fathers of Law and Economics and one of the great, innovative, and continuously surprising legal minds of our day,[3] as a prophecy coming true,[4] Holmes' essay placed a great number of the core treats of the coming legal evolution before his readers' eyes—over 110 years ago.

Where Holmes pointed to the rising significance of science and economics for the theory and practice of law,[5] the ensuing legal evolution seems at a minimum to have proven him right. What sets the present apart from the past, however, is that precisely this transformation of legal science into its present-day conundrical mixture of legal theory and philosophy, regulatory theory ('governance'[6]) and economic theory[7], not only goes beyond the initially sketched parameters, but fundamentally undermines a view that would conceive of law as a field together with its 'neighbour' disciplines.[8] 'The centre cannot hold'[9]—law's autonomous status within a densely structured context of social order theories is undermined, already by Holmes himself, by exposing it to a complex set of questions touching on the nature, function, and form of law, eventually challenging the boundaries

[2] Holmes (1897), n 1.

[3] *Flomo v. Firestone Nat. Rubber Co., LLC*, 643 F.3d 1013 (7th Cir. 2011), 1017: 'And suppose no corporation had *ever* been punished for violating customary international law. There is always a first time for litigation to enforce a norm; there has to be.'

[4] R. A. Posner, 'The Path Away from the Law' (1997) 110 *Harvard Law Review* 1039–43, 1043.

[5] See also O.W. Holmes Jr., 'Law in Science and Science in Law' in O.W. Holmes Jr. (ed), *The Collected Legal Papers* (Mineola: Dover Publications Inc, 2007) 210: 'A hundred years ago men explained any part of the universe by showing its fitness for certain ends, and demonstrating what they conceived to be its final cause according to a providential scheme. In our less theological and more scientific day, we explain an object by tracing the order and process of its growth and development from a starting point assumed as given.'

[6] Arguably, the new paradigm in administrative sciences. See, e.g., C. Franzius, '*Governance und Regelungsstrukturen*' (2006) 97 *Verwaltungsarchiv* 186–219; P. M. Defarges, *La Gouvernance [Que sais-je? no. 3676]* (Paris: Presses Universitaires de France, 2003); O. E. Williamson, 'The Economics of Governance' (2005) 95 *American Economic Review* 1–18; both on the national as on the global level: F. E. Johns, 'Global Governance: An Heretical History Play' (2004) 4 *Global Jurist Advances* Art. 3 (available at <http://ssrn.com/abstract=603232>); H. Willke, *Smart Governance. Governing the Global Knowledge Society* (Chicago, Ill: University of Chicago Press, 2007); P. Zumbansen, 'Governance from an Interdisciplinary Perspective' in D. Levi-Faur (ed), *Oxford Handbook on Governance* (Oxford: Oxford University Press, 2012); T. Hale and D. Held (eds), *Handbook of Transnational Governance* (Cambridge: Polity Press, 2011).

[7] A. K. Dixit, *Lawlessness and Economics. Alternative Modes of Governance* (Princeton, NJ: Princeton University Press, 2004); O. Williamson, 'The Lens of Contract: Private Ordering' (2002) 92 *American Economic Review* 438–42.

[8] See, e.g., D. Grimm (ed), *Rechtswissenschaft und Nachbarwissenschaften Band II* (München: C.H. Beck, 1976).

[9] W. B. Yeats, *The Second Coming* (1920) (available at <http://www.poetryfoundation.org/poem/172062>).

between law and non-law. And this, precisely, proved to be the aftermath and legacy of Holmes' and his colleagues' anti-formalist attack, a powerful engagement with the assumptions, theories, and policies of legal argument.[10]

This context provides promising, if not intimidating entry points for law's engagement with itself and all that it might—and might not—be. Lawyers like Holmes were well aware of the vulnerability of the edifice of norms, court rooms, and law school curricula long before the advent of globalization and the much lamented exhaustion of the state's regulatory capacity.[11] With this in mind, we should today appreciate the earlier stages of the currently very vibrant and vociferous challenges of law coming from economists and sociologists, as well as from geographers and anthropologists, among others. To reflect on origins of interdisciplinary thinking of and around law is especially crucial at a time when scientific advances propel a rapidly growing knowledge base with regard to just about anything connected to legal reasoning with the potential of the ubiquitous excitement about 'law and…'[12] having an almost overwhelming effect on us as regards an awareness and appreciation of much older engagements with law's interdisciplinary foundations.

The current interest in law's psychological[13] and behavioural economic[14] dimensions gives the undisputable triumph of law and economics over other 'law and society' movements yet another twist—with important consequences for our understanding of the embeddedness of law in a rich context of theoretical and empirical studies of human—individual and collective[15]—as well as institutional behaviour.[16] To be sure, the dialogue between economics, sociology[17] and

10 R. Pound, 'Law in Books and Law in Action' (1910) 44 *American Law Review* 12; R. Pound, 'The Call for a "Realist" Jurisprudence' (1931) 44 *Harvard Law Review* 706; F. Cohen, 'Transcendental Nonsense and the Functional Approach' (1935) 35 *Columbia Law Review* 809–49; D. Kennedy, *The Rise and Fall of Classical Legal Thought* (Frederick: Beard Group Inc, 1975).

11 K. Llewellyn, *Bramble Bush* (New York: Oxford University Press, 1950).

12 See, e.g., the scholars and related specialized programmes ranging from Law and Psychology (<http://www.law.stanford.edu/program/degrees/joint/psychology/>) to Law and Geography (<http://www.sfu.ca/~blomley/research.html>) to Law and Biology (<http://digitalcommons.law.yale.edu/fss_papers/2216>) to Law and Ethics (<http://www.trinity.utoronto.ca/Current_Students/esl.htm>) to Law and Science (<http://web.mit.edu/~ssilbey/www/pdf/Silbey_I_fnl.pdf).

13 See, e.g., the brilliant work by R. Aguilera, D. Rupp, C. A. Williams, and J. Ganapathi, 'Putting the S Back in Corporate Social Responsibility: a Multi-Level Theory of Social Change in Organizations' (2004) 32 *Academy of Management Review* 836–63 (also available at <http://papers.ssrn.com/sol3/papers.cfm?abstract_id=567842>).

14 C. Sunstein (ed), *Behavioural Law & Economics* (Cambridge: Cambridge University Press, 2000).

15 E. A. Posner and C. R. Sunstein (eds), *Law & Happiness* (Chicago: University Press of Chicago, 2010).

16 D. Rodrik, 'Institutions Rule: The Primacy of Institutions Over Geography and Integration in Economic Development' (2004) 9 *Journal of Economic Growth* 131–65; see also D. C. North, *Institutions, Institutional Change and Economic Performance* (Cambridge, Cambridge University Press, 1990).

17 See, e.g., V. Nee and R. Swedberg, 'Economic Sociology and New Institutional Economics' in C. Ménard and M. M. Shirley (eds), *Handbook of New Institutional Economics* (Berlin Heidelberg: Springer Verlag, 2005) 789–818; D. Baecker, *Wirtschaftssoziologie* (Bielefeld: transcript Verlag, 2006).

evolutionary theory[18] has considerable roots, out of which have arisen a number of very promising research avenues, altogether fostering a more expansive and interdisciplinary interest in norm-creation[19] and societal ordering.[20] Building on but going beyond the legal realists' attack of the impenetrable judicial mindset[21], law and psychology scholars and behavioural economists alike have more recently taken us a good way towards a better understanding of the motivational forces behind not only legal but also wider social decision-making.[22] It is this general context in which we find ourselves engaging with the insightful comments made by Kameda and his colleagues in Chapter 2.

II. Invest–Do Not Invest? Eat–Do Not Eat? Do–Do Not? Happy–Not Happy?

Kameda and his colleagues make a forceful argument for an appreciation of the psychological and neural underpinnings of collective human behaviour. They are particularly interested in developing a better understanding of 'herding' behaviour, evidenced by crime and obesity as well as bank-runs, stock markets, and other collective hysteria and fashion trends. Evidence for the necessity to study the psychological-neural conditions of such occurrences is found—inter alia—in literature, where the authors draw our attention to Hans-Christian Andersen's tale of the 'Emperor's New Clothes', which they interpret as telling a story about 'pluralistic ignorance'. The relevance of this allusion is made clear by likening the mindset of the Emperor's followers to that of the clients engaging in a bank-run—originally initiated by an (unwarranted) individual panic withdrawal. And, the link to present day collective behaviour is further and most helpfully emphasized by referring to the animal spirits which seem to determine our behaviour beginning with Keynes[23] and into the present day.[24] Tracing

[18] R. R. Nelson and S. G. Winter, *An Evolutionary Theory of Economic Change* (Harvard: Belknap Press of University Harvard Press, 1985); P. Zumbansen and G.-P. Calliess, 'Law, Economics & Evolutionary Theory: State of the Art and Interdisciplinary Perspectives' in P. Zumbansen and G.-P. Calliess (eds), *Law, Economics & Evolutionary Theory* (Cheltenham: Edward Elgar Publishing, 2011).

[19] R. A. Posner, 'Social Norms, Social Meaning, and the Economic Analysis of Law' (1998) 27 *Journal of Legal Studies* 553–65; C. Sunstein, 'Social Norms and Social Roles' (1996) 96 *Columbia Law Review* 903–68; and the contributions to J. N. Drobak (ed), *Norms and the Law* (Cambridge: Cambridge University Press, 2006).

[20] E. Ostrom, 'Challenges and Growth: the Development of the Interdisciplinary Field of Institutional Analysis' (2007) 3 *Journal of Institutional Economics* 239–64.

[21] See only R. Pound, 'Mechanical Jurisprudence' (1908) 8 *Columbia Law Review* 605.

[22] See, e.g., R. Thaler and C. Sunstein, *Nudge. Improving Decisions about Health, Wealth and Happiness* (New York: Penguin Group, 2008).

[23] J. M. Keynes, *The General Theory of Employment, Interest, and Money [1936]* (New York: Prometheus Books, 1997) 161: 'Most, probably, of our decisions to do something positive, the full consequences of which will be drawn out over many days to come, can only be taken as a result of animal spirits – of a spontaneous urge to action rather than inaction, and not as the outcome of a weighted average of quantitative benefits multiplied by quantitative probabilities.'

[24] G. A. Akerlof and R. J. Shiller, *Animal Spirits. How Human Psychology Drives the Economy, and Why It Matters for Global Capitalism* (Princeton, NJ: Princeton University Press, 2009).

relatively straightforward but as such no more desirable or, at least regrettable, patterns of herd behaviour—as in the example of information cascades arising around an initial (wrongful?) rejection of a paper submitted to a scientific journal, which eventually unleashes a seemingly unstoppable wave of rejections—the authors draw our attention to the importance of in-depth empirical research of collective behaviours. Among such studies, the authors point to experiments conducted with honeybees scouting the next best hive[25] as well as to research on music-downloading behaviour. Kameda and his colleagues deliver a convincing proposal for a much more serious engagement on the part of economists as well as social scientists with neural, psychological, and behavioural mechanisms. Their central contention is that while we need to recognize that these mechanisms have been playing crucial roles in the evolution of man's life on earth, they are also the potential cause of 'serious errors in modern environments, in which connectivities of individuals are much denser and externalities accruing from individual behaviours are much greater and more far reaching, as compared to ancient environments in which the human mind evolved.'[26]

III. Lessons Learned?

The message to economists seems clear, but how clear is it to a broader range of regulatory theories, including law? Here, the picture needs to be more accentuated. Lawyers in different areas such as, but not limited to, criminal law, tort law, constitutional law, or even international law[27] have long been addressing structures and effects of collective behaviour. At the basis of such engagement has been the recognition that the attribution of different legally scrutinizable forms of guilt, responsibility, or accountability but also—in international law—authority[28] requires a particular legal theoretical effort to address, for example, incomplete or inchoate chains of causation and to make sense of the intertwined nature of individual and collective behaviour in either extreme circumstances[29] or in, say, organizational corporate contexts.[30] Already against this background, the emphasis on the study of herding behaviour and a serious consideration of neural-psychological underpinnings promise to increase our analytical tools when engaging in the assessments of causation and responsibility.

But the work on herding behaviour has a number of further applications that deserve our attention. Such applications become apparent where we return to

[25] T. D. Seeley, *Honeybee Democracy* (Princeton: Princeton Universtiy Press, 2010).

[26] See Chapter 2, Section IV.

[27] See, e.g., B. Rajagopal, 'International Law and Social Movements: Challenges of Theorizing Resistance' (2003) 41 *Columbia Journal of Transnational Law* 397–433.

[28] C. Schreuer, 'The Waning of the Sovereign State: Towards a New Paradigm for International Law?' (1993) 4 *European Journal of International Law* 447–71.

[29] C. Browning, *Ordinary Men: Reserve Police Battalion 101 and the Final Solution in Poland* (New York: HarperCollins Publishers, 1992).

[30] *Canadian Dredge & Dock Co. Ltd. v. The Queen* [1985] 1 S.C.R. 662.

the earlier projects undertaken primarily by law and society scholars to render a more complete picture of the *embeddedness* of legal regulation in a heterogeneous normative and institutional setting. The path breaking work with relevance for the presently pursued project was carried out in the area of contract law.[31] Legal pluralists,[32] for that matter, as well as sociologists[33] were among those who pointed to the myriad forms in which informal norms governed behaviour in far more subtle and sophisticated ways than a formalistic legal model would imply. Standing on the shoulders of legal sociological scholars who explored the interaction between formal and informal order systems,[34] legal theorists were able to draw an impressively more layered and differentiated picture of 'contracts in action'.[35]

These evolutionary steps are important to keep in mind today when we learn that a new breed of 'social norms theorists' harbour deep scepticism vis-à-vis allegedly incompetent or overzealous judges when adjudicating complex contractual arrangements.[36] In fact, serious attempts to make sense of the formal/informal regulatory environment, which characterized, shaped and informed contractual governance had been undertaken not only through extensive empirical research but also with particular scrutiny of the economic dimensions of these regulatory patterns—already a long time ago.[37] What this work produced, among other insights, was a growing awareness of the layers of contractual bargaining that could not fully be explained by reference to either the (subjective) will of the parties on the one hand, or to an established (objective) purpose dimension of the arrangement on the other. Instead, an economic sociology and empirical legal studies approach taken to the scrutiny of contractual arrangements revealed both long-term[38] as well as organizational[39] dimensions which prompted a fundamental reconsideration of the confines of a contractual agreement. This shift in

[31] S. Macaulay, 'Elegant Models, Empirical Pictures, and the Complexities of Contract' (1977) 11 *Law & Society Review* 507–28.

[32] S. F. Moore, 'Law and Social Change: the Semi-autonomous Field as an Appropriate Subject of Study' (1973) 7 *Law & Society Review* 719–46.

[33] M. Granovetter, 'The Strength of Weak Ties' (1973) 78 *American Journal of Sociology* 1360–80.

[34] E. Ehrlich, *Fundamental Principles of the Sociology of Law* (New York: Russel & Russel, 1962) (orig. published in German as *Grundlegung der Soziologie des Rechts* (München, Leipzig: Duncker & Humblot, 1913)); G. Gurvitch, *Sociology of Law* (New York: Philosophical Library Inc, 1942).

[35] S. Macaulay, 'Non-contractual Relations in Business: A Preliminary Study' (1963) 28 *American Sociological Review* 55–67; as well as the landmark casebook: S. Macaulay, J. Kidwell, and W. C. Whitford, *Contract Law in Action* (New York, NY: Matthew Bender & Co, 1986).

[36] E. A. Posner, *Law and Social Norms* (Cambridge, Mass: Harvard University Press, 2000) 156; R. E. Scott, 'The Death of Contract Law' (2004) 54 *University of Toronto Law Journal* 369–90.

[37] See, e.g., I. R. Macneil, 'Contracts: Adjustment of Long-Term Economic Relations Under Classical, Neoclassical, and Relational Contract Law' (1978) 72 *Northwestern University Law Review* 854–905; D. Campbell, 'The Incompleteness of our Understanding of the Law and Economics of Relational Contract' (2004) 2004 *Wisconsin Law Review* 645–78; P. Zumbansen, 'The Law of Society: Governance Through Contract' (2007) 14 *Indiana Journal of Global Legal Studies* 191–233 (available at <http://ssrn.com/abstract=988610>).

[38] I. R. Macneil, 'Relational Contract: What We Do and What We Do Not Know' (1985) *Wisconsin Law Review* 483–525.

[39] T. Daintith and G. Teubner (eds), *Contract and Organisation. Legal Analysis in the Light of Economic and Social Theory* (Berlin: de Gruyter, 1986).

perspective eventually gave way to an increasingly differentiated understanding of the adaptive and, arguably, *constitutionalizing* dimensions of contract.[40]

IV. Interdisciplinarity and Contract Governance

Today, in a world where the 'materialization of contract law' has a sour ring to it, because even stern adepts of consumer protection law have grown aware of the intricacies of judicial engagements with fast-evolving, sensible areas of social organization[41], contract theorists have begun to turn their curious minds to an even more layered analysis of contractual governance, aiming at a political critique of power relations[42] in order to develop a more adequate understanding of contractual networks.[43] Again, these developments are crucial elements in the formation of a new regulatory landscape, which can be described neither with reference to the state as sole law-producer nor with reference alone to *legal* rules when we attempt to depict present and emerging regulatory structures.[44] It should be against the background and in light of legal scholars' attempts to make sense of the legal sociological, legal pluralist, and evolutionary theories as well as prospects of an emerging transnational normative order[45] that we continue to posit the project of 'contract governance'[46] vis-à-vis complementing bodies of theory interested in social ordering. A confrontation between legal and non-legal approaches to contract governance should be mindful of the questionability of law's boundaries as such—today as in the past. As Holmes said:

> It is perfectly proper to regard and study the law simply as a great anthropological document. It is proper to resort to it to discover what ideals of society have been strong enough

[40] R. Wiethölter, 'Privatrecht als Gesellschaftstheorie?' in F. Baur, J. Esser, F. Kübler, and E. Steindorff (eds), *Funktionswandel der Privatrechtsinstitutionen. Festschrift für Ludwig Raiser zum 70. Geburtstag* (Tübingen: Mohr Siebeck, 1974) 645–96; see also K. Llewellyn, 'What Price Contract? - An Essay in Perspective' (1930) 40 *Yale Law Journal* 704–51.

[41] R. Damm, '*Privatautonomie und Verbraucherschutz. Legalstruktur und Realstruktur von Autonomiekonzepten*' (1999) 50 *Versicherungsrecht* 129–41.

[42] R. Kreitner, 'Frameworks of Cooperation: Competing, Conflicting, and Joined Interests in Contract and its Surroundings' (2005) 6 *Theoretical Inquiries in Law* 59–111.

[43] G. Teubner, *Networks as Connected Contracts. Edited and with an Introduction by Hugh Collins (translated by M. Everson)* (Oxford: Hart Publishing, 2011); see already S. Grundmann, '*Die Dogmatik der Vertragsnetze*' (2007) 207 *Archiv für die Cilivilistische Praxis* 718–67, and M. Amstutz, 'The Constitution of Contractual Networks', in M. Amstutz and G. Teubner (eds), *Networks. Legal Issues of Multilateral Co-operation* (Oxford: Hart Publishing, 2009) 309–46.

[44] K. -H. Ladeur, 'Towards a Legal Theory of Supranationality - The Viability of the Network Concept' (1997) 3 *European Law Journal* 33–54; for transnational private law see, e.g., G.-P. Calliess and P. Zumbansen, *Rough Consensus and Running Code: A Theory of Transnational Private Law* (Oxford: Hart Publishing, 2010).

[45] See, e.g., C. M. Schmitthoff, 'International Business Law: A New Law Merchant' (1961) 2 *Current Law and Social Problems* 129–53; R. Cranston, 'Theorizing Transnational Commercial Law' (2007) 42 *Texas International Law Journal* 597–617; see also R- Cotterrell, 'Spectres of Transnationalism: Changing Terrains of Sociology of Law' (2009) 36 *Journal of Law and Society* 481–500; W. Kerber, 'Transnational Commercial Law, Multi-level Legal Systems and Evolutionary Economics' in P. Zumbansen and G. -P. Calliess (eds), *Law, Economics and Evolutionary Theory* (Cheltenham: Edward Edgar Publishing, 2011) 297–321.

[46] K. Riesenhuber and F. Möslein, 'Contract Governance: A Draft Research Agenda' (2009) 5 *European Review of Contract Law* 248–89.

to reach that final stage of expression, or what have been the changes in dominant ideals from century to century. It is proper to study it as an exercise in the morphology and transformation of human ideas. The study pursued for such ends becomes science in the strictest sense.[47]

With that in mind, it will simply not be enough to confine ourselves to a renewed and reinvigorated engagement between law *and* economic sciences as long as we understand each as a solidly circumscribed body of scientific endeavour. Instead, it becomes obvious merely from a cursory account of the historical transformation of both law and economics that were we to embark into a fresh collaboration between these two fields, we would have to take into account the ways in which both fields have been undergoing fundamental change. Both fields—law as much as economics—have evolved along both the lines of internal systematic differentiation and external pressure. This 'outside' pressure arises from 'crisis' in a very real way, but also in terms of the collapse of theoretical disciplinary boundaries.[48] It is the latter, which describes the evolution of law in relation to the emergence of 'governance' and 'regulatory theory' over the past decades. This development is clearly propelled by 'visible' changes in the outside world, observed and described for example as processes of 'globalisation' or 'denationalisation'.[49] But, it also is the result of an internal differentiation of scientific imagery of the 'world'.

As regards the emerging research, policy, and regulatory field of 'contract governance', we need to remain aware of the powerful grip of traditional demarcations between market self-regulation and political intervention in this area. This continues to be the case despite a seemingly wide appreciation of a new nature of connectivity between human and systemic interaction.[50] That the world is becoming more complex, that the 'state' is allegedly 'no longer' able to do what it used to do, that not only legal rules but also social norms govern complex societal constellations, or that the law is about to implode under the pressure from diversity, fragmentation, and pluralism, is—above all—an observation which applies to the way in which the law depicts itself and the world 'around it'. As such, however, it might or might not be based on an adequate description of the 'world' itself. Similarly, it might or might not be an adequate understanding of law 'in' that world. In the end, however, there is no one to make that call. It is the way the law describes itself and itself in relation to the world, and the evolving state of this description is *the law*. There is no final arbitrator to say whether the law 'got

[47] Holmes, n 5, 212.

[48] See M. Amstutz, 'Eroding Boundaries: On Financial Crisis and an Evolutionary Concept of Regulatory Reform' in P. Kjaer, G. Teubner, and A. Febbrajo (eds), *The Financial Crisis in Constitutional Perspective. The Dark Side of Functional Differentiation* (Oxford: Hart Publishing, 2011) 223–68; see also C. M. Reinhart and K. S. Rogoff, *This Time is Different. Eight Centuries of Financial Folly* (Princeton, NJ: Princeton University Press, 2009).

[49] S. Sassen, 'Globalization or Denationalization?' (2003) 10 *Review of International Political Economy* 1–22.

[50] See, e.g., S. Schwarcz, 'Systemic Risk' (2008) 97 *Georgetown Law Journal* 193 (available at <http://papers.ssrn.com/sol3/papers.cfm?abstract_id=1008326>); C. Parker, 'The Pluralization of Regulation' (2008) 9 *Theoretical Inquiries in Law* 349–69, 351: 'No one regulator, including law, has any monopoly or final authority across a whole regulatory "space".'

it right'. The law, as is true for economics, politics, and religion, constructs and reconstructs the 'outside' by connecting an ever growing and sophisticated body of 'legal' artefacts with each other.

V. Law, Economics, and More: Systemic Risk and Governance

Contract governance comes onto the scene with considerable baggage. This inheritance expresses itself in the double dimension of contract governance itself—which can either mean that contracts *govern* or that we are concerned with the governance *of* contracts. Traditional law and economics scholars would likely embrace the former interpretation, while progressive lawyers interested in the materialization of law[51] would tend to focus on the scope of adjudication and judge-made contract law.[52] Contract governance is an ingenious proposition in terms of a research enterprise because it—of course—captures both of these dimensions. And because of this it is possible to see the 'inside' and the 'outside' of contract governance, which illustrates the complex assumptions that go into the project from the start. The idea of contract governance understood as governance *by* contract renders invisible and instantaneously summons the 'basis of contract'[53], in other words the nature of contractual relationships. This certainly precedes law and economics scholars' translation—or, should we say 'abduction'—of contract governance into 'social norms theory'. Contract governance, long before the discovery of social norms by law and economics scholars[54] could be understood as part of a comprehensive, 'embedding' theory of a liberal society.[55] This embeddedness at the same time ensured that the connection between society and the practice (and theory) of contracting never was left out of sight. That connection is severed by playing contract governance off against the governance of contract, as is done by social norms theorists and adepts of a neo-formalist approach to contract law. But, contract governance is not new. The genius of contract governance has always been the recognition that these two dimensions cannot be separated such that one would potentially trump the other. To do so would render the fact that contracting is part of societal interaction absurd. To recognize contractual governance (as governance through contract) as part of society, however, connects the theory of contract governance with the theory of society. And the latter is far more complex than to be captured in the scrutiny of this or that instance, where courts wandered into the judicial resolution of complex contractual relationships.

[51] K. Renner, *The Institutions of Private Law and their Social Functions* (London: Routledge & Kegan Paul, 1949) (orig. published in German as *Die Rechtsinstitute des Privatrechts und ihre Soziale Funktion* (Tübingen: J.B.C. Mohr, 1929)).

[52] J. N. Adams and R. Brownsword, 'The Ideologies of Contract' (1987) 7 *Legal Studies* 205–23, 213.

[53] M. R. Cohen, 'The Basis of Contract' (1932) 46 *Harvard Law Review* 553–92.

[54] R. C. Ellickson, 'Law and Economics Discovers Social Norms' (1998) 27 *Journal of Legal Studies* 537–65.

[55] H. Collins, *Regulating Contracts* (Oxford: Oxford University Press, 1999) 3.

Contract governance cannot be reduced to a theory of social norms independent from the theory of society, in which it is embedded. This theory, however, is not fully accessible for the law itself, as it has its own—legal—'rhymes and reasons'. But the differentiation of the legal system occurs as the law 'reacts to the world' over time. In doing so, it receives impulses from economics, politics, and religion and these perturb, impregnate, and challenge the law and its toolkit. This is where we are.

For lawyers, to be taking 'on board' economics, be that in the way that economists engage with psychology and neurosciences, or the way that they have been pushing our imaginations to understand 'institutions' or 'norms', can be fruitful and rewarding in that it reminds us of the complex enterprise that law should be seen as. The promise lies in connecting social norms theory, new institutional economics, behavioural economics, and evolutionary theory with law's earlier engagement with sociology[56] or political theory[57] in order to unfold the true potential of a historically evolving interdisciplinary exploration of this area of law—and social, economic, and political theory. An enterprise of such ambitious nature alone would be positioned to address the types of challenges that arise from the diversity of materials, questions of method, and avenues of conceptualization—and to which we are not yet fully accustomed to in the law and economics approach to corporate law.[58] With this richer canvass in sight, we can draw more effectively on the offers made by the new directions in economic theory. It then becomes more visible how this particular interest in herding patterns is in fact relevant to concurring work on social norms, lawlessness, and economic governance on the one hand, and on the evolutionary challenge of game theory on the other.[59] This research fills gaps left by both institutional analysis and economic sociology. These gaps might exist, as neither approach seems sufficiently appreciative of the *dynamics* of information transfer and behavioural patterns such as those at the centre of psychological work on herding today. With a better understanding, then, of how behaviour influence occurs in societal practice, we are further building on the longstanding explorations of the non-contractual foundations of contract[60] and the tension between 'status' and contract[61] emerges in sharper

[56] E. Durkheim, *The Division of Labor in Society* (New York: Free Press, 1984) (orig. published in 1893; transl. by W. D. Halls); M. Mauss, *The Gift* (London: Routledge & Kegan Paul, 1990); M. Weber, *On Law in Economy and Society* (Cambridge, Mass: Harvard University Press, 1957) (transl. from the orig. in German by E. Shils and M. Rheinstein (M. Rheinstein (ed)) *Wirtschaft und Gesellschaft* (Tübingen: Mohr Siebeck, 2nd edn, 1925).

[57] S. Macaulay, 'Private Government' in L. Lipson and S. Wheeler (eds), *Law and the Social Sciences* (New York: Russell Sage Foundation, 1986) 445–518.

[58] See, e.g., F. H. Easterbrook and D. R. Fischel, *The Economic Structure of Corporate Law* (Cambridge, Mass: Harvard University Press, 1991); for suggestions to widen the hitherto pursued dialogue between economics and corporate law, see K. J. Hopt, 'Comparative Company Law' in M. Reimann and R. Zimmermann (eds), *Oxford Handbook of Comparative Law* (Oxford: Oxford University Press, 2006) 1161–91, 1186`.

[59] S. Deakin, 'Legal Evolution: Integrating Economic and Systemic Approaches' (2011) University of Cambridge Legal Studies Research Paper Series Paper No 41/2011 (available at <http://ssrn.com/abstract=1934738>).

[60] Durkheim, n 56, 158: 'For in a contract not everything is contractual.'

[61] H. S. Maine, *Ancient Law. Its Connection with the Early History of Society, and its Relation to Modern Ideas* (London: John Murray, 1861); see also C. Joerges, 'Status and Contract in Franchising

relief. At the same time, economic studies based on psychological and neural insights carry the promise of providing for a clearer picture of, say, the dynamics of emerging, competing, and evolving informal legal orders—which have been at the heart of law and economics scholars as well as legal pluralists for a long time.[62]

A caveat is, however, in order. It originates from the individualistic assumptions that appear to inform some of the current interest in herding behaviour, but that also have been underlying other law and economics approaches, for example in lawyers' engagement with game theory.[63] Such focus on individual or collective (again seen as divisible into individual actors) behavioural patterns suggests that there is still a widely held belief in the possibility of tracing results back to *choices*—however 'irrational' these might be. Contrast this assumption with the lessons we are beginning to draw from the financial crisis. The latter illustrates the shortcomings of governance and 'intervention' theories that are oriented around linear cause-effect and responsiveness relations between 'problem' and 'solution'.[64] Indeed, if we consider the current research into the 'origins' and 'causes' of the economic and financial crisis, we find that the analytical regulatory theory toolkits of cause-effect relations as well as market-state distinctions[65] are at odds with the indeed more 'systemic' grounds for the crisis. The consequences of this shift in perspective, however, are still far from clear. But, what is emerging is a sense of a need to seriously reflect on regulation on the basis of recognizing complex systemic boundaries, spheres, and co-evolutionary dynamics. On the basis, then, that there is a fundamental inability to fully 'translate' rationalities of one system—law, economics, politics, religion, among others—into another, would prepare for a perhaps more adequate understanding of how regulatory approaches that aim at universalizing the rationality of one system by imposing them on others are bound to fail. This can be illustrated by taking the example of law as a social system. 'Legal forms encode information about coordination strategies which have proved more or less successful in particular social settings, including the economic domains of the market and the business enterprise.'[66] This, however, does not mean that the economic system is able to either incorporate, let alone understand this particular approach to the framing of coordination strategies

Law' in C. Joerges (ed), *Franchising and the Law: Theoretical and Comparative Approaches in Europe and the United States* (Baden-Baden: Nomos, 1991) 11–66.

[62] L. Bernstein, 'Opting out of the Legal System: Extralegal Contractual Relations in the Diamond Industry' (1992) 21 *Journal of Legal Studies* 115–57; H. W. Arthurs, *Without the Law: Administrative Justice and Legal Pluralism in Nineteenth Century England* (Toronto: University of Toronto Press, 1985).

[63] See, e.g., A. van Aaken, 'Effectuating Public International Law Through Market Mechanisms?' (2009) 165 *Journal of Institutional and Theoretical Economics* 33–57; for a critical discussion of lawyers' usages of game theory, see Deakin, n 59.

[64] See the exchange between E. Blankenburg, 'The Poverty of Evolutionism: a Critique of Teubner's Case for 'Reflexive Law' (1984) 18 *Law & Society Review* 273–89, and G. Teubner, 'Autopoiesis in Law and Society: A Rejoinder to Blankenburg' (1984) 18 *Law & Society Review* 291–301.

[65] For a refreshing deconstruction, see R. Steinzor, 'The Truth About Regulation in America' (2011) 5 *Harvard Law & Policy Review* 323–46.

[66] Deakin, n 59, 1.

within its own reference system—nor that this would work the other way around. 'Law and Economics', as an engagement between both systems based on 'shared' concerns about 'efficiency', 'costs', 'externalities', or, of course, 'rights'.[67] Surely, though, each means different things to this or that system.[68]

It seems clear, then, that contract governance offers a welcome opportunity to reach out—but also to reach back. This is not novel for lawyers, who are known to be constantly labouring on *models* of law, which are developed in response to what has been perceived as a heightened complexity of society. While this endeavour is in fact too often understood as one that lies within the primary competence area of public lawyers, contract lawyers have continued to claim that their field cannot be understood in separation from an encompassing understanding and theorizing of social complexity.[69] The emerging research field of 'contract governance'[70] promises to shed some new light[71] on the interaction and overlap between contractual and organizational governance dynamics by exploring the governance function of contract and corporate law as parallel regulatory paradigms, tightly interwoven in the face of highly volatile markets.[72]

It becomes clear that contract *law* needs to be adequately structured in order to be able to take on board the specific contextual particularities that characterize *contract governance*, in particular where its function consists of dealing with complexity, in particular with various forms of risk. What would this mean and how would this be innovative? That there is a perceived need to both contextualize *and* politicize contract governance, might account for the continuing difficulties around a proper demarcation of contract law and social norms, above all as regards the possibility to adapt contractual arrangements over time and in response to changed circumstances. This is illustrated, for example, in the area of relational and multi-party contracting. Such forms of contracting exist both in private market contexts and in public-private regulatory and collaboration contexts, and it is the transformation of the surrounding regulatory landscape towards further decentralization and proceduralization, which prompts a renewed interest in exploring what we might want to call the 'public dimension' of such contractual

[67] R. Coase, 'The Problem of Social Cost' (1960) 3 *The Journal of Law and Economics* 1–44, 15: 'But it has to be remembered that the immediate question faced by the courts is *not* what shall be done and by whom but *who* has the legal right to do what.'

[68] See, e.g., D. Kennedy, 'Cost-Reduction as Legitimation' (1981) 90 *Yale Law Journal* 1275–83; D. Kennedy, 'Law-and-Economics from the Perspective of Critical Legal Studies' in P. Newman (ed), *The New Palgrave Dictionary of Economics and the Law* (New York: Palgrave Macmillan References, 1998) 465–74, 466–67.

[69] See, e.g., J. P. Esser, 'Institutionalizing Industry: The Changing Forms for Contract' (1996) *Law and Social Inquiry* 593–629; D. Campbell, 'Breach of Contract and the Efficiency of Markets' in S. F. Copp (ed), *The Legal Foundations of Free Markets* (London: Institute of Economic Affairs, 2008) 140–57.

[70] See Riesenhuber and Möslein, n 46.

[71] See here in particular the contributions to T. Daintith and G. Teubner (eds), *Contract and Organisation. Legal Analysis in the Light of Economic and Social Theory* (Berlin, New York: de Gruyter, 1986).

[72] F. Möslein, '*Contract Governance und Corporate Governance im Zusammenspiel. Lehren aus der Globalen Finanzkrise*' (2010) 65 *Juristenzeitung* 72–80, 78.

arrangements. But, this quarrel does not yet illuminate the limits inherent to our approaching 'external' dimensions of contract governance as, say, 'political'.[73] What is 'political' about contract governance, just as about corporate governance or the regulation of labour markets, is anything but a mappable landscape of different 'interests'. The here repeated fallacy of methodological individualism turns out to trigger highly undesirable consequences, as it falls dramatically short of capturing the complexity that ties contracts, corporations, and labour markets 'together'—to stay with our current example. What is needed is a methodology, which appreciates the fundamental differences in systems' description and construction of the world in order to imagine a non-unifying, pluralist approach to making sense of governance, regulation, and of the 'and' in law *and* economics.

It follows, that an enhanced interdisciplinary study of the non-contractual 'foundations' of contracting cannot stop at the sociological analysis of *how* and *between whom* promises are made and how they are implemented, enforced, and institutionalized. Instead, as we have seen, it is of great relevance to take into account the individual and collective dispositions of market actors but also the larger patterns and mechanisms of information transmission, such as those that underlie herding behaviour. The cautionary tale here, particularly for the legal and economic scholars who have recently begun to embrace 'social norms' and institutional economics as the foundation of a social theory of regulation, however, is that to focus on just this side of market behaviour might too easily provide a platform for a one-sided, that is de-contextual, focus on 'what people do'. One risk with such a disembedded behavioural analysis from the larger societal context in which human behaviour occurs, is that we cut the ties between longstanding sociological research into societal change and our present interest in contracts as prime modes of governance. Another one is that we risk severely underestimating the nature of the norms we are referring to under the umbrella of 'social norms'. Building, say, on legal sociology and legal pluralism on the one hand and on new institutional economics on the other, will go some way towards a more differentiated understanding of norms in the evolving complex regulatory landscape that characterizes the interaction of public, private, state-originating and non-state, informal norms today. But even that approach would have to take much more seriously different alternative types and shapes of norms, be these cultural, symbolic, or in other ways non-legal. In other words, a more suitable methodological approach would attempt to see beyond and in between individual 'motivations', 'beliefs', or 'rationales' driving people's behaviour in order to overcome the focus either on market versus non-market spheres or the breaking up of a complex environment into different 'interests'. If, to reiterate the 'context' in which our current investigations are embedded, complexity is one, if not the, crucial determinative challenge facing any attempt at a regulatory *response* to the crisis, then it is important the core trait of complexity—namely

[73] See, e.g., J. N. Adams and R. Brownsword, 'The Ideologies of Contract' (1987) 7 *Legal Studies* 205–23.

that it cannot be broken down into, or explained entirely through, their constituent parts.[74] Rather than trying to devise a meta-code oriented around a particular central or dominating goal or value, regulation will have to take into account the need to devise a process that appreciates the different functional rationalities at work within a particular regulatory 'problem'. Such an approach would include a fundamental shift from normative to cognitive expectations in the structure—and the understanding—of regulatory processes.[75] While this proposal was made with particular reference to the challenges facing legal theory in the context of a fragmented global legal order[76], it forcefully applies to the currently faced conundrum of 'financial regulation' as much as it does to the emerging field of contract governance.[77] The latter areas constitute formidable examples of complex regulatory arenas in that they each defy categorizations along traditional forms of political versus non-political, state versus non-state, public versus private regulation. Both areas are both at the same time—and more. They are neither national nor international, neither formal nor informal. Our distinctions can only go so far in illuminating the component structure of financial regulation or contract governance. What the exhaustion of said distinctions illustrates, however, is the inadequacy to try to associate these governance processes with structures of either 'regulation' or 'self-regulation'. This association would only make sense if the boundaries between both demarcated self-standing structures of norm generation and implementation. That, however, is not the case, where we base our distinction in the end on the appreciation of a particular level of deference or 'autonomy'. In the case of 'regulation', this ordinarily depicts the state as having the choice to or not to 'intervene'. By contrast, 'self-regulation' depicts actors—individual or institutional—as exercising norm-generating authority on an autonomous basis, in other words one that is free from regulation *as intervention*. The fragmentary nature of this depiction has long been pointed to[78], but beyond the clarification of the rights basis of the exercise of authority, there is the problem of over-individualizing who in fact is regulating or self-regulating. The current attempts to push regulatory theory towards a framework that can incorporate systemic linkages[79] underline the importance of moving

[74] Deakin, n 59.

[75] For more background, see M. Amstutz, 'Globalising Speenhamland: On the Transnational Metamorphosis of Corporate Social Responsibility' in C. Joerges and J. Falke (eds), *Karl Polanyi, Globalisation and the Potential of Law in Transnational Markets* (Oxford: Hart Publishing, 2011) 359–93, 373–74.

[76] Amstutz, n 75; see also G. Teubner, '"Global Bukowina": Legal Pluralism in the World Society' in G. Teubner (ed), *Global Law Without A State* (Aldershot: Dartmouth, 1997) 3–28.

[77] See Chapter 12.

[78] R. L. Hale, 'Coercion and Distribution in a Supposedly Non-Coercive State' (1923) 38 *Political Science Quarterly* 470–94; M. R. Cohen, 'Property and Sovereignty' (1927) 13 *Cornell Law Quarterly* 8–30.

[79] M. Amstutz, 'Eroding Boundaries: On Financial Crisis and an Evolutionary Concept of Regulatory Reform' in P. Kjaer, G. Teubner, and A. Febbrajo (eds), *The Financial Crisis in Constitutional Perspective. The Dark Side of Functional Differentiation* (Oxford: Hart Publishing, 2011) 223–68.

beyond 'interests' and 'stakeholders'[80] and towards a more differentiated system of 'affectedness'[81] as one of the keys in thinking about regulation and governance.

Contracts can well be seen as having been crucial instruments and *fora* of societal governance for a long time. But, that has never meant, nor should it mean today, that they can be studied in isolation from the context in which they perform regulatory functions. Parties do not just simply enter into agreements outside or 'in the shadow of the law', because they deem it efficient. The 'turn to contract' occurs in the context of a richly structured field of public, and private, intersecting modes of governance. To celebrate either contract or social norms as the (late) expressions of economic liberalism, will give little guidance to the questions we face today. Economic governance must correctly be understood as a call to arms—not *against* the alleged interventionist fervour of zealous governments or activist judges, but rather for the building of a comprehensive, interdisciplinary theory of (market) governance today.

[80] See also P. Zumbansen and S. Archer, 'The BCE Decision: Reflections on the Firm as a Contractual Organization' (2008) CLPE Comparative Research in Law & Political Economy Research Paper (available at <http://ssrn.com/abstract=1160094>).

[81] See the important work by R. Cotterrell, 'Spectres of Transnationalism: Changing Terrains of Sociology of Law' (2009) 36 *Journal of Law and Society* 481–500 and D. Held, 'Democratic Accountability and Political Effectiveness from a Cosmopolitan Perspective' (2004) 39 *Government and Opposition* 364–91.

3

Moral Hazard and Herd Behaviour in the Financial Crisis

Bruno S. Frey and Reto Cueni***

I. Repressed Voice and Costs of Non-herding

After the outbreak of a crisis, a large number of people often say that they foresaw the imminent disaster. When asked why they did not warn someone before it happened, they usually say they did but got attacked and silenced or they feared the negative consequences of predicting a disaster. The reasons given are interesting because they reveal the underlying costs of being critical, and they show that information can get lost due to these costs.

The last financial crisis provides many examples of employees who expressed their pessimistic view of the oncoming market and got mobbed and sidelined until they resigned or were fired.[1] The financial industry profits the most when the market prices of securities rise or are presumed to rise. Thus, the financial industry's best interests are served when positive economic outlooks persist and negative forecasts are rejected.

From an economic point of view, this mechanism leads to a waste of resources because it generates biased information in favour of positive ratings about future economic trends. This asymmetry generates distorted asset and resource allocations. In financial markets, there is ample evidence that such an asymmetry exists.[2]

* Senior Professor of Economics, Zeppelin University, Friedrichshafen.
** Department of Economics, University of Zurich.

[1] See, e.g., in E. Robinson, 'Research Renegades' (2009) 18(11) *Bloomberg Markets Magazine* 32–44, three equity analysts tell their stories of being punished by peers and supervisors because they forecasted a negative economic trend in their industry sectors; *ex post*, all of them put forth a correct analysis, but they all resigned because they could not stand the pressure. An article in *The Economist* ('Please do Feed the Bears', *The Economist*, 1 October 2009, p 16) describes the problems of negative forecasts and how they are suppressed by the financial industry.

[2] L. D. Brown, 'A Temporal Analysis of Earnings Surprises: Profits Versus Losses' (2001) 39 *Journal of Accounting Research* 221–41 shows that financial forecasts are generally overly optimistic. I. Welch, 'Herding among Security Analysts' (2000) 53 *Journal of Financial Economics* 369–396 finds that the herding of security analysts is stronger in periods when recent stock returns have been positive in contrast to bad times. S. Bikhchandani and S. Sharma, 'Herd Behavior in Financial

In order to understand this asymmetry, it is important to see why so many people involved in the financial industry are punished for speaking up or why they mask their negative expectations. An employee's cost of speaking up and not herding with the others has to be elicited. Once this cost is defined, it is important to identify institutional factors that can reduce this cost. Furthermore, the link between the herding behaviour of employees in a specific company and the herding behaviour of the various companies in the financial market has to be examined. If a link can be established, the individual costs of non-herding can be seen as one of the crucial factors in the origin of financial crises. These individual costs could lead to herding behaviour in many companies in the financial market.

We identify the possible costs of non-herding. At the bottom of the cost range, the subtle psychological pressure of individual co-workers arises and induces the social pressure of a team or whole department. At the top, when the pressure gets very high, workers may even feel compelled to resign their jobs or may be dismissed.

In the spirit of Blinder and Choi, we conducted a series of interviews with high ranked executives and chairpersons of banks, insurers, and hedge funds of different sizes in order to attain a comprehensive picture of the financial industry.[3] We use the statements of those we interviewed to explain, contrast, and challenge our theoretical approach and hence to connect the ideas developed to real world examples. A comprehensive analysis of an extended sample of interviews is provided in Cueni and Frey.[4]

This Chapter is organized as follows: in Section II, a brief literature review is presented. In Section III, we explain the phenomenon of the costs that lead to herding behaviour in the decision processes of companies. In Section IV, different types of non-herding costs are expounded. In Section V, we formulate several propositions about the non-herding costs and confront them with statements from the interviews of the practitioners; Section VI concludes.

II. Literature on Herding-behaviour

An important precursor is Le Bon, a famous French sociologist, who discussed the problems arising from herding behaviour and the psychology of the crowd in 1895.[5] Four years later, Thorstein Veblen, the first economist who dealt explicitly

Markets' (2001) 47 *IMF Staff Papers* 279–310 explain generally how herding and informational cascades can destabilize markets and increase the fragility of financial systems.

[3] A. S. Blinder and D. H. Choi, 'A Shred of Evidence on Theories of Wage Stickiness (1990) 105 *The Quarterly Journal of Economics* 1003–15 and later T. F. Bewley, *Why Wages Don't Fall During a Recession* (Cambridge, Mass: Harvard University Press, 1999) conducted a series of interviews in order to understand why wages do not fall during a recession as expected by classical economic theory.

[4] See R. Cueni and B. S. Frey, *The Costs of Non-Herding* (Mimeo, Zurich: University of Zurich, 2011).

[5] See G. Le Bon, *The Crowd: A Study of the Popular Mind* (London: Ernst Benn, 1895).

with herding behaviour, analysed mass consumption and tried to explain why people tend to buy what others buy.[6] His idea was further developed by Harvey Leibenstein and his famous study about 'bandwagon effects'.[7] At that time, the phenomenon of herd behaviour was mainly studied by sociologists and social psychologists, most prominently by Asch, Festinger, and Bandura.[8] Also important are the sociologists, as Granovetter's and Burt's work on collective behaviour, threshold models, and reference groups helps us to understand when and why herd behaviour can emerge.[9]

Focusing closer on our topic of herding behaviour in organizations, we identify four important approaches based on sociology and social psychology literature. In the context of decision-making processes, Janis' theory of groupthink explains why individuals perceive pressure not to dissent.[10] Noelle-Neumann's theory of the 'spiral of silence' points in the same direction; her thinking in particular treats mass communication and the origin of majority opinions in public debates.[11] The concept of diversity addresses the same problem from the opposite perspective: Bantel and Jackson propose diversified teams in order to integrate ways of collecting and processing information into a decision process.[12] Finally, the research on hidden profiles contributes important insights to the problem of collecting information in groups in order to reach a correct decision: Schulz-Hardt and colleagues demonstrate that dissent in teams is a facilitator for decision quality.[13] This finding reveals the relevance of the present analysis of non-herding costs.

[6] See T. Veblen, *The Theory of the Leisure Class: An Economic Study of Institutions* (New York: Dover, 1899).

[7] See H. Leibenstein, 'Bandwagon, Snob and Veblen Effects in the Theory of Consumers' Demands' (1950) 64 *The Quarterly Journal of Economics* 183–207.

[8] See S. E. Asch, 'Effects of Group Pressure Upon the Modification and Distortion of Judgements' in H. Guetzkow (ed), *Groups, Leadership and Men* (Pittsburgh, PA: Carnegie Press, 1951) 177–90; L. Festinger, 'A Theory of Social Comparison Processes' (1954) 7 *Human Relations* 114–40; and A. Bandura, 'Influence of Model's Reinforcement Contingencies of the Acquisition of Imitative Responses (1965) 1 *Journal of Personality and Social Psychology* 589–95.

[9] See Bandura, n 8 above; M. S. Granovetter, 'The Strength of Weak Ties' (1973) 78 *The American Journal of Sociology* 1360–80; R. S. Burt, *Toward a Structural Theory of Action: Network Models of Social Structure, Perception and Action* (London, NJ: Academic Press, 1982).

[10] I. L. Janis, *Victims of Groupthink* (Boston: Houghton Mifflin, 1972) defined the term of groupthink in his seminal work; R.S. Baron, 'So Right It's Wrong: Groupthink and the Ubiquitous Nature of Polarized Group Decision Making' in M. P. Zanna (ed), *Advances in Experimental Social Psychology* (San Diego: Elsevier Academic Press, 2005) provides a critical approach to the theory.

[11] See E. Noelle-Neumann, 'The Spiral of Silence: A Theory of Public Opinion' (1974) 24 *Journal of Communication* 43–51; E. Noelle-Neumann, *The Spiral of Silence: Public Opinion - Our Social Skin* (Chicago, Ill: Chicago University Press, 1984).

[12] K. A. Bantel and S. E. Jackson, 'Top Management and Innovations in Banking: Does the Composition of the Top Team Make a Difference?' (1989) 10 *Strategic Management Journal* 107–24 wrote the seminal paper; R. J. Ely, 'A Field Study of Group Diversity, Participation in Diversity Education Programs and Performance' (2004) 25 *Journal of Organizational Behavior* 755–80 reviewed the current literature.

[13] The term 'hidden profile' originated from the work by G. Stressed and W. Titus, 'Pooling of Unshared Information in Group Decision Making' (1985) 48 *Journal of Personality and Social Psychology* 1467–78; S. Schulz-Hardt, F. C. Brodbeck, A. Mojzisch, R. Kerschreiter, and D. Frey, 'Group Decision Making in Hidden Profile Situations: Dissent as a Facilitator for Decision Quality' (2006) 91 *Journal of Personality and Social Psychology* 1080–98 define the idea of the experiment: 'The correct solution was not identifiable on the basis of the members' individual information and could be detected only by pooling and integrating the members' unique information.'

From an economic perspective, herding behaviour can be studied by analysing payoffs and network externalities.[14] Interestingly, one of the best examples of an analysis of a payoff interaction between rational and truly selfish individuals stems from socio-biology: Hamilton's[15] study of selfish herds revealed that the clumping of animals is an indirect outcome of the selfish behaviour to put another member of the herd between itself and a predator. As in the case of decision-making in teams, the individual's concern is to refrain from being outside the herd. As long as an individual goes along with the opinion of the majority, he can hide in the herd, especially if the decision was wrong *ex post*. If anticipated, this herd behaviour serves as an individual risk-reducing strategy that creates negative externalities for the other individuals in the organization.

Connecting the mechanism of hiding in the herd and the agency problems between supervisors and subordinates, or clients and managers, leads us to reputational herding. In 1990, Scharfstein and Stein provided a seminal model that considered two managers whose abilities were not known to any observers (e.g., clients or supervisors). The observers inferred the managers' abilities by comparing the investment decisions of the managers. After each period, the observers updated their information according to the investment payoffs from the managers' strategies. The managers were paid based on the observers' assessment of their abilities. The outcome of the model is always that one manager follows the other's lead. The strategy results in a loss of information because the manager who follows ignores his private information. As the observers do not know, *ex post* or *ex ante*, what they should expect as the best investment strategy, they compare the two managers. As long as the managers take the same action, neither of them is blamed for a bad payoff.

The institutional setting of an organization's performance measurement is therefore a crucial point whenever non-herding costs are analysed. Zwiebel's extension makes the model even more realistic because in Zwiebel's version it is not always better to fail conventionally than to succeed unconventionally.[16] The benchmarking of the managers' performances allows mediocre managers to hide in the herd, but the most able managers still have an incentive to deviate and build up an outstanding reputation.[17]

Similarly, Prendergast and his theory about 'yes men' directly explore how conformity can emerge when firms use subjective performance evaluations. Instead of collecting and communicating important information about a project, the workers will try to elicit and represent their supervisor's opinion in order to please him and to further their careers.[18]

[14] See, for example, D. Hirshleifer and S. H. Teoh, 'Herd Behaviour and Cascading in Capital Markets: A Review and Synthesis' (2003) 9 *European Financial Management* 25–66.

[15] W. D. Hamilton, 'Geometry of the Selfish Herd' (1971) 31(2) *Journal of Theoretical Biology* 295–311.

[16] This saying is attributed to John Maynard Keynes.

[17] See J. Zwiebel, 'Corporate Conservatism and Relative Compensation' (1995) 103 *The Journal Political Economy* 1–25.

[18] See C. Prendergast, 'A Theory of "Yes Men"' (1993) 83 *The American Economic Review* 757–70.

There is also empirical evidence for the existence of herding behaviour due to reputational and career concerns. Graham explicitly tested and supported the model of Scharfstein and Stein empirically.[19] Hong, Kubik, and Solomon showed that there were reputational incentives for herd behaviour of equity analysts.[20] If a younger analyst deviates from the consensus forecast and does not succeed, he has a much higher probability of being dismissed than a senior analyst. This suggests high pressure for beginners to build up their reputations with conventional forecasts. Also, the newer experimental literature demonstrates in the lab how reputational concerns of managers can lead to distorted decisions.[21]

Rajan provided evidence that there is a link between the herding behaviour of individuals in an organization and the herding behaviour of organizations in the market. During an economic upturn, managers start to relax their standards for loans and to set aside rules for loan-loss reserves.[22] In order to reach the same profitability, other bank managers imitate these actions. As Rajan shows, in case of an economic downturn, the loans of the skilled managers also do poorly and thus neither of the managers is punished reputationally as they can hide in the herd.

The literature about informational cascades has to be mentioned in this context too.[23] However, this strand of the economic literature is only important in the present context as informational cascades demonstrate how information can be lost. This happens because the first mover in a cascade randomly makes a decision, whereas the following movers ignore their private signals and imitate the decision of the first mover, assuming that he had better information than they did. Kuran and Sunstein combine the idea of informational cascades and reputational concerns with the concept of availability cascades.[24] They explain how availability cascades are used in the political process of opinion formation.

19 See D. S. Scharfstein and J. C. Stein, 'Herd Behavior and Investment' (1990) 80 *The American Economic Review* 465–79.

20 See H. Hong, J. D. Kubik and A. Solomon, 'Security Analysts' Career Concerns and Herding of Earnings Forecasts' (2000) 31 *The Rand Journal of Economics* 121–44.

21 See, e.g., J. D. Hey and A. Morone, 'Do Markets Drive out Lemmings, or Vice Versa?' (2004) 71 *Economica* 637–59, M. Cipriano and A. Guarino, 'Herd Behavior in a Laboratory Financial Market' (2005) 95 *The American Economic Review* 1427–43, or M. Drehmann, J. Oechssler, and A. Roider, 'Herding and Contrarian Behavior in Financial Markets: An Internet Experiment (2005) 95 *The American Economic Review* 1403–26.

22 See R. G. Rajan, 'Why Bank Credit Policies Fluctuate: A Theory and Some Evidence' (1994) 109 *The Quarterly Journal of Economics* 399–441.

23 A. V. Banerjee, 'A Simple Model of Herd Behavior' (1992) 107 *The Quarterly Journal of Economics* 797–817 and S. Bikchandani, D. Hirshleifer, and I. Welch, 'A Theory of Fads, Fashion, Custom, and Cultural Change as Informational Cascades' (1992) 100 *The Journal of Political Economy* 992–1026 are the seminal papers in this strand of the economic literature; C. Avery and P. Zemsky, 'Multidimensional Uncertainty and Herd Behavior in Financial Markets' (1998) 88 *The American Economic Review* 724–48 provide an important extension, and K. A. Kim and J. R. Nofsinger, 'Institutional Herding, Business Groups and Economic Regimes: Evidence from Japan (2005) 78 *The Journal of Business* 213–42 exhibit new empirical evidence. A fundamental problem of this literature is to distinguish 'spurious herding' from 'intentional herding'; not all movements, for example in stock markets, are due to real herding behaviour but might be caused by truly new information (see Bikhchandani and Sharma, n 2 above, for a comprehensive discussion).

24 See T. Kuran and C. R. Sunstein, 'Availability Cascades and Risk Regulation' (1999) 51 *Stanford Law Review* 683–4.

The literature of whistle-blowing also deals with a closely related topic. Although studies about whistle blowing are mostly focused on negative topics such as unfair treatment of employees or even criminal behaviour, they discuss the process of speaking up in organizations.[25] In general, this literature belongs to the broader phenomenon of 'voice and silence in organisations'.[26] The mainly theoretical literature was recently extended by empirical studies, which provide better insight into the incentives and rational choice behaviour of employees when they have to decide to blow the whistle or not.[27]

The Section III focuses on the costs of non-herding and distinguishes the various links to the literature on herd behaviour.

III. The Costs of Non-herding

Whenever several people make a decision, the costs of non-herding arise. In a typical situation, one could imagine an investment committee in a bank, consisting of eight members. Assume that these members are equally ranked (later, we also discuss the case when there are people of different hierarchy levels). These eight members of the committee have to decide about a specific investment with one of them being in charge of the investment project. This manager makes a presentation about the anticipated assets and drawbacks of the investment. Subsequently, the usual question and answer round starts, but nobody asks any crucial questions, the questions only scratch the surface of the possible problems. After having answered the harmless questions, the committee votes on the investment and unanimously adopts it. All of this happens although the investment project is not at all above suspicion, a fact that the project leader is well aware of.

Why did the committee members not ask more critical questions about the project? The individual members of the committee have several reasons not to mention any fundamental issue: nobody wants to prolong the meeting, nobody wants to raise his or her voice against the project because an explanation would be required, nobody wants to be the loner, and as long as no other member of the committee speaks up, all members keep quiet. Because this happened several times before, nobody feels like taking a stand against the investment project this time around.

These are only a few examples of the possible costs members of committees could face during a decision-making process. We want to show, however, that such situations reveal typical characteristics and mechanisms. First, if a committee member raises his voice, he or she faces the costs of doing so immediately. In contrast, the possible benefits lie in the future and can only be

[25] See, e.g., the new review of the topic by M. P. Miceli, J. P. Near, and T. M. Dworkin, *Whistle-blowing in Organizations* (New York, NY: Routledge, 2008).

[26] See therefore the special issue of the *Journal of Management Studies* (2003).

[27] See A. Dyck, A. Morse, and L. Zingales, 'Who Blows the Whistle on Corporate Fraud' (2010) 65 *The Journal of Finance* 2213–53.

calculated after the project is realized. The member does not know in advance whether he or she ever will get any benefit out of it while the costs are imminent. This shows two types of asymmetries: one in the temporal dimension between short-term costs and long-term benefits, another in the probability of the costs and the benefits. The costs are rather clear, whereas benefits are very uncertain and difficult to calculate.

Secondly, the costs of non-herding have to be borne alone by the individual member of the committee, at least at an early stage, until other members join in the critique. The critic cannot benefit from a cost- and risk-sharing mechanism and hide in the herd.

If we add to the typical situation described above that the committee members are of different rank, principal-agent problems arise. Assume that the supervisor of a committee member presents an investment project. To argue against this project gets even more costly for the subordinate member. The supervisor is likely to decide future promotions of the inferior member as well as his future pay. These costs illustrate that any dependency on a supervising person can influence the costs not to herd dramatically for a specific committee member.

For the organization itself, the problem of the non-herding costs is twofold. On one hand, the costs not to herd induce other members to imitate such behaviour. By doing so, the individual members do not contribute their private information during the decision-making process and vote for decisions, which do not align with their personal evaluations. The imitating behaviour results in a loss of information, which is the major cost of herding behaviour for the organization. On the other hand, the non-herding costs depend on a self-reinforcing process. The longer the committee members do not raise any issues, the higher the costs not to herd and the lower the incentives to speak up. The costs of non-herding create a vicious circle, which can harm the organization in several ways. Chosen paths cannot be changed, and new and better investments are missed or ignored. As the decision involves many steps and is designed as a bottom-up process, there are non-herding costs on each level reinforcing the herding behaviour in the organization. These two mechanisms are responsible for the problems that arise from the non-herding costs in organizations. Therefore, organizations should try to reduce the costs of non-herding.

IV. Different Types of Non-herding Costs

The costs of non-herding can arise from various sources, affecting all individual employees. We pool these different sources into three categories: costs due to personality, costs due to conflicts between equally ranked employees, and costs between employees and their superiors.

Depending on self-perception, role behaviour, and identity, the costs of non-herding can affect the individual employee in different ways. People who like to expose themselves or see their role as the devil's advocate perceive the non-herding costs to be lower than assumed.

Another source for non-herding costs lies in the relationship between the employee and his co-workers or peers. In order to function, teams or committees experience a pressure to be uniform, and the members create their own social identity. The more homogeneous a team is with respect to important aspects (professional background, education, gender, etc) the more likely groupthink occurs. These diverse phenomena of social interactions in teams influence the individually perceived costs of non-herding; the more conformity is needed to be accepted as a member of the team, the higher are the costs if the individual employee deviates from the prevailing opinion. The employee is usually in competition with his peers, which can reduce the costs not to herd as it provides an incentive for the employee to speak up and distinguish himself. In contrast, competition can also raise the costs if the employee and his peers are rated by a superior manager, as shown later.

The last source of non-herding costs stems from the character of the principal-agent relationship. In addition to the above-mentioned sources, an employee and his superior's supervisor's relationship as well as the employee's personality have a massive influence on the costs of non-herding. The costs of non-herding to an employee can vary heavily. If the superior has to evaluate the employee's performance and if this evaluation determines bonus payments, future project assignments, or promotions, the employee's non-herding costs strongly increase. Due to career and reputational concerns, the employee's incentive to raise an issue about a project supported by his supervisor is likely to vanish. If the superior is accorded much respect in the committee due to his or her impressive track record and large amount of experience, the employee's costs to be critical increase even further.

These sources spawn a wide range of non-herding costs for the critical employee starting with small hostilities to mobbing and sidelining or even towards a career-ending transfer of the employee or his dismissal. After having discussed the types, perils, and sources of the costs not to herd in organizations, we analyse the possibilities to reduce them. Several propositions are developed in Section V.

V. How to deal with the Costs of Non-herding in Organizations

This Chapter suggests that the institutional setting is a major factor influencing the non-herding costs for organizations. There are fundamental principles shaping the rules of the game in organizations.[28]

We first identify factors at the micro level and then move to the macro level. At the micro level, which covers the committee and its decision-makers, there are seven different factors:

(1) the composition of the committee;

(2) agenda setting in meetings;

[28] See, e.g., D. North, *Institutional Change and Economic Performance* (Cambridge: Cambridge University Press, 1990).

(3) information flow about the projects;
(4) formal communication procedure (order of speaking);
(5) informal communication (informal pre-meeting);
(6) decision rules (voting procedure); and
(7) allocation of responsibility (to the head of the group or to each member equally).

These factors define the design of the committee and the rules therein. They have a strong direct influence on the costs of non-herding for an individual committee member. Assume that the project leader has the power to select the members of the committee or to set the agenda of the meeting. This enables him to raise the costs for a possible critic by electing a higher number of supporters of the project (or even exclude all possible critics). He could also place the vote on the most critical project at the very end of the meeting's agenda in order to minimize the time available for a proper discussion. The project leader can also heavily regulate the flow of information about the project. In addition, the formal communication rules—like the order of speaking in a meeting—the decision-making procedure and the allocation of the responsibility for the decisions taken are factors that take place at the micro level of an organization. Nevertheless, they can be influenced by decisions and settings at the macro level of the organization.

We distinguish four institutional factors at the macro level:

(1) hierarchical structure of the organization;
(2) wage policy;
(3) human resource policy; and
(4) ownership.

The first point captures the intuition that the stronger the hierarchical structures in an organization, the higher the costs not to herd. If there are only a few workers or managers on the same hierarchy level, the allocation of power and responsibility is so clearly defined that there are few incentives to be critical and speak up. If the organization is dedicated to a more cooperative or participatory style of management, then there are fewer levels of hierarchy, and more employees are on the same level. This provides a platform for discussion among equals and thus may help to reduce the non-herding costs.

The second element deals with the problem of how to remunerate the employees in order to reduce the costs of non-herding. The literature of reputation-based herding suggests that if a large part of the salary is performance-related and performance is measured relative to other employees or another benchmark, behaviour that deviates from the benchmark is very costly.

An organization's human resource policy reduces the non-herding costs by selecting the right employees. If the organization is able to select open-minded people who are unafraid to stand up for their opinions, the cost of non-herding is reduced, as one can assume that these people perceive lower costs of non-herding due to their psyche.

Finally, we propose that personally liable partners in banks are more interested in carefully aggregating information, therefore reducing the costs of non-herding in order to reveal as many critical issues as possible. In contrast, we assume that in a stock corporation with a large free-float few employees have the incentive or the power to raise critical issues due to the diffusion of responsibility.

The propositions introduced in this Section are now compared to statements made in interviews by practitioners.

VI. Costs of Non-herding in Practice

To check if our theoretical approach to influence the costs of non-herding is also valuable in practice, we conducted interviews with practitioners of the financial industry. From June to August 2010 during the first wave of our study, we interviewed six practitioners in the greater area of Zurich, Switzerland's banking capital.[29] To attain a reasonably broad insight into the various types of financial institutions, we interviewed two managers from big Swiss banks, two managers from a mid-sized regional bank, one manager of a small investment boutique who was also a former CEO of one of the larger Swiss private banks, and a CEO of a small fund of hedge funds. In addition, our sample varies with respect to the sector and the position of the person. Two analysts worked in the investment banking sector, two managers in the private banking sector, one person was involved in the top management of a universal bank, and the remaining manager leads a company in the hedge fund industry. The sample comprises one woman and five men. The sample includes companies ranging in size from 30 to over 60,000 employees. The median number of employees is 5,000 and the mean around 20,000.

An outline was used in all the focused interviews, but the order in which the questions where posed varied depending on the course of conversation.[30] The shortest interview lasted about an hour, the longest about one-and-a-half hours. The interviews were analysed by applying scaled and structured content analysis.[31]

In general, all participants confirmed that there was a problem of repressed voice in the decision-making processes of organizations. They agreed that there were individual costs involved leading to silence and herding behaviour. Explaining the various costs to non-herding employees, all managers stated that they experienced a wide range of costs during their careers starting with delicate psychological

[29] A comprehensive analysis of an extended sample of interviews is provided in Cueni and Frey, n 4 above.

[30] The term was coined by R. K. Merton and P. L. Kendall, 'The Focused Interview' (1946) 51 *The American Journal of Sociology* 541–57; the procedure is explained in S. Kvale, *Interviews: An Introduction to Qualitative Research Interviewing* (Thousand Oaks: SAGE, 1996).

[31] See P. Mayring, *Qualitative Inhaltsanalyse: Grundlagen und Techniken* (Weinheim: Beltz, 2003) and J. Gläser and G. Laudel, *Experteninterviews und qualitative Inhaltsanalyse* (Wiesbaden: VS Verlag für Sozialwissenschaft, 2006).

pressure to conform and culminating in dismissals. Several respondents offered such remarks as the 'bears got mobbed'[32] or 'everybody knew the critics and sooner or later they were not anymore invited into the important work shops' or 'from then on your days are numbered.' Responses like these reveal additional types of costs such as a deterioration of career opportunities and reduced bonuses due to criticism and conflicts.

All six interviewees mentioned various institutional factors to reduce the non-herding costs when asked broadly how to deal with these costs. To the question about the characteristics of the costs of non-herding, all managers responded that they perceive the costs to be self-enhancing over time; other characteristics were also addressed such as the temporal asymmetry between short-term costs and long-term benefits. An equity analyst explained that sometimes he does not speak up in order not to force others to stay longer in the meeting, 'just as a matter of kindness,' although he does not fear any consequences.

The majority of the respondents supported the hypothesis that there is a link between the non-herding costs of individuals in the organization and herding behaviour of the organization in the financial market. On the question of why every member of the leading top management level is exposed to the costs of non-herding, the interviewees responded that these managers also have career concerns and therefore must maintain their reputation. Whenever they deviate strongly from their benchmark, they immediately face the costs of non-herding. Subordinates, shareholders, and the media will ask for explanations.

Four of the six interviewees spontaneously brought up several points at the micro level when asked which institutional factors influence the costs of non-herding in meetings. All seven factors mentioned at the micro level were addressed by at least one respondent. Surprisingly, although the answers took many forms, the interviewees stressed the importance of informal communication before or after the meeting (whenever a decision has not yet been made) in order to reduce or avoid the costs of non-herding. Without asking, the CEO of a small hedge fund company explained the company's rules on how to proceed in investment committee meetings: they try to rule out every imbalance by randomising the order in which the topics are discussed or who starts the discussion. In addition, all of the members of their investment committee have veto power. Interestingly, over the period of four years, a veto was only cast once. The respondent stated that the mere existence of the veto leads them to consider each member's opinion.

The majority of the respondents were aware of the importance of institutional factors at the micro level. However, in their companies, rules about the procedure of meetings or other decision-making boards are ill-defined (except in the hedge fund firm). The former CEO of a large Swiss bank mentioned that during his time in office every member of the executive board had to sign a declaration that

[32] The term 'bears' refers to people who forecast an economic downturn, see, e.g., *The Economist* (2009).

obliged him to dissent from other members whenever he had a different opinion. Although this was not a credible move, the CEO wanted to make clear that dissent is important in order to find the right solutions and to take proper decisions.

Concerning our propositions of institutional factors at the macro level, the respondents exhibited a more heterogeneous picture. The question regarding the hierarchical structure of the organization and the style of management was affirmed by five of six respondents: the more cooperative or participatory style of management, the lower the costs not to herd. Only two interviewees argued that the size of the company has an influence on the non-herding costs. Interestingly, one of these two respondents worked with a mid-sized universal bank in the investment banking division, whereas the other respondent worked in the private banking division of a large Swiss bank. One respondent claimed, '[t]his is not a matter of size, normally even in big banks the daily work environment does not differ between a big bank and an institute of small or medium size.'

On the issue of an organization's wage policy, four of six respondents were convinced that a large performance-related part of the salary increased the costs of non-herding. One interviewee explained his view by stating that contributing private information was a public good and the existence of large personal incentives sabotaged the provision of these kinds of goods. One of the two negative respondents noted that only the existence of performance pay kept the employee attentive as he could lose much money when he does not provide all of his private information. Only two managers reported that they were aware of a human resource strategy to select self-confident people in order to maintain critical thinking in the organization; one of them even introduced such a policy in his firm.

When asked if ownership structure can influence non-herding costs, an unclear picture was revealed: four of six responses affirmed that it might be better to have a strong and influential main shareholder who has a potential downside risk and thus is mostly interested in aggregating all possible information. A former CEO of one of the larger Swiss private banks argued that it depends heavily on the intention of the main shareholder, saying '[a]s long as he is truly interested in the firm, this might help to further critical thinking in the organization, if not, it might even be counterproductive.' There is also no clear evidence on the question of whether the existence of a personally liable partner in a firm can influence non-herding costs. Half of the respondents confirmed the proposition and half of them denied it.

VII. The Costs of Not Going with the Financial Herd

The outbreak of a financial crisis reveals an oddity: before the crisis sets in, only a few people warn of its imminence. Whenever the crisis strikes, many say that they saw the disaster coming. When asked why they did not warn anyone before the outbreak, they usually say that they feared negative consequences. Anecdotal evidence from the financial industry suggests that co-workers and supervisors mobbed and punished employees who made critical statements about the economic trend. Several employees noted that they faced a wide range of different costs, starting from social pressure to conformity and culminating in dismissals. By hindering agents in financial markets from speaking up and revealing their true opinion about future economic trends, non-herding costs waste resources, resulting in distorted allocations of assets. In addition, the individual costs of non-herding can lead to a herding behaviour of organizations in financial markets.

This Chapter sheds light on the costs of not going with the financial herd. Two important characteristics of the non-herding costs are identified: they are self-enhancing and hold an asymmetrical relationship to possible benefits—the costs are imminent and foreseeable whereas possible benefits lie in the future and are uncertain. We propose various institutional factors in organizations aimed at reducing the costs of non-herding. In order to analyse if the problem of non-herding costs exists in practice and to challenge our theoretically derived propositions, we conducted several interviews with practitioners working in the financial industry. The respondents cover a wide range of the various types of financial companies such as big universal banks, mid-sized private banks, or small hedge fund firms.

All the practitioners affirmed that the existence of the costs of non-herding in today's financial companies leads to problems with aggregating information and proper decision-making. They support the use of institutional factors to reduce non-herding costs. The managers and financial analysts identified several propositions at the micro level of the decision-making process and at the macro level of the overall organizational setting, which are already deployed in practice or must be considered in the future.

Whistle-blowing in the Stampede?

Comment on B. Frey and R. Cuenis, 'Moral Hazard and Herd Behaviour in the Financial Crisis'

*Gunther Teubner**

I. Mismatch

Public support for whistle-blowing—this is what I see as Frey's and Cuenis' important contribution to the debate on herd behaviour. Whistle-blowing is one of the strongest countervailing forces in a situation where everybody agrees with a wrong corporate decision and nobody dares to protest. Frey's and Cuenis' ambition is to strengthen the civic virtues of dissent, protest, opposition, and *Zivilcourage* against the stifling atmosphere of corporate hierarchies and against strong market pressures for rigid conformity. Their diagnosis plausibly makes prohibitive costs of non-herding responsible for the lack of publicly raised opposition in the firm and in the market, and they can successfully claim empirical support from interviews with managers. Three main factors are singled out as raising the costs of non-herding: conflicts and problems of justification, deterioration of career opportunities, and social pressure by colleagues (groupthink). Their therapy aims to reduce these costs of dissent, among other things by strengthening institutionalized diversity in decision-making organizational bodies. Corporate governance reforms, either via private ordering or via corporation law, could play a decisive role in encouraging a culture of dissent in the corporate world. In my view, these are promising strategies.

However, of what help is whistle-blowing in a stampede? The recent financial crisis unleashed collective turbulences of such violence that the suggested cost-lowering devices would remain unheard. The herding behaviour during the recent financial crisis belonged to this especially turbulent kind, as a British observer noticed: '[t]he fastest-spreading contagion known to humankind swept through Britain this week causing raised blood pressure, spiralling stress hormone levels and rash economic actions galore. The contagion is an outbreak of mass

* Professor Emeritus of Private Law and Legal Sociology, Goethe-University, Frankfurt am Main.

panicked anxiety'. 'Contagion'—this is the key concept in the new discipline of financial epidemiology which has been developed by economists like Claessens, Forbes, and Haldane and by sociologists like Staeheli. Finance theory conceives of contagion as a 'spread of market disturbances . . . from one country to another',[1] or as a 'spill-over' effect. Contagion is based upon (too) close inter-dependencies of different markets or market sectors. The measure of contagion is defined by a change in correlations: '[c]ontagion is best defined as a significant increase in cross-market linkages after a shock.'[2] Both the speculation boom before the crisis and the panic reaction in the midst of the crisis are attributed to processes of contagion in financial markets which made both resistant to cost-conscious incentives. When Alan Greenspan discovered that this contagion in the finance markets was irresistible even for rational institutions, it came as a shock: 'those of us who have looked to the self-interest of lending institutions to protect shareholder's equity, myself included, are in a state of shocked disbelief.'[3] He would never have believed that banks would act against their own interests by imitating thoughtlessly high-risk 'gambling' practices to the point of self-destruction. It brought Greenspan to the painful realization that his 'whole intellectual edifice . . . collapsed'.

My argument in a nutshell: public support for whistle-blowing alone is helpless in a situation that the new financial epidemiology describes as the rapid processes of social contagion. Since reduction of dissent costs relies only on incentives for individual action, it cannot combat two crucial dynamics in the crisis. One is the overwhelming affective dynamic—vulgo: greed and fear—under the influence of which cost arguments are silenced. The other is a genuine collective dynamic in financial herding, a maelstrom which sweeps away individual resistance. Both dynamics require considerably widening the search for public reactions—to engage in the politics of contagion.

II. Collective Dynamics of Herd Behaviour

As is well-known, greed and fear—the affective dynamics of social contagion—greatly diminish the effects of a strategy that tries to reduce the costs of dissent. For a long time, criminological research has demonstrated that effect-related deviance cannot be prevented either by cost-raising negative sanctions or by cost-reducing positive incentives.[4] More recent risk analyses show that even when cost considerations do play a role, strong affective engagement changes the risk perception so drastically that cost reductions become marginalized. In any case, the regulatory resources needed to block herding behaviour via cost incentives

[1] S. Claessens and K. Forbes (2001) *International Financial Contagion* (Dordrecht: Kluwer, 2001) 22.

[2] Claessens and Forbes, n 1, 46.

[3] A. Greenspan, *New York Times*, 24 October 2008.

[4] For a devastating critique see P. -A. Albrecht, *Der Weg in die Sicherheitsgesellschaft: Auf der Suche nach staatskritischen Absolutheitsregeln* (Berlin: Berliner Wissenschaftsverlag, 2010) 153.

for individual dissent will be prohibitively high in the highly emotionalized situations of speculation booms or panic reactions in financial crises comparable to 2008.

A cost reduction strategy seems even more problematic when it comes to influencing the collective dynamics in herd behaviour in financial markets. Here, theories that try to identify a collective subject, a 'crowd spirit', a *conscience collective* in the Durkheimian tradition, are clearly misleading. Methodological individualism has successfully criticized such a mystification of collective entities. But for methodological individualism itself, the collective phenomenon of herd behaviour is difficult, if not impossible, to grasp. At best, methodological individualism can reconstruct herd behaviour by taking up elements of the old mass psychology and interpreting herd behaviour as the aggregation of irrational individual behaviour in a mass situation where massive stress induces individual actors to act erratically. But the sheer aggregation of individual motives cannot explain the fast-spreading contamination, be it the mechanics or the dynamics. It looks only to its effects on individuals and is not able to identify the medium of contagion itself, the channels of contamination and its inner dynamics.

The decisive step beyond this misplaced alternative is to identify the collective dimension of financial herding behaviour in a different way. Neither a simple aggregation of individual motives will do nor will the erratic movements of one trans-individual collectivity. Instead, it is the autonomous flow of financial communications itself that represents the mediality of contagion. Communication, the triad of information, signalling and understanding financial transactions, is the carrier of the contagious process on which empirical research, theory constructs, and institutional reforms should concentrate.[5] '*Contagio*' (which means touching) does not take place in the complex motivation structure of individual actors which is then supposed to be transferred in the meeting of minds from actor to actor. Instead, the contagious spreading happens much more directly in the concentration of one financial communication—money transfers as well as financial information—to the other. Social contagion gains its enormous speed and power by deviating from the usual time-consuming mode of interaction in which two actors exchange information in a complex ego-alter-relation. Instead, decisions are based on unilateral observation and pure and rapid imitation. In situations of social contagion, 'communication becomes an uncontrollable cascade of events'.[6]

The overwhelming dynamic of financial contagion is fully understood once it is seen in its interaction with other components of excessive growth compulsion within financial markets. The material component is an excessive multiplication of symbols, of ever-new financial instruments. The temporal component is

[5] *Locus classicus:* N. Luhmann, *Social Systems* (Stanford, CA: Stanford University Press, 1995) 139–45.

[6] U. Stäheli, 'Political Epidemiology and the Financial Crisis' in P. F. Kjaer and G. Teubner (eds) *The Financial Crisis in Constitutional Perspective: The Dark Side of Functional Differentiation* (Oxford: Hart Publishing, 2011) 123–42, 140.

acceleration of financial transactions, mainly via information technologies. And the social component is contagion which is reinforcing the temporal and material components and is reinforced by them.[7]

This shifts the attention away from individual motives of investors to the links between financial communication flows and the institutional structures that influence these flows. Instead of analysing in depth the 'infections' of individual actors, the inquiry should ask how the 'channels of contamination' are structured and how the infection is transmitted. Of course, flows of information are always accompanied by individual motivation, but the dynamics of contagion do not take place in the reduced psychic state of greedy or angst-ridden individual investors, rather in the connectivity of financial communication chains. In short:

> The epidemiological framework is not primarily interested in processes of subjectification (which would look to motivations of individuals and the influences of sanctions and incentives, G.T.), but in the control of network structures and topologies. What is in the foreground are the flows of communication and their media infrastructure, network links and the organisation of connectivity.[8]

III. Financial Epidemiology

If the dynamics of contagion in speculation bubbles and panic behaviour cannot be combated by individual cost incentives alone, does this then mean *lasciate ogni speranza*? Indeed, as one observer rightly notes, it is very 'difficult to control the spread of panic behaviour... Within the financial system, robustness is something that emerges; it cannot be engineered.' Contagious dynamics cannot be fought directly, one must make recourse to indirect measures that restructure the channels of contamination. One needs to go beyond measures of regulation that attack the causal influence of one or another factor responsible for the crisis, as well as beyond strategies that influence individual motives of behaviour. The financial markets need changes in the connectivity of communication channels, transformations of their capillary constitution. Indirect control means 'creating network conditions which prevent the quick spreading of contagious dynamics'. The key is what Luhmann called *Interdependenzunterbrechung*, i.e. interrupting too close interdependencies.[9]

In this vein, Haldane, one of the directors of the Bank of England and the main representative of financial epidemiology, recommends two strategies that would have the capacity to block the channels of financial contamination: (1) restructuring

[7] G. Teubner, 'A Constitutional Moment? The Logics of "Hit the Bottom"' in P. F. Kjaer and G. Teubner (eds) *The Financial Crisis in Constitutional Perspective: The Dark Side of Functional Differentiation* (Oxford: Hart Publishing, 2011) 3–42, 9. For more details, see G. Teubner, *Constitutional Fragments: Societal Constitutionalism and Globalization* (Oxford: Hart Publishing, 2012) 78–81.

[8] Stäheli, n 6, 138. On legal regulation of network structures, see G. Teubner, *Networks as Connected Contracts* (Oxford: Hart Publishing, 2011) chaps 4–6.

[9] Luhmann, n 5, 38, 476.

of financial networks and (2) de-homogenization of financial information. Both would change the 'capillary constitution'[10] of the finance sector, but each would target a different contagion process. The first strategy tries to reduce contagion between primary operations, i.e., in the flow of financial transactions themselves. The second strategy counteracts contagion between secondary operations, i.e. information, models, instruments, rumours, stories, and narratives that influence financial transactions.

As for the first strategy—restructuring of financial networks—Haldane argues that the massive deregulation of the last decades swept away banking segregation and, with it, decomposability of the financial network. The upshot was a predictable lack of network robustness in financial markets. He recommends that this massive growth of uncontrollable interdependencies should be blocked by measures similar to Glass-Steagall which should now be back on the international policy agenda. Even if it is too narrow an answer, he thinks this is asking the right question: can network structure be altered to improve network robustness which would block financial contagion?

He recommends reshaping the financial network so as to reduce the chances of future systemic collapse. He pleads for learning from experience with engineering networks through intra-system netting arrangements, which reduce the financial network's dimensionality and complexity. And regulation should ensure appropriate control of the damaging network consequences of the failure of large, interconnected institutions. Since financial networks are asymmetrically structured insofar as they have only few central nodes and numerous peripheral nodes, financial epidemiology should realize that these central nodes are super-hubs with increased connectivity and may well become 'super-spreaders' of the contagion. His advice, then, is to actively seek to vaccinate the 'super-spreaders' to avert financial contagion.

The second strategy—de-homogenization—is even more indirect, because it restructures not the payment flows themselves, but the information channels on finance instruments and risk management. Perhaps they even represent the most 'contagious' dynamics' of public perceptions and asset valuation';[11] they are responsible for a dangerous homogenization of financial models across financial sectors and within them. Simultaneously the information about potential risks, auditing, and risk management became homogenized in their turn. And even regulatory measures like Basel II amplified this homogeneity. They provided a prescriptive rule-book ensuring a level playing-field. Ratings were hard-wired into regulation. These information channels in finance models and risk management opened the way for the waves of informational contagion. From this follows the

[10] Derrida introduces this term contrasting it to the 'capital constitution' of the state which is not capable of changing the inner processes of the economic and other discourses: J. Derrida, *The Other Handing: Reflections on Today's Europe* (Bloomington: Indiana University Press, 1992) 34. For an elaboration of the concept, see G. Teubner, n 7, 83–6.

[11] R. M. May, S. A. Levin, and G. Sugihara, 'Complex Systems: Ecology for Bankers' (2008) 451 *Nature* 895.

policy recommendation to change information channels in such a way that the chance to *heterogenize finance products, risk strategies and regulation* will increase.

Again, the important thing is to change the 'capillary constitution' of the network. The suggestion is to introduce Central Counterparties (CCPs) which interpose themselves between every trade and transform the complex but fragile web from a highly decentralized heterarchical network into a more hierarchical network that consists of bilateral relationships with the central counterparty. This would be needed for all kinds of financial instruments, including a broad range of over-the-counter financial instruments, both cash and derivatives.

It is at this point that Frey's and Cuenis' cost lowering strategies and Haldane's and Staeheli's network restructuring strategies show a certain complementarity. Both strategies aim at legal policies that institutionalize dissent and diversity of opinion, different financial instruments, methods of risk analysis, and regulatory interventions. But only if the networks in the financial markets are restructured so that they create a sufficient amount of heterogeneity of operative and informational channels can the prohibitively high costs for individual actors be reduced to allow them to express their disagreement within the corporate hierarchies.

4

Herd Behaviour and Third Party Impact as a Legal Concept

On Tulips, Pyramid Games, and Asset-backed Securities

*Hans-W. Micklitz**

I. Tulips, Pyramid Games, and Asset-backed Securities—the Dramatic Implications of Herd Behaviour

1. Tulips

In the 1620s, tulip prices[1] were high because supplies of the most sought after new varieties were extremely limited. The supply of the most famous tulip of the time, the Semper Augustus, was in the hands of a single owner, who withheld the bulbs as prices offered rose from 1000 gulden per bulb in 1623 to 3000 gulden per bulb in 1625.[2]

When a Semper Augustus bulb was finally sold some time later, the owner attached the stipulation that the buyer could sell neither the bulb itself nor any of

* Professor of Economic Law, European University Institute, Florence. A number of colleagues supported me in the preparation of this Chapter to whom I would like to express my gratitude: Rozeta Karova, Antonio Marcacci, Andreas Oehler, Lucia Reisch, Gerald Spindler, Yane Svetiev, Lécia Vicente, and in particular Stefan Grundmann for inspiring discussions on firms and markets in a seminar on contract theory at the European University Institute (EUI) and at the HU in 2010 to 2012. The responsibility for any error remains mine, of course.

[1] An extract from A. M. van der Veen, 'The Dutch Tulip Mania: The Social Politics of a Financial Bubble' (March 2009) (available at <http://maurits.myweb.uga.edu/Research/TulipMania.pdf>).

[2] E. -H. Krelage, *Bloemenspeculatie in Nederland: De Tulpomanie van 1636-'37 en de Hyacintenhandel 1720-'36* (Amsterdam, NL: P.N. van Kampen & Zoon, 1942) 31–3; N. van Wassenaer, *Historisch Verhael Alder Ghedenck-weerdichste Geschiedenisse* (Amsterdam, NL: Jan Evertsz. Cloppenburgh & Jan Janssen, 1625). The Dutch currency at the time was the gulden, often translated as guilder. The annual earnings of a skilled artisan such as a carpenter around 1630 were about 300 gulden (A. Goldgar, *Tulipmania: Money, Honor, and Knowledge in the Dutch Golden Age* (Chicago, Ill: Chicago University Press, 2007) 225). At 3000 gulden, the Semper Augustus was valued at about ten times the annual income of someone in the lower middle class, quoted in van der Veen, n 1.

its offspring, i.e., small bulbs that grew on the external of the main bulb, without permission of the original seller.

Though the historical data are limited and the available price evidence is both thin and somewhat uncertain, they quite clearly indicate a rapid rise in prices accelerating through December 1636 and January 1637, followed by a steep and sudden decline after the first week of February 1637. The key factor was the social connectedness among tulip traders, who were linked to one another by religion, marriage, trade, and so on. As a result, market participants assigned greater weight to the decisions of other traders than if they had interacted only through the arms-length transactions of the market.

The number of different varieties of tulips increased very rapidly during the 1620s and 1630s—far too rapidly for any consistent naming scheme to evolve. Though there were dozens of highly prized varieties, the total supply for any given variety was frequently only a handful of bulbs, in turn the property of an even smaller number of growers. Until the early 1630s, the market for tulips was composed almost entirely of the mostly wealthy merchants whose financial fortunes would not be negatively affected by the occasional disappointing purchase of a bulb that turned out to be less refined than expected.

The futures market developed shortly thereafter: people began to sell bulbs for which they had signed a contract even though they did not yet have the actual bulbs in their possession. It took little time for speculators to enter the market. As prices began to rise and new less knowledgeable traders entered the market, transactions began to make explicit reference to a bulb's weight. The first recorded disputes to refer to bulb weights concerned contracts signed in the late summer of 1635, and bulbs began to be sold in bulk by weight. The archives record many deals for 1000 *azen* of a particular variety—usually about three–six bulbs. Lesser-valued types could also be traded by the pound, roughly 30–60 bulbs.

It became possible, therefore, to engage in transactions in which neither party had any idea about the ultimate source of the bulbs. Moreover, no real knowledge of either tulips or bulbs was required, only a sense of the going rate per *azen* for a particular tulip variety. Even though prices had risen gradually but steadily over the preceding years, the rise accelerated once these bulk contracts were introduced into the market.

The elimination of the necessity of knowledge for tulips drew new entrants into the tulip market in increasing numbers beginning in the Autumn of 1635. The real speculative bubble did not last very long. Prices began to rise faster once the bulbs had been planted in October 1636. Bulk contracts became increasingly common by December 1636, giving the market a final boost. Peak prices were paid during the last few days of January and first few days of February 1637. During this three-month period, some individual bulbs were sold as many as five–ten times, and increased more than ten-fold in price, while bulk quantities of cheaper goods increased as much as twenty-fold. By 7 February, it had become clear throughout the main trading centres that the market had crashed.

2. Pyramid games in Albania

Here is a definition of pyramid games:[3]

(1) A system under which a person gives any valuable consideration and receives the right to sell goods, services or rights of participation, and can legitimately expect to receive an advantage from recruiting other persons into this system where such recruitment is unrelated to the sale to final consumers who do not have to have to purchase in order to join the system, shall be prohibited. This prohibition covers in particular:
   (a) systems in which the participants receive a bonus for introducing a new participant into the system;
   (b) systems in which the participants receive a commission related to the initial investment (e.g. starter kits, training courses) which the new participant whom they have introduced undertakes;
   (c) systems in which the participants receive a commission related to continuous purchases of the new participants whom they have introduced in the system.

(2) A scheme which is not centrally organised and in which there exists no central beneficiary is prohibited unless the consideration is of minor value.

In the 1990s, the inadequacy of the financial system was one of the main reasons for the growth of the pyramid schemes in Albania.[4] The three main state-owned banks were unreliable intermediaries of savings and private banks were slow to emerge. Therefore, the public tended to keep a high proportion of their money in cash and looked into alternative investment opportunities, while businesses used the informal credit market, consisting of foreign exchange dealers and companies taking deposits and making loans.

The pyramid schemes grew out of a credit system-based on private loans from migrant workers to friends and family, but were illegal as these persons were not licensed to take deposits. The lending rates were high—ten per cent in 1993—but fell to six per cent in 1995. To the Albanian authorities and foreign observers (the International Monetary Fund (IMF) and the World Bank), they were seen as important contributors to growth, given the deficiencies of the formal banks.

Operating alongside them were deposit-taking companies that invested on their own account instead of making loans. These companies were the ones that

[3] Based on a study we undertook in 1999 on behalf of the European Commission: H.-W. Micklitz, B. Monazzahian, and C. Rößler, 'Door to Door Selling—Pyramid Selling—Multilevel-Marketing, A Study Commissioned by the European Commission' (Volume I and II, November 1999) (available at <http://ec.europa.eu/consumers/cons_int/safe_shop/door_sell/sur10_02.pdf >).

[4] C. Jarvis, 'The Rise and Fall of Pyramid Schemes in Albania' (1999) 99/98 IMF Working Paper (available at <http://www.imf.org/external/pubs/ft/wp/1999/wp9998.pdf>); R. Morozza della Rocca, 'Socio-cultural aspects of the Albanian Crisis' (1998) 33 *The International Spectator* 69–78, in the broader context: World Bank, *Albania Beyond the Crisis: A Strategy for Recovery and Growth, Report No. 18658-ALB, December 7* (Washington DC: World Bank, 1998).

turned into pyramid schemes. The interest rates offered in 1995 were four–five per cent. Their activities were uncertain and it was not possible to establish whether they were solvent or not. The difference between the informal credit market and the pyramid schemes was unclear to both the Albanian authorities and to foreign observers.

Two events set the stage for the pyramid-scheme mania of late 1996. First, at the end of 1995, UN sanctions against the former Yugoslavia were suspended, eliminating an important source of income (smuggling) for the companies. Secondly, the uncertainty created by approaching parliamentary elections the following May prompted the deposit-taking companies to raise their rates again, this time to eight per cent per month, or a real annual rate of well over 100 per cent. During the same period, new schemes entered the market, offering even higher rates. In January 1996, the three leading companies increased their interest rates from four–five per cent to six per cent a month, or almost 100 per cent annually in real terms, whereas the new entrants offered rates of 12–19 per cent and had no real investments.

These new schemes attracted more depositors: although VEFA (an investment fund)[5] had the largest liabilities, it had only 85,000 depositors. Xhafferi and Populli (two further investment funds) had within a few months attracted nearly two million depositors in a country with a population of three-and-a-half million. In addition, the different investment funds started to compete and began to offer higher interest rates on deposits. In July, Kamberi raised its monthly interest rate to ten per cent. In September, Populli began offering more than 30 per cent a month. In November, Xhafferi offered to triple depositors' money in three months; Sude responded with an offer to double the principal in two months. By November, the face value of the schemes' liabilities totalled US$1.2 billion.

In August 1996, the Bank of Albania expressed its concerns to the IMF and the IMF and World Bank warned the country's officials. It was only in October 1996 that the actual size of the schemes was discovered. But it was too late. On 19 November, Sude defaulted on its payments, and the collapse began. Sude's collapse shook public confidence in all of the companies and new deposits were not made. It took four months for the other schemes to collapse. An attempt by VEFA, Kamberi, Silva, and Cenaj to convince depositors of their soundness by lowering monthly interest rates to five per cent failed. In January 1997, Sude and Gjallica declared bankruptcy, triggering riots. The other schemes soon after ceased to make payments.

Reacting to the crisis, the Government implemented two important measures. First, it refused to compensate depositors for their losses, and secondly, it began to move against some of the companies. In January 1997, it froze the bank accounts of Xhafferi and Populli, the sum of which amounted to US$250 million (ten per cent of GDP). However, by March 1997 Albania was in a state of chaos. The

[5] There were a number of different funds involved. I use the original names.

Government had lost control of the south. Many members of the army and police force had deserted their duties, and one million weapons had been looted from the armouries. Evacuation of foreign nationals and mass emigration of Albanians began. The Government was forced to resign and new parliamentary elections were held before the end of June 1997. In the meantime, an interim coalition government was appointed.

3. The subprime crisis and next steps

During the 2000s, mortgages were sold to subprime customers, that is, customers whose credit bureau index was under the sufficient creditworthiness threshold, while the threshold of lending money reached beyond 100 per cent. The reason for this was two-fold: securitization of loan contracts and large bonuses for bankers who sold subprime mortgages either themselves or via intermediaries. As securitization of loan contracts was profitable, in-firm compensation schemes for bankers were designed in order to promote the sale of subprime mortgages by encouraging them to offer credit to businesses and households with poor credit ratings. It was a combination of elements of traditional market/bilateral contracts (subprime loans-based securitization) with elements of firm/organization-like contracts (incentive-designed schemes), where the former were fuelled by the latter. Moreover, firm/organization-like contracts were characterized by both compensation incentive-based herding and, to a lesser extent, reputation-based herding. Unfortunately, these incentive-driven contracts did not entirely take into account the inherent risk of subprime loan-based securitization. Within the above-mentioned combination of contracts, it was tricky to determine legal responsibilities. Who was responsible? Was it the bankers for selling subprime mortgages encouraged by bonuses or the massive buying and selling of securitized subprime mortgages?

Moreover, securitization of subprime mortgages is just *one* of the causes of the 2007–2010 economic crisis. Defining what kind of financial contracts and practices led to the economic crisis is a daunting task which is clearly beyond the scope of our analysis. Instead, we focus on who carries the legal liability burden as regards the retail credit downturn, which was a negative externality produced by the above-described network and which steeply affected retail consumers (small investors), in particular those who were not prepared to engage in highly risky economic transactions.

In economics, a negative externality occurs when an individual or firm making a decision does not have to pay the full cost of that decision, but rather externalizes these costs to the environment or society. In the subprime crisis, the compensation-incentive-based herding along with the securitization phenomenon contributed to generating the current world recession. In other words, we have witnessed a market failure with no immediate legal liability. However, in the given circumstances of the subprime crisis can we speak of herding? What is herding? And how is herding linked to negative externalities?

II. Analysis of Herd Behaviour

1. Herd behaviour in behavioural economics

The phenomenon of herd behaviour arises either when investors change their investment decision after learning what other investors have already done, or when third parties (such as corporate governance procedures) indirectly encourage investors to follow the behaviour of others. This behaviour tends to have one of four causes: (1) an investor thinks that the other investors know more than s/he actually does; (2) an investor may have an intrinsic inclination to imitate (the so-called 'sake of conformity'); (3) an investor may make decisions looking only at recent returns, thus selling recent losers and buying recent winners (however, it is not easy to determine how far this kind of irrational behaviour can be included within the herd behaviour phenomenon or not); or (4) bonuses, compensation schemes, and terms of employment for money managers give incentives to imitate (for money managers who invest on behalf of others).[6]

Three kinds of identified behavioural herding are relevant for our analysis: information-based herding and cascade, reputation-based herding, and compensation-based herding. Information-based herding argues that, where an individual's assessment of the quality of publicly available information is only privately known to him,[7] and individuals can observe each other's actions but cannot review the private information or signals that each player receives, individuals will herd according to decisions made by others.[8]In this situation, assuming rational herd behaviour, '[a]n individual will be in an 'invest cascade' ('reject cascade') if and only if the number of predecessors who invest is greater (less) than the number of predecessors who do not invest by two or more.'[9] This individual and all subsequent individuals, acting rationally, will then invest regardless of what their private signal tells them about the value of the investment. Once a cascade starts, an individual's action does not reflect his/her private information. Consequently, once a cascade starts, the private information of subsequent investors is never included in the public pool of knowledge.[10]

[6] See for exhaustive presentation of the reasons why investors engage in herd behaviour S. Bikhcchandani and S. Sharma, 'Herd Behaviour in Financial Markets: A Review' (2001) 47 IMF Staff Papers279–310 (available at <http://www.imf.org/External/Pubs/FT/staffp/2001/01/pdf/Bikhchan.pdf>); I. Welch, 'Herding Among Security Analysts' (2000) 58 *Journal of Financial Economics* 369–96; A. Ary and B. Mittendorf, 'Using Disclosure to Influence Herd Behaviour and Alter Competition' (2005) 40 *Journal of Accounting and Economics* 231–46; from a German perspective see A. Oehler, M. Rummer, and S. Wendt, 'Portfolio Selection of German Investors: On the Causes of Home-biased Investment Decisions' (2008) 9 *Journal of Behavourial Finance* 149–62; A. Oehler and St. Wendt, 'Herding Behavour of Mutual Fund Managers in Germany' (available at <http://papers.ssrn.com/sol3/papers.cfm?abstract_id=1343470>). The first, the last, and Welch provide an overview of the different approaches in the related literature.

[7] Bikhcchandani and Sharma, n 6, 279, 284–5.

[8] Bikhcchandani and Sharma, n 6, 279, 284–5.

[9] Bikhcchandani and Sharma, n 6, 279, 285.

[10] Bikhcchandani and Sharma, n6, 279, 285.

The second type of herding, reputation-based herding,[11] argues that if both an agent and employer are unaware of the agent's capability of selecting stocks, they mimic other agents, thereby preserving the fog, that is, the uncertainty surrounding the ability of the manager to manage the portfolio. Thus, the idea is that 'if a bad outcome occurs, but the action was consistent with approved conventional wisdom, the hit to the manger's reputation from an adverse outcome is reduced.'[12] This is because bounded rationality and information asymmetry play a crucial role: '[u]nder conditions of complexity and uncertainty, actors who perceive themselves as having limited information and can observe the actions of presumptively better-informed persons may attempt to free-ride by following the latter's decisions.'[13]

Finally, we turn to compensation-based herding. When the compensation of an investment manager 'depends on how her performance compares with that of other similar professionals, then this distorts the agent's incentives and she ends up with an inefficient portfolio. It may also lead to herd behaviour.'[14]

2. Legal implications of herd behaviour

a. Third party impact of contract making in the subprime crisis

There are all sorts of reasons given for the crisis. What matters in our context is the deeper analysis of herd behaviour and how herd behaviour, through synchronous contract conclusion, affected the financial markets. In this arena, (contract) lawyers discuss the following four ways bilateral contracts affected third parties:[15]

(1) the *unreasonable supply of credits* to private parties (consumers for buying houses) produced long-term effects on the availability of credits;

[11] D. S. Scharfstein and J. C. Stein, 'Herd Behavior and Investment' (1990) 80 *The American Economic Review* 465–79, 466; already J. M. Keynes, *The General Theory of Employment, Interest and Money* (London: Macmillan Cambridge University Press, 1936) 158: 'Wordly wisdom teaches that it is better for reputation to fail conventionally than to succeed unconventionally (available at <http://ebooks.adelaide.edu.au/k/keynes/john_maynard/k44g/>).

[12] S.M. Bainbridge, 'A Behavioral Economic Analysis of Mandatory Disclosure: A Thought Experiment Turned Cautionary Tale'(2000)University of California Los Angeles Law School Working Paper(available at <http://papers.ssrn.com/sol3/papers.cfm?abstract_id=329880>) 13. Quoting K. Marcel and K. Michael, 'Path Dependence in Corporate Contracting: Increasing Returns, Herd Behavior and Cognitive Biases' (1996) 74 *Washington University Law Quarterly* 356.

[13] Bainbridge, n 12, 13.

[14] Bikchandani and Sharma, n 6, 279, 292.

[15] S. Grundmann, '*Welche Einheit des Privatrechts? Von Einer Formalen zu Einer Inhaltlichen Konzeption des Privatrechts*' in S. Grundmann, B. Haar, H. Merkt,*et al* (eds) *Festschrift für Klaus Hopt zum 70 Geburtstag am 24. August 2010, Unternehmen, Markt und Verantwortung* (Berlin: de Gruyter, 2010) 61–92; in the same direction, see F. Möslein, 'Contract Governance and Corporate Governance im Zusammenspiel' (2010) *Juristenzeitung* 72, 74–5 making reference to S. Grundmann, C. Hofmann, and F. Möslein (eds)*Finanzkrise und Wirtschaftsordnung* (Berlin: de Gruyter, 2009).

(2) the *transformation of mortgages into tradable rights* and the further sales between special purpose vehicles/companies and investors enhanced the preparedness of the original creditor to take risks;[16]

(3) the *unreasonable rating* not only of corporate companies but also of consumers/small investors[17] damaged third, fourth, and fifth parties;[18] and

(4) the suggested *herd behaviour* which transformed the normal risk inherent in this kind of transaction into a systemic risk.

With these four situations in mind, we take a closer look at the legal implications of herd behaviour in the context of third-party impact.

b. What is a 'herd' and what is 'herd behaviour'? The legal implications

If we consider the four parameters on third party impact in the financial crisis set forth above, the following questions arise:

(1) *What is a herd?* Legally speaking, herding remains undefined. Herding is a behaviour that might be triggered by one person, but which requires the participation of many within one 'community'. We may find some similarities with *associative crimes* (*reati associativi*), but there is one huge difference: there is no intention to commit illegal actions. Herding, then, is when a group of people behaves in the same way without being aware of it. This behaviour is legally irrelevant as long as it does not negatively affect others, who eventually should prove a direct causal link. This comes close to attempts in private enforcement to define a collective entity which has suffered injuries or damages from the same wrongdoer and/or via the same action.[19] The similarities and differences will be studied in more detail later.

(2) *Who is the herd?* The creditor (banks), the investment companies (managers), the special purpose companies (probably not), the brokers in the stock market, the agents (sitting in the banks or investment firms) and the private investors who follow their advice, the supervisory authorities, and central banks as far as they follow main stream de-regulatory trends—each

[16] There was discussion in various legal orders whether and to what extent mortgages can be transferred into tradable rights. In the very end, either the legislator or the courts (e.g. the German Supreme Court) involved gave way to such a transformation. Looking back, one might wonder whether the judges really understood what they decided, see W. Wiegand, '*Bankrechtliche Aspekte der* Asset-backed Securities' (available at <http://www.wolfgangwiegand.ch/publikationen/_74_Bankrecht-schwerpunkt%20und%20Perspektiven/837_insgesamt.pdf>).

[17] I will use consumer-investor to make clear that the person I have in mind is not a professional.

[18] See, on the interplay between (bad) consumer scores and corporate credit rating, A. Rona-Tas and S. Hiß, *Consumer and Corporate Credit Ratings and the Subprime Crisis in the US with Lessons from Germany* (Wiesbaden: Schufa, 2008) (orig. published in German as A. Rona-Tas and S. Hiß, '*Das Kreditrating von Verbrauchern und Unternehmen und die Subprime-Krise in den USA mit Lehren für Deutschland*' (2010) 33 *Informatik-Spektrum* 241–61).

[19] F. Cafaggi and H.-W. Micklitz (eds)*New Frontiers of Consumer Protection—the Interplay between Private and Public Enforcement* (Belgium: Intersentia Publisher, 2009).

of them can form a herd and if they all operate together and contract in one and the same direction, as occurred within the Tulip Bubble, the Albanian pyramid game and to some extent in the subprime crisis—the herd might constitute a substantial part of a nation or of a transnational investment community.

We can use the three *standard explanations* given to herd behaviour for each of the actors in a different form:

(a) Information-based herding and information cascade—this phenomenon is constitutive for herd behaviour and it is in no way limited to a particular actor. It could be linked to natural persons and linked entities, if we assume that firms can 'behave'.

(b) Reputation-based herding—this phenomenon is linked to all those whose employment positions depend on reputation—in our scenariomainly investment managers, brokers, and agents. Reputation-based herding is personal—legal liability is linked to the behaviour of natural persons rather than to legal entities.

(c) Financial incentive-based herding[20]—the primary addressees are those whose remuneration depends on selling or buying particular financial instruments. The obvious candidates are investment managers, brokers, and agents. However, financial incentive-based herding may also be found in the cooperation between banks and investment firms or banks and special vehicle firms if the parties agreed on, for example, kick-back commissions. Even private investors may be tied in if the agent or broker shares the commission she gets with her customer,[21] which is still prohibited under German insurance law.[22]

(3) *What is herd behaviour?* Legally speaking, it is a daunting task to define herd behaviour. However, with regard to financial services and the relationship between small investor and dealer, herd behaviour can be seen as a lack of professional diligence, complete with the contract law remedies this kind of approach may provide. This does not exclude the possibility that the customer bears responsibility, e.g. if she still invests with *Kaupthing* despite several warnings on the missing deposit guarantee.

[20] One might question whether incentive-based herding is herding at all and whether it should not be regarded as a misguided—via false incentives—principal/agent issue. I am simply relying on well-established categories in behavioural economics research on herd behaviour. Principal-Agent would also shift the framework to institutional economics and would require a deeper analysis of who is the agent and who is the principal in financial markets. (The private investor is the agent, but she is also the principal when she buys the shares of the company, the bank agent is agent in her relationship towards her employer, but she is principal in her relationship to the private investor, etc).

[21] This was a common practice in the selling of life insurances, when the selling agents of the insurance companies shared the commission the agent received from the insurance company with the insured.

[22] The respective rule has been challenged before the ECJ Case C-2/91, *Meng* [1993] ECR I-5871.

(4) *Who is responsible for herd behaviour?*[23] Are there different actors who could be identified by the standard explanations of behavioural economics or are they all agents without there being an ultimately responsible entity? This would have huge implications. Behavioural economics is very much focused on the behaviour of individuals, although psychology, sociology, political science, and economics investigate group behaviour and its impact on individuals, so-called behavioural accounting. This brings the individual responsibility—and maybe even legal liability—of natural private persons to the fore. These persons, even if they can be held liable, are usually not in the position to compensate for potential damages resulting from their behaviour. This could mean that ultimately no one is responsible as everyone is doing what everybody else is doing—unless it is possible to establish organizational responsibility or liability for the ultimate beneficiaries of the financial transactions.

III. *Ex-post* Analysis of Herd Behaviour in the Subprime Crisis

1. Forms of third party impact

Against this background, I want to distinguish between the quality of the effect (positive or negative), the different actors involved in the subprime crisis, and the type of the effect (bound to the persons/legal entities or bound to the market structure).[24] I will pave the way for legal analysis by linking the three forms to respective legal implications. This might allow for some preliminary conclusions as to whether we can already speak of a legal concept.

a. Quality of the effect

In looking into the *quality of the effect,* one might want to distinguish *positive/negative* impacts of herd behaviour *on* third parties from *positive/negative* impacts of herd behaviour *via/by* third parties.[25] Such a distinction combines contract and corporate governance perspectives, contract governance being more focused at looking from the internal bilateral perspective of the outside word, corporate governance being more focused on looking from the internal organization/firm perspective of the market in which contracts are concluded. However, it is a normative concept that already integrates value judgments on the behaviour of third parties and the potential effect. Behavioural economics describes and analyses

[23] I will not use principal-agent theories here, as they start from a different theoretical background (institutional economics) which cannot so easily be made compatible with the approach of behavioural economics.

[24] Helpful, although somewhat over-sophisticated K. Riesenhuber and F. Möslein, 'Contract Governance—*Skizze einer Forschungsperspektive*' in K. Riesenhuber (ed)*Perspektiven des europäischen Schuldvertragsrechts* (Berlin: de Gruyter, 2008) 1–41 who distinguish between governance of contract law, governance of contract, governance with the means of contract law, and governance through contract. I will come back to this issue in Part IV of this Chapter.

[25] See Grundmann, n 15, 61, 84ff.

empirical effects of herd behaviour on third parties. Whether these effects are positive or negative depends mainly on particular preconceptions on the role and function of capital markets. That is why it is somewhat difficult to clearly assign 'positive' or 'negative' effects to particular forms of herd behaviour. We will nevertheless try to use such a distinction at least as a starting point of the analysis. A transfer of positive or negative findings within behavioural economics therefore implies that particular market preconceptions are literally transposed from its economic context into a legal concept. This is a very basic question which goes deep into legal methodology.

The subprime crisis has drawn attention to the negative impact of herd behaviour on third parties. The third party here is often equated with the average US small investor who lost his savings in the subprime crisis or the average European consumer investor who invested in asset-backed securities and lost his savings. Such a perspective makes sense if we take the findings of behavioural economics into account because they demonstrate that reputation-based and incentive-based herding can be found mainly on the side of managers, brokers or agents. Similar effects can be produced if private investors compare each other and compete with their successes.[26]'Value judgments' become more complicated when one takes into account that (private) investors might also speculate against the herding. Potential negative effects may then turn into positive ones. Positive effects of herd behaviour may also result from the fact that herding investors did not have to invest in information searches. Here, information-based herding ties in. Consumer-investors simply relied on the recommendation and behaviour of others, of investment managers, brokers, agents, and last but not least advertising and sales promotion campaigns, regardless of the private information they might have had. In the political debate, consumer-investors are blamed, accused of being greedy, although one might wonder whether greed was not a factor on all sides and that it might more appropriate to refer to collusion to assess the behaviour of the parties involved.

The potential effects—perhaps better called the opportunities that third parties might have had to influence, from the outside, the contractual relationship between the investment manager and his investment firm, or the bank agent and his bank—are more complicated to evaluate. The traditional mechanisms of influence are competition exercised through takeovers or the Wall Street Rule. But both obviously failed in the subprime crisis.[27] In theory, third parties could have influenced reputation-based or financial incentive-based herding by challenging the (herd) behaviour of investment managers, brokers, and agents. This would presuppose that they are aware of these proven effects (reputation and financial incentives), i.e., that the information on reputation behaviour and financial

[26] As it happened after the 'dot com crisis' through so-called interest snapping (*zinsschnäppchen*) or through IPO snapping before and during the 'dot com crisis'.

[27] This is not only a problem that is related to the influence of third parties. There is empirical evidence of shareholders putting pressure on company boards to take even more risky actions (eg takeover bids, which were very much involved in the financial crisis).

incentives is disclosed to them, and once they have this information, they reconsider their investment decision. Simple disclosure, however, does not suffice. The information has to be disclosed at the right moment. There is a long-standing debate in capital market theory as to when information should be disclosed, a debate focused on insider trading. Disclosure can also produce negative effects for individual investors who have benefited from private information.

The barriers to different forms of external influence are obvious for both the creditors/sellers and the buyers/investors. The incentive-based remuneration systems of investment managers, brokers, and agents were not made publicly available. The existing corporate governance system did not provide for disclosure, something I would regard as a failure to take external economic effects into account in drafting corporate governance schemes.[28] On the other hand, it is highly doubtful whether investors would have changed their behaviour even if they had known about the incentive-based remuneration system and received the information at the right moment.

b. The actors

The *different actors* in our scenario are linked by all sorts of bilateral contracts concluded between the various actors—banks, investment companies, special purpose vehicles, private investors. Because of the particularly dense network of contracts in the case at hand, the network appears more like a chain of contracts as opposed to a true network. These contracts are shaped under the privity of contract doctrine, and do not take into consideration their effect on third parties, including contracts concluded between third parties.[29]

Any evaluation of the impact of bilateral contracts on third parties might distinguish between those *directly* affected—such as banks that no longer lend money, financial service providers who lose business contacts, intermediaries who miss profit-making opportunities, private investors who are cut off from the consumer credit market—and those who are only *indirectly* affected—such as other market participants who are not in a direct competitive relation with the actors of the contract chain/networks, including banks, investment firms or investors who are not involved in the particular kind of business that triggered the subprime crisis.

Particular attention should be devoted to the role of financial supervisory bodies. They are the ones who have been put in charge of overseeing the stability of

[28] Contrary to Grundmann, n 15, 61, 84–5; Möslein, n 15 above, 72, 75 making reference to OECD 'Corporate Governance and the Financial Crisis—Key Findings and Main Messages' (2009) (available at <http://www.oecd.org/dataoecd/3/10/43056196.pdf>) 1, 14–16 and E. Wymeersch (2008) 'Corporate Governance and Financial Stability'(2008) Financial Law Institute Working Paper No 11/2008 (available at <http://papers.ssrn.com/sol3/papers.cfm?abstract_id=1288631>) 1, 13.

[29] One may wonder whether contracts concluded between third parties matter for the assessment of the effects of bilateral contracts on the formation of herd behaviour because they are also part of this contractual chain. However, I will focus on the relationship between B2I (business to investors) in the direct contractual relationship.

the capital markets and taking action if the stability is endangered by, for example, systemic risks resulting from herd behaviour. Without going into detail, as this reaches beyond this Chapter, I would assume that the financial supervision institutions have to assume their share of responsibility in the subprime crisis. Whether this is due to herd behaviour in following deregulatory mainstream ideology; the lack of appropriate instruments or enforcement structures, which incidentally is what US and EU politics would have us believe, given that they are currently reshaping the institutional architecture and introducing new supervision instruments; or enforcement failure under the existing scheme[30] remains to be discussed.

It is neither completely true nor untrue that financial supervisory bodies do not have to oversee contract-making in the respective field. It is true in that it is not the task of supervisory authorities to 'approve' contracts on the financial markets. It is untrue in that the supervisory authorities in Europe, already under the existing regulatory framework before the subprime crisis, were a European law-based organization in existence for the purpose of surveying the potential effects of contract-making on the markets.[31] This includes the need to look at third parties affected by bilateral contracts. Any prospective design of a new governance structure should take the role and function of supervisory bodies into account.

c. External personal and structural relationship

The possible externality may affect either the external *personal* relationship between the parties to the bilateral contracts and *third natural persons* and/or *third legal entity* in their economic, social, and legal position, or it may affect the external *structural* relationship in which the parties to the bilateral contracts, as well as third natural persons or third legal entities, operate.

The most well-known and widely discussed external *personal* relationship of bilateral contracts is the famous contract with protective effects with respect to a third party (*vertrag mit schutzwirkung zugunsten dritter*) that breaks down the privity doctrine. This might also be called the *positive* third party effect. Rights are granted under contract law even with respect to third persons who do not form part of the contract. In our context—the subprime crisis still as blueprint—the legal construct of contracts with third party effect is of little, if no, help.[32] In particular, in the aftermath of the bankruptcy of Lehman Brothers, (private) investors have filed all sorts of actions against intermediaries who traded in asset-backed securities.

[30] For an analysis from the private retailer perspectivesee J. Keßler, H.-W. Micklitz, and N. Reich (eds)*Institutionelle Finanzmarktaufsicht und Verbraucherschutz, Eine rechtsvergleichende Untersuchung der Regelungssysteme in Deutschland, Italien, Schweden, dem Vereinigten Königreich und der Europäischen Gemeinschaft* (Baden-Baden: Nomos, 2010).

[31] Keßler, Micklitz, and Reich, n 30.

[32] See more generally, with regard to the UK, S. Banakas, 'Intruding into Contracts between Others—The English Way' in K. Boele-Woelki and W. Grosheide (eds)*The Future of European Contract Law* (Köln: Kluwer, 2007) 231–46; with regard to France, see J.-S. Borghetti, 'Breach of Contract and Liability to Third Parties in French Law' (2010) *ZEuP* 279–303.

However, none ever argued that the bilateral contracts concluded in the distribution chain established enforceable rights to their benefit.[33] The whole discussion on investor rights and remedies took a different direction—whether and to what extent liability is not limited to Lehman Brothers but could be extended to intermediaries that sold Lehman Brothers certificates. Going back to the classification of bilateral contracts, we would classify this type of impact of bilateral contracts as negative. What is a stake here is some form of joint liability imposed on third parties who are not part of the bilateral contract. Retail banks offered and advised their customers on most of the insurance products backed by Lehman Brothers' bonds during the 12–24 months before Lehman Brothers was declared bankrupt. Many investors later claimed that those policies were presented to them as 'safe investments' fully backed by their own retail banks' capital and assets. Banks that sold the insurance products structured on Lehman Brothers' bonds might thus be held liable for misleading commercial practices and for false or misleading prospectuses. Indeed, by highlighting the sales process, the claims in the commercial brochure and the disregard for investor profiles, claimants have argued that misleading commercial practices are bound to civil law sanctions. Lower courts in Austria even used the advertising strategies of the intermediary to justify joint liability.[34] In Italy,[35] one of the major banks has been required to reimburse those customers who bought Lehman Brothers-backed policies because it had not completely disclosed the real risk of the investment, thus disregarding the investor risk profile.

The external *structural* relationship is said to remain outside the potential third-party effects of bilateral contracts, be it in providing rights that benefit of third parties, in duties in the form of liability rules with respect to third parties or in the degree to which third parties may influence the content of the bilateral contract. In Europe, the policy of the European Commission and the regulatory measures taken by the EU aim to guarantee access to the financial markets and remove all sorts of barriers that might restrict access. Therefore, investors are encouraged to switch the financial service provider at low or no cost in order to enhance competition on the market. Such a regulatory approach may clearly be associated with a particular market structure, which may be classified as governance through contract law.[36] The bankruptcy of Lehman Brothers may serve to explain how courts, when faced with the fact that third parties had indeed no knowledge of the incentive-based remuneration system and therefore had no chance to shield themselves against potential detrimental effects or, to put it the other way around, in pushing to change the detrimental incentive-based remuneration system, are developing arguments to link two contracts or to compensate

[33] The Consumer Law Enforcement Forum organized a working seminar on the consequences of Lehman Brothers in September 2009 where representatives of consumer organizations from various Member States reported on the way in which their national courts handled complaints (on file with the author).

[34] See references in C. Ghelli, 'Luserna di Rorà, Investor Protection after the Lehman Brothers Case', LLM Thesis, EUI Florence, October 2011.

[35] As reported by *Plus 24 - Il Sole 24 Ore*, 27 March 2010, 15.

[36] Riesenhuber and Möslein, n 24, 1, 35.

the third party for the missed opportunity, i.e. changing the detrimental rules. The German Supreme Court decided that the non-disclosure of the kickback provisions that the intermediary bank received from Lehman Brothers for the sale of their certificates to investors does not entitle the private investor to claim compensation, thereby rejecting a link between the firm and the market, the organization, and the contract.[37]

d. *First intermediary remark*

What can be learnt from the analysis of the third-party impact as inspired by law and economics and contract governance? What is the added value of applying these theoretical frameworks to litigation in the aftermath of the subprime crisis? In Table 4.1, we can see what the findings look like. We can get a clearer picture from the link between the forms of third party impact and the three types of herding by taking into account the difficult distinction between positive and negative *effects* on third parties respectively via/by third, thereby paving the way for tentative *conclusions* on the responsibilities of the actors involved, respectively on the personal and structural relationship.

Table 4.1

Quality of effect—positive/negative	Information-based herding	Reputation-based herding	Incentive-based herding
On third parties Via/by third parties	Positive saving costs for private investors, but speculation against the herd Making information public at the right moment and to the right people	Negative on private investors On mangers/agents Disclosure	Negative on private investors On managers/agents Disclosure
Actors involved Directly/indirectly	a) Debtors b) Investors	a) Debtors, managers, brokers, agents b) Investors: advertising the bank, the brand	a) Debtors, managers, brokers, agents b) In case of commission sharing
Impact on Personal relationship Structural relationship	Conflict of interest ?	Liability of intermediaries, of managers and banks ?	? Firms and markets

[37] The lower court of Hamburg had decided in favour, the court of appeal rejected the claim, see OLG Hamburg, 23.04.2010—Az. 13 U 117/09 (2010) *Betriebs Berater* 1945, just as the German Supreme Court 27.9.2011 AZ XI ZR 178/10 and 182 /10 (available at <http://juris.bundesgerichtshof.de/cgi-bin/rechtsprechung/document.py?Gericht=bgh&Art=en&Datum=2011-9-27&nr=58208&pos=19&anz=23>).

Broadening the analysis of third-party impact via law and economics allows for a deeper understanding of the relationship between firms and markets permitted by contract governance. It becomes clear that the legal—judicial system—as it stands in the Member States and on the European level—cannot handle the wider dimension of third-party impact outside the notion of contracts with third-party benefits (*verträge mit schutzwirkung zugunsten dritter*). There are exceptions. Lower courts are using references to advertising and sales promotion measures as a means to justify the establishment of enforceable rights against intermediaries.

What is absent thus far is a systematic investigation into the relationship between third party impact and herd behaviour. The legal—judicial—system and even the theoretical framework of law and economics or contract governance do not provide a particular insight into such a relationship. The legal—judicial—system singles out the rights and duties of parties. They do not look into the systemic dimension, or if they do, they hide it behind case-related considerations. It is plain that courts, when they decide a case like the one against Lehman Brothers, are aware of the floodgate effect. It requires little imagination to predict that courts will not solve the third-party impact question. Courts might feel tempted to prevent private investors from 'herding', in the sense that private investors might want to benefit from promising and successful litigation.[38]

Herding has a collective dimension, which runs counter to individualistic philosophy between markets and contracts, which is, however, much more developed in firms/organizations. This brings us to collective actions which I will discuss in Section III(2).

2. Third party impact in herd behaviour

From a legal perspective, we have four questions that require an answer with regard to the potential liability for third-party impact in herd behaviour. I refer to the distinctions already developed above: (1) what constitutes a herd, (2) who is the herd; (3) what is herd behaviour; and (4) who is ultimately responsible?

a. *The 'what' question*

A herd is a collective entity. Translated into the context of the subprime crisis, the herd must reach a size large enough to trigger systemic risks to the financial markets. This sets a rather high benchmark, which is obviously different from attempts to define the 'class' in collective actions. The reference

[38] See, from the US context, *Stoneridge Inv. Partners, LLC v. Scientific-Atlanta* 552 US 148 [2008]—only limited 'scheme' liability as an example where the court discusses the potential risk of courts being overburdened by individual claims.

point for discussion is nevertheless Rule 23(a) of the Federal Rules of Civil Procedure which ties the class to three requirements: *numerosity, commonality* and *typicality*.[39] These criteria may serve as a starter for conceptualizing the herd, although it has to be borne in mind that the regulation on collective litigation serves a very particular purpose. The definition of the class shall distinguish the potential claimants from those who are not given standing, whereas the herd phenomenon is not bound to a distinction between claimants and defendants:

- *Numerosity*: The number of plaintiffs must be so large that a combination of lawsuits would no longer be practical. There is no fixed benchmark. However, if the number of group members mounts up to hundreds or thousands, the combination of lawsuits does apparently not constitute a possible alternative for the group action lawsuit. Even if we reduce the threshold to mere effects on financial markets, we would still need a substantial number that could constitute a herd.
- *Commonality*: The asserted claims must show legal or factual similarities. The courts apply a qualitative rather than a quantitative standard. Contrary to the wording, a single common dispute question is sufficient, as long as it is significant (*one significant common question*). Here, the differences between a class and a herd become clear. Each individual in the class, albeit not necessarily, bases his claim on the same event which triggered the injury or the damage. Quite to the contrary, herd behaviour is based on consecutive action. It implies that somebody is taking the lead and the others follow. Class actions might also apply to consecutive behaviour of class members, but here the individual circumstance of the case might differ to a greater extent, downgrading the commonality.
- *Typicality*: The claim must be typical for the whole group. The prerequisite is closely linked to the *commonality* requirement. The *typicality* requirement exists to avoid having different objectives of the group representative (the lawyer, the consumer organisation or any other, even public, agency) and the group members despite the basic existence of underlying similarities.

At first glance, the normative framework which serves to determine the class seems equally applicable to herd behaviour. A closer look, however, reveals the picture to be more complicated if we take the three forms of herding into account. While information-based herding can be found at the starting point of numerous efforts to come to grips with herd behaviour, the strong consecutive dimension of this form of herd behaviour might cause a problem in classifying this variant as a class. The situation seems less complicated in the case of reputation-based and

[39] There is endless literature on these parameters, I refer to what I produced for a European environment, , 'Collective Private Enforcement—the Key Questions' in W. van Boom and M. Loos (eds)*Collective Enforcement of Consumer Law, Securing Compliance in Europe through Private Group Action and Public Authority Intervention* (Groningen: European Law Publishing, 2007) 13–33.

incentive-based herding because at least here the trigger mechanism is identical in both circumstances.

The true problem results from the definition of the threshold. Herd behaviour can be found whenever human beings get together in commercial, political or social transactions. However, the context is different. I am interested in herd behaviour that affects the financial markets to such an extent that the whole system becomes unstable. I am not discussing the requirements under which a class action against the unlawful behaviour of banks, investment firms etc. can be filed.[40] What is at stake is compensation for systemic failure resulting from herd behaviour. Put this way, the dimension of compensation claims becomes clear. As the herd amounts to thousands and thousands of people, not contained in one country, maybe millions all over the world, compensation claims easily reach a dimension – at least in theory—that renders them unmanageable and shifts the focus from private enforcement to public regulation. Therefore, findings of behavioural economics may be more appropriate to correct certain rationality assumptions so as to prevent herding.

b. The 'who' question

We have different 'herds', and in theory, all the different actors involved in the subprime crisis may form a separate herd, and all the separate herds may be united in a 'super herd' which covers all the different sub-herds. These separate herds include (a) banks which too readily grant credits, (b) purveyors of special purpose vehicles, (c) debtors (loan, mortgages, credit cards), (d) investors (investment services), and (e) supervisory authorities and central banks.

Herd behaviour by banks may create a situation where debtors or investors who should not get credit obtain credit. The sales of mortgages might become highly risky when all banks get involved in mortgage sales and do not take into account the real credit-worthiness of a consumer-investor. As there is no 'right to credit', providing evidence of a conflict of interest might be the only way to demonstrate that banks have been pushed to grant subprime mortgages. However, what kind of conflict of interest arises if such herd behaviour has led to bankruptcy? More than conflict of interest, are we not confronted with professional negligence? Herd behaviour that harms the investors occurs, for example, when many brokers make the same investment because their compensation schemes '*suggest*' that they do so. Here, one needs to prove a conflict of interest. This is easy in theory, even though it may turn out to be difficult in practice.

[40] For the US context, see, e.g., J. Coffey, 'Reforming the Securities Class Action—An Essay on Deterrence and its Implementation' (2006)Columbia Law and Economics Working Paper No 293(available at <http://papers.ssrn.com/sol3/papers.cfm?abstract_id=893833>) for Europe, see A. Stadler and H.- W. Micklitz, 'The Development of Collective Legal Actions in Europe, Especially in German Civil Procedure' (2006) *European Business Law Review* 1473–503; F. Reuschle, '*Das Kapitalanleger-Musterverfahrensgesetz—Eine erste Bestandsaufnahme aus der Sicht der Praxis*' in N. Caspar, A. Janssen, R. Pohlmann, and R. Schulze (eds)*Auf dem Weg zu Einer Europäischen Sammelklage* (München: Sellier, 2009) 277–92.

The question, however, is whether a diffuse conflict of interest can generate a wide-ranging impact (negative externalities) on third parties? The subprime crisis seems to suggest such links, though not via hard legal evidence. But the question is whether this is still an issue for contract governance or corporate governance or whether it rises to the level of concerning the regulation of the financial market as a whole. Alternatively, and in a *prospective* perspective, one might think of 'contractual' or 'non-contractual duties' to prevent herding, for example via protecting the creditor against engaging in unreasonable and absurd credits agreements.[41]

c. *The 'behavioural' question*

I have used the threefold distinction of herd behaviour developed by behavioural science throughout the Chapter, but so far only as a factual and not as a normative concept. In translating behavioural findings of herd behaviour into a normative concept, collective responsibility/liability springs to mind. *Ex post* analysis looks for the person ultimately responsible who can be identified and sued in court for triggering the collective herd behaviour.[42] This necessarily implies the need to distinguish between different herds and to investigate the relationship between those herds. If one looks at the herd as a whole, it is plain that sub-groups involved in the subprime crisis have played their role in the herding process. This is particularly true with regard to information-based herd behaviour. The group share in herd behaviour should not, however, automatically be equated with legal responsibility or with contributory negligence. Certainly, one might blame banks for their ease in engaging in credit transactions, special purpose vehicles for setting aside the potential effects of a massive sale of under-securitized bonds on the markets, on the buyers, managers, brokers, and agents for only considering their incentives instead of looking at the consequences, and last but not least investors for simply following the herd. However, is a particular financial player legally responsible and even liable if she has not taken action to swim against the current? Would the answer to this question differ if she had in her possession valid personal information that urged her to take a different action, and if yes, how can this be proved?

People who live in glass houses should not throw stones—in common parlance. Is this the logic of herd behaviour translated into a legal regime or does the question rest on whether we have to more closely distinguish between the different sub-herds and their particular contribution to the herd behaviour of another sub-herd?

[41] See J. Whitman, 'Consumerism vs. Producerism. A Study in Comparative Law' (2007) 117 *The Yale Law Journal* 340–406(available at <http://digitalcommons.law.yale.edu/cgi/viewcontent.cgi?article=1643&context=fss_papers&sei-redir=1#search="J.+Whitman,+Consumerism+vs.+Producerism.+A+Study+in+Comparative+Law'> who argues that German and French Laws tend to assume more paternalistic patterns of consumer/investor protection than the US, and Section IV(3).

[42] I will not discuss if there is a cause for manipulation of the person addressed as being responsible for triggering the herd behaviour.

d. The 'who is responsible' question

From a normative perspective the *key* question is to find out who is responsible for herding. Therefore, one has to distinguish between those who triggered the herd behaviour and those following the herd although they have private information/ signals at hand that tell them the contrary. The difficulty is that we have different herds, and within each herd, actors that might have triggered the herd behaviour and actors who should be classified as mere followers. In theory, a supervisory authority could trigger herding as easily as a creditor, a rating company, or an individual investor. Each of them could, similarly, be a mere follower. What makes it even more difficult is that the joint activities of different actors may deliberately or involuntarily trigger herd behaviour. So while the legal analytical question is clear, the answer very much depends on a complex set of facts that have to be carefully analysed and then proven when litigation arises. Again, I am using the three standard explanations of herd behaviour as a yardstick for clarifying responsibilities.

Information-based herding and information cascades—the point is whether disclosure of private information would help stop herd behaviour. If the first actor follows her right/positive signal, and if the others follow, the herd effect can produce negative external effects even if the right signal were disclosed. If the second or third follows the first, although she has private information that is equivalent to the private information which the first based her particular decision on, how can you hold this person responsible if she decides not to follow her signal/information? The assessment does not change if the second or third actor actually does disclose the private information, which suggests that she should not follow the herd. Legally, the only way to determine responsibility is to find out who spread the first/wrong information/signal. This is at least true *cum grano salis*.[43]

Reputation-based herding—can you hold the manager or agent responsible who mimicks other managers and other agents because this is the safest way for the manager and the agent to reject any potential critique against not following the herd? Such behaviour could become legally relevant only if the claimant can provide evidence that the managers/agents are still following the herd although they positively know or they should have known (negligence) that following reputation-based herding at this particular point would lead to detrimental effects on third parties. Most of the post-subprime litigation falls under this category. What is the link between negligence and conflicts of interest? The concept of conflict of interest is a key issue in understanding how the retail financial market works as regards consumer welfare. Banks mostly sell what they need to sell although the customer risk profile might suggest less profitable options. In such a case, the link between negligence and conflict of interest is evident.

[43] It seems that there is a very thin line separating purely psychological reasons for this behaviour from other reasons, namely the ones related to market dynamics, which include strong manipulation and speculation of the markets.

Compensation incentive-based herding (remuneration of managers)—responsibility here is tied to at least two major requirements: a) that the claimant knew or can provide evidence of the remuneration scheme (here the problem is access to information and disclosure of remuneration schemes) and b) that the claimant can demonstrate that the principal negligently set the wrong incentives. Here, the situation seen through the eyes of the claimant is not much different from the case of reputation-based herding.

In sum, information-based herding as understood by behavioural economics does not lead to clear responsibilities. This might only be different if a firm discloses misleading or irrelevant information which then causes herd behaviour effects.[44] The situation is different with regard to reputation-based and incentive-based herding. Here, the ultimate responsibility is much easier to detect—at least in theory.

The question, however, remains whether the last two forms of herding lead in the right direction when it comes to determining responsibilities. One might argue that bank managers or bank agents would have relied on the information they received from the market even without reputation-based and compensation-based incentives. Is the decision to invest and follow the herd not a question to be determined under the business judgment rule? The point then is to define and lay down appropriate requirements on the basis of what information managers and bank agents rely on when they follow the herd. Does it suffice to rely on what are considered to be trustworthy sources, like some sort of ratings for example, or is more needed, for instance, proper investigation of the information basis?[45] Such a way of thinking permits a parallel with product liability, i.e., to what extent can the producer rely on his dealers in ensuring the quality and the safety of the delivered products? An obligation to check the trustworthiness of foreign information would set incentives against herding.[46]

3. Herd behaviour in networks

What remains to be done is to look into network theory in order to find out whether this particular construct is capable of providing safer results with regard to the identified forms of herding. While there is no agreement on whether networks should be regarded as new entities which will develop their own rules and maybe even turn into a new legal concept, there is agreement that networks contain elements which cut across the distinction of firms and markets. My approach is pragmatic; I am simply testing the network model and its feasibility in the

[44] These are the telecom cases, see Reuschle, n 40.

[45] Much could be said on the principal-agent relationship in particular with regard to rating agencies and the potential role of private law liability, see P. Korth, *Quasivertragliche Haftung von Ratingagenturen gegenüber Investoren aufgrund fehlerhafter Bewertung von Unternehmensanleihen* (Baden-Baden: Nomos, 2009) but on the limits of such attempts to make a particular actor responsible for systemic risks, see G. M. Hodgson, 'The Great Crash of 2008 and the Reform of Economics' (2009) 33 *Cambridge Journal of Economics* 1205–21, 1205, 1213.

[46] I would like to thank Gerald Spindler for this important clarification.

particular circumstances of managing the third party effects in herd behaviour resulting from the subprime crisis.

The key question is whether financial instruments of the type at stake in the subprime crisis can be regarded as a *network of contracts* that combines elements of firm/organization and market/contracts and may generate legal responsibilities. Teubner,[47] who has most prominently argued in favour of network responsibilities, has defined three criteria for the assumption of the existence of a network:

- Reciprocal reference of bilateral contract*s* to one another, either found within the document and/or distilled from contractual practice (*multi-laterality*),
- a contractual reference to the overall project of connected contracts (*relational purpose(vertragsverbund)*), and
- a close and significant cooperation between the participants within the multi-lateral relation (*economic unity*).

The three criteria provide guidance against which the findings from the subprime crisis could and should be measured. The existence of the first can be deduced from practice. It remains at the bilateral level, which dominates the contract shaping in the subprime crisis. The second requires a deep knowledge of and insight into the ways in which the different contracts are interconnected. This criterion approaches the common objective which unites firms and contracting partners in long-term agreements. Economic unity is a normative concept that may be found in all legal orders, though to a different degree. In EU legal speech, economic unity may be equated with linked contracts, a concept which has been codified in various consumer contract law directives.[48] The Draft Common Frame of Reference (DCFR) does not provide input which reaches beyond the current debate.

Unlike firms where at least basic information on the structure, the statute, etc, is available via the commercial register or via publicly available balance sheets, contracts are not made public. Access to information on the content of the contract therefore becomes an issue.[49] What would theoretically be needed is a look into the various bilateral contracts concluded between the various actors—banks, investment companies, special purpose vehicles, private investors—in order to find out whether there is evidence which allows us to test whether the three criteria are met.

As a hypothesis I would formulate—even without knowing the content of the different contracts, we might assume that contracts may foresee information duties—that the relationship between the different actors in the subprime crisis

[47] G. Teubner, '*Coincidentia Oppositorum*: Hybrid Networks Beyond Contract and Organization' in M. Amstutz and G. Teubner (eds)*Networks, Legal Issues of Multilateral Co-operation* (Oxford/Portland, Oregon: Hart Publishing, 2009) 3, 20.

[48] P. Rott, 'Maximum Harmonisation and Mutual Recognition versus Consumer Protection, The Example of Linked Credit Agreements in EC Consumer Credit Law' (2006) (E) 2-3 *The European Legal Forum* 61–8 (available at <http://www.simons-law.com/library/pdf/e/677.pdf>).

[49] Access to information has not yet really reached the European level, neither with regard of access to information saved in public agencies nor with regard to private companies. The Member States' laws differ considerably.

varies considerably in the degree to which multi-laterality, relational purpose, and economic unity can be presumed. It seems difficult to understand the set of contracts concluded in and around asset-backed securities as a specific network that is entirely bound to such a financial transaction. However, the overall link might be identified in the overall purpose to widen the extension of credit for poorer people while spreading the risk more widely. This would mean the equation of the *relational* purpose with the production, trading, and marketing of asset-backed securities in the interests of an overall policy objective.[50] It would further mean that we might speak of a network if an economic transaction reaches beyond bilateral transactions and triggers market behaviour, i.e., herding. I hesitate to draw such a conclusion, although it might be tempting to link the concept of networks to particular types of transactions.

What would be the consequence if we start from the premise that no such overall network existed? Instead of one network, there might be several networks, and the question then becomes whether and how the different networks are interconnected—or to put it the other way round, whether we can link the different networks to sub-groups of the herd! It is suggested that the first network relation exists between the banks and the special purpose vehicles. Such a conclusion does not reach beyond available insight into long-term relationships in law and economics. Combined with the findings on herd behaviour, the question is whether the parties to the bilateral long-term contract assumed responsibilities to third parties potentially affected by these transactions, such as investors. This is another variant of bilateral contracts that generates rights that benefit of third parties. The second network could be the relationship between the investor and the bank in situations where the investments are credit financed. Here, the concept of economic unity is highlighted, albeit not necessarily in B2C relations, as the investors may be companies.

If we assume for the moment that a *network* existed, one that stood behind the subprime crisis, which meets the three above-mentioned criteria, what would be the consequences of its existence when handling third party impact in herd behaviour? Taken to the extreme, every sub-herd or even every natural person or legal entity could be responsible to any other sub-herd, natural person, or legal entity. *Universal responsibility* is just the flipside of *organized irresponsibility*. This sounds somewhat polemic, but is the direct result of a transfer from information-based herding to the concept of network. Reputation-based and incentive-based herding allow for a more sophisticated solution, as it might yield responsibilities for the managers, brokers, and agents to parties with whom no direct bilateral contractual relation exists. (I set aside vicarious liability, i.e., liability of firms for the behaviour of managers, of agents, or of intermediaries who are legally independent such as brokers)[51].

[50] Easy credit is regarded in the US as a means of social policy. This begs the question to what extent the relational purpose in private networks can be associated to wider public policy considerations.

[51] See in this context the Heininger Saga: H.W. Micklitz, 'The Relationship between National and European Consumer Policy—Challenges and Perspectives' (2008) *Yearbook of Consumer Law* 35–66; G. Spindler, '*Aufklärungspflichten eines Finanzdienstleisters über eigene Gewinnmargen?—Ein 'Kick-Back' zu viel*' (2009) *WM* 1821–8.

However, when public regulation fails to avoid the occurrence of negative externalities for third parties and when neither company law nor contract law can provide appropriate solutions, not even in the ambitious concept of networks ranking between firms/organizations and market/contract, tort law may play an ancillary role. This is quite a residual position but it may have an important function whenever the market becomes so complicated that *ex-ante* regulation cannot provide guidance.[52] For more than 20 years now, tort lawyers have discussed the concept of *organizational liability*,[53] which should be understood as a direct answer to diagnosed '*organized irresponsibility*' to be found in modern networks that constitutes the structural answer to the increased inefficiency of the old market and pure firm model. Brüggemeier has formulated a proposal of how organizational liability in the form of enterprise could work. Whereas even the DCFR concerns only the concept of personal liability, Brüggemeier advocates a model according to which the economic entity, the enterprise, is the direct addressee of the liability. The proposal is very much designed to handle potential defects in industrial production, but it could equally serve as a blueprint for discussing organizational liability in the production of services within networks. It reflects the more legal side of Corporate Social Responsibility. I quote:[54]

Art. 3:101 Basic Rule of Enterprise Liability,

(1) Enterprises are liable for injury to the legally protected interests of others, which is caused by inadequate operational activities and processes...
(2) Enterprises are business organizations of whatever legal form, which operate in the market and offer commercial performance for remuneration. The practice of a self-employed professional activity is considered equivalent to that of an enterprise.
(3) The operational activity or the operational process is inadequate if the injury to interests could have been avoided through the observance of organizational and technical possibilities, as well as reasonable economic standards...

Art. 3: 102 Owner of a Business Enterprise

Liability applies to those carrying out a business enterprise. In respect of affiliated enterprises, the holding company will be liable for the operational activity of the subsidiary company in justified cases.

The enterprise is not to be automatically equated with a legal entity, as Article 3:102 makes clear. I will not enter into the discussion of the relationship between tort and contract law in general. I restrict myself to demonstrate that tort law may serve, even in its current form, as a fallback position to deal with liability issues in networks. However, organizational liability via tort law can only deal with

[52] M. Wellenhofer, 'Third Party Effects of Bilateral Contracts within the Network' in M. Amstutz and G. Teubner (eds)*Networks, Legal Issues of Multilateral Co-operation* (Oxford/Portland, Oregon: Hart Publishing, 2009) 119.

[53] G. Brüggemeier, '*Organisationshaftung*' (1991) 191 *AcP* 33.

[54] G. Brüggemeier and Z. Yan, *Entwurf für ein chinesisches Haftungsgesetz* (Tübingen: Mohr Siebeck, 2009) 120.

reputation- and incentive-based herding, as it requires that ultimate responsibilities be associated with a particular entrepreneurial entity.

The attempts to transform third party impact and herd behaviour into a legal concept demonstrate the difficulties inherent in the current legal system that is based on bilateral contracts and that knows of linked agreements only in exceptional circumstances. But even attempts in legal doctrine to reach beyond the distinction of firm and market, of organization and contract, be it long-term contracts or networks, do not provide promising answers for the *ex-post* handling of the litigation which arose or might arise in the aftermath of the subprime crisis.

The initial reaction would be to transfer the set of well-developed disclosure rules from the firm to the market, from organization to contract. It is true that when access to information on the content agreed is not publicly available, information remains private. But would mandatory disclosure of contractual information between parties in a network or in chain contracts or in bilateral contracts that are tied together under one common objective change the behaviour and avoid the herding? One might conclude with hindsight that the set of contracts concluded does not form a network, not even in its most ambitious form, as there is no common objective and no economic unity.

There are two possible conclusions to be drawn from these findings: first that a crisis of the current calibre which comes near to the Dutch tulips and the Albanian pyramid game cannot be handled *ex-post* via designing responsibilities. A crisis of such a dimension oversteps the boundaries of what a civil law system is capable of managing, i.e. above and beyond individual compensation claims, the civil law system cannot cover the damage which results from systemic failure. The immediate answer to such a conclusion would be, and indeed is, the call for public regulation. One might wonder whether public regulation is better suited to deal with systemic risks resulting from herd behaviour. This is not, however, my topic for today.[55]

The second observation is that it might make more sense to associate the subprime crisis and the management of risks resulting from herd behaviour with the concept of regulated markets. This does not allow for designing liabilities, but it takes a comprehensive view of the field. This would mean—at least retrospectively speaking—that herd behaviour and third party impact cannot be regarded as a legal concept. Solutions to demarcate liabilities would have to be derived under traditional legal regimes insofar as they allow for assigning liabilities, be they based on contract or tort law, thereby taking the particular regulatory environment into account in which contract and tort is embedded.

[55] See, on the *ex-ante* management of uncertainty via public regulation in the aftermath of the crisis, K.-H. Ladeur, 'The Financial Market Crisis—A Case of Network Failure?' in P. Kjaer, G. Teubner, and A. Febbrajo (eds) *The Financial Crisis in Constitutional Perspective, The Dark Side of Functional Differentiation* (Oxford: Hart Publishing, 2011) 63–92.

IV. *Ex-ante* Prevention of Herd Behaviour via Contract Governance

While herding can be observed everywhere in society, I will remain within the purview of financial services. This allows for greater consistency in the envisaged confrontation of *ex post* versus *ex ante* analysis.

I start from a number of assumptions that I will make explicit to avoid being misunderstood. Financial services belong to the field of regulated markets, an area where there is less room for private autonomy and for private contract-making. I see private law and contract governance as operating within a regulatory framework, which is, in the case presented here, to a large extent a European one. I will take a European perspective and I will not delve deeper into the issues of multi-level governance. Further, I link contract governance to what has been labelled as co-regulation,[56] the coming together of public and private regulation. I equally start from the premise that B2B and B2C relations cannot be measured against the same yardstick. This is abundantly clear in view of the subprime crisis. The choice is not between autonomy in B2B and regulation via public authorities, in essence we have to deal with a triangular relationship: B2B, B2C, and their relation with public authorities.

I start from the premise that the search for new mechanisms via contract governance to avoid systemic risks resulting from herd behaviour should not bring us back to a contract design that relies on the rational well-informed investor.[57] It is my understanding that EU law has gradually designed all market actors as omnipotent entities guided by rational market behaviour. This is even true for the private investor, the consumer-investor, who much more closely resembles a small businessman than a human being in need of protection. The other side of the coin is that a new contract design, even in the form of co-regulation, cannot openly recognize, incentivize or promote irrational behaviour.[58] But this does not exclude consideration of the limited capacities of receiving and processing information, the deficits in rational decision-making and the well-known phenomenon of unselfish behaviour,[59] more generally the limits of mandated disclosure.[60]

I will proceed in three steps. First I will analyse the modes of contract governance that could be framed in a regulated market, I will then develop a contract

[56] F. Cafaggi (ed)*Reframing Self-Regulation in European Private Law* (London: Kluwer Law, 2006).

[57] With regard to consumer protection, see S. Issacharoff, 'Disclosure, Agents and Consumer Protection' (2011) 167 *Journal of Institutional and Theoretical Economics* 56–71 (available at <http://papers.ssrn.com/sol3/papers.cfm?abstract_id=1640624>).

[58] H. Eidenmüller, '*Der Homo Economicus und das Schuldrecht: Herausforderungen durch* Behavioral Law and Economics' (2005) *JZ* 216, 217.

[59] H. Eidenmüller, n 58, 216, 218.

[60] O. Ben-Shahar and C. E. Schneider, 'The Failure of Mandated Disclosure', University of Chicago, The Law School John M. Olin Law & Economics Research Paper No 516/University of Michigan Law School Law & Economics, Empirical Legal Studies Center Paper No 10-008.

governance design for the prevention of third party impact through herd behaviour, and finally I will examine the procedural requirements that contract governance should meet.

1. Modes of contract governance in a regulated market

The convenors of the conference propose to distinguish between four modes of *contract governance*:[61] governance of contract law (the framework in which the rules are elaborated, public/private, national/European/international), governance of contract (study of good order in a market society versus private law society), governance with the means of contract law (regulation through contract law, combination of different policy objectives), and governance through contract (supplementing the framework via autonomous rules). Personally, I think the four categories can be merged into two. The first two concern the structural level of governance (the institutional framework in the case of financial services), the second two deal with the interplay of regulation and autonomy (what I call '*regulated autonomy*'). What is missing in this distinction is the procedural dimension of governance (accountability, transparency, legitimacy) which connects the structural to the content level.

The *structural* level of governance—the institutional framework of financial services in Europe is shaped and elaborated by the EU. The overall purpose of EU rules is to establish a European capital market via common market access rules for financial services providers and their customers, via standardized financial supervision through public authorities and via minimum standards on contracts. The regulatory setting is guided by a strong reliance on the rational market behaviour of all participants which has to be secured through information regulation and best practices. Contract governance as a bottom-up approach seems beyond the political considerations of those involved in EU law-making. The Lamfalussy procedure is very much a top-down mechanism designed to elaborate market rules and guarantee their enforcement.[62] In theory, this would be the standard design for coming to grips with herd behaviour at least as a potential systemic risk. Since Lamfalussy, however, no new approach or regulation has been developed, such as, for example, the one established in the Service Directive,[63] which advocates and sets incentives for private rule-making in our field of interest through national

[61] Risenhuber and Möslein, n 24.

[62] There is an obvious conflict between the more horizontal bottom-up design of the Lamfalussy procedure which has gained much support, see, e.g., E. Posner, 'The Lamfalussy Process: Polyarchic Origins of Networked Financial Rule-Marking the EU' in C. Sabel and J. Zeitlin (eds)*Experimentalist Governance in the European Union: Towards a New Architecture?* (Oxford: Oxford University Press, 2010) 43–60 and the way the mechanism is working in practices, see for an evaluation of the practice under inclusion of the so-called third level, E. Ruffing, *Europäische Wertpapierregulierung Zwischen Input- und Output-Legitimität: Das Lamfalussy Verfahren* (Baden-Baden: Nomos, 2010). Whether and to what extent the amended procedure will strengthen a more horizontal approach that enhances participation remains to be seen.

[63] Directive 2006/123/EC of the European Parliament and of the Council of 12 December 2006 on Services in the internal market (OJ 2006 L 376/36).

and European standard bodies within a statutory regulatory framework in the EU capital market. Public regulation and private regulation are institutionally separated. This does not, however, prevent the rule-making authorities from using contract law as a regulatory device.

The *content* level: EU contract law in the field of financial services builds on a basic distinction between B2B and B2C relations which has become ever clearer over time. The distinction, however, is not one between autonomy in B2B and regulation in B2C. Both forms of contracts are subject to regulation, though to a different degree. The existing rules do not provide much guidance on herd behaviour and third party impact from a normative perspective. The few attempts to discuss the overall reach of linked contracts, or even further, to introduce network liability, failed already in the law-making process.[64] The same is true with regard to the elaboration of standard contract terms through business and consumer/investor organizations which belongs to the standard repertoire of rule setting via new (old) modes of governance. Initially the European Commission had promoted such a concept within the European codification project. Commissioner Redding seemed ready to revitalize the idea.[65] However, the draft proposal of a European Consumer Sales Law does not, contrary to previous drafts, provide for a particular article on the promotion of standard contract making via stakeholders.[66]

The *procedural* level: The EU tends to combine public and private law-making via new forms of governance. This process started in 1985 with the New Approach on Technical Standards, which served as a blueprint for the Lamfalussy procedure in financial services and culminated in the Open Method for Co-ordination in social policies. All these models suffer from one major deficiency that was inherent in the new approach and has never been remedied. The models do not discuss the three parameters which have dominated the governance debate from the beginning—accountability, transparency, legitimacy—and they do not provide guidance on the three requirements which are said to be crucial for the success or failure of the governance programme *in concreto*. I will not embark on the debate concerned with what is behind the three parameters as one can find an abundance of literature discussing governance, not only as a theoretical concept, but also in terms of its concrete implications in public administrative law and contract law. Accountability may be translated into reporting duties and self-assessment, transparency into access to information and legitimacy into rights to participate in making and assessing the results.[67]

[64] Despite strong lobbying from the consumer side, no charge back system was established in Directive 2007/64/EC of the European Parliament and of the Council of 13 November 2007 on payment services in the internal market, amending Directives 97/7/EC, 2002/65/EC, 2005/60/EC and 2006/48/EC and repealing Directive 97/5/EC (OJ 2007 L 319/36).

[65] Green Paper from the Commission on policy options for progress towards a European Contract Law for consumers and businesses COM(2010)348 Final, 1 July 2010.

[66] COM (2011) 635 Final,10 October 2011.

[67] F. Scharpf, *Governance in Europe, Effective and Democratic* (Oxford: Oxford University Press, 1999) distinguishing between in-put/out-put legitimacy, see N. Walker, 'The White Paper in

The visible expression of the blatant shortcoming in EU co-regulatory models is the missing mechanism that would link access to information and the right of stakeholders to participate in the new approach on technical standards.[68] Here, the infamous story starts with the EU granting access to information and participation to public interest groups in the law-making process 'at discretion' only. This deficiency has neither been overcome by the Lamfalussy procedure nor by the OMC. The co-regulatory models are either run by businesses or by the executive, both within a given regulatory framework where access to information and participation in the respective fora are generously 'granted' but not legally secured.[69] This means it is for those involved in the law-making process to create and establish appropriate mechanisms to meet the threefold requirements and for courts and academia to decide whether judicial review mechanisms are needed as a means of last resort.[70] Policy-makers and the EU legislator are obviously not willing (or able?) to draft a framework for the development of co-regulation which sets standards for accountability, transparency and legitimacy. The point is whether contract governance in the capital markets will be successful without such a framework. Both the co-regulatory framework and the governance dimension bear a much more general dimension which reaches beyond the purpose of this Chapter.

2. Herd behaviour, systemic risks, and risk categorization

Three approaches are possible: (1) the integration of contract governance into regulated markets—which is not my topic and which would raise several conceptual issues; (2) the definition and the role of contract governance as a means to prevent system risks and third party impact resulting from herd behaviour; or (3) the avoidance of herd behaviour which yields negative effects, not necessarily systemic risks, on third parties.

System risk is the highest benchmark possible. On 22 September 2010, the EU decided on a new architecture for financial supervision following the onset of the financial crisis.[71] A European Systemic Risk Board (ESRB):

> ...will be established which will monitor and assess potential threats to financial stability that arise from macro-economic developments and from developments within the

Constitutional Context Mountain or Molehill? A Critical Appraisal of the Commission White Paper on Governance' (2001) Jean Monet Working Paper No 6/2001, 10/27 (available at <http://centers.law.nyu.edu/jeanmonnet/papers/01/011001.html>); N. Walker, 'Europe's Constitutional Momentum and the Search for Polity Legitimacy' (2005) 4 *International Journal of Constitutional Law* 211–38.

[68] Council Resolution of 7 May 1985 on a new approach to technical harmonization and standards, (OJ 1985 C 136/1).

[69] F. Cafaggi and H. M. Watt (eds)*The Regulatory Function of European Private Law* (Cheltenham: Edward Elgar Publishing, 2009) 16.

[70] M. Dawson, *New Governance and the Proceduralisation of European Law: The Case of the Open Method of Coordination.European University Institute* (Florence: Thesis European Union Institute, 2009).

[71] See the press release on Financial Supervision package (available at <http://ec.europa.eu/internal_market/finances/committees/index_en.htm>).The final texts were adopted in late 2010; OJ 2010 L 331/12 (European Banking Authority); OJ 2010 L 331/48 (European Insurance and

financial system as a whole ('macro-prudential supervision'). To this end, the ESRB will provide an early warning of system-wide risks that may be building up and, where necessary, issue recommendations for action to deal with these risks. The creation of the ESRB will address one of the fundamental weaknesses highlighted by the crisis, which is the vulnerability of the financial system to interconnected, complex, sectoral and cross-sectoral systemic risks.

However, while it might be crucial to define the role of contract governance in the prevention of systemic risks, in order to find out whether public regulation suffices or whether the newly established board needs input and cooperation with the private sector via the development of new modes of governance, I am concerned with the impact of herd behaviour that leads to or enhances systemic risks. In a nutshell, that similar conceptual questions arise as the benchmark of systemic risk demonstrates the strong link between contract governance and public regulation. If we lower the benchmark and look into detrimental herd behaviour or herd behaviour that negatively affects third parties, we run into difficulties in separating 'negative' from 'positive' herd behaviour. If, for example, the herd invests into highly rewarding bonds, it might very well make sense to follow the herd, thereby implicitly strengthening the potential risk for the emergence of all sorts of negative effects, as discussed earlier. The point is how to define the benchmark where herd behaviour moves tilts from a 'positive' arena into a 'negative' one, from highly rewarding into finally risking the collapse of the whole financial system. Economics tells us that excess volatility in the stock market might be an indicator.[72] I wonder, however, whether empirical findings on volatility[73] can be translated into a normative concept.

Therefore, I will seek inspiration in classifying and ranking risks from a different area, where much experience is available on how to normatively shape risks. In the regulation of health and safety, there is a well-established three pronged approach on ranking risks: (a) the accepted state of the art (*allgemein anerkannter stand der technik*), (b) state of the art (*stand der technik*), and (c) state of science (*stand der wissenschaft*). It goes without saying that the criteria developed for product regulation cannot be literally transferred to financial risks. However, the idea of proceduralizing risks and linking the different responsibilities of different actors to different levels of risk might be useful. In the field of product safety, a distinction is drawn between the responsibilities of engineers (technicians) and those of natural scientists. The former establish the generally recognized rules and standards, the latter look into the future and make use of the most developed research experience in the respective field. One might distinguish, therefore,

Occupational Pension Funds Authority); OJ 2010 L 331/84 (European Securities and Market Authority); OJ 2010 L 331/120 (amending the powers of the respective three new agencies).

[72] A. V. Banerjee, 'A Simple Model of Herd Behavior' (1992) 107(3)*The Quarterly Journal of Economics* 797–817, 800.

[73] As summarized by K.D. West, 'Bubbles, Fads, and Stock Price Volatility Tests: APartial Evaluation' (1988) 43 *Journal of Finance* 639–56; T. Lux, 'Herd Behaviour, Bubbles and Crashes' (1995) 105 *The Economic Journal*, 881–96.

between 'generally accepted systemic risks' and 'pure systemic risks'. The classification of risks does not serve to determine responsibilities of supervisory authorities. In the field of product safety, the distinction addresses the responsibilities of producers and users of dangerous products too.

If we narrow the definition of risks to such a rough confrontation between at least two types of risks, we can easily associate financial regulators and private companies to the first type of financial risks. This means that financial regulators may legitimately, based on their experience and knowledge, define a threshold for intervention against risks. A similar type of thinking applies to financial service providers. They must, at the very least, respect the established standards on how to manage generally accepted systemic risks. Non-compliance with these standards implies liability. The second threshold is much higher. The newly established ESRB must go beyond 'well established systemic risks'. It has to observe market developments and in addition monitor scientific research in the field of economics which could be used in the development of an appropriate early warning system.[74] Liability for pure systemic risks, here the ESRB, might result from neglecting available research. (Let us set aside the question whether a board like ESRB might be legally responsible and (!) might have the resources to compensate for possible losses of the collapsing financial system). The legal criterion for liability is 'foreseeability'. If we use product liability as a yardstick, financial service providers might be held liable for not taking measures against systemic risks if scientific knowledge is available worldwide that requires them to take counter-measures.

3. A possible scenario to prevent herding via contract governance

What does this all mean for contract governance and herd behaviour? In light of the distinction between different types of systemic risks and in taking into account the lessons from the *ex-post* analysis of the subprime crisis, a first scenario of risk prevention could be established. The set of indicators for identifying systemic risk in the making are distilled out of the *ex post* analysis of the subprime crisis. In a more generalized form, they may serve as a yardstick against which the potential third party impact can be measured and potential preventive measures of regulators, private parties (businesses), and private parties (consumers or investors) can be designed. The indicators as well as the four parameters are certainly

[74] There is, however, some doubt, as to whether and to what extent systemic risk is manageable ex-ante at all. K.H. Ladeur, n 55, writes: 'A systemic approach to the systemic risks of the financial markets could somehow draw upon the strengthening of the openness of the search process and the diversity of modelling approaches. This could mean, for example that non-capital requirements, as such, may be given preference. In contrast standardisation and public control should be more focused on the formulation of second order models which do not compete with the complexities of financial modelisations, but instead focus on the risks of the homogeneity of financial strategies which could be answered with more hetereogeneity, or if this proves too difficult, with the imposition of additional insurance or more information with a perspective on strengthening the control functions of both the financial markets and the owners of the bank in particular.' (at 89–90).

subject to further review, in particular with regards to the specific assumptions on third party impact and the preventive measures to be taken.

However, incomplete and insufficient this scenario might be, it provides deeper insight into the task pro-active contract governance has to manage. More specifically, it allows for a series of preliminary conclusions:

- private parties, businesses, and consumer-investors cannot be put into the same box, as they do not share the same interests and do not bear the same responsibilities;
- the public/private law divide is useless, since a design for contract governance has to include all relevant actors, private parties (b and c) as well as supervisory authorities;[75]
- supervisory authorities cannot limit their activities to securing access of financial service providers but they have to monitor the market, including contract-making;[76]
- supervisory authorities cannot restrict their activities to guaranteeing the functioning of the capital market—in contract governance design, they have to take the interests of the private parties, the financial service providers, and the consumer-investors into account;[77]
- the private parties, the banks, the investment firms and the private investors have to cooperate in a spirit of trust and confidence,[78] they have to accept that with regard to systemic risks, they are in the same boat;
- the measures to be developed by private parties reach beyond the individual interest of a firm or a consumer-investor, therefore collective activities are needed; and
- the measures have to take the limited capacities of receiving and processing information of natural persons and of small and medium-sized firms into account.

This is quite an ambitious design for contract governance that transgresses the boundaries of bilateral contracting. It means that public authorities and trade and investor protection organizations are involved in drafting rules, that they do

[75] This goes along with the analysis of new modes of governance in European private law of F. Cafaggi and H. Muir-Watt (eds) *Making European Private Law, Governance Design* (Cheltenham: Edward Elgar Publishing Ltd, 2008).

[76] The MiFID 2004/39 points in this direction, see J. Keßler, H.-W. Micklitz, and N. Reich (eds)*Institutionelle Finanzmarktaufsicht und Verbraucherschutz, Eine Rechtsvergleichende Untersuchung der Regelungssysteme in Deutschland, Italien, Schweden, dem Vereinigten Königreich und der Europäischen Gemeinschaft* (Baden-Baden: Nomos, 2010).

[77] There is no agreement in Europe as to whether public agencies should regulate the market or whether they should also look into the particular interests of the regulated parties. EU law in regulated markets moves into a comprehensive approach where supervisory agencies are obliged to look after private investors. See in more detail at Section 1 below.

[78] One may refer to recent developments in the case law of the ECJ, where the court imposes public policy demands on the holder of economic rights, see L. Azoulai, '*Sur un Sens de la Distinction Public/Privé dans le Droit de l'Union Européenne*' (2010) 4 *RTD Eur* 853.

take into account the links between public supervision and private contracting, that they operate in an atmosphere of mutual trust and that they have a realistic vision of the behaviour and the decision-making process of the actors in mind. Currently, this vision is far from reality, at least if contract governance reaches beyond cooperation between supervision authorities and the financial service providers involved.

Keeping the overall purpose of avoiding systemic risks in mind, a possible design for contract governance should take the aspects into account, as detailed in Table 4.2.

Before I illustrate some of the envisaged safeguard measures, I will highlight the incentives needed to create a climate in which contract governance, herein understood as a joint effort by public and private entities, could blossom. The safeguard rules themselves follow the logic of Table 4.2. Each indicator leads to

Table 4.2

Indicators	Third party impact	Preventive measures of regulators	Preventive measures of private parties (businesses)	Preventive measures of private parties (consumer-investors)
Unusual supply of credits	Easy availability of credits	Market surveillance and access control	Denial of unreasonable credit Responsible lending	Creditworthiness, renunciation of access to credit
Market dominating financial instruments	Down-grading of non mainstream instruments	Market surveillance, quality control, prohibition	Standardizing risks of financial instruments	Risk classification and risk labelling of financial instruments
Reliance on externalquality assessment (rating)	Delegation of monitoring and surveillance	Market surveillance, investigation	Responsibility for external quality management	Exploring external competence
Herding of all or several actors	Shortage of qualified information	Disclosure of public (administrative) information	Disclosure of private (trade secret) information	Access to and evaluation of private/ public information
Internal and external incentives	Wrong guidance and false advice	Disclosure of information and correction of incentives	Monitoring the external structural effects of internal (firm) incentives	Access to information and advice driven incentives
(Excessive) public promotion and private advertising campaign	Creation of an investment climate into market dominating instruments	Surveillance and restriction	Self-control of unreasonable advertising campaigns	Counter promotion

particular measures which should ideally be jointly elaborated. The benchmark we have to keep in mind is how to prevent the risks to the financial system, which result from herd behaviour and third party impact.

(1) Incentives for cooperation (between whom?)

Regulated market negotiations between parties—public and private—will usually take place in the shadow of the law. If we start from the assumptions that public and private actors cooperate in drafting rules, then the supervisory authorities must accept responsibility for market surveillance and contract monitoring. This is to some extent enshrined in the MiFID Directive 2004/39.[79] Supervisory authorities must also be prepared to engage in negotiations not only with the financial service providers, but also with private investors, i.e., consumer organizations. Thus far there is no agreement on a two-pronged approach, one where supervisory agencies not only guarantee the functioning of financial markets but also look after the interests of businesses and private investors-consumers. The overall trend in EU law-making seems to pave the way for a two-pronged approach. The newly established *European* supervisory authorities[80] will have to develop their own approach which paves the way for a common understanding.

As EU law does not set incentives for cooperation between the different private parties and/or the supervisory authority, why should they cooperate to fight risks resulting from herding? Why should businesses cooperate with consumer organizations and why should consumer organizations cooperate with businesses in drafting rules against the third party impact of herd behaviour? Does the overall danger of new herding with disastrous effects for financial markets suffice to unite the conflicting interests? Does such a potential scenario create a distinctive feature that enhances the preparedness of all those private and public actors to co/operate, even though they usually do not?

Here, Europe cannot be regarded as a homogeneous entity. The degree to which cooperation between businesses and consumer-investors occurs largely depends on differences in the cooperation culture, which is roughly speaking more developed in the UK and the Nordic countries and less so in central and southern Europe. So additional incentives are needed such as suspension of supervision such that certain basic requirements in cooperation and drafting are met or, to take another example, the suspension of the possibility for consumer-investors to take collective action against businesses, for example, injunctions in the field of unfair terms and commercial practices or compensation claims as long as they are foreseen in the Member States.

[79] Directive 2004/39/EC of the European Parliament and of the Council of 21 April 2004 on markets in financial instruments amending Council Directives 85/611/EEC and 93/6/EEC and Directive 2000/12/EC of the European Parliament and of the Council and repealing Council Directive 93/22/EEC (OJ 2004 L 145/1).

[80] T. Tridimas, 'Community Agencies, Competition Law and ECSB Initiatives on Securities Clearing and Settlement' in P. Eeckhout and T. Trimidimas (eds)*Yearbook of European Law 2009* (New York: Oxford University Press, 2010) 216.

(2) Responsible lending and responsible investment

Consumer organizations and consumer activists have established 'The European Coalition of Responsible Credit'.[81] The overall objective is to establish a spirit of cooperation in financial transactions where neither autonomy nor accountability are regarded as the dominating preoccupation in contractual relations, but where the creditors accept responsibility for the conditions under which they grant credit to consumer-investors. Responsible lending was one of the bullet points in the legislative debate around the revision of the Consumer Credit Directive 2008/48.[82] In the adopted version, responsible lending is downgraded to the supply of appropriate information. Somewhat stronger language survived in the recitals of the Directive:

> ... [i]n the expanding credit market, in particular, it is important that *creditors should not engage in irresponsible lending*or give out credit without prior assessment of creditworthiness, and the Member States should carry out the necessary supervision to avoid such behaviour and should determine the necessary means to sanction creditors in the event of their doing so.[83]

The concept of responsible lending can easily be transferred from consumer credit to consumer investment. The regulatory framework suffices to prompt collaboration between public authorities and private actors, to engage in a much more concrete discussion of what exactly is expected from both sides in a spirit of cooperation.

Thus far the debate is very much focused on b2c relations. However, the subprime crisis tells us that the concept of responsible lending and/or responsible investment might eventually reach further and should be applied to b2b relations. This is particularly true when all actors in the market are tied together in order to avoid one particular detrimental effect: herding and the third party impact. Joint responsibilities in both types of relations would allow for tying all parties together in one overall 'relational purpose'.

(3) Ranking and labelling of risky financial instruments

There is a strong link between the development of an appropriate concept of systemic risk that defines different levels of danger and associates them with different types of action on the one hand, and the ranking and labelling of risky financial instruments on the other. Ideally, it should be possible to identify and classify potential financial instruments as being of systemic relevance for the financial market system. Provided such an undertaking turns out to be successful, this particular instrument or a group of instruments could be identified as bearing the inherent risk of producing herding that yields more than societal behaviour and triggers a stop-order mechanism. Such an instrument would, or at least could,

[81] See the website of the *Institut für Finanzdienstleistungen*, Hamburg, Director Prof. Dr. U. Reifner.

[82] OJ 2008 L 133/66.

[83] Consumer Credit Directive 2008/48, Recital 26. Emphasis added by the author.

shed new light on information cascades. The signal the market participants could receive via public or private organization would then have the character of a warning not to herd. I am well aware of the limited effects of such warnings, which may even produce a counter effect inviting investors to speculate. However, ranking and labelling is just one element in a series of safeguard measures.

The establishment of a differentiated risk classification implies a learning process, i.e., that there are different grades of risks which could be associated to particular financial instruments and to different measures, be they statutory or private. The subprime crisis triggered a political debate on whether financial instruments bearing systemic risks should be prohibited. With a few exceptions,[84] none of the developed countries have gone down that road. The overwhelming opinion was to keep these products in the market but to keep a very close check on them. The establishment of a European Systemic Risk Board is linked to this understanding. Leaving products with systemic risk potential on the market puts even stronger pressure on finding ways and means to categorize and classify financial instruments according to their risks. The financial sector, at least in Europe, developed a rather ambiguous approach with regard to ranking and labelling risky financial instruments.[85] Officially, the sector rejected any possibility of ranking financial instruments according to their risks. Unofficially, however, at least parts of the sector were engaged in attempts to do exactly what they officially rejected. Ranking and labelling seems promising for contract governance provided the process includes supervisory authorities and consumer organizations. The parallel to the standardization of products and services through standards bodies is obvious.

(4) Access to, and disclosure of, information versus advice

If we take the findings of behavioural economics on information-based herding and information cascades seriously, we need to be extremely sceptical of the potential positive effects of stopping herding through the disclosure of information on financial instruments which bear a systemic risk. One may wonder, however, whether contract governance can lead to better and more appropriate results than mandated disclosure through public regulation.

Contract governance that reaches beyond bilateral agreements and that enters into the network of contracts, which is needed to establish appropriate means against herd behaviour and third party impact, requires a spirit of cooperation based on exchange of information and mutual trust. This does not mean full disclosure, but at least disclosure of standardized, i.e., de-personalized information, relevant for the design of appropriate contract law rules. Collective negotiation between different actors cutting across the public/private and the business/consumer-investor divide opens

[84] Germany in prohibiting short sales (*leerverkäufe*).

[85] Hearing at the German Ministry for Agriculture, Nutrition and Consumer Protection. See also the Position Paper of the Scientific Advisory Board to the respective Ministry: A. Oehler, D. Kohlert, and H. Jungermann, '*Zur Qualität der Finanzberatung von Privatanlegern, Probleme des Beratungsprozesses und Lösungsansätze*' (with comments from L. Reisch and H.-W. Micklitz) (November 2009) (available at <http://www.bmelv.de/cae/servlet/contentblob/850226/publicationFile/52526/2009_11_Finanzberatung.pdf>).

up perspectives for the design of information disclosure which takes into account the deficits of current disclosure rules as defined by the legislator or regulator and which are shaped so as to allow the addressees of the information to manage and process the received information. Thus far, both business and consumer-investors have delegated the responsibility of defining disclosure rules to the legislator, both for different reasons. The legislator, in particular the European legislator, continues to make extensive use of information-based financial market regulation. The result, then, often is that neither businesses nor consumer-investors are satisfied with the result. Businesses criticize the costs and consumer organizations complain that the information rules are useless as they do not take into account the real behaviour of consumer-investors. The Consumer Credit Directive provides ample evidence of a misguided legislature.[86] Bringing information regulation back to the private parties would, at least in theory, allow for the development of rules that are much more finely tuned to the mutual needs involved. The design of rules that help to break down or stop herd behaviour through targeted information could become a prominent field.

One reservation has to be made. As far as consumer-investors are concerned, information must be coupled with competence advice. The overwhelming evidence of the deficits built into mandated disclosure demonstrates the need for the receipt of advice, even more so in financial matters.[87] Here the intermediaries come into play—bank agents and brokers. The EU has adopted a common regulatory framework for agents operating in the insurance sector,[88] but the EU has not (yet) managed to develop standards for the rights and duties of bank agents.[89] This field is largely left to the Member States, where the rules still differ considerably. In the aftermath of the subprime crisis, bank agents have been criticized for recommending the sale of financial products for which they received the highest commissions. This critique has triggered a debate on the status of bank agents, appropriate remuneration schemes and the question of whether these have to be disclosed. The solution might equally come from a joint effort from all parties concerned. In an early stage of herding, full knowledge of financial incentives might raise the awareness of the advice-seeking customers, thereby setting the end of or slowing down herd behaviour.

(5) Contract and corporate governance

Herd behaviour can be prevented by setting the correct incentives for the remuneration of managers, bank agents, and brokers. This seems to be the common

[86] P. Rott, 'Broad Economic Analysis of the Impact of the Proposed Directive on Consumer Credit' (2007) IP/A/IMCO/FWC/2005-58/LOT 4/SC1 (available at <http://www.europarl.europa.eu/comparl/imco/studies/0704_consumercredit_en.pdf>).

[87] O. Ben-Shahar and C. E. Schneider, 'The Failure of Mandated Disclosure'University of Chicago, The Law School John M. Olin Law & Economics Research Paper No 516/University of Michigan Law School Law & Economics, Empirical Legal Studies Center Paper No 10-008.

[88] Directive 2002/92/EC of the European Parliament and of the Council of 9 December 2002 on insurance mediation (OJ 2003 L 9/3).

[89] In its action plan, the European Commission has announced it will take action in that field. No proposal was been presented so far.

understanding in empirical research undertaken by behavioural economics. Much of the debate in Europe focused on exactly how to set the correct incentives in the remuneration of managers in order to avoid herding and systemic risks. Some Member States have adopted legislation, others have not. EU rules on bonus systems for mangers do not exist. In such a heterogeneous legal environment, contract governance could serve as a means to overcome differences and to set a common standard of information—not of incentives.

(6) Communication (advertising and sales promotion)

One might argue that advertising and sales promotion forms the core of business. However, what I am concerned with is advertising and sales promotion within the boundaries set by EU law. One might argue that advertising and sales promotion does not belong to contract governance, as private law draws a clear distinction between advertising and sales promotion on the one hand, and contract law on the other. I have explained elsewhere that such an understanding is deeply flawed, conceptually and even under the *acquis communautaire*.[90] Contract governance as a concept leaves more room than strict doctrinal boundaries.

Advertising and sales promotion in the EU is highly regulated in B2B and B2C relations. Directive 2005/29[91] deals with B2C relations and aims for full harmonization, whereas Directive 2006/114[92] concerns B2B only. To the dismay of many lawyers, there are no common rules that apply independent of the type of relation. Whether this difference really matters or whether the more developed Directive 2005/29 might set standards which apply to B2B too remains to be seen. This is all the more important as Directive 2005/29 is one of the few pieces of EU legislation which promotes the elaboration of European self-regulation and sets standards of compliance. However, the Directive does not lay down a regulatory framework for the procedure under which these rules have to be applied.

There is overall agreement that advertising and sales promotion constitutes a promising field for cooperative self-regulation. Thus far, no such rules exist in the field of financial services, at least not at the European level. Self-regulatory measures could be tied to the category of financial instruments that bear systemic risk. Here, advertising and sales promotion rules should be intertwined with rules on targeted disclosure.

[90] See, on the external effects of advertising law as a challenge for traditional contract law, M. Leistner, *Richtiger Vertrag und Lauterer Wettbewerb* (Tübingen: Mohr Siebeck, 2007) 137–9; Möslein, n 15, 72, 76; in more detail H.-W. Micklitz, 'Unfair Commercial Practices Law and European Private Law' in C. Twigg-Flesner (ed)*Cambridge Companion to European Union Private Law* (Cambridge: Cambridge University Press, 2010) 229–42.

[91] Directive 2005/29/EC of the European Parliament and of the Council of 11 May 2005 concerning unfair business-to-consumer commercial practices in the internal market and amending Council Directive 84/450/EEC, Directives 97/7/EC, 98/27/EC and 2002/65/EC of the European Parliament and of the Council and Regulation (EC) No 2006/2004 of the European Parliament and of the Council (OJ 2005 L 149/22).

[92] Directive 2006/114/EC of the European Parliament and of the Council of 12 December 2006 concerning misleading and comparative advertising (OJ 2006 L 376/21).

4. Addendum: on the role and function of consumers-investors

In Europe, the immediate reaction to the scenario I have drafted with regard to managing risks resulting from herd behaviour is the call for more public regulation. This is particularly true when it comes to defending the consumer and/or the interests of private investors. In contrast to this initial reaction, I explored the ways and means private parties, in particular consumer-investors, may contribute to a new contract design that uses market enhancement mechanisms. It is here that Europe suffers from a backlog.

I start from the premise that the individual consumer-investor is either not in a position or is unwilling to master a growing stack of disclosure documents, be they public or private. There might be more important things to do in life than spending one's scarce free time studying information on the stock market. I will use the concept of democratized markets as initially developed by Issacharoff.[93] The idea behind it is that in modern markets information exchange is not limited to private parties bound by long-term arrangements built on mutual trust. With the expansion of market transactions beyond the local or regional business, even across borders, the advantages of institutional actors to generate and to process information grew considerably. This is true on both sides of the market, suppliers of financial services and consumers/private investors. The EU relies heavily on switching as a market incentive to enhance competition between service providers. Issacharoff uses mobile phone contracts and car insurance as examples to demonstrate that the service provider—the contracting telephone company (or the rival vendor) in the case of insurance contracts—disposes of and manages information on the individual consumer-investor which enables her to make a better choice at no cost. Here, the market functions as an ally to the consumer. The market generates information which can be used and enforced to the benefit of the consumer by the contracting partner or by the supplier.

Financial services do not fit into such categories. If anything, they may be treated as long-term contracts. It is a well-known phenomenon that consumers-investors often engage in a life-long relationship with their bank, which will also execute investment decisions. Switching is still the exception to the rule.[94]Thus using switching as a device to enhance market mechanisms and to impose the burden of information processing on the financial service provider does not really work. In theory, the consumer/private investor could declare her intention to switch to rival providers and seek advice on the quality of the existing investment and/or envisaged investments. The mere supply of the information the consumer-investor has at her own disposal does not enable the potential rival to get a full picture of

[93] S. Issacharoff and I. Samuel, 'The Institutional Dimension of Consumer Protection in New Frontiers of Consumer Protection: Combining Private and Public Enforcement' in F. Cafaggi and H.-W. Micklitz (eds)*New Frontiers of Consumer Protection—the Interplay between Private and Public Enforcement* (Belgium: Intersentia Publisher, 2009) 47.

[94] In countries with a high inflation rate (e.g. Balkan countries) consumer credits are granted only on a short-term basis. The expiry date then serves as a trigger for the lender to raise interest, i.e., to adapt them to the inflation rate. The revolving credits considerably increase the costs for the consumer.

the consumer. In order to be able to assess the potential consumer-investor and to evaluate whether the chosen investment fits her particular needs, information, which is usually in the hands of the contracting partner of the consumer-investor, i.e. the long-term bank/investor, is required. The contracting partner of the consumer-investor has the information on the customer at hand—know your customer—as well as on the products—know your products—but she will jealously protect this information by claims of privacy and business secrecy. It might be possible to overcome this barrier by introducing a standard format that sets aside information which allows for uncovering the identity of the particular company, but which enables the consumer-investor to voluntarily decide whether to transfer the standard format information to the rival.[95] Thereby, both barriers—trade secrets and data protection—could be overcome provided the parties are ready to engage in serious cooperation.

One problem remains: without switching, the market will not produce the necessary results as the incentive is missing on the side of the contracting partner, as well as on the side of rivals. That is why in financial services an additional ally is needed, an institution that could serve as an intermediary between the consumer-investor and the financial service provider. According to European understanding—prejudice, ideological preconception?—natural candidates for such an intermediary are either consumer protection agencies and/or consumer organizations—depending on the country concerned. This brings us to the role and function of consumer protection agencies and consumer organizations in the elaboration of an appropriate governance design.

V. Conclusions

What can we learn looking back from the subprime crisis over pyramid games to tulips? Herding appears to be an old phenomenon. We know that it can cause dangerous systemic effects, but we still face difficulties identifying the individuals and the institutions that could be held liable. Linking the three events to the *ex-post ex-ante* distinction, we may associate the Albanian pyramid game with the lack of the appropriate *ex-ante* regulation, at least if we start from the premise that it is possible to draw a clear line between pyramid games that may produce systemic risk and other forms of gambling that resemble pyramid games but have more ambiguous effects. Tulips and asset-backed securities do not bear the systemic dimension right from the beginning. The distinction between *ex-ante* and *ex-post* fades away once the herding passes an imaginary threshold that triggers the systemic risk. One might argue that the discovery of 'systemic' 'risk' and the first attempt to set up a regulatory frame should be understood as a conceptual breakthrough in the search for appropriate governance rules and mechanisms.

[95] The ESRB will operate on the basis of a similar distinction.

However, is it already possible to speak of a legal concept arising from the implications of herd behaviour as discussed here? I hesitate. Contract governance still looks much more like a policy programme which sheds new light on old problems, but which allows, through its much broader perspective, for the breaking down of boundaries in the legal system between public law and private law, between firms and markets, between contract and corporate governance. I admit that there are elements of a legal concept, in particular if one links contract governance to regulated markets, to co-regulation and to the need for a statutory framework within which contract governance could develop. In this sense hit might be possible to speak of a legal concept in the offing.

Summary of the Discussions in Part II: Third Party Impact and Contract Governance Problems in Herd Behaviour

*Isabelle Wildhaber**

Chapter 2: The Concept of Herd Behaviour: Its Psychological and Neural Underpinnings

Authors: *Tatsuya Kameda, Keigo Inukai, Thomas Wisdom, and Wataru Toyokawa*
Discussant: *Peer Zumbansen*

Clayton P. Gillette started the discussion by referring to Peer Zumbansen's statement that the issue of context should be raised for any inference drawn about the relative capacity of bees and humans. Agreeing that decisions are made in different contexts, Gillette asked whether the difference is not rather a function of the fact that it takes thought and commitment to the enterprise to take the right decision. He concluded that teenagers are more willing to engage in herd behaviour because it does not take a lot of commitment to the enterprise for them to decide which music to download. This made him conclude that regulators often suffer from the same defects as the parties being regulated. He called this the 'compared-to-what question' which must be raised when discussing mechanisms for regulating contractual conduct. Important decisions need external checks and balances because of herd behaviour in contracting, and therefore, contracts need regulation.

Zumbansen stated that research on herd behaviour deals with understanding the influences leading people to particular contracting behaviours, and not so much with how to regulate contracting. Thus, he suggested that the question to be asked is not what regulation is needed, but how regulators can learn and study the decision-making patterns which unfold. In this context Zumbansen underlined the importance of the social norms theory, but pointed out that social norms and self-regulation are still in need of further explanation.

* Assistant Professor at the University of St. Gallen.

For Gunther Teubner the crucial factor in decision-making seemed to lie in the interconnection of the individuals, not so much in the psychological realms. Futhermore, Teubner pointed out that a herd could also be treated as a collective actor, a collective whole, a concept which might be useful under certain circumstances.

Van Aaken, Tatsuya Kameda, and Stefan Grundmann then discussed the independence of a decision which may be relevant for herd behaviour to turn into the wisdom of the crowds. Kameda confirmed that, from a scientific point of view, it is still unclear how human minds are designed to deal with independent decisions. He speculated that the teenagers in his example are very interdependent, which might be due to the fact that humans' tendency to rely on social information has added to their success in evolutionary history.

Richard Swedberg and Zumbansen analysed the relationship between legally regulated behaviour and herd behaviour, one being rather slow, the other being fluent by nature. The role of the law nowadays being to shape and guide behaviour, law-making—in their view—has become much more framework-regulating and permissive for constant adaptation and change. In a liberal society, there is no need for the regulators to know the results of the regulation, but the regulation's aim is to empower and enable what the liberal society is about to do. For this purpose, hard laws and soft laws are often being made in collaboration between public and private actors. Therefore, the law gives certain impulses to societal behaviour and then the collective mind sees the result. The evidence of contract-making in the last two years has shown that contract-makers were acting much faster than regulators, even though they often did not have a thorough understanding of the possible results.

Hugh Collins, Kameda, and Grundmann drew analogies between the discussion about corporate governance and contract governance. Both types of governances have similarities. First, different fields of law are discussed in conjunction with each other, secondly, a whole array of disciplines is used to analyse how people take their decisions, and thirdly, there is an international, comparative law aspect to the discussion. The three agreed that it is therefore interesting to find a way to integrate certain features or paradigms of company law into the contract law discussion.

According to Urs Schweizer, the discussion on herd behaviour should focus on the local interaction between individuals which coordinates and gives rise to the phenomenon of herding, since herding is a multi-layered phenomenon, an imagined property affecting individual behaviour. Schweizer further pointed out that in the financial crisis fixed contracts, i.e. legal behaviour, stimulated herding behaviour on behalf of the banks and others who bought these contracts. Furthermore, the very process of law-making may also be explained as a herd phenomenon.

Wolfgang Kerber came back to the difference between herding as a defective social process and the wisdom of the crowds. According to him, whether an individual's actions lead to highly intelligent or to defective behaviour depends on the institutional structure between these individuals and is therefore a governance problem. When analysing institutional structures, the question is if herding behaviour is based on imitation, and furthermore whether the process of imitation is a rational decision or a psychological process. In any case, this process needs to be taken into account in addition to an analysis of incentives from an economic perspective.

Kameda finished the discussion by stating that humans have highly adaptive abilities which surely helped their evolutionary success. However, he pointed out that the circumstances in which humans used to acquire these imitating capacities are different from the current modern environment which features many externalities. He concluded that different levels of rationality need to be thought through in order to understand the emergence of imitation and its outcomes.

Chapter 3: Moral Hazard and Herd Behaviour in the Financial Crisis

Authors: *Bruno S. Frey and Reto Cueni*

Discussant: *Gunther Teubner*

Horst Eidenmüller started the discussion with a question on Chapter 3: were there people among the 12 interviewees who not only voiced their concern but had betted on declining markets? The betting might have had a significant potential benefit, which could have counterbalanced the costs associated with the prophecy-making. Reto Cueni confirmed that there were hedge fund managers and funds of hedge fund managers who were interviewees and that at least one of them made a significant amount of money. Strangely enough, though blamed in the financial crisis, they did not follow the herd. Cueni also mentioned the example of Paulson who had made an off-benefit speculating. He added that, according to Harrison Hong of Princeton University, there was a big risk for Paulson's bet to collapse.

In Gerard Hertig's view, it was not the risk appetite, but rather the risk management and the principal-agent problem within the firm causing the problem in the financial crisis. Having analysed how risk management is usually dealt with, Hertig concluded that maybe efficiency requires herding rather than non-herding. Frey agreed with Hertig's point. To Frey, however, herding is not only the result of principal-agent relationships, but of groupthink and other phenomena even among equals.

Gillette stated that, in his view, inter-firm behaviour causes principal-agent problems rather than herd behaviour problems, because there is a centralized identity orchestrating behaviour within a firm. He expressed his astonishment about Frey's thesis against performance incentives and pointed out that there is a gap in current structures between short-term benefits/short-term compensation and the long-term costs the firm might suffer. Frey's response to this was that performance cannot be measured in any reasonable way in the given situation, because people react to the definition of performance and undermine it immediately.

Schweizer underlined that herding behaviour is not bad per se. When looking for institutional responses, he suggested that one must be careful not to prevent good herding behaviour, but one must aim at promoting good and preventing bad herding behaviour, which would mean finding a distinction at the individual decision taking level.

Teubner indicated that the point he was making in his contribution was quite different. He explained that a strong distinction should be made between psychological motivations of individuals and the micro-operations of a society in which information plays a vital role. Applied to financial operations, this means that the centre of gravity should be shifting from psychological operations to communication and to information. Teubner concluded that there are individual decisions guided by institutional incentives and sanctions as well as parallel processes of psychological operations and social operations.

Marc Amstutz noted that Teubner had avoided the expression 'system' in his talk. He advocated against Teubner's proposal for regulatory reform and stated that the main question is what spreads contagion where. In the theory Teubner had presented, it seemed that the contagion happens between the networks, and that therefore networks should be regulated. According to Amstutz, however, this is difficult since this would require criteria allowing a differentiation between informational functional networks and informational dysfunctional networks. Amstutz suggested turning to another way of conceiving of this contagion: networks are the media which infect the systems and which erode the boundaries of systems. Therefore, regulation should focus on systems contagion rather than on network contagion. He proposed to protect the autonomy of systems instead of trying to make the difficult differentiation between functional and dysfunctional networks. He concluded that from a political perspective it was clever to avoid the word system, not so, however, when focussing on the regulatory target, i.e. the autonomy of the systems.

In response to Amstutz' argument, Teubner explained that he had intended to avoid jargon and the use of technical system theory arguments. He suggested not to distinguish between good and bad networks, but rather to interfere with the speed, the violence and the breadth of the process of contagion.

Katharina Pistor underlined the importance of the development from a normal system into a contagious one. She noted that there is a lack of a good dynamic model for this purpose. She suggested reflecting on whether the frameworks currently employed are really useful.

Van Aaken thought about different types of institutional mechanisms existing to reduce dissent, i.e. the Warburg Report on Financial Market Regulation, which suggests taking away discretion from supervisors and putting it into legal norms. Van Aaken related this back to herding behaviour and suggested that by including 'non-herding' in the norms, costs could be reduced.

In the end Swedberg, Teubner, and Frey discussed whistle-blowing, especially what the help of cost incentives is. How much do cost-lowering incentives help against rational herding if the profit they expect is very high? When herding is rational, cost-lowering strategy is difficult to attain. Also, cost-incentives play a rather minor role in effect-driven situations.

Chapter 4: Herd Behaviour and Third Party Impact as a Legal Concept

Author: *Hans-W. Micklitz*

Discussant: *Michael Klausner*

Dominique Demougin and Michael Klausner started the discussion by stating that in the financial crisis the information of market leaders was badly researched and by asking whether this should not lead them to lose their position. Furthermore, they suggested that bad disclosure and bad products were the root of the problem, as opposed to herd behaviour. Liability based on incorrect disclosure should apply regardless of whether people buy because they copy each other or because they read the prospectus.

Schweizer, Hans-W. Micklitz, Klausner, and Pistor then discussed the issue of organizational liability in the context of the financial crisis. Tort law is based on the idea that it is possible to identify one single entity that is liable. The question whether a more comprehensive liability system would make sense (including all those who have a share in the potential risk and damage) is purely academic. It has, for example, not been taken up in the debates on the European Draft Common Frame of Reference. Furthermore, in the financial crisis it was not the herd behaviour, but the banks' fragility and the contagion of failed banks which caused the problem. Pistor underlined that she finds it more helpful to identify issues than to necessarily label them and then deconstruct the label. Analysing whether a given situation involves herd behaviour or not is not always helpful. One should rather try to understand the systematic problem identified in the crisis and to think about what legal mechanisms there are or there should be. One of the major issues identified was that the transaction costs of information have been lowered to such an extent that information has become meaningless.

Collins agreed that herd behaviour is not always the issue. In the sub-prime mortgage market there seemed to exist a rational free-riding on information, ignoring the risks. That, to Collins, seemed to fit the definition of herd behaviour. Collins argued for some sort of legal principle of responsible lending and expressed doubt that lending on the assumption that prices will keep going up is responsible lending. In Klausner's view, legal intervention would be proper as a consumer protection mechanism, independently of whether the mortgage is packaged or not, bought by herds or non-herds.

Micklitz expressed his belief that the major lesson learned in the financial crisis should be that there is a new legal category of 'systemic risks'. It entails a mechanism he called 'proceduralization', with the question being, when is the risk at a stage where it might become systemic. Furthermore, he added that in his view the purpose of this work was to underline that it does not suffice to delegate precautionary risk management to supervisory authorities and leave it to them, but that it is necessary to take the parties on board.

Micklitz argued that responsible investment matters when it might have a third-party impact, and proposed to think about classifying or ranking financial instruments according to the risks. As to Roberto's question of how to know the next risk, Micklitz stated that there is no mechanism available securing or guaranteeing the prevention of such risks, but that mechanisms to monitor risks resulting from systemic dimensions should at least be explored.

Klausner pointed out that legal intervention should occur where 'bad things can develop into worse things', but not at the stage of the decision process. Trying to control the herd mechanism, to him, should not be the aim of legal intervention.

Hertig criticized that on the legal side, the argument is either that it is too complicated and not much can be done, or that nothing can be done anyway. According to Hertig, simple things can always be done, for example aligning the incentives of home-buyers with those of lenders by asking the latter to keep a liquidity tranche on their balance sheet. He expressed the opinion that political economy should be at the centre of the regulation discussion.

Grundmann agreed with the example concerning the alignment of incentives. As a further example, he mentioned rating contracts involving herd behaviour and asked where the contractual liability should really end. He pointed out that the passing on of risks can be achieved not only by prudential supervision, but also by contractual devices, which is why he thought the topic of the conference to be very interesting.

Klausner concluded that in the end, after having aggregated all of these concepts about what the content of a contract should be, a question to be asked is whether the government should specify the content of a contract. When looking at the way credit agencies work in their contractual context, one should ask the following questions. Are there gains or synergies from combining a number of contract-related issues in a number of contexts? Are there gains from combining those or should one talk about credit rating contracts, lending contracts, and securitization contracts? Should they be kept as separate substances of conversation?

In Micklitz' opinion, regulators seem too focused on regulating the past, instead of identifying common elements of the past for the future. He further suggested one should look beyond financial markets to learn, for example to the REACH program of the EU on how to manage unknown risks of chemicals. He underlined that the contract governance perspective allows a prospective rather than a purely compensation-driven view. The question is whether the cooperation of private parties and public institutions allows for a new form of risk management, accepting systemic risks as a benchmark. In Micklitz' view, herd behaviour amounts to no more than an indicator to raise awareness. It is the law itself that can and must offer a mechanism to avoid a financial crisis.

PART III

GOVERNANCE OF NETWORKS OF CONTRACTS

5

Contract, Uncertainty, and Innovation

Ronald J. Gilson, Charles F. Sabel**, and Robert E. Scott****

Contract today increasingly links entrepreneurial innovations to the efforts and finance necessary to transform ideas into value. In this Chapter, we describe the match between a form of contract that 'braids'[1] formal and informal contractual elements in novel ways and the process by which innovation is pursued.

It is hardly surprising that these innovative forms of contract have emerged first in markets, and that the common law, and the theory of contract, then play catch-up. Between the time contracting practice adapts to the demands of innovation and the time contract doctrine adapts to the demands of practice, law acts as a friction on the innovation process rather than a lubricant to it. Our goal here is to reduce that lag by providing a theory that can guide courts in developing case law that addresses current forms of innovation. Put differently, we seek to provide courts the logic necessary to order the experience that Holmes, as a pragmatist, thought so central to the life of the common law.[2]

* Marc and Eva Stern Professor of Law and Business, Columbia University; Charles J. Meyers Professor of Law and Business, Stanford University; European Corporate Governance Institute.

** Maurice T. Moore Professor of Law, Columbia University.

*** Alfred McCormack Professor of Law and Director, Center for Contract and Economic Organization, Columbia University.

[1] R. J. Gilson, C. F. Sabel, and R. E. Scott, 'Braiding: The Interaction of Formal and Informal Contracting in Theory, Practice and Doctrine' (2010) 110 *Columbia Law Review* 1377–447. We draw here on this article, as well as on R. J. Gilson, C. F. Sabel, and R. E. Scott, 'Contracting for Innovation: Contracting for Innovation: Vertical Disintegration and Interfirm Collaboration' (2009) 109 *Columbia Law Review* 431–502. We are grateful to the Kauffman Foundation for research support.

[2] O. W. Holmes, *The Common Law* (Boston: Little, Brown and Company, 1881) 3. When Holmes wrote that '[t]he life of the law has not been logic: it has been experience,' he was not referring to passive process. Rather, the pattern was one in which experience driven litigation gave rise to logic—the predicative value of the court's decision. This notion that law follows from, rather than developing internally independent of, experience reflected Holmes' strongly held view, driven by his battlefield experience in the Civil War, that logic isolated from experience was ideology, from which came the carnage of the war. L. Menand, *The Metaphysical Club* (New York: Farrar, Straus and Giroux, 2001) 3–4, 61.

This Chapter provides an overview of our ongoing work. The starting point is the Knightian distinction between risk and uncertainty.[3] In our view, traditional contracting techniques and traditional contract law address problems of risk. Braiding, or contracting for innovation, addresses conditions of uncertainty. We illustrate the relevance of this distinction by describing the shift in the organizational location of innovation[4]—in particular a fundamental shift from vertical integration to contract as the organising mechanism for cutting-edge innovation.

We then describe the braiding of formal and informal contracting that has developed to organize collaboration across organizational boundaries where the desired outcome can, at best, be anticipated only very approximately. Next, we re-examine the interaction between formal and informal contracting to understand why braiding was not envisaged as a theoretical possibility before it became a salient reality, and to make theoretical sense of braiding now that it has. Finally, we look to recent case law, especially that considering preliminary agreements, to argue that the domain of braiding now includes contexts where uncertainty is not generated by technological development, and we examine the failure of courts to recognize the difference between and consequences of low-powered and high-powered enforcement in addressing braided contracts.

In particular, our analysis gives courts concrete guidance in the area of preliminary agreements, where courts for the first time are undertaking to enforce formal agreements—whether in the context of a preliminary agreement, letter of intent, or corporate acquisition agreement—that establish a process by which the parties will determine whether an innovation is possible, but do not obligate the parties to go forward with the substance of the innovation.[5] In contrast to the unpredictability currently associated with judicial accounts of how these agreements will be enforced, our development of a theory of braided contracts gives the court clear guidance: enforce the process established by the formal element of the contract through low-powered reliance damages, but *never* enforce, through high-powered (expectation) damages, the informal substantive element of the braid. This rule prevents the formal element of the braided contract from 'crowding out' the informal element, and thereby preventing the innovative activity from going forward at all.

I. Innovation, Uncertainty, and Industrial Organization

Knight's distinction between risk and uncertainty is central to understanding the role of contract in the innovative process. Risk exists when future states of the world can be estimated probabilistically. Given such estimates, a contract,

[3] F. H. Knight, *Risk, Uncertainty and Profit* (Boston and New York: Houghton Mifflin Company, 1921) 197–232.

[4] See R. J. Gilson, 'Locating Innovation: Technology, Organizational Structure and Financial Contracting' (2009) 109 *Columbia Law Review* 885.

[5] For discussion, see A. Schwartz and R. E. Scott, 'Precontractual Liability and Preliminary Agreements' (2007) 120 *Harvard Law Review* 661–707.

through a series of 'if X, then Y' clauses, can more or less specify what will occur in each realized state. Alternatively, markets can be used to hedge against particular realizations, such as the future prices of commodities, or interest, or currency exchange rates.

Under uncertainty, in contrast, future states of the world cannot be expressed probabilistically. *Ex ante*, we cannot usefully specify the desired outcome(s), or assign an option providing protection to one or another party *ex post*. In our analysis, innovation is inherently uncertain: an innovation is defined in the same process that ultimately leads to its achievement. From this perspective, the term 'linear innovation', sometimes used to describe the next step in a predictable sequence,[6] is an oxymoron.

The increasing importance of innovation in this sense can be seen in the tendency towards vertical disintegration of industry. Conventional industrial organization theory predicts that when parties in the supply chain must make transaction-specific investments, the risk of opportunism will drive them away from contracts and towards vertical integration.[7] This pressure toward sole ownership will be especially powerful in innovative industries where rapid technological change produces high levels of uncertainty in supply relationships. Contemporary contract theory concurs. In the presence of uncertainty, it offers no general solution to the problem of assuring both efficient levels of transaction-specific investment *ex ante* and adjustment to an efficient outcome *ex post* after uncertainty is resolved. So from this perspective too, firms should dominate markets as a means to organize supply relationships. For much of the 20th century, the organization of large industry tracked this account.

The dominant firms in industries such as steel, automobiles, electric machinery, and food processing—both in the United States and worldwide—used the technologies of the second industrial revolution[8] to achieve dramatic economies of scale through the mass production of standard goods with single purpose or dedicated machinery. The most conspicuous organizational feature of firms in these industries was vertical integration.

More recently, however, contemporary practice is moving away from this solution. Companies recognize that the escalating rate of change and resulting uncertainty means that they cannot themselves maintain cutting-edge

[6] M. Aoki, 'Toward an Economic Model of the Japanese Firm' (1990) 28 *Journal of Economic Literature* 1; P. A. Hall and D. Soskice, 'An Introduction to Varieties of Capitalism', in P. A. Hall and D. Soskice (eds), *Varieties of Capitalism: The Institutional Foundations of Comparative Advantage* (Oxford: Oxford University Press, 2001) 1, 50–4, distinguish between forms of national capitalism that support linear innovation (e.g., Germany and Japan) and those that support non-linear innovation (e.g., the United States).

[7] Much of this transactions cost literature is an extension of the work of Oliver Williamson. See e.g., O. E. Williamson, *The Economic Institutions of Capitalism* (New York: Free Press, 1985); O. E. Williamson, *Markets and Hierarchies: Analysis and Antitrust Implications* (New York: Free Press, 1975).

[8] M. J. Piore and C. F. Sabel, *The Second Industrial Divide: Possibilities for Prosperity* (New York: Basic Books, 1984).

technology in every field necessary for an innovative product. Accordingly, companies are increasingly electing to acquire by contract inputs that in the past they had made themselves. Instead of vertical integration, we observe vertical disintegration of firms, the expansion of collaborative research and development across firm boundaries, and at the intersection of these, the rise of platform production (where the 'operating system' and the 'applications' it integrates are co-developed by independent producers). In diverse industries ranging from contract manufacturing to pharmaceutical collaborations, these changes are accompanied by an increase in inter-firm relations with both parties expecting to innovate jointly.

In our previous work,[9] we explored three exemplars of this pattern that ranged from contracts that imposed a formal governance structure but no formally enforceable substantive obligations,[10] to collaborative research agreements that look to the development of a continuing stream of products,[11] to similar agreements limited to developing a particular product and a consequent end game.[12] None of the familiar mechanisms for coping with the problem of contractual incompleteness adequately responds to the challenge posed by structuring transactions in the face of continuous uncertainty. But these exemplars demonstrate that transactional lawyers in a number of industries apparently began responding to their clients' need to structure new relationships in light of the constraints imposed by uncertainty. We term the novel result 'contracting for innovation'. In the Section II we describe the components of this form of contracting and provide a theoretical account of why the contractual innovations that work in practice also work in theory.

II. Contracting For Innovation

Taking innovation as we have defined it, the contracting problem is to craft a structure that a) induces efficient, transaction-specific investment by both parties; b) establishes a framework for iterative collaboration and adjustment of the parties' obligations under conditions of *continuing* uncertainty—circumstances when the resolution of one element of uncertainty merely gives rise to another; and c) limits the risk of opportunism that could undermine the incentive to make relation-specific investments in the first place. The common challenges facing parties contracting for innovation across organizational boundaries give rise to solutions with common elements. In each case, a process of collaboration substitutes functionally for *ex ante* specification of the desired product—the process defines the specification, not the other way around. In each case, the parties make

[9] Gilson, Sabel, and Scott (2009), n 1, 431–502.
[10] See, e.g., the Deere-Standyne agreement, Gilson, Sabel, and Scott (2009), n 1, 431, 459.
[11] See, e.g., the Apple-SCI agreement, Gilson, Sabel, and Scott (2009), n 1, 431, 463.
[12] See, e.g., Warner-Lambert – Ligand Agreement, Gilson, Sabel, and Scott (2009), n 1, 431, 467.

relation-specific investments in learning about their collaborator's capabilities that raise the costs of switching to new partners, and so restrain either party from taking advantage of their mutual dependency.

Review of actual efforts to contract for innovation informs our understanding of how braiding is used to achieve these outcomes by relying on formal contracting to establish processes that make behaviour observable enough to support informal contracting over the substance of the (uncertain) collaboration.[13] Braiding uses *formal* contracts to create governance processes that support iterative joint effort through low-powered enforcement techniques that specify only the commitment to collaborate, without controlling the course or the outcome of the collaboration. This formal governance arrangement has two closely linked components.

The first is a commitment to an ongoing mutual exchange of information designed to determine if a project is feasible and, if so, how best to implement the parties' joint objectives. The second component is a procedure for resolving disputes arising from the first. Its key feature—the 'contract referee mechanism'[14]—is a requirement that the collaborators reach unanimous (or near unanimous) agreement on crucial decisions, with persistent disagreement resolved (or not) by unanimous agreement at higher levels of management from each firm. Together these two mechanisms render observable, and forestall misunderstandings about, the character traits and substantive capabilities that support the *informal* contracting upon which the parties rely as, working under uncertainty, they encounter unanticipated problems that can only be solved jointly. At the same time, the parties' increasing knowledge of their counterparty's capacities and problem-solving type, a direct result of the processes specified in the formal contract, creates switching costs—the costs to each party of replacing its counterparty with another—that constrain subsequent opportunistic behaviour.

The formal element of a braided contract is thus sharply and distinctively limited in what it aims to accomplish. It functions to allow both parties to learn about each other's skills and capabilities for collaborative innovation and to develop jointly the routines necessary to working together. The formal contract does not, however, commit either party to develop, supply, or purchase any product. That commitment emerges from the informal contract, where the barrier to *ex post* opportunism results not from formal enforcement of obligations created by explicit contract, but from increased switching costs generated by the collaboration process itself.[15]

[13] Gilson, Sabel, and Scott (2009), n 1, 431, 476–89.

[14] Gilson, Sabel, and Scott (2009), n 1, 431, 479–81.

[15] Only where the subject of the braided contract is a discrete project do we see formal contracting over the output of the process. In the discrete project setting, switching costs discourage opportunism during the collaborative period, but the parties have to fear opportunistic renegotiation once the cooperative stage of the project is completed and switching costs no longer provide protection. The only issue then remaining is division of the gains from prior cooperation. As a result, an explicit constraint on opportunism must be employed; but at this stage, the uncertainty having been resolved, the contract theory solution of allocating rights to decision-making is feasible.

III. Braiding and the Threat of Crowding Out

The conceptual difficulty at this point in the analysis is with our premise: that formal and informal contracting can in fact be combined. The academic literature has long recognized the two components making up a braided contract: one strand formal and legally enforceable and one strand informal and subject only to self-enforcement. However, the literature largely has either ignored the possibility of combining formal and informal contracting or treated the two techniques as mutually inconsistent substitutes. Contemporary contract theory typically assumes that formal and informal methods are separate responses to the problem of motivating relation-specific investments in a collective enterprise. If the threat of opportunism can be addressed explicitly either by specifying state contingent outcomes or by assigning decision rights among the parties, then we observe formal contracting; if not, we observe either self-enforcing informal contracts supported relationally or, when these cannot protect specific investment, vertical integration.[16] Work in experimental economics does in contrast address the possibility of formal-informal interaction, but focuses mainly on circumstances when the introduction of formal contracting degrades the effectiveness of, or 'crowds out', informal contracting.

What is broadly lacking in both literatures is a theory of when and why the parties can make use of both techniques. In this Section, we provide a first step toward developing a theory of the complementary interaction of formal and informal contracting that allows braiding.

1. The limits of formal and informal contracting

a. Formal enforcement: the verifiability problem

The capacity to compel disclosure of private information is the defining feature of formal enforcement. When a formal contract breaks down due to the opacity of the interactions or the guile of one or more of the parties, courts (or arbitrators[17]) function by assessing responsibility. To do this, courts must have better information than was available to the parties. But a judge, unlike, say, a basketball referee, cannot directly observe complex interactions on the field of play and then declare fouls. A legal referee must obtain information indirectly, from the very parties

[16] See, e.g., S. J. Grossman and O. Hart, 'The Costs and Benefits of Ownership: A Theory of Vertical and Lateral Integration' (1986) 94 *Journal of Political Economy* 691, 697–700; O. Hart and J. Moore, 'Property Rights and the Nature of the Firm' (1990) 98 *Journal of Political Economy* 1119, 1151; O. Williamson, 'Assessing Contract' (1985) 1 *Journal of Law Economics & Organization* 177–208; B. Klein and K. B. Leffler, 'The Role of Market Forces in Assuring Contractual Performance' (1981) 89 *Journal of Political Economy* 615–641; L.G. Telser, 'A Theory of Self-Enforcing Agreements' (1980) 53 *Journal of Business* 27–44.

[17] Arbitration remains a formal enforcement strategy. While arbitration displaces some of the legal rules associated with litigation, it still requires the intervention of the state to enforce the arbitration award.

who dispute the facts of their 'play'. This requires that the court have the power to impose sanctions in order to force the disputants to provide essential information known only to them. The court can then *verify* outcomes through information each party may lack individually.

Without a judicial sanction both for non-production and for misleading production favourable to a party's own position, a party would be motivated to conceal evidence known only to it: the court then would lack the ability to secure information even as good as the parties themselves possess. Breach by a party would not be verifiable.

Verification, however, is costly. As a result, formal enforcement can break down, particularly where the optimal actions for each party depend on the future state that materializes, but the future is uncertain. In that circumstance, it is prohibitively costly or impossible to specify most future states, let alone the appropriate action that is to be taken should they occur. Under these conditions, parties relying on formal enforcement are confronted with two choices: the Scylla of 'hard' terms (precise rules) and the Charybdis of 'soft' terms (vague standards). Rule-based contracts will require renegotiation after the uncertainty is resolved, because their *ex ante* allocation of rights will frequently turn out to be wrong *ex post*. This will allow the party favoured by fate to renegotiate from strength, and thus undermine incentives to invest. Similarly, the costs of verifying standards-based contracts and the corresponding risk of the court choosing the wrong proxy—the designation of what range of observable outcomes should dictate whether unobservable behaviour would be 'reasonable'—are high. To be sure, parties writing more complex contracts can lessen this problem by using combinations of standards and rules; but as uncertainty increases—precisely the circumstances of innovation—the performance of both standards and rules deteriorate.[18]

b. Informal enforcement: the observability problem

Where formal enforcement depends on court verification, informal enforcement depends entirely on private behaviour—one party's ability to observe directly the other's actions, and the capacity to sanction misbehaviour when observed. For example, parties to an agreement often can observe whether one of them has exercised 'best efforts' and can punish a slacker, even though it would be quite costly to convince a court to impose an equivalent punishment. The private, non-state sanctions that comprise informal enforcement are generally thought to take three forms, which are mutually supportive at low to intermediate levels of uncertainty, increasing the actors' capacity to enforce contracts where behaviour is directly observable to them, but outcomes are hard to verify. However, as we will see, informal enforcement also breaks down at high levels of uncertainty, making it no substitute for formal enforcement when the actors are in significant ways ignorant

[18] R. E. Scott and G. G. Triantis, 'Anticipating Litigation in Contract Design' (2006) 115 *Yale Law Journal* 814–79.

of the future they intend to create. Put differently, collaborative innovation confronts the barrier that familiar contracting strategies break down in precisely the circumstance that defines the environment of innovation.

A first type of informal enforcement is the threat that one party to an informal contract will respond to its counterparty's breach by reducing or terminating future dealings. This tit-for-tat strategy imposes losses on the defector that, in prospect, create disincentives to breach in the first place.[19] A second type of informal enforcement is normative, supported either by the morality or tastes of the contracting parties rather than their calculations of individual gain. Much experimental evidence shows that approximately half of the test subjects do not behave opportunistically even when it is in their economic interest to do so and they are not under threat of punishment or retaliation.[20] Similarly, experimental evidence also indicates a widespread, but not universal, taste for reciprocity—an inclination to reward co-operators and punish opportunists even when the subjects derive no direct and particular benefits from doing so.[21] Like character, a preference for reciprocity provides one explanation for how (and why) this informal sanctioning works. Absent a taste for reciprocity, it may be irrational for individuals to absorb the costs of shaming, boycotting, and ostracizing.

A third type of informal enforcement is normative or dispositional informal sanctions, which can operate at the level of social groups rather than among individuals. In compact and homogenous communities, for instance, the community as a whole can sanction the breach of one member's obligation to another by ostracizing the malefactor, cutting off not just business ties but all the benefits of belonging to the group. The different supports for informal contracting generally complement each other, at least while the uncertainty—and with it the complexity—of transactions remains at low to moderate levels. But informal

[19] Even where the particular parties do not expect to deal with each other in the future, the tit-for-tat enforcement structure will still work if one party will trade with others in the future—that is, if trade will be multilateral rather than bilateral—so long as the repeat play party's reputation, the collective experience of parties who have previously dealt with a person or firm, becomes known to future counterparties. The action of future counterparties then serves to discipline the misbehaving party.

[20] For a review of the literature, see E. Fehr and K. Schmidt, 'Theories of Fairness and Reciprocity: Evidence and Economic Applications' University of Zurich, Institute for Empirical Research in Economics, Working Paper No 75 (2001) 2–3 (available at <http://www.iew.uzh.ch/wp/iewwp075.pdf>).

[21] The experimental evidence on individuals' propensity to reciprocate yields two key findings. First, many people respond cooperatively to generous acts and, conversely, punish non-cooperative behaviour. Secondly, the observed preference for reciprocity is heterogeneous. Some people exhibit reciprocal behaviour and others are selfish. Taking all the experiments together, the fraction of reciprocally fair subjects ranges from 40% to 60%, as does the fraction of subjects who are selfish. For discussion see, e.g. E. Fehr, *et al*, 'Reciprocity as a Contract Enforcement Device: Experimental Evidence' (1997) *65 Econometrica* 833, 850 (finding roughly half of subjects punishing shirkers, and roughly half rewarding non-shirkers); E. Fehr and S. Gatcher, 'Fairness and Retaliation: The Economics of Reciprocity' (2000) 14 *Journal of Economic Perspectives* 159, 162 ('Many studies have carried out detailed analyses of individual decisions and found that the fraction of subjects exhibiting reciprocal choices is between forty and sixty-six percent.'). For applications of this experimental evidence to contract theory, see R. E. Scott, 'A Theory of Self-Enforcing Indefinite Agreements' (2003) 103 *Columbia Law Review* 1641, 1661–75.

enforcement depends on clear observation of the counterparty's actions: the simpler a party's action, the easier it is for the counterparty to observe and characterize. Thus, increasing complexity interferes with all three types of informal enforcement. The probability of a mistake in playing tit-for-tat increases with the difficulty of assessing a counterparty's actions. And by the same token, the capacity to assess whether one's counterparty has a taste for reciprocity, or is of a character to forgo opportunism, or is observing community norms also degrades in a complex environment: the match between a party's actual behaviour and the character of that party becomes more difficult to assess. In a mistake-prone or 'noisy' tit-for-tat environment, misreading a counterparty's actions as opportunistic first leads to retaliation, which in turn leads to responsive retaliation and a cycle of opportunistic behaviour that continues until another mistake resets the cooperative equilibrium. In such a setting, tit-for-tat is no longer the most effective strategy because it risks triggering a retaliatory cycle. The dominant strategy is more forgiving: it allows some percentage of the other party's defections to go unpunished.[22] This is where the complementarity of the supports for informal contracting becomes relevant. A significant probability that a counterparty has a taste for reciprocity, or is of a character that dictates forgoing opportunism, makes it less threatening to be more forgiving of an apparent defection. An independent reason to trust the counterparty results in a corresponding higher probability that the apparent defection was really a misunderstanding. Moreover, just as the normative modes of informal enforcement can support tit-for-tat calculations of the value of ongoing relations when counterparty's actual behaviour becomes less observable, so too can the existence of ongoing relations increase the effectiveness of normative enforcement. The presence of an ongoing relationship that allows for retaliation in the event of counterparty opportunism makes it less risky for a party to act on the probability that the counterparty values reciprocity or forgoes opportunism. In this sense, the existence of the continuing relationship allows the parties to learn about each other's tastes and character. Thus we see a virtuous cycle, in which each of the mechanisms that support informal contracting reinforces the others by making the conduct of the counterparties more observable—less subject to mistaken assessment—to each other. Indeed, given the mutually supportive relationship among the types of informal enforcement, we can think of them (at least at low to moderate levels of uncertainty) as aspects of a single informal enforcement mechanism, one rooted in ongoing relations among parties supported by a (normative) disposition to reciprocity.

The experimental evidence suggests, moreover, that informal enforcement, when it is effective, is both cheaper and better than formal enforcement. Informal

[22] The literature is well developed and uncontroversial: generous tit-for-tat strategies outperform simple tit-for-tat strategies in noisy environments. See, e.g., M. Nowack and K. Sigmund, 'Tit for Tat in Heterogeneous Populations' (1992) 355 *Nature* 250–53; H. C. J. Godfray, 'The Evolution of Forgiveness' (1992) 355 *Nature* 206–07; J. Bendor, R. M. Kramer, and S. Stout, 'When in Doubt...: Cooperation in a Noisy Prisoner's Dilemma' (1991) 35 *Journal of Conflict Resolution* 691–719; R. Axelrod and D. Dion, 'The Further Evolution of Cooperation' (1988) 242 *Science* 1385–90.

enforcement is cheaper because a party only incurs the costs of observing the other's behaviour, while formal enforcement requires the parties to expend additional resources (lawyers' fees, court costs, etc) in verifying that behaviour to a court. Moreover, when informal enforcement works, it is also better. It permits parties to make credible promises regarding observable (and perhaps only observable with repetition) but non-verifiable measures of performance, thus allowing parties to avoid the risk of opportunism arising from formal enforcement of a precise rule or the moral hazard associated with the *ex post* application of a broad standard. These advantages explain why, in commercial contracting, parties often rely on informal enforcement even when formal sanctions are available.[23] These mechanisms of informal enforcement, however, are subject to inherent limitations. Informal contracting, even that supported by taste and character, works best with repeat play in the narrowest sense: the same actors doing the same things with each other again and again, makes conduct more observable, an indispensable element of informal contracting. The more actors undertake novel things with strangers—precisely the conditions of collaborative innovation in the face of uncertainty—the greater their chances either of mischaracterizing each other's acts and intentions, or lacking the ability to characterize what the others are doing at all. When changing sequences of novel performances among unfamiliar actors dissipate the transparency necessary for informal contracting, a switch to forgiving strategies no longer interrupts the vicious cycles of mistake, retaliation and counter-response, as can occur at lower levels of uncertainty. Instead, retaliations escalate and destroy the relation.

In sum, formal contracting has an advantage where performance is verifiable *ex post* but not necessarily observable *ex ante*. Informal contracting has an advantage where performance is observable but costly to verify. But both can break down in the highly uncertain environments that are the domain of innovation. Can contract planners address such circumstances by combining the two strategies in a fashion that is more effective than either standing alone?

c. Complements or substitutes? Explaining the rivalry between formal and informal enforcement

The preceding discussion suggests that contracting parties should be motivated to capture the benefits of both formal and informal enforcement by relying on formal enforcement to solve complex problems with noisy interactions and on informal mechanisms to enforce contingencies that are difficult to verify but clear enough to be observable. A mixed strategy is feasible if formal and informal enforcement mechanisms can be complements, but not if they are substitutes in that recourse to formal contracting 'crowds out' the operation of informal contracting. Here, the existing theory and evidence offer limited guidance. Predicting when

[23] This insight was first explored in Stewart Macaulay's classic account of how commercial contractual relationships rely on informal enforcement even when the parties previously have entered into to a formal, legally enforceable contract: S. Macaulay, 'Non-Contractual Relations in Business: A Preliminary Study' (1963) 28 *American Sociological Review* 55–69.

the crowding out effect dominates requires an understanding of the mechanism through which formal enforcement degrades the operation of informal contracting. Consistent with our analysis that informal contracting depends on the observability of a counterparty's actions, we argue that crowding out occurs when the presence of a formal contract and the potential for high-powered legal sanctions *degrade* the information about the nature of the counterparties and the nature of their interactions.[24] In other words, we see crowding out when formal contracting makes the parties' actions and performance less observable. This occurs because of the effects of two interrelated factors: a) formal enforcement changes the way a party *perceives* the observed behaviour of the counterparty, and b) formal enforcement reduces the number of observations of the very behaviour that signals an intention to cooperate.

First, there is evidence that the parties' behaviour will change depending on whether they believe they are engaged in norm-based or arm's-length arrangements.[25] The most familiar example is the experiment of using formal sanctions to cause parents to be timely in picking up their children from nursery school. In an effort to improve punctuality, a fine was imposed to encourage compliance. But rather than increasing compliance, imposing a fine caused late pickups to increase. The formal fine 'crowded out' the reputation-based norm by changing the parents' perception of each others' obligation from a commitment to the community to a price for additional day care.[26]

[24] The distinction between high-powered legal sanctions that drive out informal enforcement and low-powered sanctions that, we argue later, do not result in crowding out is critical to our theory of how braiding works. High-powered enforcement consists of the imposition of standard breach of contract remedies for a failure to perform specified contractual obligations. High-powered enforcement, then, is tied to outcome variables and provides incentives that induce parties to take specified substantive actions designed to maximize expected surplus.

[25] We acknowledge that our argument could be cast entirely in terms of the conditions under which a more forgiving form of the self-interested strategy of tit-for-tat displaces a less forgiving one, without reference to the conditions under which intrinsic or moral motives are crowded out by extrinsic, gain-oriented ones. For two reasons, we choose instead to combine the two forms of argument, and, as in the preceding discussion, even to underscore their complementarity. First, we are convinced by the experimental evidence that intrinsic motivation—particularly a propensity to reciprocity—is a fact of (some) human behaviour. To be sure, we are a long way from understanding the operation and implications of such intrinsic motivation; but it seems odd to transcribe what we do know of it into a rational-choice vocabulary that denies, or least questions its existence. Secondly, to acknowledge the existence of intrinsic motivation, is hardly to abandon the postulate of rational action in economic exchanges of the kind under consideration here. Rational actors are perfectly capable of making rational choices—calculating decisions when, and in relation to whom, to rely on intrinsic motivation. Indeed, a central claim in our braiding argument is that under uncertainty it is rational for actors to design institutions that allow them to develop a counterparty's propensity to reciprocity, along with her capacities. For an earlier effort to reconcile rational-choice and intrinsic approaches to trust, see C. Sabel, 'Studied Trust: Building New Forms of Cooperation in a Volatile Economy' in R. Swedberg (ed) *Explorations in Economic Sociology* (New York: Russell Sage Foundation Publications, 1993) 104–44 For a review of the persistent tension between rational choice and intrinsic perspectives, see C. J. Paraskevopoulos, 'Social Capital' (2010) *Comparative Politics* 475–94. We are grateful to Yochai Benckler for reminding us of just how far we are from a full understanding of intrinsic motivation and its relation to institutional rather than individual behaviour.

[26] U. Gneezy and A. Rustichini, 'A Fine is a Price' (2000) 29 *Journal of Legal Studies* 1–17. An extensive literature in social psychology also considers the crowding out of intrinsic motivations.

Similar results are reported in more commercial settings.[27] Studies indicate that when offered a contract whose performance is based only on trust, a substantial number of individuals will both pay higher prices and extend higher levels of effort than narrow self-interest would dictate. But when offered the same choices *plus* the possibility of having a third party impose a monetary sanction if the promisor fails to perform, the average price offered and the average effort given declines significantly. The introduction of the formal enforcement option causes shirking to increase and trust vanishes almost completely.[28] In effect, the introduction of a formal sanction that governs all of the parties' actions under the contract results in a 'cognitive shift that crowds out norm-based social behaviour and increases the likelihood of income maximizing behaviour.'[29]

Moreover, when the introduction of formal penalties changes the parties' perception of their interaction, that change also may change the signal indicating the taste or character of the party who proposed the formal penalty. A party's willingness to expend resources to create a threat of significant damages for failure to perform the formal contract may indicate that the party is less likely to be a reciprocator. Once a counterparty's character becomes less observable and (correctly or not) the party is identified as potentially opportunistic, only fully formal contacts will be chosen.

Secondly, 'high-powered' formal enforcement contributes to crowding out by suppressing information that supports reciprocity. For example, one party's request for an adjustment of contractual duties subsequently may be found to justify the other party's declaring an anticipatory repudiation of the contract, thereby exposing the requesting party to substantial damages. A single misstep can transform a surplus-generating cooperative enterprise into a zero-sum game.[30]

This threat, in turn, deters actions—as requests for mid course adjustment of the contract—that invite a counterparty to reciprocate proportionally and informally

See E. L. Deci, R. Koestner, and R. M. Ryan, 'A Meta- Analytic Review of Experiments Examining the Effects of Extrinsic Rewards on Intrinsic Motivations' (1999) 125 *Psychological Bulletin* 627–68.

[27] See, e.g., I. Bohnet, B. S. Frey, and S. Huck, 'More Order with Less Law: On Contract Enforcement, Trust and Crowding' (2001) 95 *American Political Science Review* 131–44.

[28] E. Fehr and S. Gachter, 'Do Incentive Contracts Crowd Out Voluntary Cooperation?' University of Zurich, Institute for Empirical Research in Economics, Working Paper No 34 (2002) (available at <http://ssrn.com/abstract=313028>). A similar result is reported by D. Houser, E. Xiao, K. McCabe, and V. Smith, 'When Punishment Fails: Research on Sanctions, Intentions and Non-Cooperation' (2008) 62 *Games & Economic Behavior* 509.

[29] Houser, *et al*, n 28, 509–32.

[30] In addition to the notion that only one party can breach and that material breach results in compensatory damages as well as loss of accrued contract rights, rules governing insecurity and anticipatory breach permit one party to threaten these consequences whenever the other discloses anticipated difficulties in performance. In addition, the mitigation doctrine only operates once a party forfeits all rights by breaching. Until there is a breach, the counterparty can ignore requests for adjustments that might reduce the consequences of non-performance. The threat of the ultimate sanction thus deters parties from voluntarily revealing the information needed for the counterparty to adjust informally: C. J. Goetz and R. E. Scott, 'The Mitigation Principle: Toward a General Theory of Contractual Obligation' (1983) 69 *Virginia Law Review* 967, 1011–18.

and that can confirm a party's tastes or character. In short, high-powered penalties dramatically raise the stakes associated with observability-based informal contracting, leaving the parties to rely on verifiable formal rules.

IV. Braiding in the Courts: Preliminary Agreements

Ideally, courts would respond to the need for the parties to initially address a project's feasibility by enforcing the chosen methods of mutual cooperation on terms consistent with the arrangements themselves. Low-powered sanctions designed to encourage compliance with the information exchange regime (and the informal relations it supports) would be imposed while avoiding high-powered sanctions that crowd out informality and destroy the braid. And indeed, this is what we are beginning to see: courts in leading cases are sanctioning overtly selfish abuse of information-exchange regimes. But because the sanction relates only to the commitment to collaborate, damages are limited in principle to the reliance costs incurred in the collaboration rather than lost profits from not going forward with the project. In this way, the collaboration commitment can achieve its intended purpose of generating information and trust precisely; low-powered formal enforcement does not drive out informal enforcement.[31]

As might be anticipated in an emergent area of law, the decisions of courts called on to enforce braided contracts are not uniformly consistent with the enforcement theory we have developed here. Some decisions invite the award of damages for parties who participate faithfully in the information exchange regime but then decide that it is not profitable for them to pursue the joint project. Other decisions contemplate (or at least invite the possibility of) the award of full expectation damages—that is, high-powered enforcement—for breach of the information-exchange obligation. In both instances, courts fail to appreciate the importance of limiting formal enforcement to low-powered sanctions focused on wilful violations of the collaboration agreement itself and thereby create the kind of incentives that undo braiding by inducing strategic crowding out of informal enforcement.

In this Section, we review judicial decisions that address the contract doctrine applicable to contracting for innovation. Although pertinent cases have arisen in the context of contractual and anti-trust disputes over joint development of technology,[32] we extend the reach of our analysis by focusing on the area of preliminary agreements or letters of intent, as they are termed in the context of corporate acquisitions. In these settings as well, parties realize that the feasibility of many projects can only be established by joint investment in the production of information necessary to make that very determination, and consequently distinguish

[31] See Gilson, Sabel and Scott (2010), n 1, 1377–447.
[32] See Gilson, Sabel and Scott (2010), n 1, 1377–447.

agreement on the process of disciplined co-evaluation from final agreement on the actual project.

We see cases in these domains in which courts get it right by applying low-powered enforcement to commitments to collaboratively determine the feasibility of a potential project, and declining to enforce at all claims that a party wrongfully refused to actually pursue the project. But we also see cases where the court gets it wrong by holding out the possibility either of imposing damages on parties who participate faithfully in the information exchange regime but then decide not to pursue the joint project, or the award of full expectation damages for breach of the information exchange obligation. The divergent approaches to formal enforcement reveal that the courts lack a sound theoretical construct that informs their treatment of braided contracts.

We show here that a better understanding of theory can help courts to frame the proper contract doctrine, and thereby facilitate innovation.

1. Braiding in preliminary agreements

Assume two commercial parties agree to collaborate in investigating the prospects for what they hope to be a profitable commercial project.[33] The parties agree on the nature of the initial investment that each is to make to evaluate the project, but the terms of the ultimate project cannot be determined without that initial investment. Consequently, the parties agree to proceed with their initial investments and also agree to negotiate the remaining terms of the contract once they can observe the fruits of their efforts. These two parties have reached what the law now recognizes as a 'preliminary agreement'. Only by each party investing and sharing the information that their investment reveals can they determine collaboratively whether their project can succeed. The increased knowledge about the project revealed by the initial investments will then permit the parties to determine whether to finalize the deal with a fully enforceable contract and on what terms.

The legal question is, to what extent a preliminary agreement that looks to the future exchange of private information is formally enforceable? The question is important because the parties meet as strangers with no necessary prospect of an ongoing relationship (and so with no basis for trust). Thus the risk of opportunism is significant. This is particularly the case where the parties undertake to make preliminary investments concurrently and then to share the information that the investments yield. Suppose one party then elects instead to wait and see what comes of her counterparty's investment—in effect reneging on the mutual commitment to collaborate. Delaying a promised investment under these conditions offers several strategic advantages. First, the passage of time and her partner's investment is likely to reveal whether the project will be profitable. If so, the opportunistic party—having yet to make any investment in

33 The discussion in this Section draws on Schwartz and Scott, n 5, 661.

the project—can exploit the counterparty in a negotiation over the terms of the ultimate contract. Secondly, if the project proves unsuccessful, delay permits the opportunistic party to avoid what otherwise would have been sunk costs. Those savings will likely be larger than any offsetting losses from delay if the project instead proves profitable.

Historically, such preliminary agreements were unenforceable under the indefiniteness doctrine of the common law of contracts. Recently, however, courts have affected a major shift in doctrine by relaxing the common law rule under which parties are either fully bound or not bound at all. Instead, a new enforcement rule is emerging to govern cases where the parties contemplate further negotiations.[34] This new rule responds to the increasing importance of the search for new partners in an uncertain environment to successful collaborations. The new rule starts with the presumption that preliminary agreements typically do not create fully binding contracts.[35] This presumption rests on the traditional common law view that courts should not hold parties to contracts unless the parties intended to make them. The shift comes from courts now recognising that welfare gains can result from attaching some level of formal enforcement to agreements to collaborate that were intended to bind despite the need for further negotiation.

The new default rule thus enforces 'a mutual commitment to negotiate together in good faith in an effort to reach final agreement.'[36] Neither party, however, has a right to demand performance of the contemplated transaction. If the parties cannot ultimately agree on a final contract, they may abandon the deal. Both parties thus enter into an option on the ultimate deal, which is exercisable after the parties learn the information produced through the preliminary investments and whose price is the cost of the preliminary investment.

This new rule governing preliminary agreements to collaborate—creating a legal duty to bargain in good faith but not requiring the parties to agree—is an appropriate first step in solving the parties' contracting problem. As we argued earlier, it is helpful to attach some formal support to agreements that depend on initial learning to achieve innovation, particularly when the imposition of low-powered enforcement stimulates the mechanisms that build trust. The contemporary judicial approach to preliminary agreements of this sort appropriately

[34] The rule originated with the opinion of Judge Pierre Leval in *Teachers Insurance and Annuity Association of America v. Tribune Co.*, 670 F. Supp. 481, 488 (S.D.N.Y., 1987). Judge Leval identified two separate types of 'preliminary agreements'. He labeled as 'Type I' those cases where the parties have agreed on all material terms but have also agreed to memorialize their agreement in a more formal document. Disputes arise primarily because parties have failed to express clearly their intention as to *when* their arrangement would be legally enforceable. Here the question is solely one of timing—when have the parties manifested an intention to be legally bound? In contrast, 'Type II' agreements concern binding preliminary commitments, the preliminary agreements we analyse here. In this latter case, the parties agree on certain terms, but leave possibly important terms open to further negotiation. This requires courts to determine *whether* such an agreement had been made, *what* the duty to bargain in good faith entails, and *which* remedy should be awarded for breach of that duty. This framework has been followed in at least 13 states, 16 federal district courts and seven federal circuits. See Schwarz and Scott, n 5, 661, 676, 680.

[35] See *R.G. Group Inc. v. Horn & Hardart Co.*, 751 F.2d 69, 74 (2d Cir, 1984).

[36] *TIAA v. Tribune*, 670 F. Supp. at 481, 498.

opens the door to judicial support of mutual learning in contracts for innovation. Nevertheless, the courts' experience so far provides little normative guidance concerning the breadth of the enforceable obligation, or the consequences of its breach. This is an important shortcoming when, as we have seen, the breadth of judicial enforcement is critical to whether crowding out is the unintended consequence of formal enforcement.

Our analysis of the function of the braiding mechanism suggests that the parties to this agreement should be legally required to comply with their initial commitments to pursue promised preliminary investments (typically investments in information) that are necessary to reveal whether or not the proposed project is feasible. But formal enforcement should play no role in determining whether or not the project should go forward and on what terms. After all, rational parties will pursue efficient projects and abandon inefficient projects. The parties already have strong incentives to negotiate faithfully over the conditions for achieving success. Rather, the challenge is to discourage parties from defecting early in the relationship before a robust pattern of cooperation has developed. The threat of a legal sanction, therefore, should only be designed to give the parties sufficient opportunity to develop patterns of cooperation supported by switching costs.

How well, then, does the new legal framework governing preliminary agreements support the braiding mechanism? In our analysis, the complementary braiding of formal and informal enforcement will be successful if and only if the courts only deploy low-powered incentives; that is, courts only sanction cheating on the parties' mutual commitment to iterative collaboration but do not attempt to regulate the course or the outcome of the collaboration. Put differently, if the preliminary agreement is breached, the court should require a party to repay the price the counterparty paid for the option—the amount spent on the preliminary investment. It should not require even a breaching party to exercise the option, either by completing the transaction or by imposing expectation damages. An examination of litigated preliminary agreements suggests that courts are divided in their understanding of the breadth of their role.[37] We illustrate the lack of clarity in two manifestations of the preliminary agreement issue. The first is its application in a general commercial setting. The second is its application in a specialized form of preliminary agreement—a letter of intent in a corporate acquisition.

a. *The commercial setting*

Consider first *In re Matterhorn Group, Inc*[38] There, Swatch wanted to sell more watches in the United States by expanding its franchise operations. Matterhorn and Swatch agreed to collaborate on pursuing the possibility of a long-term relationship: the parties signed a letter of intent granting Matterhorn the exclusive

[37] For an analysis of the litigated cases, see Schwartz and Scott, n 5, 661, 691–702.

[38] *In re Matterhorn Group Inc*, 2002 WL 31528396 (Bk. S.D.N.Y., 2002).

franchise for 30 possible sites. Under the agreement, Matterhorn undertook to invest in finding appropriate locations for retailing Swatch watches from among the list of possible locations. Swatch undertook to process diligently the applications for franchises at potentially profitable locations as Matterhorn filed them, and then to seek financing and approval of franchises at chosen locations from its parent firm. Thus, in our framework the parties agreed to collaborate by making concurrent investments in pursuit of an entrepreneurial innovation: Swatch would incur opportunity costs (by granting exclusive rights to Matterhorn) and invest the human capital needed to evaluate Matterhorn's applications and to become familiar with the American business climate; Matterhorn would invest the search and information costs necessary to identifying profitable locations. The project contemplated an iterative exchange of information focused on finding profitable retail sites for selling Swatch watches in shopping malls, but precisely which locations, if any, would be mutually profitable could not be determined without the initial investments by both parties.

In this case, the parties had no prior history, did not share membership in a homogeneous community, and could not depend on the discipline of repeated exchange to constrain opportunism. As a consequence, informal sanctions were weak at the outset of the relationship and the parties were each at risk of exploitation. And, indeed, Swatch engaged in just the strategic behaviour that our framework predicts: it delayed processing several applications and failed to secure the necessary approvals.[39] The court found Swatch to be in breach of a preliminary agreement to bargain in good faith and awarded Matterhorn reliance damages based on its investment expenditures in investigating the locations in question. Importantly, however, the court denied Matterhorn's claim for expectation damages based on lost profits, holding that 'there is no guarantee that it would have opened a store in [that location].'[40] Thus, the court compensated Matterhorn for the price it paid for the option, but did not protect it from Swatch's decision not to exercise it.

The result in *Matterhorn* is consistent with the hypothesis that narrowly defined duties of good faith will complement a regime that depends primarily on informal enforcement. A properly configured braiding mechanism, such as the one that appears to have been adopted by the court in *Matterhorn,* likely will not crowd out the informal mechanisms that build trust but rather will offer a low-powered complement during the early stages of collaboration, thereby giving reciprocity and trust the opportunity to evolve.

[39] The court held: '[t]he rejection of the Vail application violated the Letter of Intent. The Letter of Intent granted Matterhorn the exclusive right to negotiate a lease in Vail despite Vail's geographical distance from Matterhorn's base of operation in the Northeast. Furthermore, it required Swatch to review the Vail application in good faith, and in a manner consistent with the criteria discussed above... [Swatch] unilaterally rescinded the exclusivity that the Letter of Intent had granted, and Swatch's [decision] to reject the Vail application was improper. In addition, Matterhorn sent the Vail letter of intent in late April 1996... Swatch took four months to complete its processing of the application... Accordingly, Swatch breached the Letter of Intent by rejecting the Vail application for improper reasons.' *In re Matterhorn Group Inc,* 2002 WL 31528396 at 16–17.

[40] *In re Matterhorn Group Inc,* 2002 WL 31528396.

b. Preliminary agreements in corporate acquisitions: letters of intent and the duty to negotiate in good faith

The pattern of preliminary agreements that contemplate concurrent preliminary investments can also be seen in the context of corporate acquisitions. We turn now to several cases that illustrate this pattern. They also illustrate the adverse consequences when courts fail to understand the interaction of formal and informal enforcement.

(1) *Tan v. Allwaste, Inc*

Tan v. Allwaste, Inc involved a claim by shareholders of Geotrack that Allwaste had breached an obligation to negotiate in good faith Geotrak's acquisition. Discussions between Allwaste and Geotrack had led to the parties executing a letter of intent that stated Allwaste's intention to make the acquisition subject to satisfactory due diligence. The letter of intent also stated that it 'does not constitute a binding agreement among the parties' and further stated that, according to the court, 'the parties do not have a deal until a formal agreement was executed.' However, the letter did contain some binding obligations. It bound the parties to pursue a deal in good faith and contained a 'no shop' clause by which Geotrack promised not to shop Allwaste's stock offer to other potential buyers. During the due diligence investigation, Allwaste discovered Geotrack had not remitted payroll and withholding taxes to the Internal Revenue Service for some time. Allwaste withdrew from further negotiations and was unwilling to buy Geotrack even after it offered to lower the price.

This preliminary acquisition agreement can be fairly characterized as an innovative effort to secure the synergies that might arise from combining the Allwaste and Geotrack businesses, whose assessment and ultimate success depends on both parties making preliminary investments in the proposed project concurrently. Here the buyer invests in information (due diligence) to determine the actual condition of Geotrack's business and to develop the information necessary to assess the potential for synergy and the difficulty in actually achieving it. In turn, this investment is protected by a no-shop clause: the seller cannot use the fact of Allwaste's interest to induce other buyers to enter a competing bid and thereby devalue Allwaste's investment in information.

Thus Geotrack makes an opportunity cost investment and incurs the potential costs of running the business without change and subject to its competitors' actions while Allwaste undertakes its investigation.[41] Concurrent investment and the passage of time together will show whether a profitable project exists, at which time the parties would be free to write a contract to complete the acquisition if the underlying innovation was feasible.

[41] Sellers in these acquisition agreements may also invest in the synergies that result from integration. See Gilson and Schwartz, 'Understanding MACs' (2005) 33 *Journal of Law Economics & Organization* 330–40.

In this case, the court correctly held that the letter agreement was a preliminary agreement obligating Allwaste to negotiate further in good faith with Geotrack: in our terms, this was a low-powered formal obligation that supported the concurrent investment that was necessary to get the parties to the point where they could assess whether synergy gains could be captured and then decide whether to complete a transaction. However, the court went a step further by also concluding that there was sufficient evidence for a reasonable jury to conclude that although the target had failed to disclose that it had not paid its payroll and withholding taxes for some time, Allwaste had declined to go forward with the deal for reasons that were unrelated to Geotrack's actions, omissions, or financial status.[42] On this basis, the court concluded that the case would go to a jury to determine whether Allwaste had breached its obligation to negotiate in good faith because it may have declined to go forward with the transactions for reasons unrelated to the target's misbehaviour.[43]

Under these circumstances, exposing Allwaste to the threat of a jury finding a bad faith failure to negotiate transforms the preliminary agreement from a low-powered formal enforcement tool that supports the diligence process necessary to assessing the potential for innovation, to a high-powered sanction that exposes Allwaste to large damages from not making the acquisition.[44] There was no allegation that Allwaste had not made its preliminary investment in assessing the potential of the acquisition; it had paid the price for its option. Rather, Geotrack alleged that Allwaste had merely concluded that the acquisition was no longer advantageous, which the court concluded would be a breach. So expansive an interpretation of the good faith obligation and the expansion of the role of formal enforcement goes much further than the low-powered enforcement associated with a braiding strategy, which contemplates only that each party is held to making the preliminary investments necessary to assess the acquisition, but neither is obligated to close the transaction. More concretely, a braiding strategy does not envision that a letter of intent shifts the risk of changes in general economic conditions or the potential buyer's circumstances or strategy to the buyer. Such an expansion of formal enforcement is precisely the shift in the relative importance of formal and informal enforcement that is associated with crowding out the development of informal patterns of cooperation necessary to exploit the potential for innovation in the first place. The court in *Tan v. Allwaste* unwisely

[42] In particular, plaintiffs noted the acquisition of Geotrack was to be debt-free, so Geotrack's tax liability should not have affected Allwaste's analysis of the deal. Plaintiffs also provided evidence that Allwaste simply decided not to conduct any more acquisitions. *Tan v. Allwaste, Inc*, 1997 WL 337207 at 4. However, Allwaste might well have concluded that a counterparty that lied about its liabilities may have been lying about other matters, such as the condition of its assets or the non-debt aspects of its financial condition that a debt free acquisition would not protect against.

[43] The court appears to have concluded that if Allwaste declined to go forward with the acquisition because it 'simply decided not to conduct any more acquisitions', *Tan v. Allwaste, Inc*, 1997 WL 337207 at 4, a jury could conclude that it breached its preliminary agreement. In other words, the court construed the obligation as prohibiting a change in one party's strategy.

[44] The court did not limit potential damages to Geotrack's reliance costs, thus leaving open the possibility that Allwaste could be held to benefit of the bargain damages.

departed from the kind of low-powered enforcement necessary to support effective braiding, and thereby restricted the range of contractual techniques available to parties seeking to innovate.

(2) *VS & A Communications and Venture Associates*

The potentially dysfunctional reasoning and result in *Tan v. Allwaste* is not simply an example of a single judge getting it wrong. The absence of a theoretically sound principle to guide judicial enforcement of a letter of intent can be seen by comparing the efforts of two distinguished jurists confronting this problem—then-Delaware Chancellor William T. Allen, and then-Chief Judge Richard Posner of the United States Court of Appeals for the Seventh Circuit. Both reach the right result in the end, but Chancellor Allen inflicted on the defendant a costly trial that he later acknowledged was unnecessary,[45] and Judge Posner, albeit in dicta, held out the possibility that the damages for breach of an obligation to negotiate in good faith contained in a letter of intent might extend to expectation damages.[46]

In *VS & A Communications*, Chancellor Allen considered the claim that an obligation to negotiate in good faith contained in a letter of intent concerning an acquisition in effect required the seller to close the transaction on terms that the buyer alleges the seller could not in good faith have rejected.[47] While the facts that give the buyer's position at least surface plausibility are complicated, Chancellor Allen's framing of the issue is not:

> In my opinion [the letter of intent] does create an implied obligation to keep the Stations off the market and not to offer to sell or negotiate with others concerning the sale. In addition, [the buyer] was obligated to continue to assist the negotiation process in specific ways: to afford information, for example. These obligations are real and they would have value to one negotiating to buy the Stations. But the obligation ... does not go so far as to constitute a concession from the seller of its right as a property owner to change its mind ... prior to the time it agrees to bind itself legally to a sale.

Markets change. Negotiating a complex transaction is always subject to the risk that a material change in a relevant market will suddenly make a proposed deal uneconomic from one side of the transaction or the other. That risk inevitably exists until a party is legally bound.[48]

Thus Chancellor Allen reaches a conclusion that is consistent with low-powered formal enforcement of a braiding strategy and the avoidance of a crowding out. However, it is important to keep in mind that Chancellor Allen was writing a post-trial opinion. As he said, '[i]t may be that, taking the view of this case that I now do, it would have been permissible to grant summary judgment of dismissal

[45] *VS & A Communications Partners, L.P. v. Palmer Broadcasting Limited Partnership*, 1992 WL 339377 (Del Ch, 1992).

[46] *Venture Associates Corporation v. Zenith Data Systems Corporation*, 96 F. 3rd 275 (7th Cir, 1996).

[47] The case is unusual in that typically it is the buyer who elects not to go forward.

[48] *VS & A Communications Partners, L.P. v. Palmer Broadcasting Limited Partnership*, 1992 W.L. 339377 at 8.

to defendants. That course would have saved the substantial effort and expense entailed in the trial that has now been completed.'[49]

The risk of trial, especially trial to a jury as opposed to the bench trial found in the Delaware Chancery Court, becomes especially significant if the potential damage remedy extends not just to reliance damages (the amount of one party's preliminary investment), but also to benefit of the bargain damages (the profits the party would have earned had the acquisition actually been completed). And here is where Judge Posner's opinion in *Venture Associates Corporation*[50] becomes relevant.

Judge Posner correctly concludes, as did Chancellor Allen, that an obligation to negotiate in good faith contained in a letter of intent does not constrain a party from changing its view of the desirability of an acquisition in light of a change in conditions:

> Since [the seller] had not agreed on the sale price, it remained free to demand a higher price in order to reflect the market value of the company at the time of the actual sale... [The seller] was free to demand as high a price as it thought the market would bear, provided that it was not trying to scuttle the deal... If the market value... rose... say to $25 million, [the seller] would not be acting in bad faith to demand that amount from [the buyer] even if it knew that [the buyer] would not go that high. [The seller] would be acting in bad faith only if its purpose in charging more than [the buyer] would pay was to induce [the buyer] to back out of the deal.[51]

Consistent with proper judicial enforcement of a braiding strategy, a party is not committed to exercising the option to close the transaction.

However, the risk of trial becomes a serious threat to crowd out informal contracting, even if the charge to the jury is correct, if the potential damages are calculated in terms of a breach of an obligation to pursue the ultimate deal. And here Judge Posner expresses the view that the threat is real: '[d]amages for breach of an agreement to negotiate may be, although they are unlikely to be, the same as the damages for breach of the final contract that the parties would have signed had it not been for the defendant's bad faith.'[52] The difficulty with Judge Posner's invitation to courts to award expectation damages is that it blurs the separation between the formal portion of the braided contract and the informal portion, thereby increasing the risk of crowding out.

The conclusion in *Tan v. Allwaste* that a party who has made the contemplated preliminary investment cannot simply decline to close the transaction, together with Chancellor Allen's subjecting such a party to trial and Judge Posner's holding

[49] *VS & A Communications Partners, L.P. v. Palmer Broadcasting Limited Partnership*, 1992 W.L. 339377 at 2.

[50] *Venture Associates Corporation v. Zenith Data Systems Corporation*, 96 F. 3rd 275.

[51] *Venture Associates Corporation v. Zenith Data Systems Corporation*, 96 F. 3rd 275 at 275, 279–80. Judge Posner does not address the broader point made by Chancellor Allen that the changed conditions that have affected the price would allow the seller in good faith simply to decline to complete the transaction.

[52] *Venture Associates Corporation v. Zenith Data Systems Corporation*, 96 F. 3rd 275 at 278.

out the possibility that the party might be subject to expectation damages premised on a breach of the final contract, illustrates the importance of a theory to explain the underlying commercial behaviour and prescribe the appropriate facilitative role for courts. No matter how sharp the intuitions of experienced judges, courts unguided by a theoretical framework are prone to error. Thus in both cases, the court failed to embrace fully the notion that an enforceable preliminary agreement only requires a party to pay the option price by undertaking a promised investment in acquiring and sharing information. Framing the obligation in this way should permit a party to properly obtain summary judgment even though it walks away from the transaction for reasons wholly unrelated to the actions of the counterparty. And even if the promised investment is not made, the defendant's liability is properly limited to the investment cost and not to the expectancy that might result from a concluded deal.

2. How courts can know braiding when they see it

An important theme emerges from the preceding discussion of some of the evolving case law governing braided contracts. It is clear that the duty to negotiate in good faith in preliminary agreements and letters of intent provides a useful doctrinal placeholder permitting courts to imply a governance structure to support agreements that rely principally on iterative investments in information. However, the new obligation to negotiate in good faith is unmoored because the cases do not indicate what the parties are supposed to bargain over, or when the refusal to agree constitutes bad faith, or just what should be the remedy for bad faith. Under contemporary legal doctrine, for example, the question of when preliminary agreements should be enforced requires a multi-factor analysis that invokes the language of the agreement, the existence and number of open terms, the extent of any reliance investments, and the customary practice regarding formalities. The court, in addition, is required to consider the context of the negotiations resulting in the preliminary agreement.[53] Such a laundry list of relevant factors leaves the decision process largely obscure. That is particularly the case when, as is typical, courts fail to attach weights to the factors or specify the relationship among them.[54] In the absence of a theory, the courts are left to interpret criteria for imposing liability that are unconnected to the operative facts that might justify formal enforcement. Our theory of how courts can best support the braiding of formal and informal contracting provides a coherent way to think about the domain and limits of the obligation to negotiate in good faith: courts best respond to the proliferation of preliminary agreements induced by innovation under uncertainty by imposing low-powered sanctions designed to encourage compliance with the information-exchange regime while avoiding high-powered sanctions that crowd out informal enforcement and destroy the braid. In short, the duty to negotiate in

[53] See *TIAA v. Tribune*, 670 F. Supp. at 481, 500–02.
[54] Schwartz and Scott, n 5, 661, 675–676.

good faith means that parties should be held to their commitment to make initial investments in collaboration and nothing else.[55] Thereafter, each party faces a choice as to whether or not to proceed to a fully enforceable, formal obligation. The key to understanding the nature of low-powered sanctions, therefore, is to recognize that an obligation to collaborate is not an obligation to bargain. Whenever a court holds to the contrary, that the dissenting party has an obligation to bargain in good faith, it follows that there must be a state of the world in which failing to reach agreement is a breach. It is precisely that trap that led the court in *Tan v. Allwaste* and Judge Posner in *Venture Associates* to error.

[55] Our principal concern has been the question of what it means to formally enforce these preliminary obligations. But, as noted earlier, the criteria for determining *when* parties have reached such an agreement are also needlessly vague: see nn 53 and 54 Since parties are always free to indicate their desire to be completely free from formal enforcement, courts should hold all commercial parties to an obligation to invest as promised whenever they agree to invest collaboratively in a letter of intent or other similar form of transaction.

Getting it Just Right

Comment on R. J. Gilson, C. F. Sabel, and R. E. Scott, 'Contract, Uncertainty, and Innovation'

*Gerard Hertig**

Building upon Knight's distinction between risk and uncertainty,[1] Gilson, Sabel, and Scott develop an innovation process theory which would make it easier for courts to properly adjudicate contractual disputes when the future state of the world cannot be assessed probabilistically.

In the past, entrepreneurs often dealt with this kind of uncertainty through vertical integration. However, such an approach had two major drawbacks. First, integration had to occur through internal growth, as acquisitions often must take place behind the veil of uncertainty. Secondly, it presupposed that firms could remain innovative on their own even in an era of major technological breakthrough.

It should thus come as no surprise that firms have developed new mechanisms to facilitate the acquisition of or cooperation with innovative firms. More specifically, as pointed out by the authors, firms '*contract for innovation*' by institutionalizing an initial collaboration process that significantly reduces uncertainty. Obviously, this kind of collaboration requires relation-specific investments, which is costly. But these investments also have the advantage of raising the costs of switching to new partners, which in turn reinforces collaboration incentives.

The authors underline that contracts for innovation generally have two formal governance components (mutual exchange of information + dispute resolution), but no product output commitment (the parties have yet to determine whether an innovation is possible). Courts, however, often fail to perceive the limited scope of these contracts. They do not limit themselves to deciding whether one party must pay reliance damages for having breached its collaboration obligations. Courts

* Professor of Law, Swiss Federal Institute of Technology, Zurich.

[1] F. H. Knight, *Risk, Uncertainty, and Profit* (Boston: Hartford Publisher, 1921).

often also venture into adjudicating lost profit awards, even though the parties have yet to move to the product stage of their relationship.

This is deemed very unfortunate, as it is likely to crowd out contracts for innovations when they are most useful, i.e. in complex environments. High-powered judicial enforcement will deter parties from investing in initial collaboration, which will make it more difficult for firms to cope with uncertainty and, thus, hamper innovation. Consequently, the authors describe the circumstances under which low-powered enforcement by the parties themselves can be preferable. They also illustrate how case law could be improved if the courts were to apply contracting for innovation theory.

The authors make a very compelling case. It would definitely be worthwhile for courts to examine whether the parties have contracted for innovation—and, if so, to consider whether the claims can be summarily rejected or, at least, to limit their review to reliance damages.

At the same time, current case law may be less flawed than one would expect and even have some advantages. As will be discussed some issues could be tackled though contract wording (Section I), crowding-out effects may be less pervasive than expected (Section II), parties may let business opportunities pass while busy exchanging information (Section III), and contracting for innovation could serve anti-competitive purposes (Section IV).

I. Contract Wording

The authors point out that courts can get it wrong by 1) imposing damages on parties who participate faithfully in the information exchange regime but then decide not to pursue the joint project, or 2) awarding full expectation damages for the breach of the information exchange obligation. Conceptually, this may be privately and socially costly should crowding-out effects follow (see Section II.). However, parties negotiating contracts for innovation can observe case law and ask their lawyers to adjust the contractual wording accordingly. This should significantly reduce the damages risk and minimize crowding-out effects.

To be sure, local contract law may forbid or restrict liability limitations and established judges may be biased against creative lawyers. On the other hand, contracts for innovation are generally of significant importance. It follows that choice of law and arbitration options are likely to be worthwhile: the parties are likely to benefit from having their relationship subject to a more innovation-friendly contract law or from empowering 'private' decision-makers to handle their disputes. Admittedly, a party that proposes to exercise the choice of law and arbitration options could also be signaling litigiousness or lack of trust, which could give the other party as good reason not to enter into a contract for innovation. But in some instances, at least, contract wording could be the best way to cope with judicial error.

II. Crowding Out

It would be hard to deny that high-powered formal enforcement can affect information exchanges or even prevent entering into contracts for innovation. This effect may, however, be more significant for the 'getting to know each other' component of a contract for innovation than for its 'information gathering' component. When it comes to the former, judicial intervention is likely to affect the participants' intrinsic motivation[2] more directly. Indeed, what is at stake is not so much whether the relevant data has been provided, but whether the participants have behaved in a trustworthy fashion.

From this perspective, it is not easy to evaluate the impact of the case law discussed by the authors. If judges focus on information-gathering, crowding out may not be as dramatic a development, as formal contracts could be an adequate substitute. The reverse may, however, be true if judges focus on trustworthiness. This is an area which deserves further research, including whether it makes a difference when the contractual parties are corporations rather than individuals.

III. Missed Opportunities

The authors emphasize that courts fail to understand the nature of contracts for innovation by awarding damages for lost profits rather than merely for reliance costs incurred during the collaboration. This very important point has a logic to it, but it does not necessarily imply that courts are fundamentally mistaken. Contracts for innovation may take time to be fulfilled, providing competitors a window to enter into competing arrangements.

It follows that when a party breaches a contract for innovation, it may impose significant opportunity costs on its counterparty. If the latter had known *ex ante* that it would not get the promised data or was contracting with an untrustworthy party, it would have devoted its time and efforts to entering into a contract for innovation with a competitor. To the extent this option is not available anymore *ex post*—competitors having entered into parallel arrangements in the meantime—awarding damages for lost profits could be the efficient approach. To be sure, it may prove difficult to establish the existence of an opportunity and its value, but this issue is not directly related to the contract being for innovation.

IV. Reducing Competition

Contracts for innovation may be valuable in connection with a diverse set of transactions, for example acquisitions, joint ventures, and research or distribution

[2] See, e.g., B. S. Frey, *Inspiring Economics* (Cheltenham: Edward Elgar Publishing, 2001).

agreements. However, the profitability of such contracts may also have its dark side. Information gathered and in particular trust-building may also aim to or result in reducing competition.

The issue here is not that this dark side is uniquely related to contracts for innovation. Anyone familiar with antitrust matters is aware that acquisitions, joint ventures, or vertical agreements may aim to or result in reducing competition. What is problematic with contracts for innovation is that they deal with uncertainty, providing a close to perfect *intent* cover for those entrepreneurs entering into them to (among others) reduce competitive pressures. This makes the task of antitrust authorities much harder, as they are left with the having to prove the anticompetitive *effect* of the (resulting) acquisition, joint venture or research/distribution agreement.

In summary, there are reasons to be both more and less optimistic than the authors about the benefits we may expect from contracting for innovation. Experience teaches us that such a conclusion generally means that the authors got it just right.

6

Contractual Networks in Socio-economic Perspective: The Case of the European Financial Crisis (2009–2010)

*Richard Swedberg**

One of the topics I will discuss in this Chapter is the role of contractual networks in socio-economic perspective.[1] By a contractual network I mean the kind of network that emerges when you conceptualize a number of actors, and the contracts between them, in the form of a network. The actors in this case are typically banks, and other financial institutions, or states may also be involved.

The role that networks of this type can play will be set in a very specific empirical and theoretical context. The empirical context is that of the second phase of the financial crisis in Europe (Autumn of 2009). During this phase, the situation came very close to a systemic crisis in late April to mid-May 2010. The theoretical context of the Chapter is informed primarily by a concern with *confidence*—a topic I have been working on for some time.[2] Confidence plays a key role in economic life, and what characterizes financial crises is, for one thing, that confidence suddenly evaporates. Confidence, in other words, is of importance for an understanding of financial crises.

* Professor of Sociology, Cornell University.

[1] This Chapter was originally presented as a paper at the conference on 'Contract Governance – Dimensions in Law and Interdisciplinary Research", Berlin, 30 September– 2 October, 2010. I am grateful for the comments made at the discussion of my paper. For help with the figures in this Chapter, I thank Jared Peifer.

[2] R. Swedberg, 'The Structure of Confidence and the Collapse of Lehmann Brothers' in P. Hirsch and M. Loundsbury (eds), *Markets on Trial: The Economic Sociology of the US: Financial Crisis* (Bingley: Emeral Group Publishing Limited, 2010) 67–110, R. Swedberg, 'The Role of Confidence in Finance' in K. K. Cetina and A. Preda (eds) *Handbook of the Sociology of Finance* (New York: Oxford University Press, 2011) 529–545 (also published as Working Paper No 54, Center for the Study in Economy and Society, Cornell University, Department of Sociology (available at <http://www.economyandsociety.org/publications/wp54_Swedberg_RoleofConfidenceinFinance.pdf>)).

I. The Role of Confidence

Let me begin with confidence. Currently there exists no generally accepted theory of confidence, be it among sociology or economics scholars.[3] Nonetheless, scholars such as Simmel in sociology and Keynes in economics have strongly argued that confidence plays a crucial role in economic life.[4] Recently there has also been somewhat of a surge of interest in the topic.[5] The key idea is that many economic actions leave the actor vulnerable to other actors, and that unless there is confidence, there will be no interaction in many cases.

This is more of a description of the role of confidence than an analytical take on the subject, but it will suffice for the moment. The next point I want to make is that certain economic actors are active in what may be called confidence-intensive areas of the economy. One such area is deposit banking, and the reason is that this type of bank borrows its resources in the form of deposits, without specifying the time when these can be withdrawn, while they lend them out with a specific deadline. The depositors, in brief, can withdraw their resources at any moment, say, when their confidence in the bank is low. Something similar is true for many modern financial institutions, including investment banks of the US type. Additionally, these borrow funds on a short-term basis, and invest them on a long-term basis, making them vulnerable to sudden demands by their creditors.

In the empirical case of this Chapter, some of the main economic actors, besides banks and other financial institutions, are states, and while these are not confidence-intensive institutions, they do rely on confidence to carry out their habitual economic activities. It should be noted that it is also hard for market actors to determine when, say, European states are worthy of confidence and when they are not. How is one to decide the value of a bond issued by a state, say, a member of the eurozone? Should one look at the rate of debt in relation to the budget, to a country's GDP? If not, then what? How do protests by the population affect the valuation? Will the EU or the eurozone countries operate as a unity and back up the debts of countries like Greece and Spain—or will these countries be left to fend for themselves?

Looking at the role of states, it is also clear that the way that confidence is managed becomes important. When Trichet makes a public statement about the situation, say, of the banks in Greece, is he describing their economic situation or is he managing confidence? Depending on the answer, investors may wish to buy or sell. The blatant way in which the notion of confidence has been used to justify the attempts to fight the financial crisis through budget cuts has also made some economist refer disparagingly to a belief in a mythical 'confidence fairy'.

[3] Swedberg (2011), n 2.

[4] G. Simmel, *The Philosophy of Money* (London: Routledge, 1978), J. M. Keynes, *The General Theory of Employment, Interest and Money* (London: Macmillan, 1936) chap 12.

[5] Swedberg (2011), n 2.

All you have to do is to say that your policy will create confidence and thereby economic growth.[6]

An important part of the argument in this Chapter will finally be played by a theory of the way that financial crises can be triggered by a loss of confidence. It draws on an idea in a classic study in the finance literature that is often mentioned when financial panics are discussed, namely *Lombard Street* (1873) by Walter Bagehot.[7] It is in this work that one finds the famous piece of advice on how central banks are supposed to operate in moments of crises, namely to infuse huge amounts of credit into the system.

According to Bagehot, what may trigger a financial crisis are *hidden costs*. Nothing unnerves investors and depositors as much, Bagehot argues, as the sudden discovery that a bank has huge hidden losses. This may either cause a sharp fall in the financial markets or bring down the whole financial system. The key passage in *Lombard Street* reads as follows:

> We should cease... to be surprised at the sudden panics [in the banking system]. During the period of reaction and adversity, just even at the last instant of prosperity, the whole structure is delicate. *The peculiar essence of our banking system is an unprecedented trust between man and man; and when that trust is much weakened by hidden causes, a small accident may greatly hurt it, and a great accident for a moment may almost destroy it.*[8]

The dynamics of a run on the bank have been nicely formulated by Robert K. Merton in his essay 'The Self-fulfilling Prophecy'.[9] A bank becomes insolvent when it is seen as insolvent by the depositors, who, in acting on the belief that it is insolvent, will end up making it so—even if the bank was perfectly sound to start out with.[10] Bagehot, in a complementary fashion, has explained what triggers a whole financial panic: a sudden loss of confidence occurs when hidden losses are suddenly discovered, which in turn unnerves investors.

While both Merton and Bagehot realized how central confidence is in economic life, neither of them defines what constitutes confidence. Neither can one say that the issue of confidence has attracted much interest among economists or that there is consensus in whatever little literature there is on the topic.[11] I will

[6] P. Krugman, 'Myths of Austerity', *New York Times*, 1 July 2010 (available at <http://www.nytimes.com/2010/07/02/opinion/02krugman.html>); P. Krugman, 'British fashion Victims', *New York Times*, 22 October 2010, p A35 (available at <http://www.nytimes.com/2010/10/22/opinion/22krugman.html>); J. Stiglitz, 'To Choose Austerity is to Bet It All on the confidence Fairy', *The Guardian*, 19 October 2010 (available at <http://www.guardian.co.uk/commentisfree/cifamerica/2010/oct/19/no-confidence-fairy-for-austerity-britain>); C. Romer, 'Now Isn't the Time to Cut the Deficit', *New York Times*, 24 October 2010, p BU 5 (available at <http://www.nytimes.com/2010/10/24/business/24view.html>); G. Soros, 'The Real Danger to the Economy', *New York Review of Books*, 11 November 2010, p 16 (available at <http://www.nybooks.com/articles/archives/2010/nov/11/real-danger-economy/>).

[7] W. Bagehot, *Lombard Street: A Description of the Money Market* (London: John Murry, 1922).

[8] Bagehot, n 7, 151–2 (emphasis added).

[9] R. K. Merton, 'The Self-fulfilling Prophecy' in R. K. Merton (eds), *Social Theory and Social Structure* (New York: The Free Press, 1968) 475–90.

[10] Merton, n 9, 476–7. [11] Swedberg (2010), n 2.

therefore suggest my own theory of confidence, and as my point of departure, I will use a statement by Mancur Olson.

Confidence, Olson once said in an interview, is all-pervasive in society as well as in the economy. When I, for example, walk on a pavement, he continued, I put down my feet in the belief that what I take to be solid concrete, is indeed solid concrete, and not, say, a piece of paper painted to look like concrete.[12]

Olson's seemingly trivial example brings to mind a comment that can be found in *Philosophical Investigations*. Wittgenstein makes more or less the same point as Olson, but also adds that confidence is closely linked to action. He says:

> When I sat down on this chair, of course I believed it would bear me. I had no thought of its possibly collapsing...The feeling of confidence. How is this manifested in behaviour?[13]

What unites these two ways of looking at confidence is that confidence is seen as consisting of what can be called a double structure. There is, on the one hand, the actual issue with which the actor is concerned (that the sidewalk is strong enough to walk on or that the chair is strong enough to sit on). There also exists, on the other hand, something that indicates that this is indeed the case to the person who is doing the walking or about to sit down. This indicator can be conceptualized as a *sign* that stands in for something else—what I will call a *proxy sign*. From this perspective, confidence can be conceptualized as something that you need to have in order to act in situations where you lack accurate information and must rely on signs instead.

The proxy sign can either correctly indicate the actual situation or not.[14] In the former case, the sign can either indicate that the situation is positive, and the situation *is* positive (+/+). Or the sign can indicate that the situation is negative, and so it is (–/–). The sign tells us that the sidewalk or the chair is sturdy, and so it is. Or that it is not sturdy, and it is not. In both cases the actor can have full confidence in the situation and adjust his or her behaviour accordingly.

But when the proxy sign and the situation are *not* aligned, there will be trouble (–/+, +/–). Merton describes what happens when the sign is negative and the situation is positive (–/+): there is a rumour that a bank is not solvent, while in reality it is solvent. And Bagehot describes the very opposite case: the sign is positive and the situation negative (+/–): a bank appears to be solvent, but in reality has hidden losses. In the case of Merton we may want to speak of a loss of confidence due to incorrect information, and in the case of Bagehot, of *false confidence*. Typically the two go together in a crisis: a situation à la Bagehot may trigger the crisis, while healthy banks are drawn into the turmoil along the lines of Merton.

[12] M. Olson, 'Interview' in R. Swedberg (ed), *Economics and Sociology* (Princeton, NJ: Princeton University Press, 1990) 167–85, 178.

[13] L. Wittgenstein, *Philosophical Investigations* (New York: Macmillan Publishing Company, 1968) 557, 579.

[14] See Figure 6.1.

		The Economic Situation is: Positive	The Economic Situation is: Negative
Proxy Sign Indicating the Economic Situation is	Positive	+ +	+ −
	Negative	− +	− −

Figure 6.1 Proxy Signs and the Nature of Confidence

Comment: Confidence can be defined as an actor's readiness to base the decision to act on *proxy signs*, in situations where the actor lacks access to better information. A proxy sign can be either aligned with the state of affairs or not. In the former case, a positive proxy sign correctly indicates a positive state of affairs, and a negative sign correctly indicates a negative state of affairs. Confidence is maintained in both of these cases, since the actor has correct information (++/−−). When, in contrast, the proxy sign and the situation are misaligned, and the proxy sign consequently misrepresent the situation, confidence will suffer.

If the proxy sign is negative, and the state of affairs positive, and this is applied to the situation of a bank, one may get a run on the bank along the lines that Robert K. Merton has outlined in his essay on self-fulfilling prophecy.[15] When the proxy sign is positive, and the state of affairs negative in the banking community, one in contrast gets a case that is closer to the dangerous situation that is described by Bagehot.[16]

II. The Trigger of the Sovereign Debt Crisis in Europe: Greece

It is often said that Greece set off the European sovereign debt crisis in the Autumn of 2009. Still, one is justified in asking how this could be done:

> Looking at Europe from afar, it must be difficult to understand the eurozone crisis. How could a small nation's refinancing difficulties—Greece constitutes only 2 per cent of the eurozone GDP—trigger a systemic crisis for the euro that brought global financial markets to the brink?[17]

In discussing what set off the European sovereign debt crisis (rather than what caused it), this Chapter will suggest that it had to do with hidden losses. More precisely, the trigger was the disclosure in late October 2009 that the projected budget deficit of Greece for 2009 (calculated as a percentage of GDP) was going to be several times larger than what the government had earlier reported. This disclosure made investors suddenly realize with a shock that Greece was in deep trouble.

Before looking at what happened in the Greek case in more detail, it should be noted that information about the economic situation of a corporation or a country (a proxy sign in our terminology) is often linked to very strong economic interests.

[15] Merron, n 9. [16] Bagehot, n 7.

[17] R. Baldwin and D. Gros, 'What To Do?' in R. Baldwin and D. Gros (eds) *Completing the Eurozone Rescue: What More Needs to Be Done?* 1 (published online by VoxEU.org and available at <http://www.voxeu.org/index.php?q=node/5194>).

If the proxy signs are wrong, the consequences can be enormous, and this affects the way that the knowledge of this type is disseminated and made known. When there are losses in a firm or a country, there exist very strong interests to let these remain unknown, so that the firm or the country can continue to get credit at a low rate or, in very serious cases, just continue to exist. Still, there is often talk and gossip.

That this situation will affect the existing networks is clear. An actor that is linked to a firm or a country that is in trouble will be in less trouble so long as the news about the loss is kept secret. It should also be pointed out that the investors have a great interest in having correct information, especially when there is some trouble in the economy. Fortunes and careers are typically at stake, meaning that there will be rumours, denials of rumours, and so on. This includes false rumours, since correct information can be hard to get. There is also the further twist that a false rumour can become true, thanks to the dynamic of self-fulfilling prophecies.

What all of this adds up to is a very complex situation, which is difficult for a researcher to document. Secrets are difficult to study and so are rumours. There exist, for example, no studies yet of the role that hidden losses have played in the case of Greece, and the account that follows makes no claim to be complete.

The following is approximately what happened. On 21 October 2009, the newly elected Greek government announced to the EU Commission that its projected budget deficit (in relation to GDP) for 2009 was three times larger than what its predecessor had claimed a few months back. The projected budget deficit was suddenly adjusted from 3.7 per cent to 12.5 per cent, according to the figures of the PASOK government. This also meant that it was four times higher than what is allowed.

The press, including the *Financial Times*, had disclosed this information one day before the report of the European Commission was published, something that illustrates the fact that this type of important economic information is often circulated in private before it is announced publicly.[18] It was also later reported that a secret memo had circulated in EU circles already in July, according to which the Greek deficit was likely to be more than 10 per cent.[19]

In the report of the European Commission that was made public on 21 October, it was said that while the EU countries practically never had made major revisions in their statistics, the Greek government had done so on several

[18] T. Barber, 'Greece Vows Action to Cut Budget Deficit', *Financial Times*, 20 October 2010 (available at <http://www.ft.com/cms/s/0/3e7e0e46-bd47-11de-9f6a-00144feab49a.html#axzz3Dei7taO9>).

[19] T. Barber, 'Saving the Euro: Tall Ambition, Flawed Foundations', *Financial Times*, 11 October 2010 (available at <http://www.ft.com/intl/cms/s/0/643daffa-d57a-11df-8e86-00144feabdc0.html#axzz2mzrAzpzK>); C. de Gruyter, 'Brussels Knew about Staggering Greek Budget Deficit in July', *NRC Handelsblad*, 20 December 2009 (available at <http://www.nrc.nl/international/article2442172.ece/Brussels_knew_about_staggering_Greek_budget_deficit_in_July>).

occasions.[20] Eurostat, the statistical agency of the EU, had been struggling with the issue of inaccurate Greek data for years: it had made more than ten visits to the Hellenic Statistical Agency (ELSTAT), and on five occasions it had made public reservations about the data. The new incidence, the report concluded, testified to 'the lack of quality of Greek statistics'.

In December 2009, the figure of 12.5 per cent was revised to 12.7 per cent. The Greek Prime Minister promised to reform the ELSTAT. He also stated that 'we have suffered a complete loss of credibility' and that this was the reason why Greece was in such trouble. 'Many of our problems have less to do with the absolute figures as with the fact that nobody believes us because our statistics are not correct'.[21]

In early January 2010, it was time for another revision, this time from 12.7 per cent to 13.6 per cent. Within a few days this was followed by another report on the problem of Greek statistics by the European Commission. This time the report spoke of 'deliberate misreporting' of data by the Greek government, and added that Eurostat had 'major doubts' about the current figures.[22] The main reason for the poor state of Greek statistics, it was noted, had to do with 'institutional weaknesses'. The Greek government responded by stating that the misleading statistics had come from the government which Pasok had replaced after its electoral victory in October 2009.[23]

No revisions were made during the month of February 2010, but there were rumours in the international press that the Greek government had used credit default swaps and similar financial instruments to hide some of its deficit, and that it had been helped to do so by none other than Goldman Sachs. The US investment bank was at the time seen as the incarnation of the evil speculator. As it turned out, Goldman Sachs and some other financial firms had indeed helped the Greek government to hide expenses—but this was several years ago, it was reported in the press.[24] And with this piece of information, the issue of using secret financial deals to hide the extent of Greek debt disappeared from public view.

In April 2010, there was another revision of the figures for 2009. This time, Eurostat suggested that the correct figure was probably higher than 14 per cent.

[20] T. Alloway, 'Greek Tragedy', *FTAlphaville*, 12 January 2010 (available at <http://ftalphaville.ft.com/blog/2010/01/12/124691/greek-tragedy/>).

[21] H. -J Schlamp and W. Reuter (transl. by P. Cohen), 'Interview with Greek Finance Minister: "Punitive Measures are not Appropriate"' *SpiegelOnlineInternational*, 14 December 2009 (available at http://www.spiegel.de/international/europe/0,1518,666912,00.html>).

[22] European Commission, 'Report on Greek Government Deficit and Debt Statistics', 8 January 2010 (available at <http://epp.eurostat.ec.europa.eu/cache/ITY_PUBLIC/COM_2010_REPORT_GREEK/EN/COM_2010_REPORT_GREEK-EN.PDF>).

[23] T. Barber, 'Greece Condemned by the European Commission for Falsifying Data', *Financial Times*, 12 January 2010 (available at <http://www.infiniteunknown.net/2010/01/13/greece-condemned-by-the-european-commission-for-falsifying-data/>).

[24] L. Story, L. Thomas Jr., and N. D. Schwarz, 'Wall St. Helped to Mask Debt Fueling Europe's Crisis', *New York Times*, 13 February 2010 (available at <http://www.nytimes.com/2010/02/14/business/global/14debt.html>).

The history of the hidden losses of Greece can consequently, so far, be summarized as follows. What had started out as a projected deficit of 3.7 per cent had first been revised to 12.5 per cent (October 2009), then to 12.7 per cent (December 2009), then to 13.6 per cent (January 2010) and finally to more than 14 per cent (April 2010).

By the Summer of 2010, it appeared that the revisions of the Greek debt were over for good. In early September, however, the Director-General of Eurostat announced in an interview that Greece had still not produced the full record of the ways in which it had been helped by Goldman Sachs and other financial institutions to hide its debt.[25] Already in 2008, it was now disclosed, some member states of the eurozone had been asked to disclose swaps and similar deals they had used for this purpose. All countries complied, except for Greece. This request was repeated in early 2010, the Director-General of Eurostat continued, when there were rumours that Goldman Sachs had helped Greece hide its debt—but Greece had yet to hand in all the records. That this could lead to another revision was clear from the fact that the 2001 deal that Goldman Sachs owned up to reduced Greece's debt in relation to GDP to 1.6 per cent. The day after the interview, it can be added, the Finance Minister of Greece stated that '[t]he statistics now reflect the guarantees which have been called, they reflect swaps that were not reflected and there is a clear and complete break with past practices.'[26]

In mid-November, Eurostat, after lengthy investigations in Greece, declared that a final figure for the 2009 deficit had finally been decided upon. The figure that was now presented was 15.4 per cent.[27] Presumably this is the final-final figure.

What were the effects of the disclosure of the hidden losses of Greece? One way to find out is to look at the cost for Greece to borrow money, which is typically done by studying the spread between the cost for German 10-year bonds and Greek 10-year bonds. In doing so, it is clear that many factors probably caused the rise of interest rates besides the revision of the Greek statistics. Many investors, for example, probably looked to the three major rating agencies for guidance. There is also the fact that the sudden discovery of hidden losses may cause more losses to take place through the process of self-fulfilling prophecy.

If one inspects the price for 10-year bond yields in the case of Greece, it seems to have taken the investors awhile to register the disclosures made 21 October

[25] A. Katz and E. Martinuzzi, 'Greek Deals Hidden from EU Probed as Bonds Show Doubt', *Bloomberg News*, 8 September 2010 (available at <http://www.bloomberg.com/news/2010-09-07/greek-debt-deals-hidden-from-eu-probed-as-400-yield-gap-shows-bond-doubts.html>).

[26] M. Petrakis, 'Greece Says Bonds Now an "Opportunity" as Budget Deficit Falls', *Bloomberg News*, 9 September 2010 (available at <http://www.bloomberg.com/news/2010-09-09/greece-says-its-bonds-now-investment-opportunity-as-budget-deficit-falls.html>).

[27] Petrakis, n 26; Eurostat Press Office, 'Euro Area and EU27 Government Deficit at 6.3 per cent and 6.8 per cent of GDP Respectively (2010) 170 *Eurostat NewsRelease*, (available at <http://epp.eurostat.ec.europa.eu/cache/ITY_PUBLIC/2-15112010-AP/EN/2-15112010-AP-EN.PDF>).

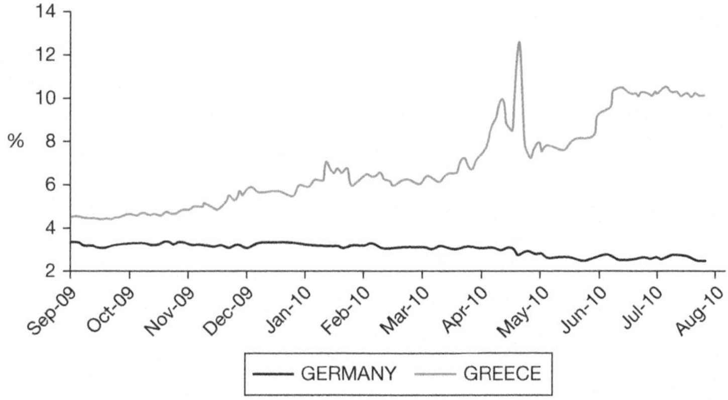

Figure 6.2 Ten-Year Bond Yield for Greece and Germany, September 2009–August 2010
Comment: The Greek statistics scandal took place in late October 2009 and on 2 May 2010, a loan of 110 billion euro was arranged for Greece.
Source: Bloomberg Terminals

2010.[28] One reason for the delay may have been confusion, another that Greek and German bond yields had been close for many years. When a norm or habit is broken, the reaction may take awhile. In any case, by the second half of November 2009, the price was clearly rising on the yield Greece had to pay. The financial press also began to pay more attention to Greece.[29] In December 2009, its bonds were also downgraded by Fitch as well as by Standard and Poor's (from AA- to BBB+).

Downgrades and warnings by the rating agencies continued during the Spring. These were also extended to the country's banks, which by now had no access to the international market but had to rely on the ECB for funds. This was a first sign that not only states, but also banks were involved in the new phase of the crisis.

From late April to early May, the yield rose dramatically on Greek bonds. The downgrade of Greek bonds to junk status on 27 April 2010 by Standard and Poor's added to the difficulty. The situation was so bad that the decision by the EU on 2 May 2010 to lend Greece 110 billion euro on a coordinated bilateral basis failed to stop the rise. It was not until a decision was made to establish a 750 billion euro facility on 10 May 2010 that the situation stabilized. Since then, however, the yield started to climb again, and it remained high far into the Autumn of 2010 (when this Chapter was originally written).

Since the October 2009 disclosure, the Greek government has tried to restore confidence in its bonds in several ways, but this has been a difficult

[28] See Figure 6.2.
[29] S. Juko, 'Have the Media Made the Greek Crisis Worse? An Inquiry into the Credit Crisis of the State' (2010) 12 *Economic Sociology – The European Electronic Newsletter* 2841 (available at <http://econsoc.mpifg.de/archive/econ_soc_12-1.pdf>).

task for a number of reasons. One is that Greece has been handing out false information for a very long time in the EU, including when it applied for membership in the eurozone in 2001.[30] Jacques Delors has, for example, recently stated that 'we have long been aware that the Greeks had concealed the real figures'.[31] According to a former commissioner, pretty much every statistic that the Greeks supplied was faulty, and this was commonly known. 'It was a case of: "We all pretend to believe them and they all pretend to be doing enough for us to believe them".'[32]

Adding to the problems for Greece is the fact that investors tend to regard countries that have often defaulted differently from those who have not. From 1800 to 2008, Greece spent more than half the years in default; it also went through five defaults or restructurings.[33]

One way in which the Greek government has tried to restore confidence is by reforming its statistical agency, ELSTAT.[34] This project was announced in the Autumn of 2009 and carried out the following Spring. Instead of falling under the finance department and reporting directly to it, ELSTAT was to be independent and report to the Greek parliament. By June 2010, ELSTAT's board had several new members, including a former statistician from the International Monetary Fund (IMF) and a board member of Eurostat.

The main effort of the Greek government to restore confidence has, however, been to make cuts in the government budget. In general, however, little is known about how investors react to this type of action. It is also difficult to evaluate a country's economy, since it is not only a question of how the state acts, but also how the population does as well. Greece, for example, has had a number of strikes since its troubles began in October 2009.

Since these problems began, the Greek government has made cuts and changes in its budget several times, most radically in connection with the 110 billion euro loan on 2 May 2010. These changes include a rise in the age at which people may retire and an attempt to open up a number of closed jobs and professions, from lorry drivers to medical doctors. None of this, however, has been able to stop the downward spiral of the Greek economy, which is projected to shrink 1.5 per cent during 2010. Unemployment is also high and still rising.

30 BBC News, 'Greece Admits Fudging Euro Entry' (available at <http://news.bbc.co.uk/2/hi/business/4012869.stm>).

31 'Just Trust Europe!' Interview with J Delors, *Die Zeit*, 20 May 2010, p 3 (transl available at <http://www.atlantic-times.com/archive_detail.php?recordID=2187>).

32 Barber, n 19.

33 C. Reinhart and K. Rogoff, *This Time is Different: Eight Centuries of Financial Folly* (Princeton, NJ: Princeton University Press, 2010) 98.

34 Katz and Martinuzzi, n 25.

III. How the EU Managed the Greek Crisis

Not only did Greece itself try to restore confidence in the country after the debacle in October 2009; the EU also put in considerable effort because Greece is one of its member as well as a member of the eurozone. The latter in particular is significant, since it meant that Greece had the same currency as the other eurozone countries, and that a threat to its economy could affect that of the other eurozone countries. Since it joined the eurozone in 2001, Greece has had the advantage of using a strong currency despite its high level of debt, but on the other hand, has been unable to devalue its currency, as it used to do when faced with mounting debt.

The choices open to the eurozone countries in dealing with Greece were either a bailout or allowing Greece to go bankrupt. The latter would mean a loss of prestige for the EU and for everyone who owned Greek bonds, especially banks. Today we also know that this option was already firmly ruled out in the Autumn of 2009.[35] The legal basis for any bailout would have been problematic: according to Article 125 in the Lisbon Treaty,[36] no bailout of a Member State is allowed.

But it is also true that another article in the treaty allows extraordinary measures to be taken under extraordinary circumstances (Article 122). This can possibly be interpreted to mean that the EU can bail out one of its members in especially urgent situations. This is in any case what happened on 2 May 2010, when the EU and the IMF arranged for a loan on 110 billion euro to Greece.

The choice between bailout and bankruptcy, however, is not what made it so hard for the EU to help Greece between October 2009 and May 2010. Something else was involved, namely the conflict between two opposing tendencies in the EU, one of which wanted the EU as a whole to assist Greece and the other of the mindset that all aid should be bilateral.

The leader of those wanting the EU to act on its own was France, led by Sarkozy. And the leader of the opposing tendency, arguing that the individual states should be the key actors, was Germany, led by Merkel. The differences between these two approaches are very deep seated and linked to two very different visions of what the EU should be: a new and independent entity or just the existing Member States, working together.

The difficulty that this opposition entailed for the EU helps to explain why aid to Greece was postponed for half a year, until 2 May 2010. For one thing, it made things very hard for the German leadership. The more that Germany insisted on a bilateral solution, the more its own contribution to the loan was

[35] M. Walker, C. Forelle, and B. Blackstone, 'On the Secret Committee to Save the Euro, a Dangerous Divide', *The Wall Street Journal*, 24 September 2010 (available at <http://online.wsj.com/article/SB10001424052748703467004575464113605731560.html?mod=WSJEUROPE_hps_LEFTTopWhatNews>).

[36] Treaty of Lisbon Amending the Treaty on European Union and the Treaty Establishing the European Community, 13 December 2007 (2007/C 306/01).

emphasized—and the more it also became obvious to the German citizens that they were supposed to pay for 'other people' rather than for 'their own'.

Merkel had an important election in North Rhine-Westphalia on 9 May 2010, and commentators early began to say that this made her want to postpone any concrete decision to give aid to Greece. The hostility to Greeks that emerged in the German mass media during the Spring of 2010 also shows how difficult the political situation was for Merkel.

While it is clear that the delay in helping Greece until 2 May 2010 was very costly for Europe, it should also be noted that it was probably less Merkel herself than the combination of aid opponents (such as Merkel) and aid proponents (such as Sarkozy) that made the situation deteriorate in the Spring of 2010. I have earlier argued that for confidence to be stable, you need an alignment of proxy sign with the economic reality (+/+ or -/-). In this case, however, there was a non-alignment of a special kind (+/-). Some political actors first said 'yes, aid has been decided and will come', which was then followed by other actors who said 'no' and stopped the EU from providing the aid.

Before looking at the way that the EU reactions unfolded after the Greek statistics scandal in October 2009, it must be emphasized that we currently know very little about what actually made the various EU actors act as they did. The situation is even harder to read since many actors said one thing, just to calm the markets, and then acted in a different way. Archival research, interviews, and autobiographical accounts of what happened at the various meetings of EU leaders and their Finance Ministers will eventually make it possible to piece together the story. In the meantime, one has to rely on fragments—while also noting that this is about as much information as the markets actors typically have.[37]

It seems that it took awhile after October 2009 before the EU understood the danger that Greece represented. The European Central Bank (ECB), for example, cut off some of its facilities for banks, which it had installed during the first round of the financial crisis in the late Autumn of 2009. One reason was no doubt that the ECB did not realize how vulnerable Greece was. Like other members of the EU, Greece had for a long time been able to draw on the strength that came from being associated with the EU. In its capacity as a member of the eurozone, Greece had also for years been able to sell its bonds at practically the same low rates of interest as Germany.[38]

Eventually, however, the EU began to act, and in December 2009, EU countries expressed their verbal support for Greece. By this time rumours also began to circulate that a loan would eventually be made. At this early stage it was made clear by the leading EU countries that the IMF would not be involved. The French associated the IMF with US supremacy and the Germans viewed its potential

[37] This Chapter draws primarily on the international press (especially *The New York Times, The Wall Street Journal*, and the *Financial Times*). I have also consulted *Bloomberg News*, various EU documents, and some other writings.

[38] See Figure 6.3.

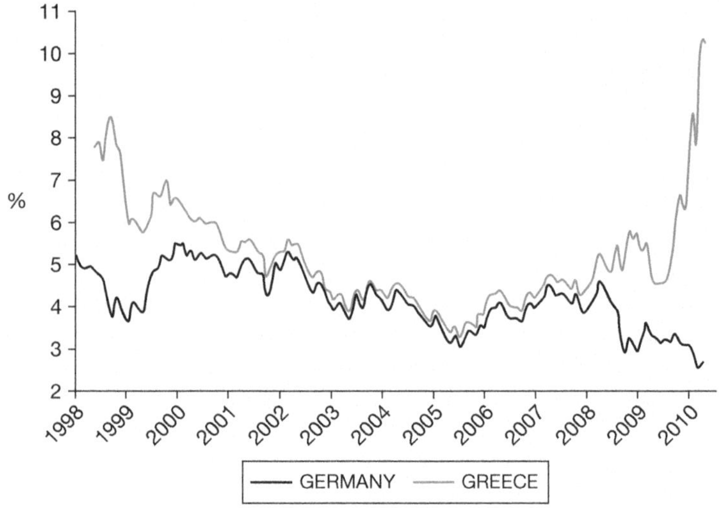

Figure 6.3 Ten-Year Bond Yield for Germany and Greece, January 1998–August 2010

Comment: Greece joined the euro in 2001, the financial crisis began in August 2007, and the Greek statistics scandal broke in late October 2009.

Source: Bloomberg Terminals.

participation in a loan as a loss of prestige. 'We don't need the IMF', to cite Axel Weber, the powerful President of the Bundesbank.[39]

Despite the talk of a loan in December 2009, no concrete measures were taken. During January and early February 2010, the rumours that the EU was going to offer Greece a loan intensified. On 11 February 2010, Van Rompuy, the President of the European Council, said on CNBC that 'there is an agreement', and a few days later the EU Finance Ministers announced their intention to assist Greece. According to leaks and rumours in the international press, the loan was to be in the range of 20–25 billion euro and to be managed in a strictly bilateral fashion. The credit was going to come both from states (in the form of loans via state controlled banks) and from private banks in the respective countries. Germany especially insisted on the bilateral nature of the loan.

But just as insistent as these rumours were in early to mid-February, equally insistent were the denials by Merkel and the European Commission some time later. Greece can manage very well itself, was one line; another that Greece had not asked for help.

During the month of March, Greece's need for aid was getting close to desperate, and the rate of interest it had to pay was shooting up rapidly. During the first part of the month Germany countered with the idea of creating a

[39] 'No the IMF Aid Expected for Greece: EU to Solve Financial Fiasco Alone', *SpiegelOnlineInternational*, 14 December 2009 (available at <http://www.spiegel.de/international/europe/0,1518,669215,00.html#ref=rss>).

European equivalent to the IMF, a European Monetary Fund. The European Commission endorsed the idea, while some market actors wondered if the whole thing was not really meant as a signal to Greece that it would not get a loan for a long time. The delay that the creation of a new EU institution meant did not, however, seem to deter Merkel, who said that 'a quick act of solidarity is definitely not the right answer. Rather, the right answer is to seize the problem at the roots'.[40]

During the second half of March, key EU members changed their view of the IMF and now decided that they wanted it to participate in a loan to Greece. The IMF itself was eager to get in on the action. On 25 March 2010, a loan to Greece was announced, and it amounted to 45 billion euro at a few percentage points lower than the market price.

The loan could only be used as a last resource, however. This meant that the loan was not distributed, and that the project of providing Greece with some resources therefore continued to be on the agenda in April. During this month, the economic situation of Greece continued to deteriorate and was soon close to catastrophic. Greece was at this point described as 'a sinking ship' by its Prime Minister.[41]

By the time that the negotiations for the 45 billion euro loan had become concrete and everything was set to go, however, the situation had changed dramatically. More than twice the amount was now needed to take care of Greece's needs, and the figure had risen to 110 billion euro. The loan was hastily put together and agreed upon on 2 May 2010, with the IMF contributing 30 billion euro.

The 2 May 2010 agreement made it possible for Greece to roll over its debts for the next few years without having to use the international financial market. It did this at a very steep price—by adding 110 billion euro at 5 per cent to its debt. Greece, as already mentioned, also had to undertake a number of radical reforms and cut its budget. The key issue for Greece—how to increase the productivity of the economy so it could pay off its debts was not addressed in the loan. The 110 billion euro loan was a stop-gap measure and nothing else.

IV. The Peak of the European Debt Crisis (late April—early May 2010)

While the disclosure of the hidden losses of Greece may have triggered some of the development that led the 2 May 2010 loan, it is clear that the major cause of

[40] 'Merkel Wants Scope to Expel Eurozone Troublemakers', *EurActiv.com*, 18 March 2010 (available at <http://www.euractiv.com/priorities/merkel-wants-scope-expel-eurozon-news-354178>).

[41] N. Kitsantonis and M. Saltmarsh, 'Greece, Out of Ideas, Requests Global Aid', *New York Times*, 23 April 2010 (available at <http://www.nytimes.com/2010/04/24/business/global/24drachma.html>).

the decline of the Greek economy had to do with its own economic state and how it had been affected by the financial crisis. Two of the main sources of income of the country, tourism and transportation, had been especially hard hit by the turmoil in the European economy from the Autumn of 2008 onwards.

During 2009 it was gradually realized that the financial crisis had also had a very severe impact on the EU countries in general, including the eurozone countries. Already in the Autumn of 2008, emergency measures had to be taken to save many individual banks as well as entire national banking systems. At a meeting on 12 October 2008, it was also decided that each country in the EU should guarantee its own banking system.

Many of the losses in the financial sector that now came about were allowed to remain hidden, in the hope that things would improve. The general economic development in each country was also, to repeat, deeply affected by the financial crisis. The average rise in deficit in relation to GDP for the year 2008–2009 was 4.3 per cent for the EU countries and 4.5 per cent for eurozone countries.[42]

In January 2010, the spread for Greek ten-year bonds was going up and the same also started to happen with Spanish bonds. For the first time since the introduction of the euro in 1999, voices began argue that the eurozone might fall apart and the euro go down with it. Nouriel Roubini, for example, told Bloomberg News in an interview around this time that a very dangerous development had been set in motion by the Greek debacle, and that in a few years it could lead to 'a break-up of the monetary union'.[43] He described the fiscal difficulties that the eurozone countries found themselves in as 'a new phenomenon'. He noted that the bond investors so far 'have been asleep at the wheel', but that they were about to wake up.

Trichet countered by labelling the idea of the EU breaking up as 'absurd'; he also stated that the difficulties of Spain and Ireland did not constitute a threat to the eurozone.[44] Soros, who was following the financial crisis very closely, took an intermediary stance and noted that while the economic crisis in Greece had made it clear that the eurozone had its weak points, there also existed a 'strong force' that held it together.[45]

Bond investors, however, continued to worry, and as the aid to Greece from the EU was postponed over and over again, the costs to borrow money on the international market continued to rise. As with Greece, the downgrades of the bonds of Spain, Portugal and Italy by the three major rating agencies accompanied and probably worsened this development. In brief, the problems of Greece had set off a contagion process that was now threatening to engulf the EU as a whole.

[42] 'Euro Area and EU27 Government Deficit at 6.3 per cent and 6.8 per cent of GDP Respectively' (2010) 55 *Eurostat NewsRelease* (available at <http://epp.eurostat.ec.europa.eu/cache/ITY_PUBLIC/2-26042011-AP/EN/2-26042011-AP-EN.PDF>).

[43] T. Keene, 'Roubini Pessimistic on Euro Area, Calls Spain a Risk', *Bloomberg News*, 27 January 2010 (available at <http://www.bloomberg.com/apps/news?pid=newsarchive&sid=aVW11LBGT.08>).

[44] Keene, n 43. [45] Keene, n 43.

At this point, it may be useful to return to the topic of the legal and socio-economic networks. Banks and states are linked to each other in a complex way in the eurozone as well as in the EU as a whole, and the crisis that was now beginning, was spreading through this network. How it was spread was partly decided by its structure.

Many of the links in this network were of the legal kind, constituting a deposit, a loan, or some new financial product. While this may seem straightforward enough and make the situation easy to conceptualize and analyse in network terms, this is not the case. The size and type of the transactions matter—and so do the size and the solvency of the actors. To this should be added a number of other factors, including the geographical location of the actor, and if the actor is a subsidiary or owned by another actor. Most of this information is currently not only lacking for Europe during the Spring of 2009, it is unlikely to ever be available.

At a more abstract level, one can nevertheless distinguish certain ways through which an economic crisis, such as the euro crisis, spreads and does damage. The longer the chains of links between the actors are, for example, the more the actors can be affected negatively by a loss at one end of the chain. This may be referred to as *a domino effect*. One may also speak of *an integration effect*, since the more integrated an area is—and the eurozone has become more integrated since 1999—the more it will be affected by a major loss suffered by one actor. And the more a geographic continent is linked to other continents, the more these latter are likely to be affected—something we may term *the globalization effect*.

There also exist so-called contingent contracts, and these add further complexity to the network dynamics involved. One may speak of *contingent legal debts*, and one example of this would be a credit default swap, which is only activated under certain circumstances. One may also speak of *contingent social debts*; an example would be what economists call moral hazard. If a major bank goes down, the state where it is situated may be under pressure to step in and cover its debts. These contingent debts may affect existing networks in unpredictable ways, especially if these debts were not previously known but just suddenly appeared.

Finally, when hidden debts are suddenly disclosed, market actors tend to panic and play it safe by not doing business with any actor who belongs to the same category as the actor who got into trouble in the first place. This happened, for example, with the money market after Lehman Brothers went bankrupt. One of the firms in this market was linked to Lehman Brothers and when it experienced trouble, the whole money market froze up. While this type of reaction can probably be conceptualized in terms of networks, it may make more sense to cast it in terms of reacting to *categories* of actors, as opposed to specific individual actors.

We currently know very little about the way that the contagion accelerated and spread in Europe during the Spring of 2010. It is clear, however, that as the Greek bonds were devalued, all banks and other financial institutions that owned some of these were faced with the situation that they might have to acknowledge these losses. It is also clear that the ECB's policy of accepting the bonds of all member states as equally valid collateral had encouraged banks in different EU countries to buy bonds with a slightly higher yield, in order to earn a small but (seemingly) safe profit.[46] This way the bad debt was spread around.[47]

It is obvious that the economic difficulties that the eurozone countries experienced after the first round of the financial crisis (2008–2009) played an important part in the contagion that took place in the Spring of 2010. Money represents a form of interest; like water, it will tend to flow where it can.

Another important factor may also have been at play and it was of an even more sociological character. This was the investor perception of the EU and the eurozone as one single unit. European unity is often discussed in terms of how its citizens view the EU, but a group's unity is also decided by the way that it is seen by outside actors. In evaluating eurozone bonds, the investors oriented their actions to the EU or the eurozone, rather than to its individual members (to use Weberian language). This is evidenced by the strong convergence in the spread for ten-year bonds of such countries as Spain, Portugal, Italy, and Germany from the very creation of the euro in 1999.[48] This is also true for Greece, which joined the EU in 1981 and the eurozone in 2001.[49]

What the spread for 1ten-year bonds also shows is that once the crisis began, the convergence ended and each country now started to be seen—and evaluated—as its own separate entity by the investors.[50] From a sociological perspective, it would seem that as the higher and emergent social unit was broken up, attention was switched to its parts, and the orientation of the investors went from the overall unit to its parts. Also this time a new evaluation took place of each country by itself. 'New' costs suddenly appeared, when eyes were turned from the EU to individual countries, such as Italy, Spain, Portugal, and so on.

[46] G. Soros, 'The Sovereign Debt Problem', Lecture given at the World Leaders Forum, Columbia University, 5 October 2010 (transcript available at <http://www.georgesoros.com/interviews-speeches/entry/the_sovereign_debt_problem/>).

[47] Soros, n 46, writes: '[s]o even though member countries [in the euro zone] share a common currency, when it comes to sovereign credit they are on their own. Unfortunately, this fact was obscured until recently by the willingness of the European Central Bank to accept the sovereign debt of all member countries on equal terms at its discount window. This allowed the member countries to borrow at practically the same interest rate as Germany and the banks were happy to earn a few extra pennies on supposedly risk-free assets by loading up their balance sheets with the government debt of the weaker countries. For instance, European banks hold more than a trillion euro of Spanish debt, of which more than half is held by German and French banks. The large positions came to endanger the creditworthiness of the European banking system, depriving them of the capacity to add to their positions.'

[48] See Figure 6.4. [49] See Figure 6.3. [50] See Figure 6.5.

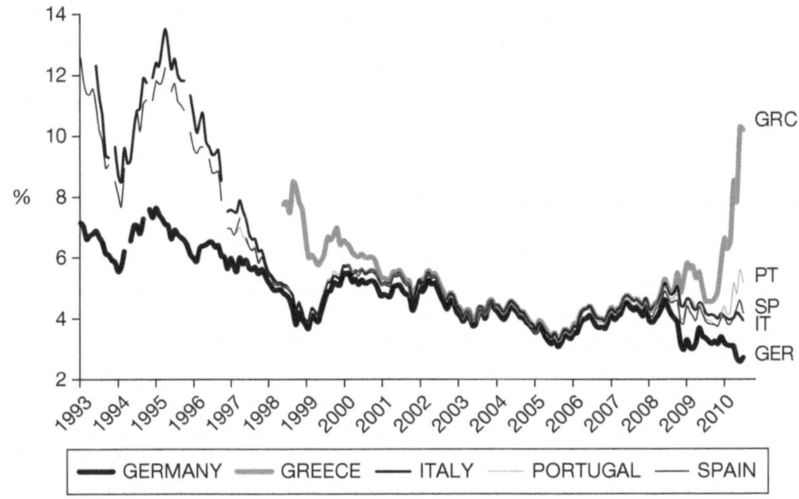

Figure 6.4 Ten-Year Bond Yield for Germany and GIPS Countries, January 1993–August 2010

Comment: The euro was created in 1999 and the Greek statistics scandal took place in late October 2009.

Source: Bloomberg Terminals.

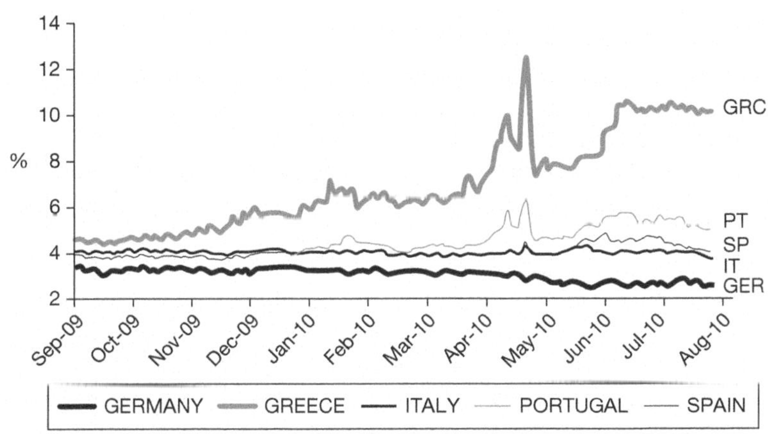

Figure 6.5 Ten-Year Bond Yield for Germany and GIPS Countries, September 2009–August 2010

Comment: The Greek statistics scandal took place in late October 2009 and the 750 billion euro facility was arranged for on 10 May 2010.

Source: Bloomberg Terminals.

We here see another side of the problem mentioned earlier: the federal view of Europe versus the bilateral or intergovernmental view. To decide whether to act in unison or separately is a problem that has plagued the EU from the very beginning of the financial crisis. Shortly after the collapse of Lehman

Brothers in September 2008, attempts were made, primarily by France, to coordinate the European response to the crisis.[51] Germany, however, firmly opposed it and demonstratively acted on its own to insure its banks on 5 October.[52]

The official decision to let each country fend for itself was announced at a meeting of the European leaders on 12 October. George Soros describes the situation in the financial world at the time of the meeting in the following way:

> Conditions in the financial system continued to deteriorate. The commercial paper market grounded to a halt, LIBOR rose, swap spreads widened, CDSs blew out, and investment banks and other financial institutions without direct access to the Federal Reserve could not get access to overnight or short-term credit. The Fed had to extend one lifeline after another. It was in this atmosphere that the International Monetary Fund (the IMF) held its annual meeting in Washington, starting on October 11, 2008. The European leaders left early and met in Paris on Sunday October 12. At that meeting they decided to guarantee, in effect, that no major European financial institution would be allowed to fail. They could not agree, however, to do this on an inclusive Europe-wide basis, so each country set up its own arrangements.... After a heated debate in which Germany resisted a Europe-wide solution, it was decided that each country should guarantee its own financial system.[53]

With this in mind, let us move back to the Spring of 2010. The contagion that had begun in January 2010 made a qualitative leap in April, and towards the end of this month, and in the first few days of May, many feared that the very financial system of Europe and perhaps of the whole world would come apart. After the collapse of Lehman Brothers in September 2008, systemic risks emerged several times in the US. It also did so during the period between the end of April and early May 2010, and this time it took place in Europe.

One can cite many examples of important actors who thought that a systemic crisis was present. According to the IMF, there were 'tensions [during these days] threatening a financial meltdown'. And according to OECD's General Secretary, the crisis had begun 'threatening the stability of the financial system'.[54] The EU's President would later say that 'we were on the edge of a breakdown. At a certain moment it could have become a world crisis'.[55] Trichet said that 'it looked somewhat like the situation in mid-September 2008 after the Lehman Brothers'

[51] N. Kulish and G. Bowley, 'Facing a Financial Crisis, European Nations Put Self-Interest First', *New York Times*, 7 October 2008 (available at <http://www.nytimes.com/2008/10/08/world/europe/08unity.html>).

[52] D. Gow and A. Chrisafis, 'German Deposits Guarantee Blows Hole in EU's Action Plan' *The Guardian*, 6 October 2008 (available at <http://www.theguardian.com/business/2008/oct/06/europe.germany>).

[53] G. Soros, *The Crash of 2008 and What It Means* (New York: Public Affairs, 2009) 162, 212.

[54] 'Euro Area Policies: 2010 Article IV Consultation—Staff Report', IMF Country Report No 10/221, July 2010 (available at <http://www.imf.org/external/pubs/ft/scr/2010/cr10221.pdf>) 7; A. Davis and E. Ross-Thomas, 'Merkel Vows Faster Greek Aid as Spain Shows Contagion', *Bloomberg.com*, 28 April 2010 (available at <http://www.bloomberg.com/apps/news?pid=newsarchive&sid=aoEjq.BGmM2o>).

[55] T. Barber, 'A Tent to Attend To', *Financial Times*, 17 June 2010 (available at <http://www.ft.com/cms/s/0/49b000ae-79a7-11df-85be-00144feabdc0.html>).

bankruptcy'. He also added that 'contagion...can occur quickly. Sometimes it is a question of half days'.[56]

The actors who were involved in arranging the 110 billion euro loan to Greece on 2 May 2010 understood very quickly that they had failed to stop the crisis. From this point until the early hours of 10 May 2010 when the EU announced the creation of a 750 billion euro facility to fight the crisis, a truly dramatic set of events took place. During the first ten days in May, the EU was the eye of the storm, as the French Minister of Finance put it.[57]

While many details of what happened during these days are not yet known, the broad outlines of what took place are clear enough.[58] On 6 May 2010, the flash crash took place in New York and the Greek bonds tumbled even further. On Friday, 7 May 2010, the eurozone leaders met in Brussels and understood that they had to act forcefully. On Sunday and Monday morning, 9–10 May 2010, the actual deal was hammered out by EU Finance Ministers.

On 7 May 2010, Sarkozy arrived early to the meeting in Brussels and spent the extra time rounding up support for making a forceful intervention in the crisis in the name of the EU as opposed to a bilateral deal. By the time that Merkel arrived, much had already been decided, to her great dismay. 'When she was told [what had happened]', according to one source, 'she looked like a boxer who had been punched in the chest'.[59]

Things, however, would get worse and not only for Merkel. Trichet was present during the meeting and handed out material that showed how the markets were diving all over the world, set off by the eurozone crisis. One participant recalls Trichet saying, 'this isn't only a problem for one country [Greece]. It's several countries. It's Europe. It's global. It's a situation that is deteriorating with extreme rapidity and intensity.'[60]

The audience was stunned by Trichet's message. According to an EU ambassador 'Sarkozy was white with shock. I've never seen him so pale.'[61] Some of Sarkozy's anger was immediately directed at the ECB and its policy of not buying member states' bonds. One participant recalls how 'Sarkozy was screaming [to Trichet]: "Come on, come on, stop hesitating".'[62] Trichet, however, did not budge,

[56] Interview with Jean-Claude Trichet, 19 May 2010, *Frankfurter Allgemeine Zeitung*, 20 May 2010 (available at <http://www.ecb.europa.eu/press/key/date/2010/html/sp100521.en.html>).

[57] L. Kassenaar and M. Deen, 'France's Power Broker', *Bloomberg Markets*, August 2010, pp 44–7 (available at <http://www.scribd.com/doc/33952087/Bloomberg-Markets-201008>).

[58] M. Walker, C. Forelle, and B. Blackstone, 'Currency Union Teetering, "Mr Euro" Was Forced To Act', *The Wall Street Journal*, 26 September 2010 (available at <http://online.wsj.com/article/SB10001424052748703904304575497871279626904.html?mod=WSJEUROPE_hps_LEFTTopStories>).

[59] L. Baker, 'Timeline: The EU's $ 1 Trillion Rescue: How It Happened' *Reuters*, 10 May 2010 (available, on 25 August 2010, at <http://in.biz.yahoo.com/100510/137/bavkaq.html?utm_source=twitterfeed&utm_medium=twitter>)

[60] T. Barber, 'Saving the Euro, I: Dinner on the Edge of the Abyss', *Financial Times*, 10 October 2010 (available at <http://www.ft.com/intl/cms/s/0/190b32ae-d49a-11df-b230-00144feabdc0.html#axzz1a10hSrrW>).

[61] Barber, n 61. [62] Barber, n 61.

since he wanted the EU leaders to commit to a major intervention before revealing his decision to let the ECB buy member states' bonds.

With Trichet impossible to move, Sarkozy again started to push for his view that it was the EU that must act, not the individual states.[63] 'This is the moment of truth', he said, 'we must act'. Having arrived late, Merkel was at a clear disadvantage, but she nonetheless tried to block a decision until she knew the details of Sarkozy's plan. When she realized that these were quite hazy and that the deal itself was much too federally minded for her taste, she went against Sarkozy's proposal.

The deadlock between Merkel and Sarkozy was broken by the EU President Van Rompuy, who proposed the creation of a 'stabilization fund', with the details worked out by the Finance Ministers over the weekend.[64] This was accepted by the participants who directed the European Commission to design a 'stabilization mechanism' to be later worked out by the Finance Ministers.[65]

When the meeting was over, Sarkozy felt like a winner and held a triumphant press conference, while Merkel quickly disappeared looking 'utterly humiliated'.[66] S Sarkozy told the assembled world press that 'today we face an attack on the whole of Europe, not just Greece. We had to respond with community mechanisms, not just bilateral loans as it was the case of Greece'.[67] He announced that the whole deal would be in place on Monday morning and that he had imposed his will '95 per cent'.[68]

The sense that the market was endangering the whole project of the EU as well as the euro was very strong among the Finance Ministers who assembled in Brussels on Sunday, 9 May 2010. The Swedish Finance Minister told the press in an oft- quoted statement that 'we now see... wolf pack behaviour [in the financial markets], and if we will not stop these packs, even if it is self-inflicted weakness, they will tear the weaker countries apart'.[69]

Once the meeting began, however, strong differences in opinion soon emerged between those who were for and those who were against a federal solution. Germany and Spain refused to accept the Commission's proposal, which was defended by France and the Nordic countries. The discussion got so heated that at one point one of the participants bit off a tooth. After a few hours of discussion, the French Finance Minister also privately told her delegation that the eurozone was on the verge of breaking up.[70]

[63] M. Walker and D. Gauthier-Villars, 'The "Opposite Twins" Clash Over the Future of Europe', *The Wall Street Journal*, 2 July 2010 (available at http://online.wsj.com/article/NA_WSJ_PUB:SB10001424052748704853404575323142895146902.html>).

[64] Walker, Forelle, and Blackstone, n 59. [65] Barber, n 61.

[66] Charlemagne, 'The Euro Crisis: Glimmers of a Plan for Saving the Euro', *The Economist*, 9 May 2010 (available at <http://www.economist.com/blogs/chalemagne/2010/05/euro_crisis_1>).

[67] A. Willis and V. Pop,'Euro Area Races to Set up Crisis Fund', *EUObserver.com*, 8 May 2010 (available at <http://euobserver.com/9/30038>).

[68] Walke and Gauthier-Villars, n 64.

[69] N. Hume, 'Stopping the Wolfpack', *Financial Times*, 9 May 2010 (available at <http://ftalphaville.ft.com/blog/2010/05/09/224426/stopp8ing-the-wolfpack/>).

[70] Walker, Forelle and Blackstone, n 35.

After a break to cool things down, suggested by the French Finance Minister, an agreement was finally reached. The German line had won on all major points. The deal was sealed in the early morning hours of 10 May 2010, just a few minutes before the markets in Asia opened. By this time the results from the important North Rhine-Westphalia election were also in, which made it easier for Germany to back the deal.

Trichet, who had refused to move before a deal had been made, now made an announcement that the ECB was ready to buy bonds of member countries.[71] His announcement that the ECB was ready to go for its 'nuclear option' was met with relief by the Finance Ministers, since it was believed that without an active intervention in the markets by the ECB, the markets might continue to go down.[72]

The amount involved in the 10 May 2010 deal—750 billion Euros—was a testimony to the attempt of the EU leaders to stop the crisis through a big blow-out ('shock and awe'). The strategy succeeded. The prices for European bonds immediately shot up, as did prices on the world's stock markets. The VIX, or the fear index, took a sharp dive.

But it was also clear that those who had wanted to see the deal as a manifestation of European unity had failed, and that the bilateral strategy of Merkel and her supporters in the EU had won. The European Commission was not, as it had wanted, in charge of the new European Financial Stability Facility (EFSF), and no Eurobonds were to be issued to finance it.

The actual aid package looked very different. It consisted of three separate parts. There was first of all the EFSF itself, with a capacity to make 440 billion euro in loans, drawn from resources from individual member countries. Then there was the 60 billion euro to be raised and controlled by the European Commission, and then 250 billion euro from the IMF. The EFSF did not become a permanent institution linked to the EU, as the federalists had wanted. Instead it was to be a temporary organization, lasting only three years and housed in Luxembourg. Its loans were to be bilateral in nature, with each country (including the ones in deep economic trouble) contributing a proportional part of every loan.

The 10 May 2010 deal was hastily put together, and it was well understood by the actors involved that it would not solve the difficult economic situation that faces the EU and the eurozone countries. A short time after the deal had been announced, the yield for the bonds of countries such as Greece, Spain, Italy, and Portugal began to rise again. This would also be the case for some time.[73]

Since 10 May 2010, two major attempts to deal with the difficult situation in Europe and restore confidence have been made: radical budget cuts and bank stress tests. The first is that severe budget cuts were announced in a number of EU and eurozone countries. A debate was also started up as to whether these will improve the situation or endanger it by negatively affecting economic growth. Trichet, as well as the EU countries, have come out very strongly in favour of

[71] Walker, Forelle, and Blackstone, n 59; Barber, n 61. [72] Barber, n 61.
[73] See Figure 6.5.

moving ahead with radical budget cuts. At a meeting of G-20 in Toronto on 26–27 June 2010, the EU succeeded in getting the advanced economies to unite around the project of budget cuts, despite strong resistance from the US.

There exist some problems with this position, one of which is that there exists little knowledge of what actually determines the prices of state bonds. Or, to phrase it differently, we have little knowledge of what it is that makes investors in the international bond market behave as they do. At what point, for example, do the so-called bond vigilantes decide to lay off a specific country, and what difference does it make to have the EU as a whole guarantee its member countries rather than each country being on its own? It also remains unclear how you can simultaneously make deep cuts *and* increase economic growth. During the early Autumn of 2010, the push for budget discipline has continued.

The stress tests on European banks were conducted in the Summer of 2010 and the results made public on 23 July 2010. It was at this time well known in financial circles that the European banks were in bad shape and had plenty of hidden losses, thanks to the difficulties they had experienced after the collapse of Lehman Brothers. As a result, many of the banks were, by the Spring of 2009, unable to borrow in the international markets and had to rely on the ECB for funds. The idea with the stress tests was that by laying bare the weaknesses of the European banks, investors would regain confidence in them.

The actual tests, however, did not probe very deeply into the financial state of the banks. All government bonds, including those from Greece, were evaluated at full value, as long as they were kept off of the trading books of the banks, which they typically were. Other ways of concealing the actual state of the banks were also allowed in the tests.

On 23 July 2010, the authorities in charge of the stress tests nevertheless announced that the state of European banks was fine. Only seven out of 91 banks had failed the tests, and these only needed 3.5 billion euro in extra capital rather than the tens of billions that many expected. Several banks that no investor wanted to touch were declared healthy. Confidence in the banks was nonetheless somewhat restored, even if it is clear that problems remain—in Germany, Ireland, Spain, and so on.

V. Concluding Remarks: Contracts, Confidence, and Contagion

> My main message is that the centre must be given a greater role in national fiscal policy if EMU is to become a more effective, and more resilient, monetary union. But of course I recognize that such a delegation of fiscal powers to the centre could meet political resistance in some countries, where the appetite for ceding further control to Brussels is already weak.[74]

[74] D. Strauss-Kahn, Managing Director of the IMF, 13 October 2010, cited after T. Barber, 'Saving the Euro, III: Bound Towards a Tense Future', *Financial Times*, 13 October 2010, p 9 (available at <http://www.ft.com/intl/cms/s/0/c5fcc1e4-d643-11df-81f0-00144feabdc0.html#axzz1a10hSrrW>).

What does the future of Europe look like from the perspective of this Chapter? The international financial system has been very unstable since the decline of the Bretton Woods system in the early 1970s.[75] The amount of money that flows forth and back in the world is today truly astronomical, and the number of financial crises has accelerated during the last few decades.[76] There is also the fact that the European countries have been seriously weakened by the first round of the financial crisis (2008–2009) as well as by its second round (Spring of 2010 and onwards). The projections for growth in Europe are not positive, and its banks have huge amounts of hidden losses. To judge from experience, it will take something like a decade for Europe before there will be vigorous growth.[77]

It would also seem that there exists no easy solution to the ongoing fight between those who want a federal Europe and those who want a more bilateral and intergovernmental one. If one or the other of these two tendencies could win out, it would be easier to re-establish confidence, something which is very difficult in any case.

If each country was on its own, investors could evaluate it exclusively on its own merits. And if the federalists won out, investors would probably once again start to view individual countries as part of a larger emerging whole, a bit like they did during 1999–2009, when the bond yields for eurozone countries strongly converged. In this case, it would not matter so much if an individual country was in poor economic shape, since it would be seen as a part of a whole. The community, to speak in Durkheimian terms, would protect it.

But a decisive victory for one or the other of these two tendencies does not seem very likely. To this should be added the way that the eurozone is currently constructed, with a common central bank but little else in terms of common economic governance. From the sociological perspective of this Chapter, this practically amounts to an institutionalization of the contradiction between the parts and the whole. And we know from experience today that this is particularly dangerous in difficult economic times and can even lead to systemic crises.

The link between confidence and contagion in networks is also worth exploring in detail. I have pointed out that from a networks perspective, there is a difference between ordinary legal contracts and contingent contracts, and also that legal networks and social networks may overlap but are by no means always identical. Hidden costs help to create a very special networks dynamics and, in doing so,

[75] J. Buchanan, 'The Constitutionalization of Money' (2010) 30 *Cato Journal*, 251–8; J. Eatwell and L. Taylor, *Global Finance at Risk: The Case for International Regulation* (Cambridge: Polity Press, 2000).

[76] Reihnart and Rogoff, n 33.

[77] C. Reinhart and V. Reinhart, 'After the Fall', paper presented at the Federal Reserve Bank of Kansas City Economic Policy Symposium, *Macroeconomic Policy: Post-Crisis and Risks Ahead*, Jackson Hole, Wyoming (available at <https://ideas.repec.org/a/fip/fedkpr/y2010p17-60.html>).

create new losses. Markets can freeze up, as they did after the collapse of Lehman Brothers, when investors were unnerved by hidden losses and decided to be cautious and not do any business. In short, confidence, contracts and contagion are all closely interrelated—and present the social scientist studying networks with formidable challenges.[78]

[78] Attempts are currently being made to conceptualize situations such as the current financial crisis in network terms. One of these is described as follows: Andrew Lo, a Professor and Director of the Laboratory for Financial Engineering at the Massachusetts Institute of Technology, sees the global financial system as the universe, where each financial centre is a galaxy: a collection of stars, planets, and other celestial objects held close to each other by their own gravity—in this case, the trades and contracts that tie them together. If you could chart the entire universe and measure all the forces connecting every object inside it, you would have what economists and other scientists call a network map. To Lo, fully understanding what's going on in the markets requires the entire map—not just one value-at-risk number, but every major transaction that connects one entity to another, reported daily (D. Altman, 'The Network: How a Map Can Prevent the Next Financial Crisis', *The Nation*, 9 October 2009 (available at <http://www.tnr.com/article/ecnomy/the-network?page=0,1>). Setting up a solid information base capturing global financial exposures is imperative. There is a long list of exposures that are not transparent today, for example the cross-border links between large, complex financial institutions (LCFIs) and the whereabouts of credit default swaps, collateralized debt obligations and other asset-backed securities. Putting together a global 'risk map' displaying financial links among LCFIs as well as the most important risk drivers, such as asset price changes and yield spread dynamics, would enable authorities to carry out financial system stress tests. Otmar Issing and Jan Krahen are working on a similar project, which would entail constructing a global 'risk map'. They describe it as follows: '[s]etting up a solid information base capturing global financial exposures is imperative. There is a long list of exposures that are not transparent today, for example the cross-border links between large, complex financial institutions (LCFIs) and the whereabouts of credit default swaps, collateralised debt obligations and other asset-backed securities. Putting together a global "risk map" displaying financial links among LCFIs as well as the most important risk drivers, such as asset price changes and yield spread dynamics, would enable authorities to carry out financial system stress tests. The basis for the risk map would be a global database. We have proposed that standards be defined by a task force of experienced international agencies, such as BIS, the European Central Bank, the Organisation for Economic Co-operation and Development and the International Monetary Fund, allowing the data to be aggregated by region or by product. Data privacy conditions and capacity limits mean data collection must be defined on a discrete – for example, quarterly – basis. The risk map project could be chaired by the IMF. Data sharing could be on an aggregated level to preserve data privacy and to maintain a level playing field for international competition. Furthermore, data analysis would focus on an early warning methodology and a general assessment of systemic risk, which in turn could feed directly into the minimum capital requirement of international banks. Such a hard-wiring of systemic risk analysis to capital standards would allow supervisors to carry out counter-cyclical policies.' (O. Issing and J. Krahnen, 'Why the Regulators Must have a Global "Risk Map"', *Financial Times*, 18 February 2009 (available, on 18 February 2009, at <http://www.rediff.com/money/2009/feb/20bcrisis-why-the-regulators-must-have-a-global-risk-map.htm>).

Networks in Socio-economic Perspective: A Proposal for Financial Regulatory Reform

Comment on R. Swedberg, 'Contractual Networks in Socio-economic Perspective: The Case of the European Financial Crisis (2009–2010)'

*Marc Amstutz**

I. Swedberg on Confidence in the Financial System

Swedberg has given us a sobering account of the first year in the European sovereign debt crisis, the seriousness of which became apparent in the Autumn of 2009, when it emerged as a new phase in the continuing global financial crisis. Based on this account, he has proposed the following hypothesis: financial crises are a *problem of confidence*. And the problem with this problem is that we do not yet have a generally accepted theory of confidence in crisis situations. Because of this, Swedberg has taken it upon himself to sketch out the foundations for such a theory. His point of departure is the following 'core idea', as already articulated in an earlier work:

> [C]onfidence has to do with people's tendency to base their actions on...*proxy signs* for what some situation is like, in those cases where they lack direct knowledge of the situation.[1]

* Professor of Business Law, Economic Law, and Legal Theory at the University of Fribourg School of Law.

[1] R. Swedberg, 'The Structure of Confidence and the Collapse of Lehman Brothers' in M. Lounsbury and P. M. Hirsch (eds) *Markets on Trial: The Economic Sociology of the U.S. Financial Crisis* (Bingley: Emerald, 2011) 71–114, 102; this is a slightly revised version of a paper of the same name, delivered at the Markets on Trial Workshop, 23–5 October 2009 (Evanston, IL) and published online as CSES Working Paper Series, Paper No 50 (2009) (available at <http://www.economyandsociety.org/wp-content/uploads/2013/08/wp50_Swedberg_LehmanBrothers.pdf>).

It follows from this idea that confidence exhibits a *double structure*, which Swedberg explains as follows:

By this I mean that human beings are able to make important judgements about some topic X, by relying on some proxy sign or proxy information about X, that we may call Y... This means that we have *confidence* in Y.[2]

What is the connection between confidence defined in this way and the financial crisis? Swedberg distinguishes between three possible constellations of circumstances:

(1) Where *proxy signs* correspond correctly to the economic situation, this inspires 'full confidence' among investors.[3]
(2) Where *proxy signs* are negative, even though the economic situation is, in fact, positive, this leads to the situation described by Merton as resulting from a *self-fulfilling prophecy*.[4]
(3) For Swedberg, however, the scenario in (2) above is not the most central problem in financial crises. The real cause of panic reactions is what Bagehot has termed *hidden losses*:
[W]hen hidden debts are suddenly disclosed, market actors tend to panic and play it safe by not doing business with any actor who belongs to the same category as the actor who got into trouble in the first place.[5]

In this connection, Swedberg emphasizes two points of great importance for the way in which relationships between the actors in financial markets function. He first notes that 'in a so-called *confidence relationship*, one actor has confidence that the other actor will do something, based on a proxy sign.'[6] Implicit in this relationship is the possibility—though certainly not the necessity—that there will be no direct or formalized contact between the market participants:

A confidence relationship can also include a *third party*—someone who guarantees the quality of the proxy sign, by virtue of his or her objectivity, special knowledge or the like. This is typical for a modern financial system, and rating agencies are an example of such a third party.[7]

Swedberg's second provocative observation relates to the cross-sectoral dimension of this confidence relationship:

Confidence in the financial system is not only economic, it is also political in nature and can be used as a political tool.[8]

By emphasizing specifically these two aspects of the confidence relationship, Swedberg focuses in on the role of *networks* in the financial system. The conclusion

[2] Swedberg, n 1, 71, 74. [3] Swedberg, n 1, 71, 75.
[4] Swedberg, n 1, 71, 75, referring to R. K. Merton, 'Self-Fulfilling Prophecy' (1948) 8 *Antioch Review* 193–210 (see R. Swedburg, *Social Theory and Social Structure* (New York: Free Press, 1968) 475–90).
[5] See Chapter 6; see also Swedberg, n 1, 71, 73–6. [6] Swedberg, n 1, 71, 103.
[7] Swedberg, n 1. [8] Swedberg, n 1.

to be drawn from this is that, in Swedberg's view, the smooth functioning of the capital markets is contingent upon the existence of *properly formatted* networks.

Swedberg's notion of a properly formatted network, it may be inferred, is one that is *so designed as to be able to produce* proxy signs *that correspond accurately to the actual state of the financial markets*. Within this hypothesis lies regulatory dynamite. For, if it is correct, the challenge it raises for regulators is nothing short of awe-inspiring, requiring simultaneous and coordinated intervention on two entirely different fronts:

- Swedberg's concept is constructed around an *actor-oriented* methodological approach, that is, a model of 'methodological individualism', which assumes rational behaviour on the part of the *individuals* who are active within a given sphere of activity—in this case, in the financial markets.[9, 10]
- Swedberg's methodological approach also relies on a specific *theory of networks*, that is, his thesis is constructed on the basis of an analysis of the relations between different actors who come, in part, from different sectors within the society (that is, the economic, political, legal or other such spheres). The regulatory problem here lies in the conceptualization of such networks.

In the following, I would like to elaborate somewhat further on the nature of these two, very real, regulatory problems.

II. Methodological Individualism: A Fallacy of Composition

In the foreword to the 11th ICMB-CEPR Geneva Report on the World Economy one reads the following:

The crisis which began in the US sub-prime mortgage market in early 2007... was not the first banking crisis. It was closer to the 100th. We can draw a few important implications

[9] Swedberg has elsewhere explained his approach to the analysis of social mechanisms as follows: 'proper explanation of change and variation at the macro level entails showing how macro states at one point in time influence the behavior of *individual* actors, and how these actions generate new macro states at a later time. That is, instead of analyzing relationships between phenomena exclusively on the macro level, *one should always try to establish how macro-level events or conditions affect the individual* (Step 1), how the *individual* assimilates the impact of these macro-level events (Step 2), and how *a number of individuals*, through their actions and interactions, generate macro-level outcomes (Step 3)' (emphases added); P. Hedström and R. Swedberg, 'Social Mechanisms: An Introductory Essay' in P. Hedström and R. Swedberg (eds) *Social Mechanisms* (Cambridge: Cambridge University Press, 1998) 21–2.

[10] The literature on methodological individualism is vast. For a recent treatment of the subject, which provides both an overview of the issues involved and argues sensibly that a proper understanding of sociological events requires simultaneous analysis from different perspectives, see R. Jepperson and J. W. Meyer, 'Multiple Levels of Analysis and the Limitations of Methodological Individualisms' (2011) 29 *Sociological Theory* 54–73; from a legal perspective, see R. Ahdieh, 'Beyond Individualism in Law and Economics' (2011) 91 *Boston University Law Review* 43–85; M. S. Zouboulakis, *The Varieties of Economic Rationalities: From Adam Smith to Comtemporary Behavioral and Evolutionary Economics* (London/New York: Routledge, 2014) 84–91, 125–38.

from this observation. If an event with widespread and severe economic and social consequences keeps on repeating itself, the onus is surely on the authorities to change something.[11]

The last sentence is worth reflecting upon. The statement that the burden of revising the design of the regulatory system is 'surely' incumbent upon the authorities is by no means absurd. At the same time, however, it is a simplification of the situation that calls for further explanation. It must be recalled, namely, that the authorities do not act randomly. Their operations are based on a certain vision of reality which has its origins in the social sciences.[12] This circumstance has even been recognized, with surprising frankness, by the authors of the Geneva Report:

> The current approach to systemic regulation implicitly assumes that we can make the system as a whole safe by simply trying to make sure that individual banks are safe. This sounds like a truism, but in practice it represents a fallacy of composition.[13]

The choice of words is felicitous: 'fallacy of composition' nicely articulates the flaw that renders Swedberg's meticulous analysis of confidence at the individual level inadequate as an explanation of systemic dysfunctions in the financial markets. The simple observation that there is a lack of confidence in the reliability of proxy signs on the part of individual investors or other financial actors does not logically permit any conclusions concerning the function of confidence in the financial system. Swedberg is, of course, fully aware that there is a gap in his thinking here. He attempts to bridge it by placing particular stress, as already mentioned, on the network-theoretical aspect of the role played by confidence in the financial system.

This does not change the fact, however, that Swedberg's analysis of the function of the networks that 'support' confidence in the financial system is grounded in the assumption that there is a direct connection between individual behaviour and systemic effects—a conception still firmly rooted in methodological individualism: macroscopic phenomena are seen as aggregates of microscopic behaviour. This may, at times, be the case, but in order to determine that, there is a need to differentiate between two types of aggregates. Some aggregates have a *simple* cumulative structure and represent nothing more than the sum of their parts. Where that is the case, the macroscopic picture is indeed an accumulation of individual behaviours.[14] By contrast, however, other aggregate effects have a *complex* structure, so that a discrepancy emerges between the motives of

[11] M. Brunnermeier, A. Crocket, C. Goodhart, A. D. Persaud, and H. S. Shin, *The Fundamental Principles of Financial Regulation: Geneva Reports on the World Economy 11* (Geneva: International Center for Monetary and Banking Studies (ICMB)/London: Centre for Economic Policy Research, 2009) xi.

[12] For a fuller treatment of this issue, see M. Amstutz, 'The Constitution of Contractual Networks' in M. Amstutz and G. Teubner (eds) *Networks: Legal Issues of Multilateral Co-operation* (Oxford/Portland, Oregon: Hart Publishing, 2008) 310–20.

[13] Amstutz, n 12.

[14] On the '*effets de composition*', see R. Boudon, 'Action' in R. Boudon (ed) *Traité de sociologie* (Paris: Presses Universitaires de France, 1992) 21–55, esp. 44–50.

individual behaviour and the macroscopic consequences they provoke. Here, the collective effects of the aggregate are of a different nature than that of a simple multiplication of the individual behavioural characteristics.[15] Something new emerges, the effects of which *cannot be foreseen* by simply observing the behaviour of individuals.[16] Swedberg's confidence theory is based on the simple, cumulative model of aggregate behaviour. In the highly complex environment of the financial system, however, such a paradigm is deceptive. For this reason, if Swedberg's approach is to be developed further, it will require a different foundation, one that takes into account the systemic component of network behaviour. One possible way of addressing the question is to consider the sociology of systems.[17]

III. Network Theory: The Erosion of Systemic Boundaries

While modern systems theory is in a better position to elucidate *systemic effects* more precisely than methodological individualism has thus far been able to do, it does not yet have a ready response to the problems under discussion here. On the contrary—the functioning of networks is still a great and unexplained mystery to the sociology of systems.[18] Nevertheless, what such an approach can offer is the possibility of widening the range of possible means of intervention through which financial market regulation could become more systemically effective. Systems theory can develop Swedberg's network approach further by suggesting a paradigm for financial market regulation that incorporates a qualitative concept of systemic risk. Implicit therein is a regulatory regime that uses *indirect means* to deploy its effects. This is a necessary consequence of the very nature of networks, which makes it impossible to deal with them as 'targets' of directly interventionist regulatory measures. I will return to this point shortly.

First, however, there is another question that must be addressed: how is it methodologically possible to describe the networks identified by Swedberg in such a way as to render their effects apprehensible? In attempting a response, the hypothesis

[15] Boudon, n 14, 47–50.

[16] This is the fundamental premise underlying the burgeoning field of network studies—the number of publications emanating from which has been rising exponentially in recent years. Much of the literature, having its origins in departments of mathematics and physics, is highly technical. A brief, comprehensible, and much-cited overview of the issues is given by S. H. Strogatz, 'Exploring Complex Networks' (2001) 410 *Nature* 268–75; a more thorough treatment is provided by M. E. J. Newman, 'The Structure and Function of Complex Networks' (2003) 45 *SIAM Review* 167–256. On the application of network science to the study of social phenomena, see the contributions in P. J. Carrington, J. Scott, and S. Wasserman (eds) *Models and Methods in Social Network Analysis* (Cambridge: Cambridge University Press, 2005).

[17] For an overview of the modern sociological theory of systems, see M. King and C. Thornhill, *Niklas Luhmann's Theory of Politics and Law* (London: Palgrave Macmillan, 2003) 1–33.

[18] See M. Amstutz, V. Karavas, and G. Teubner, 'Preface' in M. Amstutz and G. Teubner (eds) *Networks: Legal Issues of Multilateral Co-operation* (Oxford/Portland, Oregon: Hart Publishing, 2008) vii–xviii.

recently articulated by Ladeur—in the form of a question—offers a useful point of departure: *The Financial Market Crisis—a Case of Network Failure?*[19] Ladeur assigns a cognitive role to networks. This makes it possible to accurately address the informational problem at the centre of the financial crisis, as identified by Swedberg: the proper alignment of proxy signs with the actual economic situation. Ladeur's suggestion is that financial regulation should concentrate on the cognitive function of networks. In other words, Ladeur's argument is that regulatory law should aim to influence the communication structure of networks so as to allow for the satisfaction of Swedberg's 'alignment' requirement. The difficulty, of course, lies in the fact the possibilities available to the law for directly influencing the communications structures of financial networks tend to be limited. Networks, as Ladeur rightly notes, are 'hybrid forms of communication.'[20] It follows from this that ambivalence is intrinsic to information production in networks. Because of that ambivalence, the perfect *alignment* that Swedberg seeks is, as such, a systemic impossibility. Even in the event that such an alignment were, by a combination of circumstances, to accidentally come about, it would be unknowable.

Thus, for purely practical reasons, the law will never be able to distinguish between financial networks that are to be considered *functional* and those that are *dysfunctional*. Because of the informational complexity of such networks, a sufficiently precise modulation of their structures cannot be achieved using only those means at the disposal of the law. This by no means implies that the concept of networks in connection with the regulation of financial systems is of no use at all. The salient point is that the emergence of networks tends to increase the permeability of the boundaries between the systems those networks connect. And this occurs at various levels. Networks can form links not merely between the subsystems of a single social domain—as, for example, between the production, distribution, and financing systems of the economy. They can also lead to the formation of interchanges between the major functional systems of society, that is, between the economic, political, and legal systems, for example. The danger inherent therein is that the communication loops that necessarily form between these various systems no longer simply provide for an exchange of information, as Swedberg describes it; instead, is possible that they will begin to *erode the boundaries that separate those systems from each other* and, in this way, impair the ability of those systems to perform their respective social functions.[21] As we were able to observe in the current crisis, for example, the differentiation between the narrow and the broader banking systems—as subsystems of the overall financial

[19] K. -H. Ladeur, 'The Financial Market Crisis—a Case of Network Failure?' in P. F. Kjaer, G. Teubner, and A. Frebbrajo (eds) *The Financial Crisis in Constitutional Perspective: The Dark Side of Differentiation* (Oxford/ Portland, Oregon: Hart Publishing, 2011) 63–92.

[20] K. -H. Ladeur, n 19, 63, 80.

[21] For a fuller treatment of this issue, see M. Amstutz, 'Eroding Boundaries: On Financial Crisis and an Evolutionary Concept of Regulatory Reform' in P. F. Kjaer, G. Teubner, and A. Frebbrajo (eds) *The Financial Crisis in Constitutional Perspective: The Dark Side of Differentiation* (Oxford/ Portland, Oregon: Hart Publishing, 2011) 223–68.

system—was almost completely eradicated, giving rise to serious malfunctions in both.[22] Similarly, interactions between the financial sector and various political institutions have made it increasingly difficult to distinguish the operations of one from those of the other.[23]

The importance of this phenomenon, from a regulatory point of view, is crucial. If, in fact, the functional disturbances to which we give the name 'crisis' result from the erosion of systemic boundaries, then it is here that regulation is required. What I am suggesting is this: as long as the formation of network linkages between systems does not impinge upon the individual autonomy of those systems, such networks may be said to further a socially virtuous exchange of information. Where networks threaten to compromise the autonomy of their component systems, however, they constitute a social danger, and must be regulated. The point at which the law must step in, therefore, is not in the formation or structuring of communication links between networks—with the goal, for example, of achieving a correct alignment of proxy signs, as Swedberg would wish—but at the ongoing operational level. The aim must be to counteract the tendency of the constantly evolving networks active in the financial markets to erode the boundaries of the systems they connect.

IV. A Systemic Approach to the Financial System: Code Regulation

In order to better explain this, it will be useful first to briefly recall some of the underlying assumptions of a systemic approach. The point of departure is that in a complex society such as ours, the process of functional differentiation leads to the emergence of various subsystems within society (such as the economy, the law, politics, etc).[24] Within each of these systems, specific functions can then be assigned to subsystems. A subsystem of the economic system, for example, would be the financial system, within which there are further, even more specific subsystems, such as the narrow and broader banking systems.[25]

[22] Amstutz, n 21, 229–33, following C. Goodhart, 'The Boundary Problem in Financial Regulation' (2008) 206 *National Institute Economic Review* 48–55.

[23] Amstutz, n 21, 233–40.

[24] The approach here is largely based on that developed by Niklas Luhmann, as expounded at large in his various publications. An overview of that approach, in English, is provided in N. Luhmann, *Social Systems* (Stanford: Stanford University Press, 2004).

[25] See, e.g., H. Willke, *Systemtheorie I: Grundlagen* (Stuttgart: Lucius & Lucius, 7th edn, 2006) 68–80. The process of systems differentiating into subsystems with spiraling effect is skillfully described from a non-systems-theory perspective by Bourdieu on the example of the legal system: 'a process of circular reinforcement goes into action: every step toward the "juridisciation" of a dimension of practice creates new "juridical needs," and thus new juridical interests among those who, possessing the specific qualifications necessary... find in these needs a new market. Through their intervention, such practitioners cause an increase in the formalism of legal procedures, and thereby contribute to increasing the need for their own services and products': P. Bourdieu, 'The Force of Law: Toward a Sociology of the Juridical Field' (1987) 38 *Hastings Law Journal* 814–53, 836.

In order for each system, or subsystem, to properly perform its designated function, it must be able to operate with complete, so-called 'autopoietic', autonomy.[26] The idea is quite simple: economic decisions should be made on the basis of economic considerations, financial decisions on the basis of financial considerations—and so on down the line. The process by which the various systems distinguish themselves from each other is that of 'functional differentiation', which refers to the process by which each system defines its own specific function.[27] Where this process of differentiation has been successfully completed, one speaks of 'systemic closure', meaning that the system has fixed its own boundaries and operates autonomously as a closed system—in interaction with, but independently of, other social systems.[28] Thus, in more complex societies, each of the major social domains is governed by its own system, which is clearly distinguished from the others and which operates, ideally, with unconstrained autonomy.

The process of differentiation is set in motion when there develops a need in the society to classify events, as a means of coming to terms with them. A political system emerges, for example, in response to a need to distinguish between events in the public weal and those that are of only private interest. Following the stock market debacle of 1929, for example, it was decided by the political system of the United States that certain financial dealings were no longer to be considered as simply private matters, but had a direct bearing on the well-being of the polity, with the result that a system of financial regulation was instituted.[29]

[26] On systemic autonomy and its relation to the autopoiesis of systems, see H. Baxter, 'Autopoiesis and the "Relative Autonomy" of Law' (1997–1998) 19 *Cardozo Law Review* 1987–2090, esp 2003–14; see also N. Luhmann, 'Law as a Social System' (1989) 83 *Northwestern University Law Review* 136–50; J. Mingers, 'Can Social Systems be Autopoietic? Assessing Luhmann's Social Theory' (2002) 50 *Sociological Review* 278–99; from a stoical perspective, see P. Fuchs, *Der Sinn der Beobachtung: Begriffliche Untersuchungen* (Weilerswist: Velbrück 2004) 53–61.

[27] The concept of functional differentiation is developed in N. Luhmann, *Die Gesellschaft der Gesellschaft* (Frankfurt am Main: Suhrkamp, 1998) 595ff, esp 707ff; a summary of the theory, in English, can be found in N. Luhmann, 'Differentiation of Society' (1977) 2 *Canadian Journal of Sociology* 29–53, esp 35ff; on the social consequences of functional differentiation, see R. Stichweh, '*Inklusion/Exklusion: Funktionale Differenzierung und die Theorie der Weltgesellschaft*' (available at <http://www.fiw.uni-bonn.de/demokratieforschung/personen/stichweh/pdfs/17_36stichweh_6.pdf>) (this is a revised version of an earlier article of the same name, originally published in (1997) 3 *Soziale Systeme* 123–36); see also, generally, W. Rasch, *Niklas Luhmann's Modernity: The Paradoxes of Differentiation* (Stanford: Stanford University Press, 2000).

[28] On systemic closure and the interaction between closed systems, in particular as they relate to legal systems, see M. Amstutz, 'Métissage: On the Form of Law in World Society' (2013) 112 *Zeitschrift für Vergleichende Rechtswissenschaft* 336–60, 343; N. Luhmann, 'Operational Closure and Structural Coupling: The Differentiation of the Legal System' (1991–1992) 13 *Cardozo Law Review* 1419–41; G. Teubner, *L'ouvert s'appuye sur le Fermé: Offene Fragen zur Offenheit Geschlossener Systeme—Replik auf Klaus von Beyme*' (1991) 31 *Journal für Sozialforschung* 287–91.

[29] On the history of financial regulation in the US, see J. Seligman, *The Transformation of Wall Street: A History of the Securities and Exchange Commission and Modern Corporate Finance* (New York: Aspen, 3rd edn, 2003); in a review of Seligman, B. Longstreth notes that underlying efforts to regulate Wall Street was 'a belief that without the intervention of a governmental agency charged with oversight, and armed with the power to force change in the Exchange's rules of operation, the Exchange's self-interest would prevent it from aligning its practices with the public interest': see B. Longstreth, 'The SEC After Fifty Years: An Assessment of its Past and Future' (1983) 83 *Columbia Law Review* 1593–613, 1596; see also M. Friedmann and A. Jacobson Schwartz, *The Great*

Common to all systems is the primary process of differentiating between those events that are relevant to the system and those that are not. For this, each system uses what is referred to in systems theory as a binary 'code': a set of two categories into which the system divides all that it encounters in its environment. And it is by this code that the function of each individual system is defined. Just as the political system distinguishes between what is political and what is not, and the legal system distinguishes between what is lawful and what is not. The criteria on the basis of which these decisions are made are particular to each given system.[30]

The hypothesis I am proposing here is that crises result from the corruption of these codes, that is, from an erosion of the boundaries that separate the functions of these systems. Thus, for example, under the influence of private economic forces, the political system may no longer be able to distinguish between what is in the interest of the public and what is only of private interest.[31] Or again, the legal system may begin to term unlawful acts as lawful, based on political or economic criteria that are, by their nature, extrinsic to the legal system.[32]

It is precisely such a breakdown of systemic borders, I would argue, that we have witnessed in the present crisis—which began as a crisis of the financial system, but which has, in the meantime, taken on far wider social and political ramifications. The social function of the financial system, as a subsystem of the economic system, is to quantify risk. In other words, the financial system differentiates between those events that bear risks capable of being quantified and thus also of being adequately compensated, and those that are not subject to quantification and compensation. Quantifiable risks are then subjected to the operations of the financial system and assigned a price, making risk a distributable commodity—a 'financial product' and thus a part of the larger economic system.[33] The present financial crisis occurred when non-financial factors were used both in determining which events bore risks capable of quantification and in assigning prices to

Contraction 1929–1933: With a New Preface by Anna Jacobson Schwartz and a New Introduction by Peter L. Bernstein (Princeton/Oxford: Princeton University Press, 2008).

[30] On the concept of codes see N. Luhmann, '*Einführende Bemerkungen zu einer Theorie Symbolisch Generalisierter Kommunikationsmedien*' (1974) 3 *Zeitschrift für Soziologie* 236–55; D. Chernilo, 'The Theorization of Social Co-ordinations in Differentiated Societies: The Theory of Generalized Symbolic Media in Parsons, Luhmann and Habermas' (2002) 53 *British Journal of Sociology* 431–49; see also Amstutz, n 21, 244–6.

[31] An analysis of the case of UBS in Switzerland is given in Amstutz, n 21, 233–40 and 250–28.

[32] Typical cases of political considerations overruling the law may be seen in such institutions as diplomatic immunity, or again in court orders permitting otherwise unlawful wiretapping, with the concomitant dangers of abuse. Bribes are one of the most common examples of economic considerations overruling the law; the granting of construction permits to large companies, in breach of environmental law—in the hope of lowering unemployment or increasing tax revenues—is another. This phenomenon has been aptly termed 'structural corruption': see for an elucidation of this concept, G. Teubner, '*Ein Fall von struktureller Korruption? Die Familienbürgschaft in der Kollision unverträglicher Handlungslogiken* (BVerfGE 89, 214ff.)' (2000) 83 *Kritische Vierteljahresschrift für Gesetzgebung und Rechtswissenschaft* 388–404.

[33] On the function and functioning of the financial system, see J. Benjamin, *Financial Law* (Oxford: Oxford University Press, 2007) esp. 3–4.

those risks. To take the most blatant example: the risk involved in granting mortgages to people clearly incapable of repaying them is inherently not quantifiable, or must be quantified as being astronomically high. The price of such risk, denoted in the form of interest, is thus incalculable, or, at the very least, astronomical as well. The fact that such loans were granted—at low interest rates, without any relation to the actual risk assumed by the banks—was possible only by the banks adopting loan criteria fully—and woefully—alien to the code of the financial system.

In this connection, it is worth recalling that the social function of the financial system is, as already mentioned, the distribution of risk as a subsystem of the overall economic system. The very real failure of confidence that Swedberg has noted was a natural consequence of the failure of the financial system to perform this function. Confidence in what Swedberg terms 'proxy signs' plays a role only *after* the conversion of risk into a commodity: it is an important factor in determining whether the financial products created will be successfully marketed or not. While properly aligned ratings—as 'proxy signs'—can certainly be helpful in preventing unsuitable products from reaching the market, the source of the problem lies clearly with the failure of the financial system to correctly distinguish between quantifiable and non-quantifiable risks—that is, the failure of the financial system to perform the social function defined by its code.

Seen in this way, it is clear that the risk posed by the banks that were touted as being 'too big to fail'—and therefore deserving of taxpayer aid—lies not in their size, but in their manifest inability to perform the function required of financial institutions by the society at-large, that is, to properly estimate and distribute risk. This being the case, the aim of regulation must be to contribute to the differentiation of the financial system from other systems and return it to its social function. The difficulty lies in the fact that the events that the financial system deals with are not isolated, but are, in fact elements of extensive networks that connect the functions of various systems. A decision by a central bank to set interest rates at a certain level is a political decision intended to exert influence on the financial system in the public interest. That decision has financial implications, however, which must be taken into account when evaluating certain risks and assigning prices to them. Those financial decisions may then affect the sale of houses, for example, with resultant effects for other subsystems of the economy. It is this very complexity that makes it essential for each system to function within the parameters set by its code. It is only if the financial system performs its function properly that the desired economic and political effects of intervention can be achieved.

Because of the number of factors involved in financial calculations, however, it is illusory to believe that fixed rules or algorithms can be invented for the calculation of risk. And it is for this reason that an understanding of the role of codes in the functioning of systems takes on practical regulatory importance. Regulation must be structured so as to oblige financial institutions to eliminate extrinsic factors from their risk calculations. Practical suggestions as to how this might be achieved do exist. John H. Walsh, for example, has noted that there is an emerging trend in transatlantic financial market regulation, which he describes as 'institution-based'.[34] The strategy behind this new regulatory model consists of requiring that financial firms establish certain internal 'institutions'—such as compliance officers—which operate along guidelines furnished by regulators and are granted sufficient power and autonomy within the corporate structures to monitor the other operations of the company. By internalizing this 'watchdog' function, it should—at least in theory—be possible for financial institutions to develop self-correcting mechanisms whenever extrinsic considerations begin to interfere with their proper operations.

Whether Walsh's regulatory model is more widely adopted, or whether another paradigm must be sought, one thing is clear as I have tried to show in my foregoing remarks on the systemic origins of crisis: any attempt to mitigate or avoid such crises must attack the problem at that the root level. A way must be found to ensure that financial institutions fulfil their social function rather than serving solely as a means of achieving private ends. The alignment of proxy signs, and with it, a restoration of confidence, would follow naturally from such a correction and would not need to be imposed from the outside.[35]

[34] J. H. Walsh, 'Institution-Based Financial Regulation: A Third Paradigm' (2008) 49 *Harvard International Law Journal* 381–412; a critical consideration of this approach is offered by A. I. Anand, 'Rules v. Principles as Approaches to Financial Market Regulation: Responding to John H. Walsh, *Institution-Based Financial Regulation: A Third Paradigm*, 49 HARV. INT'L L.J 381 (2008)' (2009) 49 *Harvard International Law Journal* 111–15; see also F. D'Souza, N. S. Ellis, and L. M. Fairchild, 'Illuminating the Need for Regulation in Dark Markets: Proposed Regulation of the OTC Derivatives Market' (2010) 12 *University of Pennsylvania Journal of Business Law* 473–516, 501.

[35] It is perhaps worth noting that while it is true that one of the possible characteristics of 'confidence' lies in its reliance on what Swedberg has termed proxy signs, a more useful definition, specifically with regard to the financial system, but also in general, would be that confidence is the willingness to assume risk in exchange for compensation of some kind. A loss of confidence, in other words, is a diminution of the willingness to take on risk. This may well occur because of a realization that the proxy signs, in reliance upon which there existed a given level of such willingness, were not, in fact reliable. The defining element of confidence, however, is not that it is based on one sort of information or another, but that it provides the impulse for a certain form of behaviour, that is, for the assumption of risk. It is because the taking of risk is so essential to, indeed defines the very function of, the financial system that confidence is, rightfully, given such prominence in discussions of the financial markets. The definition of confidence as a willingness to assume risk is, however, also applicable in other situations: by saying we have confidence in a bridge, for example, we are simply indicating euphemistically that we are willing to risk our lives traversing it for the reward of getting to the other side.

7

Governance Mechanism in Long-term Contracts

*Michael Klausner**

When parties contemplate entering into a long-term contractual relationship, their contracts often establish coordination processes, create financial incentives, and limit the parties' freedom to conduct business outside the deal. In keeping with the theme of this book, one could describe such contract provisions as 'contractual governance'. These arrangements, which supplement direct commitments to supply goods or services, mirror corporate governance mechanisms. Like corporate governance mechanisms, these processes respond to the potential for moral hazard. In addition, they respond to the conceptually distinct danger of 'hold-up' associated with asset-specific investment. This Chapter examines how governance provisions in long-term contracts address these economic phenomena and provides two case studies—one, a long-term supply contract in the semiconductor industry, and the other, a biotech collaboration—in which contractual governance plays an important role.

I. Corporate Governance

Corporate governance refers to arrangements designed to align the interests of a corporation's top management, or its controlling shareholder, with those of its dispersed shareholders. In publicly held companies, corporate governance mechanisms include, for example, the presence of independent directors on a company's board, the use of incentive compensation for top management, the power of shareholders to bring a lawsuit for mismanagement, and exposure of the firm to a hostile takeover or a proxy fight brought by an activist investor seeking to replace the board in order to change the company's strategy. In a corporation with dispersed shareholders, such mechanisms address the agency costs associated with the separation of management and shareholders. Where there is a controlling

* Nancy and Charles Munger Professor of Business and Professor of Law, Stanford Law School.
Thanks to Ron Gilson and George Triantis for comments on an earlier draft of this Chapter.

shareholder, the primary agency cost is between the controlling shareholder and public shareholders. In either context, corporate governance mechanisms, ideally, are designed to assure public shareholders that the corporation will be managed to promote their interests, which generally means maximizing the value of their shares.[1]

The agency cost inherent in a public corporation is a specific case of moral hazard. Actions that managers take, and the impact of their actions on firm performance, are largely unobservable to shareholders. If managers' actions and their effects were observable, readily subject to evaluation, and verifiable by a court or arbitrator, then shareholders and managers could simply enter into contracts providing that managers would take actions reasonably designed to maximize the value of the company's shares. If a manager failed to adhere to the contract, shareholders could sue for damages. The threat of liability would deter breach, and when breach nonetheless occurred, the shareholders would be compensated.[2] No governance apparatus would be needed.

Corporate governance mechanisms are used because the inability to observe, evaluate, and verify management action, as well as the difficulty of specifying in advance how the company should be managed, makes both writing and enforcing such contracts impracticable. Governance mechanisms are designed to accomplish the same objective—albeit imperfectly—by creating incentives that align managers' interests with those of shareholders, subjecting the results of managers' actions (if not the actions themselves) to a degree of exposure, and committing management to orderly decision-making processes. Stock-based compensation for management, commitments to have financial statements audited and disclosed to the public, holding board meetings on a regular basis, and the power of shareholders to replace a company's board and thus management are examples of corporate governance mechanisms designed to induce those in control of the corporation to act in the interest of shareholders.

Corporate governance mechanisms in a public company context are not contractual in the conventional sense. There is no formal offer or acceptance of an actual contract providing for governance arrangements. Indeed, some corporate governance arrangements are mandated by law. Nonetheless, the governance structures of public companies have characteristics of contract, and can be conceptualized as contractual. When the owners and managers of a private company take their company public in an initial public offering, they have ample scope within which to adopt governance mechanisms, and they disclose those mechanisms to the market. Some of those mechanisms cannot be changed without the consent of shareholders. Others can later be changed by management unilaterally but at some cost, through a decline in the value of shares they

[1] Management may take actions motivated by corporate social responsibility as well. Such actions are often expected to benefit shareholders.

[2] Because this is an entirely unrealistic scenario, there is no need to get to the question of whether managers could cover the losses shareholders suffer, whether insurance might cover the losses, or other ancillary questions.

own or perhaps through reputational damage. While investors do not negotiate governance arrangements, they are free to buy a company's shares or not, and in buying them, they receive whatever protection the company's governance structures provide. The market is understood to include the quality of a company's governance mechanisms—the extent to which agency costs will be reduced—in the company's share price so that shareholders, in effect, pay for the quality of governance they receive when they buy shares. There is thus an exchange. Pre-IPO shareholders reap the benefit of good corporate governance commitments through higher IPO share prices, and they bear the cost of bad governance commitments through lower IPO prices. Whether this contract-like mechanism promotes optimal governance is a matter of debate, but it is generally agreed among economically oriented corporate law scholars that, where markets are reasonably efficient, the market provides at least some inducement for pre-IPO shareholders and managers to consider adopting effective governance arrangements at the time of the IPO.[3] Once a company goes public, the contract characterization is more attenuated. There are mechanisms in place that allow shareholders to impose changes on management—for example, through a proxy context that replaces the board—and there are actions that management can take unilaterally that may not be in the shareholders' interest. But to the extent changes in governance are reflected in share prices and to the extent management holds shares in the company, management will reap some gain from higher quality governance and pay a cost for lower quality governance.[4]

II. Contractual Governance

The relationship between parties to a long-term contract mirrors that between shareholders and managers in a corporation, and the mechanisms used to maximize the value of long-term contractual relationships often mirror corporate governance mechanisms. Governance mechanisms in long-term contracts, however, address a broader set of challenges than corporate governance mechanisms.

[3] See F. Easterbrook and D. Fischel, 'The Corporate Contract' in Easterbrook and Fischel (eds) *The Economic Structure of Corporate Law* (Cambridge, Mass: Harvard University Press, 1991) 1-39 setting out the purist view of the connection between the market and optimal governance. For doubts regarding the purist view, see M. Klausner, 'Corporations, Corporate Law, and Networks of Contracts' (1995) 81 *Virginia Law Review* 757; M. Klausner, 'The Contractarian Theory of Corporate Law: A Generation Later' (2006) 31 *Journal of Corporate Law* 782; R. Daines and M. Klausner, 'Do IPO Charters Maximize Firm Value? Antitakeover Protection in IPOs' (2001) 17 *Journal of Law, Economics, & Organization* 83. In countries with a baseline of weak corporate governance, studies have shown that the adoption of stronger mechanisms increases share value. B. Black, 'The Corporate Governance Behaviour and Market Value of Russian Firms' (2001) 2 *Emerging Markets Review* 89; B. Black and W. Kim, 'The Effect of Board Structure on Firm Value: A Multiple Identification Strategy Approach Using Korean Data (2012) 103 *Journal of Financial Economics* 203–26 (available at <http://ssrn.com/abstract=968287>).

[4] Whether management pays a *net* cost or reaps a *net* gain depends on how many shares it holds and private costs or benefits that it incurs from a change in governance.

Long-term contracts, and the governance provisions that many contain, must accomplish what is already accomplished within a corporation; they must facilitate the integration of the parties' businesses to the degree necessary to accomplish the parties' objectives. In a corporation, integration occurs by virtue of the firm's ownership of a set of complementary assets—factories, equipment, and intellectual property—that are used to produce particular products. This amalgamation of assets provides workers with an opportunity to create value that they could not create on their own, and to earn a portion of that value for themselves. Workers are thus attracted to the firm and become an integral part of the amalgamation. A well-run corporation provides workers with incentives to work diligently, to develop firm-specific human capital, and to stay with the firm for as long for as the relationship remains productive.[5] In the context of a long-term relationship between two companies, the parties often seek integration as well, although not necessarily as complete as the integration that occurs within a corporation. The parties invest in complementary assets or skills, and they become interdependent with one another, thereby enhancing the value of their relationship. For example, in the case study discussed in Section II(2)(a), a supplier of semiconductor testing equipment had to build a production line specifically to produce customized testing equipment integral to the buyer's manufacture of a new semiconductor. In another case study, a biotech company and a pharmaceutical company entered into a long-term agreement under which the former attempted to develop a drug that, if successful, the latter would manufacture and sell. In this relationship, there is relatively little reconfiguring of the parties' businesses, but each party is dependent on the other over a long period of time for success of the venture. The fundamental function of a contract in such a long-term business relationship is to provide the assurance necessary to promote the formation of an interdependent, and hence integrated, relationship that creates value for both parties. Governance mechanisms are commonly used to help accomplish this objective.

1. Underlying economics

In some business relationships, the assurance of future performance that the parties seek may be specified by contract. Consider, for example, the following contract: 'Party A will supply 10,000 class A widgets to Party B on the first day of each month for the following five years, in return for which Party B will pay Party A $1 million per month ($100 per widget), payable within 30 days of delivery (with late payments accruing interest at LIBOR plus 2 per cent).' So long as the delivery of class A widgets is easily observable and verifiable by a court if a dispute arises this contract may provide all the assurance the parties need. Party A may feel sufficiently

[5] What is described in this paragraph is a summary of what is known as the 'property rights' theory of the firm: see S. Grossman and O. Hart, 'The Costs and Benefits of Ownership: A Theory of Vertical and Lateral Integration' (1986) 94 *Journal of Political Economy* 691–719; O. Hart, 'An Economist's Perspective on the Theory of the Firm' (1989) 89 *Columbia Law Review* 1757–74; B. Holmstrom, 'The Boundaries of the Firm Revisited' (1998) 12 *Journal of Economic Perspectives* 73–94.

confident that it will have at least $1 million in sales per month to invest in a class A widget manufacturing facility. Similarly, Party B may be sufficiently certain that it will have access to another 10,000 widgets per month that it is willing to expand its own manufacturing operation, which uses widgets as an input.

Often, however, parties to a long-term contract cannot specify each other's obligations or observe each other's performance to such an extent that they can fully rely on legal enforcement to provide the assurance they need. In this situation, two challenges can arise which, unless met, may prevent a business relationship from being formed in the first place. Those challenges are the danger of hold up, which is associated with asset-specific investment, and moral hazard. Where either challenge is present, governance arrangements can complement the (imperfect) specification of ultimate commitments to provide a degree of assurance that those commitments will be performed in a diligent manner. Such governance arrangements include financial incentives, limits on the parties' activities outside of the contract, and processes by which the parties share information and coordinate with one another.

a. *Hold-up and asset specificity*

The integration that parties seek in a long-term business relationship often entails customization, whereby one or both parties configure their facilities or develop specialized skills in order to serve the other. In some cases, customization is so extensive that the assets or skills involved have no significant use outside the parties' relationship. For example, in the case study discussed in Section II(2)(a), the production line that the manufacturer of semiconductor test equipment had to build had essentially no use other than to produce equipment customized for the buyer. The line is thus an example of an asset-specific investment, meaning that once the asset has been built, the cost of redeploying it outside the context of a particular transaction is substantial, and often prohibitive—or, put differently, the value of the asset to parties other than the counterparty is very low. A party that makes an asset-specific investment must rely on its counterparty to recoup the cost of the investment plus a reasonable return. The concern associated with asset specificity is that once the investment has been made, the owner of the asset can become vulnerable to holdup by its counterparty—that is, the counterparty may attempt to renegotiate a better price under threat of terminating the relationship. Without protection against hold-up and with the cost of the investment sunk, the seller could find itself agreeing to a new price that covers only its variable cost. (If its variable cost is not covered, the seller will not produce.) Thus, unless a party can be reasonably assured that it will not be held up after making an asset-specific investment, it will not make the investment in the first place.

The classic response to the challenge of ensuring a return on a major asset-specific investment is vertical integration.[6] For example, the semiconductor manufacturer

[6] O. E. Williamson, *Markets and Hierarchies: Analysis and Antitrust Implications* (New York: The Free Press, 1975); O. E. Williamson, *The Economic Institutions of Capitalism* (New York: The Free

and the manufacturer of test equipment would merge. Assuming the merged company is well managed and that those in control of the previously separate businesses cooperate with one another, the managers of the merged company will ensure that the test equipment production line is built and that the semiconductor is manufactured.

Vertical integration, however, is not the only response to asset specificity. In fact, there are costs to vertical integration, such as difficulty creating incentive structures and coordinating activity within a firm.[7] Long-term contracts can provide an alternative means of providing assurance against hold-up in order to motivate valuable asset-specific investment.[8] Some contracts do so solely through the specification of legally enforceable contractual commitments, as in the class A widget contract discussed earlier. Such a simple contract, however, may be unattractive to one or both parties because circumstances may arise that make performance excessively costly. At the other extreme, it is often impracticable for parties to anticipate all circumstances that may arise during their relationship and to specify all obligations under all circumstances. In economic terms, an efficient, completely state-contingent contract may be infeasible. Pricing, quality, quantity, delivery location, or other elements of the deal may need to change in response to unanticipated, changed circumstances, and the parties may want to leave room for such changes in the contract. The result will often be gaps in the contract, sometimes large gaps. If circumstances arise that the contract does not address, disputes may occur, one or both parties may fail to perform, and the value of the relationship may deteriorate. Litigating the dispute is often unattractive because of the expense and uncertainty involved. At that point, a party that has made an asset-specific investment may be vulnerable to being held up by its counterparty. The counterparty might make an offer that the owner of the asset-specific investment is better off accepting rather than continuing with a deteriorating relationship or risking litigation, even if payments under the offer will not cover the cost of its investment. The possibility of being held up, however, may mean that the asset-specific investment—and therefore the business relationship—will not be formed from the start, and the value that would have been created would be lost. In order to ensure that the relationship is formed, the parties must find a way to provide the assurance needed for the asset-specific investment to be made. To the extent they cannot do so directly by specifying commitments, they may be able to do so by designing governance mechanisms that provide incentives and opportunities to cooperate despite gaps in their contract.

Press, 1985); B. Klein, R. G. Crawford, and A. A. Alchian, 'Vertical Integration, Appropriable Rents, and the Competitive Contracting Process' (1978) 21 *Journal of Law and Economics* 297–326.

[7] J. Roberts, *The Modern Firm* (Oxford: Oxford University Press, 2004) 74–117.

[8] For a discussion of the factors that lead to contractual alliances rather than vertical integration, see S. H. Chan, J. Kensinger, A. Keown, and J. Martin, 'Do Strategic Alliances Create Value?' (1997) 46 *Journal of Financial Economics* 199–221; P. Smith Ring and A. Van De Ven, 'Structuring Cooperative Relationships Between Organizations' (1992) 13 *Strategic Management Journal* 483.

b. Moral hazard

Moral hazard can be a challenge in long-term business relationships as well. Again, if the parties' expectations are clear from the start, and if their actions are observable and verifiable by a court, specific contract terms may address moral hazard adequately. If this is not feasible, however, the parties might have to rely on broad contractual standards such as commitments to exert 'best efforts' or 'commercially reasonable' efforts in lieu of specific obligations. Consequently, disputes may arise, in which case there will be uncertainty regarding whether a court will conclude that one's counterparty has fully complied with a contractual commitment. Has the counterparty exerted best efforts or commercially reasonable efforts, or has it shirked in performing its commitments? Not only are the counterparty's actions less than fully observable and verifiable—and hence, subject to dispute—but there may be a dispute as well regarding what the contract requires. The prospect of legal enforcement, therefore, may be insufficient to quell concerns over moral hazard. Moral hazard poses a threat to the formation of long-term business relationships both where asset-specific investment is needed and where it is not.

Without other means of providing assurance that one's counterparty will perform as expected, long-term business relationships will not be formed. If an asset-specific investment is needed, shirking by one's counterparty can mean the loss of the investment, just as being held up would. In a hold-up situation, the counterparty openly asks for a better deal when the opportunity arises, after an asset-specific investment has been made. In a moral hazard scenario, the counterparty underperforms in a way that cannot be discerned, or that at least cannot be verified by a court. For example, in the semiconductor case discussed in Section II(2)(a), if the test equipment manufacturer had committed to exert 'best efforts' to improve the quality of its equipment within two years, and the buyer was not satisfied with the results two years later, the buyer would have difficulty determining whether the supplier had breached its best efforts commitment, and greater difficulty proving to a court that it had. To the extent moral hazard threatens the prospect of earning a return on an asset-specific investment, a party will be hesitant to make the investment from the start. Hence, for the long-term relationship to be formed, the parties must find a way to protect the party being asked to make that investment.

Where no asset-specific investment is involved, the long-term contract itself can create a situation of reliance analogous to that of a party that has made an asset-specific investment. Once a party has made a contractual commitment, it is precluded from pursuing alternative opportunities because they may constitute anticipatory breach. That party is vulnerable to its counterparty's failure to perform. Moral hazard is thus a concern. Where a counterparty's actions are unobservable or unverifiable, one cannot count on legal enforcement to ensure diligent performance (or compensatory damages). Consequently, as in the case of an asset-specific investment, the contract may not be formed at the outset. The greater the degree of reliance on the counterparty's performance, the more important it is to address moral hazard. In the biotech collaboration examined in Section II(2)(b), for example, once the biotech firm entered into the collaboration agreement, it was dependent on the pharmaceutical company to sell the drug it developed. If the pharmaceutical company shirked in its marketing and sales effort, the biotech firm would suffer. The parties had to find a way to provide the biotech firm with sufficient assurance that the pharmaceutical company would perform. As will be seen, the solution was broad contractual language defining the pharmaceutical company's obligation to 'maximise operating profits' plus governance mechanisms that provide it with an incentive to do so.

c. *Contractual governance mechanisms*

What a long-term contract cannot accomplish by specifying ultimate performance obligations alone, it can often accomplish by setting out governance mechanisms that complement those obligations. These governance arrangements might include any or all of the following: (a) structured financial payments that respond to moral hazard and hold-up concerns; (b) limitations on one or both parties' freedom to do business with third parties; and (c) processes by which the parties share information, coordinate their actions and make joint decisions. These types of mechanisms promote the formation of commitments that are self-enforcing and that the parties can adjust as circumstances change.

Structured payment mechanisms in long-term contracts are commonly designed to ameliorate the threat of hold-up and to align the parties' incentives with their ultimate goals. Particularly with respect to the latter, these arrangements are analogous to executive compensation in the corporate governance context. Where the parties' actions are unobservable to one another or unverifiable to a court, a system of rewards and penalties based on observable outcomes can address moral hazard. For example, payments can be made as a party meets specified performance benchmarks, or parties can share profits from jointly produced products. Payments can also be structured to reduce the threat of hold-up where an asset-specific investment is involved. One approach is to provide for progress payments to the party making the asset-specific investment. To the extent progress is identifiable, payments can coincide with the investment, thereby eliminating or at least reducing concern over hold-up. Construction firms, for example, are paid on this basis as construction proceeds. Escrow arrangements are another approach where progress is not sufficiently observable as a project proceeds.

Contractual limits on a party's freedom to act outside the contract are another mechanism by which long-term contracts can respond to moral hazard and hold-up concerns. Such limits may relate to a party's business activities with third parties or to unilateral activities that could threaten diligent performance of the contract. The parallel in the corporate governance context are the limitations imposed on managers by the corporate opportunity rule and the general practice of requiring managers to work full-time for the corporation. Limiting options outside the contract addresses moral hazard in two ways. First, it can ensure that a party will not have divided loyalties that lead it to favor a competitor over its counterparty. Secondly, limitations on outside options reduce the possibility that a party will divert its attention and resources from performing the contract to pursuing more attractive—even if unrelated—opportunities that arise. As a response to hold-up, a restriction on a counterparty's outside options converts a unilateral asset-specific investment into a bilateral relationship-specific investment. One party is locked into a relationship by virtue of its asset-specific investment, and the other is locked in by contract. As a result, each party is dependent on the other, and hold-up is less of a concern. Limitations on options outside the contract have the virtue of being subject to relatively straightforward legal enforcement—limits are relatively easy to specify and actions that violate them are fairly observable and verifiable. Consequently, along with financial incentives, such limitations can promote an alignment of interest between the contracting parties.

Processes established by contract for information-sharing, coordination and decision-making are analogous to those followed by a corporation's board of directors. They often involve the formation of one or more joint committees with responsibility for performing these functions on behalf of the parties. Governance processes facilitate mutually beneficial adjustment in the parties' performance over time. Where specific commitments cannot be made at the outset, they often can be made incrementally as the parties' performance and the business environment evolve. Regular processes of information-sharing and coordination promote incremental adjustment where the parties have a mutual interest in continuing to work together—a mutual interest that may have been created in part by the incentives and limits on outside options that the contract creates. To the extent there is a mutually beneficial path forward in the parties' relationship, these processes provide a structured opportunity for the parties to find it and to demonstrate good faith and engender trust.[9] Governance processes also address moral hazard by increasing the visibility of the parties' conduct, thereby reducing the scope of unobservable and unverifiable action. With action more observable and potentially verifiable, shirking becomes more difficult and mutual assurance of diligence becomes easier. Moreover, increased observability reduces the danger of value-destroying tit-for-tat spirals in which each party punishes the other for perceived misconduct. On the other hand, if a party is determined to engage in misconduct—to shirk or to hold up its counterparty—these processes alone are not a solution. Their virtue lies in their ability to facilitate good faith performance and reduce misunderstandings. Biotech collaborations, including the one discussed later, typically make use of governance processes.

Gilson, Sabel, and Scott are particularly interested in these types of processes in the context of very open-ended collaborations, where the objective is not even known at the time the collaboration begins. Their prototype example is a

[9] Gilson, Sabel and Scott emphasize the potential for these processes to engender trust: see R. Gilson, C. Sabel, and R. Scott, 'Braiding: The Interaction of Formal and Informal Contracting in Theory, Practice, and Doctrine' (2010) 110 *Columbia Law Review* 1377.

collaboration between Pharmacopeia, Inc and Bristol-Myers Squibb Co in which the parties agreed to conduct joint research to produce compound libraries to be used in drug discovery. The parties did not have any compounds in mind when they began their collaboration. Finding such compounds was their first objective. They agreed that, if the collaboration resulted in the discovery of any commercializable products, Bristol-Myers Squibb would have the right to produce and sell those products subject to a royalty payable to Pharmacopeia. The parties' collaboration agreement provided for a set of governance processes that would facilitate a sharing of information. Those processes included the creation of a Research Steering Committee that would develop annual research plans, a commitment by each party to submit quarterly reports to the Committee on all inventions related to the collaboration, and to provide reciprocal access to all data, research materials, and labs. All decisions of the Research Steering Committee had to be unanimous and all disputes were elevated first to the parties' senior vice presidents and then their CEOs. As the authors explain, these formal processes were designed to knit the parties' research efforts together in a way that became self-enforcing—where each party found it in its own interest to continue working with the other, first to define research objectives, then to conduct joint research, and then to commercialize the results of the research.

2. Case studies: long-term supply contract and biotech collaboration

The following case studies illustrate the principles described earlier. Each case involves a long-term business relationship in which contractual governance mechanisms address concerns over hold-up or moral hazard, and thereby promote value-enhancing interdependence and integration. These are actual contracts. The details and identities of the parties, however, are changed in order to preserve confidentiality.

a. Supply contract for semiconductor testers

TestCo, a young privately held company, developed a new technology for testing advanced semiconductors. TestCo entered into a long-term supply contract with SemiCo, a large publicly held semiconductor manufacturer, to provide testers for a semiconductor that SemiCo had just developed and planned to manufacture for several years. Testers are critical to the semiconductor manufacturing process. Especially at the high end, they are customized for particular semiconductors, and are designed in conjunction with the design of the semiconductor. Taking into account the high fixed costs of production as well, testers' upfront costs are substantial. Consequently, a producer of testers must have assurance in advance that a semiconductor manufacturer will order a sufficiently high volume of testers to amortize its development costs and its fixed cost of production. Conversely, because testers are essential to the production of semiconductors, a semiconductor company must be assured of a timely supply of testers. An interruption in supply would mean a delay in production, which would have a devastating effect on a semiconductor company's business. Pricing is also important in the supply of testers. Semiconductor prices tend to decline over time. Because testers are a significant factor in the production of semiconductors, it is important that a tester declines in price as well.

In short, TestCo had to make a large asset-specific investment in order to supply testers to SemiCo and therefore needed assurance that SemiCo would buy enough testers to justify the investment. SemiCo, on the other hand, was at risk of becoming highly reliant on TestCo once the two companies entered into a supply contract. In addition, SemiCo did not know what the future demand for its semiconductors would be and wanted to avoid buying unneeded testing equipment. The parties' long-term supply contract, then, combines specific purchase and sale commitments with governance arrangements to address these concerns.

The basic elements of the parties' commitments are as follows. First, TestCo commits to devote its entire production facility to SemiCo testers for the first two years of their contract, and thereafter to devote a portion of its production facilities solely to SemiCo. The capacity set aside for SemiCo is tied to SemiCo's projections of order flow nine months in advance. Secondly, TestCo is required to deliver in a timely fashion all testers that SemiCo orders up to the volume that SemiCo has projected. Thirdly, SemiCo in turn is committed to purchase all the testers it needs from TestCo, except for those purchased from the second source described later. Fourthly, SemiCo is committed to specified minimum purchases regardless of its actual needs. Finally, the parties agree to a price schedule tied to purchase volumes for an initial period of time. After that initial period, there is a schedule of price reductions and a commitment from TestCo to provide SemiCo most favored nation treatment tied to 'substantially similar testers', a provision that makes legal enforcement uncertain since the tester customized for SemiCo is unique.

These commitments create vulnerabilities for each party. SemiCo has an incentive to inflate its projections in order to ensure an adequate supply, and inflated projections will result in costly unused capacity at TestCo. On the other hand, especially in the event of an unexpected increase in demand, TestCo may be unable to fulfill SemiCo's orders on a timely basis, causing SemiCo to slow down production and turn away orders. TestCo is a young company using new innovative technology, which is precisely why it is attractive to SemiCo, but there is a risk that TestCo's technology will fall short, leaving SemiCo exposed to potentially serious disruption.

The supply contract provides that SemiCo will exercise 'commercially reasonable' judgment in making its projections, and that TestCo will make 'commercially reasonable' efforts to meet SemiCo's purchasing requirements. It is clear to the parties, however, that legal enforcement of those commitments offers little if any assurance of protection.

To supplement the necessarily limited assurances that explicit purchase and sale commitments could provide, the supply contract establishes governance arrangements designed to promote coordination between TestCo and SemiCo. Those arrangements include financial incentives, a 'second source' option that gives SemiCo limited freedom to purchase testers from a third party, and joint management processes.

Financial incentives provide TestCo with a degree of assurance against hold-up and moral hazard. During the pre-manufacturing period, as TestCo was developing its technology to meet SemiCo's needs, SemiCo had to make payments to TestCo as development reached certain easily identifiable milestones. These payments put SemiCo in the position of sharing a substantial portion of TestCo's asset-specific investment. The possibility that SemiCo would hold-up TestCo, therefore, became less of a concern. In addition, upon closing, SemiCo made a substantial equity investment in TestCo. This not only provided TestCo with necessary financing, but it also gave SemiCo an interest in TestCo's success. Since the company's success in the long-run would turn largely on its success with this contract, the investment ameliorated SemiCo's incentive to inflate its projections and increased its incentive to share information and coordinate with TestCo so that both parties' needs were met. These incentives were probably strengthened by SemiCo's interest in having TestCo serve as a supplier of testing equipment in the future as well.

Protection of SemiCo's reliance on TestCo came primarily from the deal the parties struck with respect to creating a second source from which SemiCo could purchase testers. As is common in the semiconductor sector, SemiCo insisted that it not be entirely reliant on TestCo. This meant that TestCo would have to license its tester technology to a third party and allow that party to produce testers for SemiCo. TestCo, not surprisingly, was concerned about sharing its technology and negotiated a somewhat complex process for selecting such a second source. TestCo had the right to designate the company that would serve as the second source—presumably a company that it trusted not to steal its technology. But if a TestCo-designated second source was not up and running by a certain date, SemiCo would have the right either to manufacture its own testers with a license and technical assistance from TestCo or to designate a third party to manufacture TestCo's testers, again with a license and technical support from TestCo. So long as TestCo was meeting its production and delivery requirements, SemiCo could purchase no more than 15 per cent of its tester requirements from the second source. If, however, TestCo failed to meet its obligations or if TestCo went bankrupt, SemiCo had the right to either purchase all its requirements from the second source or purchase TestCo's own production facility line at TestCo's cost plus 20 per cent. This right to purchase TestCo's production facility plays a role similar to that of a hostile takeover in the corporate governance context: if TestCo is ineffective, SemiCo can acquire it.

Finally, information flow, particularly with respect to SemiCo's future orders, was central to maximizing the value of this relationship. To facilitate information flow, representatives of each company were required to hold monthly management meetings at which SemiCo provided rolling six-month, four-quarter and eight-quarter projections of its purchases. In addition, the parties were expected to discuss inventory, product innovation, and pricing. SemiCo also had a right to have a member of its management team attend all TestCo board meetings.

In sum, the governance mechanisms to which TestCo and SemiCo agreed complemented the supply agreement's necessarily incomplete purchase and sale commitments. Together, these governance mechanisms and the purchase and sale commitments supported the substantial asset-specific investment that each party had to make to form a mutually valuable relationship.

b. Biotech collaboration

Big Pharma and Biotech were engaged in a contractual collaboration to develop, manufacture, and distribute Reduxit, a drug for the treatment of prostate cancer that promises to be more effective than current treatments with less severe side effects. Big Pharma was a publicly held pharmaceutical company with large-scale manufacturing facilities and a worldwide distribution system. Its pipeline of internally developed drugs, however, had not kept pace with its past success and did not fully utilize the company's manufacturing or distribution capacity. Biotech was a privately held, venture-backed firm that has developed Reduxit and successfully taken it through much of the clinical trial process required for regulatory approval in the US and Europe. Biotech needed funding to complete the development of Reduxit, and it had no commercial-scale manufacturing facilities or sales force. The two companies entered into a collaboration agreement under which Biotech would continue to develop Reduxit with funding from Big Pharma and bring it through the remaining trials required for approval in the US and Europe. The collaboration agreement provides that if Reduxit received regulatory approval, Biotech would begin small-scale manufacturing in its own facilities while transferring manufacturing technology and know-how to Big Pharma. Big Pharma would then take over large-scale manufacturing and distribution of Reduxit.

As is typical in alliances of this type, Biotech's performance would come first and Big Pharma's efforts to commercialize the results of its work would come later. Biotech, therefore, needed assurance that if Reduxit were successful from a scientific perspective, Big Pharma would do all it could do to make the drug a commercial success. Biotech was concerned that during the period in which Big Pharma was expected to manufacture and sell Reduxit, it might have other priorities—at worst, drugs that would compete with Reduxit, but also other drugs that would simply be more profitable for Big Pharma. In either case, Big Pharma could choose not to devote appropriate resources and effort to Reduxit, a classic case of moral hazard. Unless Big Pharma's shirking was extreme, Biotech would have no way of evaluating the effort that Big Pharma put into commercializing Reduxit.

Big Pharma had moral hazard concerns as well. It would be financing the development of Reduxit with limited visibility into Biotech's efforts. Big Pharma did not want to fund research at Biotech for the development of drugs in which it would have no interest. Big Pharma was concerned, particularly if Biotech's scientists became pessimistic about Reduxit, that Biotech might use its financing to research other drug prospects, particularly those with similar underlying science.

The parties' collaboration agreement provides that each party will perform its role by exerting 'commercially reasonable and diligent efforts to develop and bring Reduxit to market as soon as practicable and to commercialize Reduxit in such a manner as to maximise its operating profits.' This commitment is vague enough to make legal enforcement a very lose and uncertain constraint on the parties' efforts to have the collaboration succeed. But anything more specific would be impractical. The parties could not effectively specify the steps Biotech would take in the lab or in clinical tests to maximize the likelihood of making scientific discoveries or of obtaining regulatory approval. Nor could they map out how Big Pharma would manufacture or market Reduxit in order to maximize profits.

Governance mechanisms, however, provided sufficient assurance to each party. Those mechanisms include a system of financial payments, limits on the parties' outside options, and a decision-making process. The agreement also provides for an exit option under certain circumstances.

The payment structure provided for in the collaboration agreement addresses both parties' concerns regarding moral hazard. It addressed Big Pharma's concern that its funding not be diverted to research from which it would not benefit. It also addresses Biotech's reliance on Big Pharma for a return on its investment in Reduxit. Biotech's investment was not asset specific. It could have contracted with any of several pharmaceutical companies to manufacture and sell the drug. But once it entered into the collaboration agreement giving Big Pharma an essentially exclusive[10] right to distribute Reduxit, Biotech's fortunes were tied to Big Pharma's efforts. The payment structure addresses this vulnerability.

During Reduxit's development phase, Big Pharma was required to make cash payments to Biotech as well as equity investments in Biotech as Biotech reached certain milestones. The milestones were easily identifiable indications of progress, such as regulatory approvals and patent grants. Thus, Big Pharma paid a portion of Reduxit's development expenses essentially as they were incurred, which mitigated the extent to which Biotech continued to incur costs in reliance on Big Pharma's later commercialization efforts. In addition, by keying the payments to observable milestones, Big Pharma's exposure to Biotech's diversion of its research efforts was mitigated as well.

Once responsibility shifted to Big Pharma to begin large-scale manufacturing, the collaboration agreement provides that the parties would share profits, with Biotech getting 35 per cent of the profits and Big Pharma getting 65 per cent. Thus, Big Pharma had an incentive to manufacture and distribute the drug to the extent its 65 per cent profit share warrants.

The collaboration agreement further addresses the parties' incentives by limiting their opportunities outside the development and commercialization of

[10] As discussed later, there is a last-resort exit option, but that option is not considered attractive.

Reduxit. Rather than preventing the parties from developing or selling other drugs, however, the agreement provides that if Biotech develops a similar drug or if Big Pharma sells such a drug, that drug will be brought into the collaboration subject to the same terms as Reduxit. This arrangement provided Big Pharma with further comfort that it would share the benefit of the research that it financed. It also provides Biotech with some protection against Big Pharma diverting its resources or attention away from Reduxit—at least with respect to similar drugs.

There was still the concern that Big Pharma's 65 per cent profit share could lead Big Pharma to divert its attention and resources to an unrelated drug for which it did not share profits (or that Big Pharma would develop a blockbuster drug that would divert a disproportionate share of the company's resources). As protection against this possibility, or any other situation in which the parties' interests diverged, the collaboration agreement provides an exit mechanism that either side can trigger under certain circumstances. Once commercialization begins, if profits from Reduxit decline on a year-to-year basis by more than a specified percentage, a buy-sell process can be invoked. Under that process, the party that triggers the process must make an offer to buy out the other party. The offeree can then either accept the offer or make a higher offer to buy out the offeror. (The counteroffer price must be higher after correcting for the 65:35 division of profits.) This mechanism, like SemiCo's option to purchase TestCo's production line, plays a function similar to that of a hostile takeover in the corporate context. But the parties view it as a risky and costly last resort.

The collaboration agreement also establishes an organizational structure for the collaboration, consisting of four committees that oversee the development and commercialization of Reduxit: a Management Committee, a Development Committee, a Commercialization Committee, and a Finance Committee. Each committee has an equal number of Biotech and Big Pharma members, which suggests that the parties intend to work by consensus but that each party can veto decisions of the other, subject to a dispute resolution process described later. The Management Committee is required to meet at least once per quarter and is responsible for setting and overseeing strategy in all phases of the collaboration. The Development Committee is responsible for overseeing clinical trials, compliance with regulatory processes necessary to gain approval to market Reduxit in the US and Europe, initial manufacturing by Biotech, and post-approval research. The Commercialization Committee is responsible for selecting trademarks and reviewing marketing plans. The Finance Committee is responsible for budgeting. The collaboration agreement sets out a dispute resolution process that will take effect if members of any committee cannot agree on a decision. As a first step, the Management Committee is given 30 days to resolve the dispute. If it is unable to do so, the CEOs of Biotech and Big Pharma have 14 days in which to engage in 'good faith negotiation'. If they fail to reach an agreement, the dispute goes to binding arbitration according to standard procedures specified in the contract. Consistent with the discussion earlier, this organizational structure has promoted the free flow of information between the parties and the creation of trust. This committee structure has proved to be effective in coordinating the parties' actions and providing visibility for each other's performance.

III. Conclusion

Long-term business relationships commonly face hold-up and moral hazard concerns. A completely state-contingent contract would resolve those concerns, but such a contract is often infeasible. Where this is true, governance mechanisms can complement performance obligations to provide the assurance to support asset-specific investment and reliance on the commitments of one's counterparty. These mechanisms include payment structures that minimize hold-up and moral hazard, limitations on the parties' options outside the contract, and processes for information sharing and decision-making. These mechanisms, which are analogous to corporate governance mechanisms, can keep the parties' interests aligned and facilitate coordination of activities that achieve the parties' mutual goals.

Summary of the Discussions in Part III: Governance of Networks of Contracts

*Florent Thouvenin**

Chapter 5 : Contract, Uncertainty, and Innovation

Authors: Ronald J. Gilson, Charles F. Sabel, and Robert E. Scott

Discussant: Gerard Hertig

Paul Davies first commented on this chapter, which he said would essentially be a comment on Coase's 'The Nature of the Firm'[1] since the chapter ends with a theoretical comment on Coase's thesis. According to Davies, Coase explained two things: first, why we have firms at all and secondly, what the boundaries of firms are.

In Coase's view, production can be organized in two ways: either across markets or within firms. His explanation as to the choice between markets and firms is, of course, based on transaction costs: coordination takes place within firms rather than across markets since the necessary coordination is less expensive this way. The main advantage Coase identifies for the firm is that the entrepreneur has the power to direct the use of the production factors, thereby economizing on contracting costs. With regard to the topic of the discussion, Davies stressed that Coase did not perceive the differences between coordination through markets and coordination within firms as being identical with the differences between coordination through contracting and coordination through some other mechanism. In fact, Coase clearly states that the power of direction that firms give to entrepreneurs is based on contract. In his view, the difference between firms and markets is vested in the different types of contracting. Accordingly, he distinguishes two types of contracting: intra-firm contracting and inter-firm contracting.

According to Coase, intra-firm contracting is essentially about an employee agreeing to obey the directions of the entrepreneur in return for remuneration

* Assistant Professor (tenure track) for Information and Communication Law, University of Zurich.

[1] R. H Coase, 'The Nature of the Firm' (1937) 4 *Economica* 386–405.

and within certain limits. This allows all production factors to be conveniently brought together into contractual relations between the parties. However, Davies indicated that Coase was much less clear about the specific characteristics of contracting taking place through the markets. Although he may have thought of market contracts as spot contracts, he seemed rather to perceive them as contracts where some specific good or service was provided in exchange for a price. According to Davies, Coase's proposition that contracts within firms are contracts in which the entrepreneur contracted for control, and contracts across markets are contracts for specific goods or services, could be challenged.

Although the notion of intra-firm contracting as contracting for remuneration in exchange for control may work for physical production factors, it would not, in Davies view, work for labour. Davies held that in this respect Coase's theory was based on a rather old-fashioned view of labour contracts and production, where labour was at best semi-skilled, a labourer was a hand and one hand was essentially replaceable with another. With the advent of highly skilled technical and professional employees, it has become far from clear that employers still have the ability to specify precisely how the work has to be done. In addition, it is known today from human resource management theory that for an entrepreneur to get the best out of their workforce requires a great deal more than a simple legal power to direct the employees. Often, the employer will wish to encourage their employees to work cooperatively without having been given detailed directions. All of this leads to the elaboration of various types of governance mechanisms for long-term relational contracts that goes well beyond the mere power of the employer to direct their employees.

With regard to contracting between firms, Davies refers to the Gilson, Sabel, and Scott chapter where the authors point out that market contracts may not only involve contracting for a specific outcome but also for coordination and cooperation, i.e. the type of contracting that Coase had identified as being the role of the firm. If cooperation can be secured through inter-firm contracting as well, the entrepreneur has an additional option and can choose from achieving the necessary cooperation by carrying out production within the firm or by spreading it across firms. Of course, this finding undermined Coase's contribution to some extent and the authors indeed went so far as to say that there was no longer a theory of the boundaries of the firm. However, Davies pointed out that this conclusion would go too far. In any event, Coase's contribution to the question of why firms exist would survive the issues raised in the Gilson, Sabel, and Scott chapter, since this chapter does not describe a world in which firms have been replaced by contracting between non-firms. Instead, it refers to a world with more extensive contracting between firms, i.e. a world in which production is disaggregated across firms rather than concentrated within firms. After all, the firm is still dominant, but the contractual links between firms have become much more important.

Roberto raised a number of issues related to direct claims and distribution of profits. He started by pointing out the differences in the perception of contracts by lawyers and economists. While economists believe that contracts just need smart lawyers and enough time to negotiate and draw up the whole agreement in long contracts of 60, 70, or even 100 pages, the real issues are different. From Roberto's point of view, the main problem with contracts is their enforceability, namely that few can afford commencing contract litigation which might last for years. Against this background, the actual content of a contract seems to be much less important than one would think. According to Roberto, this is true, now more than ever, with regard to the renegotiation clauses that can be found in most long modern contracts. As these clauses relate not only to minor aspects, but also typically to major points such as the price, the real question is what the entire contract is actually concluded for.

Roberto then addressed the issue of kickbacks using the example of a big Swiss bank which sold large amounts of Lehman papers to its clients. For every paper sold, the bank received a commission from Lehman. Against the background of the financial crisis, it is debatable whether banks should be obliged to hand over such distribution provisions to their clients in order to prevent obvious conflicts of interest. According to Roberto, this simple solution would lead to a legal problem in the field of funds, since funds are obliged to distribute all of their papers at the same price. Hence, if a bank sold large amounts of papers of a specific fund, it would receive a large kickback. If the bank had to hand over these kickbacks to their clients, the clients who bought the respective papers through this bank would have bought them at a lower price compared to others who bought the same papers through different banks and received smaller kickbacks or none at all. As a consequence, in order to comply with the requirements of a possible provision on kickbacks, banks would be legally obliged to infringe the provision on identical prices for funds' papers.

Finally, Roberto turned to the problem of liability, namely the liability of a bank that issues the papers of another financial institution. From his point of view, liability rules with regard to third parties have an undesirable impact on the market structure since banks that are held liable for other financial institutions over which they have no control tend to integrate such institutions. As a result, third party liability rules set incentives to integrate the industry, whereas, at the same time, politicians are trying to find solutions for the 'too big to fail' problem. As with kickbacks, a way out of these contradictions seems hard to find.

Gerard Hertig referred to the issue of 'make or buy', which Davies had addressed, and elaborated further on it with regard to financial innovation. To Hertig, these innovations consist of two components: financial products and information technology. If a firm wants to innovate in these fields, it can choose either a formal or an informal route. The formal route would be to go through the innovation process within the firm, and maybe decentralize some of the processes; the informal way would be to innovate together with their peers. However, regardless of which route it chooses, the firm might encounter antitrust problems. If it successfully innovates on its own it may achieve a dominant position in the respective market. If the firm collaborates with others and sets up a research network, the usual way to keep such networks together is to fix prices and quantities or to establish concerted practices. Again, there would be antitrust problems. Therefore, Hertig was not surprised that recent studies revealed that contracting for innovation often occurs bilaterally. Apart from the fact that this sort of cooperation has not yet attracted the attention of antitrust authorities, another important advantage of the bilateral solution is that the activity is efficiently concentrated and not as diffuse as it would be in a network.

Davies agreed with Hertig that the open-ended contracts which were typical for joint innovation would be easier to control and maintain, and therefore more efficient if the number of the parties were limited. Stefan Grundmann pointed out a general trend that had been described by the other discussants. As opposed to Coase's clear-cut position with regard to firms and contracts, he identified a continuum which consists of different elements. One of these elements is how much unilateral decision-making power a party has within a contract, an organizational contract, or a company. According to Grundmann, an additional element of a partnership is the sharing of input and a certain quota for the distribution of the output, whereas split accounts and no sharing of profits apply to the contractual solution.

Hans- W. Micklitz returned to the issue of kickbacks. To him, this is a perfect example of how the legislative system is used as a kind of repair service. After the failure of Lehman, retailers were looking for compensation and identified the banks that had sold the papers and received the kickbacks as potential addressees. These demands contributed to the long-standing and controversial debate as to whether and to what extent fees charged in inter-firm transactions have to be disclosed. However, even if there was an agreement in Europe that all kickback transactions had to be disclosed, Micklitz remained sceptical about the effect of such disclosure. According to Micklitz, the ultimate question is whether the Lehman transactions would not have occurred if the kickbacks had been disclosed. Roberto fully agreed with Micklitz and added that even if legislators agreed on disclosure as such, they would still have to find an appropriate solution as to how disclosure should be effected. Davies added that he could not understand why disclosure should be a problem. To him, these fees should not in any case be called kickbacks, but commissions. If a bank distributes a large proportion of a certain paper, the bank is performing a service for the originator for which it ought to be paid. Against this background, the purpose of disclosure would not be to pass the kickbacks on to the client, but to inform the client, thereby allowing it to establish whether or not the advice of the bank was biased by that commission.

Horst Eidenmüller referred to Roberto's comment on contract renegotiation duties. In his view, two different types of renegotiations must be distinguished: opportunistic renegotiations seeking to redistribute rents, and renegotiations triggered by an assessment of inefficiencies in a contract. However, if a contract does become inefficient, one would expect the parties to renegotiate it regardless of whether they had previously agreed on a renegotiation duty. From this perspective, the only effect of such a duty would be that the renegotiation process might start earlier, namely at a point in time when it was still unclear whether it was initiated for opportunistic or for honest reasons. In order to fulfil this purpose, a renegotiation clause would have to go beyond a mere duty of renegotiation and would have to establish a process enabling the party faced with a renegotiation request to discover the opportunistic behaviour of the other party, for example by imposing a duty to provide upfront information as to the cause of the renegotiation request. Hertig agreed and added that renegotiation clauses and other informal agreements only work if some sort of trust-enhancing provision exists. To him, such provisions are necessary in all kind of long-term relationships, in firms and networks alike.

Michael Klausner concluded the discussion by referring to the suggestion made in Chapter 5, according to which research on contract governance might develop in a way comparable to the established topic of corporate governance. He agreed with Hertig, pointing out that people will always try to customize their own governance arrangement, especially in long-term relationships. Therefore, Klausner assumed that research on contract governance could reveal a general set of concepts, which would not apply to all kinds of on-going relationships, but also to a set of particular aspects that might vary between different situations such as joint ventures or long-term supply contracts.

Chapter 6: Contractual Networks in aSocio-economic Perspective: The Case of the European Financial Crisis (2009–2010)

Author: Richard Swedberg

Discussant: Marc Amstutz

Dominique Demougin started the discussion by referring to the financial crisis and pointing out that some of the players in that game must have been winners and must have been interested in creating all the noise. According to him, some of the big banks were obviously winners as they were able to charge premium interest rates for debts that were in fact guaranteed by taxpayers. Richard Swedberg agreed on this point and said there was indeed empirical evidence suggesting that some players created, or at least added to, the crisis in order to benefit from it. However, he stressed that one has to keep in mind that no one has control over the international financial markets. To him, this aspect was much more important than the idea of someone creating the crisis in order to benefit from it. Swedberg agreed that over-confidence actually played a role in the crisis.

Urs Schweizer referred to Demougin's statement and questioned whether banks have really been able to dictate interest rates. From his point of view, one unpredictable aspect of the crisis was that market players expected the EU to follow the rules that excluded bailouts. At a certain point in time, however, it became quite clear that the markets did not believe that the EU would stick to those rules, which was one of the reasons why the interest rates in government bonds converged despite the obvious differences in the ability of countries to repay their debts. Swedberg gave a reminder that investors were social beings who perceived the EU as a unit, believing this unit to be some kind of guarantee. However, when unity ceased under the pressure of the financial crisis, the investors' perceptions changed and they started to look at the bad debts of some of the individual member states. From a sociological point of view, one of the problems during the crisis was that the EU oscillated between being a unit and not being a unit. Fernando Gomez then referred to Schweizer's earlier statement and disagreed to a certain extent. In Gomez's view, it was because of the crisis that the markets finally returned to a reasonable pricing of the risks concerning certain member states. The mistake had arisen during the post-euro boom and the bubble years, given that the Member States' ability to pay had always been different. What had surprised Gomez was the investors' confidence in the ability of the monetary union to eliminate the differences in the risks between the individual countries—a perception that the crisis obviously proved wrong.

Gunther Teubner turned attention back to the topic of networks by reiterating one of networks' most important characteristics: their ability to institutionalize contradictions. From his point of view, network contracts are hybrids combining the characteristics of contracts and organizations in an almost contradictory way. Network contracts usually combine exchange and coordination aspects, competition and cooperation aspects, as well as individual aspects of the different knots and the collective aspect of the network as a whole. Therefore, networks can be seen as a way out of organizational failures by transforming external contradictions into productive internal tensions. With regard to the inter-systemic networks that Marc Amstutz had mentioned, Teubner referred to the example of research projects that are often conducted as cooperative ventures between a scientific institute, a government agency, and a private firm. For such projects, he said, it could be detrimental if one had to choose between a purely contractual or organizational structure as this would result in one dominant logic. By choosing a network contract, the logics of all three entities could be combined within the network. However, Teubner also pointed out the 'dark side' of networks, which arises when the institutionalized contradiction becomes destructive, for example the panic behaviour in the economy as witnessed during the financial crisis. He therefore wondered whether this characteristic is inherent in networks as such, and whether they are—by their very nature—such precarious arrangements that it would be almost impossible to define the tipping point at which the whole institution became destructive. Amstutz agreed with Teubner as to the capacity of networks to bring contradictions together, as well as on potential harm. Given that, to date, network analysis has focused on positive aspects, Amstutz suggested that future research should look at contract networks' potentially destructive side as well.

PART IV

GOVERNANCE IN LONG-TERM CONTRACTUAL RELATIONSHIPS

8

Fairness and Reciprocity in Contract Governance

*Stefan Magen**

Contract governance, it seems, examines a set of rather different regulatory constellations.[1] In such analyses, fairness or reciprocity would be relevant in many different ways that cannot be pursued here. Instead, I examine governance for the purpose of this Chapter in a narrower and, at the same time, more general sense that cuts across the different forms of contract governance. In the following, I understand governance to be concerned (among other things) with problems of cooperation or opportunistic behaviour, i.e., situations in which it is difficult to realize mutually beneficial outcomes because actors have an incentive to deviate from cooperation.[2] The canonical model for this type of social problem is, of course, the Prisoner's Dilemma, but in fact cooperation problems take a variety of forms that pose different problems, for the analysis of which a multitude of more sophisticated and more adequate models is being applied. This Chapter looks at the role of fairness or reciprocity in solving problems of this sort, focusing more on general mechanisms than on specific results (whose external validity has to be considered with caution and care).

I. What is Fairness or Reciprocity?

Before we look at what fairness or reciprocity entails, it is important to recognize that this question can be asked at different levels: at the mental, behavioural, and

* Chair in Public Law, Legal Philosophy, and Economic Analysis of Law, Ruhr-University Bochum.

[1] F. Möslein and K. Riesenhuber, 'Contract Governance – A Draft Research Agenda' (2009) *European Review of Contract Law* 248–289, 260–87.

[2] This understanding should be covered by the use of the term by Elinor Ostrom and Oliver Williamson: see E. Ostrom, *Governing the Commons* (Cambridge: Cambridge University Press, 1990); E. Ostrom, *Understanding Institutional Diversity* (Princeton, NJ: Princeton University Press, 2005); O. E. Williamson, 'The New Institutional Economics' (2000) 38 *Journal of Economic Literature* 595–613, 601; O. E. Williamson, 'Transaction Costs Economics' (2010) 100 *American Economic Review* 673–90, 679.

social level. At the mental level, fairness can, for example, take the form of moral sentiments or of moral judgments; on the behavioural level, the form of voluntary cooperation or of a rejection of inequitable offers; and on the social level, the form of shared normative expectations (an aggregate of mental phenomena), of a pattern of sanctioning behaviour (an aggregate of behaviour), or of a combination of both aggregate behaviour and expectations. Which level one should focus on depends, of course, on the question at hand and should be delegated to different disciplines accordingly. With regard to the analysis of governance problems, it seems helpful to adopt a more comprehensive approach and to conceive of fairness as a 'social mechanism' to sustain cooperation in human interactions based on individual behavioural disposition. From this point of view, the different levels mentioned above refer to different aspects of the same phenomenon, which are somewhat independent from each other, but which also interact. Thus it becomes crucial to understand how the different—mental, behavioural, and social—aspects of fairness work together in bringing about cooperation, what their respective contributions are, how they are linked with one another, and what difficulties arise in their interplay.

1. The identification problem: moral motive or selfish strategy?

This task, however, is not easy, because any account of fairness is faced with serious identification problems. A similar pattern of observable behaviour can result from different types of motivations (for example, selfish motives, moral motives based on ethical reasoning or moral emotions, or simply the motive to follow a rule that is regarded as appropriate) and individual motivation can be differently affected by social influences (for example, via hard sanctions, refusal to cooperate further, social disapproval, role models or information about the behaviour of others or about social expectations).[3] Consider the case of a supplier in the automotive industry who has the chance to produce parts at a lower cost, but with lower quality and a slightly higher probability of deterioration. Although there is only a very small probability of detection, the supplier does not seize the opportunity to produce inferior quality and substitute it for normal quality. If we focus on the observable behaviour, the story suggests an example of fair behaviour, but in fact there might be quite different underlying motives. For example, business relations between the producer and the customer might be permanent and quite valuable or even vital for the supplier, and given the high stakes, even with a small probability of detection the expected loss might outweigh the gains to be expected from cheating. The point here is that it is often difficult to make valid inferences about the selfish or moral character of motivation from behaviour alone. Even if we knew all relevant circumstances and could determine that behaving fairly was the best strategy to maximize income, the actor could still

[3] For an overview of the psychological debate on egoism, see, e.g., C. D. Batson, *The Altruism Question: Toward a Social-psychological Answer* (Hillsdale, NJ: Erlbaum, 1991).

have chosen this behaviour out of moral concern. The opposite can also be true. There are situations where people's behaviour seems to be selfish, but their actual motivation is that they feel unfairly treated. Imagine an employee who is shirking his obligations at work. This might be because the employee knows that the employer cannot observe the quantity or quality of his work and thus minimizes his effort, or because his sense of justice is hurt because colleagues are paid higher wages (which should not, as such, bother a rational utility maximizer who is concerned only with his own payoffs). If, however, fairness and selfishness are so easily confused, then why should contract governance bother to try to tear them apart at all? The reason is that institutions have to achieve considerably different tasks, depending on whether people are solely driven by selfish or also by moral motives. Thus, with fair-minded people, institutions have to be designed differently.

2. *Homo oeconomicus* versus *homo reciprocans*

Since mental phenomena can never be directly observed (not even with brain-imaging techniques) and self-reports are notoriously unreliable, it is crucial to study the impact of fairness motives on behaviour in diagnostic situations, i.e. in situations where it can be precisely determined which actions are in the self-interest of an actor and which are not. The scientific tool that allowed for enormous progress in this regard was laboratory experiments that implemented games rooted in game theory (for example, the famous Ultimatum Game).[4] These experiments tracked participants' investment behaviour in games where real money was at stake and compared it to the game-theoretic prediction what a rational self-interested agent would do in the same situation to maximize his outcome.

Two consistent behavioural patterns emerged from numerous experiments conducted in a multitude of variations, [5] many of which were carried out by Ernst Fehr or are inspired by his seminal work.[6] In what economists call 'theories of fairness', these two behavioural tendencies have been formalized mathematically

[4] For a discussion of the experimental method and its methodological merits and problems, see, e.g., S. Gächter and C. Thöni, 'Micromotives, Microstructure, and Macrobehavior' (2011) 35 *Journal of Mathematical Sociology* 26; F. Gula, *The Methodology of Experimental Economics* (Cambridge: Cambridge University Press, 2005) 141ff; S. Levitt and J. List, 'What do Laboratory Experiments Measuring Social Preferences Reveal About the Real Word?' (2007) 21 *Journal of Economic Perspectives* 153. For a discussion of the application of experimental findings for policy-making and in the law see, e.g., H. -T. Normann and R. Ricciuti, 'Laboratory Experiments for Economic Policy Making' (2009) 23 *Journal of Economic Surveys* 407; K. Zeiler, 'Cautions on the Use of Economic Experiments in Law' (2010) 166 *Journal of Institutional and Theoretical Economics* 178; commented on by C. Engel, 'The Multiple Use of Experimental Evidence in Legal Scholarship' (2010) 166 *Journal of Institutional and Theoretical Economics* 199; C. Engel, 'The Difficult Reception of Rigorous Descriptive Social Science in the Law' in N. Stehr and B. Weiler (eds) *Who Owns Knowledge?* (New Brunswick, NJ: Transaction Publishers, 2007) 169.

[5] For an overview, see, e.g., E. Fehr and H. Gintis, 'Human Motivation and Social Cooperation: Experimental and Analytical Foundations' (2007) 33 *Annual Review of Sociology* 43.

[6] Starting with E. Fehr, G. Kirchsteiger, and A. Riedl, 'Does Fairness Prevent Market Clearing? An Experimental Investigation' (1993) 108 *Quarterly Journal of Economics* 437.

as two types of preferences that have been called inequity aversion and reciprocity. However, one has to bear in mind that economic theories of fairness differ substantially from psychological theories on the same subject. Unlike the latter, the former have no intention of realistically mapping the cognitive processes that eventually lead to fair behaviour. Rather, they try to strip the complexity of mental phenomena down to those factors which are necessary to capture the general behavioural patterns resulting from moral motives. Put differently, economic fairness theories do not aim to explain fairness. Rather, they model fairness in order to explain economic behaviour. Thus, the concept of *homo reciprocans* put forward by behavioural economists[7] is just as much an artificial model of human behaviour concocted for the purposes of economic theorizing as was the old *homo oeconomicus* of neoclassical economics, whom *home reciprocans* is meant to replace.

How do both models differ? Whatever preferences *homo oeconomicus* is assumed to hold, they usually conform to the assumption of selfishness, i.e., the presumption that people are indifferent about the utility of others and care only about their own consumption. This rules out all other types of 'social preferences', for example, altruism, spite, envy, competitiveness, and fairness.[8] Preferences for fairness, on the other hand, are defined by departing from the selfishness assumption in a specific way. Preferences for fairness are social preferences in the sense that they also consider what other people get (be it more or less). However, unlike altruistic preferences, preferences for fairness are not about other people's welfare as such, but about relative differences in gains or losses between the actor and other people. That is, fairness is not about A doing something good for B, but about whether A gets more or less than B, and for what reason.

Inequity aversion—the first type of fairness preference—sees fairness as being concerned with outcomes, or more specifically with how outcomes are distributed. It assumes that payoff differences have, as such, a negative utility for those involved, and that this disutility is greater for disadvantageous rather than for advantageous inequalities.[9] Take, for example, an inequality-averse player in the famous Ultimatum Game, who is faced with a proposal that concedes to him two out of ten euro and leaves the proposer with eight euro. In his decision whether or not to accept the offer, this player would not only take the positive utility into account that he would derive from getting two euro, but also the negative utility he would experience from getting six euro less than the proposer. Depending on the strength of his aversion to inequality, this negative utility might outweigh the positive utility from getting at least some payoff. Thus, the assumption that having something is always better than having nothing does not necessarily hold

[7] E. Fehr and S. Gächter, 'Reciprocity and Economics: The Economic Implications of *Homo Reciprocans*' (1998) 42 *European Economic Review* 845; S. Bowles and H. Gintis, '*Homo Reciprocans*' (2002) 415 *Nature* 125.

[8] J. Sobel, 'Interdependent Preferences and Reciprocity' (2005) 43 *Journal of Economic Literature* 392.

[9] E. Fehr and K. Schmidt, 'A Theory of Fairness, Competition and Cooperation' (1999) 114 *Quarterly Journal of Economics* 817; G. Bolton and A. Ockenfels, 'A Theory of Equity, Reciprocity, and Cooperation' (2000) 90 *American Economic Review* 166.

for inequality-averse players. Instead, to avoid the displeasure of being treated unfairly, such a player might reject a positive offer, as can be observed in experimental games all over the world.[10] But people are not only willing to forgo considerable amounts of money to avoid unequal distributions to their disadvantage. They also tend, albeit to a lesser degree, to share equally to avoid the negative utility from having an unfair advantage.

Theories of reciprocity, as the other type of fairness theories, do not refer to unequal outcomes directly, but assume that people primarily care about the intentions of other actors, i.e., whether they are treated kindly or not. Hence, in these theories the fairness of a distribution is not relevant as such, but indicates the fairness of an actor's intentions.[11] As in theories of inequity, it is assumed that people suffer disutility from being treated unfairly or treating someone unfairly. But it is also assumed, that they gain positive utility from responding with kindness to kind people and with unkindness to unkind people. This provides a more direct explanation for why participants in experimental games are willing to reciprocate fair or kind or cooperative actions even if they have to pay a price for this or could have taken advantage of it (like in the above example of the supplier of automotive parts). The tendency to repay at a cost is particularly pronounced when it comes to punishing someone by whom one has been treated unfairly.

Both types of fairness theories do not pretend that people care solely about fairness. Rather, they take the utility from the actor's own payoff as a primary motivational force, but expect this motivation to be mediated by fairness to some degree. Thus, the interesting question arises of how fairness firs in. The outcomes that result from the interplay of fair and selfish motives depends, of course, on the specific situation. Here, the behavioural game-theoretic approach is particularly illuminating because it helps to elucidate how or in what ways different motives work together in particular strategic situations to produce certain social dynamics that lead to, say, the unravelling of cooperation in a contractual relationship or in the provision of public goods, of which we shall later speak more. Before addressing this question, we should consider the conceptual limitations of purely economic accounts of fairness.

3. Equity theory

As mentioned before, economic theories model fairness for the purposes of economic theorizing. They aim at aggregate outcomes, but do not intend to provide

[10] J. Henrich, *et al*, *Foundations of Human Sociality* (Oxford: Oxford University Press, 2004); J. Henrich, *et al*, 'Costly Punishment Across Human Societies' (2006) 312 *Science* 1767–70.

[11] M. Rabin, 'Incorporating Fairness into Game Theory and Economics' (1993) 83 *American Economic Review* 1281–302; G. Charness and M. Rabin, 'Understanding Social Preferences with Simple Tests' (2002) 117 *Quarterly Journal of Economics* 817–69; M. Dufwenberg and G. Kirchsteiger, 'A Theory of Sequential Games' (2004) 47 *Games and Economic Behavior* 268–98; A. Falk and U. Fischbacher, 'A Theory of Reciprocity' (2006) 54 *Games and Economic Behavior* 293–315. For empirical evidence, see A. Falk, E. Fehr, and U. Fischbacher, 'On the Nature of Fair Behavior' (2003) 41 *Economic Inquiry* 20–6.

a realistic account of the underlying cognitive or psychological processes. This seems a reasonable approach for many economic questions, but in order to understand the significance of fairness motives for governance problems and the way fairness motives impact on them, one has to go further. Three related issues are of particular importance here. First, it does matter how distributional concerns (inequity aversion) and relational concerns (reciprocity) relate to one another, but this relationship remains unclear in economics. Secondly, people do not oppose unequal distributions in every case, but are willing to accept differences in outcomes if there are legitimate reasons to differentiate. It is a feature of fairness judgments, first described by Aristotle[12] and well established empirically by social psychological equity theory, that just distributions also include distributions proportional to some criterion of 'worthiness' or 'being deserving', in particular proportionally to merit (especially contributions) or need.[13] On the surface, this equitable nature of fairness judgments has been recognized in behavioural economics and indeed demonstrated by many experiments. In fact, outcome-oriented fairness theories have been called theories of in*equity*. However, proportional distribution criteria have rarely found their way into these preference models, presumably to keep the models manageable.[14] Thirdly, acknowledging that fairness can also mean, and in fact very often does mean, a proportional distribution according to some criterion of worthiness brings to the fore another feature of fairness judgments that has plagued philosophical ethics for centuries, i.e., the indeterminacy of justice. When fairness can assume several forms, the question arises as to which criterion of justice is to be preferred in general or in particular situations (equality, merit, need, status, or rights?) and how it is to be operationalized and applied. In fact, much of the ethical or political debate is occupied with these questions. Each individual who articulates a preference based on concerns of fairness is faced with similar structural problems. But in everyday decisions, people rarely solve this problem by deliberate principled reasoning the way philosophers do. They rarely even are aware of it, but rather form their social preferences intuitively. It is no surprise that fairness preferences often do not operate as rationally as is required by economic theory. Instead, they are strongly influenced by personality traits, peculiarities and flaws of psychological decision-making mechanisms, social context and cultural influences. This is not to say that the actual content of fairness preferences is a random product of chaotic processes. In order to understand how context-dependent preferences are formed, one must take into account the interaction between social and psychological factors. This necessitates different kinds of theory.

[12] In Book Five of the Nicomachean Ethic.

[13] D. Messick and K. S. Cook, *Equity Theory* (Ney York: Praeger, 1983); E. Walster and G. W. Walster, 'Equity and Social Justice' (1975) 31 *Journal of Social Issues* 21–43; T. R. Tyler, *et al*, *Social Justice in a Diverse Society* (Boulder, Col.: Westview, 1997) 45.

[14] W. Güth, 'On Inequity Aversion' (2005) 524 Papers on Strategic Interaction, Max-Planck-Institute for Economics. But see R. Selten, 'The Equity Principle in Economic Behavior' in H. W. Gottinger and W. Leinfellner (eds) *Decision Theory and Social Ethics* (Dordrecht: Reidel, 1978) 289.

II. *Homo Reciprocans* Needs Governance But for Different Reasons

Let us now turn to the question of how prospects for cooperation are altered by of fairness preferences. The picture is rather mixed and certainly more complicated than with selfish individuals alone. In a population of people acting like *homo oeconomicus*, cooperation is possible if it is in the interest of the individual to cooperate, for example, in repeated interactions under the restricted conditions put down in the so-called Folk Theorem (sufficient probability of repetition and sufficiently low discount rate, in particular).[15] However, if cooperation is not incentive-compatible, the problem of opportunism may arise. In those situations, sanctions or some other mechanism have to be employed in order to make cooperation possible. By comparison, it is both easier and more difficult to sustain cooperation in situations with a considerable share of fair-minded people, as we shall see. This has been extensively studied with an experimental game called the Public Good Game, which is a variant of the Prisoner's Dilemma with multiple players (usually four).[16] Of course, the Public Good Game involves several (albeit few) actors, whereas cooperation in contractual relations is often bilateral. But seminal findings have been made with this research tool and it seems plausible that these findings will, in principle, carry over to interactions with fewer participants. In the Public Good Game, people receive an endowment that they can (in part or as a whole) keep to themselves or invest in a public good. In the latter case, because it is assumed that cooperation produces an added value, the sum invested in the public good is enlarged and distributed to all participants such that a contributor always gets back less from his own contribution than he invested, but on aggregate participants are better off. If a game of this kind is played only once, or for a known number of rounds, selfish individuals should always contribute nothing, i.e., cooperation should not occur.

1. Reciprocity and its limits

Instead, people tend to invest 40 to 60 per cent of their endowment in one-shot Public Good Games.[17] Thus, a considerable share of people does not behave selfishly right from the start. Their behaviour, however, is driven by the expectation that the others would also behave cooperatively.[18] The reciprocal nature of their

[15] E. Rasmusen, *Games and Information* (Malden, MA: Blackwell, 2nd edn, 1994) 124ff.

[16] E. Fehr and S. Gächter, 'Cooperation and Punishment in Public Goods Experiments' (2000) 90 *American Economic Review* 980–94.

[17] E. Fehr and B. Rockenbach, 'Human Altruism: Economic, Neural, and Evolutionary Perspectives' (2004) 14 *Current Opinion in Neurobiology* 784–90, 785; U. Ones and L. Putterman, 'The Ecology of Collective Action' (2007) 62 *Journal of Economic Behavior and Organization* 495–521, 496.

[18] C. Engel, S. Kube, and M. Kurschilgen, 'Can We Manage First Impressions in Cooperation Problems?' (2011) Preprint from the Max Planck Institute for Research on Collective Goods 2011/5 (available at <http://www.ts-si.org/files/SSRN-id1788915.pdf>).

motivation to cooperate becomes apparent when the game is played for several rounds. These games also start with comparable contribution rates in the first round, but cooperation then declines inescapably until only about ten per cent of participants still contribute.

a. The problem of heterogeneous populations

Judging from the result, it looks as if people were behaving selfishly in public goods situations, as can be observed in many real-life situations. However, this is not because most participants are motivated by selfishness, but rather because a majority of fair-minded people responded to the opportunistic behaviour of a selfish minority by repaying in kind. Hence, the majority refuses to cooperate further for reasons of fairness. These actors can be described as 'conditional cooperators'[19] their cooperation is conditioned on the cooperation of their fellow actors. Although considerable caution is appropriate with regard to the external validity of such estimates, the proportion of different types of behaviour seems to be roughly around 30 per cent of participants acing selfishly, 60 per cent acting reciprocally and ten per cent acting altruistically, at least in some games, and according to some experimental tests.[20]

b. Biased reciprocators

However, although reciprocal behaviour in strategic games is often in fact motivated not by purely strategic considerations, but by concerns of fairness, this motivation should not be idealized either. In particular, people do not behave as impartially as should be expected from a truly ethical point of view. For example, conditional cooperators indeed reciprocate, but they systematically tend to contribute a bit less than they suppose others will.[21] This demonstrates perhaps one of the most pervasive characteristics of human motivation, the so-called self-serving bias. It is important to recognize that the self-serving bias does not result from conscious strategic considerations or from overtly selfish motives. Instead, self-servingly biased motivations can and often do appear to the actor to be objective, impartial, and unbiased. This is so because the bias results from an unconscious distortion of implicit cognitive processes, particularly from

[19] Fehr and Schmidt, n 9; E. Fehr and A. Falk, 'The Psychological Foundations of Incentives' (2002) 46 *European Economic Review* 687–724, 692, 711.

[20] U. Fischbacher, S. Gächter, and E. Fehr, 'Are People Conditionally Cooperative?' (2001) 71 *Economics Letters* 397–404; U. Fischbacher and S. Gächter, 'Social Preferences, Beliefs, and the Dynamics of Free Riding in Public Goods' (2010) 100 *American Economic Review* 541–56; B. Herrmann and C. Thöni, 'Measuring Conditional Cooperation' (2009) 12 *Experimental Economics* 87–92, R. Kurzban and D. Houser, 'Experiments Investigating Cooperative Types in Humans' (2005) 102 *Proceedings of the National Academy of Science* 1803–07; T. Page, L. Putterman, and B. Unel, 'Voluntary Association in Public Goods Experiments' (2005) 115 *Economic Journal* 1032–53.

[21] Fischbacher and Gächter, n 20.

distorted information searching and processing, which are not accessible to or usually not accessed by introspection.[22] Even worse, while our own judgments appear authentic and objective, we are simultaneously suspicious of others and expect their judgments to be biased.[23] Now the decisive factor determining the strength of self-serving bias is ambiguity, be it with respect to factual knowledge or normative standards, because ambiguity creates the leeway in which information processing can be deflected in one direction or the other. Two survey studies provide a telling example of the unconscious nature of the self-serving bias. They were conducted with judges in the US and in Switzerland, and who could be more impartial than judges? The judges were asked to estimate how well they performed compared to other judges with regard to how often their judgments are overturned on appeal, and to rank themselves accordingly in one of four quartiles (best, second-best, etc). Of course, these judges did not have the necessary statistical information at hand to make accurate estimates and were hence confronted with ambiguity. But with errors randomly distributed, their self-evaluations should lead to the quartiles being approximately populated evenly. Instead, the upper two quartiles were heavily overpopulated: 88 per cent of US judges and 92 per cent of Swiss judges rated themselves above average (the unbiased rating would have been 50 per cent) and 56 per cent of US judges, but only 20 per cent of Swiss judges, saw themselves in the best quartile (25 per cent being the unbiased rating).[24] Unfortunately, but not unexpectedly, the self-serving bias also affects fairness judgments.[25]

2. Sanctioning for the sake of fairness

On the one hand, one lesson from standard economic theory remains: cooperation cannot be sustained without institutional intervention, as would have been predicted under the assumption of selfishness. However, on the other hand, a better understanding of why cooperation is so fragile emerges. It is due mainly to the heterogeneity of people with regard to social preferences. Cooperation does not fail because everybody is selfish, but because the selfish behaviour of some (for whatever reason) drives fair-minded people also to behave selfishly (out of fairness concerns). Thus, selfish behaviour prevails in the end despite preferences for fairness, or rather because of preferences for fairness.

[22] E. Pronin, 'Perception and Misperception in Human Judgment' (2006) 11 *Trends in Cognitive Science* 37–43.

[23] E. Pronin, 'How We See Ourselves and How We See Others' (2008) 320 *Science* 1177–80, 1178.

[24] C. Guthrie, J. Rachlinski, and A. Wistrich, 'Inside the Judicial Mind' (2001) 86 *Cornell Law Review* 777–830; M. Schweizer, '*Kognitive Täuschungen vor Gericht*' (2005) dissertation paper, University of Zurich (available at <http://www.decisions.ch/dissertation.html>).

[25] L. Babcock and G. Loewenstein, 'Explaining Bargaining Impasse: The Role of Self-serving Biases' (1997) 11 *Journal of Economic Perspectives* 109–126; J. Konow, 'The Effects of Information and Stakes on Fairness Biases and Dispersion' (2005) 18 *Social Justice Research* 349–390.

a. The balancing function of sanctions

One of the most interesting lessons to be learned from this with regard to governance concerns the role of sanctions. Insofar as behaviour is driven by reciprocity, the relationship between actors becomes paramount. This also changes the role of sanctions. Their objective is no longer confined to correcting individual material incentives, i.e., to raise the expected costs of opportunistic behaviour to such a degree that it is in the own selfish interest of individuals to cooperate. This objective exhausts the task only with regard to the small fraction of individuals that behave selfishly. With regard to reciprocal actors, sanctions assume an additional objective of a quite different nature. Their behaviour is affected by sanctions not only, and not so much as, sanctions are addressed directly to them. They are also affected indirectly insofar as sanctions regulate the behaviour of other actors. This is so because reciprocal types condition their behaviour on the perceived fairness of the behaviour of others, repaying their fairness or unfairness in kind. Correcting material incentives with sanctions is therefore less necessary and sometimes insufficient to keep up cooperation. It is less necessary because fair-minded people cooperate in order to reciprocate the cooperative behaviour of others. Here, social or moral incentives, as one might call them, provide a substantial part of the motivation to cooperation. However, if fair-minded people are faced with opportunistic behaviour on the part of their interaction partners, social or moral incentives work in the opposite direction and make cooperation even more difficult than with selfish individuals. The offense of being exploited unfairly renders such situations much worse than just losing money. Its behavioural effects, furthermore, are not constrained to silencing positive reciprocity. Being exploited regularly also triggers negative reciprocity, i.e., a strong urge to punish the malefactor, which exaggerates the destructive impact of defection on cooperation. In order to sustain cooperation among fair-minded people, sanctions thus also have to get social or moral incentives right. They have to assume the additional objective of preserving or restoring the balance in relationships between actors. Put more practically, the objective of sanctions is to sustain cooperation indirectly, that is, to preserve voluntary cooperation on the side of the majority of reciprocal actors by preventing opportunism on the side of selfish actors.

b. Decentralized sanctioning, counter-punishment, and autonomy

As we have seen, if *homo reciprocans* is involved, sanctioning of selfish behaviour becomes even more crucial. But institutions do not only have to be concerned with keeping up *homo reciprocans*' cooperative spirits by safeguarding him against exploitation. They also have to deal with *homo reciprocans*' powerful urge to punish opportunistic behaviour himself. Thus, fairness preferences in the form of negative reciprocity themselves require sanctioning. Such decentralized punishment by the parties themselves can supplement or substitute centralized sanctioning administered by the state, but negative reciprocity also creates the need to tame private punishment. A series of public-goods experiments addresses this interaction of reciprocity, sanctioning and cooperation.

As previously stated, in Public Good Games without institutional intervention, cooperation declined in a vicious circle in which reciprocal actors adjusted their contributions downwards until a baseline of almost ubiquitous defection was reached. These negative dynamics could be reversed and almost complete cooperation achieved, however, if experimental subjects were given the opportunity to punish defectors after each round of the game, as shown in a famous series of experiments.[26] With regard to the selfish minority, decentralized punishment, if sufficiently serious, fulfils the function envisioned by standard economic theory. It eliminates the incentive to defect and causes them to cooperate. With regard to the reciprocal majority, decentralized punishment provided the necessary moral or social incentives for cooperation. It eliminated defection and induced cooperation on the part of fellow actors, thus creating the basis for positive reciprocity. For standard economic theory, the puzzling question was why people punish at all, despite punishment being costly. From a traditional point of view, a system of sanctioning is a higher order public good in that it benefits everyone who benefits from the cooperative provision of the first-order public good.[27] But there is no shortage of voluntary participation in the sanctioning system, due to negative reciprocity.[28]

However, voluntary decentralized punishment is not the only good news. Because the urge to punish is so strong, an overprovision of sanctions can easily result. For example, the willingness to punish persists even when punishment becomes inefficient because the costs of sanctioning (borne by punisher and punishee) exceed gains of cooperation.[29] Moreover, it is not always cooperators punishing defectors, but also defectors punishing cooperators. Punishment is exerted not only for cooperative reasons, but also with an anti-cooperative intention. When given the opportunity to punish the punishers, punishment

[26] E. Ostrom, J. Walker, and R. Gardner, 'Covenants With and Without a Sword' (1992) 86 *American Political Science Review* 404–417; E. Fehr and S. Gächter, 'Cooperation and Punishment in Public Good Experiments' (2000) 90 *American Economic Review* 980–94; E. Fehr and S. Gächter, 'Altruistic Punishment in Humans' (2002) 415 *Nature* 137–40; the same effect shows in centralized punishment: see R. O'Gorman, J. Henrich, and M. Van Vugt, 'Constraining Free Riding in Public Goods Games: Designated Solitary Punishers Can Sustain Human Cooperation' (2009) 276 *Proceedings of the Royal Society B* 323–9; D. Baldassarri and G. Grossman, 'Centralized Sanctioning and Legitimate Authority Promote Cooperation in Humans' (2011) 108 *Proceedings of the National Academy of Science* 11023–7.

[27] Fehr and Gächter (2002), n 26, 137.

[28] Called 'altruistic punishment': see Fehr and Gächter (2002), n 26; for altruistic punishment by third parties, see, e.g., H. Bernhard, E. Fehr, and U. Fischbacher, 'Group Affiliation and Altruistic Norm Enforcement' (2006) 96 *American Economic Review* 217–21; P. Lewisch, S. Ottone, and F. Ponzano, 'Free-Riding on Altruistic Punishment?' (2011) 7 *Review of Law and Economics* 165–94; for an experiment on different possible motivations for punishment, see A. Nicklisch and I. Wolff, 'Cooperation Norms in Multiple-stage Punishment' (2011) 13 *Journal of Public Economic Theory* 791–827.

[29] A. Botelho, *et al*, 'Social Norms and Social Choice' (2005) University of Central Florida Department of Economics Working Paper No 30 (available at <http://www3.eeg.uminho.pt/publications/NIMAwp30.pdf>).

intended to induce cooperation is in turn being punished by defectors, leading to a decline in cooperation.[30] In this regard, a series of cross-cultural experiments is quite illuminating.[31] It showed that anti-cooperative punishment exists in different cultures in different intensity. Prospects for cooperation depend crucially on the (culturally varying) amount of antisocial punishment. Because cooperative punishment is deterred or foiled by anti-cooperative punishment, cooperation is doomed to fail to the degree to which antisocial punishment is common to a culture. In this regard, it has proved telling to look at the relationship between punishing behaviour (as observed in the experiments) and social norms of civic cooperation (as elicited in the World Value Survey). Social norms of civic cooperation refer to people's attitudes towards tax evasion, abuse of the welfare state, or dodging fares on public transport. These norms show a strong statistical correlation with cooperative behaviour: the stronger norms of civic cooperation in a society, the harder the cooperative punishment in the experiments. However, the weaker those norms are, the stronger the anti-cooperative punishment; that is, the harsher cooperators are being punished. It is not far-fetched to assume that strong norms of civic cooperation act as a constraint on antisocial punishment. Put more generally, the performance of formal institutions like contracts often depends on their interaction with social norms.[32]

The existence of anti-cooperative punishment also reveals that being subjected to peer punishment is not always considered a preferable environment for cooperation. This shows in experimental games where people can choose to play a game either with or without the opportunity to punish.[33] In this case, the clear majority opts against punishment at first. However, after having experienced the devastating effects of missing sanctioning, almost everybody eventually switches to the game with punishment where now almost complete cooperation is achieved.[34] Here an aversion against sanctioning becomes visible, which probably stems from

[30] L. Denant-Boemont, D. Masclet, and C. Noussair, 'Punishment, Counterpunishment and Sanction Enforcement in a Social Dilemma Experiment' (2007) 33 *Economic Theory* 145–67; N. Nikiforakis, 'Punishment and Counter-punishment in Public Good Games' (2008) 92 *Journal of Public Economics* 91–112. For spiteful and strategic punishment, see also K. Jensen, 'Punishment and Spite, the Dark Side of Cooperation' (2010) 365 *Philosophical Transactions of the Royal Society B* 2635–50.

[31] B. Herrmann, C. Thöni, and S. Gächter, 'Antisocial Punishment Across Societies' (2008) 319 *Science* 1362–7; see also S. Gächter and B. Herrmann, 'Reciprocity, Culture and Human Cooperation' (2009) 364 *Philosophical Transactions of the Royal Society B* 791–806; S. Gächter, B. Herrmann, and C. Thöni, 'Culture and Cooperation' (2010) 365 *Philosophical Transactions of the Royal Society B* 2651–61.

[32] S. Magen, 'Fairness, *Eigennutz und die Rolle des Rechts*' in C. Engel, *et al* (eds) *Recht und Verhalten* (Tübingen: Mohr Siebeck, 2007) 261–360; S. Magen, '*Zur Interaktion von Recht und sozialen Normen bei der dezentralen Bereitstellung von Gemeinschaftsgütern*' in M. Stolleis and W. Streek (eds) *Aktuelle Fragen zu Politischer und Rechtlicher Steuerung im Kontext der Globalisierung* (Baden-Baden: Nomos, 2007) 185–208.

[33] Ö. Gürerk, B. Irlenbusch, and B. Rockenbach, 'The Competitive Advantage of Sanctioning Institutions' (2006) 312 *Science* 108–11.

[34] Gürerk, Irlenbusch, and Rockenbach, n 33; M. Sutter, S. Haigner, and M. Kocher, 'Choosing the Carrot or the Stick?' (2010) 77 *Review of Economic Studies* 1540–66.

the fact that monitoring and coercion impairs one's autonomy.[35] That autonomy is a decisive factor is corroborated by research showing that cooperation increases substantially if a sanctioning mechanism is not imposed by fiat, but if people can vote for or against it.[36] If chosen autonomously, participants apparently seem to find a sanctioning mechanism more helpful than annoying. In a sense, governance is faced with a dilemma regarding punishment: in order to sustain voluntary cooperation, opportunistic behaviour has to be suppressed by sanctions, which in turn interferes with people's autonomy and signals distrust. But at the same time, one has to maintain trust and a cooperative mindset that is impaired by control and coercion. Therefore it is crucial for the success of cooperation that sanctioning mechanisms be viewed as legitimate. Procedures might be the key to provide this legitimacy.

3. Coordinating fairness

There is another important issue that should be addressed here. It concerns the indeterminacy of fairness. Our previous conclusions about cooperation based on fairness have to be qualified in this regard. They are all premised on the presumption that people at least practically settle on a common understanding of what fairness means in a given context. In the Public Good Games used in the experiments reported above, selecting a fairness standard did not pose a serious problem. Since every participant was given the same endowment and benefited from the public good in the same way, equal contributions were the obvious standard of fair behaviour. But as soon as people differ in relevant respects (wealth, income, abilities, productivity, sensitivity, etc), several standards compete. Actors then are faced with considerable leeway regarding the choice and operationalization of the criterion of justice. As always when faced with ambiguity, each party's choice of a standard is biased by self-interest. In real-life situations, which are usually fraught with differences and asymmetries, psychological indeterminacy of fairness is a permanent and serious source of conflict. It is also an important reason for institutional intervention. Considered in isolation, the selection of a standard of fairness seems to be a usual conflict over distributional questions. Viewed in the context of cooperation, this choice instead concerns a higher order coordination problem: people are better off if they settle on a common standard because they can then reap the benefits of cooperation, but their preferences differ as to which standard should be chosen.

From a behavioural perspective, it seems to me that dealing with this higher order coordination problem is one of the most important functions that

[35] For the valuation of autonomy see B. Frey and R. Jegen, 'Motivation Crowding Theory' (2001) 15 *Journal of Economic Surveys* 589–611; B. Frey and F. Oberholzer-Gee, 'The Cost of Price Incentive' (1999) 87 *American Economic Review* 746–55.

[36] S. Tontrup, W. Gaissmaier, and H. Gong, 'The Comparative Advantage of Legitimate Procedures' working paper (unpublished) (cooperation increased, e.g., from 58% to 85% average contributions); see also Baldassarria and Grossman, n 26.

institutions in general, and the law in particular, fulfil with regard to fairness and justice. But how can institutions in general, and the law in particular, shape and influence individual fairness judgments? One psychological mechanism, or rather a group of somewhat similar mechanisms, that seems particularly important in this regard is framing. The term 'framing' sometimes refers to a specific effect and sometimes to a more general effect. In its specific meaning, framing relates to prospect theory. Prospect theory posits that valuations of alternatives are not based on absolute outcomes, but depend on whether the outcome is framed as a gain or as a loss compared to a reference point, with losses carrying greater weight than gains (loss aversion), and this difference leads to risk-seeking in the face of losses and risk aversion in the face of gains.[37] Changing the reference point by describing a decision problem in a different way can thus alter individual valuations by changing the frame from gains to losses or vice versa. Similar effects, it can be assumed, occur in fairness judgments. For example, not reciprocating a gift seems to be less reprehensible than taking something of the same value from someone. Put more generally, in the context of fairness, reference points determine whether a given fairness question is a matter of positive reciprocity or of negative reciprocity.

Under a second meaning, the term 'reference point' does not refer to a turning point between losses and gains, but to social comparisons in general, for example, to the questions of what the others get in a similar situation.[38] Social comparisons of this kind have a huge impact on fairness preferences. For example, if a proposer plays several Ultimatum Games with different responders simultaneously and responders know what the proposer offers to the other players, their willingness to accept an offer as fair depends crucially on the offers made to the other players.[39] But it is not reference transactions alone that serve as reference points. Familiar social norms or salient institutions can also serve this purpose. In this more general context of social comparisons and normative expectations, framing affects behaviour by providing (direct or indirect) information about reference transactions or about relevant social norms or institutions. These cues then influence the fairness standard that individuals adopt—not necessarily in a conscious way—in forming their fairness judgment. For example, cooperation in a Prisoner's Dilemma experiment increased substantially only because the game was labelled 'Community Game' instead of 'Wall Street Game'.[40]

[37] D. Kahneman, 'A Perspective on Judgment and Choice' (2003) 58 *American Psychologist* 697–720, 703ff; for a documentation of seminal papers, see D. Kahneman and A. Tversky (eds), *Choices, Values and Frames* (Cambridge: Cambridge University Press, 2000).

[38] G. Jasso, 'The Theory of Comparison Processes' in P. Burke (ed) *Contemporary Social Psychological Theories* (Stanford: Stanford University Press, 2006) 165; D. Kahneman, J. Knetsch, and R. Thaler, 'Fairness and the Assumptions of Economics' (2003) 59 *Journal of Business* S285–S300.

[39] See, e.g., D. Alelwell and A. Nicklisch, 'Wage Differentials and Social Comparison: An Experimental Study of Interrelated Ultimatum Bargaining' (2009) 29 *International Review of Law and Economics* 210–20.

[40] L. Ross and A. Ward, 'Naive Realism in Everyday Life' in E. Reed, *et al* (eds) *Values and Knowledge* (Hillsdale, NJ.: Erlbaum, 1996) 103.

III. Fairness in Contract Governance

Contracts enable private parties to create legally enforceable obligations by mutual exchange of promises (under the conditions specified by the relevant law). A traditional law and economics point of view would consider such an institution to affect behaviour by altering selfish incentives through the expectation of enforcement, hence by sanctions. From a behavioural point of view, contracts might influence behaviour quite differently. Contracts obviously often serve as a means to institutionalize cooperation in the form of mutually beneficial exchange. With *homo reciprocans* contracting, contracts will be accompanied by expectations of fairness.[41] These fairness expectations might not be recognized by the law as relevant, but it is safe to assume that they influence the formation and execution of the contract by the parties and should hence be taken into account by contract governance. For example, a contract design proposed by economic contract theory as an efficient mechanism will be avoided if parties regard it as unjust. If chosen anyhow, it might have detrimental effects.[42] Put more generally, fairness may support or impede a contract's execution, or it may interfere with it otherwise. These questions are important for any behavioural account of contract law, but they have only begun to be addressed systematically. Thus, we have to confine ourselves to some examples that hint at the direction future research might take.

1. Statutes as reference points

In 2001, the German Distance Selling Act (now § 312b (1) of the German Civil Code) implementing the EU Distance Selling Directive introduced a mandatory withdrawal right for buyers in distant selling contracts. Since most distance sellers had already granted a withdrawal right on a voluntary basis, the revision of the law did not change the rights of buyers in effect, but only the motives of their provision. Nevertheless, the rate of returns increased from 24.2 per cent to 35 per cent.[43] For example, clothes were increasingly ordered in different sizes, with people sending back the unfitting ones. Georg Borges and Bernd Irlenbusch examined the reason for this change of behaviour with the help of an experiment.[44] Their results suggest that a voluntary provision of a withdrawal right is

[41] E. Fehr, S. Gächter, and G. Kirchsteiger, 'Reciprocity as a Contract Enforcement Device – Experimental Evidence' (1997) 65 *Econometrica* 833–60.

[42] E. Fehr, A. Klein, and K. M. Schmidt, 'Fairness, Incentives and Contractual Incompleteness' (2001) Institute for Empirical Research in Economics, University of Zurich, Working Paper No. 72; see also E. Fehr and A. Falk, 'Wage Rigidity in a Competitive Incomplete Contract Market' (1999) 107 *Journal of Political Economy* 106–134.

[43] G. Borges and B. Irlenbusch, 'Fairness Crowded Out by Law: An Experimental Study on Withdrawal Rights' (2007) 163 *Journal of Institutional and Theoretical Economics* 84–101, 88; for a discussion of the phenomenon and its implications, see S. Bechtold '*Die Grenzen zwingenden Vertragsrechts*' (Tübingen: Mohr Siebeck, 2010) 110ff.

[44] Borges and Irlenbusch, n 43.

perceived as friendly, such that buyers reciprocate by not exploiting sellers too heavily. However, if withdrawal rights are obligatory under the law, buyers may feel entitled to return goods, eliminating the need to reciprocate. Also, sellers now lack the opportunity to show friendly intentions. As a consequence, Borges and Irlenbusch argue, the motivation to treat distance sellers fairly is crowded out by the law.[45] In my view, this interpretation does not exactly hit the point. The law presumably did not turn consumers into selfish beings, but changed the content of their fairness expectation such that they now felt morally entitled to return purchases. According to their (maybe biased) perceptions, their reaction was not selfish, but righteous. So what the revision of the Distance Selling Act did in behavioural terms was to change the reference points relative to which consumers formed their fairness preferences.

This research is but an example of what has been called the 'expressive function' of the law.[46] In standard law and economics, this function is confined to providing focal points in coordination problems,[47] but cannot contribute to the solution for problems of cooperation. With preferences for fairness, expressive aspects of the law assume a much more prominent and maybe crucial role.[48] They correspond to the need to coordinate individual standards of fairness if cooperation is to be sustained among reciprocal actors. The behavioural mechanism by which the law may achieve this end is by providing salient and legitimate reference points and by framing interactions that take place in the shadow of the law. As the above example of the Distance Selling Act teaches us, the law has expressive effects regardless of whether or not they are intended.[49] It also tells us that ignoring these effects may foil the purpose of the law or may inadvertently produce otherwise undesired results. Thus, contract governance seems well advised to take them into account.

2. Contracts as reference points

According to standard incomplete contracts theory, it can be advantageous for parties who want to enter into a long-term contract but are faced with uncertainty about relevant aspects of the future state of the world to form an incomplete contract first and leave the completion of contractual terms to future renegotiations when the actual state of the world has been revealed. If *homo oeconomicus*-like behaviour is assumed, these renegotiations will be conducted in a Coasian way leading to an (*ex-post*) efficient bargain.[50] However, (*ex-ante*) inefficiencies can

[45] Borges and Irlenbusch, n 43, 84, 96ff; for motivation crowding theory, see Frey and Jegen, n 35.

[46] R. McAdams, 'An Attitudinal Theory of Expressive Law' (2000) 79 *Oregon Law Review* 339–90; on the meaning of the term 'expressive' in this regard see also L. A. Kornhauser, 'No Best Answer?' (1998) 146 *University of Pennsylvania Law Review* 1599–1637, 1624ff.

[47] R. McAdams, 'A Focal Point Theory of Expressive Law' (2000) 86 *Virginia Law Review* 1649–1729.

[48] S. Magen, *Gerechtigkeit als Proprium des Rechts* (2009) habilitation thesis, University of Bonn, 183ff.

[49] See, e.g., B. Depoorter and S. Tontrup, 'The Legal Endowment Effect' (2011) Hastings College of Law, San Francisco, Working Paper; B. Depoorter and S. Tontrup (2011) 'Contract Entitlement', Hastings College of Law, San Francisco, Working Paper.

[50] On incomplete contracts, see P. Bolton and M. Dewatripont, *Contract Theory* (Cambridge, Mass: MIT Press, 2005) 487ff; O. Hart, 'Incomplete Contracts' in S. N. Durlauf and L. E. Blume

arise because of the hold-up problem. Under the prospect of future renegotiations, rational parties will underinvest during the contractual relationship because non-contractible sunk investments will be exploited by the other party in later renegotiations.[51] It is an interesting question whether the hold-up problem is alleviated when parties care about fairness, possibly keeping them from exploiting commitments made by the other party. If, however, parties are also affected by self-serving biases and if they sometimes also punish spitefully or too much, fairness-related cooperation problems as those described earlier are to be expected in the context of long-term contracting, too.

That this is, in fact, the case has been shown recently in a very illuminating line of work,[52] which seems quite promising with regard to possible directions of future research. It empirically tests[53] a behavioural theory on renegotiations in incomplete contracts put forward by Oliver Hart and John Moore.[54] Instead of relation-specific investments, the theory considers performance. Performance, it assumes, can be perfunctory or consummate, but only perfunctory performance is verifiable before courts and hence contractible. Nevertheless, reciprocal actors will be willing to provide consummate performance as long as they feel they are getting what they are entitled to. If, on the other hand, parties feel treated unfairly, they will withhold some part of consummate performance, dubbed 'shading' by the authors. Since the self-serving distortion of fairness judgments increases with ambiguity, shading should increase with ambiguity because parties will more often feel deprived of what they are entitled to. Against the backdrop of these considerations, long-term contracts assume quite a different function of which standard contract theory is not aware: contracts, according to Hart and Moore, serve as reference points determining a party's sense of entitlement.[55] If a contract is rigid, it pins down future outcomes very precisely and leaves little room for disagreement and aggravation, parties tend not to shade on their obligations as long as they get what is specified in the contract. If, however, a contract is more flexible and allows for more than one outcome, feelings of entitlement will be exposed to self-serving distortions. Then, Hart and Moore assume, each party will feel entitled to the outcome most favourable to it, whereby fairness-expectations will diverge and shading increase. Hence, contracting parties are faced with a

(eds) *The New Palgrave Dictionary of Economics* (New York: Palgrave Macmillan, 2nd edn, 2008) 175–84.

51 See Bolton and Dewatripont, n 50, 560ff; S. Shavell, 'Contractual Holdup and Legal Intervention' (2007) 36 *Journal of Legal Studies* 325–54.

52 O. Hart and J. Moore, 'Contracts as Reference Points' (2008) 73 *Quarterly Journal of Economics* 1–48; E. Fehr, O. Hart, and C. Zehnder, 'Contracts, Reference Points, and Competition – Behavioral Effects of the Fundamental Transformation' (2009) 7 *Journal of the European Economic Association* 561–72; E. Fehr, O. Hart, and C. Zehnder, 'Contracts as Reference Points — Experimental Evidence' (2011) 101 *American Economic Review* 493–525.

53 Fehr, Hart, and Zehnder (2009), n 52 above; Fehr, Hart, and Zehnder (2011), n 52.

54 Hart and Moore, n 52.

55 Hart and Moore, n 52, 1, 2ff. For contracts and loss frames, see R. R. W. Brooks, A. Stremitzer, and S. W. Tontrup, 'Framing Contracts: Why Loss Framing Increases Effort' (2011) John M. Olin Centre for Studies in Law, Economics, and Public Policy, Research Paper No 438.

trade-off between rigidity (which reduces shading, but excludes adjustments to unforeseen contingencies) and flexibility (which allows for adjustments, but increases shading).

Experiments conducted by Ernst Fehr, Oliver Hart, and Christian Zehnder using a two-stage game support this theory.[56] In the game, participants are uncertain at the time of contract formation whether production costs will be low (good state of nature) or high (bad state of nature) at the time of performance. At a first stage, buyers can choose between a rigid and a flexible contract. Prices are then negotiated in an auction in which sellers compete for contracts. In rigid contracts, the negotiated price is fixed, irrespective of the state of nature. In flexible contracts, the negotiated price forms the lower bound of a price range (the upper bound being given exogenously) from which the buyer can choose the actual price at the second stage. After contracting, the state of nature is revealed and buyers can choose a price if the contract is flexible. When costs turn out to be high, rigid contracts are not performed because they are no longer mutually beneficial. Flexible contracts, by contrast, allow the buyer to choose a higher price and perform the contract. After the buyer has chosen the price from within the price range, the seller can choose between consummate performance (high quality) and perfunctory performance (low quality). Perfunctory performance reduces the buyer's payoffs substantially,[57] but also burdens the seller with a slightly higher (not lower!) cost.[58] Thus, the seller has no material incentive to shade because he has to pay a price for it. The second stage thus bears a certain similarity to an Ultimatum Game.[59]

The results are very much in line with Hart and Moore's hypothesis of 'contracts as reference points'. First, both with rigid and flexible contracts, competitive forces compel sellers to accept low prices (in rigid contracts) or lower price bounds (in flexible contracts) and prices and lower price bounds converge downwards on the competitive price. Competition thus leads to a markedly uneven distribution of payoffs. With rigid contracts, sellers on average earn only a quarter of what buyers earn. With flexible contracts, actual prices chosen from the price range are somewhat higher, but sellers still receive only 40 per cent of buyers' payoffs on average.[60] The question then is: how do sellers react? Selfish sellers should not punish at all, because punishment is costly (and hence not subgame perfect). Reciprocal sellers should shade when they perceive the offer as unfair. Since prices are lower in rigid contracts than in flexible contracts, inequity aversion should lead to more shading in rigid contracts. According to the 'contracts as reference points' hypothesis, however, it should be the other way around, because rigid contracts are unambiguous and thus serve as better reference points, whereas flexible contracts provide leeway for self-serving distortions, increasing perceived

[56] Fehr, Hart, and Zehnder (2009), n 52, 561, 568ff; Fehr, Hart, and Zehnder (2011), n 52, 493, 505ff.

[57] 100 instead of 140.

[58] 25 instead of 20.

[59] Further discussed by Fehr, Hart, and Zehnder (2011), n 52, 493, 519.

[60] See Fehr, Hart, and Zehnder (2011), n 52, 493, 506.

unfairness. Experiments confirm this hypothesis. Although sellers earn less from rigid contracts, they nevertheless still almost always provide consummate performance (94 per cent of the cases), whereas consummate performance drops significantly in flexible contracts (to 75 per cent of the cases).[61] However, if contracts are not formed voluntarily by the parties, but terms and parties are given exogenously, shading reappears in rigid contracts (consummate performance drops to 84 per cent) and the difference with flexible contracts is no longer statistically significant.[62] Somehow, rigid contracts seem to lose their legitimacy as reference points under these circumstances. Fehr, Hart, and Zehnder take this observation as evidence that competition legitimizes the terms of a contract. The reason they suppose is that buyers can hide their unfairness behind a 'veil of competition' because outcomes are attributed instead to market processes.[63] Although there is something to be said for this explanation, it somehow misses the point. If parties are matched and given terms by fiat, there is no contract anymore at all, but instead a forced relationship. Not only competition is missing here, but also mutual agreement and consent. Thus, consent makes reference points legitimate and highlights the crucial difference between rigid and flexible contracts: in rigid contracts, the seller consents to precisely the price he is later given. Therefore, he accepts it as fair. In flexible contracts, the seller does not consent to any particular price, but to a price floor and the buyer's right to determine the price later. Therefore, the reference point in flexible contracts is not only more ambiguous (which it is, indeed), but the contract is also referred to in a different context in which it assumes a different meaning. Flexible contracts do not serve as a reference point for performance based on a set price, but as a reference frame for deferred price negotiations. This not only entails more ambiguity, but also diminished legitimacy because the seller has not committed himself to anything more than a lower limit for future negotiations. Aside from this, there is nothing specific to which he later feels bound.

3. Commitment through promises and legal procedures

This line of argument suggests, of course, that there might be other specific motivational forces at work in a contractual relationship beyond reciprocity. Although this has not been researched in depth, there is indeed some initial evidence that the very fact of making a promise as well as the 'procedure' of doing so with reference to the law may have a behavioural effect. With standard preferences, neither the exchange of promises nor reference to the law as such should make any difference, because without the backing of sanctions, such communication remains 'cheap talk'. In experimental games, however, the mere exchange of promises usually enhances cooperation considerably. However, it is unclear whether this is due

[61] Fehr, Hart, and Zehnder (2011), n 52, 493, 506ff. An analysis of individual behaviour confirms this result, see Fehr, Hart, and Zehnder (2011), n 52, 512ff.

[62] Fehr, Hart, and Zehnder (2011), n 52, 493, 516ff.

[63] Fehr, Hart, and Zehnder (2011), n 52, 493, 497, 521.

to fairness (not letting down others' legitimate payoff expectations) or because people have an intrinsic motivation to keep their word. At least one experiment suggests that the latter is the case.[64] In another experiment, it is shown that cooperation is further enhanced when an agreement is framed as a valid contract (citing legal norms) compared to a mere promise, although enforcement is possible in neither of the cases. Hence the procedure of concluding a contract with reference to the law seems to evoke an intrinsic motivation to comply beyond the moral commitment of a promise.[65]

IV. Conclusion

The last two decades have witnessed tremendous progress towards a behavioural account of fairness and reciprocity, brought about by a combination of economic theories and empirical methods that is nowadays known as behavioural economics. The point of this research was not just to show what everyone except economists knew anyhow, that is, that people do care about justice and fairness. The point was to examine whether and how individual concerns for fairness play out in strategic interactions and thus have to be regarded as a class of preferences of practical relevance in economic and other policy-related settings. In this regard, behavioural economics was successful in showing that fairness preferences influence behaviour in a way that renders predictions based on the selfishness assumption often, but not always, misleading. However, to know that man is rather a *homo reciprocans* than a *homo oeconomicus* does not mean that his behaviour can be better foreseen, because *homo reciprocans* is a rather impressionable being and his behaviour depends heavily on the specifics of the situation and the social context in which he is acting at any given point. This characteristic of fairness motives also casts doubt on the external validity of experimental results, not so much with regard to the general behavioural tendencies and dispositions detected, but with regard to how these general behavioural mechanisms play out in real life. What is needed here is a combination of theory and experiments, corroborated by real-life data from field experiments or econometrics.[66] Thus, unfortunately, that which represents clear progress in the scientific account of human social behaviour turns out to be a nuisance for the quest for solutions to specific governance problems

[64] C. Vanberg, 'Why Do People Keep their Promises?' (2008) 76 *Econometrica* 1467–80; see also M. Belot, V. Bhaskar, and J. van de Ven, 'Promises and Cooperation: Evidence from a TV Game Show' (2010) 73 *Journal of Economic Behavior and Organization* 396–405; T. Baumgartner, U. Fischbacher, A. Feierabend, K. Lutz, and E. Fehr, 'The Neural Circuitry of a Broken Promise' (2009) 64 *Neuron* 756–70; G. Charness and M. Dufwenberg, 'Bare Promises: An Experiment' (2010) 107 *Economic Lettres* 281–3.

[65] S. Tontrup, B. Irlenbusch, and M. Kurschilgen, 'The Expressive Function of Contracts' working paper (unpublished); but see C. Vanberg, 'Voting on a Sharing Norm in a Dictator Game' (2010) 31 *Journal of Economic Psychology* 285–92.

[66] For a commendable example, see B. Frey and B. Torgler, 'Tax Morale and Conditional Cooperation' (2007) 35 *Journal of Comparative Economics* 136–59.

because with fairness these now hinge on unexpected details. Whereas traditional rational choice theory often can come up with predictions that are robust but inaccurate, predictions based on fairness preferences are more realistic, but are, at the same time, notoriously incomplete and rather fuzzy. Nevertheless, quite a bit can be said about certain generic properties of fairness and reciprocity as driving forces of behaviour.

In this Chapter, I tried to sketch some important features of these general working mechanisms of fairness based on a selective review of a small part of the literature. To understand those working mechanisms, it is crucial to distinguish mental, behavioural, and social aspects of fairness and to see how they work together and what their respective contributions are in sustaining cooperation or avoiding opportunistic behaviour. Experimental game theory has focused mainly on the behavioural level and developed two types of models of preferences for fairness: inequity aversion, concerned with the distribution of outcomes, and reciprocity, concerned with the fairness of intentions. Both assume that preferences for fairness interact with selfish preferences that remain a primary motivating force. Fairness judgments, however, also allow for several proportional criteria of distribution, as equity theory has shown. The (psychological) necessity to select among different criteria of fairness and their operationalization renders fairness judgments indeterminate and makes them receptive to social and contextual influences.

Compared to *homo oeconomicus*, cooperation is both easier and more difficult with *homo reciprocans*. It is easier because reciprocity repays cooperation with cooperation. It is more difficult because opportunistic behaviour by selfish types, usually mixed into real-life populations, triggers negative reciprocity in reciprocal actors, causing a downward spiral that eventually extinguishes cooperation. Furthermore, even fairness judgments are unconsciously biased toward self-interest if and insofar as factual knowledge or normative standards are ambiguous. Therefore, sanctions remain crucial to sustain cooperation, but they assume quite a different objective compared to *homo oeconomicus*. With *homo reciprocans*, sanctions have to provide social or moral incentives in order to sustain positive reciprocity, and they do so indirectly by preventing opportunism and thus keeping social relations fair or balanced. Negative reciprocity provides sufficient motivation to leave punishment to the parties, but excess punishment and anti-cooperative punishment combined with self-serving perceptions calls for institutional intervention in order to prevent a vicious circle. Although people in general show an aversion to punishment institutions, they are accepted as legitimate if they are chosen autonomously.

Indeterminacy of fairness creates the need to settle on shared fairness standards, if cooperation is to be based on positive reciprocity and protected against negative reciprocity. Since fairness judgments intrinsically rely on reference points and reference transactions, institutions can contribute to this higher-order coordination problem by providing those references. In contract governance, both statutes and contracts can serve this purpose through their expressive effect. For example, making a withdrawal right obligatory by law—it had hitherto been granted by distance sellers on a voluntary basis—can increase returns because the revision of the law also shifted the framing of withdrawal from a friendly concession to an action the seller is obliged to endure. In long-term contractual relations, initial contracts can serve as reference points for subsequent renegotiations. This can reduce perfunctory performance or other forms of opportunistic behaviour if contracts are unambiguous rather than flexible. Finally, the mere fact of making a promise and the 'procedure' of doing so with reference to the law induces a commitment to the contract beyond reciprocity. In short, with *homo reciprocans* as a party to the contract, contractual relationships are necessarily accompanied by expectations of fairness and reciprocity. Contract governance is thus charged with the task of institutionalizing and taming sanctions and of coordinating fairness standards by managing frames and reference points via the expressive dimension of statutes and contracts.

The Governance of Contractual Relations: A Case for Fairness?

Comment on S. Magen, 'Fairness and Reciprocity in Contract Governance'

*Gralf-Peter Calliess**

In his contribution to this volume, Stefan Magen gives a brilliant overview of the recent advances of economic analysis which came to be known under the title of 'behavioural law and economics'. In order to assess in how far fairness preferences as a feature of the proposed '*homo reciprocans*' model are relevant in the context of contract governance (see Section II), it seems to be necessary to elaborate in more detail what 'traditional' new institutional economics analysis entails with regard to the governance of contractual relations (see Section I).

I. The Governance of Contractual Relations

While there are a variety of valuable suggestions to map the governance of contractual relations, the analysis and terminology of Oliver Williamson's 'economics of governance' seems to be particularly helpful as a starting point. By equating contracts with transactions, new institutional economics approaches the issue of economic exchange in a non-juridical way. Drawing on many findings of other authors as well, in the following I develop a map of governance of economic exchange consisting of a total of 12 generic governance mechanisms which in practice are combined and recombined in manifold ways. According to a recent summary Williamson provided of his own theory:

> ... [t]he economics of governance is an effort to implement the "study of good order and workable arrangements", where good order includes both spontaneous order in the market... and intentional order... The object is to work out the efficiency logic for managing

* Professor of Private Law, International and Comparative Commercial Law, and Legal Theory at the Law Department of the University of Bremen and Director of the Centre for Transnational Studies.

transactions by alternative modes of governance—principally spot markets, various long term contracts (hybrids), and hierarchies.[1]

Williamson starts his analysis with the classical distinction between markets and hierarchies (firms).[2] An economic actor in need of a product (goods or services) faces 'the alternatives of make or buy'.[3] Economic actors employ governance mechanisms in order to cope with the intrinsic *uncertainty* involved in co-operation, which is founded in *ex ante* bounded rationality, i.e. contracting parties' inability to draft 'complete contracts', as well as *ex post* opportunism, i.e. contracting parties' ability to annihilate part of the mutual gain from co-operation in order to increase their individual share in it.[4] The relevant criteria for choosing a governance mode for a specific transaction under conditions of such uncertainty are *frequency* (occasional/recurrent) from the point of view of the buyer and *asset specificity* with regard to necessary investments made by suppliers (non-specific/mixed/idiosyncratic).[5]

1. Lawfulness

Given that the state has the monopoly to define property rights and to enforce contracts (lawfulness), *market governance* is the main governance structure for non-specific transactions, for example the purchase of standard equipment or material. Here, actors mainly rely on market alternatives (prospective exit) and legal rules and litigation (retrospective voice) to protect against opportunism, since the transaction costs of employing additional private governance mechanisms do not pay off. *Unified governance* by means of vertical integration is the most favourable governance mechanism for recurrent transactions with idiosyncratic investment characteristics, for example the site-specific transfer of an intermediate product across successive stages. If in intra-firm trade a problem arises, access to courts is denied (forbearance) and parties—who in this case are not legally distinct persons, but business units of the same firm—must resolve their disputes internally by means of hierarchy. The firm, thus, becomes its own court of ultimate appeal.[6]

Private governance comes into focus for transactions with mixed investment characteristics, for example the purchase of customized equipment or material, as well as for occasional transactions with idiosyncratic investment characteristics,

[1] O. Williamson, 'The Economics of Governance' (2005) 95(2) *American Economic Review* 1–18, 1.

[2] R. Coase, 'The Nature of the Firm' (1937) 4(16) *Economica* 386–405; O. E. Williamson, 'The Modern Corporation: Origins, Evolution, Attributes' (1981) 19(4) *Journal of Economic Literature* 1537–68, 1539.

[3] For the following see O. Williamson, *The Economic Institutions of Capitalism* (New York/London: Free Press/MacMillan 1985) 68; O. Williamson, *The Mechanisms of Governance* (Oxford: Oxford University Press, 1996) 66; Williamson, n 1, 1, 3, 11.

[4] Williamson (1996), n 3, 9.

[5] Williamson (1985), n 3, 72–9.

[6] Williamson, n 1, 1, 9ff.

as in the case of the construction of a plant. Here, specialized investments are made by the supplier, a fact which poses additional contractual hazards such as premature contract cancellation. The implied risks will either be priced out by the supplier, or the buyer has to offer credible commitments as a relief. Such credible commitments are characteristic for *hybrid governance*, which best fits long-term relational contracts. Since switching costs rise due to relation-specific investments, the exit option characteristic for market governance is of little value. In addition to reliance on the state legal system, contract parties therefore employ mechanisms of private ordering to support the exchange. These may be either bilateral or trilateral. In case of *bilateral governance mechanisms*, the immediate parties to an exchange are actively involved in the provision of order, for example by posting hostages (such as entry fees or a deposit), engaging in reciprocal trade, or otherwise embedding the transaction in a self-enforcing arrangement, where the potential benefits of opportunism with regard to a single transaction have to be set off against the disadvantages of a disruption of the long-term business relationship (exit). In case of *trilateral governance mechanisms*, trusted third parties are involved in the provision of private order, for example an escrow agent, a bank issuing a letter of credit, or arbitration institutions offering alternative dispute resolution services.[7]

Because added bureaucratic costs and lower incentive intensity accrue once a transaction is taken out of the market, Williamson concludes that vertical integration is usefully thought of as the governance mode of last resort: 'try markets, try hybrids, and have recourse to the firm only when all else fails'.[8] However, Williamson holds that while:

> ...[the] main contractual action...takes places between the parties in the context of private ordering, and court ordering appears late, if at all... each generic mode of governance (market, hybrid, hierarchy) is supported by and in significant ways is defined by a distinctive form of contract law.[9]

This is obvious for market governance, which relies on state contract law and contract enforcement, and for hierarchy, which relies on state corporate law and property rights enforcement. It is less obvious for hybrids, which, as in the case of long-term contracts, rely on state contract law, but at the same time additional private governance is crucial. Thus, the economics of governance is a theory of *private ordering in the shadow of the law*, assuming that the state has created and enforces efficacious rules of law.[10]

[7] For the distinction between bilateral and trilateral governance see Williamson (1985), n 3, 72–7. With special attention to bilateral governance mechanisms see O. Williamson, 'Credible Commitments: Using Hostages to Support Exchange' (1983) 73 *American Economic Review* 519–40.

[8] Williamson, n 1, 1, 12.

[9] Williamson (1985), n 3, 10.

[10] See the notion of 'lawfulness' in Williamson, n 1, 1–2; see also A. K. Dixit, *Lawlessness and Economics. Alternative Modes of Governance* (Princeton NJ/Oxford: Princeton University Press, 2004) 25.

2. Lawlessness

Insisting on his premise that even in well-developed countries the state's efforts to protect property rights and to enforce contracts are inherently limited, a fact inviting the use of private ordering to infuse order, Williamson acknowledges that circumstances where the state law is 'very costly, slow, unreliable, corrupt, weak, or simply absent'[11] pose *additional* private ordering challenges.[12] Drawing on a vast array of empirical studies, Avinash Dixit recently contributed comprehensive game theoretical analysis of such challenges.[13] Williamson in fact suggests that with regard to his simple scheme of contractual governance choice ('try markets, try hybrids, and have recourse to the firm only when all else fails'), in an institutional environment where the government is unable or unwilling to provide adequate protection of property rights and enforcement of contracts, one could substitute the main explaining variable of asset specificity (i.e. exposure of specialized supplier investments) with property rights (and one should add contract enforcement) hazards with equivalent results.[14]

Thus, under conditions of increasing property rights and contract enforcement hazards (lawlessness), there are three options for the organization of a non-specific transaction (purchase of standard equipment or material), which in an OECD-country (lawfulness) would be conducted on the unassisted market: (1) the hazards remain unrelieved and the implied risks will be priced out; (2) private governance mechanisms are employed in order to add institutional support through credible commitments (hybrids); and (3) hierarchy is induced by the creation of uniform ownership or other kinds of equity relations (corporate groups, joint ventures, strategic partnerships, etc).[15]

A situation of *lawlessness* is not only pervasive in developing countries and transition economies, but also, for a lack of state co-operation through multilateral treaties, in *global cross-border trade*—where even parties situated in OECD-countries with an internally well-functioning legal system face added institutional uncertainties resulting from the following questions: (a) which court will decide (jurisdiction to adjudicate), (b) which law applies (jurisdiction to prescribe), and (c) whether a judgment of a court situated in country *A* will be recognized and enforced in country *B* (mutual recognition).[16] Thus, the transaction

[11] Dixit, n 10, at 3. [12] Williamson, n 1, 1, 14. [13] Dixit, n 10.

[14] Williamson, n 1, 15, in fn 24.

[15] B. D. Richman, 'Firms, Courts, and Reputation Mechanisms: Towards a Positive Theory of Private Ordering' (2004) 104 *Columbia Law Review* 2328–67, 2349, rightly observes that it is 'one of the most glaring problems of the legal-centric private ordering literature' to focus on the alternative of public versus private ordering (at 2338) alone, and the alternative of firm versus market (at 2348) should be included in the analysis in order to get the full picture. See G.-P. Calliess and J. Mertens, 'Transnational Corporations, Global Competition Policy, and the Shortcomings of Private International Law' (2011) 18 *Indiana Journal of Global Legal Studies* 843–72.

[16] See D. Schmidtchen and H.-J. Schmidt-Trenz, 'The division of labour is limited by the extent of the law. A Constitutional Approach to International Private Law' (1990) 1 *Constitutional Political Economy* 49–71; M. E. Streit and A. Mangels, '*Privatautonomes Recht und grenzüberschreitende Transaktionen*' (1996) 47 *ORDO – Jahrbuch für die Ordnung von Wirtschaft und Gesellschaft* 73–100; G. Rühl, 'The Problem of International Transactions: Conflict of Laws Revisited' (2010) 6 *Journal of Private International Law* 59–91.

cost economics scheme introduced earlier may provide a good explanation for a governance structure of global markets described as follows:

Recent estimates suggest that there are about 65,000 TNCs [transnational corporations] today, with about 850,000 foreign affiliates across the globe... [which] account for... one-third of world exports. Moreover, if the value of worldwide TNC activities with non-equity relationships (e.g. international subcontracting, licensing, contract manufacturers) is considered, TNCs would account for even larger shares in these global aggregates...[17]

The increasing importance of intra-firm trade within transnational corporate groups (*unified governance*) and of transnational business networks (*bilateral governance*) is one important institutional facet of economic globalization.[18] However, these modes of transnational contractual governance work in the spirit of 'think global, act local' in that the mechanisms of private ordering employed are functional only in the shadow of national law: TNCs work on the assumption of efficacious state enforcement of the underlying equity and non-equity relationships, based on local contract and corporate laws enforced by local courts.[19]

The same holds true for many *trilateral governance* mechanisms employed by international commerce. One example is international commercial arbitration, the functionality of which depends on local arbitration laws as well as the recognition and enforcement of foreign arbitral awards under the 1958 New York Convention.[20] Other examples of the involvement of trusted third parties in international commercial transactions are letters of credit, escrow services, and indirect import and export.[21] These mechanisms nationalize contractual relations for the immediate parties (for example, seller and buyer) to a cross-border transaction by involving on both sides banks or merchants specialized in import and export as intermediaries. The cross-border transactions between the intermediaries, in turn, are embedded in an ongoing business relationship which makes the contracts self-enforcing (bilateral governance).[22] Thus, instead of supplier *S*

[17] UNCTAD, *World Investment Report 2002, Overview* (New York/Geneva: United Nations, 2002) 1 (available at <www.unctad.org/en/docs/wir2002overview_en.pdf>).

[18] See D. Schmidtchen and H.-J. Schmidt-Trenz, 'New Institutional Economics of International Transactions. Constitutional Uncertainty and the Creation of Institutions in Foreign Trade as Exemplified by the Multinational Firm' (1990) 9 *Jahrbuch für Neue Politische Ökonomie* 3–34; J McMillan and C Woodruff, 'Private Order under Dysfunctional Public Order' (2000) 98 *Michigan Law Review* 2421–58; T Dietz, *Global Order Beyond Law* (Oxford: Hart Publishing 2014).

[19] See G.-P. Calliess and S. von Harder, 'Intra-Firm Trade Law. Contract Enforcement & Dispute Resolution in Transnational Corporations', ZenTra Working Paper in Transnational Studies (No. 01/2012) (available at <http://ssrn.com/abstract=2161314>); in more detail, see P. T. Muchlinski, *Multinational Enterprises and the Law* (Oxford: Blackwell Publishers, 2nd edn, 2007).

[20] See N. Blackaby, *et al, Redfern and Hunter on International Commercial Arbitration* (Oxford: Oxford University Press, 5th edn, 2009).

[21] See D. Schmidtchen and H. –J. Schmidt-Trenz, 'Private International Trade in the Shadow of the Territoriality of Law: Why Does It Work?' (1991) 58 *Southern Economic Journal* 329–38; for more detail see H. -J. Schmidt-Trenz, *Außenhandel und Territorialität des Rechts, Grundlegung einer Neuen Institutionenökonomik des Außenhandels* (Baden-Baden: Nomos, 1990).

[22] A very good account of how letters of credit work is to be found at J. K. Levit, 'Bottom-Up Lawmaking through a Pluralist Lens: The ICC Banking Commission and the Transnational Regulation of Letters of Credit' (2008) 57 *Emory Law Journal* 1147–225.

contracting directly with buyer *B* across jurisdictional borders, in indirect export, *S* sells domestically to exporter *E* who has a self-enforcing long-term relationship with importer *I* who in turn sells domestically to *B*. But note that the intended transfer of the institutional uncertainties implied in cross-border commerce to specialized third parties works on the assumption that the relations between *S* and *E* and *I* and *B* take place under circumstances of lawfulness, i.e. state enforcement of sales contracts, letters of credit, and the like.[23]

In sum, the *additional* private ordering challenges resulting from the relative lawlessness implied in international commerce when compared to domestic transactions are tackled by employing bilateral as well as trilateral governance mechanisms to infuse order (hybrid governance) or by taking such transactions out of the market (unified governance), with all of these mechanisms in one way or the other taking place in the shadow of state law.[24]

3. Mapping contract governance

Decomposing the described modes of governance into their components along the lines of the classical division of state powers into the functions of legislation, adjudication, and enforcement, one can identify 12 generic governance mechanisms employed in contractual relations, an overview of which is given in Table 8a.1.

In order to explain Table 8a.1, it should be confessed that although it draws on the terminology used by Williamson, the categorization is inspired by a similar table presented by Ellickson, who in presenting his 'theory of norms' develops a 'system of social control' which differentiates between five types of controllers that make rules and administer sanctions. These controllers are first, second, and third party control, where the latter is split in the three subcategories of informal (reputation-based sanctions), organizational (exclusion), and governmental (legal system) third-party control.[25] However, where Ellickson is not specifically interested in contractual

Table 8a.1 Public and Private Governance Mechanisms in Contractual Relations

Dimension / Regulator	Legislation	Adjudication	Enforcement
Public Trilateral	Parliamentary Act	Courts	Legal Sanctions
Private Trilateral	Social Norms	Arbitration	Reputation, Exclusion
Private Bilateral	Relational Norms	Negotiation, Mediation	Exit, Hostages, Escrow
Private Unified	Internal Trading Policies	Board Decision	Property-based Instructions

[23] A fact which seems to be undervalued by Schmidt-Trenz, n 21.

[24] G. K. Hadfield, 'The Public and the Private in the Provision of Law for Global Transactions' in V. Gessner (ed) *Legal Certainty Beyond the State* (Oxford: Hart Publishing, 2009) 238–55.

[25] See R. C. Ellickson, *Order Without Law: How Neighbors Settle Disputes* (Cambridge, Mass: Harvard University Press, 1991) 123ff (especially the Table at 131).

governance, but more generally in 'order without law', I substituted his category of first-party control — meaning the self-control of an actor by personal ethics in relation to another actor — for the economically more relevant internal control of transactions within the hierarchy of the firm (unified governance). This category may be used as well to reflect the issues of corporate governance and corporate social responsibility, where a firm binds itself by means of a code of conduct in relation to actors outside the firm, such as potential investors, consumers, or the general public.

With reference to the third column of the table (enforcement mechanisms), it should be explained that rather than drawing a simple line between public (legal) sanctions and private (non-legal) sanctions,[26] I suggest distinguishing further. Namely, I suggest distinguishing between internal sanctions administered within the hierarchy of a firm, second-party sanctions of one party of a business relationship towards the other (which basically entails the termination of a (long-term) business relationship (exit), and—if hostages were provided—the commercial realization of such securities), and finally social sanctions passed upon the norm offender by third parties, where such social sanction admittedly may be administered informally (reputation) or formally by an organization such as a trade association or an exchange (exclusion).[27]

In summary, contractual relationships need institutional support by a governance regime which provides for the reliable enforcement of contractual obligations. Such regimes consist of a specific combination of governance mechanisms performing the functions of legislating, adjudication, and enforcing. However, these regimes are neither purely private nor purely public. In the practice of commerce, we find instead a pragmatic approach which combines and re-combines public and private mechanisms into effective governance regimes, while the proportion of private mechanisms increases in situations of lawlessness, for example in cross-border situations.

II. The Role of Fairness Preferences in Contract Governance

In the following, I intend to explore the degree to which fairness preferences as a feature of the proposed '*homo reciprocans*'-model—as introduced by Magen—may be relevant in the context of contract governance. Admittedly, it seems to be impossible to evaluate the potential contribution of 'behavioural law and economics' (BLE) in this commentary in a comprehensive manner.[28] There are two

[26] As proposed, e.g., by S. Panther, 'Non-Legal Sanctions' in B. Bouckaert and G. De Geest (eds) *Encyclopedia of Law and Economics Vol I* (Cheltenham: Edward Elgar Publishing, 2000) 999–1028 (also available at <http://encyclo.findlaw.com/0780book.pdf>).

[27] See Ellickson, n 25, 131; in more detail, see D. Charny, 'Non-Legal Sanctions in Commercial Relationships' (1990) 104 *Harvard Law Review* 375; on the practice of black-listing by trade associations see Dietz, n 18, 187ff, 208ff.

[28] But see, e.g., the recent contributions to H. Fleischer and D. Zimmer (eds) *Beitrag der Verhaltensökonomie (Behavioral Economics) zum Handels- und Wirtschaftsrecht* (Verlag Recht und Wirtschaft: Frankfurt am Main, 2011) which run to 177 pages without any specific reference to contract governance.

possible approaches to such evaluation, one from economic analysis of law and another from the broader perspective of interdisciplinary studies and legal theory.

1. The internal perspective of economics

The lines of argumentation within the former internal debate are already well established: BLE challenges 'conventional law and economics' (CLE) based on experimental evidence of certain biases which—it is argued—prove to be systematic deviations from the rational-choice-model of human behaviour and its assumption of selfishness. CLE does not neglect the value of the contributions of BLE, but—in turn—criticizes that the theoretical implications of the empirical evidence provided on these biases need further analysis. In the words of Jennifer Arlen:

> Behavioral economic analysis of law is unlikely to replace conventional law and economics unless it can formulate a superior model of human behavior suitable for making normative decisions about optimal legal regimes. Yet it will be difficult to construct a more realistic model of human behavior based on cognitive biases whose origins, scope, and magnitude are not well understood. Many of the behavioral results occur in some circumstances but not in other, relatively similar, circumstances. Other behavioral results are robust in the laboratory, but are not necessarily robust in the circumstances in which people find themselves in the real world. Individual learning, group dynamics, organizations, experts, markets, and government policy all can affect whether people will exhibit various biases and heuristics. In addition, people often are subject to multiple biases with conflicting effects; the effects are even more uncertain when decisions involve multiple participants who each may be subject to various biases. Finally, the task of formulating policy prescriptions based on behavioral analysis is further complicated by the fact that most observed biases are likely to affect not only the individuals we might seek to protect but any government officials brought in to protect them—giving rise to the possibility that the cure may be worse than the disease.[29]

Moreover, while BLE does not provide a superior alternative model of human behaviour, the advantage of bringing additional depth and complexity to economic analysis by adding a more psychologically realistic picture of the average person is questionable. As Richard Posner observes:

> But in theory-making, descriptive accuracy is purchased at a price, the price being loss of predictive power. The rational-choice economist asks what "rational man" would do in a given situation, and usually the answer is pretty clear and it can be compared with actual behavior to see whether the prediction is confirmed. Sometimes it is not confirmed—and so we have behavioral economics. But it is profoundly unclear what "behavioral man" would do in any given situation. He is a compound of rational and nonrational capacities and impulses. He might do anything.[30]

[29] J. Arlen, 'Comment: The Future of Behavioral Economic Analysis of Law' (1998) 51 *Vanderbilt Law Review* 1765–88, 1788.

[30] R. A. Posner, 'Rational Choice, Behavioral Economics, and the Law,' (1998) 50 *Stanford Law Review* 1551–75, 1559.

Finally, where the specific advantage of CLE, i.e. its predictive power resting in a simplification of reality (rational choice), is abandoned by BLE, the interesting question arises, how BLE performs in relation to other well established theories of society which suffer from the same level of complexity:

> If there is any theory in their [BLE] approach, it is not an economic theory. They take a psychological approach to phenomena that are sociological and psychological as much as they are economic, yet call their approach economic. It is as if they thought economics the only social science, which if true would mean that any social scientific critique of economics must itself be a part of economics.[31]

2. The external perspective of social science

Here we come to the previously addressed external approach to the evaluation of BLE, i.e. from the broader perspective of interdisciplinary studies and legal theory. If BLE from the standpoint of CLE does not provide a rigorous alternative theory, the question arises why BLE neither draws on nor borrows from the sphere of sociological and/or socio-psychological theory with respect to human interaction and communication. And indeed, as a scholar who specializes in interdisciplinary legal studies from various backgrounds,[32] I find it to be the most striking quality of BLE scholarship, that it seems to be obsessed with criticizing CLE so much that it never cites– and it is presumed never reads or is aware of—even the most popular, let alone the most advanced and elaborated sociological explanations of the issues at stake.[33]

At this point I can merely give one little example of this failure. In Section III(2) of his chapter, Magen elaborates on 'sanctioning for the sake of fairness'. Presumably, any scholar educated in criminal law, criminology, or philosophy of law would arrive at the conclusion that most of the ideas presented resemble the different functions of sentencing as established since more than a century by punishment theory.[34] However, Magen does not say so and he is not using the established punishment theory terminology (for example, retribution, deterrence, rehabilitation, education, etc.). In this context, Magen argues that BLE leads to:

> . . . a better understanding of why cooperation is so fragile [. . .]. It is due mainly to the heterogeneity of people with regard to social preferences. Cooperation does not fail because everybody is selfish, but because the selfish behaviour of some (for whatever reason) drives fair-minded people also to behave selfishly (out of fairness concerns). Thus, selfish

[31] Posner, n 30, 1558.

[32] See, e.g., G. Calliess and P. Zumbansen, *Rough Consensus and Running Code. A Theory of Transnational Private Law* (Oxford: Hart Publishing, 2010).

[33] This critique applies as well to CLE see, e.g., E. Posner, *Law and Social Norms* (Cambridge, Mass: Harvard University Press, 2000), who treats the issue of social norms as if it were a brand new topic, thus neglecting any non-economic advances in the field.

[34] See only A. Duff, 'Legal Punishment' in E. N. Zalta (ed) *The Stanford Encyclopedia of Philosophy* (Summer 2013 Edition), (available at: <http://plato.stanford.edu/archives/sum2013/entries/legal-punishment/>).

behaviour prevails in the end despite preferences for fairness, or rather because of preferences for fairness.

Furthermore, he concludes:

> ... [p]ut more practically, the objective of sanctions is to sustain cooperation indirectly, that is, to preserve voluntary cooperation on the side of the majority of reciprocal actors by preventing opportunism on the side of selfish actors.

This last sentence is exactly the point of the so-called 'positive general prevention' theory of punishment, which deals with the 'expressive function' of punishment vis-à-vis non-offenders.[35] Again, neither Magen nor other BLE scholars seem to be aware of the fact that there already exists an elaborated theory of the observed phenomenon. Instead of putting their interesting experimental findings into the context of existing theories—which would create an instance of best interdisciplinary scientific practice, they instead come up with problematic generalizations and normative policy implications. To quote Posner once again, BLE recommends:

> ... as an effective method of deterring unlawful behavior, making law enforcement "highly visible", as by replacing conventional parking tickets with "large, brightly-colored tickets that read 'VIOLATION' in large letters on the driver's side window." This is actually a risky deterrent strategy. Suppose that the police ticket only one in every hundred violators. The low probability of being ticketed will be highlighted by the increased visibility of the tickets. Ask yourself: Would deterrence be increased or decreased if law enforcement authorities informed the public of the actual probability that a given offense would result in arrest, prosecution, and conviction?'[36]

One promising alternative to such economic analysis of sanctioning is the sociological theory of law as put forward by Niklas Luhmann, who defines norms as counterfactual expectations of behaviour.[37] While cognitive expectations of behaviour are characterized by the readiness to learn in case of a frustrated expectation, any act of norm disobedience bears a communicative dimension which places the validity of the norm in question and thus creates the need for a reaction from its supporters to ensure that the norm shall prevail in the future regardless of its disobedience in an individual case. While the law has the function of stabilizing generalized counter-factual expectations of behaviour, the necessary reaction can take many forms besides sanctioning, one of the most important being the neglect of the act of disobedience by keeping the case unreported.[38]

[35] See K. Schumann, *Positive Generalprävention* (Heidelberg: C. F. Müller Verlag, 1989); C. Roxin, *Strafrecht Allgemeiner Teil, Band I: Grundlagen. Der Aufbau der Verbrechenslehre* (München: C. H. Beck, 4. Aufl. 2006) 78ff.

[36] Posner, n 30, 1553.

[37] N. Luhmann, *Rechtssoziologie* (Opladen: Westdeutscher Verlad, 3rd edn, 1987) 40ff.

[38] Luhmann, n 37, 53ff.

In summary, compared with state of the art sociology and philosophy of law, regulation, and governance, the level of argumentation with regard to sanctioning in both CLE and BLE seems quite poor and archaic.[39] If BLE intends to add complexity to CLE, it should become educated about the existing parallel universes of social science theories that successfully deal with contingency and complexity of social phenomena such as social communication. However, with regard to the governance of contracts, it is difficult to see what the analysis of fairness preferences by BLE adds to the established new institutional economics of governance as summarized in Section I. Any advances to be made here in the future should in any case be balanced against the price of BLE, i.e. the above-mentioned loss of predictive power.

[39] See Luhmann, n 37, 106ff., giving an historical evolutionary explanation for the fact that highly visible and brutal sanctioning as a form of symbolic reaction to disobedience was phased out by the advent of the modern western legal systems, where the court decision substituted for physical force as a means to prove and symbolize that the law prevails over disobedience.

9

Class Actions, Compliance, and Moral Cost

*Bruno Deffains and Dominique Demougin**

'How selfish soever man may be supposed, there are evidently some principles in his nature, which interest him in the fortune of others, and render their happiness necessary to him, though he derives nothing from it except the pleasure of seeing it.'[1]

1. Introduction

In law and economics, it is assumed that parties behave rationally making choices which maximize their respective expected utility. The rationality assumption is usually combined with a hypothesis of purely self-interested preferences focusing the attention on extrinsic incentives. However, human behaviour is also influenced by social norms and moral concern. For instance, an individual who caused harm to a third party may be plagued by feelings of remorse, guilt, regret, and/or shame.[2] Moreover, the strength of these feelings will likely be dependent on the initial precaution undertaken by the injurer; if he complied with expected norm, the injurer may feel less culpability than if he was careless. A rational individual would anticipate this potential disutility *ex ante* and include it as 'moral costs' in his decision process. This emphasizes the importance of accounting for intrinsic incentives, not only as an additional motivation for precaution but also due to a potential interaction between intrinsic and extrinsic effects.

Indeed, in the recent economic literature a number of authors have stressed the possibility that extrinsic motivation may be crowded out by intrinsic incentives.[3]

* Bruno Deffains, Paris Center for Law and Economics, University of Paris 2 (e-mail: Bruno.Deffains@u-paris2.fr); Dominique Demougin, School of Management, University of Liverpool (e-mail: dominique.demougin@liverpool.ac.uk). This chapter was originally published in (2011) 7 *Review of Law and Economics* 481–500.

[1] A. Smith, (1759) 'The Theory of Moral Sentiments' in D. D. Raphael and A. L. Macfie (eds) *The Glasgow Edition of the Works and Correspondence of Adam Smith*, vol. 1 (Indianapolis: Liberty Fund, 1982).

[2] See L. Kaplow and S. Shavell, *Fariness versus Welfare* (Cambridge, Mass: Harvard University Press, 2002).

[3] B. Frey and R. Jegen, 'Motivation Crowding Theory: A Survey of Empirical Evidence' (2001) 15(5) *Journal of Economic Surveys* 589–611.

For instance, Gneezy and Rustichini[4] performed a real experiment investigating the effect of introducing a fine for parents arriving late to collect their children from day nursery. In the experiment, a small fine (extrinsic incentive) apparently increased the incidence of parents coming late. The authors reason that their finding results from a countervailing reduction in intrinsic motivation. Intuitively, parents coming late to pick up their child feel less guilty if they 'pay' for the service. In the law and economic context, Akerlof and Dickens[5] make a similar point arguing that penalties could potentially undermine the 'internal justification' of individuals for behaving according to the law.[6]

An additional concern is that the balance perceived by an individual between his intrinsic and extrinsic motivations may depend on how other people behave. In particular, intrinsic incentives may be influenced by an externality effect.[7] For instance, in the above experiment if fewer parents are punctual when collecting their children from day nursery, it may reduce remorse and/or shame felt by latecomers. This observation may provide a possible reasoning as to why, in the Gneezy and Rustichini experiment, once the fine was removed coming late nevertheless remained high. The explanation goes as follows; the initial introduction of a fine induced a crowding-out of intrinsic motivation raising the number of latecomers. Once the fine was removed, parents' intrinsic motivation remained low because parents took into account the now contemporaneous high level of latecomers.

In this Chapter, we consider the introduction of a class action procedure in a competitive environment where decision-makers in firms have an intrinsic motivation to avoid harming others, albeit to a different degree. In other words, moral concerns for the well-being of others is taken to differ from one person to the next. Specifically, each producer is thought to suffer an individual moral disutility, or moral cost, if he under-produces care relative to first-best. Hence, each producer has a choice to either follow his intrinsic or his extrinsic incentive; the intrinsically motivated producer behaves according to his moral concern, undertaking first-best care and avoiding moral costs altogether; in contrast, the extrinsically motivated producer disregards his moral sentiments, under-produces care, and endures moral disutility. The decision of an individual to behave according to one or the other incitation depends, in particular, on his type measured by the magnitude of his moral discomfort for under-producing care.

We use the heterogeneity in moral sentiments in order to introduce a 'lemons problem' in the market.[8] Since firms implement different levels of care, goods produced by various companies will not be characterized by the same likelihood

[4] U. Gneezy and A. Rustichini, 'A Fine is a Price' (2000) 29 *Journal of Legal Studies* 1–17.

[5] O. Akerlof and T. Dickens, 'The Economic Consequences of Cognitive Dissonance' (1982) 72 *American Economic Review* 307–19.

[6] C. -C. Lai, C. -Y. Yang, and J. -J. Chang, 'Environmental Regulations and Social Norms' (2003) 10 *International Tax and Public Finance* 63–75; J. P. Conley and P. Wang, 'Crime and Ethics' (2006) 60 *Journal of Urban Economics* 107–23.

[7] See, e.g. G. Suurmond, *Enforcing Fire Safety in the Catering Industry: An Economic Analysis* (Leiden: Leiden University Press, 2008).

[8] O. Akerlof, 'The Market for Lemons: Qualitative Uncertainty and the Market Methane' (1970) 84 *Quarterly Journal of Economics* 488–500.

of damage. Suppose now that care is not discernible by buyers and that goods are otherwise homogeneous.[9] In such a context, consumers will only be willing to pay a price that reflects the average level of care in the market and, depending on the legal set-up, expected recovery in the case of damage.

Introducing class actions facilitates damage recovery in the case of mass tort. In the current environment, it raises the expected recovery that the consumer of a specific good can anticipate in the case of harm. From the point of view of producers, it increases their expected liability costs. This generates an adjustment process of the market equilibrium which affects all market participants. In the short-run—holding the number of suppliers and their respective choice of care constant—the adjustment process provides a comparative advantage for intrinsically motivated producers. In the medium-run—allowing producers to adjust care while keeping the number of market participants fixed—the average quality increases. Finally, in the long-run, additional firms enter the market and consumers' true costs of consumption (price plus expected unrecovered damage) decrease.

Consider the short-run. Due to the increase in expected damage recovery, the equilibrium price would go up. In a perfectly competitive environment, that price increase exactly offsets the improved damage recovery (i.e. true costs of consumption remain constant). However, while the price change equally affects all the producers, the increase in expected liability costs resulting from a potential class action lawsuit are type dependent. Consider an intrinsically motivated producer. His choice of care is higher than the average of the market. Hence, his increase in expected liability costs is below average. In contrast, a producer that is extrinsically motivated selects a care level below market standard. His customers are more often harmed and expected compensation from class action is above the average of other firms. Altogether, intrinsically motivated producers obtain a comparative advantage from the introduction of a class action procedure.

In the medium-run, firms are free to adjust their level of care, but there is no entry or exit in the market. The adjustment process leads to an increase in average care for two reasons. First, consider a producer with moral costs such that, before the introduction of a class action procedure, he was indifferent between undertaking first-best or second-best care; in other words, a producer whose opportunity costs generated by his moral concern are exactly offset by the advantage of ignoring the latter and under producing care. From the foregoing, we understand that the introduction of a class action procedure provides a comparative advantage to the intrinsically motivated. Thus, the producer who was initially indifferent between following or ignoring his intrinsic motivation is now no longer indifferent. Instead, he definitely favours following his intrinsic incentives, thus, raising his choice of care.

[9] In the literature about producer's liability, it is generally assumed that the perception of risk by consumers is not perfect. One argument to explain why risk calculation is extremely difficult is precisely because the care level decided by the producers is difficult to observe (see, e.g. S. Shavell, *Economic Analysis of Accident Law* (Cambridge, Mass: Harvard University Press, 1987), W. Landes and R. Posner, *The Economic Structure of Tort Law* (Cambridge, Mass: Harvard University Press, 1988), or K. Viscusi, *Regulation through Litigation* (Washington DC: Brookings Institution Press, 2002).

The second justification for an increase in average care follows the traditional reasoning as to why class action is thought to be advantageous. Consider an extrinsically motivated producer. In the absence of class action procedures, he would decide the quality level of his product by equating the marginal cost of care with the marginal benefit of a reduction in liability costs. Introducing class action makes it more likely that the producer will be sued following harm. This raises that producer's marginal benefit of augmenting care, inducing him to increase.[10]

Assuming producers only differ with respect to their moral concerns, but otherwise employ the same technology, the above set-up implies that intrinsic motivation, if acted upon, lowers profit. Intuitively, intrinsically motivated producers do not correctly minimize the sum of their care and expected liability costs. As a result, in a competitive environment where producers are free to enter or exit the market, the marginal entrant must be intrinsically motivated. In the foregoing, we argued that in the short-run introducing class action is beneficial for the intrinsically motivated. Thus, the marginal entrant's profit must go up attracting new producers into the market and lowering the equilibrium price.

As a result, in the long-run the introduction of a class action procedure should benefit consumers by raising their surplus. In addition, it should return the profit of intrinsically motivated producers to their normal level leaving them indifferent between allowing and prohibiting class actions. Extrinsically motivated producers would definitely be disadvantaged by class actions because it would erode some of their supra-normal profit; already in the short-run they would be incentivized to increase care and they would not be fully compensated by the price increase for higher damage recovery. Moreover, in the long-run entry in the market would reduce price which would further eat away at their profit. Finally, from an efficiency point of view, admitting class actions would be advantageous since firms producing second-best care initially would be incentivized to increase care.

For ease of presentation, formal arguments are kept to a minimum by a number of simplifying assumptions. The key simplification is the representation of moral concerns discussed earlier. Its main advantage is that producers can only behave in one of two ways, either following extrinsic or intrinsic motivation. In addition, the production technology is kept very simple with constant marginal costs up to a maximal quantity. Finally, the framework is designed in such a way that, absent the lemons problem, the return to scale from class action proceedings becomes straightforward. In Section V of the Chapter, we briefly discuss the effect of removing these simplifications in a more general framework.

Our Chapter is related to the standard literature on class action. For example, Che[11] analyzes adverse selection and potentially signaling effects which depend on the defendant's initial information. Marceau and Mongrain[12] develop the idea that

[10] See Shavell, n 9 and Landes and Posner, n 9.

[11] Y. -K. Che, 'Equilibrium Formation of Class Action Suits' (1996) 62 *Journal of Public Economics* 339–61.

[12] N. Marceau and S. Mongrain, 'Damage Averaging and the Formation of Class Action Suits' (2003) 23 *International Review of Law and Economics* 63–74.

a class action has the characteristics of a public good since once the class action is created against a tortfeasor, all the victims have the opportunity to join it. In particular, those who join benefit from the provision of the good without having to incur the initial cost (and risk) associated with the formation of the class action.[13] Issues associated with moral hazard and the need for incentive contracts associated with legal council have also been discussed in a number of papers. For example, Klement and Neeman[14] use a mechanism design approach to analyze the efficiency effects of the lodestar method depending on whether a court can or cannot observe a lawyer's effort. The list is obviously not exhaustive and only intended to reflect a few directions in which the law and economics literature has investigated class action procedures.

Our analysis is also related to the recent literature on prosocial preferences. In his 2009 address to the American Economic Association, Dixit stated that the role of 'prosocial preferences' for the governance of economic activities 'is important... not merely because they exist, but also because the intrinsic incentives they generate can interact with the standard monetary or other extrinsic incentives'.[15] In particular, we apply the reasoning discussed by Stout[16] who already noticed that 'other-regarding behavior is often apparently consistent with legal incentives because a variety of legal rules are designed to promote other-regarding behavior (e.g., criminal law, contract law, tort law)'.

The remainder of the Chapter is organized as follows. Section II presents the model. We then analyze the victim's choice to go to court contingent on the judicial set-up. In Section IV, we investigate the firm's decision of care. Section V derives the market equilibrium under a class action regime. Finally, Section VI offers some concluding remarks and discusses possible extensions.

II. The Model

We consider a competitive market with a large number of consumers and producers who are all risk-neutral. Producers are indexed by i, $i = 1, \ldots, N$. Each producer is characterized by a moral costs' parameter $\mu_i \geq 0$. Without loss of generality the μ_i's are taken to be increasing in the index.

A producer's pecuniary cost depends on three variables; the quantity he produces denoted by x, his per-unit care costs, c, and the associated expected liability

[13] See B. Deffains and E. Langlais, 'Informational Externalities and Information Sharing in Class Action Suits' in J. G. Backhaus, A. Cassone, and G. B. Ramello (eds) *Economics of Class Actions* (Cheltenham: Edward Elgar Publishing, forthcoming) for a countervailing argument.

[14] A. Klement and Z. Neeman, 'Incentive Structures for Class Action Lawyers' (2004) 20 *Journal of Law, Economics, & Organization* 102–24.

[15] A. Dixit, 'Presidential Address', American Economic Association, 2009.

[16] L. Stout, 'Other-Regarding Preferences and Social Norms' (2001) Georgetown Law and Economics Research Paper No 265902 and (2001) Georgetown Public Law Research Paper No 265902.

costs. With respect to production, all the producers employ the same technology generating a cost function:

Equation 1 $$C(x)=F+\begin{cases} Kx & \text{if } x\leq z \\ +\infty & \text{if } x>z \end{cases}, \quad \text{where } F,K,z>0$$

The variable z denotes the maximal number which a firm can produce using this technology. In Section III, when examining the lawsuit decision of victims, we use the working hypothesis that all producers active in the market set output to the maximal quantity, $x^* = z$. When analyzing the firm's problem, we will verify that the hypothesis is consistent with profit maximization of firms.

A product supplied by a specific firm either causes damage to all of its consumers or to none.[17] In the case of harm, we denote by δ the per-consumer damage and by $\Delta = z\delta$ the total damage. The *ex ante* probability of harm is a function of care costs, $\pi(c)$, which is assumed to satisfy standard regularity requirements, i.e. $\pi' < 0$, $\pi'' > 0$.[18] Slightly abusing language, we also refer to c as care or precaution. We assume that the level of care chosen by a firm is private information. Finally, a firm's expected liability costs depend on whether the legal system allows for a class action as well as on the injurees' decision rule to go (or not) to court. These costs will be derived in Section III when analyzing victims' incentives to initiate a lawsuit. As already mentioned in the introduction, we assume that the behaviour of a producer with respect to care also depends on his ethical attitude and the moral costs associated with under-producing care relative to first-best. The exact description of moral costs will be given subsequently, when we define the producers' exact objective function.

At the moment of buying, a consumer's true expected cost of consumption depends both on the market price, p, and on the size of expected unrecovered loss, l. The latter will depend on the legal set-up and the information available to the consumer at the moment of buying. From the foregoing, care undertaken by a specific producer is private information and is, thus, unknown by the consumer at the moment of buying. In the remaining, we assume that consumers correctly anticipate the average damage in the market. Finally, we denote with Q the total quantity sold in the market and with $D(Q)$ the inverse demand function with $D'(Q) < 0$. Hence, the following equality must be satisfied

Equation 2 $$p+l=D(Q)$$

where $p + l$ measures the consumer's true expected cost of consumption.

[17] This is a standard assumption considering mass tort litigation (see, e.g. S. Lane, 'Economics of Consumer Class Actions' (2005) 7 *Journal of Consumer Affairs* 13–22 or Kaplow and Shavell, n 2).

[18] The assumptions correspond to the standard model of 'unilateral care' accidents where the producer can only influence the risk of accident via the choice of the care level (see, e.g. Shavell, n 9).

We distinguish between two judicial environments depending on whether class action procedures are legalized or not. Moreover, we assume that consumers are protected by a standard producer liability rule. Hence, if the victim goes to court and proves her case, she recovers the incurred damage δ.

In order to keep the formal analysis to a minimum, we make the following simplifying assumptions for consumers who suffer harm. Firstly, in the case of damage the injured parties can always prove their case in court, albeit at a cost. In particular, from the viewpoint of a victim there is no *ex ante* risk associated with the court's decision. Secondly, each party to a trial pays their respective fees according to the US cost allocation rule. In other words, even if the plaintiff always has a clear-cut case, it still remains costly for them to start a lawsuit. Thirdly, court costs are case-dependent, yet equal for goods produced by the same firm (intuitively, the victims of a single firm face the exact same decision problem). Specifically, before a trial the victim's potential court costs, A, are revealed to the parties. *Ex ante* all parties view the victims' court costs as a random variable over the support $S = [o, \bar{A}]$ with $\bar{A} > \Delta$ and cumulative density function $G(A)$.

III. The Victims' Decision Problem

In this Section, we consider a group of consumers who all utilize the product from a given firm. We examine a partial equilibrium where the firm's care choice has been kept constant. We solve for the probability that the consumers would be compensated conditional on the occurrence of a damage and on the judicial environments.

1. **No Class Action:** In this case, each victim must individually decide whether to start a lawsuit against the producer. Once harm has occurred A is revealed. Since it is common knowledge that the potential parties of trial correctly anticipate the court's decision, a victim can credibly threaten the firm to start a lawsuit if $A \le \delta$. Obviously, with A being commonly observed, the victim and the firm will prefer to settle out of court, thereby avoiding court costs altogether. In contrast, with $A > \delta$, the victim is better off taking the loss and not going to court.
   Considering the decision rule of a victim *ex ante* (i.e. at the time of buying) yields the likelihood that a consumer will be compensated if harmed. Hence, in a judicial environment without class action procedures, producers and consumers will expect victims to recover damages with the probability $q^{NC} = G(\delta)$.
2. **Class Action:** In a situation where class action proceedings are allowed, we assume that all the victims cooperate on whether to initiate a lawsuit. From the foregoing, each firm produces $x^* = z$ and in the case of damage all the consumers are harmed. Hence, in the case of harm, there are z injured consumers who will all participate in a class action against the firm. Thus, the costs per plaintiff is A/z. As a result, victims can credibly threaten to start a class action against the producer if $A \le z\delta = \Delta$. Just as before, with A

commonly observable the parties will find it more advantageous to settle out of court. Alternatively, with $A > \Delta$ the victims are in a more advantageous position taking their loss.

Altogether, when class actions are authorized, market participants will evaluate the probability of damage recovery at $q^{CA} = G(\Delta)$.

Proposition 1. *In the partial equilibrium, the introduction of a class action procedure raises the probability that injured consumers will be compensated.*

Proof. $G(\cdot)$ is a *cdf*, hence, it is an increasing function. Thus, with $\Delta = z\delta > \delta$ we conclude $q^{CA} = G(\Delta) > G(\delta) = q^{NC}$.

This proposition is in line with the standard literature on class actions.[19] Intuitively, class action proceedings introduce a lawsuit return to scale for injurees. As a result, the number of harmed persons going to court increases. Moreover, overall compensation increases. Obviously, the result easily extends to environments that are less restrictive than the one described above as long as the return-to-scale feature prevails.

IV. Profit Maximization

In this Section, we consider the profit maximization problem of firm i with respect to its production decision, x, and its choice of care, c. From the viewpoint of the firm and due to the competitive structure of the environment, p is exogenously determined. Moreover, the producer takes the judicial set-up as given. Hence, it anticipates the likelihood of damage recovery, q^J which depends on whether class action procedures are legalized ($J = CA$) or are not authorized ($J = NC$).

We depart from the standard framework by introducing in the analysis moral costs if the producer under-produces care relative to first-best. Hence, the producer can behave in either of one of two ways.

1. **Intrinsically motivated producers:** Such a producer selects care to minimize the true primary costs:

Equation 3 $$c^* = \arg\min_{ci} ci + \pi(c_i)\delta$$

Thus, the expected profit of an intrinsically motivated producer is:

Equation 4 $$\Pi_{\text{Int}}(q^J, x) = \left[p - K - c^* - \pi(c^*)q^J\delta\right]x - F,$$

[19] See, e.g. K. Viscusi, n 9, Kaplow and Shavell, n 2, D. Rosenberg, 'Individual Justice and Collectivizing Risk Based Claims in Mass Exposure Cases' (1996) 71 *New York University Law Review* 210–51, or R. Nagareda, 'Autonomy, Peace and Put Options in the Mass Tort Class Action' (2002) 115 *Harvard Law Review* 747–74.

where $J = CA$ or NC. The ensuing per-consumer care and expected liability costs of such an intrinsically motivated producer are given by:

$$\text{Equation 5} \qquad C_{\text{Int}}(c^*, q^J) = c^* + \pi(c^*)q^J\delta$$

Note that we assume that, despite his moral concerns, the producer is not volunteering to compensate his victims *ex post*. Intuitively, an intrinsically motivated producer is sufficiently concerned on the base of moral to produce correct care, but not sufficiently to indemnify victims spontaneously.[20]

2. **Extrinsically motivated producers:** Alternatively, a producer may disregard his moral concern and simply minimize *his* share of the primary costs. In doing so, he neglects the externality of his decision on consumers whose court costs are sufficiently large to prevent them seeking recovery in court. Thus, an extrinsically motivated producer implements the level of care:

$$\text{Equation 6} \qquad c^J = \arg\min_{Ci} C_{\text{Ext}}(c_i, q^J) = c_i + \pi(c_i)q^J\delta$$

In either legal environment, with or without class action, injured consumers are not always indemnified, i.e. $q^J < 1$, $J = CA$ or NC. Hence, an extrinsically motivated producer under-produces care relative to first-best, $c^J < c^*$.

If producer i follows his extrinsic motivation, he suffers the moral cost μ_i. Intuitively, μ_i represents the largest monetary amount which producer i is willing to forego in order to do what is 'right'.[21] The monetary equivalent of 'profit' for a μ-producer net of his moral costs is:

$$\text{Equation 7} \qquad \Pi_{\text{Ext}}(q^J, x, \mu) = \left[p - K - c^J - \pi(c^J)q^J\delta \right] x - F - \mu$$

Hereafter, we refer to Equation 7 as the firm's 'quasi-profit'.

Proposition 2. *Both intrinsically or extrinsically incited producers either set $x^* = 0$ or $x^* = z$.*

The proof immediately follows from the participation condition of a firm. If the firm does not participate in the market, it sets $x^* = 0$. If the firm participates in the market, its profit must be non-negative. Hence, with $F > 0$ the square brackets in Equations 4 and 7 must be strictly positive. Thus, for either judicial set-up profit is strictly increasing in x and the firm chooses maximal output, i.e. $x^* = z$.

A producer has the choice between following his intrinsic or his extrinsic incitation. In order to evaluate which decision is more advantageous, he compares

[20] See B. Deffains and C. Fluet, 'Legal Liability when Individuals have Moral Concerns' (2009) CIRPEE Working Paper, UQAM for a further discussion on this point.

[21] Alternatively, μ_i can be thought as the price associated with producer i's inhibition threshold or the price of his 'moral corruptability'.

$\prod_{\text{Int}}(q^J, z)$ and $\prod_{\text{Ext}}(q^J, z, \mu)$ and selects accordingly. Alternatively, we can define the critical moral costs or inhibition threshold μ^J:

Equation 8 $$\left[p-k-C_{\text{Int}}(c^{*},q^{J})\right]z-F\left\{\left[p-k-C_{\text{EXT}}(c^{J},q^{J})\right]z-F-\bar{\mu}^{J}\right\}$$

Intuitively, in the judicial environment J the producer characterized by $\bar{\mu}^J$ is indifferent between achieving the lower profit $\prod_{\text{Int}}(q^J, z)$ or obtaining a larger profit but suffering the moral disutility $\bar{\mu}^J$. Hence, producers with moral costs $\mu_i > \bar{\mu}^J$ will prefer to follow their intrinsic incitation implementing c^*, while those characterized by $\mu_i < \bar{\mu}^J$ will disregard their moral sentiments and produce c^J.

We denote with k^J the largest index such $\mu_{KJ} < \bar{\mu}^J$. Since firms have been indexed in such a way that the μ_i's increase in the index, the natural number k^J also denotes the total number of extrinsically motivated producers.

Assumption: There are more than k^J firms active in the market where $J = CA$ or $J = NC$.

The assumption guarantees that, whether class actions are permitted or not, the market has both type of producers: firms 1 to k^J follow extrinsic incentives ($c = c^J$), while active firms with an index $i > k^J$ are intrinsically motivated ($c = c^*$). Rearranging terms in Equation 8, we can directly solve for the critical inhibition threshold:

Equation 9 $$\bar{\mu}^J=\left[C_{\text{Int}}(c^{*},qJ)-C_{\text{Ext}}(c^{J},q^{J})\right]z$$

Applying the definitions for $C_{\text{Int}}(c^*, q^J)$ and $C_{\text{Ext}}(c^J, q^J)$, and differentiating with respect to q^J, yields:

Equation 10 $$\frac{d\bar{\mu}^J}{dq^J}=\left[\pi(c^{*})-\pi(c^{J})\right]\Delta-\left[1+\pi^{J}(c^{J})q^{J}1\right]\frac{\partial c^{J}}{\partial q^{J}}<0$$

In order to verify the sign, first observe that the term in the second square bracket measures the marginal effect of care of an intrinsically motivated producer. Since the latter minimizes his share of the primary costs, this term must be zero. Secondly, extrinsically incentivized producers are more likely to induce a damage than intrinsically motivated ones, hence $\pi(c^*) < \pi(c^J)$.

Finally, Δ is positive verifying that the critical threshold μ^J is decreasing in q^J.

Proposition 3. *The introduction of a class action procedure:*

(*i*) *reduces the number of extrinsically motivated firms,* $k^{CA} \leq k^{NC}$, *and*

(*ii*) *raises the care level undertaken by those remaining extrinsically incentivized,* $c^{CA} > c^{NC}$.

Proof. Since $q^{CA} > q^{NC}$, we have $\mu^{CA} < \mu^{NC}$:

(*i*) As a result k, i.e. the largest index such μ_k is less than the critical threshold, is reduced by the introduction of a class action procedure.

(*ii*) Extrinsically incentivized firms undertake care q^J which solves:

$$1+\pi'(c^{J})q^{J}\delta=0$$

Implicitly differentiating verifies the result since:

$$\frac{\partial c^J}{\partial q^J} = -\frac{\pi'(C^J)\delta}{\pi'(c^J)q^J\delta} > 0$$

The proposition has a simple intuition. Suppose we start with an environment where class action proceedings are not allowed. Consider the critical producer, $\bar{\mu}^{NC}$, who is indifferent between undertaking the care level c^* and/or c^{NC}. From Section IV, we know that the probability of harmed consumers recovering damages goes up ($q^{CA} > q^{NC}$). As a result, extrinsically motivated producers increase care to $c^{CA} > c^{NC}$. This decreases the quasi-profit of extrinsically motivated producers, thereby reducing the difference in profit between undertaking first-best and second-best care. Consequently, the μ^{NC}-producer is no longer indifferent; he now strictly prefers following his moral sentiments setting $c = c^*$.

V. Market Equilibrium

In this Section, we assume that the market is initially in a long-run equilibrium in a judicial environment without class action. Next, we change the legal framework by authorizing a class action proceeding and examining the adjustment process. Firstly, we study the medium-run equilibrium assuming the participating firms can adjust their choice of care, but that their number is temporarily fixed. Secondly, we examine the long-run equilibrium where the marginal firm is constrained to make zero profit.

1. The partial equilibrium

Denote with $N^{NC} > k^{NC}$ the number of active firms in the initial long-run equilibrium without class action. From Section IV, we know $\prod_{\text{Ext}}(q^J, z, \mu) > \prod_{\text{Int}}(q^J, z)$. Hence, the marginal producer must be intrinsically motivated. Moreover, since all the intrinsically incentivized producers are in the same situation, they must all make zero profit. The fractions k^{NC}/N^{NC} and $1 - k^{NC}/N^{NC}$ are the respective proportion of extrinsically and intrinsically motivated producers. Given the respective care choices and the associated probability of damage $\pi(c^{NC})$ and $\pi(c^*)$, we can write the expected unrecovered damage for a consumer as:

Equation 11 $$l^{NC} = \left[\frac{k^{NC}}{N^{NC}}\pi(c^{NC}) + \left(1 - \frac{k^{NC}}{N^{NC}}\right)\pi(c^*)\right]\delta(1 - q^{NC})$$

The term in the square bracket is the average likelihood of damage over the entire market. However, from the point of view of a consumer, he only carries the damage, δ, if he is not indemnified which happens with the probability $(1 - q^{NC})$.

If class actions are allowed, a similar logic yields the consumer's expected unrecovered damage

$$\text{Equation 12} \quad l^{CA} = \left[\frac{k^{CA}}{N^{NC}}\pi(c^{CA}) + \left(1 - \frac{k^{CA}}{N^{NC}}\right)\pi(c^*)\right]\delta(1 - q^{CA})$$

where the number of firms has been kept constant at the initial level N^{NC}.

Proposition 4. *In the partial equilibrium, the introduction of a class action procedure lowers consumers' expected unrecovered loss at the time of buying,* $l^{NC} > l^{CA}$.

Proof. From Proposition 1, we know that $1 - q^{NC} > 1 - q^{CA}$. The claim holds if:

$$\frac{k^{NC}}{N^{NC}}\left[\pi(c^{NC}) + \left(1 - \frac{k^{NC}}{N^{NC}}\right)\pi(c^*)\right] > \frac{k^{CA}}{N^{NC}}\pi(c^{CA}) + \left(1 - \frac{k^{CA}}{N^{NC}}\right)\pi(c^*),$$

or, equivalently:

$$\frac{k^{NC}}{N^{NC}}\left[\pi(c^{NC}) - \pi(c^*)^1\right] > \frac{k^{CA}}{N^{NC}}\left[\pi(c^{CA}) - \pi(c^*)^1\right]$$

From Proposition 3, we know $k^{NC} \geq k^{CA}$ and $c^{CA} > c^{NC}$. The latter inequality together with $\pi' < 0$ implies $\pi(c^{NC}) > \pi(c^{CA})$ verifying the claim.

The result has a straightforward intuition. From Proposition 3, we know that with class action proceedings more producers undertake first-best care. In addition, from Proposition 1 class action guarantees that injured consumers are more frequently compensated. The latter effect also induces intrinsically motivated producers to improve second-best care. All of these changes have a similar influence, lessening consumers' expected unrecovered loss at the time of buying.

To conclude this subsection, we now investigate the profit of intrinsically motivated producers in the partial equilibrium. The effect of changes in expected unrecovered loss, $l^{NC} - l^{CA}$, on the market price aside, intrinsically motivated firms would lose from the introduction of a class action procedure because consumers who buy their products and are harmed are now more often compensated.

However, the increase in compensation implies that *ex ante* unrecovered loss goes down. Thus, holding the buyer's expected cost of consumption constant

$$\text{Equation 13} \quad p^{NC} + l^{NC} = P_m^{CA} + l_m^{CA}$$

means that the price which firms charge goes up, $p^{CA} > p^{NC}$.[22] This provides a countervailing effect. We now verify that for intrinsically motived firms the countervailing effect dominates the increase in expected liability costs.

Proposition 5. *In the partial equilibrium, holding the number of active firms constant at N^{NC}, the introduction of a class action procedure increases the profit of producers that were initially intrinsically motivated.*

Proof. In the short-run, the number of active market participants N^{NC} is given. Hence, total output is fixed at $Q^{NC} = zN^{NC}$. We denote with $D^{NC} = D(Q^{NC})$ the ensuing inverse demand.[23] Thus, in the respective judicial environment, we have:

$$p^{NC} = D^{NC} - l^{NC} \text{ and } p_m^{CA} = D^{NC} - l_m^{CA}$$

Substituting p^J into Equation 4, we show that in the partial equilibrium the profit of an intrinsically motivated producer goes up. This holds if

$$m - K - c - \pi q \quad \delta^1 z - F > \left[D^{NC} - l^{NC} - K - c^* - \pi^* q^{NC} \delta^1\right] z - F$$

or, after canceling common terms and dividing by z, if

$$l_m^{CA} - l^{NC} < \pi(c^*)\delta q^{NC} - q^{CA}$$

Substituting in the inequality l^{NC} and l^{CA} from Equations 11 and 12 respectively, and dividing by δ the inequality becomes

$$\left[\frac{k^{CA}}{N^{NC}}\pi(c^{CA}) + \left(1 - \frac{K^{CA}}{N^{NC}}\right)\pi(c^*)\right](1 - q^{CA})$$
$$-\left[\frac{k^{NC}}{N^{NC}}\pi(c^{NC}) + \left(1 - \frac{K^{NC}}{N^{NC}}\right)\pi(c^*)\right](1 - q^{NC}) < \pi(c^*)\left(q^{NC} - q^{CA}\right)$$

or, equivalently

$$\frac{K^{CA}}{N^{NC}}\pi(c^{CA}) - \pi(c^*)^1(1 - q^{CA}) < \frac{K^{NC}}{N^{NC}}\pi(c^{NC}) - \pi(c^*)^1(1 - q^{NC})$$

From Proposition 3, we know $k^{CA} \leq k^{NC}$, from the proof of Proposition 4, we have $\pi(c^{CA}) - \pi(c^*) < \pi(c^{NC}) - \pi(c^*)$, and finally from Proposition 1, we also have $1 - q^{CA} < 1 - q^{NC}$, hence verifying the claim.

[22] The index m indicates adjustments in the medium-run.
[23] Hence, we have $N_m^{CA} = N^{NC}$ and $D_m^{CA} = D^{NC}$.

To better understand the intuition of the result, imagine a situation where all the producers undertake first-best care in the judicial environment without class action proceedings. Changing the legal set-up to allow class actions would, nevertheless, reduce consumers' *ex ante* expected unrecovered loss because victims would be more often compensated. However, the profit of producers would remain unchanged because the price would adjust to exactly offset the consumer's reduction of expected loss. If not all producers initially undertake first-best care, introducing class action has two additional effects; firstly, it induces some producers to switch behaviour from extrinsic to intrinsic motivation. Secondly, the producers who remain intrinsically motivated nevertheless improve their choice of second-best care. From the point of view of initially intrinsically motivated producers, both effects create a positive externality. In contrast, the quasi-profit of the extrinsically incited producers decreases. For these producers, the price increase does not fully compensate them for the change in expected recovery from harmed consumers.

2. The long-run equilibrium

In this Section, we consider the adjustment process of introducing class action proceedings on the long-run equilibrium where firms are free to enter or exit the market. In the outset situation without class actions, the market equilibrium included N^{NC} active firms, out of which $(N^{NC} - k^{NC})$ were intrinsically and k^{NC} extrinsically motivated. Moreover, from Section IV we understand that the former firms were making zero profit while the latter had a positive quasi-profit.

In the medium-run, shift in care production and incitation behavior triggered the following adjustments. Firstly, the profit of the initial $(N^{NC} - k^{NC})$ intrinsically motivated firms was raised above zero. Secondly, producers with a moral cost $\mu \in [\mu^{CA}, \mu^{NC}]$ switched behaviour away from extrinsic incitation, thereby, raising the number of intrinsically motivated and active firms to $(N^{NC} - k^{CA})$. Thirdly, the remaining k^{CA} extrinsically incited producers obtained a lower quasi-profit.

The positive profit of the marginal producer in the medium-run implies that new firms will be enticed to enter the market. The entry process will continue until the profit of the marginal firm returns to zero. Hence, in the long-term the number of active firms increase to $N^{CA} > N^{NC}$ and the total quantity traded is raised from $Q^{NC} = zN^{NC}$ to $Q^{CA} = zN^{CA}$. Naturally, the increase in equilibrium output means that consumers' true expected cost of consumption

Equation 14 $$p^{CA} + l^{CA} = D(Q^{CA}) < D(Q^{NC}) = p^{NC} + l^{NC}$$

declines. Moreover, producers who decide to enter the market must have moral costs larger than μ^{CA}. Hence, entrants must be intrinsically motivated. Consequently, the adjustment process triggered by the introduction of a class action procedure should raise average care and lower expected unrecovered damage.

Proposition 6. *Comparing the long-run equilibrium between a legal environment with and without class action, we find that the introduction of class action:*

(i) attracts new entrants, thereby lowering the buyers' true cost of consumption,
(ii) the new entrants are intrinsically motivated, thereby reducing the proportion of firms that produce second-best care, $^{kCAkN\ C}$, and increasing average care in the market.

In summary, we can conclude that the introduction of a class action procedure should benefit customers in the long-term because it increases the consumer surplus. From the point of view of producers, the verdict is mitigated. Although intrinsically incited producers initially benefit from class action, in the long-run their profits return to zero. Thus, it should leave them indifferent between endorsing or disapproving the introduction of class actions. Extrinsically motivated producers are likely to be disadvantaged by class actions. In the medium-run, their quasi-profit should go down because the price increase following the introduction of a class action proceeding would not fully compensate them for the raise in liability and care costs. Moreover, in the long-run market entry should reduce price which would further eat away at their profit. However, there is a countervailing effect; with entrants being intrinsically motivated consumers' expected unrecovered damage goes down. Hence, the exact size of the price change is not obvious and will depend on the elasticity of the demand function. Finally, from the point of view of cost efficiency, admitting class actions is definitely advantageous since firms producing second-best care initially would be incentivized to increase care.

VI. Conclusion

The foregoing conclusions were derived using a theoretical model and were based on a number of simplifying assumptions. In this Section, we discuss probable effects of removing some of these simplifications. Finally, we briefly discuss possible extensions of our analysis.

The preceding analysis studied the adjustment process following the introduction of class actions in market environments when producers have moral concerns, albeit to a varying degree. Formal arguments were kept to a minimum by five simplifying restrictions. Firstly, production either harmed all or none of the customers of a firm. Secondly, going to court is costly, but there is no uncertainty about the outcome. Thirdly, production costs are linear up to a maximum quantity. Fourthly, producers only suffered moral costs by under-producing care relative to first-best.

The first two assumptions greatly simplify the victims' trial decision while maintaining the key characteristic that authorizing class actions would raise damage recovery. Any generalization which keeps this feature would extend the above conclusions. The third assumption is a purely technical requirement introduced to avoid an issue which is not at the core of our analysis. Specifically, with increasing marginal costs the producers face an additional trade-off between quantity and care. Considering this possibility would not seriously affect the conclusion, but considerably clutter the analysis.

The fourth assumption is the key restriction. The central simplification is that in equilibrium firms behave in only one of two ways; some produce first-best care while all the other producers choose the exact same level of second-best precaution. More generally, one could model moral costs as a function of the producer's type and the difference between actual and first-best care or alternatively between actual and average care. In either case, a firm's choice of precaution would become a monotonic function of its type.

Such an environment would generate similar results to Propositions 5 and 6. Specifically, in the medium-run authorizing class actions would benefit producers with an intrinsic motivation above a critical value while it would hurt all the others. It would also remain true that the marginal entrant is the producer with the highest intrinsic incentive. Such a producer would certainly be above the critical value. Hence, in the medium-run the profit of the critical firm would go up. Just as in the earlier analysis, it would attract new entrants over the long-run. Finally, a similar argument to the one discussed in Section V(2) implies that consumer surplus and average cost efficiency increases.

Our analysis is a first attempt to study the interplay between intrinsic and extrinsic motivations in a tort model with class actions. Intrinsic motivation conceived as empathy for the victim is modeled as a cost for non-compliance (linked to behaviour). A possible extension is to model intrinsic motivation as a cost, K, based on outcomes. In that case, the firm faces an additional cost associated with non-compliance only if a product harms a consumer. One can also observe that the use of class actions may serve as alternative corrections of enforcement problems. The model abstracts from any procedural rule and does not consider the role of litigation costs.[24] In the case where regulation introduces punitive damages instead of class action, it may be worth analyzing the changes in the results. Another important remark is that class action produces a kind of 'backlash effect', in the sense that it renders intrinsic motivation and self-interest indistinguishable. So, we could anticipate that if there are additional social rewards for intrinsic motivation, for instance customer loyalty, those effects would be certainly undermined. Finally, imperfect enforcement is caused by a variety of factors, such as insolvency and disappearing defendants, court errors on causation, errors, and caps on damages. Class actions do not correct these imperfections. The wedge between intrinsically and extrinsically motivated firms would not be eliminated by class actions if other imperfections exist. Under all these circumstances, the 'good equilibrium' identified in the Chapter may be wiped out and intrinsically motivated firms would be selected out of the market.

[24] M. Cenini, B. Luppi, and F. Parisi (2013), 'Incentive Effects of Class Actions and Punitive Damages Under Alternative Procedural Regimes' *European Journal of Law and Economics*.

Intrinsic and Extrinsic Motivations to Comply with Legal Rules

Comment on B. Deffains and D. Demougin, 'Class Actions, Compliance, and Moral Cost'

Fernando Gomez and Mireia Artigot i Golobardes***

I. Designing Incentives for Compliance

This Chapter explores the relationship and role between intrinsic and extrinsic motivations when individuals or firms decide whether to comply with legal rules.

The law and economics literature has focused mostly on the role of legal rules in creating incentives for compliance with certain standards of behaviour. Such an incentive mechanism is based on a normative design that makes compliance a preferred alternative to non-compliance for the individual or firm subject to the rule. When compliance is preferred to non-compliance, compliance is achieved through the agent's incentives to choose what is best for herself, given her private interests—or self-regarding preferences. Legal rules, in this sense, are an instrument in which compliance is achieved through an extrinsic incentive mechanism.

But extrinsic incentives are not the only mechanism to induce compliance with some desired standard or goal. The chapter by Deffains and Demougin emphasizes the role of intrinsic incentives for compliance as well as the potential relationship between intrinsic and extrinsic motivations for compliance. Specifically, the paper explores the impact and effects of introducing class actions in a perfectly competitive market setting where some firms have intrinsic motivations to invest in care.[1]

Deffains and Demougin find that the introduction of class actions would increase the average care level adopted given that in the short-run intrinsically motivated firms benefit from the introduction of class actions while in the long-run, new intrinsically motivated firms enter the market.

* Professor of Law and Economics, Pompeu Fabra University, Barcelona.
** Professor in the Department of Law, Pompeu Fabra University, Barcelona.

[1] Deffains and Demougin assume a heterogeneous level of intrinsic motivation across the different firms.

II. Context

This Chapter explores a setting in which firms have a heterogeneous degree of concern about 'doing the right thing' and 'not harming others' when producing goods that may be harmful to consumers. When consumers are harmed, the legal system is imperfect in providing compensation so that it is possible that some of the harm goes undercompensated and is then not fully internalized by the firms causing it.

Such under-deterrence will not affect firms with higher moral concerns because they will take an optimal level of effort regardless of whether or not they are legally compelled to compensate their victims, an obligation that would result from legal liability. In contrast, those with lower levels of moral concern will take insufficient care resulting from the imperfect internalization of harm, and their market position will not be affected because consumers cannot distinguish one type of firm from the other.

The effects of the introduction of a legal device that increases the chances of consumers recovering the harm caused by the product are analyzed at three different points in the time sequence: the short-term, the medium-term, and the long-run.

In the short-term, when changes in firm's techology and market entrants are not possible, consumers will have a higher willingness to pay for the products they buy given that their valuation of such products will be higher due to the higher level of compensation they expect for the harm they may suffer. This will result in an increase of the equilibrium price for all producers given that consumers cannot distinguish between the different types of firms—'moral' versus 'immoral' firms. The problem of this price increase is that it would have asymmetric effects depending on the type of firm. The introduction of class actions is an extrinsic incentive mechanism that increases the firm's liability exposure. Given that moral firms, due to the force of their intrinsic incentives, take higher care and hence are less exposed to the liability increase, the price increase resulting from the consumer's higher willingness to pay might be outweighed by the simultaneous increase in liability costs.

In the medium-run, the firm's care choices may vary so that the firm's precautions could increase for two main reasons: (i) more firms will be induced—by the external incentives—to adequately invest and choose the socially optimal level of care, and (ii) given higher, albeit still imperfect, levels of internalization of harm by firms, the 'immoral' firms would raise their level of care with respect to the previous equilibrium, given their higher expected levels of liability.

In the third stage presented in the Chapter—the long-run—the entry of new market participants is allowed. Since the marginal firm is a 'moral' firm, new entrants will be of that same kind, that is, 'moral' firms, which leads to higher levels of care in the market, a higher proportion of 'moral' firms, and with the resulting increase of market entrants and hence suppliers, a lower equilibrium price and greater consumer surplus.

III. Main Contributions

The Chapter by Deffains and Demougin nicely combines two different strands of the law and economics literature. On one hand, it addresses the role of intrinsic motivation when adopting decisions and the moral concerns of complying with legal rules, along with incentives resulting from firms' goals of avoiding liability for consumer harm and maximizing profits. On the other, it deals with the consequences of improving consumer protection through enhancing the legal tools available to consumers when seeking compensation for the harm suffered, using class actions as a 'representative institution' of the latter.

The Chapter shows how strengthening extrinsic incentives through higher liability exposure based on the increased likelihood of being held liable positively interacts with intrinsic motivations based on 'moral' concerns.

Early literature on the relationship between intrinsic and extrinsic motivations focused on the positive effects of extrinsic motivation when there are already intrinsic motivations in place as well as on the possible crowding out of intrinsic motivation by extrinsic incentives.[2] The main novel contribution of this Chapter stems from showing the comparative advantage intrinsically motivated firms enjoy when class actions—as an example of an extrinsic motivation mechanism—are introduced or become more viable.

IV. Comments

We present three major comments on the Chapter by Deffains and Demougin. The first refers to the Chapter's assumptions and their relevance for the Chapter's results, the second relates to the definition of intrinsic motivations and its relevance on the Chapter's conclusions, and the third refers to the scope of the Chapter's results regarding the impact of the introduction of class actions upon already intrinsically motivated firms.

1. Assumptions

Some of the assumptions regarding market structure, production, and the litigation game are simplifying but innocuous given the focus of the Chapter.

[2] U. Gneezy and A. Rustichini, 'Pay Enough or Do Not Pay at All' (2000) 115 *The Quarterly Journal of Economics* 791–810; B. S. Frey and R. Jegen, 'Motivation Crowding Theory' (2001) 5 *Journal of Economic Surveys* 589–611 and I. Bohnet, B. Frey, and S. Huck, 'More Order With Less Law: On Contract Enforcement, Trust, and Crowding' (2001) 95 *American Political Science Review* 131–44. See also D. Sliwka, 'Trust as a Signal of a Social Norm and the Hidden Costs of Incentive' (2007) 97 *The American Economic Review* 999–1012 analyzing the crowding-out effects of extrinsic motivations through the introduction of a third group of agents who derive utility from norm adherence but who will 'do the right thing' as long as they believe a significant fraction of the other agents will also 'do the right thing'.

But other assumptions included in the Chapter might be important when analyzing the Chapter's results. For example, the authors assume that parties can always file a legal claim and meet their burden of proof and that courts do not make mistakes. The possibility that potential victims file frivolous claims is hence ruled out.

But a well known side-effect of class actions is that they increase the leverage of those considering filing frivolous claims while simultaneously increasing their chances of reaching a settlement even when the underlying claim is spurious.[3] As a result, liability imposed is higher than it should be, and the number of frivolous claims filed increases remarkably.

2. Characterizing intrinsic motivations

The difference between intrinsic motivations and rightfulness, in addition to being challenging, is relevant for the purpose of the Chapter.

Firms are assumed to aim to maximize their profits. But when introducing intrinsic motivations in a firm's decisions, the firm's objective function includes 'doing the right thing' when choosing a care level in addition to including a profit-maximization goal.

However, the moral concept of 'doing the right thing' may not necessarily entail equivalent conduct that would require complying with the legal rule—being a law-abider. In other words, not harming others based on moral considerations may not be equivalent to complying with the level of care required by the legal system. Such difference may be of special importance because firms, regardless of their intrinsic motivations, will have to compensate injured victims *ex post* whenever they failed to comply with the level of care required by the legal rule. However, moral considerations may require a higher investment in care based on, for example, the firm's private information regarding product risks and might involve *ex post* monetary compensation of an injured victim in cases where the level of care adopted fell below the one required by moral considerations.

Hence, being legally righteous, in addition to being a different concept than being moral—or 'doing the right thing'—might have different economic consequences and hence might be relevant when determining the firm's level of care.

This issue reaches beyond the question of labeling preferences: experimental literature shows that individuals are more concerned with doing the right thing

[3] An extreme example of the perverse effects of class actions regarding incentives to file frivolous claims is the case against William S. Lerach, a plaintiff's attorney and partner in the law firm Milberg Weiss, who pleaded guilty for paying potential plaintiffs to become members of a class so that they would file and pursue class actions based on frivolous claims against major US corporations that were willing to—and in fact did—settle such claims for millions of dollars in order to minimize their legal costs resulting from the judicial procedure. Mr Lerach pleaded guilty in 2007 to conspiring to obstruct justice and to make false statements under oath. See the Press Release from the United States Attorney's Office, Central District of California (available at <http://www.justice.gov/usao/cac/Pressroom/pr2008/012.html>). See also Y. -K. Che, 'The Economics of Collective Negotiation in Pretrial Bargaining' (2002) 43 *International Economic Review* 549–76 and Y. -K. Che, 'Equilibrium Formation of Class Action Suits' (1996) 62 *Journal of Public Economics* 339–61.

when others may observe their behaviour.[4] But when considering the framework defined by Deffains and Demougin, the firms' behaviour and level of care adopted is not observable by consumers, and hence the intrinsic incentive of 'doing the right thing' would be remarkably weakened.

The Chapter assumes that firms produce goods of different quality but that consumers cannot observe the producer's level of care, so that goods are perceived as being homogeneous. But such an assumption could easily be made more realistic if the firm's decisions were framed within a setting in which potential injurors were concerned about signaling their moral type.[5]

In order to make the Chapter's model more realistic, one could assume that 'moral' or 'righteous' firms are able to signal—even if imperfectly—their being more concerned and careful with their products, especially assuming they are competing in a perfectly competitive environment where there is an infinite number of profit-maximizing firms offering a perfectly substitutable product and where information is generally assumed to be perfect.

Thus, introducing reputation seems to be the natural feature of the setting defined in the Chapter by Deffains and Demougin. Considering reputation would allow for distinguishing between 'moral' and 'immoral' firms. In the Chapter firms are identical except for their moral disutility parameter μ. However, it is likely that μ will be correlated with other factors that may hinge upon the liability question, such as the size or the level of the firm's assets, the firm's experience or market share, and the cost effectiveness in the use of technology.

Some of these correlations may reinforce the Chapter's findings that an increase in the level of legal liability through the introduction of class actions would harm 'moral' firms less than others, but other correlations could also work in the opposite direction and hence should be considered. For example, class actions may be more likely to be pursued against well-established and large firms that might also be those with higher μ. If that were the case, 'moral' firms would be more adversely affected by the introduction of class actions than other firms. Furthermore, 'moral' firms, in order to keep the promises of being 'moral', would be weaker in settlement negotiations given that they would be willing to compensate victims more easily and more generously than other firms.

If some of these arguments were true, then the argument against class actions or against any other legal instrument that would involve an expansion of consumer rights raised by 'moral' firms should be considered given that they may anticipate that 'nastier' firms will be more likely to not be the target of the increased liability involved in such reforms and will be able to avoid their consequences. But it should be remembered that it might be the 'not so nice' firms who would be the ones opposing expanding liability though legal reforms.

[4] Although there is also anonymous other-regarding behaviour: see B. S. Frey and S. Meier, 'Pro-social Behavior in a Natural Setting' (2004) 54 *Journal of Economic Behavior & Organization* 65–88.

[5] B. Deffains and C. Fluet, 'Legal Liability When Individuals Have Moral Concerns' (2009) CIRPEE Working Paper No 09–51 (available at <http://ssrn.com/abstract=1516337>).

Two further issues regarding the Chapter's assumptions should be highlighted: on the one side, possible heterogeneous incentives regarding care, and on the other, the importance of whether the interaction between firms and consumers is a one-time interaction or a repeated one.

a. Heterogeneous incentives of care and extrinsic and intrinsic motivations

One of the implicit assumptions of the Chapter by Deffains and Demougin is the difference between the incentives for care created by extrinsic mechanisms and intrinsic motivations. However, such mechanisms may not affect the same kind of dimensions when the firm determines the level of care to be adopted.

Incentives might be heterogeneous and have different dimensions—observable or not. From this perspective, extrinsic incentives—here with observable or non-observable dimensions—might create distortions when they affect certain dimensions of care where there are already intrinsic incentives for care without affecting those for which there are no intrinsic incentives.[6]

This issue is of particular importance when considering observable and non-observable dimensions of care by the consumer. If some investments in care are observable while others are not, firms might be more willing to comply with extrinsic incentives in observable dimensions. At the same time, firms may already have intrinsic incentives for these observable dimensions or for non-observable dimensions. If that were the case, the role, impact, and effects of extrinsic incentives on the level of care adopted by the firm would be contingent on the dimensions in which it would operate as well as on whether firms had intrinsic incentives for care with respect to such dimensions.

Related to this question is the issue of defining the tasks—or required level of care—subject to extrinsic incentives.[7] In the context of employee compensation, literature on multi-tasking shows that compensating any subset of tasks will result in focusing on these and substituting the uncompensated activities for activities with extrinsic incentives for compensation.[8] At the same time, the required level of effort for tasks might involve different levels of effort and some there might be a misallocation of effort among tasks caused by extrinsic incentives.

Applying these considerations to the context of the Chapter, the firm's level of care might have different dimensions that may involve different costs and that may or may not be subject to extrinsic incentives. In such cases, firms concerned

[6] See C. Pendergast, 'The Provision of Incentives in Firms' (1999) 37 *Journal of Economic Literature* 7–63 studying the different mechanisms of creation of incentives in firms and focusing mostly on contracts.

[7] D. M. Kreps, 'Intrinsic Motivation and Extrinsic Incentives' (1997) 87(2) *American Economic Review* 359–64, Papers and Proceedings of the Hundred and Fourth Annual Meeting of the American Economic Association.

[8] See B. Holmstrom and P. Milgrom, 'Multi-Task Principal-Agent Analysis' (1991) Special Issue 7 *Journal of Law, Economics, & Organization* 24–52 noting that jobs with high intrinsic motivation often involve a remarkable task ambiguity. See also Kreps, n 7, 359–64 noting that in order to evaluate performance, a combination of subjective as well as objective parameters should be used.

with 'doing the right thing' might have incentives for investing in those observable dimensions that involve lower cost levels. Imposing extrinsic incentives upon these dimensions could be counterproductive.

b. One time versus repeated interactions between consumers and firms

The impact of incentives, compliance with legal norms, and reputation is strongly conditioned by the nature of the interaction between the parties in the transaction. Repeated interactions allow for honest behaviour and for higher intrinsic incentives while static, one-time relationships allow for higher levels of cheating.[9]

In order for firms to have lasting intrinsic incentives with their customers and hence allow for reputation, customers must have the ability to react whenever the level of care of the product does not meet the expectations to which the customer was entitled to. Whenever the interaction between a firm and its customers is a one-time interaction, the firm's incentives to comply with intrinsic as well as extrinsic incentives are remarkably diluted given that customers cannot react to the firm's lack of compliance. In contrast, whenever the interaction is repeated, if customers are able to observe whether the firm might have intrinsic incentives for care, there is a possibility of creating trust in light of the firm's intrinsic incentives to 'do the right thing'. As a result, repetition of the relation might imply better outcomes for firms with intrinsic incentives for care whenever customers can observe performance and they subjectively evaluate such performance.[10] On the other hand, as has recently been shown, legal liability may be able to reduce the cost of ensuring reputation in a repeated interaction between firms and consumers.[11]

3. Scope of the results

As explained above, defining, modeling or just characterizing intrinsic motivations in the context of firms is quite challenging. Moral concerns or moral considerations do not seem to easily fit the standard definition and characterization of firms that suggests a profit-maximizing goal without further concerns. But other elements, such as the firm's ownership structure, might also be important when analyzing the results of the Chapter.

Firm's owners—shareholders—might not necessarily have intrinsic motivations regarding levels of care especially in cases where the corporation is large and ownership dispersed. But corporate managers could be sensitive to intrinsic motivations as well as extrinsic motivations. Further, corporate managers could be considering intrinsic motivations when deciding on care levels that need not

[9] See also Kreps, n 7, 359–64.

[10] For an analysis of the impact of repeated versus one-time interactions in the context of employment relationships see Kreps, n 7, 359–64.

[11] See J. Ganuza, F. Gomez-Pomar, and M. Robles, 'Product Liability vs. Reputation' (2011) Working Paper, Universitat Pompeu Fabra (available at <http://ssrn.com/abstract=1986237>).

necessarily aim at maximizing the firm's profits. In such cases, shareholders could decide to replace such managers for others seeking maximum profits or could file a derivative suit on behalf of the corporation claiming compensation for the harm suffered by the corporation as a result of the manager's breach of duty of maximizing shareholder value.

If shareholders would replace, or aim to hold liable, 'moral' corporate managers for breaching their fiduciary duties on account of their non-profit maximizing decisions, the shareholders would drive out corporate managers who act based on intrinsic motivations.

If this were true, the market would only be populated by one kind of firms: firms with managers following purely extrinsic motivations. In this sense, the Chapter's assumptions that two types of firms—a first type of firms with managers with intrinsic motivations and a second type of firms with extrinsic motivations—coexist in the market would not hold and hence would have to be additionally justified.

Another side effect resulting from the assumption that firms—or more precisely, corporate managers—could act based on intrinsic motivations when adopting corporate decisions with respect to care towards consumers should be considered. Assuming, as the Chapter does, that 'moral' and 'immoral' firms would coexist in the market, another factor is whether the relationships and joint performance of intrinsic and extrinsic motivations is different when one introduces utility considerations to the decision-making process. If firms derive some positive utility from acting according to their intrinsic motivations, it is well settled in the literature that once extrinsic motivations are imposed, the individual's—in this case the firm's—utility function changes and such change might result in a disutility for adopting care. The idea is that whenever an individual performs a task, he rationally justifies such a task and will attribute some enjoyment to performing such a task. Such enjoyment in 'doing the right thing' will also create incentives to continue 'doing the right thing' and doing it even better—if possible. When extrinsic incentives are put in place, the individual's perception of the task or the effort will change, and he will attribute his effort to the extrinsic incentive mechanisms imposed, developing, then, a distaste for the required effort that could easily result in an unwillingness to continue performing the task or in a decrease of the effort devoted to such task.[12]

Psychologists and sociologists attribute the disutility created by extrinsic incentives once intrinsic incentives are in place to the agents' lack of confidence in their own abilities or in their willingness to perform a certain task as a consequence of the effects resulting from extrinsic motivations.[13]

[12] See Kreps, n 7, 359–64.

[13] See Kreps, n 7, 359–64. See also R. Bénabou and J. Tirole, 'Intrinsic and Extrinsic Motivation' (2003) 70 *Review of Economic Studies* 489–520 showing the conditions under which rewards and punishments work and under which circumstances they could be counterproductive and claiming that the reaction to such 'hidden costs' of extrinsic motivations is rational.

Hence, the voluntariness element of the behaviour based on intrinsic incentives is crucial. The literature has suggested the use of economic incentives to complement the intrinsic incentives of performing certain tasks and to avoid the disutility that extrinsic incentives would create.[14]

It seems difficult to justify the role of the firm's utility functions in the context of market transactions between firms and consumers. The standard assumption is that firms have a profit-maximizing goal and that utility functions, as modeled for individuals, are not the instrument to model the firm's decisions.

However, the idea that extrinsic incentives diminish the importance and role of intrinsic motivations for adopting a certain care level also seems applicable in the context of firms, especially when it is assumed that the firm type—'moral' or 'immoral'—is observable by the consumer and reputation is introduced. In a market situation, firms might be interested in letting consumers know that the level of care of their products is different from other firms not because they are legally required to adopt such a level of care, but because they believe they are concerned about the welfare of consumers and thus feel internally compelled to adopt such a care level. In this sense, trust should arise between firms and customers as long as the latter can observe and have information on the level of care, as well as on the motivations for adopting such a level of care. If these two elements were not observable by consumers, then firms could be tempted to cheat given that consumers would not able to distinguish between 'moral' and 'immoral' firms.

V. The Complex Interaction Between Intrinsic and Extrinsic Mechanisms when Creating Incentives for Care

This Chapter by Deffains and Demougin contributes to the law and economics discussion on the creation of incentives. In addition to well-studied extrinsic mechanisms such as class actions, this Chapter analyzes the role of intrinsic mechanisms in incentive creation and their relationship with extrinsic mechanisms that might also be in place.

This valuable contribution by Deffains and Demougin turns on the finding that the introduction of class actions—an extrinsic mechanism—would increase the average level of care adopted in the short-term while also encouraging new intrinsically motivated firms to enter the market in the long-run.

[14] See T. Ellingsen and M. Johannesson, 'Pride and Prejudice: The Human Side of Incentive Theory' (2208) 98 *American Economic Review* 990–1008 introducing the role of esteem—an external reward—in normative compliance and in claiming that under certain conditions, extrinsic incentives such as control systems or pecuniary incentives erode intrinsic incentives to perform while explaining that unconditional high pay might result in agents' motivation.

10

Legal Supervision of Commercial Opportunism

*Clayton P. Gillette**

I. Introduction

Opportunism, in Oliver Williamson's felicitous phrase, consists of 'self-interest seeking with guile.'[1] The phrase elegantly captures the sense that, while commercial actors are expected to pursue personal gain, when they enter into contracts they implicitly allocate to themselves risks that they may regret having accepted when the time for performance has arrived. Market prices may have changed, obstacles to performance may have materialized, and transactions that *ex ante* seemed like a good gamble may turn out to look like sure losses. At that time, commercial actors may attempt to recapture contractual benefits that neutral observers and the counterparty may have reasonably thought were surrendered in the initial bargain. In that sense, opportunism shares with the absence of good faith the idea that parties guilty of such behaviour inappropriately attempt to reclaim forgone opportunities.[2]

Ideally, commercial parties would specify the risks each takes with sufficient precision to avoid opportunistic efforts to reclaim forgone risks. But the range of activities that may constitute opportunistic behaviour—from blatant lying to more subtle forms of chiselling on performance—is too broad to permit complete contracting. Parties will necessarily be unable to specify and thus explicitly to prohibit all activities that fall within the scope of opportunism, even those activities that they would agree *ex ante* falls outside of commercial propriety. Indeed, contracting explicitly against guile seems superfluous insofar as opportunism involves behaviour so inconsistent with the contractual risk allocation that the parties would have thought that no such specification was necessary. Parties in long-term, repeat-play situations may be less concerned about incomplete

* Max E. Greenberg Professor of Contract Law, New York University School of Law.

[1] O. E. Williamson, *The Economic Institutions of Capitalism* (New York: The Free Press, 1985) 47.

[2] See S. J. Burton, 'Breach of Contract and the Common Law Duty to Perform in Good Faith' (1980) 94 *Harvard Law Review* 369–404.

contracting because they can rely on course of performance to fill in contractual gaps and on reputational sanctions and the capacity for retaliation to control some misbehaviour by counterparties. But subtle forms of opportunism are likely to be either non-observable—that is, undetectable to the counterparty—or non-verifiable—that is, difficult to prove to third parties—so that reliance on extra-legal sanctions may provide less of a constraint than in the case of obvious misconduct.

In theory, commercial law can compensate for the high transactions costs implicit in specifying acts of opportunism by creating default rules that replicate what parties would have bargained for had they negotiated about the issue. But the array of acts that might be deployed by a party who regrets the prior risk allocation and the sensitivity of a finding of opportunism to the context in which a contract is performed means that drafters of legal rules will have no more success than the parties to a specific contract in identifying with precision the acts that would constitute opportunism. Instead, characterizing particular conduct as opportunistic is likely a matter that can only be determined *ex post*. Default rules can only provide the roughest of proxies for opportunistic behaviour, with the details to be completed by courts on an *ad hoc* basis. Legal doctrine can facilitate that inquiry in either of two ways. First, legal doctrine may require behaviour that is deemed to be consistent with the absence of opportunism and prohibit conduct that has characteristics of opportunism. That is, legal doctrine can create rough proxies for appropriate behaviour and require parties to comply with the proxies, even though doing so creates both false positives (parties will sometimes act non-opportunistically even though they have violated the legal doctrine) and false negatives (parties will sometimes behave opportunistically even though they satisfy the requirements of legal doctrine). Secondly, legal doctrine may create vague standards that permit third party arbiters to make very fact-specific inquiries into the conduct of parties to determine whether one of them has exhibited conduct that the parties would have avoided explicitly had transactions costs permitted negotiation about it.

Either of those mechanisms requires substantial intervention by courts or arbitrators to assess whether the behaviour of one of the parties transcends mere self-interest and enters the prohibited realm of 'guile'. In this Chapter, I suggest that such interventions are more costly and less effective than is typically recognized. In the first instance, the selection of rules to stifle one form of opportunism may invite alternative forms of opportunism. In the latter case, intervention requires arbiters (by which I mean judges, arbitrators, or administrative regulators) to reverse engineer the parties' transaction in ways that are often beyond a third party's capacity in all but the most obvious cases of commercial misconduct. In doing so, arbiters purport to enforce the initial bargain of the parties. But therein lies the difficulty. In order to enforce that bargain, arbiters must have the capacity to understand the scope of the parties' own risk allocation. Arbiters may fail to understand the commercial purpose of particular contractual allocations and trade-offs, and thus mistake opportunism with exploitation of opportunities that the party paid to enjoy. Thus, I conclude that efforts to control opportunism through legal intervention create a substantial risk that arbiters will frequently reallocate risks rather than enforce the parties' bargain. The result is that arbiters would generate results more consistent with parties' intent if they apply legal rules and contractual language strictly, rather than interpret rules and language through a filter laden with judicial conceptions of appropriate commercial conduct.

Judicial restraint in the face of colourable misconduct does not mean that commercial parties have no capacity to constrain opportunism. To the contrary, I suggest that even though arbiters are limited in their ability to reverse engineer transactions, parties have greater capacity than is often realized to employ contract to constrain opportunism. While contracts are necessarily incomplete, parties can craft clauses that discourage deviations from original understandings. However, bargained-for clauses that, from an *ex ante* perspective, provide an at-risk party with reasonable protection against opportunistic behaviour may, from an *ex post* perspective, appear to impose inappropriate restrictions on the counterparty. As a result, the very arbiters that can only afford limited protection against opportunism end up invalidating the self-help efforts of parties who are more capable of understanding and bargaining about the risks implicit in their transaction.

In Section II of this Chapter, I will indicate how efforts to fashion legal rules that constrain opportunism are only partially successful. That is, they may, indeed, limit opportunism of a particular type by reducing the ability of parties to engage in behaviour that is frequently associated with strategic behaviour. But in doing so, those same rules provide opportunities for the counterparty to exploit the restrictions on the first party, that is, to replace one form of opportunism with another. Unless we think that one party is more likely to engage in opportunism than another, these legal restrictions cannot readily be seen as creating a net reduction in strategic behaviour. I then explore the capacity of courts to apply vague legal standards that presumably have as their purpose the regulation of opportunistic behaviour. Finally, I turn to contractual efforts to constrain opportunism. I focus primarily on hold-up problems in which parties who have made relationship-specific investments are vulnerable to exploitation by counterparties. A variety of commonly considered contract clauses can limit the ability of counterparties opportunistically to force the investing party to reallocate the contractual surplus in order to avoid loss of its investment. At least in Anglo-American law, however, I find that attempts by parties are subject either to arbiter invalidation or to misapplication that frustrates the efforts of parties to do what arbiters presumably cannot.

II. Legal Rules to Restrict Opportunism: Perfect Tender versus Substantial Performance

A common dispute in commercial law involves the circumstances under which less than full performance by one party justifies the other party in terminating the contract. In the US, conditions for termination vary with the type of contract.

In the case of a sale of goods, formal legal doctrine embodies a perfect tender rule under which any nonconformity, regardless of its severity, justifies rejection of the goods in whole.[3] In the case of other contracts, such as construction contracts, a substantial performance rule applies. Under that rule, as long as the project that was the subject of the contract substantially conforms to contractual specifications, the aggrieved party may recover damages for the difference between the project as contracted for and the project as completed, but the aggrieved party is not entitled to terminate the contract or to avoid paying for the value of what was delivered.[4]

In each case, the rule might be viewed as an effort to minimize the threat of opportunism. One might distinguish between sales contracts and construction contracts by considering the complexity of the performance and the consequences of allowing termination.[5] Goods may involve relatively simple characteristics that are easily identifiable so that conformity is readily determined. In addition, goods typically are exchanged in relatively thick markets, so that the risk of forfeiture in the event of contract termination may be relatively minor, since even nonconforming goods may be resold. Construction projects are both relatively complex and highly individualized. As a result, termination of the contract for minor nonconformities may cause substantial forfeiture by a party whose performance deviates insubstantially from contractual requirements.

These distinctions suggest that one overriding consideration in formulating a legal rule for the termination of goods or other contracts is the likelihood that parties to goods contracts and construction contracts are subject to different risks of opportunism. The seller in a fixed-price goods contract may come to regret its agreement where the cost of producing the good has increased between the time of contract and the time of performance. Under those circumstances, sellers are likely to chisel on performance by offering goods of lower quality than was contractually specified. A perfect tender rule reduces the risk of seller opportunism by allowing the buyer to reject proffered goods that deviate even minimally from contractual requirements. The risk that goods will have to be retrieved and resold presumably discourages seller opportunism. As I explain later in this Chapter, provisions that offer the seller an opportunity to cure any nonconformity before termination may perversely reduce the incentive to perform perfectly in the first instance. But the possibility of cure may not substantially induce seller misbehaviour, because even a seller who cures a nonconformity must bear the cost of undoing the initial performance and completing a second one.

That explanation, however, does not easily explain the prevalence of a substantial performance rule with respect to goods in other legal systems. The United Nations Convention on Contracts for the International Sale of Goods (CISG), for instance, allows a buyer to avoid the contract only if the seller's nonconforming

[3] See Uniform Commercial Code (UCC) § 2-601.

[4] See *Jacob & Youngs v. Kent*, 129 N.E. 889 (1921).

[5] See, e.g., T. Muris, 'Opportunistic Behavior and the Law of Contracts' (1981) 65 *Minnesota Law Review* 521–90, 573–5.

performance amounts to a 'fundamental breach'.[6] That phrase, in turn, is defined as a breach that results in such detriment to the other party that it substantially deprives that party of what it was 'entitled to expect under the contract.'[7] Minor deviations from contractual requirements will not justify termination, although the aggrieved party will be able to collect damages or procure other remedies that compensate the buyer for the loss of expectation.[8] The justification for the 'fundamental breach' rule is simply the mirror image of the justification for the perfect tender rule. Buyers who enter into a transaction may come to regret their transaction between the execution of the contract and the time of performance, perhaps as a result of intervening reductions in market prices for the goods that are the subject of the contract. Armed with a perfect tender rule, buyers who suffer regret may seize on technical nonconformities that do not adversely affect the performance of the goods in order to avoid acceptance or at least to force a renegotiation of the contract price. Indeed, non-opportunistic buyers might actually prefer a substantial performance rule, because sellers who anticipate strategic buyers under a perfect tender rule are likely to charge more for their goods in order to defray some of the costs related to the cost of renegotiation or of recovering or curing nonconformities related to opportunistic rejections. Thus, buyers who do not expect to act strategically might prefer the anticipated discount in price related to a substantial performance rule. But the fact remains that the very existence of a perfect tender rule that is intended to constrain seller opportunism can be exploited by opportunistic buyers.

Of course, non-strategic sellers will have just the opposite preference. To the extent that they are willing to forgo the opportunity to impose nonconforming goods on a buyer under a substantial performance rule, sellers may be able to command higher prices for their goods by accepting a perfect tender rule. But, as noted earlier, that rule simply displaces a risk of seller misbehaviour with one of buyer misbehaviour. In light of the reciprocal risks that the alternatives present, whether a perfect tender rule or a substantial performance rule is superior would appear to depend on whether we believe that buyer opportunism or seller opportunism is more prevalent. An initial assignment of the entitlement either to the buyer (a perfect tender rule) or to the seller (a substantial performance rule) that depended on which party was least likely to exploit its advantage would presumably reduce transactions costs and satisfy the criterion of creating commercial default rules that reflected the parties own preferences.[9] It is rational to believe, in short, that parties who fully negotiated their contracts would place the risk of opportunism on the party least likely to engage in it. There is little reason, however, to believe that either buyers or sellers are more or less likely than the other to act strategically. Indeed, since commercial actors typically engage as both buyers and sellers (for example, buying raw materials

[6] See CISG, Art 49. [7] See CISG, Art 25. [8] See, e.g., CISG, Arts 75, 76.

[9] G. Calabresi and A. D. Melamed, 'Property Rules, Liability Rules, and Inalienability: One View of the Cathedral' (1972) 85 *Harvard Law Review* 1089–128.

and selling finished products), selecting one rule over another as a means of reducing the sum of opportunistic behaviour in sales transactions entails the improbable belief that the same parties act opportunistically when they are acting in one capacity, but not in the other.

One might contend that the combination of a perfect tender rule and a seller's right to cure—a combination offered in the Uniform Commercial Code (UCC)[10]—does effectively constrain buyer opportunism. A buyer may be less likely to exploit a technical breach if a seller victimized by that effort will have another opportunity to hold the buyer to the contract. Buyers would have little reason to invest in technical rejection of goods for nonconformities that sellers can easily cure. But the conditions of permissible cure are sufficiently narrow and costly that a buyer who is otherwise inclined to invoke the perfect tender rule opportunistically may at least threaten to impose the costs of cure on the seller in order to renegotiate a price reduction. Moreover, just like the prefect tender and substantial performance rules pose reciprocal risks, the possibility of cure increases the risk of seller opportunism at the same time that it decreases the risk of buyer opportunism. A seller who has an additional opportunity to perform, albeit a more costly one given the need to undo and replace the first transaction, may discount the benefits of an initial conforming performance. A seller who has a right to cure may expect to exercise it only in a small percentage of cases of minimal nonconformity. Buyers may not always detect minor defects and may not always complain of minor defects that they do detect. Therefore, assuming that minor defects reduce seller costs (for example, lower quality control costs) a seller with a right to cure may be induced to chisel on a large number of contracts in the reasonable belief that any costs it incurs by the occasional demand for cure will be offset by the gains on contracts in which no such demand is made notwithstanding the presence of nonconformities.

This is not to say that all legal rules will generate the same level of opportunism. Indeed, one of the puzzling aspects of the CISG is that its combination of a fundamental breach standard and a right to cure could increase opportunism above what one might expect from a perfect tender/cure regime. The CISG permits cure even after the seller has tendered goods that fail to satisfy the more forgiving substantial performance rule. Thus, under both regimes, an opportunistic seller can tender imperfect goods in the hope that the buyer does not complain, but then demand a right to cure if the buyer does complain. But under the UCC, the right to cure after the time for performance has expired is contingent on the seller's having had reasonable grounds to believe the initial tender would have been acceptable with or without money allowance.[11] The seller bears some risk that a tender that fails substantially to conform to contract specifications will not satisfy that condition, because a reasonable buyer might treat such a breach as grounds for termination. The CISG, on the other hand, permits the seller to cure even a fundamental breach as long as it can do so without unreasonable delay and without

[10] See UCC § 2-508. [11] UCC § 2-508(2).

causing the buyer unreasonable inconvenience.[12] One might conclude, therefore, that a seller whose transaction is governed by the CISG will have less incentive to comply with contractual requirements in the first instance.

That does not mean, however, that even an increased amount of seller opportunism under the CISG would exceed the level of buyer opportunism that might materialize under a perfect tender rule. Again, there seems little reason to conclude that, as an empirical matter, buyers or sellers are less likely to exploit the advantages granted by the assignment of a legal entitlement. As a result, it seems implausible that assignments of entitlements can be expected to reduce the net amount of strategic behaviour in transactions.

III. Judicial Administration of Broad Standards

If the assignment of specific entitlements cannot reduce opportunism, then allowing third-party arbiters broad authority to police parties' conduct against opportunism on an individual basis appears to be a reasonable alternative. Broad standards such as the obligation of good faith performance, often said to be implied in every contract, typically are invoked for this purpose. Indeed, some courts and commentators suggest that the UCC's perfect tender rule does not really permit rejection for any nonconformity, notwithstanding the statutory language to that effect. Instead, commentators suggest, buyers are restricted to good faith rejections for nonconformities, a category that excludes rejection for technical breaches where the buyer appears to be dissatisfied with the deal that it struck rather than with the seller's performance.[13]

Vague admonitions that constrain the permissible scope of transactional behaviour such as good faith, commercial reasonableness, and best efforts certainly provide courts with standards for monitoring the conduct of commercial parties and penalizing conduct that smacks of opportunism. The problem, then, lies not in the existence of authority, but in its exercise. Judicial intervention does not solve the problem of incomplete contracting if the judiciary is no more able to observe or verify deviations from anticipated behaviour *ex post* than the parties were able to specify *ex ante*. Thus, the principle of good faith may be useful to prohibit very specific acts that one would have thought all parties would agree

[12] CISG, Art 48(1). As a technical matter, the seller's right to cure a fundamental breach is subject to the buyer's right to declare the contract avoided. See CISG, Art 49(1)(a). But the combination of the two provisions sets up a difficult analytical cycle. While Art 49(1)(a) allows the buyer to avoid a contract where the seller has committed a fundamental breach, if the buyer can cure a nonconforming tender without unreasonable delay and inconvenience to the buyer, the buyer arguably is not deprived of its expectation under the contract. See CISG, Art 25. As a result, there would be no fundamental breach if a cure occurs. Oddly, therefore, the right to avoid, and thus to disallow a proposed cure, depends on a fundamental breach; but the existence of a fundamental breach may itself depend on whether the seller can cure in accordance with Art 48(1).

[13] See J. J. White and R. S. Summers, *Uniform Commercial Code* (St. Paul: West Publishing Co, 6th edn, 2010) 415–16.

were inappropriate even though the contract did not mention them, presumably because the intent to prohibit them was so obvious that explicit clauses would be superfluous. Charles Fried, for instance, explored the application of good faith in the classic case of *Patterson v. Meyerhofer*,[14] in which the defendant agreed that plaintiff should acquire land at auction and then resell it to her at a specified price. She then successfully bid against the plaintiff for the land, and the plaintiff sued for non-performance. The court granted the claim on the ground that 'implicit in [plaintiff's] contract with defendant was an obligation not to take actions interfering with her contractual partner's performance.' Notwithstanding the absence of any explicit bar in the contract against plaintiff bidding for the property, and in the absence of a contrary usage governing the situation, Professor Fried concludes that the judicial filling of the gap was simply implementing the parties' intent:

> [T]he defendant/broker must have been more than a little surprised to see the plaintiff at the auction, bidding against him. Surely one of the things he would say in his defense would be that had he thought of the matter, he would certainly have precluded the possibility explicitly in the contract. He would say he had not thought of it just because it seemed so obvious.[15]

The concept of good faith in these situations, however, does not appear to be doing any independent work in analysing the content of the contract. Instead, the prohibition on plaintiff bidding would appear to be an implied term of the contract, agreed to by each of the parties, because both parties would presumably have agreed that neither could frustrate the efforts of the other to perform its obligations. The parties need not include a clause to that effect in their contract to give it effect any more than they need to include a clause measuring damages for breach by the expectation standard if they intend to include that within the contract. In either case, the default rule created by custom (in the case of not frustrating the counterparty) or by law (in the case of the expectation damage measure) becomes part of the contract without explicit mention. But once one casts the analysis in those terms, the additional admonition that the misbehaving party also acted in bad faith adds nothing.

Similarly, courts have employed the CISG's good faith obligation to observe 'good faith in international trade'[16] to create more specific behavioural rules that might be deemed 'obvious' to parties within the trade. For instance, German cases deploy the good faith obligation to require parties who rely on standard terms to make those terms available to the counterparty.[17] But again, the invocation of 'good faith' appears to be doing little of the analytical work in assigning the risk associated with standard terms. Instead, the relevant decisions seem

[14] *Patterson v. Meyerhofer*, 204 N.Y. 96 (1912).

[15] C. Fried, *Contract as Promise* (Cambridge, Mass: Harvard University Press, 1981) 87.

[16] See CISG, Art 7(1).

[17] See Court of Appeals (*Oberlandesgericht*) Celle, 24 July 2009 [13 W 48/09] (available at <http://cisgw3.law.pace.edu/cases/090724g1.html>) and also at (2010) *NJW-RR* 136; Federal Supreme Court (*Bundesgerichtshof*) 31 October 2001 (available at <http://cisgw3.law.pace.edu/cases/011031g1.html>) and also at 149 *BGHZ* 113.

predicated on a view that the party who has drafted the standard terms and who desires to incorporate them into the contract is in a better position to make them known than the counterparty. Regardless of whether one agrees that imposing on one party the obligation to volunteer standard terms is less costly than imposing on the counterparty the obligation to inquire about them, once risk allocation is predicated on that belief, the additional argument that failure to provide terms would violate good faith again seems to add little to the analysis.

Using vague standards of good faith to augment alternative standards of analysis may be superfluous, but do not necessarily interfere with the parties' assignment of contractual risk. But applying vague standards such as good faith can be problematic because they implicitly assume that the contract has not allocated a risk in a manner that allows one party to take advantage of a condition, even though doing so inflicts a substantial harm on the counterparty. Even courts that employ standards such as good faith would seem to agree that sophisticated actors are entitled to accept, and be compensated for, risks that they subsequently regret taking. Thus, an implicit risk of vague standards is that courts will fail to recognize that what looks like exploitation of an unfortunate situation is instead the manifestation of a risk that a party was paid to take. In that case, judicial evaluation of commercial propriety can end up reallocating risks rather than enforcing allocations to which the parties would have bargained had transactions costs permitted.

The problem can be exemplified by one of the standard US examples of judicial allegations of bad faith performance. In *T.W. Oil, Inc. v. Consolidated Edison Co*,[18] the plaintiff had sold oil to the defendant under a contract of 24 January 1974 that stipulated delivery by 30 January 1974 of oil with a sulphur content of 0.5 per cent. The defendant was permitted to burn oil with a sulphur content of up to one per cent and often mixed oil from different shipments to maintain that figure. The oil tendered by the buyer actually contained sulphur in excess of 0.9 per cent. The defendant rejected the tender, notwithstanding that the plaintiff offered both to reduce the price and to cure the defects with a delivery of oil that was scheduled to arrive on 28 February, and that did arrive on 4 March—about four weeks after the delivery time specified in the original contract. The defendant was apparently willing to take the oil only at the then-prevailing price, which was 25 per cent below the market price at the time the contract was executed. After reselling the oil, the plaintiff brought an action for breach of contract to recover the difference between the contract price and the lower resale price. The court concluded that the seller had offered cure within the meaning of the relevant UCC provision and thus was entitled to recover. But the court also implied that the defendant's rejection was motivated by the intervening price movements, and thus violated its obligation to act in good faith. Not content to conclude that the conditions of post-delivery date had been satisfied, the court implied that the defendant's failure

[18] *T.W. Oil, Inc. v. Consolidated Edison Co* 443 N.E.2d 932 (NY, 1982).

to accept the subsequent delivery demonstrated 'sharp dealing' and that the judicial role included employing the remedy of cure to 'thwart [...] the chiseler.'[19]

The very conditions that the court suggests evince a lack of good faith, however, may also be interpreted as defining the scope of the parties' bargain. The court notes that the contract coincided with a period of extreme price volatility, as evidenced by the 25 per cent decline in oil prices subsequent to execution of the contract. But that same volatility also suggests that the parties were allocating to themselves a variety of price risks in a manner that appears to have escaped the court's notice. Con Ed may have been willing to purchase oil at a particular price on 24 January and taken a one-week risk that prices would decline prior to delivery. But, aware of volatile price fluctuations, it may have been unwilling to take the risk of a fixed-price contract for a longer period of time, and certainly not until 4 March. In effect, the court, by extending the time for performance from one week to four weeks, reallocated any such price risk from the seller to the buyer. In short, even if the defendant could have used the oil in late February, it is by no means clear that under the market conditions that prevailed on 24 January it would have paid the same for a late February delivery as it was willing to pay for a late January delivery. If that is the case, then it does not follow that the buyer was acting in bad faith in refusing to accept the late delivery, even if it could have used the oil as the court suggested. Had it taken the oil at the contract price, it would have been accepting a risk that it was not compensated to take.

To test that proposition, assume two contracts. In the first, the buyer agrees to purchase oil to be delivered within one week. In the second, the buyer agrees to purchase the same amount and quality of oil to be delivered within six weeks. Would we expect the buyer to pay the same amount for the two deliveries? If not, that suggests that the buyer is taking on some risk about market price movements during the intervening period. If the buyer is subsequently required to purchase in four weeks at the one week price, then the buyer will have been obligated to bear that risk without compensation. The court was certainly correct to interpret the UCC's cure provision as an effort to thwart chiselling by those who hope to escape bad bargains. But whether the court was correct in finding that the defendant was engaged in sheer opportunism rather than rejecting the imposition of a risk that it had not agreed to accept is a more difficult inquiry.

It is, of course, impossible for courts to ignore its impressions about the reasonableness of commercial behaviour when interpreting statutes that allocate entitlements between commercial actors. The provision that the court was applying in *T.W. Oil* allows for post-delivery date cure if, but only if, the seller had reasonable grounds to believe that the non-conforming tender would be acceptable.[20] Even then, the buyer has only a 'further reasonable time' to substitute a conforming tender. These conditions provide courts with substantial latitude in determining whether the conditions for cure have been satisfied in a specific case. For instance,

[19] *T.W. Oil, Inc. v. Consolidated Edison Co* 443 N.E.2d 932, 934, 938.
[20] UCC § 2-508(2).

a court that considered the defendant's conduct consistent with the contractual risk allocation could have concluded that four weeks was too long to constitute a 'further reasonable time' to provide a substitute. Thus, my argument is not that courts can or should ignore the conduct of commercial actors. Rather, my argument is that courts, especially courts of general jurisdiction, often have difficulty reverse engineering the risk allocations of the transactions that they are analysing. As a result, they are prone to confuse behaviour consistent with initial risk allocations with inappropriate conduct when the former permit conduct that, from an *ex post* perspective, appears to be opportunistic. In short, courts are likely to find false positives for opportunism. That possibility is increased by the use of vague standards of conduct, such as good faith, that permit courts to police commercial contracts generally rather than to apply statutory standards. For instance, had the court in *T.W. Oil* focused on the explicit conditions for cure rather than viewed the issue through the lens of good faith, it would have had to grapple with the issue of whether the proffered substitution had been available within a 'reasonable time' after the period specified in the contract. That might have led it to investigate the pricing risks inherent in the contract and thus to a better understanding of the parties' transaction.[21]

The same proclivity for substituting moral judgment in place of addressing contractual risk allocations can be found in other doctrines that courts employ in an apparent attempt to constrain opportunism. In Anglo-American law, perhaps the doctrine best suited to control strategic behaviour falls under the category of duress. The commercial situations in which the elements of duress are likely to be at issue involve conditions consistent with the economic concept of 'hold-up'. That term indicates a situation in which one party to a contract agrees to highly disadvantageous demands made by the counterparty because the former has substantial needs that can only be satisfied by resources over which the latter holds a situational monopoly.[22] In the economic and commercial law literature, hold-up is typically associated with proposed modifications by one party in order to extract a previously uncontracted-for share of the contractual surplus after the counterparty has made an investment the cost of which is not recoverable unless the contract is performed. Such investments, known as relationship-specific transactions,[23] are

[21] Two additional points are worth making here. First, it may be churlish to blame the court for the omission. The defendant's attorneys must share some of the responsibility if they did not point out the risk allocation in the contract. Secondly, the court did pay significant attention to ambiguity in the statutory requirement that post-delivery date cure is permitted only if the seller had reasonable grounds to believe that the initial tender would be acceptable. That analysis was more consistent with efforts to comprehend the transactional risk allocation. Ultimately, however, the court believed that 'reasonableness' had to be filtered through the vagaries of 'good faith' rather than through an understanding of the risks inherent in the contract.

[22] See, e.g., P. W. Schmitz, 'The Hold-Up Problem and Incomplete Contracts: A Survey of Recent Topics in Contract Theory' (2001) 53 *Bulletin of Economic Research* 1–17; B. Klein, 'Transaction Cost Determinants of "Unfair" Contractual Arrangements' (1980) 70 *American Economic Review* 356–62.

[23] See, e.g., V. Crawford, 'Relationship-Specific Investment' (1990) 105 *Quarterly Journal of Economics* 561–574; P. L. Joskow, 'Contract Duration and Relationship-Specific Investments: Empirical Evidence from Coal Markets' (1987) 77 *American Economic Review* 168–85.

inherently at risk where the parties must act sequentially and one party must invest before the other party puts assets at risk. Think, for instance, of an electric generating plant constructed nearby a mine-mouth that is to serve as the source of coal for the plant. Once the plant is constructed in a particular location, the coal supplier has an incentive to renegotiate coal prices, since the plant operator cannot easily relocate to obtain better contractual terms elsewhere. Under these circumstances, the party who has made the relationship-specific investment can be held up in an amount up to the value of the non-transferable investment by the counterparty's refusal to perform the contract without some alteration of the initial allocation of contractual benefits. In theory, judicial invalidation of modifications under those circumstances will have beneficial effects both *ex post* and *ex ante*, as the threat of judicial invalidation dilutes the incentive to seek opportunistic modifications.[24]

But not all modifications are motivated by a desire to hold-up a counterparty. Changes in circumstances that materialize subsequent to execution of the contract may justify a reallocation of risks and benefits that both parties believe is appropriate, notwithstanding that it requires some redistribution of the initial contractual surplus. Under these circumstances, judicial invalidation of the modification would remake a deal that the parties entered into through arm's length bargaining and without any of the characteristics of economic coercion associated with a 'duress' defence. Thus, one would anticipate that courts inclined to supervise commercial opportunism would use a duress doctrine to invalidate modifications that emerged from hold-up, but would validate those that emerged from a change in circumstances that warranted contractual reallocation.

Unfortunately, the actual motivations of the parties will frequently be unverifiable to a court. Thus, there is reason to question judicial capacity to distinguish between opportunistic and appropriate contract modifications. One of the traditional cases in Anglo-American law that considers the propriety of modification reveals the difficult nature of the relevant inquiry into opportunism. In *Alaska Packers' Association v. Delmonico*,[25] labourers who had agreed to be transported to Alaska to serve as sailors and fisherman at a salmon cannery for a specified wage refused on arrival at the destination to work without a pay increase. The employer's agent acceded to the demand, but the employer refused to honour the modification when the labourers returned from Alaska to obtain payment.

Initially, the collective refusal of the workers to comply with their agreement appears to be a classic example of hold-up implemented through a bad faith modification. The fishing season was short, the location of the enterprise was remote, and no alternative source of labour was available. Thus, the scenario shares many of the characteristics of a situational monopoly in which a party that has made relationship-specific investments—about US$150,000 in the cannery plus the costs of transporting the labourers to Alaska—is vulnerable

[24] See, e.g., S. Shavell, 'Contractual Holdup and Legal Intervention' (2007) 36 *Journal of Legal Studies* 325–54.

[25] *Alaska Packers' Association v. Delmonico*, 117 F. 99 (9th Cir, 1902).

to exploitation by the counterparty.[26] Thus, it may not be surprising that the court refused to enforce the modification. At first glance, the court's nullification of the modification appears to be an appropriate intervention that negates the incentive to act opportunistically. There would be no reason for the labourers to threaten to quit or to strike if they knew that the adjustments they extracted would not be enforced.

On reflection, however, the propriety of the invalidating the new wage term is more questionable. This is true for two reasons. First, courts (at least in Anglo-American legal systems) tend to address the hold-up problem inherent in modification by resorting to doctrines such as consideration. Courts that reject one-sided modifications, such as a change in wage rates, will frequently conclude that there has been no consideration for the alteration from the initial contract. But the doctrine of consideration is itself sufficiently subject to manipulation that it offers few barriers against opportunistic practices. For instance, the court in *Alaska Packers* concluded that the employer's consent to the increased wage was unenforceable because it had been given without consideration. In return for the additional pay the workers agreed only 'to render the exact services, and none other, that they were already under contract to render.'[27]

But sophisticated, albeit opportunistic commercial parties can circumvent the consideration problem by providing some minor modification of their own performance in return for the extorted contractual adjustment. The doctrine that courts will not look behind the adequacy of consideration should provide an effective shield against weighing the value of the trade.[28] Assume, for instance, that the labourers in *Alaska Packers* had agreed to stay for an additional day in return for the increased wage during their entire period of employment. Presumably, that exchange would have been sufficient consideration to mandate judicial enforcement of the modified agreement. Of course, the consideration doctrine is also subject to manipulation by courts. For example, notwithstanding the doctrine that courts do not evaluate the adequacy of consideration, courts are permitted to ignore mere nominal consideration or the mere pretence of a bargain,[29] and the court itself would be the ultimate arbiter of that difficult distinction between adequate and nominal. The point, therefore, is not that courts lack the doctrinal tools to foreclose opportunism. Rather the point, again, is that courts lack the institutional capacity to determine with confidence and systematic accuracy when opportunism rather than appropriate risk allocation better explains the parties' conduct.

The shibboleth of good faith could enter here as well to limit the effectiveness of modifications, even those accompanied by new consideration. Indeed, the UCC employs just such a test, in lieu of one mandating consideration. UCC

[26] See R. A. Posner, 'Gratuitous Promises in Economics and Law' (1977) 6 *Journal of Legal Studies* 411–26.

[27] *Alaska Packers' Association v. Delmonico*, 117 F. 99 (9th Cir, 1902) 102.

[28] See, e.g., *Apfel v. Prudential-Bache Sec.*, 616 N.E.2d 1095 (NY, 1993).

[29] See E. A. Farnsworth, *Contracts* (New York: Aspen Publishers, 4th edn, 2004) 71–2.

§ 2-209(1) states that an agreement modifying a contract within Article 2 needs no consideration to be binding; Official Comment 2 to that section provides, however, that modifications must meet the test of good faith imposed on all contracts, and 'extortion of a "modification" without legitimate commercial reason is ineffective' as a violation of the good faith obligation.[30] But the limited capacity of courts to reverse engineer transactions and to detect noncompliance with vague obligations such as good faith applies with particular force here. Parties who demand modifications typically provide explanations for their demands by alleging that some change in circumstances subsequent to the original transaction justifies reallocation of contractual benefits and risks. If true, those allegations would typically satisfy the obligation to perform in good faith. But the veracity of those claims can be difficult to evaluate. Return, for example, to *Alaska Packers*. The labourers in that case did not allege that they were attempting to exploit a situational monopoly. Rather, they insisted that the equipment that the employer furnished was defective. As a result, they alleged, the original exchange, in which wages were based on the size of their catch, would not provide the income that they reasonably anticipated. In effect, the labourers did not deny that the situation involved the exploitation of a situational monopoly; rather, they maintained that they were the victims of the employer's opportunistic in sending them to Alaska without easy means of return or alternative employment, and then strategically provided equipment that would reduce the employer's exposure for wages.

The court implied that the employer would have no incentive to provide substandard equipment, because a lower catch for the labourers would also mean lower profits for the cannery. But concluding that the employer cannot have acted as alleged because it would have been economically irrational proves too much.[31] One might equally conclude that the employees could not have been acting opportunistically because it would have been irrational for them to refuse to work, thus leaving themselves both without a source of income and arguably with limited means for returning from Alaska. Hold-up frequently occurs in situations of bilateral monopoly, so that the players face a structure similar to a chicken game that in which each party is credibly willing to engage in personally negative-sum behaviour as a means of extorting gains from a counterparty. Efforts by courts to distinguish the exploiter from the exploited on the basis of rational behaviour is unlikely to provide much in the way of certainty in such situations, as they are inherently characterized by broader views of irrationality.

There may be circumstances in which courts can detect and invalidate opportunism with greater certainty. Shavell, for instance, notes that some efforts to

[30] See UCC § 2-209, Official Comment 2 (2002).

[31] In addition, there is an economically rational explanation for the employers' alleged behaviour. The labourers may, with superior equipment, have caught more fish than the employer could use, especially in an era in which there was no means of preserving the catch. As a result, the employer would have an incentive to reduce the catch below the maximum that was technologically possible. See D. L. Threedy, 'A Fish Story: *Alaska Packers' Association v. Domenico*' in D. G. Baird (ed) *Contracts Stories* (St. Paul: Foundation Press, 2006) 335, 353.

exploit take place against a background of market prices.[32] The existence of a market price may provide a more objective reason to believe that a party charging a supra-competitive price is attempting to exploit a situational monopoly, at least in the absence of some alternative explanation. But outside of those cases, there is little reason to have confidence in the ability of arbiters to accurately designate behaviour as opportunistic.

IV. Contractual Efforts to Constrain Opportunism

My argument to this point has been that arbiters cannot reliably distinguish opportunism from commercially reasonable risk allocations, and thus their efforts can frequently constitute a reallocation of reasonable risks rather than a constraint on strategic behaviour. Any assumption that the problem of incomplete contracting can be solved by *ex post* legal intervention must consider whether the costs imposed by arbiter error are sufficiently great to outweigh the benefits of external monitoring of contractual conduct. The willingness to allow judicial supervision of commercial opportunism, therefore, cannot be resolved without consideration of alternative means for constraining misconduct. Certainly parties will not exploit all opportunities to act strategically, even if legal intervention is not a threat. If opportunism is observable to the counterparty, even though not verifiable to a third-party arbiter, then parties are likely to restrain themselves from exploiting opportunities in order to maintain a good reputation with the counterparty or with others in the industry, or to induce cooperation and reciprocity where there will be continued interactions between the parties.[33]

Even in an environment of incomplete contracting, however, parties may be able to take matters into their own hands by designing contract terms that address the risks of opportunism. Certainly, parties who must make relationship-specific investments recognize their exposure to exploitation. Examination of contracts negotiated in those circumstances reveals that parties incur significant drafting costs in order to reduce incentives for opportunism. The resulting contract may be incomplete in the sense that it only indirectly prohibits inefficient behaviour. But these same clauses reveal that parties are not helpless against opportunism—at least (and this is the important caveat) to the extent that courts are willing to enforce the clauses that parties include in order to reduce the risk of opportunism. Such clauses, however, frequently take forms that grant substantial discretion to one party or that appear to impose substantial disadvantages on the counterparty. Here again, courts may misinterpret the reasonable nature of the parties' bargain and conflate rational risk allocations intended to forestall opportunism with contract terms that result from unequal bargaining power or other perverse incentives in the bargaining process. As a result, courts may invalidate such clauses or

[32] See Shavell, n 24, 325.
[33] See, e.g., C. P. Gillette, 'Reputation and Intermediaries in Electronic Commerce' (2002) 62 *Louisiana Law Review* 1165–98.

construe them in a manner inconsistent with their plain meaning. The result of such judicial intervention is to frustrate the parties' own self-help remedies against opportunism.

A few examples illustrate the ability of commercial actors to negotiate around problems of opportunism. Compensation arrangements are the most obvious clauses on which parties may focus in order to avoid strategic behaviour. Royalty arrangements, for instance, typically confront problems related to asymmetric information and slack. Agents, especially in the case of independent contractors, may be retained because they have specialized knowledge about a matter of importance to a relatively ignorant principal. The superior knowledge of the agent makes it difficult for the principal to monitor the agent's quality of performance. The principal presumably will not know which level of inputs are appropriate to complete the agent's task in a manner that optimizes the principal's interests, and the principal will likely be unable to monitor the agent's effort level directly.[34]

Assume, for instance, that a relatively new firm involved in oil exploration desires to investigate an area to determine whether it is prospective for hydrocarbons. The firm may hire as an independent contractor an expert to identify specific parcels within the area. Effort level, however, will affect the accuracy of the expert's evaluation of parcels and thus affect the return to the firm. The very fact that the firm has decided to employ an independent contractor rather than use an employee to make the relevant investigation reflects the firm's relative inability to monitor effort levels of the agent. Presumably, if the firm were aware of the optimal effort level, it would direct someone under its control, an employee, to exercise that effort and pay an appropriate salary to that person. But that same inability suggests that the firm must find some reasonable substitute for monitoring effort levels in order to ensure that the independent contractor does not shirk. An hourly wage, for instance, might induce the independent contractor to spend too much time on the project exploring parcels with a low probability of containing marketable hydrocarbons. Alternative compensation arrangements, however, could align the agent's interests with the firm's own. For instance, while a flat payment would provide no upside risk to the agent, a royalty based on hydrocarbon production from identified parcels would increase the expected reward from additional effort. Even a self-interested agent would then balance personal costs against higher personal expected benefits in a manner that supported a higher level of effort.

Courts have revealed sensitivity to such principal-agent problems and have developed a series of doctrines to address them. For instance, even where parties have failed to include provisions that align the interests of principals and agents, courts may imply a 'best efforts' clause in order to preclude an agent from claiming that it had either no obligation under the contract or only an obligation that could be satisfied by substantially subordinating the principal's interests to its own.[35] At best,

[34] See L. Kaplow and S. Shavell, *Contracting* (St. Paul: West Publishing, 2004) 26–31.

[35] See, e.g., *Wood v. Lucy, Lady Duff-Gordon*, 118 N.E. 214 (NY, 1917); *Bloor v. Falstaff Brewing Corp.*, 601 F.2d 609 (1979).

however, these judicially created doctrines only foreclose claims that an agent can devote zero effort to the principal's task or that the agent is required to serve as a fiduciary to the principal. In short, these doctrines at best can exclude the extremes along the spectrum of possible obligations that the agent may owe to the principal. Within those extremes, the inability to monitor or observe agent effort means that arbiters can provide little guidance to commercial actors about the level of effort that the transaction requires. Even when measured against an objective standard, judicial inquiry is typically made with insufficient information to allow accurate conclusions about the propriety of agent behaviour. For instance, some commentators suggest that best efforts should be defined in terms of that level of agent effort that maximizes the joint interests of the parties. It thus treats the venture between the parties as if it had been implemented by a single firm, which would presumably balance total costs against total marginal net revenue.[36] The underlying assumption is that, in a zero transactions costs world, the parties would have contracted for the arrangement that maximizes joint profits; thus, courts should employ that same standard when implying a best efforts term in the contract or when interpreting such a term that the parties included in their contract.

In theory, joint maximization does appear consistent with the presumed intent of commercial actors to create the largest possible surplus, and thus provide an opportunity for each to extract the maximum benefit from their transaction. The problem is that application of the joint maximization standard requires the ability to convey to an arbiter verifiable information about the marginal cost of agent performance at different effort levels and the concomitant rewards to both agents and principals. Faced with these practical obstacles, many courts appear to adopt an interpretation of 'best efforts' that is consistent with verifiable variables, even

[36] See, e.g., C. J. Goetz and R. E. Scott, 'Principles of Relational Contracts' (1981) 67 *Virginia Law Review* 1089–150, 1119–26. To see how the standard would be applied, assume that a manufacturer would receive different returns from different levels of effort by a distributor charged with distributing the manufacturer's products.

Effort Level	Marginal Costs to Distrib.	Marginal Revenue to Distrib.	Marginal Revenue to Manuf.	Total Marginal Net Revenue
1	7	10	12	15
2	10	12	14	16
3	10	10	17	17
4	12	10	20	18
5	14	0	21	7

Presumably, the manufacturer would prefer that the distributor exercise effort level 5, because that maximizes manufacturer revenues. The distributor would prefer to exercise effort level 3, because the marginal cost of exercising additional effort after that point exceeds the marginal return to the distributor. The joint maximization principal would require the exercise of effort level 4, which maximizes the total marginal net revenue to the 'enterprise' taking into account the costs and revenues of both the manufacturer and the distributor.

if those variables deviate from the actual marginal costs that agents incur or marginal benefits that principals and agents enjoy from different effort levels.[37]

The problem with contractual efforts to solve principal-agent problems, however, is not simply one of vagueness. Instead, the legal doctrines may miscomprehend the commercial propriety of clauses intended for these purposes. In construction contracts, for instance, the purchaser of services typically suffers from asymmetric information in that contractors have superior information about the quality of materials necessary to meet contract specifications. Absent the ability of purchasers to evaluate the full range of options available to them, contractors have incentives to maximize profits by providing components of lower quality (and hence, lower cost to the contractors) than purchasers would prefer. That incentive is arguably exacerbated in flat fee contracts because any savings that the contractor can obtain in purchasing materials increases the residual that the contractor retains as profit.

One way for the purchaser to minimize the contractor's opportunistic use of low-price, low-quality components is to enter into a cost-plus contract that essentially guarantees the contractor a specific profit and thus induces the contractor to use components of a quality that the buyer would approve. This is not to say that cost-plus contracts perfectly align the interests of purchasers and contractors; the contractor may, under a cost-plus contract, purchase components of higher quality, and thus of higher cost, than the purchaser would require if she had perfect information. But purchasers may limit their exposure under cost-plus by using price caps or requiring advance approval of items that cost more than a stated minimum. The point, therefore, is not that either a cost-plus or flat fee contract is an ideal solution to the threat of opportunism. Rather the point is that both types of contracts are plausible under certain conditions and that different parties could reasonably select different contracts for similar projects, depending on their level of risk preference and their ability to monitor contractor behaviour. Thus, one would expect to see different clauses used in different contracts, depending on the relative capacities of the parties to monitor different inputs and outputs. In each case, the parties would be adjusting contractual terms to constrain a specific form of opportunism.

Given that different parties would have different preferences for different contractual arrangements, and that each of the arrangements could be effective to constrain opportunism of a particular type, it would seem peculiar to find law intervening to prohibit any of these contractual allocations, at least where sophisticated actors are concerned. Nevertheless, in the United States, governmental contracts are frequently subject to a prohibition on cost-plus contracts.[38] In short,

[37] See C. P. Gillette and S. D. Walt, *Sales Law: Domestic and International* (St. Paul: Foundation Press, 2nd edn, 2009) 144–50.

[38] See, e.g., 48 CFR § 216.306, which provides:

> (c) Limitations. (i) Except as provided in paragraph (c)(ii) of this section, annual military construction appropriations acts prohibit the use of cost-plus-fixed-fee contracts that—
>
> (A) Are funded by a military construction appropriations act;

far from facilitating parties in their efforts to constrain opportunistic behaviour, law may actually exacerbate the problem by removing from the parties' arsenal one weapon for aligning their interests. While the legal intervention in this situation takes the form of administrative regulation or statute, rather than judicial supervision of the contract, the effect is the same. A useful term that parties might reasonably have included in their contract to address the risk of opportunism is invalidated, presumably because the term is thought to have been imposed in a manner that systematically exploits one of them.

That same disconnection between legitimate commercial efforts to constrain opportunism and legal doctrine is exacerbated when courts fail to understand the function of clauses that parties might use reduce the risk of strategic behaviour. For instance, a court that failed to understand the inducements inherent in royalty arrangements might too narrowly construe the reach of the royalty, perhaps, in my example, limiting it in time or geographical area in a manner not intended by the parties. Alternatively, a court might misunderstand the joint maximizing nature of the royalty arrangement. Assume, for instance, that a publisher of Author A attempts to publish a competing title by Author B. Author A may successfully object that the competing publication will adversely affect her royalty earnings and thus publication of the competing title would violate the publisher's implied obligation to exercise best efforts in marketing Author A's work.[39] But if Author B's work would otherwise have been published by an alternative publisher, then the adverse effect on Author A's royalties would have materialized in any event, so that the joint profits of Author A and the publisher would be greater if the latter publishes both than if some alternative publisher does.[40] In short, judicial misconception of the scope of opportunistic behaviour may affect the ability of parties to contract about it.

The same problem is apparent when courts fail to enforce clauses that plausibly have been inserted into contracts to restrict the ability of counterparties to exploit the counterparty's relationship-specific investment. As I argued, such investments render parties vulnerable to the threat of non-performance or reduced performance unless the investing party agrees to renegotiate the initial allocation of the contractual surplus. This was the court's understanding of what the labourers had intended in *Alaska Packers*, notwithstanding that alternative, less malign

(B) Are estimated to exceed US$25,000; and
(C) Will be performed within the United States, except Alaska.

(ii) The prohibition in paragraph (c)(i) of this section does not apply to contracts specifically approved in writing, setting forth the reasons therefor, in accordance with the following:
(A) The Secretaries of the military departments are authorized to approve such contracts that are for environmental work only, provided the environmental work is not classified as construction, as defined by 10 U.S.C. 2801.
(B) The Secretary of Defense or designee must approve such contracts that are not for environmental work only or are for environmental work classified as construction.

[39] See, e.g., *Van Valkenburgh, Nooger & Neville, Inc. v. Hayden Publishing Co.*, 281 N.E.2d 142 (NY, 1972); *Joyce Beverages of New York, Inc. v. Royal Crown Cola Co.*, 555 F.Supp. 271, 275 (SDNY, 1983); *Polyglycoat Corp. v. C.P.C. Distribs., Inc.*, 534 F.Supp. 200, 203 (SDNY, 1982).

[40] See R. E. Scott and J. S. Kraus, *Contract Law and Theory* (New York: Matthew Bender & Co, 4th edn, 2007) 351.

explanations were also plausible. In theory, parties should be able to avoid the uncertainty of judicial intervention in such circumstances by including a contractual prohibition on renegotiation in their agreement. Such a prohibition may be over-inclusive in that it precludes modifications in the face of unanticipated circumstances that justify reallocation of the contractual surplus as well as modifications induced by opportunism. But if parties calculate that the need for good faith modifications during the course of their contracts is sufficiently small, then barring both good faith and bad faith modifications could be jointly beneficial. In short, parties may rationally agree that *ex ante* commitments should not be subject to *ex post* modifications, even if those modifications appear reasonable at the time that they would be entered into. Indeed, a party who might be disadvantaged by such a clause because it places a positive value on the probability that it might subsequently require a modification could still agree to such a prohibition, because assent to the clause creates a strong signal of fidelity to the original terms of the transaction and thus induces the counterparty to invest optimally in the transaction as well.

Nevertheless, parties who desire to pre-commit against subsequent modification of their contract are essentially barred from doing so by doctrines that invalidate 'no modification' clauses.[41] Courts that invoke these doctrines presumably do so in the name of maintaining the autonomy of the parties during implementation of the contract and a fear that non-modification clauses themselves are typically extracted under duress or as the result of some form of unequal bargaining power. The autonomy justification, however, cannot logically bar individuals from binding themselves to a particular form of contract any more than it can bar individuals from entering into enforceable contracts at all. Nothing in autonomy theory denies the ability of individuals to enter into binding agreements and thus to limit their future choices. Autonomy theory, that is, does not render unenforceable an agreement by which I promise today to purchase ten apples from you tomorrow at a price of US$1 per apple, even if tomorrow I regret my decision because of a change in my tastes or in market prices. To the contrary, the underlying assumption of contract law is that by allowing me to commit today to a future performance, I expand my set of transactional choices and thus enhance, rather than reduce the scope of autonomy, because more people are willing to deal with me if they understand that I am committed to the bargain at the risk of paying damages for breach. But if that is the case, there seems no reason why I cannot also commit today not to modify my contract with you tomorrow, even if the

[41] *Beatty v. Guggenheim Exploration Co.*, 122 N.E. 378, 387–88 (NY, 1919). See, e.g., K. Davis, 'The Demand for Immutable Contracts: Another Look at the Law and Economics of Contract Modifications' (2006) 81 *New York University Law Review* 487–549, 518; C. Jolls, 'Contracts as Bilateral Commitments: A New Perspective on Contract Modification' (1997) 26 *Journal of Legal Studies* 203–38, 208–09; E. Talley, 'Note, Contract Renegotiation, Mechanism Design, and the Liquidated Damages Rule' (1994) 46 *Stanford Law Review* 1195–244. There is some argument to the effect that enforcing clauses that prohibit renegotiation would create perverse incentives for agents to reduce their effort. See P. W. Schmitz, 'Should Contractual Clauses that Forbid Renegotiation Always be Enforced?' (2005) 21 *Journal of Law, Economics, & Organization* 315–29.

market price of apples has decreased to US$0.50 per apple by the time that I am supposed to perform and even if you would otherwise be inclined to agree to the modification.

The concern that arbiters will fail to enforce a no-modification clause has generated some ingenious efforts to circumvent the legal doctrine. For instance, parties that seek to limit renegotiation, and thereby lock their counterparties into an agreed performance that would justify a relationship-specific investment, may seek to insert a clause that substantially inhibits renegotiation, even if the clause does not purport to create an outright prohibition. Maskin and Tirole suggest that parties could contractually impose a penalty on any party that suggests renegotiation.[42] But it is plausible that an arbiter otherwise disposed to avoid a no-modification clause would pierce the form of that alternative and invalidate it as the substantive equivalent of an invalid prohibition on renegotiation. Thus, the main effect of such suggestions is to indicate the length to which parties may go to avoid legal doctrines that misunderstand the utility of contractual agreements and instead strike deals that optimally constrain opportunism. Judicial enforcement of the parties' intended no-modification without any additional investigation into the circumstances that generated it provides a less costly alternative for achieving the same end. Unless we conclude that the majority of no-modification clauses arise out of exploitative relationships that cannot be constrained by other legal doctrines, there seems little reason to take the significant risk that courts will confuse legitimate clauses with inappropriate ones.

Alternatively, the parties might attempt to preclude hold-ups by explicitly contracting for specific performance as a remedy for breach. Indeed, at least one commentator has suggested that renegotiation of athletes' contracts should be prohibited, and the contract specifically enforced on this ground, notwithstanding the traditional admonition against employing specific performance in personal services contracts.[43] More generally, Edlin and Reichelstein suggest that, under a set of assumptions about bargaining power and sharing of the contractual surplus, an expectation of specific performance provides an investing party with an incentive to choose a first-best investment.[44] Nevertheless, at least in Anglo-American jurisdictions, parties may be reluctant to bargain for specific performance, again because they fear that arbiters are reluctant to enforce such a remedy, even where the parties have expressly contracted for it. Moreover, parties may eschew specific performance clauses, notwithstanding that they implicitly signal fidelity to the transaction, because such clauses simultaneously constrain even efficient breaches of contract, that is, those breaches worth committing even after full damages are paid. A party that could otherwise efficiently exit a

[42] See E. Maskin and J. Tirole, 'Unforeseen Contingencies and Incomplete Contracts' (1999) 66 *Review of Economic Studies* 83–114, 99.

[43] See A. M. Johnson, Jr, 'The Argument for Self-Help Specific Performance: Opportunistic Renegotiation of Player Contracts' (1989) 22 *Connecticut Law Review* 61–128.

[44] A. Edlin and S. Reichelstein, 'Holdups, Standard Breach Remedies, and Optimal Investment' (1996) 86 *American Economic Review* 478–501, 482–6.

transaction can be precluded from doing so by a decree of specific performance, and thus can be exploited by a counterparty who demands supra-compensatory damages in exchange for forgoing the specific performance option. As a result, use of the clause to induce optimal investment could simply displace one hold-up problem by creating another.

Finally, parties might attempt to avoid opportunism in relationship-specific transactions by reducing the expected benefits from threatening breach unless a counterparty agrees to a modification. Where one party must make a relationship-specific investment, and thus is susceptible to hold-up, the non-investing party's willingness to exploit the investment is bounded in part by its exposure for breach of contract. The non-investing party, that is, does not have a credible threat to walk away from the contract if damages exceed the savings it would enjoy if it can extract a reallocation of the contractual surplus. As a result, a clause that imposes high damages on a breaching party may have the desired inhibiting effect. An investing party, for instance, might not fear the opportunistic party's threat if breach obligated the latter to pay the former the full cost of its investment. But it is by no means clear that such costs would be recoverable. A court might interpret recoverable expectation damages as including those amounts that would place the aggrieved party in the same position as performance, but only insofar as those amounts reflect profits lost from implementation of the contract and not necessarily the investments necessary to implement the contract.

In theory, parties could signal their willingness to pay high damages, and thus to induce relationship-specific investments, by specifying the damages to be paid in the event of breach. But, as noted by other commentators who have sought to facilitate relationship-specific investments, courts may also be reluctant to enforce liquidated damages clauses.[45] If, at the time that damages are payable, a court classifies the liquidated damages clause as a penalty, it will refuse to enforce it.[46] Arbiters that refuse to enforce liquidated damage clauses agreed to by sophisticated parties may be acting in a paternalistic manner that is inconsistent with the lessons of contract design or the preferences of the parties. Indeed, many courts have recently displayed a greater willingness to enforce liquidated damage clauses.[47] But sophisticated parties who fear that their liquidated damages clauses will be scrutinized and invalidated are less likely to include such clauses in their contracts, notwithstanding their utility in constraining opportunism and inducing optimal investment.

A final example of legal intervention that has the perverse effect of reducing contractual constraints on opportunism also involves damages. As I indicated

[45] See D. Markovits, 'Making and Keeping Contracts' (2006) 92 *Virginia Law Review* 1325–1374, 1344; R. E. Scott and G. G. Triantis, 'Embedded Options and the Case Against Compensation in Contract Law' (2004) 104 *Columbia Law Review* 1428–91, 1452.

[46] *JMD Holding Corp. v. Congress Financial Corp.*, 828 N.E.2d 604 (NY, 2005).

[47] See *XCO International Inc. v. Pacific Scientific Co.*, 369 F.3d 998, 1002 (7th Cir, 2004) ('[t]he rule against penalty clauses, though it lingers, has come to seem rather an anachronism, especially in cases in which commercial enterprises are on both sides of the contract').

earlier, the ability of a party to threaten breach in order to force a reallocation of the contractual surplus is limited by the damages that the breaching party will have to pay. In theory, expectation damages plus reliance damages that fully compensate for all harms would deter opportunistic threats of breach. Perhaps in consequence, the traditional Anglo-American rule is that the breaching party is responsible for all damages caused by the breach, including consequential damages, which usually consist of lost profits. That rule, however, is subject to a caveat that renders unrecoverable any damages that the breaching party did not have reason to foresee as a probable result of the breach when the contract was made.[48] The same principle also appears outside of Anglo-American jurisdictions, either directly or through a standard of adequate causation.[49]

The problem with the foreseeability rule is not necessarily that it limits damages and thus provides some area within which an opportunistic actor may threaten breach without paying full damages. That consequence does exist, but the alternative might be worse, insofar as liability for unforeseeable damages could require non-strategic breaching parties to bear losses whose risk was not priced into the contract. In addition, liability for consequential damages appears inconsistent with efficient risk allocations because the materialization of such damages tends to be in the control of the aggrieved party, rather than the breaching party. The aggrieved party controls the degree to which it will rely on the contract to make investments that might be lost in the event of breach and has better information about the benefits it anticipates receiving from full performance of the contract. Recovery of consequential damages poses a moral hazard problem insofar as their recovery induces the aggrieved party to ignore the breacher's costs in deciding how much reliance is appropriate.[50] As a result, rational parties would tend to allocate the risk of consequential damages to the aggrieved party.

The allocation of consequential damages, therefore, poses a stark choice for sophisticated commercial actors. If they are primarily concerned about strategic behaviour, they might allocate those damages to the breaching party, as the risk of paying high damages deters opportunism that could be interpreted as a breach. If they are more concerned about placing losses on parties best positioned to avoid them, they might allocate those same damages (including foreseeable consequential damages) to the aggrieved party. As a practical matter, most commercial actors appear to take the latter route. The evidence for that proposition is the near-universal observation by commentators that sophisticated commercial parties systematically opt out of the default rule that awards at least foreseeable

[48] See, e.g., Restatement (2d) of Contracts § 351(1); CISG, Art 74.

[49] See B. Zeller, *Damages under the Convention on Contracts for the International Sale of Goods* (New York: Oceana Publications Inc, 2005) 54–7, 89–90.

[50] S. Shavell, 'Damage Measure for Breach of Contract' (1980) 11 *The Bell Journal of Economics* 466–90. For efforts to address the overinvestment problem, see, e.g., R. Cooter and M. A. Eisenberg. 'Damages for Breach of Contract' (1985) 73 *California Law Review* 1432–1481; A. S. Edlin, 'Cadillac Contracts and Up-Front Payments: Efficient Investment Under Expectation Damages' (1996) 12 *Journal of Law, Economics, & Organization* 98–118.

consequential damages.[51] Indeed, this observation suggests that the default rule of allowing recovery of consequential damages is inappropriate, at least as measured by the objective that default rules should reduce transactions costs and thus should reflect the majoritarian preferences of commercial actors.[52]

But even if, as a general matter, sophisticated commercial parties do not wish to place the risk of consequential damages on breaching parties, one could imagine that parties in transactions with characteristics that are particularly indicative of potential opportunism would prefer a damages standard that was closer to full expectation damages in order to deter breach. As I noted earlier, situations in which those concerns arise are frequently characterized by relationship-specific investments that are vulnerable to hold-up. Thus, one might expect courts to employ the default rule to allow consequential damages systematically in cases that involved such investments. At least in US jurisdictions, however, there is no sense that courts are more likely to determine that damages were 'foreseeable' and thus recoverable because the underlying transaction involved a relationship-specific investment. Instead, foreseeability is predicated on objective standards of what reasonable actors would have anticipated at the time the contract was executed—not on the characteristics of the transaction.[53]

There was a time when courts appeared to be gravitating towards an interpretation of foreseeability that would be more consistent with parties' efforts to constrain opportunism. In the first third of the 20th century, both English and American interpretations of foreseeability focused on those damages from breach that were deemed to be 'in the contemplation of the parties' at the time the contract was executed. That phrase, however, was not intended to convey what was in the contemplation of the parties by virtue of what was foreseeable to a reasonable person. Rather, parties 'contemplated' damages in the sense that they agreed to accept liability for them either tacitly or explicitly. In US jurisprudence, the position was put most directly by Justice Holmes in *Globe Refining Co. v. Landa Cotton Oil Co.*[54] Recoverable damages were limited to those 'the defendant fairly may be supposed to have assumed consciously, or to have warranted the plaintiff reasonably to suppose that it assumed, when the

[51] See, e.g., A. Schwartz and R. E. Scott, 'Market Damages, Efficient Contracting, and the Economic Waste Fallacy' (2008) 108 *Columbia Law Review* 1610–69, 1612. See D. G. Baird, 'The Boilerplate Puzzle' (2006) 104 *Michigan Law Review* 933–52, 940; R. Danzig, '*Hadley v. Baxendale*: A Study in the Industrialization of the Law' (1975) 4 *Journal of Legal Studies* 249–284, 281; D. J. Smythe, 'Commercial Law in the Cracks of Judicial Federalism' (2007) 56 *Catholic University Law Review* 451–502, 491; R. A. Epstein, 'Beyond Foreseeability: Consequential Damages in the Law of Contract' (1989) 18 *Journal of Legal Studies* 105–38, 108.

[52] For the position that the reflection of majoritarian default rules is the primary objective of commercial law, see, e.g., C. J. Goetz and R. E. Scott, 'The Limits of Expanded Choice: An Analysis of the Interactions Between Express and Implied Contract Terms' (1985) 73 *California Law Review* 261–322, 321; A. Schwartz, 'The Default Rule Paradigm and the Limits of Contract Law' (1993) 3 *Southern California Interdisciplinary Law Journal* 389–420; C. P. Gillette and R. E. Scott, 'The Political Economy of International Sales Law' (2005) 25 *International Review of Law and Economics* 446–86.

[53] See Restatement (2d) of Contracts § 351(1); UCC § 2-715(2).

[54] *Globe Refining Co. v. Landa Cotton Oil Co.*, 190 U.S. 540 (1903).

contract was made.'[55] This followed from Holmes's conception of contract as a means by which each party takes the risk 'of an event which is wholly, or to an appreciable extent, beyond his control.'[56] The willingness to take a contractual risk was necessarily contingent on one's exposure should the risk materialize. Thus, when one decides to enter a contract, 'the extent of liability... is likely to be within his contemplation,'[57] so that a reasoned decision about whether to take the related risk can be made. 'Contemplation', therefore, did not entail the objective or knowledge-based standard of what a reasonable person would foresee as the consequence of the breach. Rather, it meant what the breaching party explicitly agreed to bear as damages or, where the contract was silent, 'terms which it fairly may be presumed he would have assented to if they had been presented to his mind.'[58] This was the 'tacit agreement' test in which consequential damages could be awarded only to the extent that parties had agreed a breacher would be responsible for them.

In light of the near-universal disclaimer of liability for consequential damages, one might reasonably ask, what are the conditions under which a party would not disclaim them, that is, when would a party agree to accept liability for consequential damages over which it had no control? A plausible response is that, much as in the case of liquidated damages or specific performance clauses, parties would accept such liability in order to signal an intent not to exploit a relationship-specific investment by the counterparty. Indeed, a party who desired to signal its intention not to act opportunistically might prefer acceptance of consequential damages to a liquidated damages clause or a specific performance remedy that, if enforced, would have the same effect. The reason is that the agreement to pay consequential damages is unlikely to be invalidated by a court, for the very reason that it is consistent with the (non-majoritarian) default rule. A tacit agreement test that looked at the underlying transaction to determine whether parties would have agreed to such an award in order to signal fidelity to the transaction arguably would be consistent with parties' intent to design a contract that optimally limited opportunism. Nevertheless, arbiters have missed that opportunity. They have instead largely repudiated the tacit agreement test in favour of one that is quite intentionally oblivious to the intent of the parties and that looks instead solely to what reasonable people would have foreseen as the consequences of a breach.[59]

[55] *Globe Refining Co. v. Landa Cotton Oil Co.*, 190 U.S. 540 (1903) 544.

[56] *Globe Refining Co. v. Landa Cotton Oil Co.*, 190 U.S. 540 (1903) 543.

[57] *Globe Refining Co. v. Landa Cotton Oil Co.*, 190 U.S. 540 (1903).

[58] *Globe Refining Co. v. Landa Cotton Oil Co.*, 190 U.S. 540 (1903) 543.

[59] In English law, see, e.g., *Heron II (Kaufos v. C. Czarnikow, Ltd)* [1967] 3 All ER 686 (HL) 691; *Victoria Laundry (Windsor), Ltd v. Newman Indus., Ltd* [1949] 1 All ER 997, 2 KB 528. In US law see, e.g., *Native American Reclamation and Pest Control, Inc. v. United Bank Alaska*, 685 P.2d 1211, 1219 (Alas, 1984); *R. I. Lampus Co. v. Neville Cement Products Corp.*, 378 A.2d 288, 292 (Pa, 1977).

V. Conclusion

Commercial opportunism will always remain a difficulty for commercial parties. Nothing I have said implies that legal actors should be oblivious to its presence. But they should also be sensitive to the comparative institutional competence to address the issue. Legal rules cannot easily create entitlements that foreclose opportunism by one set of actors without simultaneously enabling the entitled set of actors to engage in a similar array of opportunistic behaviour. Arbiters who seek to police transactions with blunt instruments such as good faith will inevitably have difficulty distinguishing opportunistic behaviour from appropriate exploitation of the parties' initial risk allocations. The parties themselves are best positioned to assess and contract about the threat of opportunism. That effort, however, can be undermined by interpretative styles that inject arbiters of disputes into policing contractual terms without fully comprehending the basis for the parties' own risk allocation. Arbiters who fail to recognize the function of clauses that parties employ to constrain opportunism or who fail to enforce those clauses out of a sense that something is amiss in the bargaining process exacerbate rather than redress the very problems that their interventions are intended to solve.

Commercial Opportunism from an Incentive Perspective

Comment on Clayton P. Gillette, 'Legal Supervision of Commercial Opportunism'

*Urs Schweizer**

I. The Vague Notion of Opportunism

Due to prohibitive costs, real contracts typically have to remain incomplete. Commercial law can create default rules that fill in the gaps. Such rules specify, in particular, rights of a party to terminate under less than full performance by the other party. Legal doctrine can create vague standards to also substitute for complete contracting. Broad standards include the obligation of good faith performance, commercial reasonableness, and best effort. Yet these approaches require substantial intervention by courts or arbitrators. Worse, the own efforts of the contracting parties may well be mitigated by interpretations of third parties who police contractual terms without fully comprehending the original intentions behind these terms.

Gillette reports on interesting casual facts from legal practice to exemplify the potential as well as the danger that comes with the different mechanisms.[1] His analysis of the trade-offs seems well balanced. My only criticism concerns his way of organizing thoughts along the vague notion of opportunism.

What is *opportunistic* behaviour? Is opportunistic behaviour synonymous with strategic or selfish behaviour? What are the normative implications that follow from opportunistic behaviour? Is opportunistic or strategic behaviour bad per se?

Williamson defines opportunism as self-interest seeking with guile.[2] I do not think that this definition clarifies much. Gillette adds that commercial actors are expected to pursue personal gain when they enter into contracts, but they should not inappropriately reclaim forgone opportunities. In spite of all such attempts,

* Professor of Economics, Rhenish Friedrich-Wilhelms-University, Bonn.

[1] See Chapter 10.

[2] See O. E. Williamson, *The Economic Institutions of Capitalism* (New York: The Free Press, 1985).

the notion of opportunism remains vague, and it may come at the price of losing the normative criterion of efficiency.

Williamson likes alluding to Simon, who initiated the theory of bounded rationality.[3] No doubt, modern behavioural economics can be traced back to Simon. But so far, behavioural economists have not been able to come up with a more precise definition, let alone with experimental tests that allow separating self-interest seeking with and without guile. Again, while behavioural economics may improve prediction of human actions, it lacks the normative criterion of (Pareto) efficiency whenever human decision-making cannot be guided by subjective preference orderings.

Hence, for good reasons, traditional economic analysis of contract law still relies on risk-neutral agents, such that efficiency simply means maximizing the sum of all payoffs. Quite likely, Gillette could also have made many of his points by referring to the more traditional approach without referring to any vague notion of opportunism. In fact, in the following, I report on a few results based on traditional economic analysis and compare them with the arguments brought forward by Gillette.

II. Notions from Welfare Economics as a Substitute

Let me begin with the comparison of perfect tender versus substantial performance. I happened to be the official discussant when Grundmann praised the fine-tuning of termination in sales contracts on efficiency grounds.[4] Grundmann supports the rule that the creditor must allow for an additional period of time of reasonable length before she may invoke the remedy of termination. In other words, the creditor has to tolerate delayed performance.

On that occasion, I challenged Grundmann's view vehemently. From the efficiency perspective, it remains unclear why this solution should be superior to the one that allows the creditor to terminate immediately after the debtor has failed to perform in full accordance with the terms regulating his obligation. In fact, with respect to performance incentives, the comparison between the two rules remains ambiguous. I later repeated this view when I became a member of the economic impact group that had to evaluate the economic consequences of the Draft Common Frame of Reference (DCFR).[5]

Gillette, in contrast, has worked out the trade-offs between different perfect tender and substantial performance rules to illustrate the difficulties inherent in constraining opportunism by entitlements. His findings remain ambiguous. But

[3] See H. A. Simon, *Administrative Behavior* (New York: The Free Press, 2nd edn, 1961).

[4] See S. Grundmann und A. Hoerning, '*Leistungsstörungsmodelle im Lichte der Ökonomischen Theorie—Nationales, Europäisches und Internationales Recht*' in T. Eger and H. B. Schäfer (eds) *Ökonomische Analyse der Europäischen Zivilrechtsentwicklung* (Tübingen: Mohr Siebeck, 2007).

[5] See U. Schweizer, '*Remedies for Non-Performance: Chapter 3 of Book III of the DCFR from an Economist's Perspective*' in P. Larouche and F. Chirico (eds) *Economic Analysis of the DCFR* (München: Sellier, 2010).

while my argument was phrased in clearly defined concepts of traditional game theory and welfare analysis, Gillette sticks to the bloomy term of opportunism. What does he gain? He certainly loses rigor.

Or look at the main conclusion Gillette draws from his analysis: the parties themselves are best positioned to assess and contract about the threat of opportunism. In Section IV, on contractual efforts to constrain opportunism, he focuses primarily on hold-up problems where parties have made relationship-specific investments. I follow him by also elaborating on such a hold-up problem though from the perspective of traditional welfare analysis. My example is based on Shavell's over-reliance framework.[6]

By non-contingent contract, the seller promises to perform at some later date in consideration for which the buyer promises to pay a fixed price to the seller. *Ex ante*, the buyer undertakes reliance investments in anticipation of the seller's due performance. *Ex post*, it becomes known what are the actual benefits and costs of performance.

At that stage, however, a contingency may arise under which performance would be inefficient. The seller may then decide on purely selfish grounds to pay expectation damages instead of performing. By doing so, he certainly acts in a strategic way. But would such behaviour already classify as opportunistic and, if so, should it be constrained and on what normative grounds?

From the welfare perspective, the damages regime provides efficient performance incentives, and there may be no reason to enforce inefficient performance. In fact, common law does not view the concept of efficient breach as a sacrilege against the nature of contracts. Would the opportunism perspective change this view? Or was it even the very fear of opportunism that supports specific performance as the primary breach remedy in civil law countries?

In any case, non-contingent contracts in combination with expectation damages as the only default rule provide efficient incentives *ex post* as far as the performance decision is concerned. This regime fails, however, to generate efficient investment incentives *ex ante*. In fact, compared with first best, the buyer has excessive reliance incentives as is well known from the over-reliance result formally established by Shavell. But notice, Shavell does not have to allude to opportunism or other vague concepts. He simply refers to the notion of efficient outcomes in a setting with risk-neutral parties.

So do Edlin and Reichelstein, a paper Gillette also refers to, the main difference to Shavell's setting being that, instead of a binary performance choice, a continuous quantity choice follows the investment stage.[7] In such a context, Edlin and Reichelstein establish that a non-contingent contract specifying a suitably fixed quantity and a suitably fixed price per unit in combination with expectation damages as a default rule allow generating efficient reliance incentives. In other words,

[6] See S. Shavell, 'Damage Measures for Breach of Contract' (1980) 11 *Bell Journal of Economics* 466–90.

[7] See A. S. Edlin and S. Reichelstein, 'Holdups, Standard Breach Remedies and Optimal Investment' (1996) 86 *American Economic Review* 478–501.

Shavell's over-reliance result disappears if the performance decision is of continuous instead of binary nature and if parties specify a non-contingent quantity and price appropriately.

Ohlendorf has managed to generalize the result to two-sided investments by both the buyer and the seller in spite of Edlin and Reichelstein, who have entertained conjectures to the contrary.[8] In other words, the simple default rule of expectation damages allows for efficient investment incentives by a simple, non-contingent contract, provided that the performance decision is continuous and the parties have specified the non-contingent quantity of trade properly.

But even in Shavell's setting of binary performance choice, efficient investment incentives can be generated if a suitable performance excuse is available which allows constraining the buyer's reliance incentives.

III. Commercial Impracticability

The starting point for my work on this topic was a legal debate on the commercial impracticability doctrine as introduced by the 2002 reform of German obligation law.[9] To admit the defence, the promisor's costs of performance must be *disproportionate* to the promisee's benefits. The formulation of the provision remains vague. Worse, as Ackermann has pointed out, a literal interpretation of the provision would, in terms of the promisor's payoff, be inconsistent with the much less controversial physical impossibility defence.[10] He argues in favour of a more consistent interpretation according to which the impracticability defence should be admitted whenever the promisor's costs of performing exceed the price as specified in the contract.

Köndgen, in contrast, requires performance to be excused when performance happens to be inefficient.[11] In terms of *ex post* efficiency, Köndgen's position seems well taken, but also rather straightforward. More challenging is an analysis of the resulting reliance incentives. Is it possible to generate efficient reliance incentives with a non-contingent contract and expectation damages combined with a performance excuse as default rules?

Surprisingly enough, the answer unambiguously depends on the condition under which the seller is granted the excuse. In fact, a non-contingent contract

[8] See S. Ohlendorf, 'Expectation Damages, Divisible Contracts, and Bilateral Investments' (2009) 99 *American Economic Review* 1608–18.

[9] See U. Schweizer, '*Breach Remedies, Performance Excuses, and Investment Incentives*' (2010) 28 *Journal of Law, Economics, & Organization*717–37.

[10] See T. Ackermann, '*Die Nacherfüllungspflicht des Stückverkäufers*' (2002) 8 *Juristenzeitung* 378–85.

[11] See J. Köndgen, '*Die Entlastung des Schuldners wegen Unmöglichkeit der Leistung—Versuch einer Ehrenrettung des § 275 Abs. 2 BGB*' in T. Eger, C. Ott, J. Bigus, and B. von Wagenheim (eds) *Internationalisierung des Rechts und Seine ökonomische Analyse* (Wiesbaden: GWV Fachverlage GmbH, 2008) 275–96.

is sufficient to generate efficient reliance incentives if the seller is excused whenever performance fails to be profitable (Ackermann's interpretation of the law). If, however, he is excused if performance happens to be inefficient, reliance incentives remain excessive (Köndgen's interpretation).

In order to provide a rough intuition for this unexpected result, let me look at the seller's payoff as a function of the buyer's benefits from performance which, in turn, depends on the buyer's reliance investments. If this function decreases, then the buyer's reliance investments impose a negative externality on the seller and, for that reason, the legal regime in place generates excessive reliance incentives.

Under expectation damages in isolation, the seller's payoff is decreasing indeed as a function of the buyer's benefits because the quantum of damages obviously increases with these benefits. If the seller is excused from inefficient performance, his payoff still decreases and, hence, reliance incentives are still excessive. If, however, the seller is excused from unprofitable performance, the seller's payoff increases for all contingencies where the price as specified in the contract is smaller than the costs of performance which, in turn, are lower than the benefits from performance.

Since, in such contingencies, the seller would be excused from performance, he can credibly threaten not to perform in spite of the fact that performance would be efficient. In the shadow of this threat, parties voluntarily renegotiate leaving part of the renegotiation surplus to the seller. Therefore, in such contingencies, the seller's payoff becomes an increasing function of the buyer's benefits. The resulting positive externality can be exploited to constrain the buyer's reliance incentives to their efficient level.[12]

As a consequence, a non-contingent price for performance can be specified by the parties such that the buyer has efficient reliance incentives if expectation damages are combined with a performance excuse based on non-profitability of performance. In other words, a suitable non-contingent contract combined with the appropriate default rules from contract law solve the hold-up problem, the reason being that equilibrium payoffs become contingent even if the contract itself was not. It remains the task of the parties to find the appropriate non-contingent price for performance. The rest is done by default rules of contract law. But notice, in this case, default rules are based on rather clear-cut standards if unprofitable performance were excused indeed as suggested by Ackermann.

This leaves judicial administration of broad standards as a means to constrain opportunism as discussed by Gillette. Mandates of transactional behaviour such as good faith, commercial reasonableness, and best effort rest on notions that remain almost as incomprehensible to a traditional economist as commercial opportunism itself it does. For that reason, I feel unable to comment on that part of Gillette's Chapter.

[12] For details of a proof, the reader is referred to Schweizer, n 9.

IV. Conclusion

To sum up, Gillette provides great insights and casual inference from legal practice on the trade-offs between default rules, broad standards and contractual efforts. While he sees constraining opportunism as the major goals of such mechanisms, I have argued that traditional economic analysis allows for similar conclusions, the advantage being that traditional analysis does not have to rely on the notoriously vague notion of opportunism and instead can make use of the well-established normative criterion provided by welfare theory. While I fully subscribe to Gillette's conclusion that parties are in a good position to generate efficient incentives even by making use of simple, non-contingent contracts, I have argued that the appropriate default rules must be in place. Such rules may include standards to be administered by third parties. Yet they are far less broad than the ones discussed by Gillette.

Summary of the Discussions in Part IV: Governance in Long-term Contractual Relationships

*Stefan Wichary**

Chapter 8: Fairness and Reciprocity in Contract Governance

Author: Stefan Magen

Discussant: Gralf-Peter Calliess

Horst Eidenmüller started the discussion. Regarding the issue of fairness and contract governance he agreed with Gralf-Peter Calliess that the present experimental studies have focused specifically on outcomes and have neglected the process issues. But between intentions and outcomes there is the process of negotiation. Eidenmüller suggested that experimental economist should focus much more on the design of process issues. Transparency of the process and involvement of parties, who are affected by a potential agreement, could play a role. Bruno Frey agreed that procedural aspects are very important and pointed to the literature about procedural fairness, and especially to the work of Tom R. Tyler. With respect to the issue of the interplay between fairness and law, Eidenmüller cautioned against the normative conclusion that something has to be wrong with the law, because nobody wants fairness crowded out by the law. This is ambiguous and would depend very much on the setting in which the experimental studies were done, he argued. The paper entitled 'Fairness Crowded out by Law' by Borges and Irlenbusch[1], which Stefan Magen mentioned, is about consumers' right to withdraw a particular contract. Eidenmüller suspected that somebody who is confronted with this study, would conclude that there would be a need to increase the exercise of withdrawal rights and crowd out this 'phony' fairness

* Department of Private Law, German, and European Commercial and Economic Law, Ruhr-University, Bochum.

[1] G. Borges and B. Irlenbusch, 'Fairness Crowded Out by Law: An Experimental Study on Withdrawal Rights' (2007) 163 *Journal of Institutional and Theoretical Economics* 84–101.

thing. But possibly businesses that have voluntarily offered a withdrawal right to their consumers, succeed in supplicating the consumers to not exercise it.

Magen agreed that Eidenmüller was right and that something that is fair isn't necessarily good. But he mentioned the paper of Borges and Irlenbusch to make another point: if you want to understand the effect withdrawal rights have or, in general, understand the mechanism by which the law influences behaviour, you have to take fairness into account even if you do not exactly know the mechanisms by which fairness actually drives behaviour.

In Frey's opinion experimental economics has absolutely no relevance for anything in real life. So if experimental economists found out in law experiments that 40 per cent of people were selfish and 60 per cent were conditional co-operators, this would only tell you that not 100 per cent of people were selfish because the result depends on institutional conditions and the law itself sets a lot of these conditions. So the number of people acting selfishly would depend strongly on the law. Frey recommended lawyers read Ostrom's 'Governing the Commons'[2] or her Nobel Prize lecture[3]. Ostrom demonstrate about 25 conditions under which the public goods problem is overcome and her work has incredible amounts of empirical evidence ranging from India to the Swiss Alps. Frey added that he noticed a strong decrease of laboratory experiments. The new thing, he said, is field experiments and, even better, natural experiments. Magen agreed with Frey that experiments have their limits. There can't be any direct transfer from experiments to real life, but experiments can come up with explanation as to how cognitive processes and motivation drive individual behaviour, and so form the basis for hypothesises about social mechanisms. Of course, these hypothesises would have to be tested in field experiments and with survey studies.

Richard Swedberg then asked Magen for his opinion about the status of field experiments versus the old fashioned form of experiments. Magen doubted that there would be a lot of field experiments in the coming years, because they are very difficult to conduct, they need a lot of craftsmanship, and they are very time expensive. Calliess disagreed that conducting natural experiments is very difficult. He said that as lawyers and politicians are involved in law, then law is a natural experiment.

Klaus Hopt asked Magen to explain the meaning and the concept of expressive law so Magen stated that law could affect behaviour without changing material incentives—only by communication. Fairness research could help us to understand which mechanisms near communication influence preferences, and thereby behaviour. Magen regretted that economists' model of fairness preferences don't have the ability to capture the expressive effects. As a consequence, adaption of more cognitive standards to fairness preferences would be needed.

[2] E. Ostrom, *Governing the Commons: The Evolution of Institutions for Collective Action* (Cambridge: Cambridge University Press, 1990).

[3] E. Ostrom, 'Beyond Markets and States: Polycentric Governance of Complex Economic Systems' (2010) 100 *American Economic Review* 641–72.

Anne van Aaken confirmed the problems with capturing the effect of communication between people and its influence on how people perceived fairness. Some experimental economists have already admitted that under controlled situations they could not capture communication in the correct way. So Frey could be right and there could be a need for more field studies or maybe for taking a more psychological approach.

Finally, Florian Möslein got back to the importance of institutional design for fairness behaviour and to the relevance of these institutions. Möslein supposed some kind of interplay between the behaviour of the parties and the evolution of the institutional design. Magen agreed and added that according to Ostrom successful commons management is successful because people adapt rules very specifically to concrete commons problem and this adaption would be close to making institutions variable.

Chapter 9: Class Actions, Compliance, and Moral Cost

Author: Bruno Deffains and Dominique Demougin
Discussant: Fernando Gomez

Paul Davies considered the duty to take reasonable care as the substantive rule, as discussed by Dominique Demougin. But that is a rule which is particularly open to hindsight bias. Accordingly, the judge could think *ex post* that a higher level of precaution should be taken, than was intended by the—*ex ante* operating—legislature. So in the end a higher level of care would be imposed. But consumers would have to incur the additional price in order to get that level. First and foremost, Davies warned, that the hindsight bias operates in an unpredictable way so actor's firms, which have exercised appropriate levels of care, nevertheless are adjudicated subsequently not to have taken it. In that case the 'good guys' are liable. Furthermore, if it isn't costless for the 'good guys' to reject a claim, which is brought by someone against their firms, there are incentives for them to settle just to get the claim to go away. So, again, the 'good guys' are paying out the compensation.

Clayton P. Gillette followed up on Davies' comment and suggested taking additionally the class action lawyer (instead of the consumer) as a real party in interest more into account. Fernando Gomez looked at the extrinsic and intrinsic motivations of the firms and at the deviations. On the one side he assumed that there is no deviation. The consumers would simply want to get compensated for the injuries they have suffered. But the real party in interest in the class action on the other side would not be the consumer but the class action lawyer. Gillette guessed that there would be deviations between extrinsic and intrinsic motivations on the class action lawyer's side. 'Bad guys' on the class action lawyer's side would dramatically change the results of Demougin's model, which thus would become much more interesting and, as Gillette also admitted, much more complicated. Demougin agreed that his model would not cover problems like mistakes by courts or bad motivation of lawyers. But these would not only apply to class actions but also to individual lawsuits, though maybe not in the same extension.

Katharina Pistor argued that producers might not be such wonderful managers. Strategic actors could diversify their risk by taking different corporate strategies. Even the 'good guys' could source out some of the activities that might create the greatest harm into a subsidiary. So the quantity of harm producers can do, and the varieties they can choose, has a major impact. Demougin admitted that this kind of diversification of the risk to the rest of the world mights often happen. To avoid liability, managers find a firm which would go bankrupt in case of damage or loss. Demougin had no response to this or, at least, not in his model.

Hans- W. Micklitz remarked that in the national laws of European countries there are enormous differences between the class action and group action systems but according to the current political message of Commissioner Viviane Reding in European law there soon won't be any harmonized system of class action. Nevertheless Gomez expected that the debate about class actions was not likely to stop. In the last years European countries have introduced different models of class action or—to be accurately termed—collective or aggregate litigation. Gomez was confident that you learn something from experimenting with different solutions. Micklitz highlighted the Dutch system of class action, whereupon the parties to a class action type of conflict have first to agree on a settlement and then the settlement has to be approved in the court. Thus parties come together on a voluntary basis and there are a number of cases where this mechanism works. In Micklitz' opinion Demougin's model suggests that it would make sense to introduce a class action on a voluntary basis and to combine it with a kind of settlement. The consumers would be ready to pay something on top to get the security of benefitting from the class action type of solution. An opt-in/opt-out solution, where the consumers would have to choose, would be possible too. Finally, Micklitz put attendees in mind of the history of the right to withdrawal, which was voluntarily introduced in the 1970s and then widely imposed by the European Directive on Distance Selling (Directive 97/7/EC). Demougin pointed out that he did not know the Dutch system and would not be able to immediately demonstrate how the model could be adapted to consider class action on a voluntary basis.

For injury type of damages caused by product defects Vito Roberto doubted any need for class actions in European countries. He pointed out the huge difference in handling these damages between the legal systems in Europe and in the US. If somebody is hurt in Germany, France, Italy, Switzerland, and most other European countries, first social security pay treatment expenses then settlement takes place between social security and the producer, i.e. between social security and the insurance company of the producer. So for class actions only the area of economic losses will still remain. Moreover, Roberto invited the others to look at the results of the class action system in reality in the US. He answered his own (rhetorical) question, whether in the US there would be a higher standard of care or a better quality of products than in Europe, with another question: if reality could not cope with the model, what was wrong with the reality? Demougin thought this was a good question but he reminded the group that a model-based reality would be so much simpler than the real world and that a model would abstract from a lot of the elements of reality. Maybe one way to think about Roberto's objections would be to think about whether pro-social references play a role or if pro-social preferences have eroded more in one environment than in other. Maybe you are slightly more immoral, if you have nothing to lose than if you have a lot to lose.

In Michael Klausner's opinion, Demougin's model was not only about class actions but also about liability actions, so it would be also an interesting model, when looking at why we are in the liability system.

Gerard Hertig explicitly agreed and added that class actions could be a market driven instrument for enforcing product liability but you could have fines, too, for example imposed by an agency. He referred to the competences of the European Commission in the competition area, which aren't subject to so much manipulation by lawyers' incentives. Finally, Hertig remarked that on the basis of empirical studies, the class actions system in the US looks much more benign than some previous speakers have pretended. Demougin agreed with Klausner's opinion. He clarified that he was not talking about classes in that sense. For the way his model works classes would be 'miraculously' put together, without looking at the incentives for creating a class. Gomez added that any kind of comparison between levels of care or levels of consumer protection on both sides of the Atlantic specifically, and any kind of comparison between legal systems or between institutions in general would be very difficult. Class actions are only one particular feature of the legal system. You can't know if it will always be *ceteris paribus*. Maybe in the US, levels of consumer protection and levels of care are lower without class actions but this is doubtful elsewhere.

Urs Schweizer argued that even in cases of violation of antitrust law private enforcement could be pushed, but apparently with little success. In these cases a single consumer usually has very low damages and thus only a low incentive to ask for compensation. But from a social perspective the damages could be huge so there would be a need for class actions to summarize the claims of many affected consumers. Demougin confirmed that antitrust cases were discussed at length during some of the hearings on class actions. In one case that was mentioned a cartel of three mobile phone providers in France created at least 1.7 billion Euros in losses, but no single consumer has asked the providers for any compensation.

Chapter 10: Legal Supervision of Commercial Opportunism

Author: Clayton P. Gillette

Discussant: Urs Schweizer

Karl Riesenhuber did not share Gillette's pessimistic view about courts determining the parties' interests. He argued that there usually is an adversarial procedure and therefore the parties usually have a chance to give their story. Of course they could still behave opportunistically but this would be a chance to get close to the truth and Riesenhuber doubted there would be any better opportunity. Moreover, many of the given examples would be treated similarly in German law. So the question is whether not only courts, but also legislators, can get it wrong as a matter of policy. Gillette remarked that he had also asked himself why courts, even in an adversarial setting, could not get this right. Looking only at US experiences he laid the blame on the lawyers. Business lawyers may write contracts but on the rare occasion when something breaks down, the litigators must resolve this and maybe those litigators do not fully understand the business under discussion. Often only contract lawyers could explain to litigators why a contract clause was there, so the litigators would not be able to explain this to the courts. Finally, in the US legislators do not get involved in the process that much, because there is no kind of explicit commercial codes.

Anne van Aaken wondered why the reputation should be affected. Reputation would come into play if you have some kind of standard—social norms, some kinds of behavioural standard, or even the law—against which you are judged. Even though Gillette doubted the importance of law he did not underestimate the law as a standard against which your reputation is judged. Gillette stated that if you are able to explain what really went on, your reputation is not necessarily hurt, even if you are judged against the law. Maybe the story would be non-verifiable to any third party that is in the group within which the reputation counts. He added, however, that it would be hard to send a reputational signal in these disputed accounts—when each party has their own story—because it would depend on who actually believes you. Van Aaken turned towards non-modification clauses and mentioned the works of Kevin E. Davis, a colleague of Gillette at New York University School of Law.[4] It seemed to her that courts would obviously invalidate these clauses in purely contractual settings between firms but they would uphold them in settings where a state and a company have a contract. She wondered if courts would maybe try to take account of an, at least assumed, inequality of negotiating power. In Gillette's opinion unequal bargaining power would actually get over-utilized. Benjamin Klein, an economist, has already cautioned against evoking doctrines of unequal bargaining power.[5] In the *Alaska Packers'* case[6], that he discussed, the party seemed to have run into unequal bargaining power in the sense that there was a big firm against a single employee, but you would need to know a lot more about the facts of the case before drawing any conclusions.

Horst Eidenmüller agreed with Gillette's analysis that parties could do a lot in order to curtail the policing of opportunism by designing appropriate contractual arrangements. He stated that maybe the more the parties to a particular contract

[4] See, e.g., K.E. Davis, 'The Demand for Immutable Contracts: Another Look at the Law and Economics of Contract Modification and Renegotiation' (2006) 81 *New York University Law Review* 487–549.

[5] See, e.g., B. Klein, 'Transaction Cost Determinants of 'Unfair' Contractual Arrangements' (1980) 70 *American Economic Review* 356–362.

[6] *Alaska Packers' Association v. Delmonico* 117 F. 99 (9th Cir, 1902).

have done to constrain opportunism on each side the less some form of intervention by courts can be justified. So in the *Alaska Packers'* case the court would probably have correctly interfered because they could not have done much in terms of contractual arrangements with respect to curtailing opportunism. Gillette was sure that in the *Alaska Packers'* case there would not be any bargaining at all about the wage but he was sceptical about what to infer from the fact that the labourers were paid a wage they did not individually negotiate. If a market wage was paid, there would not be any need for bargaining but a situation in which everyone is paying the same wage could be explained by two diametrically opposed phenomena—a perfect competition or a perfect oligopoly. Gillette highlighted the difficulty in working out which one is happening and doubted that courts could manage this.

Michael Klausner agreed largely and turned attention to the inability of judges to understand the underlying economics of complex transactions. At least in the US, judges as well as lawyers, would be poorly educated in this context. Therefore, Klausner suggested that limiting the number of claims might not be a wise idea to police opportunism. Judges would be no better at making this distinction than at resolving other disputes. Gillette stated that in a subset of cases, where you have some sort of a benchmark—for example a market price—courts would be pretty good at making this distinction. Steven Shavell demonstrated this interrelation.[7]

Eidenmüller continued that in many jurisdictions there are doctrines that allow courts to police opportunism. He took the notion of economic duress and the notion of undue influence as examples in English law and the doctrine of unlawful threat that allows you to resign the contract, as an example in German law. Some doctrines give courts certain flexibility other force courts to intervene in such circumstances. The doctrine of unlawful threat would be problematic. In the *Alaska Packers'* case, for example, it would be difficult to argue that this would not be an unlawful threat, because the workers had threatened breach of contract. So under German law the other side would have been able to resign the contract. In contrast, the doctrine of undue influence, or the doctrine of economic duress, would enable courts to take more account of the specific circumstances of the case. Gillette agreed. Nevertheless he referred to the dangers for the law. If there are too many doctrines that courts can use to resolve a case, then the court can choose a doctrine that gives the desired results. So the doctrine of economic duress, for example, could be seen as a strike-breaking mechanism. In the past, US courts have been very resistant when faced with efforts by labour to organize. In this context Gillette pointed out that economists use the synonymous term hold-up instead of opportunism. So the very same lack of definition in opportunism is also a lack of definition in hold-up. Schweizer dissented, so Grossman

[7] S. Shavell, 'Contractual Holdup and Legal Intervention' (2007) 36 *Journal of Legal Studies* 325–54, 334ff.

and Hart[8] gave an exact meaning to the hold-up problem: at the investment stage, there is uncertainty about the future and the question is whether parties can conclude a contract in which they anticipate everything and that provides efficient incentives.

Pistor cited another paper by Shavell[9] about the private versus the social costs and benefits of litigation and wondered whether there should not also be private versus social costs of certain general norms. So in a very individualistic analysis the outcome might be inefficient, but there could be strong incentives for cooperative behaviour, or certain other social benefits, that might not be taken into account. Gillette agreed completely on the incentives for cooperation.

[8] S. Grossman and O. Hart, 'The Costs and Benefits of Ownership: A Theory of Lateral and Vertical Integration' (1986) 94 *Journal of Political Economy* 691–719.

[9] S. Shavell, 'The Fundamental Divergence of Social and Private Benefits of Litigation' (1997) 2 *Journal of Legal Studies* 575–612.

PART V

CONTRACT GOVERNANCE AND RULE-SETTING

11

Private Regulation and Industrial Organization: Contractual Governance and the Network Approach

Fabrizio Cafaggi and Paola Iamiceli***

I. Transnational Private Regulations: Trends and Challenges

The internationalization of markets and trade is transforming the regulatory space and reshaping the structure of supply chains.[1] States, as global regulators, increasingly reveal their weaknesses while private players, both market actors and NGOs, often take the lead introducing stricter standards. Private regulatory regimes are emerging and consolidating, often as a complement to public regulation, sometimes even as a substitute, when treaty-making entities and international organizations are unable to regulate effectively cross border activities.[2]

The driving factors for the growth of Transnational Private Regulation (TPR) are numerous. Amongst them, we can highlight (1) higher concentration at the retail level related to increasing disintegration at production level; (2) the multiple crises connected with product safety in food and non-food sectors and the

* Director of the Centre for Judicial Cooperation and former Professor of Comparative Law at the European University Institute, Florence, and at the University of Trento.

** Associate Professor at the University of Trento. This Chapter is part of a broader research project on 'Transnational Private Regulation (TPR) and System Level Innovations in Global Food Value Chains' realized in collaboration with Turku University of Applied Sciences (Finland, 2011–2013). A previous version was presented and discussed at the VIII Annual Conference of the Euro-Latin Study Network on Integration and Trade (ELSNIT) in Paris (15–16 October 2010). The Chapter is the result of a joint contribution by the authors both in terms of the analysis of background literature and practices and the elaboration of derived implications. However, Sections I, II, III, IVII, and VIII have been drafted by Fabrizio Cafaggi and Sections V, VI, and sub-sections have been drafted by Paola Iamiceli.

[1] S. Ponte and T. Sturgeon, 'Explaining Governance in Global Value Chains: A Modular Theory-building Effort' (2014) 21(1) *Review of International Political Economy* 195–223, 197.

[2] For an overview see F. Cafaggi, 'A Comparative Analysis of Transnational Private Regulation: Legitimacy, Quality, Effectiveness and Enforcement' (2014) (available at <http://papers.ssrn.com/sol3/papers.cfm?abstract_id=2508684>) and F. Cafaggi, 'New Foundations of Transnational Private Regulation' (2011) 38 *Journal of Law and Society* 20–49; T. Buthe and W. Mattli, *The Global Rulers* (Princeton, NJ: Princeton University Press, 2011).

resulting consumers' demand for stronger, more effective and coordinated monitoring and control; and (3) the inability of states to deal with cross-boundary risk assessment and management.

The difficulties for effective regulation, as far as states are concerned, relate not only to standard-setting but also, and even more importantly, to implementation and compliance monitoring. In this domain, it has become clear that a 'one size fits all' strategy is ineffective, and in several areas, a supply chain approach to regulation has been proposed by legislation. Such evolution has generated a significant, primarily informal, regulatory delegation to private actors along the supply chain. Strategies of delegation to private actors concern both standard-setting and standard implementation via risk management schemes; compliance monitoring across jurisdictions is very costly and might require significant coordination costs. Delegation to supply chains with external oversight permits reducing costs and increasing efficacy. This approach assumes that firms and more generally private actors, including non-governmental organizations (NGOs), can provide more effective and often cheaper implementation of public regulation related to product safety and quality, environmental protection.[3] The primary set of regulatory instruments is drawn from contractual governance including bilateral, multiparty contracts, and corporate organizations. Contracts are used for the adoption of standards by single firms and groups of businesses, for labels licensing, to monitor compliance, for the enforcement of (contractual) duties to comply with standards and licensing rules. Different types of contracts are used to design standards, monitor compliance, and enforce regulatory obligations.

Compliance monitoring via contractual governance differs across sectors and, even within the same sectors differences emerge depending on the commodity, the nature of the hazard, and its spreading pathways. Thus, even in the area of food safety, one of the subjects of this Chapter, the different types of supply chain and market structures influence the effectiveness of the 'supply chain regulatory approach' and the need to differentiate both objectives and instruments.[4]

Contractual governance influences the selection of regulatory strategies.

The supply chain regulatory approach demonstrates a radical change in perspective: the shift from product to process standards driving to more intense chain regulation.[5] Process standards regulation has moved away from the product and focused much more on the organizational dimensions of processes including

[3] See, e.g., in the food sector, Commission Communication,'EU Best Practice Guidelines for Voluntary Certification Schemes for Agricultural Products and Foodstuffs' (2010 C 341/04) and, in the US, the Food Safety Modernisation Act (2010) and the Consumer Product Safety Improvement Act (2008).

[4] See F. Cafaggi (ed) *The Enforcement of Transnational Regulation* (Cheltenham: Edward Elgar Publishing, 2012), C. Parker and V. Lehman Nielsen, *Explaining Compliance: Business Responses to Regulation* (Cheltenham: Edward Elgar Publishing, 2011); M. B. Hutter, 'Understanding the New Regulatory Governance: Business Perspectives' (2011) 33 *Law & Policy* 459–76; N. Gunningham in D. Levi Faur (ed) *Handbook on the Politics of Regulation* (Cheltenham: Edward Elgar Publishing, 2011).

[5] See ISO Economic Benefits of Standards, ISO Methodology v 2.0, 14ff (available at <www.iso.org>).

social and environmental standards.[6] Process standards increase interdependencies among chain's participants. For example the unit of analysis in risk regulation has shifted from the single organization to the chain. Risk assessment and risk management can be coordinated by a single actor but have to involve the entire chain and its participants. Contracts represent the main instruments for regulatory coordination but within contract a wide variety of tools is available. This Chapter tries to single out some determinants of the choice among different contractual technologies focusing on network contracts.

The choice between a product or a process standard, between an input or an output standard, and the degree of interdependence of standards compliance can influence the relationships among firms located along the supply chain and affect their contractual relationships. The choice and design of the contractual network will reflect the relevance of these variables. Regulatory choices influence contractual governance.

A safety standard related to the production process and the product necessarily involves many nodes of the supply chain. As will be illustrated, information regulation concerning risk assessment and risk management of dangerous products may require the creation of inter-firm networks so as to increase communication and effectiveness. Thus, the creation of regulatory networks to produce information about new risks concerning drugs, food, feed, or even financial services may be the result of a regulatory strategy based on the assumption that strong risks' interdependence calls for coordination and cooperation. 'Command and control' regulatory strategies may work in the context of vertically integrated firms (where hierarchy is available) or paradoxically with single firms among their divisions, when risks can be parcelled out and the leader has complete information. By contrast, risks' interdependence of conducts related to firm's involved in the same chain requires the abandonment of 'command and control' and the adoption of responsive strategies, which often call for network-based organizational models.[7] Responsive regulation works better than command and control when no single actor has full information about the risk and its spreading pathways. Monitoring compliance requires different modes of interaction between regulators and regulated entities and among regulated when interdependencies of regulated entities' conduct is high.

The features of the supply chain affect the choice of regulatory strategies, but the selection of the regulatory strategy in turn may require or induce changes in the supply chain.[8] We observe this mutual interaction between regulatory strategies

[6] See the increasing reference to sustainability and the integrate approach as it appears in the FAO SAFA Guidelines.

[7] F. Cafaggi, 'The Regulatory Functions of Transnational Commercial Contracts: New Architectures' (2013) 36(6) *Fordham International Law Journal* 1557–xxx; F. Cafaggi, 'Transnational Governance by Contract—Private Regulation and Contractual Networks in Food Safety' (March 2011) (available at <http://ssrn.com/abstract=1874749>), published in a revised version in A. Marx, M. Maertens, J. Swinnen, and I. Wouters (eds) *Private Standards and Global Governance: Legal and Economic Perspectives* (Cheltenham: Edward Elgar Publishing) 195–234.

[8] G. Gereffi and J. Lee, 'A Global Value Chain Approach to Food Safety and Quality Standards' (February2009) GlobalHealthDiplomacyforChronicDiseasePreventionWorkingPaperSeries (available at <http://www.cggc.duke.edu/pdfs/GlobalHealth/Gereffi_Lee_GVCFoodSafetyl_4Feb2009.

and organizational models but how they interplay and influence each other is still significantly under-investigated. Those who theorize about regulation, even when advocating market-friendly schemes, do not consider market structures and vertical (dis)integration of the supply chain as significant variables to be internalized in the definition of objectives and choice of instruments. Those who study the evolution of industrial organizations rarely consider regulation, whether public or private, as a significant factor affecting the selection of models.[9]

In this Chapter we claim that the correlation between regulation and models of industrial organization, is reciprocal and varies both across and within sectors. We want to investigate the relationship between regulation and industrial organizations at the transnational level, focusing on the correlation between contractual governance and product safety transnational regulation. Within this broad framework we analyse the relationship between monitoring compliance and transnational contractual governance showing when networks perform better as regulatory instrument and how various forms of networks can be explained by the adoption of different monitoring strategies whose common denominator is the use of private actors along the supply chain.

We adopt a broad definition of regulation which includes both public and private regulation while leaving out the regulatory function of civil liability. In a separate paper, we integrate *ex ante* (regulation) with *ex post* (liability) instruments.[10]

The Chapter proceeds as follows. In Section II, we address the influence of different forms of the supply chain and market structures on regulatory choices. In Sections III–VII, we examine how regulation influences the choice of supply chain models between markets, hierarchies, and networks. We focus in particular on contractual governance and the role of networks as a means to enhance the effectiveness of compliance with private standards and compare different regulatory schemes in order to identify possible correlations between regulatory models and network models. Concluding remarks, in Section VIII, follow the definition of a future research agenda on transnational regulation and contractual governance.

II. How do Supply Chains Affect the Choice of Regulatory Strategies and Instruments at Transnational Level?

Supply chains are facing relevant changes due to the enormous growth of global value chains, often boosted by emerging economies.[11] Global value chains and

pdf>); F. Cafaggi and P. Iamiceli, 'Supply Chains, Contractual Governance and Certification Regimes' (2014) 37 *European Journal of Law and Economics* 131–73.

9 This conclusion cannot be generalized. For some considerations in this respect see, e.g., Ponte and Sturgeon, n 1.

10 See F. Cafaggi and P. Iamiceli, 'The Effects of Civil Liability on Supply Chain Architectures' (unpublished).

11 G. Gereffi and T. Sturgeon, 'Global Value Chain-oriented Industrial Policy: the Role of Emerging Economies in 'Global Value Chains in a Changing World' in D. K. Elms and

global production and distribution networks have become the 'core features' of international political economy.[12] Different structures concerning the relationship among supply chain participants have been identified (1) Market-type relations, enabling for low switching costs for all parties, are compared with (2) modular value chains, where production is sourced from specialized suppliers using standardized components and technologies; (3) with relational value chains, characterized by specific investments and high interdependence between the parties; (4) with captive supply chains, in which the buyer exercises intense control over the seller, which faces high switching costs; (5) with vertical integration, based on hierarchical relation between headquarter and subsidiaries and affiliates.[13] Moving from this framework, this Section addresses the following, apparently rhetorical, question: can the choice of regulatory strategies ignore the structure of the supply chain, the degree of vertical integration or disintegration, the level of market concentration, or the distribution of power along the chain among the various enterprises? This question is relevant both when there is delegation of regulatory functions to private actors and also when public regulators exercise direct oversight over firms operating in global supply chains across jurisdictional borders assuming regulatory burdens via due diligence.

Our answer is that both the level of market competition and the degree of vertical integration strongly affect the choice of supply chain regulation (the type of standard) and its distributive effects (how costs and benefits are allocated along the chain).[14]

For the relationship between market competition and choice of regulation, differences emerge between competitive and oligopolistic markets. Clearly the oligopolistic nature of the market suggests that market players will endeavour to preserve the *status quo* and use private regulation as a barrier to entry. The potential anti competitive effects of TPR will be more limited in a highly competitive market where private regulation primarily affects the entry costs for newcomers.[15]

P. Low (eds) (2013) WTO—FGI 329ff, available at <http://www.wto.org/english/res_e/booksp_e/aid4tradeglobalvalue13_intro_e.pdf>; G. Gereffi, 'Global Value Chains in a Post-Washington Consensus World' (2014) 21(1) *Review of International Political Economy* 9–37, 15.

[12] J. Neilson, B. Pritchard, and H. Wai-Chung Yeung, 'Global Value Chains and Global Production Networks in the Changing International Political Economy: An Introduction' in (2014) 21(1) *Review of International Political Economy* 1–8.

[13] G. Gereffi, J. Humphrey, and T. Sturgeon, 'The Governance of Global Value Chains' (2005) 1 *Review of International Political Economy* 78.

[14] One of us has addressed the distributional effects of transnational private regulation elsewhere: see F. Cafaggi and K. Pistor, 'Regulatory Capabilities: A Normative Framework for Assessing the Distributive Effects of Regulation' (2014) *Regulation and Governance*. We shall not address the distributive question in this Chapter.

[15] On the impact of competition on regulation, as here examined, see also Gereffi and Lee, n 8, in which the authors maintain that the higher the concentration at both the production and distribution level (bilateral oligopolies), the more likely the emergence of comprehensive private standards (process and product standards); the higher the concentration at the level of the producers without a similar concentration at the distribution level (producer-driven chains), the higher the emergence of private standards concerning process (more than products); the higher the concentration at the level of retailers without a similar concentration at the production level (buyer-driven chains), the higher the emergence of private standards concerning products (more than process);

Hence the use of public regulation, including competition law, should be favoured over private when markets are thin and access is costly.

The choice between regulatory strategies and instruments depends also on the degree of vertical integration and competition between firms along the supply chain.[16] Here, the argument we present, unlike the previous one, is descriptive rather than normative. In limiting the analysis to TPR, it seems that a high degree of vertical integration is compatible with 'command and control' since the use of hierarchy as a regulatory device is made possible by the existence of a controlling actor, being it a single firm or the controlling entity of a pyramidal multinational group. Vertically integrated chains primarily use contractual technologies based on standard clauses, protocols, and guidelines unilaterally drafted by the chain leader. Chain's participants are often only given a 'take it or leave it' option to enter the chain and to participate to the regulatory process.

Vertical disintegration implies a longer and more fragmented chain which requires a stronger, albeit more expensive, coordination mechanism. In this case 'command and control' might be a very costly and highly ineffective strategy. Responsive regulation—where the different firms along the supply chain are requested to coordinate and each one acts on the expectation that the others have adequate incentives to cooperate—appears to be more suitable to supply chains characterized by high level of specialization and less hierarchical relationships when assessing and managing risks. The emergence of private standards and more broadly of TPR is linked to supply chains that are not vertically integrated including both captive, relational, and modular.[17] Contractual governance characterizes the three types with the use of different instruments. Contractual networks can play a role in each type of supply chain but their forms differ depending on the chain's structure.

An additional factor is related to competition both along the chain and among players positioned at the same level within the chain.[18] The degree of competition within the chain primarily concerns vertically disintegrated supply chains.[19]

the higher the fragmentation at both levels (traditional markets), the more limited the production of private standards, while public standards remain limited and less comprehensive.

[16] On this aspect see also Gereffi and Lee, n 8, 1, 15, who maintain that it is exactly when a producer moves from a vertically integrated model to vertical disintegration that he/she has higher incentives to codify standards and ensure compliance, while, with vertically integrated production, retailers show higher incentives to produce standards.

[17] See Ponte and Sturgeon, n 1, 205.

[18] See G. Gereffi, R. Garcia-Johnson, and E. Sasser, 'The NGO-Industrial Complex' (2001) 125 *Foreign Policy* 56, 64 ('While competition can foster higher industry standards, less pressure will leave companies room to dictate their own terms of compliance.').

[19] This is not to say that chain leaders do not use competition even within highly integrated supply chains to select their partners and to distribute power and costs. We are here not referring to regulatory competition but economic competition among chain participants. See, for an example concerning the Illycafè supply chain, F. Cafaggi, C. Ferrari, P. Iamiceli, K. Sorsa, and L. Swensson, 'Transnational Private Regulation (TPR) and System Level Innovations in Global Food Value Chains: Evidence from the Coffee Sector (Brazil, Italy, Finland)' Research Project Draft Report, November 2014, prepared in collaboration by Turku University of Applied Sciences, Turku, Finland and European University Institute, Florence, Italy, within a research programme funded by Tekes (Finland).

Strong competition may bring about instability: a race to the bottom driven by costs which may be at odds with coordination.

Competition may open different possibilities in terms of regulation strategies:

(1) A high degree of competition within the chain suggests that 'command and control' may not be operationalized and that responsive regulation, which requires coordination, might be difficult to achieve. More market-based strategies might better reflect internal equilibria associated with high levels of chain's internal competition.

(2) A low degree of competition along the chain suggests that both 'command and control' and responsive regulation may be usefully deployed.

III. The Impact of Regulation on the Structure of the Supply Chain

A second set of questions concerns the relationship between the structure of the supply chain and the nature of the regulatory instruments deployed in the domain of private regulation. In particular the correlation between the regulatory functions of supply chains, the form and content of contracts.[20]

There is evidence that both contractual architectures and practices are correlated with the regulatory functions they perform.[21] In particular, when contracts are used as a monitoring device to ensure compliance with transnational regulation, different monitoring strategies result in different contractual technologies. Here again various supply chains require different monitoring strategies. However current private standards do not seem to acknowledge these distinctions and assume uniformity of chains.

Let us first begin with type of standards and then analyse the corresponding contractual technologies. Standards may result from three different complementary regulatory sources:

- transnational public regulation (for example European regulations, inter-state conventions, CAC standards, FAO guidelines, and codes of practice, etc);
- domestic public regulation applicable to the contracts (mandatory requirements of final market destination);
- transnational private regulation (for example codes of conduct, guidelines, other standards as set and implemented by single firms, enterprise organizations, or other private entities, mainly through contracts).

We address the questions of whether and how different regulatory instruments influence the organizational features of the supply chain, producing changes in

[20] See Cafaggi, n 5.

[21] See F. Cafaggi, 'The Regulatory Functions of Transnational Commercial Contracts. New Architectures' (2013) 36 *Fordham Journal of International Law*, 1557–618.

contractual relationships among enterprises. In particular, we investigate when networks arise in response to the adoption of one or more regulatory strategies.

IV. Supply Chain Structures and Regulatory Strategies

We now analyse how transnational regulation and in particular private standards influence the structure of supply chains and the relationships within them: the other side of the coin. Economic literature, drawing widely on empirical studies, extensively analyses the changes in the supply chain as directly or indirectly induced by the increase in number and sophistication of private standards.[22]

Two main perspectives are considered: one related to the market structure, the other concerning the organization of the firm and its strategies for inter-firm collaboration.

In relation to market structure, it is contended that the increasing diffusion of private standards creates entry barriers for suppliers who have insufficient skills and resources to comply with these standards or drives them away from global markets.[23] This phenomenon is particularly striking in developing countries, although it might emerge in other countries as well.[24] Depending on the context, the proliferation of standards may either force exit from the market or create a dual system in which compliant production is distinguished from 'un-regulated' production with higher safety risks.[25] The exclusionary effects of regulation are

[22] S. Henson and J. Humphrey, 'The Impact of Private Food Safety Standards on the Food Chain and on Public Standard-setting Processes' (May 2009) paper prepared for FAO/Who (available at <http://ec.europa.eu/food/international/organisations/sps/docs/private_standards_codex_en.pdf>); Joint FAO/Who Food Standards Programme (5–9 July 2010, Geneva) '*Codex Alimentarius* Commission, 33rd Session, Consideration of the Impact of Private Standards' (available at <ftp://ftp.fao.org/codex/Meetings/CAC/cac33/cac33_13e.pdf>.

[23] WTO Committee on Sanitary and Phytosanitary Measures, 'Private Standards and the SPS Agreement' (January 2007) (available at <http://ec.europa.eu/food/international/organisations/sps/docs/g-sps-gen_746.pdf>). See also I. Maher, 'Competition Law and Transnational Private Regulatory Regimes: Marking the Cartel Boundary' in C. Scott, F. Cafaggi, and L. Senden (eds) *The Challenge of Transnational Private Regulation: Conceptual and Constitutional Debates* (Berlin: Wiley Blackwell, 2011) 119–37; Henson and Humphrey, n 23; A. Marx and D. Cuypers, 'Forest Certification as a Global Environmental Governance Tool: What is the Macro-effectiveness of the Forest Stewardship Council?' (2010) 4 *Regulation & Governance* 404–34; A. Marx, 'Global Governance and the Certification Revolution: Types, Trends and Challenges' in D. Levi-Faur (ed) *Handbook on the Politics of Regulation* (Cheltenham: Edward Elgar Publishing, 2012) 590ff, 600; D. Fuchs, A. Kalfajanni, and T. Havinga, 'Actors in Private Food Governance: the Legitimacy of Retail Standards and Multi-stakeholder Initiatives with Civil Society Participation' (2011) 28 *Agriculture and Human Values* 353–67, 353, 354. On the issue of the impact of food safety standard on free trade see also J. Wouters, A. Marx, and N. Hachez, 'In Search of a Balanced Relationship: Public and Private Food Safety Standards and International Law' (June 2009) Leuven Centre for Global Governance Studies Working Paper No 29 (available at <http://www.law.kuleuven.be/iir/nl/onderzoek/wp/wp139e.pdf>).

[24] See O. De Schutter, 'Contract Farming and Inclusive Business Models in the Food Chains,' Interim Report of the Special Rapporteur on the Right to Food to the 66th Session of the General Assembly, UN Doc A/66/262, 4 August 2011.

[25] Fuchs, Kalfajanni, and Havinga, n 24, 353, 356.

described by some scholars having regard to so called techno-economic networks (TEN), these consisting in organizational forms composed of links between heterogeneous actors (including, for example, standard setters, certifiers, and certified firms) who collectively participate in the development of procedures for producing goods or services, some of which give rise to market transactions.[26] Smallholders unable to comply with standards would have no access to the network and therefore to the relevant market.

Still in the first perspective, the divide between fragmentation and harmonization of standards is considered. On the one hand, excessive fragmentation of standards increases the costs of compliance, compounding the risk of market exit.[27] It might also favour captive relations between the standard-setter (usually the buyer/retailer) and the standard-taker (seller), increasing the risk of opportunism.[28] On the other, harmonization of standards might lower competition among enterprises who would otherwise be prone to invest in higher quality standards to gain competitive advantage.[29]

Looking more specifically at the structure and the boundaries of the firm as well as at the models of the supply chain, the impact of private standards on the choice between vertical integration and contractual collaboration has been analysed with a specific focus on the choice between different types of inter-firm collaboration within the chain.

Availability of standards may help to codify the relevant knowledge, while potentially increasing the complexity of the transaction and the level of capabilities necessary for a supplier. Within this theoretical framework, higher and more complex standardization would generate modular chains (if suppliers' capabilities are adequate) or vertical integration (if availability of skilled suppliers is lacking).[30] From the authors' perspective the latter would be the most diffuse in developing countries, though gradual knowledge transfer may take place and leave room for relational collaboration at some point.[31]

Elaborating on this theoretical approach, others question why in fact vertical integration is not so widely practised as expected in the context of low sophistication of suppliers and high demand of standard compliance. According to this view, one possible explanation could be identified in the role of 'third party assurance systems' as institutions in charge of scrutinizing and monitoring potential and actual suppliers. This scheme would lower the costs of outsourcing, reducing

[26] See A. Loconto and L. Busch, 'Standards, Technoeconomic Networks, and Playing Fields: Performing the Global Market Economy' (2010) 17(3) *Review of International Political Economy* 507–36, 521ff.

[27] Joint FAO/Who Food Standards Programme, n 23.

[28] L. Fulponi, 'Private Voluntary Standards in the Food System: The Perspective of Major Food Retailers in OECD Countries' (2006) 31(1) *Food Policy* 1–13; Fuchs, Kalfajanni, and Havinga, n 24, 353, 354.; The World Bank, *Agricultural Innovation Systems: An Investment Sourcebook* (Washington DC: The World Bank, 2012).

[29] Joint FAO/Who Food Standards Programme, n 23.

[30] On the correlation between standards and vertical integration, see Gereffi, Humphrey, and Sturgeon, n 13.

[31] Gereffi, Humphrey, and Sturgeon, n 13.

the incentives for vertical integration. Its concrete efficiency would not remain uncriticized, however, given the lack of competence and the risk of corruption that have been observed in practice with some third party assurance systems.[32]

In all these approaches, however, the role of inter-firm networks seems to be under-investigated, and bilateral contracting remains the reference point.

In the first approach, that distinguishes five models of supply chains, the emergence of modular chains as a result of codification through standardization is emphasized, while the option of vertical integration remains a strong alternative, given the high cost of compliance for unskilled suppliers.[33] This analysis could be complemented by observing how the emergence of relational value chains based on collaboration and mutual knowledge transfer may require different organizational forms and more specifically different models of contractual governance. In fact, standards may need to be reviewed and adapted to actual contexts and unforeseen circumstances, including changes in technology within the chain. Even assuming unchanged standards, compliance requires an exchange of knowledge and information which may or may not be codified. From this perspective, organizing relational value chains through networks may be desirable.[34]

In the second approach described earlier, having regard to the impact of certification systems on outsourcing, the role of third party assurance operators is seen more as a substitute for active control by buyers than as a source of interdependence and collaboration among the several hubs in a network.[35] Certification is still primarily entrusted to individual operators with whom the certifier concludes a service contract. But coordination among suppliers in the chain is necessary to meet certification requirements and group certification is growing.[36] Looking at how private certification systems promote the creation of networks among producers or between producers and distributors may be promising. Collaborative contracts may imply a different network shape that ensures effective cooperation among the certified, especially when certification includes a significant number of supply chain participants. Moreover, the costs of certification, which increase the overall cost of regulation, may be too high to be borne individually, while the adoption of network forms may contribute to better spreading out the costs, thereby increasing fairness as well as efficiency. As we see in the analysis below,

[32] M.M. Blair, C.A. Williams, and L.W. Lin, 'The New Role for Assurance Services in Global Commerce' (2008) 33 *Journal of Corporation Law* 325–60.

[33] Gereffi, Humphrey, and Sturgeon, n 13.

[34] As indirectly suggested by Gereffi, Humphrey, and Sturgeon, n 13, about evidence concerning Kenya. On the role of networks, see Section VI.

[35] Blair, Williams, and Lin, n 33.

[36] Henson and Humphrey, n 23, 1, 30. On the role of farmers' cooperatives in fostering farmers' capability to comply with standards, see M. Hatanaka, C. Bain, and L. Busch, 'Third-party Certification in the Global Agrifood System' (2005) 30 *Food Policy* 354–69, 361. On the different but connected issue of the role of small scale farmers networks as a means to allow farmers to appropriate a larger share of value along the chain, see UN General Assembly, 'The Right to Food', (2011) 1, 15ff (available at <http://www.ohchr.org/Documents/Issues/Food/A.66.262_en.pdf>).

group certification represents an organizational response which may take different forms from a cooperative to a multiparty contract with or without legal personality.

As networks increasingly incorporate the 'value chain approach', the benefits of effective standard implementation aim to reach consumers at large. How profits and costs of these mechanisms are, in concrete terms, distributed along the value chain is a more critical issue. Such distribution in turn strongly influences the choice of networks as to standard implementation devices and the choice of models and forms of networks if adopted.

The following analysis will elaborate on the observation of some network dynamics that are emerging within standard implementation mechanisms, particularly in the area of third party certification systems. More specifically, the observation of concrete cases will address the issue on *whether both the emergence and the form of networks depend on the characteristics of regulation*. While doing so, special attention will be given to: (i) the distinction and relation between standard-setter and certifier; (ii) the scope of application of the certification scheme (whether involving a specific segment of the production chain or extending beyond production towards the trading phase); (iii) the characteristics of the regulatory implementation system whether involving, besides monitoring, service provision (including technical assistance in compliance) and/or additional enforcement mechanisms including sanctioning (see Section VI).

V. Where do Networks Emerge and Stand? Some Guidelines

Sections I–IV have shown that structure and instruments of supply chain coordination are influenced by regulatory strategies both in terms of design and implementation. In particular examples of correlations between supply chain structures and contractual technologies were provided. We now focus on a particular set of instruments: contractual networks.

According to the previously examined literature, on the one hand, increasing vertical disintegration would boost private standards' production; on the other hand, at some point complexity of standards and costs of compliance would lead to a higher level of vertical integration in order to increase harmonization and reduce costs. Where might networks stand within contractual governance? Does transnational regulation favour the creation of networks and/or influence their functioning? When 'regulatory' networks implementing private standards are set up, how do they influence the inter-firm relationships along global supply chains?

In this Chapter, the focus is not on the design of standards but rather on the use of networks for regulatory implementation. Given that quality and or safety regulation involves all or at least many participants to the supply chain, effective implementation would require a network structure rather than a sequence of bilateral contracts. Not only the multiplicity of actors but also the interdependence of their actions to prevent or mitigate risks suggest that network form may perform better than bilateral contracts. The notion of interdependence does not merely refer to the link among connected exchange contracts along the chain.[37] Rather, it relates to compliance by multiple actors along the chain of safety obligations concerning the process and the characteristics of the final product. In this perspective interdependence stands at the core of emerging modes of regulation, which are more and more focused on processes and establishment of control points along the production chain. Interdependence calls for a cooperative approach in identifying hazards and providing effective responses. This specific need for joint problem solving and for coordinating standard implementation represents an additional driver for the formation of networks along the supply chain.[38]

The concept of network is a complex one that may be examined according to several perspectives.[39] Within this Chapter we mainly refer to networks aimed at facilitating the implementation of standards along the chain. Like other types of networks, these tend to promote synergies and govern complementarities among critical resources and capabilities (for example skills related with risk management at different stages of the production chain)[40]; they reduce inefficiencies linked to specific investments related risks of opportunistic behaviour (for example in the adoption of a new information technology enabling traceability along

[37] However, this reference is relevant in contract theory and legislation. For an examination in the perspective of French law as regards the legislation on 'ensemble contractuel', see C. Aubert de Vincelles, 'Linked Contracts under French Law' in F. Cafaggi (ed) *Contractual Networks, Inter-firm Cooperation, and Economic Growth* (Cheltenham: Edward Elgar Publishing, 2011) 163ff, 168ff.

[38] This effect is already prompted by relevant changes in market relations between suppliers, manufacturers, traders, retailers, as shown in the recent analysis of H. Collins, 'The Weakest Link: Legal Implications of the Network Architecture of Supply Chains' in Amstutz and Teubner, n 40, 193ff, observing changes in the mechanisms of purchasing decisions, marketing decisions, information disclosure along the value chain, joint design, and the use of software as a tools for determining and coordinating choices within contractual relations.

[39] The issue has also been recently revisited by G. Teubner, '*Coincidentia Oppositorum*: Hybrid Networks Beyond Contract and Organisation' in M. Amstutz and G. Teubner (eds) *Networks. Legal Issues of Multilateral Cooperation* (Portland: Hart Publishing, 2009) 3ff, starting from the contribution of R. M. Buxbaum, 'Is Network a Legal Concept?' (1993) 149 *Journal of Institutional and Theoretical Economics* 698–705. Within the present Chapter, by inter-firm networks, we mean all those collaborative structures that enterprises establish, either through contracts or organizations, in order to realize common interest projects and to coordinate interdependent activities or interdependent modes of using resources (often complementary resources, innovative knowledge, or intangibles in general). This definition is intended to show the intrinsic inter-disciplinary essence of the concept of a network, as influenced in recent decades by economic and sociological studies more than legal ones. Though in different perspectives reference should be made to O. E. Williamson, *The Mechanisms of Governance* (Oxford: Oxford University Press, 1996) 93ff; C. Ménard, 'The Economics of Hybrid Organizations' (2004) 160 *Journal of Institutional and Theoretical Economics* 345–76; A. Grandori, *Interfirm Networks: Organizations and Industrial Competitiveness* (London: Routledge, 1999). In the field of sociological studies, see W. W. Powell, 'Neither Market Nor Hierarchy: Network Forms of Organizations'(1990) 12 *Research in Organizational Behavior* 295–336; S. Helper, J.P. MacDuffie, and C. F. Sabel, 'Pragmatic Collaborations: Advancing Knowledge While Controlling Opportunism' (2000) 9 *Industrial and Corporate Change* 443–88. Combining the sociological approach with the legal one, see Teubner, 3–30. In the recent legal debate, see G. S. Geis, 'Business Outsourcing And The Agency Cost Problem' (2007) 82 *Notre Dame Law Review* 101–46; F. Cafaggi (ed) *Contractual Networks, Inter-firm Cooperation, and Economic Growth* (Cheltenham: Edward Elgar Publishing, 2011); S. Grundmann, 'The Contractual Basis of Long-Term Organisation—The Overall Architecture' (forthcoming).

[40] Powell, n 40.

the chain)[41]; they enhance collaborative practices, co-determination, mutual learning, internal monitoring (for example in implementing a product recall).[42] As we see later, the monitoring function of networks may be crucial for standard compliance when the actions of chain's participants are interdependent.

High degree of interdependence along the chain cannot be effectively managed by bilateral contracts in fragmented supply chains. Interdependence has to be governed in a setting which often includes a combination of cooperative and competitive relationships among multiple actors.[43] This peculiar mix between competition and cooperation might assume different features and intensity depending on the type of network. We will distinguish accordingly between contractual and organizational networks and vertical and horizontal networks.

In previous contributions, we have shown how the choice between contractual and organizational structures can affect the functioning of inter-firm networks in terms of power allocation and collaborative practices.[44] The former are governed either through a multilateral contract (for example a contractual joint venture or a multilateral framework contract as a source of technical standards) or a set of linked bilateral contracts (for example subcontracting networks, franchising, cross licensing, etc).[45] The latter are established through the creation of a new entity, normally a corporation or an interest group.[46] As shown in Figure 11.1, the organizational network does not imply full ownership integration but rather the creation of a new company, where several firms along the supply chain organize the production process maintaining their individual legal independence. Each firm will continue to produce individually but the coordination is ensured by organizational law rather than contracting.

As will be demonstrated later, with reference to networks directed to manage standard implementation, contractual networks show higher flexibility and the ability to tailor bilateral relations to specific circumstances and characteristics as they arise at any single point in the supply chain. On the other hand, homogeneity and convergence among different bilateral relations may be more costly to attain; the role of a leader enterprise, if any, is crucial here as is her/his ability to exercise authority. Unlike what could be expected following institutional economics,

[41] See O. E. Williamson, *The Economic Institutions of Capitalism* (New York: Free Press, 1985); Williamson, n 34, 93ff; L. Zingales, 'In search of New Foundations' (2000) 55 *Journal of Finance* 1623–53; Grundmann, n 40.

[42] Helper, MacDuffie, and Sabel, n 40; G. S. Geis, 'The Space Between Markets and Hierarchies' (2009) 95 *Virginia Law Review* 99; Collins, n 39, 187, 199.

[43] Teubner, n 40, 25ff.

[44] See F. Cafaggi and P. Iamiceli, *Reti di Imprese tra Crescita e Innovazione Organizzativa. Riflessioni da una Ricerca sul Campo* (Bologna: Il Mulino, 2007).

[45] See F. Cafaggi, 'Contractual Networks and the Small Business Act: Towards European principles?' (2008) 4 *European Review of Contract Law* 493–539. On contractual networks based on the link among bilateral contractual relations see also R. Brownsword, 'Network Contracts Revisited' in Amstutz and Teubner, n 40, 31ff, 33; Teubner, n 40, 31: 'The reference of one contract to another entails the inclusive acceptance by the contractual partners of a foreign private order'. With specific reference to production and distribution chains, see S. Grundmann, n 40, 111–62.

[46] See Council Regulation (EEC) No 2137/85 of 25 July 1985 on the European Economic Interest Grouping.

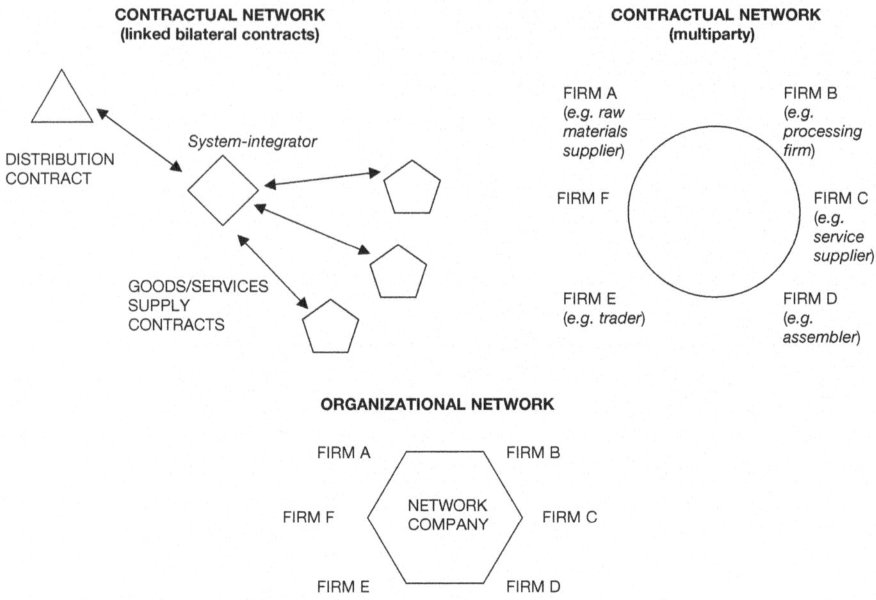

Figure 11.1 Contractual and Organizational Networks

empirical research shows that organizations are often used when power is and has to be evenly distributed or is consensually delegated to designated bodies, whereas bilateral sequential contracting is used when power is unevenly distributed.

Multilateral contract networks and sometimes organizational networks tend to distribute decision-making power more evenly and to allow decision-making practices based on consensus, majoritarian view, or delegation of power depending on the legal form.[47] In organizational networks and especially in 'incorporated' forms, segregation of assets as well as more sophisticated agency mechanisms allow the network to deal with third parties at lower transaction costs and to separate financial risk from the entrepreneurial risk of single participants.[48]

A second important distinction, addressed in Figure 11.2, is the one between horizontal and vertical networks. Vertical networks, as created among enterprises that play a different role along the chain (for example farmers, manufacturers, certifiers, retailers) normally face a lower threat in terms of internal competition, as compared with horizontal networks (for example as among retailers), where participants are definitively competitors.[49] In practice, vertical networks are mainly contractual and

[47] F. Cafaggi, 'Contractual Networks and Contract Theory: a Research Agenda for European Contract Law' in F. Cafaggi (ed) *Contractual Networks, Inter-firm Cooperation, and Economic Growth* (Cheltenham: Edward Elgar Publishing, 2011) 66ff, 100ff.

[48] See H. Hansmann and R. Kraakman, 'The Essential Role of Organization Law' (2000) 110 *Yale Law Journal* 387–440; E. M. Iacobucci and G. G. Triantis, 'Economic And Legal Boundaries Of Firms' (2007) 93 *Virginia Law Review* 515–70.

[49] Cafaggi, n 48.

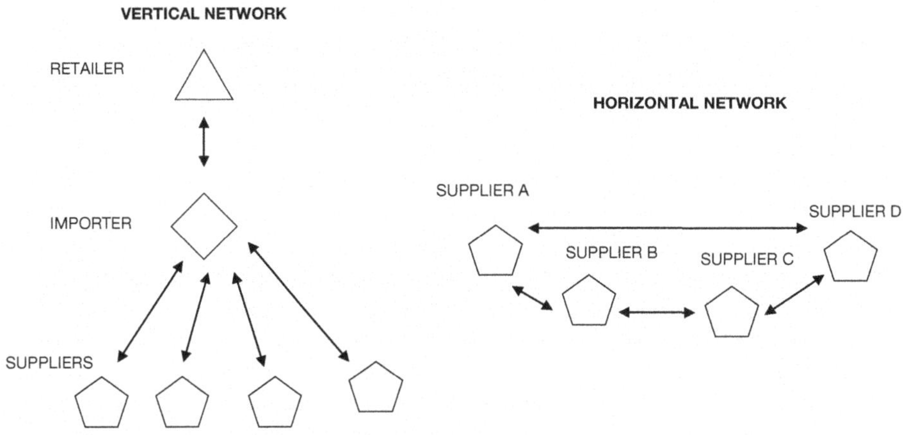

Figure 11.2 Vertical and Horizontal Networks

based on bilateral linked contracts, while horizontal networks tend to be organizational or based on a multilateral contract.[50]

We submit that the increasing regulatory function concerning standard's implementation with global chains may be effectively achieved through contractual networks whose shape will vary depending on the regulatory strategy that parties want to adopt to monitor compliance.

In this Chapter, we want to show that both private and public regulation stimulate the creation of new networks or deploy current networks to implement regulatory standards. With special reference to private regulation, we will focus on compliance monitoring and certification systems. Within this area we will examine whether networks within supply chains play any role in complementing the monitoring function of certifiers or other players in the regulatory scheme. Hence the remaining part of this Chapter concerns how new regulatory standards influence the choice of contractual governance and in particular promote the creation of contractual networks within chains complementing or implementing certification schemes.

More particularly the observation of concrete cases will enable to verify *the hypothesis for which the need for hierarchical monitoring leads to the formation of vertical networks, mainly based on linked bilateral contracts, while organizational networks combine cooperative methods and hierarchy and often play a more complex role, aimed not only at monitoring compliance but also at providing instrumental services (including technical assistance and training) and sometimes enforcing the standards through an internal sanctioning system* (see Section VI).

[50] F. Cafaggi and P. Iamiceli, 'Interfirm Networks in the Wine European Industry' (2010) EUI Working Paper No 2010/19 (available at <http://cadmus.eui.eu/bitstream/handle/1814/15654/LAW_2010_19_rev.pdf?sequence=5>).

VI. The Role of Networks in Standards Compliance: The Case of Third Party Certification

When supply chains have to implement transnational regulatory standards they use primarily contractual governance. Within the wide array of contractual instruments networks provide collaborative tools that may warrant effective cooperation across jurisdictional boundaries. The architecture of these networks will depend, among other factors, on the regulatory choice concerning monitoring compliance with safety, social, or environmental obligations.

In particular differences are related to the alternative between first-, second- and third-party monitoring[51], the use of certification schemes and the impact on the use of networks and the choice of network forms. Certifiers may help enabling this cooperation signalling the existence of risks or spotting mistakes that can be corrected through cooperative practices.[52]

They may trigger learning processes in which certified firms become gradually capable to comply with additional standards that are not mandatory in a former stage.[53]

We shall focus on third party certification schemes as monitoring devices and investigate their effects on the structure of regulatory networks partaken by final producers and/or suppliers.

More particularly, we will focus on regulatory networks that are either established or practically oriented to manage compliance mechanisms with transnational standards (mainly private standards) related to safety and environmental protection. In this context, two types of monitoring are compared: *peer monitoring*, where enterprises participating to the network (the nodes) are expected to monitor each other in order to protect the network's interest to comply with

[51] Conventionally, a distinction is made between first party certification (as provided by suppliers), second-party certification (as provided by paid technicians employed by retailers) and third-party certification (TPC) (as provided by independent certifiers, the cost of which is normally borne by the supplier). Gereffi, Garcia-Johnson, and Sasser, n 18, 56ff; F. Ciliberti, G. de Groot, J. de Haan, and P. P. 'Pontrandolfo, Codes to Coordinate Supply Chains: SMEs' Experiences with SA8000' (2009) 14 *Supply Chain Management: An International Journal* 117–27, 119; Joint FAO/Who Food Standards Programme, n 23, 1, 7; Hatanaka, Bain, and Busch, n 37, 354, 357.

[52] On this perspective of analysis, see Cafaggi, n 22 and Cafaggi and Iamiceli, n 10.

[53] See, e.g., the UTZ Core Code of Conduct Version 1.0 for Group and Multi-group Certification (2014) (available at <http://www.utzcertified-trainingcenter.com/home/images/stories/library_files/EN_UTZ_Core_Code_for_Individual_Certification_2014.pdf>). The Core Code includes four blocks of control points, concerning: management, farming practices, working conditions, and environment. Two types of control points are provided: mandatory control points and additional control points, subject to the express choice by the certified entity. A certification period of 4 years is foreseen, during which some control points become mandatory only at the second, third, or fourth year. The latest edition of the UTZ scheme, issued in 2014, comprises this Core Code of Conduct, which is applicable to all UTZ certified commodities, and modules that contain specific requirements for each commodity. This structure supersedes the former commodity-based approach, in which all relevant standards and control points were established separately for coffee, tea, rooibos, and cocoa. It also opens to the possibility to extend the scheme to other commodities in the near future.

standards; *hierarchical monitoring*, where control is ensured through a single authority and power is asymmetrically allocated between the monitor and monitored. Although in principle both contractual and organizational networks may perform each type of monitoring function, we shall examine whether there is any correlation between forms of monitoring and forms of networks.

The view suggesting that hierarchical settings different from networks tend to provide for monitoring and detecting breaches along the chain, while networks which primarily ensure flows of coordinated information reject hierarchy in favour of an 'acephalous or heterarchical' form of inter-firm collaboration is not supported by the analysis provided in this Chapter.[54] In fact, evidence shows that both hierarchical and peer monitoring may emerge within networks as built along the supply chains. Moreover, compliance with standard implementation requires both inspection practices and prompt information flows along the chain, well beyond the conventional setting of bilateral exchange contracts.[55] Information flows play a major role to enable effective correction in order to prevent rather than compensate the economic consequences of violation of regulatory provisions. Correction and adaptation of economic behaviour leading to non-compliance may call for cooperation by several actors along the chain, sometimes irrespective of the existence of a contractual relation under which they exchange goods or service for a price. Failure to detect hazard at an early stage of the production process may impose additional tasks to downstream suppliers both to identify and remove the hazard or mitigate the consequences stemming from its emergence.

Regulatory networks may complement the role of certifiers in several ways, for example by (i) providing technical services aimed at enhancing producers' capability to deal with risk management and regulatory compliance; and (ii) ensuring enforcement of standards through the administration of measures and sanctions reacting to violation by network participants. Both these functions are very relevant to favouring producers' access to global supply chains.

High certification costs may prompt group certification in order to share the economic burdens among the group participants. Group certification is managed through a joint control system administered by a leader enterprise or, more often, an organization, e.g. a cooperative, composed by the group participants. The emergence of the network form is thus linked to both efficiency (cheaper and more effective) and distributional (fair allocation of monitoring costs) drivers. Coordination among parties reduces transaction costs related to inspection and audits. In addition, if one enterprise along the chain is non-compliant, it can influence the ability of the final producer to earn certification. Corrective measures have to be taken on behalf of the whole chain and the producer group may combine *cooperative methods* in providing technical assistance and enacting

[54] For this correlation see Collins, n 39, 187, 200, and 203 (about a comparison between retailers' driven networks and franchise networks).

[55] On the network dimension of inspection rights as well as of information duties in contractual networks see also Grundmann, n 40, 111, 149ff, who tends to apply restrictively the former and extensively the latter.

action plans due to correct mistakes, with a more *hierarchical role* in monitoring and sanctioning violations of standards. Network certification can reduce and redistribute the costs and make certification available for small enterprises that want to access international markets and would not be able to do it individually.

In order to show these dynamics, we consider examples from food and non-food sectors; within the latter textile has been chosen where private standards and Third Party Certification (TPC) have grown significantly in recent years.[56] Illustrations are conceived as providing hints for analysis without necessarily being representative of widely diffused practices. More structured and extended empirical research would be necessary to add material evidence and a strong foundation to our hypothesis.

Three cases are selected in order to compare the main governance options. In all of them certification is provided through a third-party certification scheme aimed at ensuring compliance along the (whole) chain by means of monitoring and sanctioning powers assigned to certifiers and, possibly, regulators. Regulatory networks formed among chain participants (suppliers, final producers, sometimes retailers) may complement the role of certifiers and standard-setters in ensuring compliance. The cases differ with respect to:

- (having regard to the regulatory scheme) the *relation between regulator and TPC, in particular the level of independence between the standard-setter and the monitor*. When the former is an institution whose membership is not composed by producers and retailers (for example an independent research institution), then third-party monitoring and sanctioning may be assigned to the regulator itself (Case I); when the regulator is also composed of producers and retailers, then the TPC scheme is run by a separate group of certifiers who may cooperate with the regulator in monitoring and sanctioning, provided that the certifiers' independence in ensured (Cases II and III);
- (having regard to the structure of the supply chain and the role of regulatory networks in ensuring compliance) the *type of monitoring*, taking place within the supply chain and complementing the monitoring function provided by certifiers and, possibly, standard-setter; from this perspective, in order to examine the correlation between regulatory/monitoring strategies and the form of networks, we distinguish between:
  - *peer monitoring*, mainly enacted by each chain participant by conveying to the certifier appropriate information on chain participants and their compliance with given standards (Case I and, combined with other mechanisms, Cases II and III);
  - *hierarchical monitoring* as enacted by a chain leader (for example the final producer) or a producer group, who is responsible, vis-à-vis the certifier and regulator, for chain participants' compliance (Cases II and III); this type of monitoring may be coupled with the use of cooperative methods

[56] See Marx, n 24, 596ff.

of compliance capacity building through technical assistance and management of action plans (Case III);

- (having regard to the role of networks in the enforcement of standards through sanctions) the *type of sanctioning powers* possibly assigned to players different from certifiers and regulator: whereas, in Cases II and III, chain leaders may resort to contractual remedies (such as requesting specific performance or threatening termination of contractual relation), more specific sanctioning powers may be observed in Case III, when a producer group is at stake.

By providing a brief description of each case, the analysis that follows will show how different types of networks may help supporting the just described functions in terms of regulation, monitoring and sanctioning.

Some comparative remarks on the three Cases will be presented in Section VI(4).

1. Integration between standard-setting and monitoring as delegated to independent actors. Case I: the *Oeko-Tex* case

The first case relates to the textile sector. It is a case of private regulation where both standard-setting and compliance assurance are performed by an international body composed of specialized research and test institutions (neither producer-, nor retailer-based).[57] Indeed, the private standard scheme is elaborated by textile research and test institutes in Europe and Japan and implemented by the same association through its member institutes.[58]

The declared purpose of this scheme is to iron out the global differences relating to the assessment of harmful substances in the textile industry and to equally spread out the costs of standard implementation[59]. This goal is mainly attained through a multiplication of tests along the chain: tests are conducted whenever a textile product is processed further or a chemical change is made. Then every producer, who is in a position to materially alter the use of the chemicals or similar substances, has to undergo certification. As shown in Figure 11.3, certification includes the license to use the logo/label. The regulatory network takes the form

[57] For a full description, see the Oeko-Tex Association website (available at <https://www.oeko-tex.com/en/manufacturers/philosophy/why_oeko_tex/why_oeko_tex.html>): 'The Oeko-Tex® Standard 100 was introduced at the beginning of the 1990s as a response to the needs of the general public for textiles which posed no risk to health. "Poison in textiles" and other negative headlines were widespread at this time and indiscriminately branded all chemical across the board used in textile manufacturing as negative and dangerous to health.'

[58] For full details see the Oeko-Tex website (available at <http://www.oeko-tex.com/oekotex100_public/content5.asp?area=hauptmenue&site=gruendefuereinfuehrung&cls=0>).

[59] The concrete allocation of costs may generate some weaknesses as regards the incentive to cooperate. In fact, there might be an unbalanced relation between costs (which are connected with idiosyncratic factors related with the technical features of process and product as controlled by each applicant enterprise) and benefits of certification, which will not necessarily be spread along the chain following the same idiosyncratic factors and will possibly be concentrated in the last part of the value chain in favour of final producers and/or retailers.

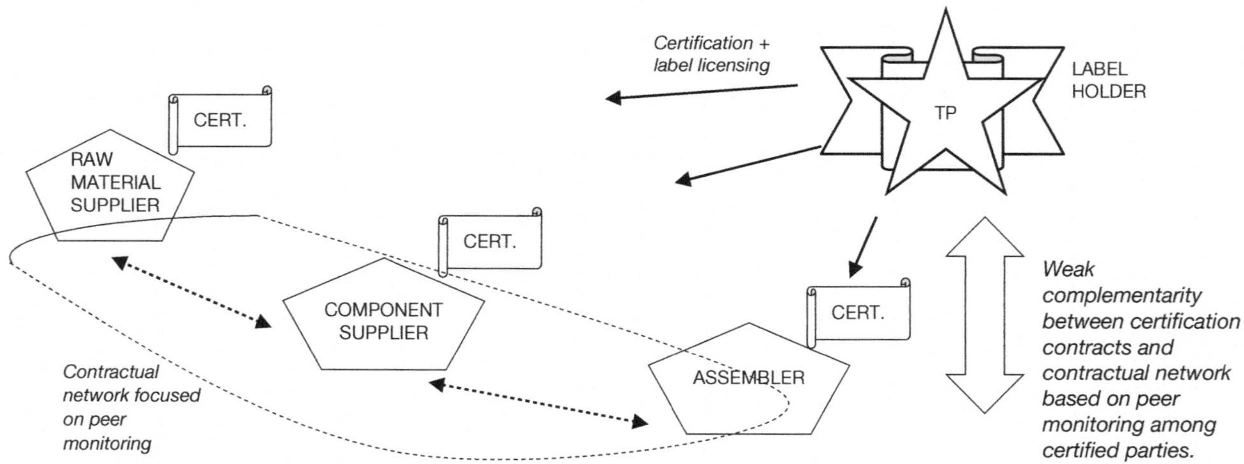

Figure in bold: coordination role; the degree of coordination is indicated by the thickness of the line (weak coordination model)

Figure 11.3 The Oeke-Tex Regulatory Network

of a contractual network involving all certified producers along the chain and the institution playing as both standard setter and certifier.

Comprehensive control separately involving each stage of the chain is possibly attained thanks to:

- the role of third party certifier, to whom enterprises have to disclose the list of suppliers so as to verify the continuity of tests along the chain;
- the pressure that each applicant places on his/her suppliers, requesting certification in order to benefit from the certification and the consequent label award; and
- a peer monitoring system among enterprises involved in this network: indeed, whoever, within the chain identifies irregularities among partners or competitors is requested to report to the relevant member institute (certifier). Whistleblowing within the certification scheme may be considered a form of monitoring among peers due to induce the adoption of appropriate measures by the competent authority (the certifier).

This is a case in which the integration between standard setting and certification within a single institution triggers concentration of regulatory functions played by this institution, whereas, at the level of the supply chain, the only visible impact consists in requesting peer monitoring among chain participants subject to certification;moreover, no specific measure is provided by the certification protocol to effectively ensure that such monitoring takes place. The network among producers does complement the function of the certification scheme, whereas, unlike in Cases II and III, no specific role is played by chain leaders to complement the monitoring function of standard-setter and certifier.

2. The partial separation between standard-setting and monitoring. Case II: the *Global Organic Textile* case

A second option has also been identified in the textile sector.[60] Here, standard-setter and certifiers are separate entities, because the standard-setter is an organization including representatives of the industry (subject to certification). In these circumstances the very nature of a TPC scheme, as based on certifier's independence from due-to-be certified producers, would request a separation between standard-setter and certifier. [61]

[60] Global Organic Textile Standard, version 3.0 (March 2011) (available at <http://www.global-standard.org/images/stories/gots-version3_01march2011.pdf>): '[T]he aim of the standard is to define world-wide recognised requirements that ensure organic status of textiles, from harvesting of the raw materials, through environmentally and socially responsible manufacturing up to labelling in order to provide a credible assurance to the end consumer.' Though the focus is on quality and environmental standards, safety is an important concern when toxitocity comes into question (e.g., among environmental criteria, the following is included: 'prohibition of critical inputs such as toxic heavy metals, formaldehyde, aromatic solvents, functional nano particles, genetically modified organisms [GMO] and their enzymes.').

[61] In this case, the holder of labelling rights on the logo (a registered trademark) that are (sub) licensed to certified enterprises is a limited liability company established by three industry

Indeed, in terms of regulatory strategy, there is a producer-based system (the main 'owners' being trade organizations) delegating standard-setting to an internal technical committee and compliance assurance to external players as accredited and independent certifiers. Unlike in Case I, producers directly or indirectly exercise control over the regulatory strategies.

While certifiers are independent from the standard-setter when exercising inspection and monitoring powers, they may cooperate with the standard-setter once defection is detected. Then, indeed, both standard-setters and certifiers can pursue legal remedies against unauthorized or misleading use. In this respect, special emphasis is given to corrective measures and to remedies that safeguard the scheme's credibility.[62] As we see later, this mix between standard-setter's and certifier's monitoring is then complemented with a more structured monitoring scheme along the supply chain: this is based not only on peer monitoring, like in Case I, but also on hierarchical monitoring, as explained later.

A second element of the regulatory scheme affecting the supply chain regards the the scope of application to the chain. Indeed, in this case all players acting along the supply chain must hold a valid conformity certificate (processors, manufacturers *and traders*).[63] More specifically, while retailers who receive and sell ready pre-packed and labelled products directly to end consumers are exempt from the certification requirement, traders (who buy and sell products to other retailers) are not.[64] This induces traders to actively take part in the implementation system, as they are charged with verifying the authenticity of certified products and ensuring

organizations in the world and one charity in the UK. Standards are elaborated by a technical committee composed of experts appointed by the members. Licenses are awarded to enterprises on the basis of certified compliance with standards. Certifiers are third parties as accredited under the rules of the standard-setter. See also GOTS, Licensing and Labelling Guide (June 2009) § 3.1 (available at <http://www.global-standard.org/images/stories/gots_licensing&labelling_guide-issue_02june09.pdf>): 'With the completion of GOTS certification by an *Approved Certifier* the *Certified Entity* acquires a sub-licence which entitles it to participate in the GOTS programme, including use of the standard and the GOTS logo on its respective GOTS Goods in accordance with the provisions of this labelling guide and as long as the certification remains valid.'

[62] See GOTS, n 63, § 5: 'The IWG [standard-setter] and/or the Approved Certifiers will pursue all legal remedies for any unauthorised or misleading use of the GOTS logo on product declarations, in advertisements, catalogues or other contexts, including actions such as corrective and/or legal action and/or publication of the transgression so as to safeguard credibility of the GOTS identification.'

[63] See Global Organic Textile Standards, n 62, § 1: '[T]his standard covers the processing, manufacturing, packaging, labelling, trading and distribution of all textiles made from at least 70% certified organic natural fibres... Processors, manufacturers and traders that have demonstrated their ability to comply with the relevant GOTS criteria in the corresponding certification procedure to an Approved Certifier receive a GOTS conformity certificate (= operational certificate, scope certificate) that lists the certified products (and the production stages) that are in compliance with this standard.'

[64] See Global Organic Textile Standards, n 62, § 4.1 and Annex (A) for the definition of 'Trader' as 'Entity trading with (= buying and selling) GOTS Goods in the supply chain between the producer of the fibre and the retail merchant of the final product regardless whether the goods are physically received or not (e.g. an import, export or wholesale trading entity). Agents that do not become proprietor of the goods and retailers only selling to the end consumer are not considered as traders.' See also C. Coglianese, A. M. Finkel, and D. Zaring (eds) *Import Safety, Regulatory Governance in the Global Economy* (Philadelphia: University of Pennsylvania Press, 2009).

integrity of goods. This also contributes to spread compliance costs along the distribution chain discouraging inefficient forms of chain fragmentation where new intermediaries cannot effectively contribute to higher safety and control.[65]

The application of the certification requirements to the down part of the chain favours the assignment of a monitoring function to the chain leader, then creating the space for a form of hierarchical monitoring within the supply chain. Indeed, in this case, the entity under whose name or brand the certified goods are sold to end consumers is responsible for *exercising due care* in ensuring product compliance with the requested standards,[66] meaning that, at least indirectly, this entity is induced by the liability regime to exercise monitoring power along the chain. As shown in Figure 11.4, a contractual vertical network is formed, including all suppliers possibly affecting on the integrity of the product and contributing to compliance with standards; this network assumes a specific role in monitoring through hierarchy.

Compared with Case II, Case III shows a different type of network in which coordination in compliance is attained through an organizational structure, playing a more complex role, including not only monitoring but also providing technical assistance and taking measures to correct or to sanction violations of standards.

3. The group certification model. Case III: the case of GlobalG.A.P.

The third example concerns the food safety standard area and in particular the implementation mechanism designed under the GlobalG.A.P. (EurepGap), a private sector body setting voluntary standards for the certification of the production processes of agricultural produce around the world. This initiative was initially promoted by major retailers and is still strongly influenced by them, though producers now participate as well.[67] Therefore, in terms of regulatory strategy, this case can be presented as a retail-based model, though open to a certain degree of multi-stake participation within the industry. Like in Case II, certification occurs through a separate network of accredited certifiers, in some instances cooperating with the standard-setting while playing their monitoring function. Also like Case II, the monitoring functions played by standard-setter and certifiers

[65] Exemptions or exceptions are foreseen for a) small-scale subcontractors with a low risk potential and b) traders with less than 5000 euro annual turnover with certified goods, provided that they do not re-pack and/or re-label goods. This occurs provided that these suppliers have a contract with a certified entity (that is responsible for their compliance with the standard) and are clearly identified so that they may be subject to inspection by certifiers. Further requirements include that they are anyway registered with a certifier and full information is granted in case of excess of the 5000 euro threshold: see Global Organic Textile Standards, n 62, § 4.1.

[66] See Global Organic Textile Standards, n 62, § 4.1.

[67] Henson and Humphrey, n 23, 1, 22. On the current structure of the organization see the GLOBALG.A.P. (EUREPGAP) website (available at <http://www.globalgap.org/uk_en/who-we-are/governance/>).

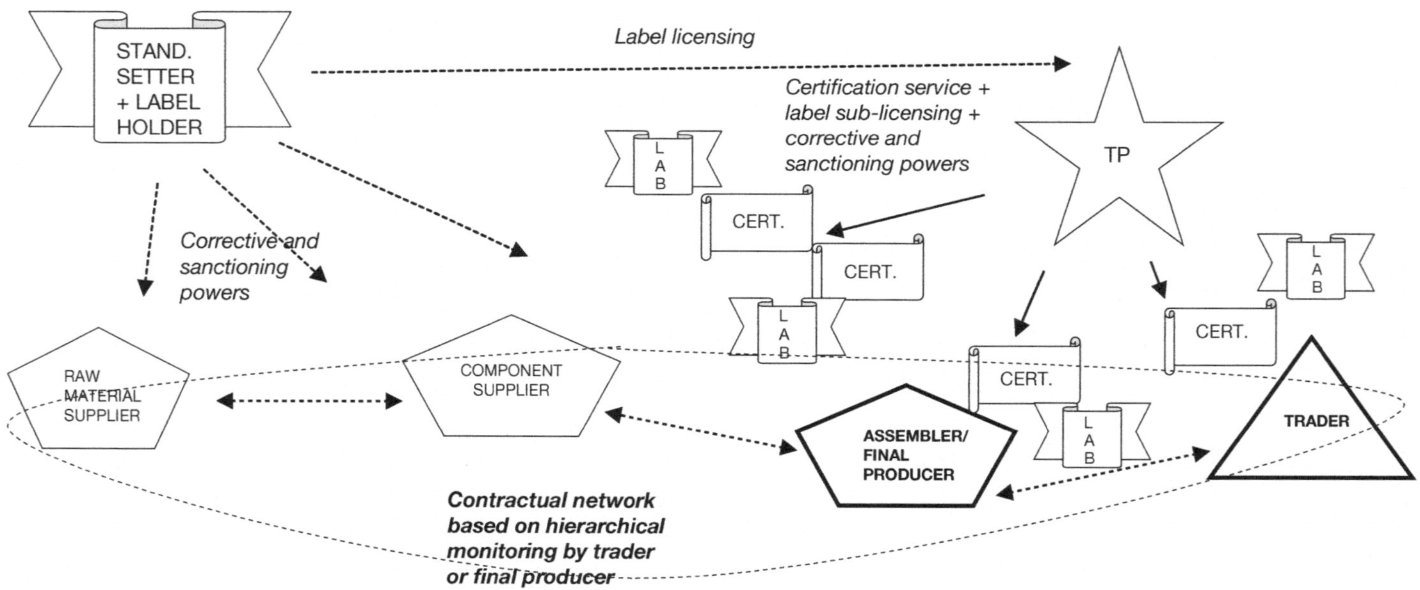

Figure(s) in bold: coordination role; the degree of coordination is indicated by the thickness of the line (stronger coordination model, if compared with model I)

Figure 11.4 The Global Organic Textile Regulatory Network

are then coupled with a complementary monitoring scheme enacted within the production chain via regulatory networks composed by producers and their suppliers. However, unlike in Case II, we here observe a mix of vertical contractual networks and horizontal organizational networks. Not only the form of these latter networks is different, but their function is wider, including the provision of technical services (that are instrumental to compliance with standards) and the exercise of sanctioning powers.

Indeed, compliance with standards along the chain is implemented through two different mechanisms that may be combined or alternatively used: one in which certification is awarded to individual applicants, and one in which certification is awarded to producer groups.[68] Individual certification follows the general structure described in Case II, triggering the formation of vertical contractual networks based on hierarchical control by the chain leader.[69] Group certification triggers the formation of horizontal organizational networks.

In the case of group certification, the certification is assigned to a producer group which proves capable of running a quality management system for all the group's participants. Typically, this would be a cooperative company where many producers, each an independent legal entity, join the cooperative.

The producers' participants are then subject to the same type of internal control, so that they cannot sell their product outside the group. Indeed, the collective audit and certification system oblige participants to sell their produce certified under the group option exclusively through the group.[70] The consolidation of the quality management system not only reduces costs, but also enhances the efficiency and effectiveness of the audit by favouring an exchange of information, mutual learning, and diffusion of best practices.

In order to enact such a system, the group must dispose of a specific organizational structure. Indeed, it must be an entity, legally separate from its own members. The legal 'incorporation' of the group enables the organization to act on behalf of its members and to administer a sanctioning system that reinforces the effectiveness of the implementation mechanism.[71]

[68] On this option, see also Henson and Humphrey, n 23, 1, 30.

[69] In the case of individual certification the applicant producer must ensure (by providing correspondent documentation) that any subcontractor is either (a) certified by a third party certification body or (b) assessed by the producer as compliant in accordance with the same criteria. See GLOBALG.A.P. (EUREPGAP), Control Point and Compliance Criteria in Section AF 4 (available at <http://www.globalgap.org/export/sites/default/.content/.galleries/documents/130315_gg_ifa_cpcc_af_cb_fv_v4_0-2_en.pdf>). This combination between being subject to third party verification and active monitoring of its own production cycle emphasizes the interdependence and coordination of compliance modes along the chain, favouring mutual learning and risk prevention. According to this model, the producer becomes liable for the chain and has to monitor the different tiers to ensure compliance. This type of liability, even if not necessarily combined with legal liability, very likely triggers the creation of a network, led by the producer, to monitor compliance. This scheme is similar to the one observed under Case II.

[70] GlobalG.A.P., General Regulations, Part II (March 2013) § 1.1.2.1.

[71] GlobalG.A.P., General Regulations: Part I, General Rules (March 2013) §§ 3.2 and 5.2 (available at <http://www.globalgap.org/export/sites/default/.content/.galleries/documents/130315_gg_gr_part_i_v4_0-2_en.pdf>).

Members are allowed to leave the group and register with another group provided that they have respected the rules laid down by the group and no sanction process is pending against them.[72]

The organizational structure here, however, is not the only governance device deployed. Indeed, this is an organizational network complemented by a contractual scheme.

First, as applicant and then certificate holder, the group is contractually liable vis-à-vis the standard-setter.[73] Secondly, the label license contract is conditional upon certification as provided under the certification service contract with an accredited certifier.[74] Thirdly, each member signs a contract with the group agreeing to comply with G.A.P. standards and to be subject to audits and the sanctioning power of the group.[75] Fourthly, each member must include in any service level agreement or contract with any subcontractor clauses obliging this subcontractor to comply with G.A.P. standards.[76] This compliance may be assessed either by the group's participant outsourcing the service or by an accredited TPC (whose report must be received by the group as well).[77] Thus, the certification applies to the producer groups and also captures the whole chain by requiring monitoring commitment of single participants to monitor its own sub-chain. This means that, although often in practice the producers' group can be seen as a horizontal sub-network (for example among strawberry producers), because of the required compliance with certain standards, this sub-network can assume a vertical dimension involving the upper part of the value chain.

The producer group has sanctioning power which has to be specified in the individual contracts with the scheme participants.[78] In case of non-compliance, corrective measures have to be taken by the non-compliant party. Responsibility for implementing and resolving corrective actions should be defined in the contracts.[79] If non-compliance persists, an escalating system based on warning, suspension, and cancellation will have to be contractually defined.[80] A similar sanction scheme is applied by the certifier to the group. As with the Case II, the standard-setter may also exercise some sanctioning power without referring to the certifier.[81]

[72] GlobalG.A.P., n 73, § 4.4.2.

[73] GlobalG.A.P., General Regulations: Part II, Rules for Option 1 and Option 2 Multisites with QMS (March 2013) § 1.1.1 (available at <http://www.globalgap.org/export/sites/default/.content/.galleries/documents/130315_gg_gr_part_ii_v4_0-2_en.pdf>): 'The legal entity will enter into a contractual relationship with GLOBALGAP (EUREPGAP) through the signature of the GLOBALGAP (EUREPGAP) Sub-Licence and Certification Agreement with a GLOBALGAP (EUREPGAP) approved CB, and becomes the sole holder of the GLOBALGAP (EUREPGAP) certificate.'

[74] GlobalG.A.P., n 75, § 1.1.1.

[75] GlobalG.A.P., n 75, § 1.1.2.1.

[76] GlobalG.A.P., n 75, § 1.10: 'Procedures shall exist to ensure that any services subcontracted to third parties are carried out in accordance with the requirements of GlobalGAP standard.'

[77] See GLOBALG.A.P. (EUREPGAP), n 71.

[78] GlobalG.A.P., General Regulations, Part II (March 2013) § 1.1.2.1.

[79] GlobalG.A.P., General Regulations, Part II (March 2013) § 1.1.2.1.

[80] See GlobalG.A.P., n 73, § 6.4 and GlobalG.A.P., n 75, § 1.7.

[81] See GLOBALG.A.P., Sublicense & Certification Agreement, Version 1.2, § 10 (available at <http://www1.globalgap.org/north-america/upload/CBs/130111_GGNA_CB_Sublicense_and_Certification_Agreement_v1.2.pdf>): 'In the event of the CP's willful or negligent infringement of the obligations under the GLOBALG.A.P. System, in particular obligations that CP has contractually undertaken, GLOBALG.A.P. NA is entitled to enforce the measures described in the List of Sanctions within the General Regulations in its latest version.'

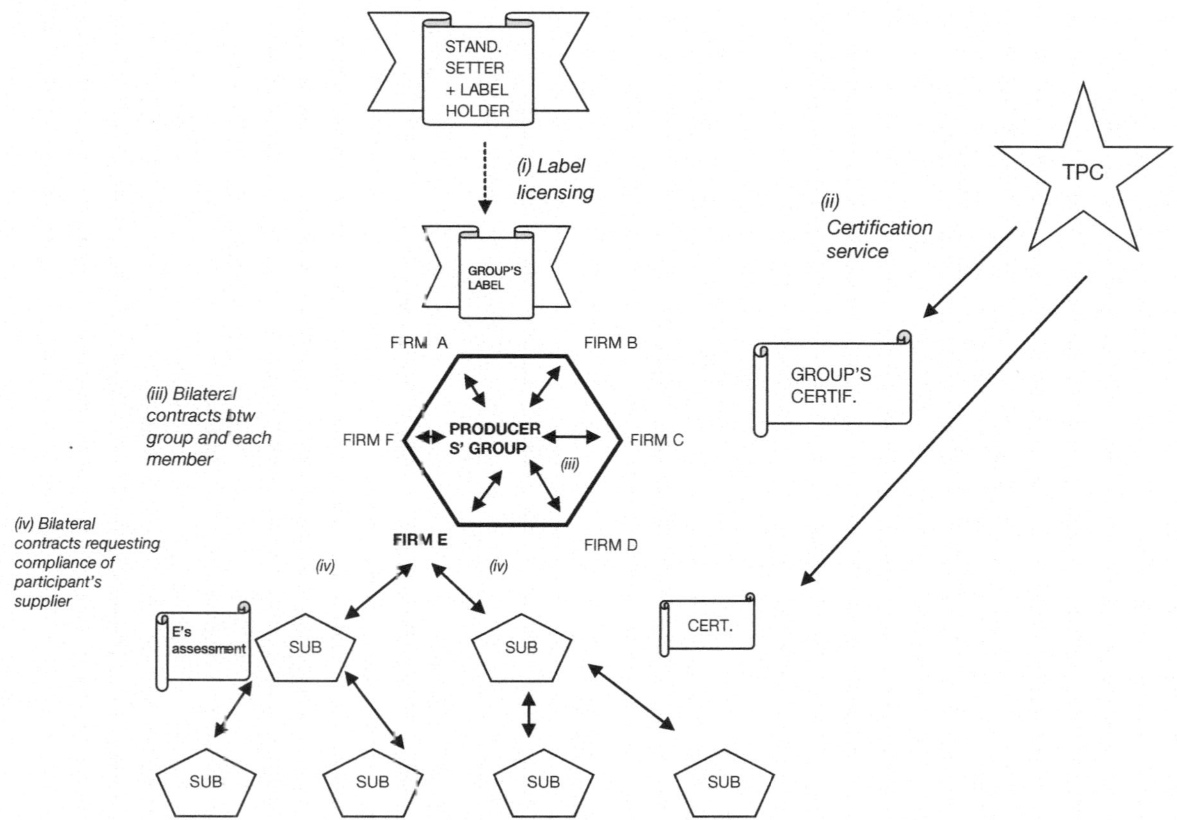

Figure 11.5 The Global G.A.P. Regulatory Network

Figure 11.5 provides an example in which a complex mix between contracts and organization offers a 'chain design' of compliance. The costs of risk assessment, management, and communication are collectively borne within the group, reduced by economies of scale and optimized in terms of efficiency. Flexibility is maintained through the use of contracts, both inside and outside the organizational network, enabling the group to share the coordination role with individual participants who are able and willing to govern compliance along 'their own' chain.

Thus, the combination between organizational and contractual devices within the same network enhances its efficiency and effectiveness: the organization process reinforces the possibility of harmonizing the enforcement system and spreading the costs of a professionalized internal audit scheme, while the contracts allow an adequate level of flexibility, as requests can be made to adapt the common management system to a number of different settings.

Here, a regulatory scheme driven by retailers (also open to the participation of producers) has generated a model of network coordinating compliance with high ability to govern interdependence and foster cooperation along the chain and a high degree of responsibility placed on producers if adequately organized.

When is this network likely to arise? Probably where a certain number of producers share similar needs in terms of risk analysis and are simultaneously able to take significant advantage from cooperation and competition.

4. Comparing the three cases

The examination of third party certification schemes sheds some light on the impact of private regulation on the contractual governance of the supply chain. A 'network response' to the need for effective compliance along the whole processing and, sometimes, distribution chain can be observed. Different types of networks emerge depending on the model of standard regulation and the adopted third-party certification scheme.

In developing this analysis particular attention has been paid to (1) the relation between standard-setting and different modes of monitoring (by the standard-setter and/or certifiers) and (2) the extent to which standards and compliance mechanisms are applicable along the value chain or in more restricted segments of it.

Under the former perspective, different schemes of third party certification have been compared depending on the involvement of producers and retailers in the standard setting: the lower this involvement (being the standards set by independent actors, for example, research institutions[82]) the more integrated may be standard setting and monitoring functions without infringing the independence requirement for TPC schemes.[83] The observation of Case I would suggest that such

[82] In this respect, the analysis partially builds on the conventional distinction between state-driven, company-driven, and NGO-driven standards, as elaborated in K. Abbot and D. Snidal, 'Strengthening International Regulation through Transnational New Governance: Overcoming the Orchestration Deficit' (2009) 42 *Vanderbilt Journal of Transnational Law* 501ff.

[83] This independence is intended as independence from enterprises acting along the value chain, namely producers, traders, and retailers: see Hatanaka, Bain, and Busch, n 37; Gereffi,

a concentration of the monitoring functions within the single regulatory institution is in fact coupled with a relatively dispersed monitoring scheme within the supply chain taking the form of mere peer monitoring. This case would suggest an hypothesis deserving further investigation, for which the higher the concentration of monitoring power within a single regulatory institution, the lower the delegation of monitoring powers to chain participants. This approach would lead to the formation of contractual networks along the chain based on mere peer monitoring without a clear definition of the consequences of peers' failure to comply with monitoring requirements. Formalization of networks introduces legal obligations to peer monitoring. If the duty to monitor among peers is not enforced in fact, then a collective action problem may arise and hinder the attainment of an adequate level of compliance. Sanctions of this duty are generally extralegal and the purpose is to clearly define the power of peers rather than their responsibility. The role of the standard-setter/certifier in ensuring compliance is more stringent in this case and the complementarity between certification scheme and contractual network partaken by certified producers is weaker than the one described for Cases II and III.

A different setting emerges when standard-setters are institutions in which producers and/or retailers directly or indirectly participate.[84] This is the case with the examples described under Cases II and III. Then the TPC scheme needs to ensure the certifiers' independence by introducing some level of separation between standard-setting and monitoring. The separation between standard-setting and certification induces the formation of a more complex scheme at the regulatory level, in which the certificate holder is responsible vis-à-vis both the standard-setter and the certifiers and is subject to sanctioning power by both institutions.

The comparison between Case I, on the one hand, and Cases II and III, on the other, also suggests that, when monitoring is articulated within a more complex structure (being certifiers separate from standard-setters), a more intense coordination of monitoring mechanisms within the supply chain may be needed. This may lead, within the supply chain, to a shift from mere peer monitoring to a more structured monitoring scheme in which some key actors along the supply chain bear liability for other actors' non-compliance or in which cooperation is triggered among several participants in order to prevent or correct irregular behaviours.

Different models of networks correspond to Cases II and III. Indeed, the structure of the network may depend on the scope of the regulatory scheme as regards the extent of the value chain due to be monitored. The need for ensuring compliance along several and interdependent segments of the supply chain may require the introduction of some level of hierarchy. As Case II suggests, hierarchical features may be assumed by contractual vertical networks assigning a monitoring function to a 'chain leader', who is then responsible for 'chain compliance' vis-à-vis both the standard-setter and the certifier. Comparatively,

Garcia-Johnson, and Sasser, n 18, 56, 58. See also Marx, n 24, 592, where a distinction between standard-setter and independent certifiers seems to be assumed in TPC.

[84] On the distinction between state-driven, company-driven, and NGO-driven standards, see n 84.

Table 11.1 The Main Comparative Elements

	Oeko-Tex	Global Organic Textile	GlobalG.A.P.
Monitoring			
regulatory level	Standard-setter = certifier (same institution)	Certifier (and standard-setter as separate institution)	Certifier (and standard-setter as separate institution)
production chain level	Peer monitoring [contractual network]	Hierarchical monitoring by chain leader [contractual network]	Producers group monitoring, combining cooperation and hierarchy [organizational network]
Sanctioning			
regulatory level	Standard-setter = certifier (same institution)	Certifier (and standard-setter as separate institution)	Certifier (and standard-setter as separate institution)
production chain level			Producers group
Technical assistance			Producers group (PG's quality management system)

Case III shows that monitoring over producers' compliance may be also ensured through organizational regulatory networks (for example producers groups in group certification) whenever certified enterprises share similar needs in terms of resources and capabilities requested by their participation in certification schemes. In these cases the regulatory network tends to combine hierarchical monitoring and sanctioning with cooperative practices focused on service provision and capability building.

Table 11.1 provides a summary of the main comparative elements observed through the analysis above.

VII. The Impact of Private Regulation and Certification Systems on Contractual Governance

The described combination of monitoring systems internal and external to the value chain helps shed light on the correlation between private regulation and contractual governance of the value chain. Indeed, private standards schemes influence not merely the formation of networks to enhance coordination about compliance by different actors along the chain; but by doing so, they also influence the modes of the 'value chain contractual governance'. Monitoring compliance with private standards by many participants requires the creation of a network that strengthens cooperation and maximizes coordination in detecting and mitigating risks of default.[85]

The incorporation of clauses and terms referring to regulatory standards, both public and private, changes the monitoring structure of the exchange contract which becomes embedded in a network framework. Contractual performance of the regulatory provision constitutes, at the same time, an obligation owed to the other contractual parties and a duty to implement the regulatory regime of which the party is a member.

Furthermore, external and independent actors (for example certifiers) help monitoring performance, improving the visibility of compliance.[86] In many cases, given the nature of the standards, tangible and intangible aspects of performance become observable (especially when safety standards are joined with social standards, concerning labour practices or similar).[87] Compliance with regulatory provisions can be subject to second party monitoring by the buyer, and/or third party monitoring by the certifier and the regulatory body, which has promoted/imposed compliance with the code of conduct.[88] Certifiers become new intermediaries playing a pivotal role in supply chain governance especially in group and chain of custody certification.[89]

As in other collaboration contracts, characterized by high interdependence among performances by different parties along the chain, information exchange, error detection practices, and performance adjustments play an important role within the contractual relation along the chain.[90] Benchmarking mechanisms become more and more common as a means to operationalize standard compliance.[91] Contractual governance hence includes new monitoring techniques coming from transnational private standards and certification schemes.

The resulting architecture influences the visibility of performance in commercial contracts, increasing monitoring costs but potentially decreasing the risk of default or at least mitigating its consequences. While the main focus is on regulatory compliance, clearly the overall contractual performance is subject to higher monitoring than the normal commercial contract.

[85] This approach is consistent with regulatory objectives within the safety domain. Public and private transnational safety regulation must respond to the emergence of hazards over time and take corrective measures when mistakes are made. Compliance is the combination of measures to define ex ante the hazard control system and to ensure its proper functioning over time. Coordinated responses along the chain have to be promptly offered and certification schemes have to ensure that the organizational structure of regulated firms is adequate to meet regulatory requirements. The goal is broader than abiding by the rules; the objective is to comply with regulatory objectives. See F. Cafaggi, 'A Comparative Analysis of Transnational Private Regulation: Legitimacy, Quality, Effectiveness, and Enforcement' (2014) available at <http://ssrn.com/abstract=2449223>).

[86] See Cafaggi, n 22.

[87] Ciliberti, de Groot, de Haan, and Pontrandolfo, n 52, 117, 118.

[88] For a broader discussion see Cafaggi n 22.

[89] See Cafaggi, Ferrari, Iamiceli, Sorsa, and Swensson, n 19.

[90] Geis, n 40; M. Blair, M. O'Hara, E. O'Connor, and G. Kirchhoefer, 'Outsourcing, Modularity, and the Theory of the Firm' (2011) *Brigham Young University Law Review* 263–314.

[91] WTO, n 24.

Moreover, effectiveness in reacting to standards' violation is more easily ensured than in ordinary commercial contracts.[92] Indeed, the TPC scheme tends to provide corrective measures more than compensatory ones; it tends to prioritize and rank measures with respect to type of violation to a larger extent if compared with conventional regimes for breach of contracts.[93]

Moving out of the logics of conventional theory on contractual breach and remedies, the subscription of regulatory and certification schemes obliges participants to monitor over risks' occurrence irrespective of their direct involvement in causing the risk. Fault and to a broader extent liability inquiries lose their key role. Parties have to be engaged in addressing defaults regardless of their degree of liability. If seen in the limited perspective of a single bilateral relation between buyer and seller, this approach leads to expand the role for duties to cure and duties to mitigate well beyond the boundaries commonly known by contractual liability. In other words, assuming that both buyer and seller are subject to the certification rules and a dispute arises on the consequences of goods non-conformity, the buyer will be confronted with a less disputable right to cure in favour of the seller and a more stringent duty to mitigate if he, rather than the seller, is in the best position to address the risk.[94]

If the TPC scheme expands along the chain, as seen in the examples earlier, similar cooperation duties are extended to subcontractors either because they are requested by their clients to get certified or because compliance with standards is imposed via contract when incorporating private regulation.[95] This incorporation often comes together with the supplier's duty to establish an ad hoc monitoring structure along the chain.[96]

Cooperation in risk assessment and risk management may even reach higher levels of enforcement when several chain participants take part in a common TPC

[92] For further evidence in the food sector, see F. Cafaggi and P. Iamiceli 'Remedies Against Breach' in Unidroit (2014) 'FAO, Legal Guide on Agricultural Production Contracts' (available at <www.unidroit.org>).

[93] More specifically on this comparative analysis see Cafaggi, n 22, and Cafaggi and Iamiceli, n 51.

[94] More specifically on this comparative analysis see Cafaggi, n 22, and Cafaggi and Iamiceli, n 51.

[95] In addition to the examples described in Section VI see, among other schemes, UTZ Certified Certification Protocol, version 3.0 (September 2012) para 2.1, specifying that the entity that is responsible for implementing and monitoring the requirements of the UTZ Certified Code of Conduct can be a group of producers (organized in an association or cooperative) or another entity (such as a processor or exporter) that buys the product from the producers and organizes contracts and/or trains the producers according to the UTZ Certified Code of Conduct. In this instance the internal control system is delegated by the certifier the task of making inspections and ensuring compliance (see para 5) (available at <http://www.utzcertified-trainingcenter.com/home/images/stories/library_files/EN+UTZ+Certification+Protocol+v3.0.pdf>).

[96] See, e.g., the Code of Business Conduct of Ferrero (available at <http://goo.gl/0CtnAR>) which states (at 7): 'Ferrero reserves the right to conduct unannounced inspections of suppliers and their business practices, records and facilities as well as private interviews with employees. Each supplier shall designate staff responsible for also monitoring the factories of their subcontractors used in production for Ferrero. In case of non-compliance, Ferrero will demand corrective measures and reserves the right to terminate any agreement. Ferrero uses independent third parties to assess compliance with this Code.'

scheme by means of a multi-party contract[97]. In this case each actor has a contractual duty to cooperate in taking any useful measure to prevent risk occurrence and/or reduce its consequences.

When the multi-party risk management scheme takes the form of an organizational network, monitoring and sanctioning powers are often assigned to network's managers or directors, leaving space for a more hierarchical structure compared with the one of a multi-party contract.

Further empirical research is needed to analyse the correlations between regulation in a broad perspective and the evolution of organizational models within and across sectors. On the one hand, along the lines indicated by economic sociology and neo-institutional economics, attention should be paid to the correlation between different types of supply chains and regulatory outputs, considering not only the type of standards, but also their modes of implementation. On the other hand empirical research is needed to document how the adoption of a particular regulatory regime affects the formation of networks or groups and the degree of vertical integration or disintegration of the chain.

VIII. Concluding Remarks

In this Chapter we have addressed the relationship between transnational regulation and industrial organization suggesting that they are mutually influential. In particular we have focused on the influence of transnational regulation on contractual governance examining the reasons for the emergence and differentiation of networks to ensure compliance along global supply chains.

Implementation of transnational standards by private actors require monitoring compliance within supply chains deploying different forms of contractual governance among which stand networks. Networks take different forms and reflect different distribution of powers. Unlike the conventional view we have shown that often organizational networks are used to monitor when power is evenly allocated among chain participants while contractual networks are deployed when monitoring power is unevenly distributed and a chain leader prevails.

We have shown that the structure of the supply chain influences the selection of regulatory strategies, in particular the choice between hierarchical command and control and responsive or market-based strategies. At the same time the regulatory approach influences the selection of instruments and the type of contractual governance with different power distribution. The promotion of private compliance monitoring within transboundary supply chains leads to the creation of networks

[97] See, e.g., the 4C Association, Code of Conduct and its guidelines (available at <http://www.4c-coffeeassociation.org/>) and specifically the case of the 4C Association establishing a 'Common Code for the Coffee Community' whose guidelines provide that a 4C Unit can be a group of small-scale farmers who agree to register jointly. Other options include: an already organized group such as a cooperative or a farmers' association, a collecting station, a mill, a local trader, an export organization, or even a roaster, and that such a unit is mainly in charge of managing internal monitoring.

characterized by diverse allocation of regulatory power. In some instances hierarchical monitoring prevails while in others peer monitoring dominates.

We have provided a few concrete examples in the field of safety regulation, distinguishing between food and non-food, and highlighting that different types of regulation generate networks with different forms of monitoring, i.e., peer and hierarchical. In particular, examining certification, we have shown that networks with different organizational complexity are generated, ranging from light contractual to a complex mix between organizational and contractual, in order to cover the upper part of the supply chain.

The analysis shows that, in practice, differences between networks aimed at monitoring regulatory compliance may depend on who establishes the regulatory schemes; whether these are led by producers, retailers, or independent actors (like research institutes); how monitoring power is distributed among the chain participants, particularly when group or chain certification is in place; and on the extent to which the certification requirements are imposed along the chain, whether including also traders and sometimes retailers. The distinction between individual and group certification has proven to be rather relevant.

These illustrations are meant to highlight a correlation between the regulatory function of supply chains and different forms of contractual governance.

The forms of contractual governance related to monitoring are dependent on the type of regulatory strategy and the structure of the supply chains. Hence, the main lesson of this Chapter is: when designing group certification schemes or chain of custody more attention should be given to the choice between organizational and contractual arrangements depending on the degree of interdependencies of chain participants and the allocation of sanctioning power in case of non compliance and the monitoring strategy that implementation of transnational standards requires.

Private Regulation and Networks in Transnational Supply Chains

Comment on F. Cafaggi and P. Iamiceli, 'Private Regulation and Industrial Organization: Contractual Governance and the Network Approach'

*Wolfgang Kerber**

I. Introduction

The Chapter by Cafaggi and Iamiceli is an extremely interesting and rich study about recent developments in the institutional structure of complex transnational supply chains. These developments are triggered by the increasing internationalization of supply chains as well as mounting regulatory requirements with regard to product safety and environmental and social standards. The main problem the authors are dealing with is the difficult question of how compliance with the regulatory requirements can be ensured over the entire supply chain consisting of many firms in different countries (including producers of primary goods in developing countries). The main thesis of the authors is that there is a strong correlation between the regulatory strategies on the one hand and the industrial organization structure of the supply chain on the other. In this respect, they turn to network-based organizational structures to solve the complex informational problems and ensure an industrial and institutional structure which is sufficiently responsive to emerging compliance problems. Their Chapter is based both on a complex theoretical analysis and on three case studies, each of which represent a different type of this kind of network with its own advantages and problems. My comments will refer primarily to an analysis of the theoretical reasonings, which—from an economic perspective—are based on a highly sophisticated but also complex combination of different theoretical approaches.

* Professor of Economics, Department of Business Administration and Economics, Philipps University Marburg.

II. Three Theoretical Dimensions: Structure, Regulations, and the Transnationality of the Supply Chains

How can we characterize the different dimensions of this complex problem from a theoretical perspective? The first dimension is the existence of a supply chain consisting of a number of firms, each of which contributes to some extent to the final product which is sold via retailers to consumers. This refers to the theoretical question of the optimal structure of the supply chain, with respect to the degree of vertical (dis)integration or outsourcing as well as the organizational or contractual relationships between the firms. Theoretically, this is linked to transaction cost economics but also to other reasons (as economies of scale and scope, flexibility, etc) which might favour a longer or a shorter chain of independent firms as well as tighter or looser contractual relations between the firms in the supply chain. This is the industrial organization dimension that has been emphasized so strongly by the authors. Using the network approach for analysing inter-firm structure in the supply chain is fitting because networks can be understood both as an industrial structure (from the perspective of industrial organization) and as an institutional arrangement (from the perspective of institutional economics). It is rare and very helpful that Cafaggi and Iamiceli analyse their specific networks from both perspectives and, in particular, that they also explicitly take into account the contractual relationships between the firms in the network. The reason that networks as a group of intermediate solutions between hierarchies ('command and control') and pure markets might be good solutions, can only be understood after considering the regulatory dimension of the problem.

Why do we need regulation at all in these cases? If the consumers could recognize with low costs whether the products they want to buy comply with certain safety, social, or environmental standards, then we would not assume market failure problems, and no specific regulatory strategies would be necessary. However, in many supply chains, a huge number of information problems can be expected, leading to many information asymmetries and complex principal-agent problems, both with regard to the consumers and between the firms in the supply chain. These information problems can lead to complex market failure problems with respect to health risks (for example in the case of food) as well as to violations of social and environmental standards whose satisfaction is important for the consumers. From that perspective the question arises of how compliance with the relevant standards can be ensured along the entire supply chain. Since each firm has incentives for saving costs by not complying with these standards, and monitoring costs can be assumed as positive, sophisticated institutional structures are necessary to solve the compliance problem at reasonable costs. Therefore, information problems are the ultimate reason underlying the need for regulation, and these regulations can be seen as part of consumer policy.

Cafaggi and Iamiceli leave open whether the regulations that should be complied with are public regulations (as, for example, European regulations of inter-state conventions) or private regulations, i.e. standards set up and implemented by single firms or organizations of firms or private certification agencies. On first glance this is surprising, because the former are mandatory regulations enacted by states, whereas the latter are institutional solutions, which have been developed in the market (private regulation). To a certain extent, both kinds of regulations are very different: whereas the requirements for standards enforced by private regulations can usually only reflect the preferences of the individual consumers (regarding health risks, social, and environmental standards) who buy these products on competitive markets, the mandatory standards in public regulation can be influenced by all kinds of political objectives, which may or may not correspond to the preferences of the consumers of these products. However, Cafaggi and Iamiceli are right in ignoring these differences because they want to focus on the compliance problem within the supply chain, irrespective of the kind of regulatory standard.

The other (perhaps more important) argument for treating both kinds of regulation in a similar manner is based upon the transnational character of the supply chain. As the authors emphasize at the beginning of their Chapter, one important (third) dimension of the problem is the fact that the firms within the supply chain are located in different countries. Why is this important? Public and private regulations are to some extent always alternative policy options, even in domestic settings. Insofar as private regulations (as, for example, certification solutions or the reputation mechanism) as market solutions can sufficiently solve the market failure problems through information problems, mandatory public regulations should be avoided from an economic policy perspective. But there might be situations where mandatory public regulations (for example safety standards for food) are necessary. However, the proper line between using public and private regulation might be different in transnational and domestic settings. Since it is much harder (or even impossible) to enforce domestic public regulations in other countries, the relative advantage of private regulation compared to public regulation might be much greater in transnational settings. This much greater importance of private regulations for ensuring compliance with certain standards is the reason why the transnational character of the supply chain is so important for Cafaggi and Iamiceli. What is missing in their analysis, at least explicitly, is the problem that, in a transnational context, the enforcement of private contractual relationships within the networks of firms might also raise a lot of problems if the firms are located in different countries. This is a well-known problem in the discussion of transnational law, and there are a number of possible solutions. A comprehensive analysis of all relevant aspects of the institutional aspects of the networks should also consider this problem because some types of networks might solve these enforcement problems better than others.

Cafaggi and Iamiceli are right in discussing the impact of the structure of the supply chain, especially market competition and the degree of vertical integration, on the choice of regulatory strategies, as well as the opposite question about the impact of regulation on the structure of the supply chain. It is clear that there are considerable effects in both directions. It can be presumed that, in the short-term, the effects of the market and supply chain structure on regulatory strategies might be stronger, at least in the case of private regulations. However, in the long-term, the regulatory requirements might dominate, requiring a market and supply chain restructuring, and engendering new institutional solutions for enforcing proper compliance with the regulatory standards. The different types of networks the authors are emphasizing might be the outcome of such an adaptation process in the market. We should be aware, however, that such an outcome within markets requires a high level of competition in all intermediate markets along the entire supply chain. Without effective competition, it is doubtful whether the forces of the market are strong enough to lead to appropriate processes of restructuring the supply chains in order to ensure cost-efficient forms of fulfilling the regulatory requirements. The liberalization and globalization processes of the last 20 years might have helped significantly to strengthen competition on many international markets and have therefore facilitated the emergence of more suitable supply chain structures, as, for example, those different forms of inter-firm networks. But such a positive result cannot be taken for granted, as the authors have also emphasized by hinting at competition problems and unevenly distributed powers in the supply chain.

III. Problems and Advantages for Small- and Medium-sized Producers

At this point, it might be appropriate to discuss the problem that both private and public regulations might lead to higher entry barriers for small- and medium-sized producers and firms, especially in developing countries, who are not able to invest enough money to meet all the certification requirements of the regulatory standards, which usually are defined in developed countries. Here, the argument is that heightening the regulatory standards (or the necessity of certifying the compliance with these standards) can lead to negative distributional effects on small producers and firms in developing countries who are already at a disadvantage in the global division of labour.[1] Raising regulatory standards for products or production processes can lead to higher entry barriers, which, however, might be justified by market failure problems. But negative effects on these small firms can still exist. One can think about specific policy solutions (such as subsidies); however, we should also understand, that in competitive markets the firms on the buyer side within such a supply chain have significant incentives for keeping these entry barriers for small (but otherwise efficient) firms as low as possible, for example, by helping them to fulfil the compliance requirements. The reason is that these small suppliers increase competition and therefore have a price-dampening effect which

[1] See, e.g., D. Prévost, 'Sanitary, Phytosanitary and Technical Barriers to Trade in the Economic Partnership Agreements between the European Union and the ACP Countries' (2010) ICTSD Issue Paper No 6.

is in the interest of the whole supply chain. If, however, the certification requirements lead to strong economies of scale effect (as it is often the case with regulations), the danger increases that these small firms might no longer be competitive. Thus, on one hand, certification requirements can be an entry barrier, but on the other hand, certification can also lead to a lot of export opportunities for small firms because it reduces the uncertainty of potential buyers in other countries. In that respect, it can also lower entry barriers considerably.

IV. Network Structures and the Implications of the Specific Complexity of Information Problems

The main analysis of Cafaggi and Iamiceli focuses on the study of different options for how networks can ensure compliance with standards in the supply chain by using third party certification. In information economics, it is well known that certification is one of the most powerful market solutions for solving market failures arising from information asymmetry. The most important economic advantage of certification is that certified firms do not need to build up reputation capital of their own (via, for example, advertising), but can use the reputation of the certification agency. This is particularly interesting for small- and medium-sized firms. Therefore the economic rationale of certification depends on the credibility of the certification agency with regard to the quality of its standards and the monitoring of the compliance of all participating firms with these standards. Labels as legally protected signs are an important legal instrument for the effectiveness of the reputation mechanism of the certification instrument.[2]

Starting with basic building blocks of networks distinguishing two types of contractual networks (with bilateral or multilateral contracts) and organizational networks as well as vertical and horizontal networks, Cafaggi and Iamiceli compare three different options for the role of networks in solving compliance problems by installing regulatory standards along the supply chain via third-party certification in different ways. I cannot discuss here in detail this very sophisticated and rich analysis, which is based upon their three case studies. From a theoretical perspective, I only want to emphasize one point: what the best structure of this network of suppliers, standard-setter, label-holder, and certification agency is, and what kind of contractual/organizational relationships between these entities is most suitable for ensuring cost-efficient and responsive compliance with regulatory standards depends on the specific structure of the information problems and asymmetries as well as the (relative) costs of monitoring the performance of the suppliers, either mutually or by the certification agency or a dominant firm (as, for example, the final retailer) in the supply chain. Different

[2] For the general problem of monitoring in regard to certifications see G. Jahn, M. Schramm, and A. Spiller, 'The Reliability of Certification: Quality Labels as a Consumer Policy Tool'(2005) 28 *Journal of Consumer Policy* 53–78.

structures of information problems and information costs within the supply chain will lead to different optimal structures of the supply chain and different optimal institutional arrangements. Therefore, it is not surprising that the authors find a wide variety of solutions for the implementation of compliance mechanisms in supply chains. Cafaggi and Iamiceli have made an important contribution with many new insights to this under-researched problem of the relationship between the structure of a supply chain and regulation. However, ultimately the specific structure of the complex information problems determines the specific need for regulation as well as the optimal structural and institutional characteristics of the network of firms along the supply chain.

12

Flipping Wreck: *Lex Mercatoria* on the Shoals of *Ius Cogens*

*Hugh Collins**

I. The Lacuna of Private Transnational Law

This is a tale of two jurisdictions, a global market, and a lacuna. In this story, the courts of New York and London reached diametrically opposite conclusions regarding the enforceability of a term in a contract. In New York, a term that conferred a charge over property by way of security for a loan was held to be invalid;[1] whereas in London, the court ordered that the identical charge in the same contract be enforced.[2] The litigation arose as a consequence of the recent crisis in financial markets and the insolvency of some investment banks. In the context of insolvency, it becomes vital to establish which among the many creditors of a debtor has a priority right to a particular asset. Yet these two jurisdictions that provide the axis around which global financial markets transfer, restructure, leverage, metamorphose positions, and reuse billions of dollars and pounds every day could not agree on this basic question of the enforceability of a charge over valuable assets. Whilst the financial market is fluid and global—as evidenced by the international cast of characters in this case of an Australian fund manager, a British subsidiary of an American bank, special purpose vehicles formed in the Republic of Ireland and the Cayman Islands, and US investment banks, the applicable law for the contract appears resolutely fractured by national boundaries. The financiers of these two cities operate as the hubs of a single network of capital markets, but from the viewpoint of the courts the global transaction must be understood as a local contract, governed and regulated by the applicable state law.

* Vinerian Professor of English Law, University of Oxford and Fellow of All Souls College, Oxford. I am very grateful to Jacco Bomhoff, Jo Braithwaite, Jeff Golden,, and Sarah Worthington, for their enormous assistance in helping me understand aspects of this topic.

[1] *Re Lehman Brothers Holdings Inc*, 422 BR 407 (US Bankruptcy Court, SDNY, 2010).

[2] *Belmont Park Investments PTY Ltd v. BNY Trustee Services Ltd, Lehman Brothers Special Financing Inc* [2011] UKSC 38, [2012] 1 AC 383, on appeal from *Perpetual Trustee Co Ltd, Belmont Park Investments PTY Ltd v. BNY Corporate Trustee Services Ltd, Lehman Brothers Special Financing Inc* [2009] EWCA Civ 1160, [2010] Ch 347.

So, we have identified two jurisdictions and a single global market, now what about the lacuna in this tale? This missing element comprises the absence of any explicit reference in the decisions of the courts to a global law to govern and regulate this global financial market and its contracts. Does such a global law exist? Indeed, given the historical dominance of nation states in claiming the power to make law, is the idea of global law an oxymoron? How can we conceive of this kind of transnational, even post-national, law? However puzzling we may find this notion of global law, we can observe that financial markets have governed themselves for the most part by their own rules, devised and enforced by the participants in those markets. We can discover these privately created norms in many places: in the rules of Exchanges used for the sale of financial products such as shares and commodities futures; in the decisions of arbitrators charged with resolving such disputes, decisions which perhaps reflect the customs and principles observed by participants in these markets; and in the terms of standardized contracts that govern the trading in these markets. How should we understand the authority of these privately created norms? How do they interact with the laws of states? Judging by the evidence of the two cases at the heart of this tale, these privately created norms are regarded by judges at most as terms of a privately concluded contract, which must cede authority to mandatory national laws. There is no acknowledgement that these privately created norms might serve as an alternative frame of reference to national law, a rival normative system that may conflict with national law, with the consequence, in the case of conflict, that adjudicators will be required to resolve this conflict of laws between state law and transnational law.

The principal aim of this Chapter is to examine this idea of privately created norms that provide an alternative frame of reference for the governance of contracts concluded in global financial markets. Notwithstanding the burdensome historical baggage that the terminology brings with it, it is convenient to refer to this notion of a privately created normative system in a commercial context as a *lex mercatoria*. Having analyzed some of the key features of the concept of a *lex mercatoria* in Section II, the Chapter proceeds to consider some of the special characteristics of the regulation and governance of financial markets in Section III. That perspective on the idiosyncratic features of financial markets enables us then to examine the particular regulatory and governance problems encountered by the type of transaction at the heart of the two cases in this story in Section IV. Though focusing attention on these particular cases, the issues that they raise are of more general interest, because it was transactions of this type that created the systemic risk in financial markets that finally erupted in the credit crunch. The legal reasoning, the results, and the final outcomes in the cases are then described and assessed in Section V. In the final Section, the threads of the story are gathered together with a concluding interrogation of the idea of *lex mercatoria*. Should courts ignore the presence of such sectoral transnational normative orders or should they recognize their legitimate authority to regulate transactions that fall within their scope? What principles should govern this reception of transnational private orders into national law? In particular, in the context of contractual governance, how should national law resolve conflicts between its mandatory rules (as opposed to default rules) and the provisions of the *lex mercatoria*? And finally, does the *lex mercatoria* itself contain mandatory principles, a transnational *ordre public* or *ius cogens*, which could have provided the resources to govern the international financial market in this case?

II. *Lex Mercatoria*

Lex mercatoria is a chameleon-like concept. The term originates from a time before the nation state succeeded in asserting its monopoly of legitimate authority within its territory. In the medieval period, merchants' courts, rather than the courts of kings and princes, would adjudicate disputes between traders. The court might assume jurisdiction over a particular market in a city or district or over dealings in a particular commodity in a number of locations. Its power might reside not so much in its ability to impose a remedy as in its threat to exclude a merchant from the market by damaging a trader's reputation. The normative standards applied by these courts, developed through precedents, could be described as a *lex mercatoria*, that is, a law derived neither from the political authority of a prince, nor ecclesiastical authority, but primarily from the local customs of merchants, which no doubt were viewed as part of a broader scheme of customary laws and privileges. In the absence of a clearly demarcated and supreme system of state law within a territory, and, therefore, in the absence of a sharp division between the public and the private, the *lex mercatoria*, like other customary laws and privileges, constituted part of a network of norms that provided tools for governance.[3]

Whilst remaining sensitive to these historical roots, contemporary discussions of *lex mercatoria* often diverge in their competing conceptions of its key qualities.[4] One version, which is perhaps most closely associated with German legal scholarship, stresses the existence of a coherent system of norms.[5] Accordingly, *lex mercatoria* is identified with non-state codes of commercial law or soft law codes, such as the UNIDROIT Principles of International Commercial Contracts.[6] Another

[3] In an interesting discussion of the evidence from the Middle Ages, Ralf Michaels challenges the claim that the *lex mercatoria* was autonomous from state law, but it seems to me that the notion of state law was not yet clear itself, so the boundaries would not have been evident to participants at the time: R. Michaels, 'The True Lex Mercatoria: Law Beyond the State' (2007) 14 *Indiana Journal of Global Legal Studies* 447–68, 454.

[4] For a useful overview of different views, see R. Cranston, 'Theorizing Transnational Commercial Law' (2007) 42 *Texas International Law Journal* 597.

[5] See, e.g., K. P. Berger, *The Creeping Codification of the Lex Mercatoria* (The Hague: Kluwer Law International, 1999) and 'Transnational Law Digest & Bibliography', Centre for Transnational Law (CENTRAL) (available at <http://tldb.uni-koeln.de/>).

[6] International Institute for the Unification of Private Law (UNIDROIT), *Unidroit Principles of International Commercial Contracts* (2004) (available at <http://www.unidroit.org/english/principles/contracts/principles2004/integralversionprinciples2004-e.pdf>); J. Kleinheisterkamp and S. Vogenauer, *Commentary on the Unidroit Principles of International Commercial Contracts* (Oxford: Oxford University Press, 2009).

version, which perhaps emerges most clearly in French legal scholarship, identifies *lex mercatoria* in the principles and rules developed through international commercial arbitration.[7] The arbitrators of these commercial disputes have developed, according to this perspective, transnational principles of law through their decisions and precedents. These principles, though influenced by national legal systems, are not tied to any particular national order, but serve the functional goal of justice and fairness in international commercial disputes. Yet a third conception of *lex mercatoria*, which perhaps predominates in the common law world, finds the source of its laws in the customary practices and usages of particular branches of trade, which frequently involve the use of detailed standardized documentation.[8] In the context of international financial markets, a leading example of this kind of *lex mercatoria* would be the International Swaps and Derivatives Association (ISDA) Master Agreement.

Each of these three conceptions of *lex mercatoria* can be (and have been) criticized for their defective understanding of the qualities needed for a phenomenon to be accurately or persuasively denoted as law. The Germanic conception, with its emphasis on a coherent code, seems to lack a requirement of some kind of effective adjudication or enforcement mechanism. The French conception of principles of international commercial arbitration, though possessing an adjudication mechanism, lacks the systematic and coherent body of rules that is normally found in state legal systems. The common law conception of standardized contracts may be criticized for mistaking contracts for law, thereby misrepresenting private rules as public norms, even though they lack the qualities of abstraction, system, and generality commonly associated with law. What all these criticisms have in common, of course, is the observation that the *lex mercatoria*, in whatever conception is proposed, differs in significant ways from the normal features of state law. These criticisms are indubitably correct, but also unhelpful.

They are unhelpful, because it makes no sense to insist that, to qualify as law, *lex mercatoria* must share identical qualities to state law. The point of referring to *lex mercatoria* is precisely to signal that it is not state law. Nor is it international law in the sense of rules grounded in conventions between nation states. The crucial point is that, like the mediaeval customary laws of merchants, the modern *lex mercatoria* has not been created by the political authorities of the nation state, but rather by a sector of society, functioning at a global or regional level. [9] The international financial markets behave like a global village community with their own sectoral rules. Furthermore, given this source of law in the community, it is to be expected that the form in which law is promulgated will not duplicate the patterns set by state law, such as legislation and codes. Indeed, given this origin

[7] Y. Dezalay and B. G. Garth, *Dealing in Virtue: International Commercial Arbitration and the Construction of a Transnational Legal Order* (Chicago, Ill: University of Chicago Press, 1996).

[8] R. Goode, 'Usage and Its Reception in Transnational Commercial Law' (1997) 46 *International and Comparative Law Quarterly* 1; R. Goode, 'Rule, Practice and Pragmatism in Transnational Commercial Law' (2005) 54 *International and Comparative Law Quarterly* 539.

[9] G. Teubner, 'Global Bukowina: Legal Pluralism in the World Society' in G. Teubner (ed) *Global Law Without a State* (Brookfield, Dartmouth, 1997) 3–28.

of global law in social practice, it is predictable that it might take on a variety of forms according to what a particular section of the global community might find it conducive to serve as a tool of normative guidance. One sector may try to establish a comprehensive code, while another part of the community may be satisfied by fragments of a rule system, leaving the remainder to be fixed by national laws or international conventions, and yet another prefer to promote a set of abstract principles, such as a declaration of human rights or labour rights, thereby delegating to others a margin of appreciation in how those rights should be recognized and enforced in a local context. The obvious danger posed by this insistence on differentiating *lex mercatoria* and other types of global law from state law is that we may dilute the reference to law to such an extent that we may be led by an all-embracing style of legal pluralism to label any non-state claims to make binding rules as exercises in law-making. Here we encounter the recurrent dilemma of legal pluralism of expanding the notion of law beyond any serviceable boundaries.

Our focus here is not on global non-state law as a whole, however, but rather on commercial practices and, within that category, on the specialized rules developed within international financial transactions. In this particular context, the form adopted by private norm creation has been primarily through contracts, associations, and networks.[10] The contracts take the form of standardized rules for contracts of a given type, such as an interest rate swap, perhaps combined with a currency exchange as well. The rules of the standardized contract are generated through the experience and practice of lawyers writing such contracts. This expertise and knowledge is combined through an association of these lawyers and their clients, which promulgates the standard terms of a master agreement for use by members of the association. Although there is no compulsion by an external force to adopt these master agreements, the global financial and banking network uses them to achieve efficiency and greater reach for the capital markets, and participants in the market have little choice but to accommodate the standard form contracts. Is this assemblage of contracts appropriately dignified by the term law as in *lex mercatoria*?

In answering this question, it is necessary to address the puzzle that as contracts normally depend for their validity and enforceability on rules that are external to the contract's terms, namely the law of contract of a particular state, it seems impossible for any contract to perform the trick of hoisting itself by its own bootstraps by providing the rules that govern its own validity.[11] But as Teubner has observed,[12] this paradox can be evaded, though never entirely resolved, by elaborate contractual structures. In the case of financial transactions in capital markets,

[10] For a comprehensive survey of the variety of regulatory tools, see C. Bradley, 'Private International Law-Making for the Financial Markets' (2005) 29 *Fordham International Law Journal* 127–80.

[11] Goode (2005), n 8, 539, 548.

[12] This argument follows that proposed by Teubner, n 9, 3–28 albeit in slightly different terminology; H. Collins, 'Private Production of Transnational Law through Standard Form Contracts' in H. Eidenmuller (ed), *Regulatory Competition in Contract Law and Dispute Settlement* (Munich:Verlag CH Beck/Oxford: Hart Publishing/Baden Baden: Nomos, 2013) 123–43.

the master agreement can be viewed as external to the particular contract, and this distance enables that master agreement to appear like a separate law to regulate the particular transaction, even though its effectiveness and relevance have been determined by the terms of the particular agreement. Furthermore, the master agreement may contain mechanisms within it to introduce further rule-making by the association or arbitrators, so that its content is not fixed by the terms of the particular transaction, but can evolve in the light of further experience. The organization of arbitrators into an association, with its own rules of conduct, facilitates the systematic development of legal principles.[13] In the relation between the master agreement and a particular transaction, we can observe a similar pattern to that existing between state contract law and a particular transaction: the hierarchy of the former over the particular transaction, an evolutionary capacity in the master agreement or contract law, and a separation or externalization of the standardized agreement from the particular contract. None of this complex structure of rules constructed by contracts and associations entirely resolves the bootstraps problem though, of course, the same criticism can be addressed to state law as well, because, ultimately, positive law must presuppose its own validity and authority. But like state law, the *lex mercatoria* strives to constitutionalize itself as an autonomous legal order, and insofar as it succeeds, it buttresses its claim to be regarded as law.

If it is correct that the *lex mercatoria*, or at least the part that aspires to regulation of global financial markets, can claim law-like qualities, what happens when it conflicts with the applicable state law? *Lex mercatoria* must remain soft law, at least for the foreseeable future, because it typically lacks adjudicative mechanisms that can effectively enforce its rules and judgments without depending on the force at the disposal of territorial states. But this dependence on state institutions for enforcement does not rule out the possibility that state law may choose to acknowledge the norms created by private parties through their contracts and associations. When *lex mercatoria* makes a claim to be recognized by state law, implicitly it asserts itself as a source of authority and guidance, even if it differs from state law. At this point of contact, the collision between regimes of state law and *lex mercatoria*,[14] the key question arises whether the norms of *lex mercatoria* are regarded by a court or arbitral panel that is charged with resolving a dispute as not merely the terms of a private contract, but as an authoritative source of rules or principles. In other words, the judge or arbitrator must feel under an obligation in performing his or her role to take these norms into account in determining the rights and obligations of the parties. To qualify as an authoritative source of norms, the rules must be applicable to the dispute, though not necessarily determinative, because other sources of law may also be applicable and conflict. In the conceptual framework presented by Hart,[15] this requirement of applicability

[13] G. Teubner, Review Essay, 'Breaking Frames: The Global Interplay of Legal and Social Systems' (1997) 45 *American Journal of Comparative Law* 149.

[14] A. Fischer-Lescano and G. Teubner, 'Regime-Collisions: The Vain Search for Legal Unity in the Fragmentation of Global Law' (2004) 25 *Michigan Journal of International Law* 999–1046.

[15] H. L. A. Hart, *The Concept of Law* (Oxford: Oxford University Press, 1961).

means that the rules and principles must be identified by the rule of recognition that is observed by the adjudicator both as a matter of practice and in principle. On the most favourable interpretation available,[16] Hart's theory of a legal system is dynamic in the sense that the rule of recognition may evolve as a customary law, where changes in official practice, which are supported and respected by arguments of principle, succeed in modifying this test of what should be regarded as authoritative sources of norms or law. If the non-state rules and principles satisfy this requirement of applicability by becoming qualified by the evolving rule of recognition as a source of authoritative guidance, they begin to interact with the law of the state. Soft law irritates hard law, compelling the latter to incorporate, reject, or translate soft law into its own norms.

It is only when that condition of applicability under a rule of recognition is satisfied that we may speak of a lacuna, that is, the failure of an adjudicator to acknowledge the relevance and applicability of norms to the dispute in hand. It is the absence of reference to the *lex mercatoria*, when it should have been considered, that calls the judgment into question, because it has omitted what should have been part of its normative orientation.

III. Contractual Governance and Club Markets

One of the central themes of a previous work[17] is the claim that a useful way of thinking about contract law is to view contractual agreements as a method of business self-regulation. Although this description may not fit easily everyday transactions, such as consumer purchases in a shop, this viewpoint is particularly apt for the transactions of concern here, when businesses use standard form contracts for their business arrangements or when there is a long-term business relationship or when there is a network of interdependent contracts. The lengthy (both in terms of size and duration) framework contracts in such situations produce what may be described as a short code of detailed contract provisions designed to govern the relationship between the parties. Typically in UK–US legal practice, the terms of the contract will seek to provide comprehensive regulation, dealing not only with the primary obligations of the parties such as price and main subject-matter, but also with what should happen in the event of all foreseeable contingencies, including the assessment of any compensation payable for breach of those obligations. In particular, it is normal practice for these contracts to provide a dispute resolution mechanism, often with several levels of appeal, and to decide explicitly what rules the adjudicators should apply to the dispute, which will not necessarily be the normal default rules supplied by the domestic law.

[16] For an exploration of this interpretation, see J. Finnis, 'Revolutions and the Continuity of Law' in AWB Simpson (ed) *Oxford Essays in Jurisprudence* (2nd series) (Oxford: Oxford University Press, 1971) 44.

[17] H. Collins, *Regulating Contracts* (Oxford: Oxford University Press, 1999).

From this perspective of seeing contractual agreements as a method of business self-regulation, the applicable law, the law of contract, can then be described as the 'regulation of self-regulation'. This viewpoint challenges the common perception of the basic rules of private law that determine the legal validity of contractual agreements. These rules of contract law are customarily regarded as facilitative rules that enable individuals to form binding reciprocal undertakings, rather than duty-imposing rules that control the actions of participants in markets. But in fact this regulatory viewpoint casts considerable light on the functions and objectives of the basic rules of contract law, such as those concerning the formation of agreement by 'offer' and 'acceptance'. Instead of asking, for instance, what the legal rules say should count as a valid acceptance of an offer, one can ask what constraints the rules place on the parties' choices and decisions with regard to when their conduct amounts to a binding agreement on which both can reasonably rely, at least to some extent. For instance, can the parties decide that acceptance and therefore a binding undertaking can be achieved by conduct, such as removing the wrapping around the product, or even by inaction and silence?

In some respects, the 'law and economics approach', which dominates the literature in the US adopts a similar perspective by thinking about the consequences of alternative regulatory regimes and contract law rules from a perspective of efficiency. The difference in perspective of a more comprehensive regulatory approach is that a broader range of considerations becomes applicable, not least considerations concerning processes of standard-setting, effective compliance with standards, and the variety of possible enforcement mechanisms (for example criminal law, compensatory measures of private law, collective private redress, default rules, etc).

In certain fields of commercial activity, however, this view of contract law that it comprises legal regulation that controls and steers self-regulation by businesses proves inadequate. The model describes two levels of regulation: first the self-regulation provided by the contractual terms and, secondly, the legal regulation of this self-regulation. But in some contexts, to explain social practice adequately, there seems to be a need for a more complex model that involves three levels of regulation. The paradigm of such a context is a transaction on a stock exchange or a commodities exchange. In this context, there is an agreement between the parties concerning the sale of shares or future rights to commodities, but that agreement is subject to the rules of the Exchange or 'club market'. These rules typically provide for criteria for membership of the Exchange, such as the posting of margins, rules of conduct, and dispute resolution mechanisms. The rules of the Exchange also insist upon the application of a standard set of terms to the individual contracts carried out on the trading platform. Indeed, with the exception of the price of the deal, the rules of the exchange purport to govern exclusively and with finality every aspect of the trading activity of its members. Though merely a private body comprising a club for its members, the Exchange acts like a regulatory authority itself. In this respect, there is a strong analogy between the conception of *lex mercatoria* explained earlier and the way in which the Exchange, an association constructed by contract, provides an externalized, hierarchical, and evolutionary mechanism for regulating particular transactions. The role of the state law here necessarily becomes more complex, because the law of contract has to regulate both the contractual agreement between the traders and at the same time the rules and activities of the Exchange.

The two targets of legal regulation—the individual contracts and the regulatory activities of the Exchange—are closely interlinked, because the rules of the Exchange impact on the content and effect of the individual contracts. For example, if the Exchange insists on a 'netting' of transactions through a clearing-house system, the ordinary laws of contract concerning set-off should not be applicable. Nevertheless, legal regulation has to assess the validity of the netting system of the Exchange in order to judge the effects of the individual contract. In other words, the task of regulating contracts involves an assessment of the Exchange's practice of netting through a clearing house and the limits, if any, that should be placed on this mechanism for the settlement of debts.

I have previously cautioned against significant intervention by the law in the actions of the regulatory authority of Exchanges, because these complex systems of rules use unfamiliar techniques such as netting and (at least in the common law) specific performance of contracts to achieve economic objectives that would be inappropriate in ordinary contractual relationships.[18] For instance, under a netting system, liabilities owed under a contract can disappear when netted out under the clearing house system, whereas if there is a simple contractual arrangement, the right to use set-offs may leave much of the liabilities in place.[19] The difference can prove highly significant in the event of the insolvency of one of the parties.

In sum, my argument was that Exchanges create a private legal system or system of governance for members of the club. An Exchange imposes rules that are essential to its functioning, but which may deviate from ordinary legal rules that constrain lawful activity in markets. There has always been some doubt, for instance, about whether the speculative futures trading in commodities was a form of gaming or betting, transactions which under the ordinary common law are void and unenforceable. Given the uniqueness of this self-regulation found in Exchanges, it seemed right to urge caution in devising appropriate legal regulation. The ordinary legal regulation of the self-regulation of contracts might prove dysfunctional in the context of the private governance systems of club markets. The wiser course seemed to be to abstain from detailed legal regulation of the transactions conducted through Exchanges, and to focus instead on the protection of outsiders, that is persons and businesses who were not members of the Exchange, but who relied on the Exchange, such as investors or clients of the brokers.

One of the main purposes of Exchanges and their clearing house system of managing liabilities is to avoid the risks that might arise from the insolvency of

[18] Collins, n 17, 218–21.

[19] See, e.g. *British Eagle International Air Lines Ltd v. Compagnie Nationale Air France* [1975] 1 WLR 758 (HL).

one of the members of the club. In theory, the use of variable margins should prevent the insolvency of any of the participants in the trading system from having negative consequences for any of the other participants. This diminution of the risk of insolvency permits far more risky trading to take place on Exchanges than in ordinary markets. In particular, the rules of the Exchange facilitate the trading in futures, that is, the buying and selling of commodities that do not exist yet, between parties who have no interest in acquiring those commodities, but rather who seek to speculate on the future prices of those commodities. It is sometimes argued that this speculation performs a useful social function because it permits hedging against future prices for those businesses that require more predictability of costs in a volatile market, such as an airline that wants to hedge against massive changes in the costs of fuel for aircraft. Although this facilitation of hedging does happen, an Exchange is not strictly necessary for that purpose—a forward contract or an option to purchase fuel at a fixed price at a future date will suffice to protect the airline. Exchanges seem to me to be rather more about facilitating speculation for its own sake, and they do so by providing a trading platform that minimizes standard risks such as insolvency. In particular, the Exchange and its clearing house system greatly facilitate the practice of 'shorting', where assets are sold and only subsequently purchased in the hope of obtaining a profit in a falling market.

It is also true that Exchanges facilitate legal regulation of financial markets by being publicly observable. The rules of the Exchange can be discovered, and the trading prices are observable. A regulatory authority can ascertain that adequate margins are held by the clearing house so that excessive risks are not undertaken. This 'prudential supervision' should ensure the stability of the Exchange and its interconnected banking and financial system, permitting credit to oil the wheels of commerce and speculation. But it should not be forgotten that Exchanges are created to facilitate the economic purposes of the members, not to expose them to regulatory inspection and requirements of propriety in their dealings.

IV. Over the Counter and *Lex Mercatoria*

In the years leading up to the recent financial crisis, the investment bankers thought that they could dispense with Exchanges in carrying out some aspects of their business. They believed that they could acquire the benefits of an Exchange, without the encumbrance of its transaction costs, its transparency, and its public oversight. This seemed possible to achieve by a complex contract such as the ISDA Master Agreement, which provided a standard set of terms for derivatives.[20] The detailed and dense contract, revised periodically, was supplemented by widely cited legal

[20] The ISDA documentation includes master agreements, schedules providing options, confirmations, sets of definitions, credit support documentation, annexes, protocols, bridges, netting arrangements, the use of collateral, novation agreements, and users guides: see J. Benjamin, *Financial Law* (Oxford: Oxford University Press, 2007) para 5.77.

opinions given by 'silks' (i.e. leading barristers in London) on the meaning and effects of the terms of these contracts in law. Together with some transaction-specific documentation, it was thought that this standardized umbrella contract provided the necessary self-regulation for the complicated financial deals. The framework of rules was described as 'global law',[21] 'soft law',[22] or, as here, *lex mercatoria*.

Why did bankers want to avoid the creation of an Exchange? No doubt, an Exchange for credit default swaps or interest rate swaps would have increased transaction costs, perhaps not in the simple way of adding to the costs of making and enforcing contracts, but rather in the need for the maintenance of capital requirements for members of the Exchange, capital which could be used productively elsewhere. Non-Exchange or 'Over the Counter' (OTC) transactions also had the potential advantage in that they were not disclosed publicly on an Exchange. Partly as a consequence of this privacy, these OTC transactions eluded public oversight by regulators and were not recorded transparently in the investment bank's accounts. The standardized Master Agreement did facilitate some kinds of settlement arrangements through separate clearing house businesses, but these arrangements were optional: clearing houses were used to save on transaction costs through netting-like arrangements, and only indirectly served to provide prudential regulation of the financial market.

When the financial markets went into cardiac arrest, it is not surprising that the main target of concern was these OTC transactions, which had mushroomed in the preceding years. Nor should it be unexpected that proposals for better regulation on both sides of the Atlantic have focused on the need to steer all transactions through Exchanges and clearing house netting arrangements, in order to permit both transparency and public oversight, on the one hand, and also to minimize the knock-on effects of default by one of the participants, on the other.[23] Whether or not these proposals will work must be questionable.[24] Exchanges function in the interest of their members. They were not invented to facilitate public oversight. The success of this strategy for public regulation will depend heavily on whether it prevents OTC transactions from occurring outside the framework of an Exchange. This seems extremely unlikely to me.

One example where OTC transactions seem likely to survive is the credit default swap, which is, as it happens, the second largest category of OTC transactions

[21] J. Benjamin and D. Rouch, 'The International Financial Markets as a Source of Global law: the Privatisation of Rule-making?' (2008) March *Law and Financial Markets Review* 78–86.

[22] D. Rouch, 'Law and Regulation for Global Financial Markets: If Self-regulation is Dead, Who Sets the Standards?' in R. MacCormick and D. Rouch (eds) *Public Sector Command and Control?* (London: LSE/Freshfields Bruckhaus Deringer, 2010) 1, 3.

[23] European Commission, 'Ensuring Efficient, Safe and Sound Derivatives Markets: Future Policy Actions' COM(2009) 563; House of Lords, European Union Committee, 10th Report of Session 2009–2010, 'The Future Regulation of Derivatives Markets: Is the EU on the Right Track?' (31 March 2010) HL Paper 93.

[24] J. Braithwaite, 'The Inherent Limits of "Legal Devices": Lessons for the Public Sector's Central Counterparty Prescription for the OTC Derivatives Markets' (March 2011) *European Business Organisation Law Review*.

(after interest rate swaps).[25] Here the aim of the transaction is to transfer the risk of default by a debtor onto other parties in return for a premium. It is, in effect, similar to an insurance policy against default, though unlike an insurance policy, if the event for which protection is purchased actually occurs, in this case normally the default of the debtor on the underlying debt, the purchaser of the swap must pay up even if the seller, typically a bank (or its subsidiary), has suffered no actual loss. This device is attractive to banks, because they can make risky loans such as the notorious sub-prime mortgages, but then diminish the risk to themselves considerably by transferring it to others.

The success of the OTC market depends heavily upon the reliability of the self-regulation provided by the Master Agreement. The prices and value of the contracts may depend on what is happening in an Exchange, and hence derivative from trade on Exchanges such as a currency exchange, but the OTC contracts such as interest rate swaps and credit default swaps cannot benefit from the governance system of the Exchange. It follows that for OTC contracts, the regulation is confined to the two levels of self-regulation through standardized contract terms plus legal regulation of that self-regulation. In other words, the transactions must ultimately be legally enforceable in a national court according to national rules of contract law. The OTC market lacks the benefit of an Exchange that ensures full compliance with the terms of the transaction under an independent governance system.

The OTC market seems to have flourished internationally on the basis of a belief that its standardized transaction constituted a form of *lex mercatoria*. In the international financial markets, the ISDA Master Agreement, together with its supplementary documentation, was believed to provide a comprehensive system of self-regulation. The Master Agreement was devised by the major players—that is, the banks and their lawyers—with a view to providing an appropriate system of checks and balances between the parties to the transactions. The Master Agreement rose above national legal systems because it provided a comprehensive code of self-regulation for the international financial market, which might be, and in practice invariably was, used as the documentation for these transactions. When problems occur, as happened with respect to Argentinean sovereign debt swaps, even before the litigation was complete,[26] ISDA could promptly rewrite the documents, so that they could apply appropriately, avoiding perceived ambiguities, in the different context of sovereign debt.[27] In these respects, the functioning of this branch of transnational law exhibits the features of what Callies and

[25] Bank of International Settlements, 'OTC Derivatives Market Activity in the first Half of 2009' (November 2009) quoted in House of Lords, European Union Committee, 10th Report of the Session 2009–2010, 'The Future Regulation of Derivatives Markets: Is the EU on the Right Track?' (31 March 2010). Size of market is here measured by exposure after all transactions have been netted out.

[26] *Eternity Global Master Fund Ltd v. Morgan Guarantee Trust Co of NY*, 375 F.3d 168 (2d Cir, 2004).

[27] S. J. Choi and G. Mitu Gulati, 'Contract as Statute' (2006) 104 *Michigan Law Review* 1129–74, 1142–44.

Zumbansen call 'rough consensus and running code.'[28] To the participants in the global financial community, the Master Agreement was seen as equivalent to or a good substitute for the private governance system of an Exchange. It is private law-making, by a private association, using the flexible tool of standardized documentation for contracts in a particular market sector. Its source in a private association, with a broad membership, with an aim of making the market work for all participants, probably secures its acceptance and ensures its superior welfare consequences to other mechanisms for establishing standardized terms.[29]

But of course, as has been mentioned, there are crucial differences between a standardized contract regulated by an Exchange and those that are not. The Exchange needs transparency of transactions in order to judge exposure to risk and to secure the necessary margins as a protection against insolvency. No such constraint operates in the context of OTC transactions regulated by a Master Agreement. As a result, the risks of insolvency become heightened. The chances become greater that at some point the financial bubble will burst.

V. The Flip Clause and the Anti-deprivation Principle

Stripped to its essentials, the 'synthetic collateralised debt obligation', which was involved in the two cases at the centre of my story, concerns the transfer of an income-producing financial position by a bank to investors, who in return take the risks of a downturn in the financial position in return for an income on their investment paid by the bank. But in practice the transaction is far more complicated than this simple picture of a swap of investments implies: '[t]he contract documentation is of a purgatorial complexity'.[30]

In this particular instance, Lehman Bros, through a subsidiary, Lehman Brothers Special Financing Inc (LBSF)) had an income-producing financial position. This financial position was transferred to a Special Purpose Vehicle (SPV), essentially a shell company presumably created by Lehman Bros, which was achieved (probably)[31] by the SPV entering into a derivatives contract that referenced the financial positions held by LBSF (probably some kind of 'credit default swap'). The SPV then issued Notes to investors of capital, such as Belmont Park and Perpetual Trustee, which promised a steady stream of income

[28] G. -P. Callies and P. Zumbansen, *Rough Consensus and Running Code: A Theory of Transnational Private Law* (Oxford: Hart Publishing, 2010).

[29] K. E. Davis, 'The Role of Nonprofits in the Production of Boilerplate' (2006) 104 *Michigan Law Review* 1075–103.

[30] Lord Mance, *Belmont Park Investments PTY Ltd v. BNY Trustee Services Ltd, Lehman Brothers Special Financing Inc* [2011] UKSC 38, para 138.

[31] Not all the details of all of the transactions involved are described in the cases. I rely heavily here on the description of the normal synthetic CDO provided by Benjamin, n 20, paras 18.28–18.37. She reports that the size of a typical synthetic CDO is around US$1 billion (p. 413). In the cases discussed here, there was a series of very transactions involving the issuing of notes to the total value of US$12.5 billion.

plus the return of capital at the end of the fixed term investment. These investors also took the risks of the underlying financial positions (now held by the SPV), so that, for instance, if that financial position turned out to be less profitable than expected owing to what is euphemistically called a 'credit event', the investors would suffer, perhaps by losing some of their capital or a reduced income from the investment. The SPV used the capital raised by the Notes to make a safe triple-A investment through a Trustee company (BNY Corporate Trustee Services) in what was described with some delicacy by the English court as a 'tax friendly' location. This safe investment produced an income. Then the Lehman Bros subsidiary, LBSF, agreed with the SPV that it would pay the amounts due to the noteholders as they fell due in return for the SPV paying them the sums yielded by the safe investment held by the trustee company. The cost to Lehman Bros was therefore the difference between the income produced by the safe investment and the promised steady income stream payable to the noteholders. The benefit to Lehman Bros was that a relatively risky financial position had been turned into a low risk one, backed by the capital asset purchased with the capital supplied by the noteholders. To make this point about collateral security abundantly clear, LBSF benefited from a charge (or proprietary right) over the safe investment held by the trustee in order to secure their right to the income it produced. So what once may have been a risky investment made by Lehman Bros had been transformed by the swap into one that appeared relatively safe (though for a price).[32]

But in one respect, this charge held by LBSF over the collateral held by the Trust was a kind of 'flawed asset'. There was a 'flip clause' in the documentation. Under this clause, in the event of the insolvency of LBSF (an 'Event of Default' as defined by the ISDA Master Agreement), its charge over the safe assets held by the trustee was automatically replaced by a charge in favour of the noteholders.[33] In other words, although the noteholders or investors had accepted the risk that there might be some kind of default or loss on the underlying financial positions originally entered into by Lehman Bros, they did not accept the risk of default by LBSF itself.[34] Under the terms of the investment, if LBSF became insolvent or for some other reason failed to make payments when they fell due, the noteholders

[32] It is possible that Lehman Bros in fact had held no financial position itself, but believed that it could exploit a spread in prices by entering into these transactions (i.e. arbitrage).

[33] The Trustee shall apply all moneys received by it under this Deed in connection with the realisation or enforcement of the Mortgaged Property as follows: 'Swap Counterparty Priority unless...an Event of Default...occurs under the Swap Agreement and the Swap Counterparty is the Defaulting Party...in which case Noteholder Priority shall apply.' *Belmont Park Investments PTY Ltd v BNY Trustee Services Ltd, Lehman Brothers Special Financing Inc* [2011] UKSC 38, [2012] 1 AC 383, Appendix, Supplemental Trust Deed, Clauses 5.5.

[34] Aside from protection in the event of insolvency, the charge also protected the noteholders to some extent from a decision by Lehmann to terminate the swap agreement if it was no longer to their financial advantage: see C Brown and T Cleary, 'Impact of the Global Financial Crisis on OTC Derivatives in Structured Debt Transactions' (2010) 5(2) *Capital Markets Law Journal* 218–35, 223.

could recover their original capital investment by exercising their charge, though they would be unsecured creditors like everyone else with respect to the expected income stream under the Notes.

When the insolvency of Lehman Bros occurred,[35] the question arose as to which party to the swap had the benefit of the charge over the assets held by the trustee—LBSF or the noteholders. A literal interpretation of the flip clause would transfer the benefit of the charge to the noteholders, but naturally the liquidators of Lehman Bros and its subsidiaries wanted to retain the benefit of the charge by claiming that the flip clause was invalid or ineffective. How could the clause be avoided? The answer lay in principles of insolvency law. The clause could be attacked for being a kind of fraud on creditors, thereby violating the 'anti-deprivation' principle (in England) or the '*ipso facto*' rule in the US.

Here we reach the crucial point in the story. The English courts upheld the flip clause, giving the benefit of the charge to the noteholders.[36] In contrast, the US bankruptcy court invalided the charge under the *ipso facto* rule, so that the charge remained the property of LBSF (and therefore could be exercised by the liquidators of Lehman Bros and LBSF for the benefit of all creditors).[37] Why was there this difference in outcome? The short answer is that the contrast reflects differences in the applicable national insolvency laws. In the US, the *ipso facto* rule, as codified in the law, is explicit in invaliding terms in contracts that purport to terminate or modify contractual or proprietary rights in the event of insolvency.[38] In England, in the absence of such a precise and extensive rule in its insolvency law,[39] the issue became whether the flip clause fell foul of a general 'anti-deprivation' principle of the common law.[40]

[35] This was not an isolated event, because each subsidiary had to file independently for bankruptcy, so there was a sequence of bankruptcies, the order of which became significant in the cases, but will not be considered here.

[36] *Belmont Park Investments v. BNY Trustee Services Ltd*, n 2.

[37] *Re Lehman Brothers Holdings Inc*, 422 BR 407 (US Bankruptcy Court, SDNY, 2010).

[38] 11 USC § 365(e)(1): 'an executory contract... may not be terminated or modified, and any right or obligation under such contract... may not be terminated or modified, at any time after the commencement of the case solely because of a provision in such contract... that is conditioned on... the commencement of a case under this title' 11 USC § 541(c)(1)(B): in addition to describing what constitutes property of the bankruptcy estate, also invalidates *ipso facto* clauses, providing that a debtor's interest in property 'becomes property of the estate... notwithstanding any provision in an agreement, transfer instrument, or applicable nonbankruptcy law... that is conditioned on... the commencement of a case under this title... and that effects or gives an option to effect a forfeiture, modification, or termination of the debtor's interest in property'.

[39] Ironically, of course, the US rule was based on English case law, e.g. 'there cannot be a valid contract that a man's property shall remain his until his bankruptcy, and on the happening of that event shall go over to someone else, and be taken away from his creditors', Cotton LJ *Ex p Jay; In re Harrison* (1880) 14 Ch D 19, 26.

[40] Many complex financial arrangements involving netting, clearing houses, and enforcement of security rights in financial instruments are by legislation (based on European Directives) excluded from the anti-deprivation principle: Financial Markets and Insolvency (Settlement Finality) Regulations 1999, SI 1999/2979; Financial Collateral Arrangements (No 2) Regulations 2003, SI 2003/2336.

It must be admitted that the content of this anti-deprivation principle, which must be gleaned from judicial precedents in the common law, remains opaque.[41] A leading case, *Ex p Mackay*[42] involved two transactions: the first was the sale of a patent by A to B in return for B paying royalties; the second was a loan of £12,500 from B to A. The two transactions were connected in that the parties agreed that (1) B would keep half the royalties towards satisfying the debt arising from the loan, and (2) in the event of A's bankruptcy, B could also keep the other half of the royalties. It was held that, while provision (1) was valid against A's trustee in bankruptcy, provision (2) was not. As explained by James LJ clause (1) represents 'a good charge upon one moiety of the royalties', but clause (2) 'is a clear attempt to evade the operation of the bankruptcy laws' as it 'provides for a different distribution of [A's] effects in the event of bankruptcy from that which the law provides'.[43] The analogy between this decision and the flip clause in the Lehman case is clear. Clause (2) transferred the ownership of half of the royalties from A to B in the event of the bankruptcy of A. In the Lehman Bros case, the charge held by Lehman over the safe investment held by the trustee was transferred to the noteholders in the event of the insolvency of Lehman. How could the cases be distinguished?

Judges of the Supreme Court of the United Kingdom offered different opinions on the exact scope of the anti-deprivation principle. All disliked any attempt to rely upon a distinction between the loss of a property right in the event of insolvency and a 'flawed asset' that only existed for a time and to an extent as defined by a contract. The conceptual distinction between a flawed asset, where the right has always been contingent or determinable on insolvency, and the forfeiture of an asset in the event of insolvency, what can be termed the difference between a condition precedent and a condition subsequent,[44] does not appear capable of a sharp resolution.[45] This distinction could simply turn on the form of words used in the contract rather than pointing to any difference in substance. The majority view (six of the seven judges) was that the application of the anti-deprivation

[41] 'As a number of the cases to which I have referred show, there is no doubt that the principle exists, and has been applied to defeat provisions which have that purported effect. However, it is equally clear from the authorities that there are occasions where a provision which, at least on its face, appears to offend the principle has been upheld. I do not find it easy to discern any consistent approach in the authorities as to the application of the principle. In this, I do not appear to be alone.' Per Neuberger J., *Money Markets International Stockbrokers Ltd v. London Stock Exchange* [2001] EWHC 1052, [2002] 1 WLR 1150, [2001] 4 All ER 233 (Ch) para 87.

[42] *Ex p Mackay, Ex p Brown, In re Jeavons* (1873) LR 8 Ch App 643.

[43] *Ex p Mackay, Ex p Brown, In re Jeavons* (1873) LR 8 Ch App 643, 647.

[44] Jeffrey Golden suggested this formulation to me. This is also much like the formulation of the Chancellor at first instance: 'such beneficial interest by way of security as Lehman BSF had in the collateral was, as to its priority, always limited and conditional. As such it never could have passed to a liquidator or trustee in bankruptcy free from those limitations and conditions as to its priority.' *Perpetual Trustee Co Ltd v. BNY Trustee Services Ltd and Lehman Bros Special Financing Inc* [2009] EWHC 1912 (Ch) para 45.

[45] For a different suggestion of how to draw the distinction by reference to whether or not the proprietary interest is inherently limited in time, see: S. Worthington, 'Insolvency Deprivation, Public Policy and Priority Flip Clauses' (2010) 7 *International Corporate Rescue* 28–39.

principle depended upon an examination of the good faith of the parties in not seeking to evade the normal rules applicable to insolvency. This intention could be evidenced by the commercial sense or economic logic of the transaction. In particular, in this case it was the noteholders who had provided the original capital for the collateral, so it was appropriate for them to obtain security for its repayment when the swap transaction failed. This view obtained considerable support from the earlier decision in the Court of Appeal of Lord Neuberger, Master of the Rolls, who had been impressed by the economic logic of the flip clause. Its purpose was to ensure that the noteholders did receive the return of their capital investment in the Notes, either by the SPV repaying them by liquidating the asset on the due date or, in the event of Lehman's insolvency, by exercising the flip clause and enforcing their own charge. The Noteholders were never expected to accept a risk to their capital caused by the insolvency of Lehman Bros; the risk that they had accepted was one caused by defaults or other 'credit events' created by the financial position originally created by Lehman Bros. In the Supreme Court, Lord Mance offered a different opinion, though supported the same result that the anti-deprivation principle did not apply in this case. He held that the performance of a contract can always be made contingent on events such as the bankruptcy of the other party to the contract. That contractual right to terminate the performance should not be affected by the existence of collateral designed to support performance of the contract.

But if the English court was correct in its assessment of the business logic of the deal, even if its conceptual reasoning was unconvincing, how could the US court come to the opposite result? Part of the answer lies in the breadth and clarity of the statutory statement of the *ipso facto* rule in the US bankruptcy code. There was no doubt that the alteration of the priority created by the charge was 'conditioned on' the commencement of bankruptcy proceedings. The flip clause therefore appeared to fall squarely within the statutory prohibition. Foreseeing this problem, the bankruptcy code contains limited exceptions to the *ipso facto* rule, in order to address identified commercial problems. In particular, it contains a special provision regarding derivatives, the so-called 'safe harbour', which in effect removes the *ipso facto* rule for swap agreements. It protects the right of a non-defaulting party to a swap agreement to exercise contractual rights to liquidate, terminate, or accelerate the swap agreement or to offset or net any termination values or payment amounts arising in connection with the liquidation, termination, or acceleration of a swap agreement.[46] The US court held, however, that this safe harbour did not apply to the terms governing priority over the collateral held by the trustee, because that was not part of the swap agreement itself, and, furthermore, the issue of priority over the assets held by the trustee was not concerned directly with the liquidation, termination or acceleration of the swap

[46] 11 USC § 560. This safe harbour has been criticized for creating incentives for sophisticated parties to construct financial transactions that artificially fall within the protection for their priority as creditors: see M. Roe, 'The Derivatives Players' Payment Priorities as Financial Crisis Accelerator' (2011) 63 *Stanford Law Review* 539–90.

agreement. In other words, the parties to the swap agreement were permitted in the event of insolvency to terminate it and net out their obligations without falling foul of the bankruptcy code, but this safe harbour did not apply to the slightly separate arrangements regarding the priority of charges over the investments held by the trustee. This exclusion of the safe harbour in the statutory bankruptcy code does not seem entirely convincing, because the charge over the assets and the changes in its priority according to contingencies was clearly part of the overall package involved in this type of securitization. The obscure phrase used by lawyers to describe it as 'synthetic collateralized debt obligation' does highlight the importance of the collateral (i.e. the charge over the safe assets held by the Trustee) to the business logic of the transaction.

Whatever the adequacy of the justifications given by the courts in the two jurisdictions, the upshot sent ripples of concern around the global financial markets. The contradiction at the heart of the system was plain for all to see. Whereas the English court had instructed the trustee of the security to respect the charge held by the noteholders, the New York bankruptcy court had issued a stay against any attempt to enforce that security. International Conventions and EU legislation seek to provide for cooperation between courts when disentangling rights on insolvency, especially where such a conflict arises. Courts are required to recognize foreign proceedings and to respect judgments of foreign courts when they are properly seized of a matter. The UK is governed both by the EU Regulations on Insolvency Proceedings 2000[47] and the Cross Border Insolvency Regulations 2006,[48] which are based on the UN Model Law.[49] Often these regulations will require a stay of proceedings before a national court in order to respect the bankruptcy proceedings in a foreign jurisdiction.

In this particular case, Lehman Bros and its associated subsidiaries filed for bankruptcy under chapter 11 of title 11 of the US Bankruptcy code because the US was their main place of business. A key feature of chapter 11 is that it requires a stay of all proceedings that affect the position of the insolvent debtor. But the contract in the English proceedings was governed by a choice of law in favour of English law. The English court was faced with a claim by an Australian fund manager on behalf of noteholders to enforce its charge, which it accepted as valid under English law. Lehman Bros and LBSF could have applied to the English courts to recognize the stay of proceedings issued by the US court under the Cross Border Insolvency Regulations 2006. But it is uncertain whether the English courts would have respected this stay of proceedings in such a case where, it appears, the transaction was governed by English law, the assets were in England, and those courts had reached a different interpretation of the application of the similar principle of anti-deprivation to the particular clause of this contract as that applied by the US court. In this case, the courts in both jurisdictions agreed only to issue declaratory relief pending resolution of the contradiction. One of the

[47] EC Regulation No 1346/2000 of 29 May 2000. [48] SI 2006/1030.

[49] The Model Law on cross-border insolvency as adopted by the United Nations Commission on International Trade Law on 30 May 1997.

noteholders (Perpetual Trustee) settled the claim, so this particular contractual dispute was resolved in the way that such disputes are almost invariably resolved in the common law: by the parties making another contract—a contract of settlement. Legal uncertainty affects the value of assets and the quantification of the final settlement, but does not prevent an efficient resolution of the conflict of interest.

VI. *Lex Mercatoria* and *Ius Cogens*

And here we reach the lacuna: neither court even mentions the *lex mercatoria*, aside from a brief acknowledgement of the presence of an ISDA Master Agreement in the background to the transaction. They refer exclusively to the applicable state law of their respective jurisdictions. The national rules do not admit the exception that where an international transaction regulated by a Master Agreement like the ISDA agreement is involved, the ordinary national rules of property law and insolvency law should not be applied or should only be applied in a manner that respects the authority of the Master Agreement and its purpose of regulating and supporting international financial transactions. As the bankruptcy court in the US amply demonstrated, no such exception can be countenanced: the national law is operationally closed to the transnational system of financial *lex mercatoria*. There is no *audi alterem partem* here,[50] in which the court would try to reconcile the precepts of national insolvency law with the demands of the transnational normative order.

The closest that either court approaches to the transnational normative framework provided by the ISDA Master Agreement is the reference by the English court to the desirability of giving effect to contractual terms which the parties have agreed. 'Indeed, there is a particularly strong case for party autonomy in cases of complex financial instruments…; in such cases, the parties are likely to have been commercially sophisticated and expertly advised.'[51] To that observation might be added my contention that without the comprehensive normative framework provided by the Master Agreement, such financial markets using complex financial instruments could not have become established at all, so that a court should be wary of discarding parts of the contractual framework that may serve vital commercial functions. Judicial support for party autonomy in the context of international financial markets amounts in effect to recognition of the need to respect the *lex mercatoria*, in the form of standardized documentation, even though it is not named. Yet this sophisticated body of rules remains for the judges in these cases merely a private contract, not a source of law, not a type of

[50] G. Teubner and P. Korth, 'Two Kinds of Legal Pluralism: Collision of Transnational Regimes in the Double Fragmentation of World Society' in M. Young (ed) *Regime Interaction in International Law: Facing Fragmentation* (Cambridge: Cambridge University Press, 2012) 23–54.

[51] *Perpetual Trustee Co Ltd v. BNY Trustee Services Ltd and Lehman Bros Special Financing Inc* [2009] EWCA Civ 1160 Lord Neuberger MR at para 58.

'statute' designed to regulate this sector of the financial market.[52] The attitude of the courts seems to be closest to what Ralf Michaels calls deference:[53] the courts recognize the importance of granting space or private autonomy to actors to regulate their own affairs, but the rules that they create are regarded facts, like customs and expectations, not a non-state legal order. But even viewed as a custom, the Master Agreement does not appear to have gained the authority enjoyed, for instance, by the Incoterms with respect to international trade in goods, which provide the default provisions and sources for interpretation of contracts in the field.[54] The conception of privately created transnational norms with legal effects has not yet been incorporated into the court's perspective on its governing rule of recognition for laws regarding financial markets.

Reasons for this lacuna are plentiful. State legal systems generally only recognize the validity and applicability of other legal orders under strict conditions, such as the rules of private international law. It is probably correct to say that state law has only been prepared to recognize other states as providing a source of law, because that process of mutual recognition tends to confirm the cartel of states with regard to law-making powers.[55] Beyond that central obstacle to the recognition of private transnational norms as law, it seems likely that other considerations encourage courts to limit their recognition to deference. The courts will be disinclined to award greater authority to transnational private norms if they do not comply with the principles and aspirations of the rule of law, such as transparency and consistency, or perhaps even with the requirements of the Better Regulation agenda.[56] Beyond these formal characteristics of transnational private norm creation that serve to maintain the lacuna, it is also worth considering the potential significance of substantive qualities of transnational law.

One reason for declining to regard the transnational private norms as a source of authoritative guidance may have been the silence of the Master Agreement on the issue of the anti-deprivation principle. This silence may be unsurprising. When the rules of the Master Agreement were developed, no representatives of the public were present to argue issues from the perspective of public policy. No one at the table was especially concerned about upholding the anti-deprivation principle. Everyone was focussed on the need for clarity about the allocation of risks and rights. With respect to public policy, certainly some elements would have been influential in the negotiations. The banks had to be concerned about compliance with banking regulation, especially capital requirements. In fact, this sort

[52] Choi and Mitu Gulati, n 27, 1129–74.

[53] R. Michaels, 'The Re-State-Ment of Non-State Law: The State, Choice of Law, and the Challenge from Global Legal Pluralism' (2005) 51 *Wayne Law Review* 1209–59, 1233.

[54] International Chamber of Commerce, International Commercial Terms (available at <http://www.iccwbo.org>); J. Basedow, 'The State's Private Law and the Economy—Commercial Law as an Amalgam of Public and Private Rule-Making' (2008) 56 *American Journal of Comparative Law* 703–21, 709.

[55] Michaels, n 53.

[56] J. Bomhoff and A. Meuwese, 'The Meta-Regulation of Transnational Private Regulation' (2011) 38 *Journal of Law & Society* 160–84.

of collaterized debt obligation (CDO) transaction has as one of its purposes—as well as making money—improving the capital position of the originating bank by reducing its exposure to risky investments. In this context, the flip clause is perceived as relevant to pricing of swaps by helping their credit rating and relevant to regulatory capital requirements for the bank, but the question of the validity of the flip clause in the context of insolvency rules imposed by national public policy was almost certainly not part of the conversation. The point of the collateral was rather to avoid those insolvency rules and problems that they might pose to enforceability of complex financial transactions. As Annelise Riles has observed, the collateral provides a kind of private constitution for the parties' relationship and, at the same time, it reduces the chance of legal disputes from ever arising by providing a self-help mechanism for resolution.[57] The flip clause, with its rules on priority over the collateral, provides the fulcrum for the transaction, and provides the basis for 'lift-off' for the private norm creation above state law.[58]

In such systems of private norm creation, 'the interests and values of non-participants are not part of the regulatory concerns'.[59] This point can be generalized in any discussion of contractual governance: the great virtue of contracts as instruments of regulation is that they can be tailored precisely to conform to the objectives of the parties to the exchange, and the great vice of this kind of regulation is that it systematically ignores externalities—that is, the interests of third parties such as the creditors of the participants to the transaction. In other words, what is missing from the *lex mercatoria* is a legitimation of its authority derived from its compliance or alignment with mandatory norms of public policy that reflect considerations of the general interest. Public International Law, as a sub-system of the law based originally on contracts between states, recognizes that its legitimacy and authority depends not only on conventions and customs, but also on its aspiration to comply with *ius cogens*, that is, mandatory standards of international relations and protection of human rights. With respect to particular branches of international law, the search for these qualities of legitimacy and authority has led to calls for the constitutionalization of its fragmented parts, a process that normally requires the assertion of hegemony and hierarchy over other laws for one particular normative system through the construction of general mandatory norms and a court that can make binding and authoritative determinations regarding the requirements of its normative order.[60] An important part of this process consists in asserting the conformity of the specialist regime with general principles of public policy and *ius cogens*. For instance, the WTO Appellate

[57] A. Riles, 'The Anti-Network: Private Global Governance, Legal Knowledge, and the Legitimacy of the State' (2008) 56 *American Journal of Comparative Law* 605–29.

[58] R. Wai, 'Transnational Liftoff and Juridical Touchdown: The Regulatory Function of Private International Law in an Era of Globalization' (2002) 40 *Columbia Journal of Transnational Law* 209–74.

[59] Wai, n 58, 209, 259.

[60] M. Koskenniemi, 'Global Legal Pluralism: Multiple Regimes and Multiple Modes of Thought' (2005) (available at <http://www.helsinki.fi/eci/Publications/Koskenniemi/MKPluralism-Harvard-05d[1].pdf>).

body insisted early on that customary international law applied to agreements between WTO members, thereby asserting the conformity of its rules with general principles of international law.

Is the financial *lex mercatoria*, in the form of standardized master agreements, necessarily blind to those considerations of public policy and values that occupy such an important role in state law? It is possible that this *lex mercatoria* might develop through its own evolution some principles of public policy, particularly if they concern economic and business functions, as was the case with the example of anti-deprivation principle? Must we accept the verdict that the '[t]ransnational regime law is disconnected from processes which relate to society as a whole, from processes that aim at achieving the "common welfare".'?[61] Some interesting analogies can be found in the decisions of the private arbitration panels accredited by the Internet Corporation for Assigned Names and Numbers (ICANN). In applying the association's rules on Uniform Dispute Resolution Policy to cybersquatting, the arbitration panels have developed 'general principles' for the protection of free speech, which are not based on any particular national constitution or laws.[62] Similarly, international investment arbitration within the framework of the ICSID has recognized the potential relevance of mandatory principles of public international law and has also referred to the international public policy against corruption.[63] At present, a similar development of transnational principles of public policy seems unlikely to evolve in the different context of the financial *lex mercatoria*. The absence of a specialized tribunal to deal with international financial disputes may be blocking such a development, though currently proposals for such a court are being advanced.[64]

With such a specialized tribunal in place, it is possible to imagine that it could invoke a general principle of public policy, such as the anti-deprivation principle, as a principle to be recognized within the *lex mercatoria* itself. Such a tribunal would, however, confine the anti-deprivation principle to an appropriate scope for international financial transactions, where typically the different financial positions of secured and unsecured creditors are calculated and bargained risks. For instance, the Lehman counterparty to the swap transaction in the litigation could hardly complain that it lost its security over the collateral, for the existence of the flip clause (or something functionally equivalent) was probably necessary to make the swap an attractive business proposition to the investors. The safe harbour of the US Bankruptcy Code recognizes that the anti-deprivation rule has to be excluded for derivatives. A crucial issue in the New York case was the scope of the safe harbour for the connected transactions that were designed to provide collateral. A specialized tribunal might better understand that the connected transactions

[61] Teubner and Korth, n 50.

[62] M. Renner, 'Towards a Hierarchy of Norms in Transnational Law?' (2009) *Journal of International Arbitration* 533–55, 552.

[63] Renner, n 62, 533, 544–7.

[64] J. Golden, 'The Future of Financial Regulation: The Role of the Courts' in I. MacNeil and J. O'Brien (eds) *The Future of Financial Regulation* (Oxford: Hart Publishing, 2010) 83–92.

were interdependent and that the Lehman counterparty had not been deprived of anything that it had been entitled to.

In the absence of a specialized tribunal that might develop the financial *lex mercatoria* to take into account public policy and values, an '*ordre public* transnational',[65] the current alternatives are either for the courts to apply the public policy of the law of the forum, as happened in the cases under discussion, or, more boldly, for the national courts to appreciate that, although the financial *lex mercatoria* should be given a pivotal role in determining the governance of these contracts, it is necessarily incomplete owing to its origins in private norm creation.[66] National courts should therefore approach the task of adjudication by seeking to reconcile financial *lex mercatoria* with state mandatory rules based on public policy and constitutional principles, not by granting automatic priority or hierarchy to the latter, but by trying to understand the demands of both normative systems and how they can be reconciled. This should not be a process of determining which law (state law or *lex mercatoria*) is supreme, but rather should involve the recognition of the presence of heterarchical legal orders,[67] both of which are embedded in their respective communities, the nation state and the international financial markets community, where both have valid claims to provide authoritative guidance. Using this approach, the court should ask whether the apparent evasion of the anti-deprivation principle by the flip clause really engaged the purpose of the principle or in fact that the financial position created by the documentation really created a fair balance of risks between the parties and the creditors that relied upon them. As evidenced by the cases under consideration, however, such a process of reconciliation between legal orders—between national mandatory law and transnational *lex mercatoria*—seems to be presently beyond the radar of national commercial courts.

Advocates of transnational law have long been aware of the inherent defects of private norm creation—that its rules are likely to ignore externalities, the general interest, social justice, human rights, and public policy generally. The authority of the *lex mercatoria*, particularly the rules of international financial transactions we have been considering here, depends on agreement, usage, custom, and perhaps above all, the point made earlier that the rules are constitutive of an efficient financial market. Yet this transnational law cannot forever avoid politics. When its normative system conflicts with the laws of states, the courts must reconcile the competing demands. The absence of a claim on the part of transnational law to conform to universal mandatory principles, some kind of *ius cogens*, albeit one that applies especially to financial transactions, such as respect for the anti-deprivation principle (or, going further back in time to seek the sanctification of ancient Latin principle, the *actio pauliana*), leaves the *lex mercatoria* without the normative resources with which to offer guidance to courts. Without such an additional source of legitimation, one may predict that national courts, even when

[65] Teubner and Korth, n 50.
[66] Michaels, n 3, 467–8.
[67] Teubner and Korth, n 50.

disposed to try to respect the *lex mercatoria*, will have little compunction in permitting national mandatory rules based upon clear public policy considerations to trump the *lex mercatoria*. In the absence of the integration of such transnational mandatory principles of commercial law into the *lex mercatoria*, national legal systems, which pride themselves on their comprehensive system of values and weighing of different interests, will inevitably reject the route of deferring to the specialist functional rule-system of the *lex mercatoria*.

Lex Mercatoria, The ISDA Master Agreement, and *Ius Cogens*

Comment on H. Collins, 'Flipping Wreck: *Lex Mercatoria* on the Shoals of *Ius Cogens*'

*Horst Eidenmüller**

In his elegantly written and stimulating Chapter, Hugh Collins examines *lex mercatoria* as a self-regulatory mechanism for financial transactions in general and the over-the-counter (OTC) derivative markets in particular. The principal aim of his Chapter he stipulates as follows: it is '... to examine the idea of privately created norms that provide an alternative frame of reference for the governance of contracts concluded in global financial markets'. Collins entertains a very favourable view of contracting practice with respect to OTC derivatives trading (*lex mercatoria*). He believes that this practice is, in principle, to be assessed positively—because it is flexible, cost-efficient, tailored to the interests of the parties, etc. His only cause for concern is potential externalities that might undermine the efficiency of contracting practice with respect to particular types of transactions. The Chapter then goes on to identify a problem that is characterized as a clash of jurisdictions. Litigating OTC derivatives transactions in multiple jurisdictions may lead to frictions. Conflicts between applicable mandatory laws of different states on insolvency, property, etc may occur. Collins provides the following solution:

> ... [n]ational courts should therefore approach the task of adjudication by seeking to reconcile financial *lex mercatoria* with state mandatory rules based on public policy and constitutional principles, not by granting automatic priority or hierarchy to the latter, but by trying to understand the demands of both normative systems and how they can be reconciled.

Hence, mandatory laws of different states cannot and should not automatically trump the *lex mercatoria*. There are legitimate demands of the latter that these

* Professor of Private Law, German, European, and International Corporate Law at Ludwig-Maximilians-University, Munich and University of Oxford. Hugh Collins substantially revised the paper that he had presented at the Berlin Conference for publication in this volume. References in this Chapter are to the version submitted for publication unless stated otherwise.

state systems must take into account in a reconciliation process, the details of which go unspecified, however.

In this Chapter, I will present a less favourable view of the *lex mercatoria* with respect to OTC derivatives trading than Collins. The problem of externalities is more pervasive than he seems to believe, and often there are also significant negative effects on a party to a particular financial transaction itself. Hence, rather than being part of the solution, contracting practice with respect to derivatives trading is part of the problem. I submit that the appropriate policy response is also different from the one Collins suggests. Our primary concern should not be to make state courts more responsive to the 'demands' of the *lex mercatoria* in the realm of financial markets law. Rather, we should seek to establish a new public regulatory regime for financial markets that remedies some of the fundamental deficiencies that caused the last financial and economic crisis. Further, we should seek to harmonize certain mandatory private law rules of different states to reduce the frictions that worry Collins, which are a real problem indeed. In a nutshell, I am arguing to give less weight to the *lex mercatoria* in the realm of global financial transactions instead of giving it more weight as suggested by Collins.

I. *Lex Mercatoria*: Solution or Problem?

Almost six years ago, financial markets worldwide collapsed, leading to a significant economic downturn in almost all major economies of the world. As we now know, multiple regulatory failures contributed to the development of the crisis.[1] Bank capital requirements that were too lax (over-leveraging) and poorly designed incentive structures for bank managers encouraged over-securitization. Rating agencies did not act as a significant check due to various conflicts of interest. Rapid de-leveraging of financial institutions had a pro-cyclical effect once the crisis unfolded. Rapid resolution regimes for systemically relevant financial institutions did not exist.

Thinking about the adequate regulatory response to the crisis, Collins believes that the *lex mercatoria* is part of the solution, not of the problem. In the paper that he presented at the Berlin conference, he wrote: '[t]he case of supporting the *lex mercatoria* seems clear.' In this Chapter, he takes a more cautious but nonetheless supportive position:

> ... [j]udicial support for party autonomy in the context of international financial markets amounts in effect to recognition of the need to respect the *lex mercatoria*, in the form of

[1] There are, of course, numerous accounts of the financial and economic crisis that have been published since 2008. For two particularly helpful economic analyses, see J. Stiglitz, *Freefall: Free Markets and the Sinking of the Global Economy* (New York: Penguin Books, 2010); R. G. Rajan, *Fault Lines: How Hidden Fractures Still Threaten the World Economy* (Princeton, NJ/Oxford: Princeton University Press, 2010). See also H. Eidenmüller, *Finanzkrise, Wirtschaftskrise und das deutsche Insolvenzrecht* (Berlin: De Gruyter, 2009) 9–14.

standardized documentation, even though it is not named. Hence, Master Agreements like the ISDA Agreement are portrayed as exercising... valid claims to provide authoritative guidance.

It appears that, at least with respect to international financial transactions, Collins overestimates the benefits of *lex mercatoria* and downplays its costs. First, contract practice in this field created products with no apparent social utility. This is true, for example, with respect to naked credit default swaps (CDS) or naked shorts. Buying a CDS without being exposed to any credit risk is a purely speculative transaction. It is true that such a transaction might contribute to the (informational) efficiency of capital markets. However, the sheer volume of naked CDSs and naked shorts being traded during the onset of the financial crisis suggests that any such positive efficiency effect was clearly outweighed by their detrimental influence on the rapid devaluation of certain assets. Secondly, contract practice created products with a disutility for third parties. This is true, for example, with respect to the flip clause discussed by Collins: upon the insolvency of A, a charge held by A over certain of B's assets would automatically flip to certain of A's creditors. All the remaining creditors suffer a disutility in the amount of a reduction in their *pro rata* share of A's assets. It appears that the fundamental principle of *par conditio creditorum* is violated. No wonder then that the flip clause was held to be invalid under the *ipso facto* rule by US courts, whereas English courts, being somewhat more sympathetic to the interests of the financial industry, upheld the clause and thought that it could be reconciled with the anti-deprivation rule.[2] Thirdly, contract practice in the realm of international financial transactions created products with a disutility for parties to the transaction. Arguably, for example, synthetic CDOs purchased by German public institutions such as *Berliner Verkehrsbetriebe* (BVB) or *Kommunale Wasserwerke Leipzig* (KWL) fall into this category.[3] Under these transactions, the public institutions referred to basically acted as insurers for investment banks with respect to credit risks stemming from CDOs on their books. Why a public institution that is responsible for running public transport in a particular city (BVB) or that is responsible for public water supply (KWL) should have a rational interest in insuring an investment bank against credit risks is more than questionable. *Lex mercatoria*—the ISDA Master Agreement—apparently did more to confuse these institutions about the risks they took on board than to properly inform them about these risks. Hence, Collins' statement in the paper, presented at the conference, that '[a]ll the parties to these transactions are big financial institutions, familiar with the documentation, many

[2] Cf *In re Lehman Bros. Holdings Inc.* 422 B.R. 407 versus the UK Supreme Court's opinion in *Belmont Park Investments Pty Ltd and others v. BNY Corporate Trustee Services Ltd and another* [2011] UKSC 38, affirming *Perpetual Trustee Co Ltd v. BNY Corporate Trustee Services Ltd* [2009] EWCA Civ 1160.

[3] See Case C-144/10 *Berliner Verkehrsbetriebe (BVG) v. JPMorgan Chase Bank NA, Frankfurt Branch*, 12 May 2011 (ECJ); *JP Morgan Chase Bank NA v Berliner Verkehrsbetriebe (BVG) Anstalt des Offentlichen Rechts* [2010] EWCA Civ 390, affirming [2009] EWHC 1627 (Comm); *UBS AG, London Branch & Anor v. Kommunale Wasserwerke Leipzig GmbH* [2010] EWHC 2566 (Comm)—all decisions cited concern jurisdiction in these cases.

of them having participated in its creation' is simply not true. I conclude that *lex mercatoria* in the realm of transactions conducted in global financial markets is rather part of the problem, not the solution.

II. The Appropriate Policy Response

What is the appropriate policy response? First and foremost, I believe, it lies in a new *public* regulatory regime for financial markets. This is off the radar of Collins. From his perspective, regulated markets and financial market regulation give private actors an incentive to to change their behaviour, i.e. to opt out of the public system that seeks to regulate their activities. Collins describes and, I believe, endorses to a significant extent the motives of bankers to flee Exchanges, such as reducing transaction costs or avoiding capital requirements. But clearly the main regulatory responses to the financial and economic crisis both in the US and in Europe have been geared towards reclaiming the terrain lost to non-exchange trading activities and strengthening the public regulatory regime for financial markets and, I should like to add, quite rightly so.[4] Policy issues that regulators and states are and should be concerned about are more stringent capital requirements for banks (Basel III and beyond), taxing systemically relevant banks to eliminate their financing advantage, establishing efficient restructuring regimes for banks, regulating rating agencies, possibly banning certain types of transactions (for example naked shorts), and enhancing transparency in financial markets via central counterparty clearing and reporting to trade repositories. These issues are not addressed by Collins' Chapter, but they are, I submit, more important than issues of 'contract governance'.

The second important element of an appropriate policy response lies in the continuation and strengthening of efforts to harmonize certain mandatory private law rules of different states. It is certainly correct that frictions created by conflicting mandatory private law rules of different states do exist. The flip clause and its treatment under the *ipso facto* rule in the US on the one hand and under the 'anti-deprivation' principle in England on the other provide an excellent example. Not all frictions are a problem, however. Frictions between mandatory private law rules of different states should be tolerated where they are the consequence of efficiency-enhancing regulatory competition. An example is the competition among different European states for an optimal restructuring regime for failing businesses that we are currently witnessing under the European Insolvency Regulation.[5] Frictions resulting from strategic actions to maximize individual

[4] On the Dodd-Frank Act see, e.g., D. Skeel, *The New Financial Deal: Understanding the Dodd-Frank Act and Its (Unintended) Consequences* (Hoboken, NJ: John Wiley & Sons, 2011). For the European Union regulatory reform agenda see European Commission Internal Market and Services, 'Towards More Responsibility and Competitiveness in the European Financial Sector' (2010) (available at <http://ec.europa.eu/internal_market/finances/docs/leaflet/financial_services_en.pdf>).

[5] See, e.g., H. Eidenmüller, 'Abuse of Law in the Context of European Insolvency Law' (2009) 6 *European Company and Financial Law Review* 1.

gain ('distributive motives') should be eliminated by harmonizing the relevant mandatory private law rules with respect to contracts, property, insolvency, etc. Such harmonization relates to both conflict of laws rules and substantive rules. With respect to conflict of laws rules, for example, the Rome I and Rome II Regulations[6] and the European Insolvency Regulation[7] in Europe are important cornerstones. UNCITRAL has also contributed important work in this area as evidenced, for example, by the Model Law on Cross-Border Insolvency.[8] With respect to substantive rules too, much work has been and is being done towards further harmonization both in Europe and beyond. In Europe, for example, there is the Financial Collateral Directive[9], and there is the work on the Common Frame of Reference[10]. In the insolvency field, 'Principles of European Insolvency Law'[11] were put together a few years ago. Again, UNCITRAL is quite active in this field as well. Worth mentioning are the 'Receivables Convention'[12], the 'Legislative Guide on Secured Transactions'[13], and the 'Legislative Guide on Insolvency Law'[14]. The existing state of harmonization clearly is not such that frictions resulting from strategic actions to maximize individual gain do not exist—they certainly exist in the insolvency field that is the background to Collins' analysis. But the harmonization efforts will continue to, and should be, the primary focus of our regulatory zeal.

Collins is certainly aware of the need to bring mandatory norms of public policy to bear on the regulation of transactions in international financial markets. What is missing, in his view, from the *lex mercatoria* 'is a legitimation of its authority derived from its compliance with or alignment to mandatory norms of public policy that reflect considerations of the general interest.' He hopes that

[6] Regulation (EC) No 593/2008 of the European Parliament and of the Council of 17 June 2008 on the law applicable to contractual obligations (Rome I) (OJ 2009 L 177/6 and Regulation (EC) No 864/2007 of the European Parliament and of the Council of 11 July 2007 on the law applicable to non-contractual obligations (Rome II) (OJ 2007 L 199/40).

[7] Council Regulation (EC) No 1346/2000 of 29 May 2000 on Insolvency Proceedings (OJ 2000 L 160/1).

[8] UNCITRAL Model Law on Cross-Border Insolvency with Guide to Enactment (1997) (available at <http://www.uncitral.org/uncitral/en/uncitral_texts/insolvency/1997Model.html>).

[9] Directive 2002/47/EC of the European Parliament and of the Council of 6 June 2002 on financial collateral arrangements (OJ 2002 L/168/43) as amended by Directive 2009/44/EC of the European Parliament and of the Council of 6 May 2009 (OJ 2009 L 146/37).

[10] See C. von Bar and E. Clive (eds) *Principles, Definitions and Model Rules of European Private Law, Draft Common Frame of Reference (DFCR)* (Munich: Sellier, 2009). For an analysis of the relevant policy questions see H. Eidenmüller, F. Faust, H. C. Grigoleit, N. Jansen, G. Wagner, and R. Zimmermann, 'The Common Frame of Reference for European Private Law—Policy Choices and Codification Problems' (2008) 28 *Oxford Journal of Legal Studies* 659.

[11] W. W. McBryde, A. Flessner and S. C. J. J. Kortmann (eds) *Principles of European Insolvency Law* (Deventer: Kluwer, 2005).

[12] United Nations Convention on the Assignment of Receivables in International Trade (2001) (available at <http://www.uncitral.org/uncitral/uncitral_texts/security/2001Convention_receivables.html>.

[13] UNCITRAL Legislative Guide on Secured Transactions (2007) (available at <http://www.uncitral.org/uncitral/en/uncitral_texts/payments/Guide_securedtrans.html>).

[14] UNCITRAL Legislative Guide on Insolvency Law (2004) (available at <http://www.uncitral.org/uncitral/en/uncitral_texts/insolvency/2004Guide.html>).

with the further development of sophisticated dispute resolution mechanisms such as specialized tribunals, 'it [will be] possible to imagine that [such a tribunal] could invoke a general principle of public policy, such as the anti-deprivation principle, as a principle to be recognized within the *lex mercatoria* itself.' Surely one can imagine such a scenario, but I doubt that it will ever become reality in the foreseeable future. Even if it did, specialized *private* tribunals would never be able to lend *lex mercatoria* the kind of *public* legitimation that Collins has in mind. In other words, the defects of the *lex mercatoria* as a private regulatory mechanism can only be remedied by mandatory state law rules and not by private tribunals invoking what they perceive to be principles of public policy.

The view presented in this Chapter might seem to be conservative or even conventional. But if the recent financial and economic crisis taught us one lesson, it is that stronger public regulation of financial markets and more—not fewer—mandatory rules governing private transactions are necessary. It seems somewhat odd to praise the ISDA Master Agreement as a model for innovative self-regulation. All this is not to say that *lex mercatoria* is unimportant or should be curtailed by mandatory state law rules to a maximum extent. As long as all parties to a transaction can be assumed to act rationally and there are no externalities, there is no cause for concern. However, if *lex mercatoria* is defective in these respects, a case can be made for mandatory state law rules. Even then, *lex mercatoria* is an important inspirational tool for such rules: to adequately address deficiencies in 'innovative' market practice, such practice must be fully understood, and this understanding must reflect itself in the regulatory tools applied.

13

Innovation and the Role of Public-private Collaboration in Contract Governance

Governing Global Finance: Towards Contractual Governance

*Katharina Pistor**

I. Governing Global Finance: Past and Present

It is widely accepted that whatever governance regime(s) existed for global financial markets prior to the financial crisis is in need of reform. Yet there is no consensus as to how an alternative regime should look. Most reforms that have been undertaken, or are being proposed nationally or globally, are marginal modifications of existing regimes. This Chapter argues that there is a need for a much more comprehensive overhaul of the governance of global finance. It advocates a shift from hierarchical modes of governance based on territory or membership towards open and horizontal regimes based on multi-stakeholder bargains. In the age of financial globalization, financial systems are deeply intertwined and rapidly change in scope, reflecting the mobility of capital. Contrary to assertions during the boom years that the risk inherent to any financial services can be diversified away, the global crisis has demonstrated that global finance itself is inherently fragile. In fact, the threat of contagion has arguably increased as the tradable instruments meant to diversify risk became widely held by intermediaries in countries around the globe and served as transmitters of the crisis.[1] The global financial system is characterized by interdependence, malleability, and fragility. To be effective, the governance of global finance must reflect these core features. This calls for a governance regime that is inclusive, horizontal, and cooperative. Inclusiveness refers to the need to give stakeholders who bear the costs of crisis a voice in the design of the governance regime. Horizontality requires that voice be distributed evenly to ensure that future cost bearers are not side-lined. Finally, cooperation calls for

* Michael I. Sovern Professor of Law, Columbia University.

[1] For a formal model of contagion in open systems, see F. Allen and D. Gale, 'Financial Contagion' (2000) 198 *Journal of Political Economy* 1–33.

the design of governance regimes that facilitate collective problem solving in times of uncertainty. In contrast, conventional modes of financial governance are based on territory or membership, hierarchical allocation of regulatory and supervisory powers, and the unilateral or coercive execution of such powers. In short, the features of global finance call for 'contractual' governance.

Elements of such an alternative regime can be found in the extraordinary measures central banks, fiscal authorities, regulators, and financial intermediaries took at the height of the global financial crisis. These included transnational bailouts of large financial institutions; extensive networks of foreign exchange swap lines among central banks; and a multi-stakeholder initiative to stabilize a regional market with the participation of central banks, fiscal and regulatory authorities, and private actors. While few of these measures have been institutionalized, the fact that they were adopted at all suggests that there are possibilities for alternative governance regimes. Indeed, new institutions and emergent governance systems are often born in crisis when existing governance systems fail and actors scramble for alternative solutions. This Chapter discusses these emergent modes of governance and highlights their potential as elements of a new, contractual governance regime for global finance.

A governance regime, as defined in this Chapter, is a sustained effort to coordinate actions among actors who share a common purpose.[2] Governance regimes can serve many purposes and employ different means. The purpose of financial governance may be specific (i.e. to regulate a specific type of financial service, instrument, or issuer) or open-ended (i.e. protecting the stability of the financial system, making finance accessible to a broader base, or promoting long-term investments in future technologies). A given purpose may be mutually agreed upon by all relevant stakeholders, or dictated by a power wielder,[3] i.e. a state or organization that controls critical aspects of the global financial system. The governance purposes, whether agreed upon or dictated, may be implemented unilaterally, even coercively, or in a cooperative fashion. Finally, the scope of the governance regime may be defined by territory or membership; alternatively it may be open to all relevant stakeholders who may be significantly affected by the fallout from financial market activities.

Existing governance regimes for global finance are bound by territory or membership. The dominant form of financial market governance is state regulation consisting of prudential rules and regulations that are supervised and enforced

[2] The extensive use of the term 'governance' notwithstanding, it remains notoriously under-defined in most of the literature. Dictionaries refer to governance as guiding or managing others and sometimes contrast it with governing as a specifically institutionalized form of political governance. Similarly, the corporate governance literature has used the term without paying much attention to its contents. An exception is A. Shleifer and R. W. Vishny, 'A Survey of Corporate Governance' (1997) 52(2) *The Journal of Finance* 737–83, which defines corporate governance as a set of institutions that helps investors maximize the return of their investment. This definition, however, conflates the general meaning of governance with a particular set of goals.

[3] The concept of power wielder is discussed in R. Grant and R. O. Keohane, 'Sovereign Wealth Funds and Corporate Governance: A Minimalist Solution to the New Mercantilism' (2005) 60 *Stanford Law Review* 1345–69.

by regulatory agencies and/or courts. State action, including regulatory action, is generally confined to the territory of the nation state, with two exceptions. First, the increasing transnational scope of financial markets has given rise to expansive notions of extra-territorial application of national laws,[4] although the scope and effect of extra-territoriality remains disputed; and secondly, there has been a strong trend to harmonize laws and regulations pertaining to financial markets at the regional (EU) and international levels. The latter initiatives have been spearheaded by specialized international agencies and organizations, such as the Bank of International Settlement (BIS) for banking, the International Organization of Securities Committees (IOSCO), and the International Accounting Standards Board (IASB) for accounting standards. For the most part, the harmonization efforts at the international level are intergovernmental, but the results have remained nonbinding and lack international enforcement powers. Even within the EU, which has used its law-making powers to develop rules for financial markets, enforcement is ultimately left to nation states. It is therefore fair to say that state law and territorial enforcement remains the hallmark of the formal governance system for international finance.

An alternative model for governing finance that preceded state regulation and continues to be relevant both within and across nation states is self-regulation by organizations, such as stock exchanges. Traditionally these organizations were member-based with members owning the exchange and offering exchange-based intermediation services, such as brokerage.[5] Even in the age of de-mutualization and their transformation into publicly traded corporations, stock exchanges have retained core features of self-regulation in the form of monitoring entry, setting standards for intermediation services, and establishing listing requirements for firms.[6] Membership is also the hallmark of one of the most powerful self-regulatory organizations in global finance—the International Swaps and Derivatives Association (ISDA). ISDA is based in London and calls major financial institutions in the swaps and derivatives business its primary members, and brokers, accountants, and law firms its associate members.[7] Member-based governance regimes are, not surprisingly, geared towards advancing the interests of the members. Interests of other constituencies are taken into account only to the extent that they might threaten the operations of the club.[8]

[4] A recent UN report suggests that the extra-territorial reach of national law has expanded in recent years. See United Nations, 'Report of the International Law Commission, Fifty-Eighth Session' (2006) Annex E: Extraterritorial Jurisdiction (available at <http://legal.un.org/ilc/reports/english/a_61_10.pdf>).

[5] V. E. Morgan and W. A. Thomas, *The London Stock Exchange—Its History and Functions* (New York: St. Martin's Press, 1962); R. C. Michie, *The London and New York Stock Exchanges 1850-1914* (London: Allen & Unwin, 1987).

[6] J. Köndgen, 'Ownership and Corporate Governance of Stock Exchanges' (1998) 154 *Journal of Institutional and Theoretical Economics* 224–51.

[7] G. Morgan, 'Market Formation and Governance in International Financial Markets: The Case of OTC Derivatives' (2008) 61 *Human Relations* 637–60 (for details see <http://www.isda.org/>).

[8] This threat may emanate from the failure to prevent market crashes with negative repercussions for a stock exchange or its members, or the threat to end the self-regulatory regime and replace it with state regulation. The shadow of state regulation has played an important role at the national level to ensure continuous updating of self-regulatory regimes in countries like the UK and the US.

Another hallmark of global financial governance in its current form is that regulatory standard setting for global financial markets—whether by states or self-regulatory bodies—has for the most part come from the centre rather than the periphery. The US and the UK have been at the forefront of developing standards for securities markets within IOSCO.[9] These two countries are also the home to the major stock exchanges, the London and New York Stock Exchanges, which evolved into the *de facto* standard setters for listing requirements for internationally cross-listed firms.[10] While these two markets compete with each other for business, they have as of now voiced little concern that markets in third countries might erode their pre-eminence. Indeed, while they often serve as scapegoats for one another[11] to warn against excessive regulatory intervention by the state, which is said to undermine their respective competitive edge, regulatory standards in other markets have been largely ignored.

The US and the UK have also been at the forefront of establishing standards for international banking. Amidst disagreement about the appropriate prudential standard to adopt, the UK and the US came up with a bilateral agreement and exercised their power of excluding from their markets intermediaries that did not meet these standards to effectively set global prudential standards that have become known as Basel I.[12] This has served as the benchmark for prudential regulation in banking ever since, notwithstanding the fact that it imposed substantial costs on less developed countries[13] and arguably facilitated the takeover of local banks in emerging markets by Western banks with better capital ratios. The European Union even transposed core principles of the Basel Accord into EU-wide directives, which transformed international soft law (the Accord is technically a non-binding recommendation by the BIS) into hard law not only for internationally operative banks, but also for domestic banks. The only jurisdiction from which major resistance to Anglo-American leadership in setting

See D. Philips, *Crime and Authority in Victorian England* (London: Croom Helm, 1977) for 19th century UK; see also T. L. Hazen, *Treatise on the Law of Securities Regulation* (St. Paul, Minn: West Group, 2002).

[9] IOSCO, 'Objectives and Principles of Securities Regulation' (1998) (available at <http://www.iosco.org/library/pubdocs/pdf/IOSCOPD82.pdf>); K. Pistor, 'The Standardization of Law and Its Effect on Developing Economies' (2002) 50 *Journal of Comparative Law* 101–34.

[10] Both markets are currently in merger deals with The Toronto Exchange (the LSE) and Deutsche Börse/Euronext respectively. This supports the general point made here that they occupy the centre of global finance and that expansion strategies need to include them, if not emanate from one of these exchanges. Their pre-eminence today is threatened less by markets in other countries and instead by new entrants in the US or the UK who offer lower governance standards, such as NASDAQ, or more recently, new electronic based trading platforms such as BATS.

[11] While in the past, it was typically the NYSE that lobbied against increased regulatory standards, in the aftermath of the global crisis, the London Stock Exchange feared a tightening of regulatory standards in the UK.

[12] B. Simmons, 'The International Politics of Harmonization: The Case of Capital Market Regulation' (2001) 55 *International Organization* 589–620; E. B. Kapstein, *Governing the Global Economy: International Finance and the State* (Cambridge, Mass: Harvard University Press, 1996).

[13] S. Claessens, G. R. Underhill and X. Zhang, 'The Political Economy of Basle II: The Costs for Poor Countries?' (2008) 31 *The World Economy* 313–44.

international banking standards could have come thus became a major agent for broadening the scope of these very standards.

The US (New York) and the UK (London) as the global financial centres, have thus been able to play the role of power wielders[14] in establishing the regulatory standards for international finance.[15] The thrust of the standards they have espoused is limited regulatory intervention in financial markets and a strong endorsement of the notion that financial markets not only allocate resources efficiently, but also have sufficient self-regulatory and self-disciplining capacity to avoid a major collapse. Efficiency became the hallmark of standard setting, which pre-empted any discussion about the purposes of financial intermediation in modern economies.

The International Monetary Fund (IMF) helped diffuse these efficiency standards by using 'international best practices'—a shorthand for standards derived from Anglo-American practices—for benchmarking the rules and regulations in countries around the world and advocating legal and regulatory reforms with the goal of meeting those benchmarks. The most explicit evidence of this is the International Financial Architecture the IMF promoted in the aftermath of the East Asian financial crisis.[16]

The power of exclusion combined with the EU's and the IMF's backing of regulation produced by the global financial centres made standards produced in the centre effectively binding globally—notwithstanding that technically they are 'soft' law. The most visible expression of this hierarchical system of global finance has been the G7[17]—later the G8—a meeting place of central bankers, ministers of finance, and heads of states that formed the inner circle of the global financial system. An enlarged circle of the G20[18] was established in 1999 to complement the G8, whose pre-eminence was not questioned at the time. It took the global financial crisis to elevate the G20 at least nominally to the major forum for developing global standards. Notably, however, it was the US President who invited the G20 to a meeting to take stock of the crisis in the Autumn of 2008. An explicit call for action and a series of meetings notwithstanding, the G20 has so far made little direct contribution to reshaping global financial governance.[19]

[14] See Grant and Keohane, n 3.

[15] It has been argued that, in fact, France and other European countries played a critical role in establishing these standards as global standards. See R. Abdelal, *Capital Rules* (Cambridge, Mass: Harvard University Press, 2007). While there is strong evidence of these countries playing a critical role in the diffusion of these standards, the standards themselves originated in the UK and the US.

[16] IMF, *International Standards: Strengthening Surveillance, Domestic, Institutions and International Markets* (Washington: International Monetary Fund, 2003).

[17] The G7 includes the US, UK, Canada, Germany, France, Italy, and Japan. Russia joined in 1997, making it the G8.

[18] Details about the G20 and its history are available at <http://www.g20.org/about_g20/g20_members>.

[19] C. Giles, G. Parker, B. Hall, J. Politi, D. Dombey, and M. Mackenzie, 'Bush to Call G20 Summit on Crisis', *Financial Times*, 23 October 2008 (available at <www.ft.com>).

In sum, global finance has evolved into a system that is governed by standards that were set at its core. These standards are tailored to interests represented at the core and pay scant attention to different conditions or interests in the periphery.[20] The diffusion process of standards from the centre to the periphery takes various forms, from mandatory implementation within the EU over monitoring through loan conditionality by the IMF, to voluntary implementation and re-interpretation of rules by countries at the core. Critically, once in place standards are difficult to change or amend, especially by countries on the periphery who are standard-followers, not standard-setters. The sheer complexity of the harmonization project makes this a difficult task.

Even more problematic, there is no built-in feedback loop to ensure that information about the operation of these standards in different countries is channelled back to the centre. Not surprisingly, global standards are therefore made or altered only in the aftermath of a major crisis. The Basel Concordat owes its existence to the failure of Herstatt Bank and the UK banking crisis, and the first Basel Accord (Basel I) to the aftermath of the Latin American debt crisis. Basel II is a child of the emerging market crisis in the late 1990s, and Basel III of the 2008/2009 global financial crisis.

Not only is the current governance of global finance hierarchical and overtly rigid, it also has major shortcomings in what it regulates. The major focus of these regulatory standards has been prudential regulation, in particular the establishment of standards for capital adequacy of specific financial intermediaries that fit the agreed upon definition of a 'bank'. Non-banks are not part of the regulatory agenda, and attempts to include other financial intermediaries or attach regulation to specific activities rather than institutions have had little traction.[21] This creates regulatory arbitrage opportunities, as exemplified by the rapid growth of the shadow banking system in countries at the core of the global financial system in the years leading up to the crisis.[22]

Prudential standards, specifically capital adequacy rules, are meant to prevent financial crises by establishing financial cushions at banking institutions in times of economic downturn. In case these measures fail—as they frequently do—the respective home country of the failing bank is the one to provide lender of last resort services (this is the essence of the Basel Concordat). This peculiar combination of *ex ante* regulation and allocation of *ex post* rescue responsibilities does not address the possibility that the costs created by inadequate prudential regulation, weak implementation, or the absence of any regulation of shadow banks might exceed the fiscal capacity of the country designated as lender of last resort, thus creating a major governance void.[23] The global crisis has demonstrated that this

[20] See Claessens, Underhill, and Zhang, n 13.

[21] This is not surprising given that the shadow banks—including investment banks and other intermediaries that offer bank-like services—originated at the centre of the global system and have taken advantage of the absence of regulation to expand globally.

[22] T. Adrian and H. S. Shin, 'The Shadow Banking System: Implications for Financial Regulation' (2009) 382 *Staff Report*, esp Figure 2 at 2.

[23] K. Pistor, 'Host's Dilemma: Rethinking EU Banking Regulation in Light of the Global Crisis' in H. Baum, B. Haar, H. Merkt, and P. Mülbert (eds) *Festschrift für Klaus J. Hopt* (Berlin: de Gruyter, 2010); K. Pistor, 'Sovereign Wealth Funds: Neither Market Investors nor "Imperialist

failure can destabilize the global financial system and impose major burdens on home and host countries alike. Thus, when Iceland turned out to be unable to insure British and Dutch account holders of failing Icelandic bank branches, the UK and the Netherlands stepped in to guarantee deposits in order to avoid systemic effects in their own markets. In Ireland, excessive leverage of domestic banks that had been fuelled by lending practices of foreign banks was converted into sovereign debt when Ireland offered a blanket guarantee for all bank accounts—a commitment that went beyond the means of the country. This triggered the need for a bailout by countries in the eurozone with backing from the IMF. Finally, in Central and Eastern Europe (CEE) banking groups with headquarters in Western European countries helped fuel a credit boom in the years leading up to the global crisis, which busted when the global crisis caused a retraction of capital.[24] A major financial crisis in CEE was avoided only by a multi-stakeholder response that committed banks to the region and mobilized funds from international financial institutions (IFIs) as well as foreign governments to rescue local subsidiaries of these groups (see later).

The crisis thus exposed the Achilles' heel of the existing global financial architecture: a governance regime that facilitated the externalization of financial risk to the periphery of the global financial system without allocating last resort responsibilities. It is a direct outcome of the design of the international financial architecture, which consists of a limited set of harmonized regulatory standards that offered ample arbitrage opportunities for sophisticated financial intermediaries, but are difficult to change in response to mounting problems; the aggressive promotion of capital liberalization that facilitated the rapid expansion of the financial service industry located at the core of the global financial system;[25] and the absence of transnational mechanisms to address an emerging crisis, coordinate lender of last resort facilities, and ultimately ensure a more balanced allocation of risk bearing throughout the global financial system.

II. Crisis Responses

In the context of the global financial crisis, several responses emerged to address the missing link in global financial governance: the *transnational* lender of last resort function. This Section describes three such responses: Sovereign Wealth Funds (SWFs) as lenders/investors of 'next-to-last' resort; inter-central bank foreign currency swap lines; and the European Bank Coordination Initiative

Capitalists"—A Response to Heike Schweizer' in U. Bernitz and W.-G. Ringe (eds) Company Law and Economic Protectionism (Oxford: Oxford University Press, 2010) 290–301.

[24] For a detailed analysis of the development of credit markets, the ownership structure of banks in CEE, and the limited regulatory powers of countries in the region, see the contributions in C. Enoch and I. Ötker-Robe (eds) *The Causes and Nature of the Rapid Growth of Bank Credit in the Central, Eastern and South-Eastern European Countries* (New York: Palgrave, 2007).

[25] See Adrian and Shin, n 22.

(EBCI). Section 4 will analyse in greater detail which of these responses can possibly be regarded as an emergent contractual governance regime for global finance, and why.

1. SWFs as investors of next-to-last resort

The inadequacy of the existing governance of global finance became apparent in the last quarter of 2007, when some of the largest globally active financial intermediaries found themselves vulnerable to an increasingly volatile financial market that no longer guaranteed easy access to liquidity to meet their short-term funding needs. In response, banks as well as investment banks that were technically not subject to capital adequacy rules sought to shore up their capital base to regain investor confidence. They included Barclays (UK); Citigroup, Morgan Stanley, and Merrill Lynch (US); and UBS (Switzerland). The only counterparts willing to invest in financial intermediaries at the time were Sovereign Wealth Funds from emerging markets—most prominent among them those from Singapore (Temasek and the Government of Singapore Investment Corporation), China (CIC, China's newly founded Investment Corporation) and the Gulf States (Abu Dhabi's ADIA, the Kuwait Investment Authority, and investment portfolios managed by individual Sheikhs from Saudi Arabia or the UAE).[26]

There has been much debate about the motives of SWFs, ranging from fears of mercantilism[27] to characterizations of SWFs as ordinary global investors.[28] I have argued elsewhere that neither account fully captures the nature of SWFs, especially those from non-democratic systems.[29] The important point for the argument advanced by this Chapter is that in the context of the global financial crisis, SWFs developed into stabilizing pillars of the global financial system. Whatever may have motivated them to make the first round of large investments in late 2007, they made additional investments in the same institutions in which they lost money as the crisis deepened and held on to those investments even as domestic governments stepped in as lenders/investors of last resort for financial intermediaries within their jurisdiction.[30] SWFs also responded to calls from government shareholders in the intermediaries they had invested in to convert

[26] See K. Pistor, 'Global Network Finance' (2009) 37 *Journal of Comparative Economics* 552–67 for a discussion of these transactions.

[27] R. J. Gilson and C. J. Milhaupt, 'Sovereign Wealth Funds and Corporate Governance: A Minimalist Solution to the New Mercantilism' (2008) 60 *Stanford Law Review* 1345–69.

[28] H. Schweitzer, 'Sovereign Wealth Funds: Market Investors of Imperial Capitalists?—The European Response to Direct Investments by Non-EU State-controlled Entities' in U. Bernitz and W. -G. Ringe (eds) *Company Law and Economic Protectionism* (Oxford: Oxford University Press, 2010) 250–89.

[29] Pistor, n 26; Pistor, 'Hosts's Dilemma' (2010), n 23; and K. Hatton and K. Pistor, Maximizing Autonomy in the Shadow of Great Powers: The Political Economy of Sovereign Wealth Funds (2011) 50(1) *Columbia Journal of Transnational Law* 1–81, for a comprehensive analysis of the genesis and investment patterns of these funds.

[30] See Pistor, n 26, and Hatton and Pistor, n 29, for details of these transactions.

their interest bearing debt securities into common stock in order to increase the capital of banks as a prerequisite for those banks to pass critical stress tests.[31] SWFs stepped in once again when financial intermediaries sought to raise capital to buy back their government's stakes.[32] And finally, SWFs have appeared as the most likely buyers of AIG, the insurance company the US government effectively nationalized in September of 2008 and from which the US government was planning to exit by May 2011.[33]

In essence, SWFs played a critical role as transnational lenders and investors of next-to-last resort for foreign financial intermediaries in the early stages of the crisis and are performing the role of midwives in the process to re-establish these financial giants as independent institutions. They stepped into the void left by private actors who took flight when the financial markets imploded and remained cautious even after the worst of the crisis had subsided. Importantly, their investments targeted major international banking groups headquartered outside their jurisdictions. They had no legal obligation to step in, nor did they face domestic political pressure to do so—to the contrary, the governments of Singapore and China have been heavily criticized for these loss-making investments.[34] Without doubt, stabilizing the global financial system was in the SWFs' self-interest. As funds with hundreds of billions of assets under management,[35] most of which was invested internationally, they could not afford a meltdown of the global financial system. The critical question is whether SWFs are willing or should be encouraged to play a more sustained role in stabilizing global finance in the future.

2. Inter-central bank foreign exchange swap lines

Beginning in 2007, the US Federal Reserve (the Fed), followed later by other central banks, created foreign exchange swap lines with their counterparts in other countries. Taken together, these swap lines created a global network of swap facilities with the Fed at the centre linked to 12 other central banks, with the European Central Bank (ECB) and the central banks of Japan, China, and Switzerland forming other central nodes.[36] The function of foreign exchange swap lines is

[31] Thus, GIC converted its stake in Citigroup in the spring of 2009 into common stock following an announcement of the US Treasury that it would convert its preferred stock into common stock provided that other major investors would follow suit.

[32] This has been the case for Morgan Stanley, which sought additional funds from CIC to raise enough money for paying the US government back early. In the case of Barclays, the investment by Qatar Investment Authority (QIA) even helped avert the need for government bailouts. Both transactions are detailed in Pistor, n 26.

[33] F. Guerrara, 'US Woos Sovereign Wealth Funds in AIG Sale', *Financial Times*, 13 February 2011 (available at <www.ft.com>).

[34] See Pistor, n 26.

[35] Temasek, the smallest of the SWFs that participated in those deals, has US$130 billion under management, and ADIA, the largest of all SWFs to date, is said to control over US$750 billion. See Hatton and Pistor, n 29.

[36] See R. Moessner and W. A. Allen, 'International Liquidity Provision and Currency-specific Liquidity Shortages' (2010) BIS Working Paper, esp graph 3.1 at p 8.

to give foreign central banks access to currency holdings so that they can make them available to entities within their jurisdiction that have a demand for this currency. In normal times, these banks would obtain local currency from their central banks through the discount window and engage in private market currency swaps to meet their foreign currency needs. Alternatively, their respective central bank would use its foreign currency reserves to make dollars available to domestic banks. In the context of the global crisis, both strategies became problematic. In light of increasing demand for US dollars in the volatile environment of the crisis, fuelling the sale of domestic currency would have put downward pressure on it; for the same reason, foreign exchange reserves in US dollars would have easily been depleted. By opening currency swap lines with central banks in countries that exhibited strong demand for the US dollar, the Fed effectively granted foreign commercial banks access to liquidity, which is typically reserved for domestic entities.[37] With increasing demand for other major currencies, especially the euro, the yen, and the Swiss franc, other central banks followed suit. The conditions for individual swap lines varied. Whereas the Fed accepted foreign currencies as collateral, the ECB insisted on euro currency reserves held by Hungarian, Polish, Danish, and Swedish banks when opening swap lines with them.[38] Not all swap lines were used extensively. In countries that had accumulated substantial reserves in US dollars, the impact was more symbolic than actually needed. The most critical aspect of these swap lines was to signal to markets the willingness and ability of central banks to coordinate. Most swap lines were of limited duration; however, new ones were opened when financial pressure increased once more, as in the context of the Greek sovereign debt crisis, which put the euro under pressure.[39] These differences notwithstanding, observers have called this 'one of the most notable examples of central bank cooperation in history.'[40] It provides yet another example of the responsiveness and imagination of key actors in the global financial market place in the context of a crisis. The question that will be addressed in Section 4 is whether they point beyond crisis management towards sustained cooperation, or governance.

3. The European Bank Coordination Initiative

The European Bank Coordination Initiative (EBCI) is a coordinated effort by stakeholders in the pan-European financial system that originated in a coordinated effort to avert a financial collapse in the Central and Eastern European markets when the region's financial system was threatened by the deepening of the global crisis.[41] CEE had become deeply integrated into the global financial system

[37] M. Obstfeld, J. C. Shambaugh, and A. M. Taylor, 'Financial Instability, Reserves, and Central Bank Swap Lines in the Panic of 2008' (2009) 99 *American Economic Review* 480–6, 484.

[38] Moessner and Allen, n 36, 11. [39] See Moessner and Allen, n 36, 10.

[40] Obstfeld, Shambaugh, and Taylor, n 37, 483.

[41] See K. Pistor, 'Governing Interdependent Financial Systems: Lessons from the Vienna Initiative' (2011) 2(2) Globalization and Development, Article 4 (available at <http://www.degruyter.com/view/j/jgd>).

as a result of liberalization policies and expansion strategies of banks primarily from Austria, Sweden, and Italy. Between 36 and 98 per cent of all bank assets in countries in the region are controlled by foreign banking groups.[42] When these banking groups came under pressure by the deepening global crisis and bailout packages from their own governments that were limited to domestic operations, they began to withdraw capital from the region, raising fears about the effects of an uncoordinated capital flight. Governments from the region responded by threatening to ring-fence assets and to exclude foreign-owned domestic banks from their deposit insurance schemes.

Caught between different regulators with conflicting demands, the heads of several major pan-European banking groups, led by Raiffeisenbank, petitioned the Commission of the European Union, the European Bank for Reconstruction and Development (EBRD), and the European Investment Bank (EIB) for help. While initially worded to reign in restrictive measures by governments in CEE countries, the resulting initiative evolved into a multi-stakeholder resolution of the regional crisis. After a series of meetings with individual groups of stakeholders, including banks, central banks, regulators, and ministries of finance, a joint meeting of these stakeholders was held in Vienna in March of 2009, which was also attended by representatives from the EBRD, the IMF, and the European Commission. The ECB attended as observer. This meeting established the ground rules for the Vienna Initiative, later renamed the EBCI.[43] Participants agreed to publicly commit to maintain investments in the region and not to withdraw in an uncoordinated fashion; to allow bailout funds made available by governments to parent banks headquartered in their countries to be used for stabilizing subsidiaries in CEE countries; and to coordinate rescue and stabilization efforts for each of the affected countries. This agreement was backed by a 'joint action plan' announced by the EBRD, the IMF, and the World Bank that provided additional funding for countries in the region.[44]

Over the next several months, stabilizing packages were negotiated on a country-by-country basis using the Vienna formula, and several additional meetings were convened, each with a growing number of participants. In September 2009, the EU Commission hosted a meeting in Brussels. Sixteen banking groups, up from the initial group of eight as well as government officials from home and host countries of these banks attended this meeting. In the Spring of 2010, over 100 participants attended a meeting organized in Athens that put post-crisis governance issues, such as the management of distressed assets, on the agenda.[45]

[42] See Enoch and Ötker-Robe, n 24, for data on the pre-crisis situation.

[43] W. Nitsche, 'The Vienna Initiative/European Bank Coordination Initiative: Assessment and Outlook' (2010) Austrian Federal Ministry of Finance Working Paper Series (available at <https://www.bmf.gv.at/services/publikationen/BMF-WP_4_2010-The_Vienna_Initiative-European_Bank_Coordinati.pdf?4jwmq6>).

[44] See also the final report of the joint action plan, issued in March 2011 (the first report is available at <http://www.ebrd.com/downloads/news/joint-action-plan-report-2013.pdf>).

[45] See Nitsche, n 43, for details; see also EBRD Timeline for the Vienna Initiative (April 2011) (available at <http://vienna-initiative.com/vienna-initiative-part-1/#timeline>).

The EBCI can best be described as a series of multi-stakeholder negotiations about sharing the burden for the costs of the crisis—and by implication, the costs of the failure to govern markets more effectively in the years leading up to the crisis. Every stakeholder had misjudged the potential fallout of a system from which most had benefited in the years leading up to the crisis—at least in part because of shared belief in the efficiency and self-governing capabilities of financial markets. The goal of the initiative was to avoid an uncoordinated flight from the region, which could have resulted in collapse. Experience with similar crises in other emerging markets suggested that this outcome was extremely likely. Whether in Mexico in 1994, East Asia in 1997, or Argentina in 2001, the standard response to an unfolding crisis has been for foreign bank groups to cut back investments in the region and leave it to local governments and the IMF to deal with the fallout from the crisis. Instead, the EBCI emerged as a coordinated effort to stabilize the regional markets. While IFIs played a critical role, foreign banking groups and their home governments participated in the burden-sharing exercise—notwithstanding the fact that they had no legal obligation to do so, and arguably governments may have overstepped legislative constraints on the use of bailout funds. As in the previous cases, the question left is whether these efforts are unique to crises or whether they carry the seeds of an emergent contractual governance regime.

III. From Crisis Response to Contractual Governance

The crisis responses in the Section III displayed some of the features of a contractual governance regime identified at the outset of this Chapter: inclusiveness, horizontality, and cooperation. However, these features were not evenly displayed across the different responses. Table 13.1 summarizes the classification of the responses along these three dimensions. As can be seen, only the EBCI fulfils all three criteria unambiguously. Nonetheless, each of the responses contains some features that may be deemed contractual and could serve as building blocks for an alternative global governance regime.

Table 13.1 Characteristics of Global Crisis Management

	Multi-stakeholder Bank Rescues	FX Swap Lines	European Bank Coordination Initiative
Inclusive	Partial	Partial	Yes
Horizontal	No	No	Yes
Cooperative	No	Limited	Yes

Source: Compilation by Author

1. Inclusiveness

Global financial systems consist of multiple, overlapping markets for financial services. They create effects for people in multiple countries and implicate social and economic policies in ways that trigger legitimate governance concerns in such countries. The governance regime for global finance that has been erected over the past decades has sought to minimize policy intervention with financial market development on the grounds that markets are best left to their own devices to allocate resources efficiently. The theoretical and empirical support for this proposition has always been thin.[46] The global crisis has demonstrated that however markets may allocate resources, they also allocate costs, and thus create the need for governance. Yet the allocation of regulatory powers and responsibilities is not well aligned with the allocation of costs that result from financial integration. This creates incentives for arbitrage and externalization of those costs—often by constituencies that frequently lack the resources to respond effectively to a crisis. One remedy for this misalignment has been the accumulation of foreign currency reserves by countries that had been exposed to stringent IMF conditions in earlier crises.[47] Essentially, countries are buying insurance against future crisis. These are unilateral strategies to respond to the uneven distribution of costs in the event of a crisis.

Inclusive governance, in contrast, refers to a governance regime that includes all relevant parties that are likely cost-bearers in an integrated financial system in designing strategies that better align the costs of financial market integration. In relative terms, all three response strategies discussed earlier demonstrate far greater inclusiveness than the standard IMF emergency packages that were previously dispensed to emerging markets in crisis situations. The bank bailout packages saw SWFs and home governments taking stakes in financial intermediaries whose failures were likely to destabilize the global financial system. In the most generous terms, this response strategy can therefore be described as a coordinated effort that included major stakeholders in the global financial system. Yet these measures fell short of full inclusiveness in that inclusion was conditioned on the availability of bailout funds, and taxpayers and savers, i.e., those whose resources were used in the bailout of banks, were denied explicit control rights. This is most apparent in the fact that both SWFs and governments used for the most part non-voting financial instruments, such as convertible debt or preferred stock, in the bailout packages. Thus, they denied themselves the ability to exert governance on the financial intermediaries that were bailed out in the name of those whose resources were used.[48]

[46] Lord A. Turner, *The Turner Review: A Regulatory Response to the Global Banking Crisis* (London: Financial Services Authority, 2009).

[47] See Obstfeld, Shambaugh, and Taylor, n 37, 482, showing that currency reserves were higher than predicted in several emerging markets with previous crisis experience, such as South Korea, Malaysia, and Singapore, but also in rising emerging markets, such as China and India. On the increase of foreign currency reserves in the aftermath of the East Asian financial crisis, see also FRBSF, 'Foreign Exchange Reserves in Asia: Why the High Demand?' (2003) 11 Federal Reserve Bank of San Francisco Economic Letter.

[48] Just to clarify, I am not arguing that taxpayers should be directly involved in the governance of such intermediaries, only that instruments should be used that facilitate the exertion of governance.

The scope of central bank swap lines and the number of countries included was also much more extensive than similar arrangements in the past. A total of 27 central banks participated in the network of currency swap lines.[49] The swap lines corresponded to the demand for a particular core currency—the dollar, the euro, the yen, or the reminbi—in other countries. As such, the arrangement went well beyond arrangements based on membership, such as the club of the G7 or G20, and responded to the actual scope of the market. Nonetheless, it would go too far to describe the arrangement as fully inclusive. The initiative for opening swap lines came from the central nodes in these arrangements, the central banks of the major global currencies. They too exercised the discretion to invite central banks of different countries to create such a bilateral arrangement, or not, and determine the maximum amount to be used and the duration of these arrangements. In fact, they expanded the scope of countries to be included in these arrangements only gradually—with emerging markets largely having been left out of the early arrangements, and some being left out for good.[50] It may therefore be more accurate to describe these arrangements as lowering the entry barriers to the central banks for selected countries that had previously not participated in such arrangements, rather than as a new model of inclusive governance.

Of the three arrangements, the EBCI is the most inclusive. While the initiative originated with a handful of banks, it soon mushroomed into an open forum for discussing governance needs and possible solutions for the pan-European financial market. The initiative remained in principle open to all willing to participate and included over 100 participants from across the region in the 2010 meeting in Athens.[51] Whereas bank bailouts were conducted by self-appointed lenders and investors of next-to-last and last resort, and the currency swaps depended on the generosity of the major central banks to include or not include certain countries in the arrangement, the EBCI practiced open access by stakeholders in a regional market.

2. Horizontality

Horizontal forms of governance are formed by agreement rather than dictate and imply some level of inclusiveness. The quest for a horizontal mode of governance stems from the fact that global financial markets create interdependencies among different constituencies that are all affected by how financial markets operate and share in the costs and benefits of domestic and global finance—but do so unevenly. The relevant stakeholders in the global financial

[49] See Moessner and Allen, n 36.

[50] See the comments in B. Sester, 'Where is my Swap Line? And will the Diffusion of Financial Power Balkanize the Global Response to a Broadening Crisis?' (2008) SafeHaven blog, which raises the question whether the differential access to dollars or euros might impact emerging markets that did not receive access (available at <http://www.safehaven.com/article/11625/where-is-my-swap-line>).

[51] See the EBRD timeline for the Vienna Initiative, n 45.

system include consumers and providers of financial services, regulators, fiscal authorities, and central banks from all countries with open borders to capital flows. Given that financial markets are inherently fragile and crises are fairly common, those who share the burden of a crash should be well represented in the design of governance structures. Whereas hierarchical modes of governance are built around a central authority designed to impose its will on all constituencies, horizontal governance gives multiple constituencies a voice so that promoters of certain governance solutions take into account their likely impact on those constituencies. For horizontal models of governance it is therefore not sufficient to grant some constituencies the right to be consulted; they need to have exit or veto rights to create a level playing field in the design of governance structures that take their interests into account.

The current design of global financial governance excludes such veto powers for many constituencies. Countries that do not belong to the inner circle of countries that have taken upon themselves the design of the international financial architecture are rule-followers, not rule-makers. The power of exclusion and the promotion of a financial market governance regime by the IMF, the EU, and other international bodies, such as the OECD, have effectively denied them veto rights and thereby undermined their bargaining power. Financial intermediaries are regularly consulted on domestic legislation or international standard setting, but consumers are absent and taxpayers often under-represented even by their own ministries of finance. Not surprisingly, financial intermediaries from well-established global centres are much better organized in influencing global standards than those from countries on the periphery.[52]

As indicated in Table 13.1, horizontality is embraced by the EBCI, but almost absent from the other two crisis responses. The EBCI created a forum for multiple stakeholders in countries affected by the deepening pan-European credit crisis. Specifically, the meetings in Vienna, Brussels, and Athens included transnational bank groups, their home country regulators, central banks and fiscal authorities, and their respective equivalents in the countries where they maintained operations. In addition, multinational stakeholders in the regional financial system were represented by the EBRD, the ECB, the EIB, the IMF, and the World Bank. The first multi-stakeholder meeting in Vienna set the ground rules for this initiative, which were as simple as they were powerful: an agreement to agree, open discussions with a voice for all participating stakeholders, and publicity of all commitments made.

In contrast, the multi-stakeholder bank bailout transactions reflect pre-existing vertical power relations, not horizontal bargaining. Several SWFs stepped into the fold because of an implicit commitment of mutual assistance between oil producing states in the Gulf and the US, whose major financial intermediaries

[52] This is most apparent in the European Union, where powerful lobbying organizations of West European Banks submitted their comments on regulatory guidelines to the Committee on European Banking Regulators, but countries from CEE were not represented. See Pistor, 'Hosts's Dilemma' (2010), n 23.

were implicated by the crisis.[53] Their positive response to additional requests for funding or for the conversion of their stakes into equity capital displayed their eagerness to demonstrate their commitment to the global financial system while maximizing their own autonomy against interference.[54] There is some evidence that this behaviour was rewarded, which may be taken as a sign of some bargaining behind closed doors. Thus, the Fed eased regulatory requirements for financial intermediaries from China in the fall of 2008, at a time when China's continued commitment to hold securities in Fannie Mae and Freddie Mac and potential investments in ailing investment banks was at stake.[55] However, these arrangements were not the result of transparent multi-stakeholder negotiations, but ad hoc deals, and do not reflect a shift towards a more horizontal model of governing mutual, much less multi-stakeholder, relations.

Similarly, the foreign currency swap arrangements created by central banks also took the form of bilateral agreements between the central bank granting access to its currency and a foreign central bank. However, the central banks in control of the major global currencies retained the right to unilaterally determine the scale and scope of these arrangements: they could include or exclude countries and determine the amounts made available, when to close, and when to re-open swap lines. While there is little doubt that these arrangements were made on more generous terms during the global crisis than at any time in the past, this is still a far cry from a horizontal relation with roughly equal bargaining power on both sides.

3. Cooperation

Cooperation as used in this Chapter means the establishment of a relationship based on a mutual commitment by relevant stakeholders to work together to achieve a common goal. As noted at the outset, governance regimes can be implemented by coercion or through cooperation. Coercion is meaningful in a context where the goal can be clearly circumscribed and the costs and benefits of achieving that goal are well known. In contrast, under conditions of uncertainty, governance regimes that rely entirely on hierarchy and coercion as an enforcement mechanism are unlikely to succeed and in fact may do more harm than good. They will ensure that certain objectives are achieved, but cannot easily correct for changes in the environment that may alter the balance of costs and benefits for various stakeholders when implemented. A critical feature of governance under

[53] See Hatton and Pistor, n 29, for a detailed analysis of the history of SWFs and the relation between SWF-sponsoring states and major geopolitical powers. This relation was most apparent in the bailout of Citibank by ADIA of Abu Dhabi—a deal brokered by former Secretary of the Treasury Paul Rubin who at the time occupied a top position at Citibank.

[54] See Hatton and Pistor, n 29.

[55] In August of 2008, the Fed exempted CIC, China's new sovereign wealth fund, its subsidiary Hui Jin Inc, as well as its sister organization, the state administration for foreign exchange, from bank holding status. For details see Pistor, n 26, 29.

conditions of uncertainty is the sharing of information and the creation of feedback loops so that stakeholders are aware of the possible adverse consequences of their action.

Assessing the various crisis responses on this basis, it is clear that only the EBCI was truly cooperative. The principles established at the first multi-stakeholder meeting in Vienna are quintessential features of a cooperative governance regime. The basic commitment to save the region from collapse and the meeting itself are clear signs of cooperation. The additional agreement to make commitments public elevates this to a cooperative governance regime: it allows actions to be assessed by others and creates precedents for multi-stakeholder arrangements that can be followed, thereby enhancing the probability that this governance regime will be sustained. In contrast, the other two crisis responses required some coordination between SWFs and government owners, or pairs of central banks that became parties to a swap line, but did not create the conditions for sustained cooperation. In fact, almost every one of these deals was eventually unwound. Even if new investments were made or new swap lines opened, they were made on similar terms: they were transactions deemed to be necessary and therefore beneficial for the parties at the time, but did not commit them to future cooperation.

IV. Financial Governance as Contractual Governance

Organizational theory has long grappled with the question of how different forms of organization affect outcomes. From Ronald Coase's famous inquiry about the 'nature of the firm'[56] to general inquiries into the trade-offs between hierarchy versus markets,[57] and M-Form versus U-Form organization,[58] this literature has not proven in the strict sense of the word what specific forms of organization are optimal for certain applications. Nonetheless, they have produced a number of important insights for determining in more general terms the relative superiority of hierarchy versus markets or networks in different contexts. An important insight that can be derived from this voluminous literature is that hierarchy with centralized enforcement powers works best in areas characterized by relatively high levels of certainty. In contrast, under conditions of uncertainty governance arrangements that harness the creative forces of actors from different backgrounds tend to be superior.

This Chapter starts with the presumption that financial markets are characterized by uncertainty. This refers not only to our collective ability to predict when

[56] R. H. Coase, 'The Nature of the Firm' (1937) *Economica* 386–405.

[57] O. E. Williamson, *Markets and Hierarchies, Analysis and Antitrust Implications: A Study in the Economics of Internal Organization* (New York: New York Press, 1975); see also W. W. Powell, 'Neither Market nor Hierarchy: Network Form of Organization' (1990) 12 *Research in Organizational Behaviour* 295–336.

[58] Y. Qian, G. Roland, and C. Xu, 'Coordination and Experimentation in M-Form and U-Form Organizations' (2006) 114 *Journal of Political Economy* 366–402.

and why financial markets might fail, but also to how the costs and benefits of market development as well as market failure will be allocated. The only thing that is certain is that financial markets fail on a regular basis. This Chapter suggests that this calls for a governance regime that is inclusive, horizontal, and cooperative, for which it used the shorthand 'contractual governance'. It used different episodes of fire fighting in the global financial crisis to investigate whether modes of contractual governance have emerged in the context of this crisis. The answer to this is yes, but only in one of the three responses investigated. Only the EBCI unconditionally qualifies as a contractual governance regime, and its continued existence is questioned by reforms at the EU level that call for a strengthening of hierarchical forms of governance.

Different explanations may account for this—not the least path dependency and persistence of existing power relations. Equally important, there appears to be a strong persistence in how governance is regarded in academia and among policy-makers. The quest for greater order more often than not is translated into the design of vertically integrated governance structures. Organizing as if there was certainty, however, is not a good substitute for actual certainty, but may instead exacerbate the failure to deal with uncertainty. The hope is that this Chapter has made a small contribution to rethinking the ways in which we organize financial governance within the framework of the emergent literature on contractual governance.

The Vienna Initiative: A New Mode of Governance?

Comment on K. Pistor, 'Innovation and the Role of Public-Private Collaboration in Contract Governance'

*Gunnar Folke Schuppert**

I want to comment on four points made in Katharina Pistor's very interesting and comprehensive Chapter. These are: the workings of governance by reciprocal commitments; whether the Vienna Initiative really is an institutional innovation; the need for a process manager in such situations; and the relationship between formal and informal institutions.

I. Governance by Reciprocal Commitments

In this Section I would like to assess what might be the *central message* of Katharina Pistor's Chapter. From my point of view and understanding, it discusses the advantages and disadvantages of formal and informal governance arrangements and the pros and cons of formality and informality. The answers seems to me to be quite obvious if I look at two aspects which were regarded in Pistor's Chapter as the main characteristics of the 'Vienna Initiative':

> It brought together transnational banks, regulators and central banks from home and host countries, as well as international financial institutions, and it did so in a manner *that gave each of these stakeholders a voice in an open forum that made credible the informal commitments they gave to each other*... This was made possible, because they were *reciprocated by commitments* from other stakeholders... *None* of the commitments *were legally binding*, nor were sanctions announced for defections.[1]

This informal mode of governance was—as pointed out quite convincingly– very successful, especially *in comparison with the formal structures and institutions*,

* Professor Emeritus, Humbold University, Berlin and currently Fellow at the Max-Weber-Kolleg, University of Erfurt.

[1] Vienna Initiative, 5, 17 (emphasis added).

which did not step up to handle the financial crisis; on the contrary, they remained side-line observers. In short, I would argue that Pistor was actually referring in her writing not to governance by contracts in a narrower sense, but to 'governance by reciprocal commitments'[2].

This mode of governance—as I know from other areas of informal governance—works only under two preconditions. The first one is mutual trust. If the commitments are—as Pistor points out—legally non-binding and if there are no instruments for sanctions, commitments must be based on the mutual trust of the parties involved—which may be the result of a process of communication. Hence this mode of governance by reciprocal commitments is both a mode of governance by communication (I will return to this point later on) and of governance by reputation. The second precondition is the common perception of the parties involved that the mutual commitments are balanced and fair—a conception again based on communicated trust.

II. The Vienna Initiative—An Institutional Innovation?

As to whether I believe the Vienna Initiative to be an institutional innovation, I am afraid I do not. An answer like this, so hard and running counter to the central thesis of Pistor's Chapter, must be based on convincing arguments; I draw my arguments from my knowledge about the phenomenon of institutional choice in the field of international relations.

Before I come to that, please let me briefly explain what I mean by speaking about institutional choice. Politics is—in a nutshell—about choices, and I suggest that we should distinguish between three varieties of choice. The first is institutional choice, which is the choice, say, between handling the problem by a legal command and control approach or by using economic incentives. The second variety is institutional or organizational choice, which is the choice between different institutional/organizational options like running an affair by state agencies, PPPs, outsourcing, or privatization. Finally, there is regulatory choice, of which the main example would be whether one chooses to use soft or hard law in a particular scenario.

In our case, we are confronted with an institutional choice, i.e., a choice between formal or informal governance arrangements. This is a familiar topic in the theory of international relations and I would like to refer to two articles that discuss this specific choice situation. The first is an article by Kenneth W. Abbott and Duncan Snidal discussing the question 'why states act through formal international organizations'. From their point of view, the main arguments in favour of formal organizations are the following:

> An established organization *provides a stable negotiating forum*, enhancing iteration and reputational effects. Such a stable forum also allows for a fast response to sudden developments. The Security Council, for example, is organized so that it can function on short

[2] Cf. Chapter 13, at p. 428 ("based on a mutual commitment").

notice, with each member required to maintain continuous representation at UN headquarters. A permanent organization also reinforces accepted norms: the most favored nation (MFN) principle instantiated in the WTO provides a sounder basis for state expectations than any informal arrangement.

In other ways too, centralization *shapes the political context of state interactions. IOs provide neutral, depoliticized, or specialized forums more effectively than almost any informal or decentralized arrangement.* This enables a broader range of behavior: the superpowers could discuss technical nuclear issues within the IAEA without the intrusion of high politics, even at the height of the cold war. IOs also serve as partisan forums for political coalitions: The United Nations Conference on Trade and Development (UNCTAD) for developing countries, the Organization for Economic Cooperation and Development (OECD) for industrialized states. Finally, IOs strengthen issue linkages by situating them within common organizational structures, as the WTO has done for goods, services, and intellectual property rights.[3]

The other article was published 1991 by Charles Lipson, asking this question the other way around, i.e. 'why are some international agreements informal?' He discusses this question as a *question of institutional* choice (which is an approach I find very appealing):

This article examines the strengths and weaknesses of informal agreements. It is an inquiry into the neglected institutional constraints on international cooperation—and the imperfect devices to overcome them. It considers the *basic choices between treaties and informal instruments*, as well as the *choices among different kinds of informal arrangements*, all of which can be used to express cooperation among states. Finally, it asks what these varied forms of cooperation can tell us about the more general impediments to international agreement. The aim here is to use the *choice of forms of agreement* to explore some problems of rational cooperation in international affairs and particularly their contextual and institutional dimensions.[4]

This choice is not a choice between discrete options; choosing the suitable institutional option is a *question of degree*, requiring that one select between possibilities on a continuum:

When states cooperate, they can *choose from a wide variety of forms* to express their commitments, obligations, and expectations. The *most formal are bilateral and multilateral treaties*, in which states acknowledge their promises as binding commitments with full international legal status. At the other extreme are *tacit agreements*, in which obligations and commitments are implied or inferred but not openly declared, and *oral agreements*, in which bargains are expressly stated but not documented. In between lie a variety of written instruments to express national obligations with greater precision and openness than tacit or oral agreements but without the full ratification and national pledges that accompany formal treaties. These informal arrangements range from executive agreements and nonbinding treaties to joint declarations, final communiqués, agreed minutes,

[3] K. W. Abbott and D. Snidal, 'Why States Act Through Formal International Organizations' (1998) 42 *Journal of Conflict Resolution* 3–32, XX (emphasis added).

[4] C. Lipson, 'Why Are Some International Agreements Informal?' (1991) 45 *International Organization* 495–538, 501 (emphasis added).

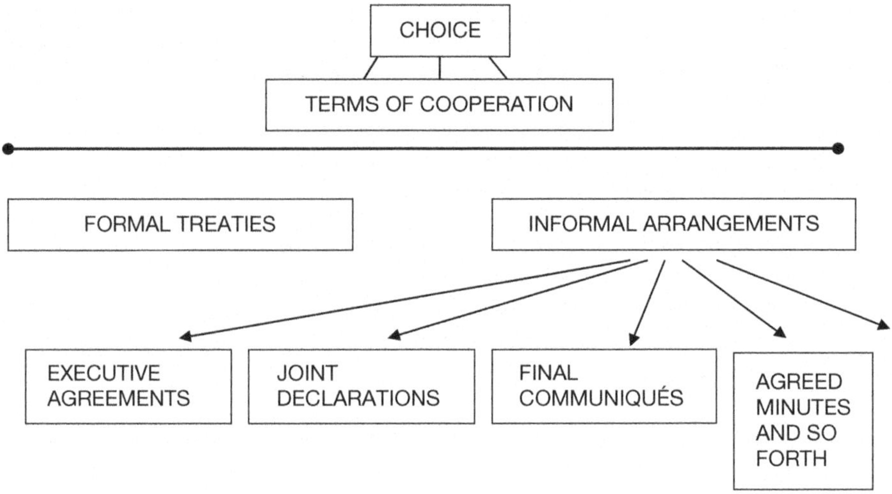

Figure 13.1

memoranda of understanding, and agreements pursuant to legislation. Unlike treaties, these informal agreements generally come intro effect without ratification and do not require international publication or registration.[5]

If we try to visualize this choice situation, it could look like the visual representation given in Figure 13.1.

Also a further look into the international relations literature comes up with a clear result: international relations scholars have observed a *trend towards informality*. Therefore, the informality of the Vienna Initiative is merely 'trendy', rather than rising to the level of an invention.

III. The Need for a Process Manager

I fully agree with the argument presented that the process of setting up an informal regime of reciprocal commitments requires a process manager or a *mediator of communication*. In the case of the Vienna Initiative, the most proactive player was the European Bank for Reconstruction and Development (EBRD), taking the role of a communication manager, a role that Pistor coined as 'anchor tenant'.

I want to back to Pistor's position with two arguments. The first argument comes from observation in the field of governance of climate change. At the very heart of this field of global governance lie *international regimes of climate protection*, like the Kyoto Protocol. If you look at the reasons for success—as in the Kyoto meeting—or for failure—as in the Copenhagen meeting—the decisive

[5] Lipson, n 3, 502 (emphasis added).

role of a *bad or good conference governance* is quite obvious. The second argument we can call 'Nudge', based on the ideas of Richard H. Thaler and Cass R. Sunstein.[6] Even if we do not follow their concept on libertarian paternalism, we can agree with their findings that soft pressure in the one or the other direction might help foster agreement on a common solution.

IV. The Relationship Between Formal and Informal Institutions: Concluding Remarks

I think that Pistor's Chapter leads us immediately to the interesting topic of the relationship between formal and informal, which I will touch upon here briefly.

By way of shorthand, I would like to refer to an article by Gretchen Helmke and Steven Levitsky[7] on informal institutions in comparative perspective, in which they present a typology of the relationship between formal and informal institutions. According to them, informal institutions can be complementary of, accommodating to, compete with, or substitute for formal institutions.

Under their analysis, *complementary informal institutions* play a *key role in making effective the formal rules of the game*:

> Examples include the myriad norms, routines, and operating procedures that ease decision making and coordination within bureaucracies, and judicial norms (such as the opinion assignment procedures and the 'Rule of Four') that facilitate the work of the U.S. Supreme Court.[8]

Accommodating informal institutions create incentives to behave in ways that alter the substantive effects of formal rules, but without directly violating them:

> They contradict the spirit, but not the letter, of the formal rules. Accommodating informal institutions are often created by actors who dislike outcomes generated by the formal rules but are unable to change or openly violate those rules.[9]

Competing informal institutions:

> ... structure incentives in ways that are incompatible with the formal rules: to follow one rule actors must violate another. *Particularistic informal institutions such as clientelism, patrimonialism, clan politics, and corruption are among the most familiar examples.*[10]

Finally, substitutive informal institutions:

> ... *tend to emerge where state structures are weak or lack authority.* During Mexico's protracted democratic transition, formal institutions of electoral dispute resolution (such as

[6] As presented in R. H. Thaler and C. R. Sunstein, *Nudge: Improving Decisions About Health, Wealth, and Happiness* (New Haven, Ct: Yale University Press, 2008).

[7] G. Helmke and S. Levitsky, 'Informal Institutions and Comparative Politics, A Research Agenda' (2004) 2 *Perspectives on Politics* 725–40.

[8] Helmke and Levitsky, n 7, xx. [9] Helmke and Levitsky, n 7, xx.

[10] Helmke and Levitsky, n 7, xx (emphasis added).

the electoral courts) lacked credibility and were frequently bypassed. In this context, officials of the national government and the opposition National Action Party resolved post election disputed through *informal concertacesiones, or 'gentleman's agreements'*.[11]

These quotations should not only remind us that we can observe a great variety in the relationship between formal and informal institutions, but also lead me to my final point, which is that there *exists no dichotomy between formal and informal institutions*. The difference between them is a question of degree. What is instead decisive is the specific institutional mix which can be found in the policy field under examination. From my experience, there is almost never just one mode of governance that is dominant in a certain field of policy. As particularly clearly demonstrated by the field of the environmental protection, there are many instruments in the policy toolbox—and again it is a question of choice of which instruments you prefer. I think it would be helpful to examine Pistor's work from this perspective.

[11] Helmke and Levitsky, n 7, xx (emphasis added).

Summary of the Discussions in Part V: Contract Governance and Rule-setting

*Susanne Augenhofer**

Chapter 11: Private Regulation and Industrial Organization: Contractual Governance and the Network Approach

Authors: Fabrizio Cafaggi and Paola Iamiceli

Discussant: Wolfgang Kerber

Christoph Möllers began the discussion by pointing out that the more important international law becomes, the more fragmented it becomes. According to Möllers, fragmentation of international law leads to a loss of relevance for general international law. However, sectoral international law (for example international economic law, international environmental law) becomes more important. Consequently, the result of fragmentation is not a loss of internationalization but in a way a win for internationalization. The second point Möllers made concerned the fact that some, although not all, of the phenomena mentioned, like the creation of international organizations, international regulators—for example the International Organisation of Securities Commissions (IOSCO)—are very much dominated by governments, but only by a few governments. This makes it very complicated because IOSCO is not beyond the US government or beyond the *Bundesfinanzministerium*. These are hegemonic projects of nation state governments not of regulators—there is no independent regulator. That has to be taken into account. In a third point, Möllers referred to the 'newness' of the discussion. In his view, when talking about newness, one has to refer to the epoch before 1914 to be able to compare current developments. If one does so, however, things do not seem as new as one might think.

Peer Zumbansen acknowledged the importance of the 'public law view' expressed by Möllers. He referred to a mirror effect as public lawyers experience

* Professor for Civil Law, European Private Law, Comparative Law, and Market Regulation through Consumer Law and Competition Law, Humboldt University, Berlin.

an erosion of sovereignty from above (from outside the state) while private lawyers experience them from below (from inside the state). The discussion reminds public lawyers that erosion has always taken place from below as well, not just globally. The mirror effect makes clear that a political analysis of the substance of the whole discussion is necessary. In the view of Zumbansen, the state can be a reference point, in the same way that contract law can be a reference point for a way of organizing society. States have existed for a relatively short period of time, when taking into account a larger time scale. Zumbansen pointed out that the 'egg or chicken' question has to be answered—in other words which came first, the state or private contracts—in order to address whether reclaiming individual liberties is possible without pushing back the state. What should not be altered, according to Zumbansen, is the state as a way of organizing society, and it is important to analyse what is at stake, which is clear for issues of legitimacy. Political issues remain to be solved even if we are more and more in favour of hybrid forms of regulation. As a last example of the erosion of sovereignty, Zumbansen pointed out that social norms and self-regulation in contracting presupposes property rights which, according to Coase and Williamson have to be well defined. However, private lawyers know that it seems almost grotesque to accept this: a property right can never be well defined as it always changes and shifts. Consequently, somebody (for instance courts, even if they perform this role inadequately at times, as Clayton Gillette had stated previously) has to define which dimension property rights should have since this question lies at the bottom of the freedom of contract. The more we hybridize contracting and social norm making, the more we forget that a vacuum is created. Zumbansen referred to Möllers' statement and agreed that it should be asked what is being gained and lost by shifting from government to governance. He also made clear that, in his view, social contracting and political philosophy of contracting should be more the focus of the debate.

Stefan Grundmann agreed on the importance of describing what separates contract governance from other forms of governance. In his view there are several differences which have to be taken into account. The first aspect he focused on was the additional complexity it brings to modern institutional economics (for example bounded rationality), stating that this will be the most difficult question to answer. His starting point was that governance has to deal with parties in a contractual setting and how their behaviour can be influenced and structured. Grundmann stated that one can learn from corporate governance and how it affects parties and stakeholders, for example in networks of contracts, or more generally third parties and how they influence the contractual setting and how they are influenced by the settings. This is, for him, the core question. He then referred to the style or paradigm how these questions are approached which is, in his view, new. With respect to corporate governance, markets are different, especially if spot contracts are taken into account: items, modes of distribution of profits, as well as default rules are different. Corporate governance, in his view, these days is mainly about listed companies and their governance. Corporate governance and contract governance easily run side by side.

Grundmann then highlighted three points: first, with reference to the differentiation between governance, government and regulation, he stated that, in his view, regulation can be seen as part of governance if the assumption is correct that the influence on the contractual setting and the different parties involved is the main issue. According to Grundmann, a new feature is to see the different areas of law as one organism. Secondly, with reference to the public/private law debate, different kinds of institutions can be compared which may have the same goals but one may achieve it better (for example mandatory rules/default rules, information/substantive regulation). It also deals with the questions of who sets the rules and who influences these rules. While this question may have previously been researched in the legislative context, it is an important aspect of governance research. The third and, according to Grundmann, most important difference is that contract governance aims at a broader meeting point of disciplines. Sociology or systems theory should not be disregarded from the beginning by lawyers. An advantage for lawyers is that field studies can be brought into play as lawyers know a lot about cases (Grundmann thereby refers to an earlier statement made by Calliess). The problem is to find borders for the research topic but the same problem exists for corporate governance and has not kept it from becoming successful.

Florian Möslein brought a new key question into the discussion by asking how much hierarchy is required for governance when coming from public to private governance. He asked whether hierarchy is a precondition for the concept of governance. He analysed hierarchy as basically the main difference between the public and the private sphere and even between the contract and corporate sphere. Even though many governance theorists argue that a spontaneous order is not governance but pure market, Möslein held that there was still some hierarchy present.

Katharina Pistor started her intervention by stating that she had thought the whole project was more subversive: economists have always claimed that markets are self-regulating. Consequently, the reason one could talk about firms was that the problems (like transaction costs) were known. But one could not talk about markets or contracts as they were said to be self-regulating. Pistor assumed that contract governance was about market governance, which she believes was an assumption also made by the World Bank in the early 1980s and 1990s: the World Bank then assumed to have something to say about issues it did not have any jurisdiction over. The World Bank was not empowered to talk about the legislative output of any of its member states. However, by shifting to output legitimacy, the World Bank no longer had to question input legitimacy but could just start measuring output. Output measures in turn create certain behaviour, thus becoming not unidirectional but completely self-referential. Pistor also agreed with Zumbansen that there are huge underlying political issues, which must be taken into account in order to completely asses the issue.

Anne van Aaken expressed disappointment regarding the public law view reported by Möllers earlier. Referring to his report, she felt that public lawyers were regarding government as good whereas the governance debate was seen to only create the challenge of sectors which was opposed the idea of democratic holism of the legislator. However in van Aaken's view, this holism has always been an illusion, an upholding of an idea. She referred to points raised by Pistor such as the developments in governance, in the legislation, and in sectoral interest policies where van Aaken felt there was nothing new but that constitutional law should be more reality-based and focus on valuable normative concepts that provide governance structures upholding certain issues we value. Van Aaken then generally invited public lawyers to take a more realistic view of the matter and to include not only economists but also political scientists in the discussion. She further encouraged the use of contract theory in public law.

Urs Schweizer illustrated how the subject developed from an economic perspective. It started with the general equilibrium theory, which then experienced problems with the Coase theorem and organizational matters. This was the reason why economists changed to game theory which can capture all kind of strategic interactions. Names were changed as well in the course of time; for example, economists first spoke of moral hazard, then about adverse selection and then about principal-agent theory. Then, at some point, in the view of Schweizer, economists started to sum up everything as contract theory. This included mechanisms legal scholars would never call contracts. But now economists even deal with market design—thus not regarding markets as self-regulatory but as a mechanism that needs designing, for instance designing auctions for UMTS-licences. Some of the findings, like the famous Myerson-Satterthwaite impossibility theorem, can be interpreted as a failure of private markets to provide the best solution in case of asymmetry of information. And the same analytical result, according to Schweizer, can be used to show that in certain settings public goods cannot be provided efficiently. He thus concluded that the analytics dictate the development of the debate.

Möllers opposed the statement of van Aaken, especially her reference to rational choice as reality. He found it naïve to assume that rational chose was a reality but democratic political theory of regulation was an illusion, seeing that there is a different epistemology for economists, private lawyers and public lawyers respectively. In his view, the reference to reality is not feasible in this kind of discourse.

He would not regard his view as over-normative, but rather in a way as positivist. To bring another aspect in the discussion, it would not be the nation state as a normative value but to egalitarian political procedures and how they are translated into multi-level processes and later described. He agreed with Pistor that the main issue for actors like the OECD and the EU when making use of governance instruments is to ignore their boundaries of jurisdiction and he quoted Bologna as an example of de-formalization of competences and jurisdictional limits, which is the political background cause of the whole discourse.

Coming back to Möslein's question of whether there was hierarchy in contracts, Möllers gave conditionality as an example of hegemony and the question where the power lies in the case of the World Bank. Even more so, it would not make any sense for Möllers to talk about governance if there was no formalized hierarchy. He therefore defined governance as the use of semi-contractual structures by hierarchical organizations to bind themselves.

With reference to Grundmann's and Zumbansen's statements, Möllers pointed out that public lawyers have the reflex to draw a distinction between governance and government due to the different mind-set.

Wolfgang Kerber remarked that, on an EU as well as on an international level, new forms of ordering are needed. 'Governance' is not useful as a general term because it is too broad. New phenomena cannot be analysed with traditional economic categories but should rather be addressed in a more specific and sophisticated way. Another aspect of the normative questions discussed was constitutional economics of the social contract, starting from the citizen's preferences as a point of reference.

Chapter 12: Flipping Wreck: *Lex Mercatoria* on the Shoals of *Ius Cogens*

Author: Hugh Collins

Discussant: Horst Eidenmüller

Gralf-Peter Calliess started the discussion by posing the question of how norms for transnational public policy are created. In his view, there are two solutions to this question: The first, as Horst Eidenmüller suggested, may be some sort of international contract. He referred to the norms cited by Eidenmüller[1] and qualified most of them as soft law norms. As a result they are, in the view of Calliess, part of public international policy and *lex mercatoria* rather than part of international law. Such norms are primarily used by arbitration courts. State courts very rarely cite such norms, for example the UNIDROIT principles, and even if they do, they only cite these principles but do not apply them as law. Calliess concluded

[1] Regulation (EC) No 593/2008 of the European Parliament and of the Council of 17 June 2008 on the law applicable to contractual obligations (Rome I) (OJ 2009 L 177/6) and Regulation (EC) No 864/2007 of the European Parliament and of the Council of 11 July 2007 on the law applicable to non-contractual obligations (Rome II) (OJ 2007 L 199/40); Council Regulation (EC) No. 1346/2000 of 29 May 2000 on Insolvency Proceedings (OJ 2000 L 160/1); UNCITRAL Model Law on Cross-Border Insolvency with Guide to Enactment (1997) (available at <http://www.uncitral.org/uncitral/en/uncitral_texts/insolvency/1997Model.html>); Directive 2002/47/EC of the European Parliament and of the Council of 6 June 2002 on financial collateral arrangements (OJ 2002 L 168/43) as amended by Directive 2009/44/EC of the European Parliament and of the Council of 6 May 2009 (OJ 2009 L 146/37); C. von Bar and E. Clive (eds) *Principles, Definitions and Model Rules of European Private Law, Draft Common Frame of Reference (DFCR)* (Munich: Sellier, 2009); W. W. McBryde, A. Flessner, and S. C. J. J. Kortmann (eds) *Principles of European Insolvency Law* (Deventer: Kluwer, 2005); United Nations Convention on the Assignment of Receivables in International Trade (2001) (available at <http://www.uncitral.org/uncitral/en/uncitral_texts/payments/2001Convention_receivables.html>); UNCITRAL Legislative Guide on Secured Transactions (2007) (available at <http://www.uncitral.org/uncitral/en/uncitral_texts/payments/Guide_securedtrans.html>); UNCITRAL Legislative Guide on Insolvency Law (2004) (available at <http://www.uncitral.org/uncitral/en/uncitral_texts/insolvency/2004Guide.html>).

that private parties like arbitrational tribunals play an essential role in creating transnational mandatory norms.

Paul Davies pointed out that Collins and Eidenmüller have used the term *lex mercatoria* in very different senses. Whereas Collins used a narrower definition which encompasses contracting practices across borders, Eidenmüller applied a wider definition, including the whole of regulation of the financial system and thereby matters which in Davies' view had little to do with the *lex mercatoria*. Davies then addressed each of the solutions proposed by the authors, regarding how to deal with the problem that courts in different countries may regard a clause in a financial contract differently. He first referred to the argument by Eidenmüller on mandatory harmonization of private law. He stated that Eidenmüller had already named all the arguments against it himself but that he wanted to add that—in EU terms—what is at stake is maximum harmonization, as all the central rules would have to be harmonized, serving as a sort of ceiling for the Member States. Such a high level of harmonization would be required in order for Eidenmüller's solution to work. With regard to Collins' solution, Davies wondered whether the proposed solution—to oblige national courts to take into account the *lex mercatoria*—was good enough. He drew a parallel to the obligation of national courts to interpret national law as far as possible in light of EU law; but if this is not possible, national courts cannot be forced to do so. He then raised the question what this meant for the *ius cogens*: how could a New York state court apply New York state law which contains a mandatory fraud on the creditor rule in the light of an international practice that goes plain against it? Davies therefore doubted whether the solution proposed by Collins presented an argument in favour of the future use of the *lex mercatoria*.

Karl Riesenhuber emphasized that Collins' main point was a structural one and then he referred to the example given by Collins: the flip clause. Riesenhuber thought that it was a valid point that there were different risks which needed to be distinguished. The one risk was that of the market changing, the other was the insolvency risk. The parties to the contract did not want to take the insolvency risk. Despite Eidenmüller's statement to the contrary, Riesenhuber thought that there were ways to insure against the insolvency risk and asked whether the flip clause really was that undesirable if insurance mechanisms were available. He then referred to the undertakings mentioned by Eidenmüller—*Berliner Verkehrsbetriebe* (BVB) and *Kommunale Wasserwerke Leipzig* (KWL)—and the fact that one manager involved did not speak English and the other is now in jail. He turned the question—whether these managers understood what they were doing—around, questioning by asking why they were engaging in this kind of transaction—buying synthetic Collaterized Debt Obligations (CDOs)—when they did not understand it. Both undertakings have to be regarded as professional players by the law and should know what they were doing. He then addressed the structural point made by Collins. In his view the insolvency problem is an example of state regulation interfering with *lex mercatoria*. The basic question is how private international law deals with *lex mercatoria*. According to Riesenhuber, in the EU the question is dealt with under national law and he claims that every single clause is subject to control under national law that goes far beyond public policy provisions. He concluded with the remark that despite his personal sympathy for the approach, mandatory rules have thus far hardly been harmonized. The draft common frame of reference (DCFR) for instance contained a lot of default rules.

Hugh Collins answered the first round of comments by referring to remarks which questioned whether his proposals did enough to bring the *lex mercatoria* into play. He first conceded that requiring courts to take the *lex mercatoria* into account was no easy solution. He referred to Teubner and agreed with him that it would be irritating to the national legal system if there were provisions against fraudulent preferences against creditors which would then not be applied because the market works differently as in the example of the New York given by Davies. He expressed his sympathy for Teubner's model of forcing the court to justify its decision. It may well be that the public policy considerations justify that the national rule on insolvency will ultimately overwhelm the *lex mercatoria*. It is nevertheless important to force the courts to think about this issue which resembles a delicate, surgical operation. Collins stressed that the *lex mercatoria* itself was suspect in terms of its failure to take into account externalities.

With regard to the comments concerning harmonization, Collins said that this was exactly what the *lex mercatoria* is supposed to be: harmonized international law, regulating financial markets. The UN does not have to invent it, as it is already there. This is why it should be taken into account, particularly because the US has agreed to these rules.

Eidenmüller first referred to the comment by Calliess and the fundamental question of public international policy and whether we should go forward the way Collins suggested or whether we should instead invest resources in harmonizing national mandatory rules. He did not see the matter as a choice between two alternatives, but rather focused on the complicated interplay between these two policy options. Eidenmüller's position would be that contract practice has a harmonizing effect but that we must not uncritically accept current international contracting practices. He questioned whether anyone present had ever read the ISDA Master Agreement or even parts of it and understood it. He thought their reaction [loud laughter] suggested that caution should be applied when using contract practice as the way forward. Instead, contract practice should be critically examined and, if there is reason for concern, efforts to harmonize mandatory state law rules should be intensified. He concluded that the interplay between these two routes is the way forward.

With respect to the comments by Davies, Eidenmüller clarified that he did not want to use a different concept of *lex mercatoria* than Collins. He agreed with Davies that harmonization of mandatory state law rules is difficult and that the goal must be maximum harmonization in order to achieve any effect. Eidenmüller then referred to the question raised by Riesenhuber as to why the managers of the BVB and KWL purchased synthetic CDOs despite not understanding that process. One of the reasons may be that they were bribed which is, according to

Eidenmüller, the reason why one of the managers is in jail. They also may have been defrauded which will have to be clarified in the English proceedings.

Zumbansen stated that, in contrast to the other comments made, in his view the proposal by Eidenmüller was more ambitious than that by Collins. He pointed out that the extensive literature published on financial questions can be seen as evidence that it is difficult to find out what people are doing and why. He found it intriguing that Collins as a private lawyer claimed the *lex mercatoria* should not be perceived as contract governance but rather a public law response was needed. However, he also expressed doubts that the two approaches could be combined, as the question of what is 'soft law' and what is 'hard law' cannot be answered that easily. Problems of externalities and harm to third parties have always led to the question of what the market could regulate and what needed mandatory rules and this question was raised long before there was cross border finance and it is part of every legal culture.

Pistor reminded the group that some of the Master Agreement provisions were actually transposed into national law. She regards the idea that there can be harmonization without interests of lobbyists coming into play as a little bit of an illusion. She also stated that where an agency is seeking to harmonize certain questions, stakeholders who try to ensure that the harmonized laws fit into their master agreements come into play as well.

Grundmann agreed that government regulation and party arrangements should not be split too strictly. He pointed out that some questions can be dealt with using either approach. For example, responsible lending can either be dealt with via regulation or through private law devices. The same is true for organizational means within a bank where, for example, it is discussed whether rules against conflicts of interest can serve as the basis of private law suits. He therefore would not concentrate on the split between the two approaches but on the comparison and or even on the combination of the two approaches.

Klaus Hopt pleaded for caution in applying the concept of *lex mercatoria*. He stated that he had always understood it in a narrow sense, as a common set of rules of international practice. If applied like this, the term is rather unclear and rather general and opaque. He reported from arbitral practice that there was reluctance to applying the *lex mercatoria* because it leaves too much leeway to arbitration tribunals. This concerned unclear substantive rules as well as procedural discretion.

In agreement with Eidenmüller, Hopt then pointed out that the financial crisis is not a problem of contracts, but of institutions, and that the financial crisis is therefore a rather bad example for contract governance and also for corporate governance. In his view, it is also wrong to see remuneration of directors as a major problem of the financial crisis; it should be seen instead as an example of wrong incentives, at which level it concerns all managers in the bank. He then referred to the contracts mentioned by Eidenmüller which do not have any apparent social utility. In this regard, he pointed out that short selling has a positive point, because it leads to speculation which ultimately leads to the right price. Hopt stressed that he was not in favour of forbidding this practice as was currently discussed in the German government. Coming back to the financial markets he underlined that there was no general problem of the banks but only of the systemic banks—however difficult it may be to define them.

Collins admitted that the term *lex mercatoria* can be rather vague. But he stressed that in the particular context, there exists a *lex mercatoria* which is written down and might be even easier to understand than the German Civil Code. He also added that in his view, the *lex mercatoria* is a workable concept.

Eidenmüller asked, referring to the comment by Hopt, how much speculation is needed with regard to short selling but otherwise agreed with all points made by Hopt. With regard to the comments made by Pistor, he agreed that harmonization may experience interference from lobbying, but he did not accept that as an argument against harmonization.

With regard to the comment made by Pistor, he agreed that lobbying can be a problem but feels this cannot be a reason to refrain from harmonization. He finally referred to the comment by Zumbansen, who was surprised that Eidenmüller distinguished between frictions he would tolerate and areas where he would advocate eliminating frictions through harmonization. It is difficult in a particular case to identify whether harmonization efforts should go forward or whether it should be left to regulatory competition.

Chapter 13: Innovation and the Role of Public-private Collaboration in Contract Governance

Author: Katharina Pistor

Discussant: Gunnar Folke Schuppert

Pistor stated that the dichotomy between formal and informal that came up in the comment to her Chapter does not seem that useful and that she therefore had not divided her presentation along these lines; her reciprocity arrangement was interpreted in the discussion as informal but Pistor clarified that this should be broadened, as even formal arrangements may be based on reciprocity. With regard to the question what kind of relationship the Vienna Initiative should have with existing institutions—complementary, substitution, accommodation, or competition—she indicated that it depends on whom you ask and when. During the crisis, it was substitution, because the EU, in the view of Pistor, did little, and she pointed out that there was speculation that the EU did so as it was hoping that national intervention would fail and it could then come forward with plans for further European integration. But there might have been other reasons too, including issues relating to competence. Now the EU regards it as competition. The Vienna Initiative advocates regard it, at least in the view of Pistor, as complimentary, if not even as substitution for current practices.

Bruno S. Frey referred to Pistor's emphasis that all stakeholders were represented in the current arrangement. In his view, that was not true but only the financial stakeholders were represented. He stressed that it was time to make clear that the financial market is not an end in itself, but that it should serve the real economy.

He then raised the question who represented the real economy—especially the taxpayers—and came to the conclusion that it was without representation. Despite Pistor's emphasis that fiscal policy must be coordinated, Frey felt she missed the point: taxation. Such a scheme, in his view, is totally biased if tax payers are not represented because it results in the taxpayers having to pay for everything. He pointed out that formal settings, although normally not favoured by him as an economist, present a certain advantage as they can help to ensure representation.

Kerber first raised the issue of whether a form of governance in order to avoid financial meltdown as presented by Pistor could work at all. To him the mechanism of unilateral commitments was unclear: do all participants have to commit or would for instance 80 per cent of all stakeholders suffice? In his second question, he pointed out that there was a certain emergency situation requiring quick decisions and that therefore there might be certain governance solutions suitable here which cannot be applied as long-term solutions. That fact might be important for the Vienna Initiative.

Eidenmüller stated that he agreed with Pistor that the Vienna Initiative was not a new process, but merely a multilateral voluntary negotiation process involving private and public actors, which is supported by a mediator (process agent or anchor tenant). It is, in the view of Eidenmüller, not contract governance, but rather a corporate process, as it is not leading to a binding contract. With regard to voluntariness, he concluded that it was voluntary despite the thread of a financial meltdown because also if the non-agreement alternatives are really bad, it does not change the fact that the parties agreed voluntarily to the process. The negotiation process is not new, since similar multilateral negotiation processes exist (for example for public infrastructure projects such as nuclear power plants and airports) with the only distinction that these already existing processes are maybe lacking an international dimension. The crucial feature in the process, according to Eidenmüller, is that a mediator was present. Usually there are three criteria a process agent (mediator) should meet. First, the mediator should be neutral. According to Eidenmüller that is not a necessary requirement but it is necessary that the parties accept the process agent in full knowledge of the interest this person might have in the outcome. Secondly, the mediator should have some substantive knowledge of the matter at hand. There will not always be one institutional person regardless of the subject matter that is best qualified to mediate the process. The third—and crucial—matter is process skills. Here, Eidenmüller stressed that organizations like the European Bank for Reconstruction and Development (EBRD) can hire mediators with the required skills ad hoc, he claims that it is therefore not necessary to install a permanent system of process agents for every potential process. Consequently, neither of these three process feature requires a change in the institutional setting.

Pistor answered the comment made by Frey by pointing out that countries who were asked to pay, like Austria, had their Finance Minister participating in the meeting. But she did not object to broadening the process on principle. With regard to the comment made by Kerber, she noted that there were no defectors on account of there being multiple stakeholders essentially monitoring one another. With regard to the question of whether there was an emergency situation that cannot be replicated in the long term, Pistor assumed the solution can work also outside an emergency situation but, but due to the fiscal interest involved it may not receive continuous support. She also added that a similar system did not emerge in the Greek crisis, probably because the financial interests involved were so overwhelming and divergent that no one had the negotiation power necessary to bring all parties together. With regard to the comments made by Eidenmüller, Pistor answered that governance structures should be changed. She expressed the view that transnational institutions for governance are necessary in order to overcome national interests. In her opinion, the Vienna Initiative may be a way to deal with transnational governmental problems which are not fully addressed. As for the question posed by Eidenmüller of whether the setting is new, she concluded that it is not new in the sense that such a phenomena has not been seen before, but it is new relative to the European financial system. A specific mediator, in her view, should not be identified, and the EBRD might not be the best mediator in the future, but rather a more flexible agent.

Gunnar Folke Schuppert thought that the emergency situation was not a crucial factor. The decisive point was that formal institutions did not want to step in and there was a governance vacuum at a certain moment. He agreed with the three points made by Eidenmüller for a communication manager. Schuppert regards process skills as the decisive feature of a mediator. He suggested that one should discuss the role of big law firms as governance actors because they are actually using the *lex mercatoria* in practice. Big law firms use contracts as templates for other contracts. In this context, he referred to an article by Sigrid Quack of the Cologne Max Plank Institute about the process of changing from simple international law practice to international norms for contracts.

Christine Windbichler referred to the notion of choice and that it requires that one has something to choose from or choose between. In her view, formal/informal is not a dichotomy but a continuum, in substance and in time. The dichotomy is just used as a tool for analysis and clarification. She also stressed the importance of providing content and explained that this is a field of trial and error. Soft law and practice provide for a wealth of possibilities and regulation and hard law have to draw from something.

Collins tried to reformulate what, in his view, Pistor's critics wanted to say. According to his understanding, they argued that, as a result of the informal meeting at the EBRD and the agreement on a massive swap-transaction produced a huge sovereign debt. This provoked its own crisis which could only be solved by the formal institutions. In other words, the Vienna Initiative looks like it solved the immediate crisis but actually just deferred and augmented the crisis.

Schweizer found the notion of governance by reciprocal commitment intriguing. He thought it would be naïve to trust institutions to follow the concept of 'be nice to others and they will be nice to you' and assumed this was not what was meant when using the term reciprocity. Another concept used was relational contracts, in particular, as economists view them as repeated games. He wondered if the idea of sub-game perfect equilibrium applied. In that case, one should look at what kinds of commitments were made and whether the participating party could retaliate in a credible way if commitments were not met.

Pistor pointed out that ad hoc responses to crises were mostly outside the formal frameworks, regardless of what example one picks, noting that the Lehman Brothers bailout works just as well as an example. She acknowledged the call for a greater number of stakeholders if a multi-state governance arrangement is truly the goal. But she emphasized that the current situation was a major improvement, as it at the very least considered Eastern European stakeholders were considered, not just Western European banks.

The question of whether reciprocal commitments are sufficient or whether sanctions are needed is difficult to answer, according to Pistor. She noted that the threat of a financial meltdown was important to get all sides to meet.

With regard to the question of whether it was a repeated game, she clarified that the game had to be set up in the first place. After the game had been set up, one had to examine whether commitments were upheld and whether a repeated game structure was created.. Pistor concluded that, at the current point, it has to be decided whether the initiative should continue along the same lines, and whether this is a credible set-up to try and govern financial markets.

PART VI

CONTRACT GOVERNANCE AND POLITICAL DIMENSIONS

14

Regulating Sovereign Bond Contracts in Europe

*Kern Alexander**

This Section analyses some of the main legal and economic policy issues involving the use of collective active clauses in EU and euro area sovereign bond contracts. The purpose of the Section is to emphasize the importance of contract design for achieving financial stability objectives and the need to regulate financial contracts so as to mitigate the negative externalities (or 'social costs') of financial risk-taking. Specifically, I shall focus on sovereign bond contracts and how they can be regulated to reduce the impact of sovereign debt restructurings and defaults whilst achieving more sustainable sovereign debt financing for EU and euro area states. In a recent report commissioned for the European Parliament, I argued that a more effective sovereign debt restructuring mechanism for EU states should require, among other things, the use of mandatory collective action clauses (CACs) in EU and euro area sovereign bond contracts and the establishment of an EU sovereign debt agency that would be responsible for overseeing the implementation of CACs and related best practice standards in EU sovereign bond contracts.[1] This Chapter contributes to the theme of 'contract governance' by analysing how sovereign bond contracts should be regulated in the eurozone to achieve financial stability objectives. The message for social scientists, economists, and lawyers who study 'contracting' in financial markets is that for too long the 'law and economics' approach to contracting in financial markets has failed to take account adequately of the problem of 'externalities' in financial markets and

* Professor at the University of Zurich and Specialist Academic Adviser to the Committee on EU Financial Regulation of the European Parliament.

[1] K. Alexander, 'Market Impact of Orderly Sovereign Default in European Parliament' in *Euro Area Governance—Ideas for Crisis Management Reform* (Brussels: European Parliament, 2010) 63–78 (available at <http://www.astrid-online.it/Dossier--d1/EUROBONDS/PE_Ideas-for-Crisis-Mgmnt_09_2010.pdf>).

how unregulated financial contracting can contribute to systemic risk and create financial instability. This Chapter offers a view of how EU—and particularly euro area—sovereign bond contracts should be regulated in order to enhance allocative efficiency in the sovereign debt market and to mitigate the impact of externalities in sovereign debt risk-taking.

Before discussing the problem of contract design in sovereign debt finance, I would like to make a few observations about the theory of regulation and transaction cost economics which are recurring themes in this volume. In a market economy, private contracting is the basis upon which economic wealth is created and the economy can grow. Economic theory, however, also recognizes that economic activity can create 'social costs' or negative externalities, which are created by the parties to a contract who have failed fully to internalize their transaction costs with the result that these costs are externalized involuntarily onto third parties (i.e. society at large) who were not parties to the contract. The Cambridge economist Arthur Pigou famously addressed the externality problem by using the metaphor of 'dirty smoke' which creates social costs because of the production activities of the manufacturer.[2] Pigou showed that when the manufacturer was able to externalise or impose some of the costs of its production onto society that it would have an incentive to produce too much and thereby pollute too much. Pigou proposed to address the externality problem by imposing 'taxes, duties and bounties' on the producer so that it would internalize more fully the costs of its production and therefore produce less of what was creating the negative externality. Coase of course trenchantly critiqued Pigou's approach of using government intervention to require the factory owner to pay a tax to cover its excess production and/or imposing legal liability on the manufacturer for any harm done by arguing that the question is not how we should restrain the manufacturer, but rather whether the value of the lost production is greater or less than the value of the product which the manufacturer's pollution of the air makes possible.[3] He argued that government intervention through taxes or restricting output would result in a misallocation of resources. Therefore what the government should permit is for those who suffer the costs of the pollution to be able to contract with the manufacturer to pay him not to pollute as much with the result that a more optimal level of production would be achieved with a lower and more socially acceptable level of pollution.

Coase's theory of allowing parties to contract around the externality problem, however, ran up against the obstacle of high transaction costs, which could prevent the parties from reaching the most efficient bargain. Coase argued that in most areas of economic activity, the transaction costs would be relatively small and not pose a serious obstacle to the parties reaching the most optimal agreement and therefore government intervention would not be necessary. In some cases, however, the transaction costs can be very high, arising from asymmetric information

[2] A. C. Pigou, *The Economics of Welfare* (London: Macmillan, 1920).

[3] R. A. Coase, 'The Problem of Social Cost' (1960) 3 *Journal of Law and Economics* 1–44, 2–3.

between the bargaining parties with the possibility of large externalities for the economy. In these limited circumstances, according to Coase, regulation had a role to play in facilitating the parties' ability to bargain in such a way that they could circumvent the transaction costs that obstructed them from reaching the most efficient agreement. The analogy of using regulation to facilitate market participants to reach the most efficient contract and allocation of risk between themselves applies, in my view, to the wholesale debt markets and in particular to the sovereign bond markets. Private contracting practices between sovereign debtor and bond investors have encountered substantial transaction costs which have prevented the parties from negotiating efficient bond contracts that allocate default and restructuring risks in such a way as to create a huge externality for the stability of financial markets. Therefore, regulation has a role to play to promote the use of sovereign bond contracts that facilitate restructuring and burden sharing with private creditors in a manner that reduces the externality for the broader financial system. The focus of my proposal for regulatory reform is the eurozone sovereign bond markets.

Outside Europe, the regulation of sovereign bond contracts for developing and emerging market economies has been an important issue for international policy-makers. In the 1980s and early 1990s, the International Monetary Fund (IMF) had discouraged sovereign debtors from restructuring their debts, even in times of crisis, by following a 'lending into arrears' policy in which the IMF would only provide financial support to a state experiencing financial difficulties if the state had agreed to a repayment plan that would include curing all of its arrears with private sector creditors.[4] The IMF policy contributed to moral hazard on the part of foreign creditors who came to believe that they could lend more on more generous terms to risky developing and emerging market countries because, if the IMF were called in to bail out the country, it would impose conditions on the borrowing state that mandated that these loans be paid in full.[5] The IMF believed that this would promote financial stability and lead to the reintegration of the ailing sovereign debtor into the international debt markets. The IMF policy, however, had the effect of encouraging private sector creditors to make more loans and investments in tradable sovereign debt with sovereign debtors, while the IMF was on standby to provide assistance to countries in financial distress under conditionality programmes that required that they cure all arrears to private sector creditors. Following the US and IMF bailout of Mexico in 1995, private sector creditors were once more assured by taxpayer institutions that their loans to risky sovereign debtors would be protected. This resulted in the risk

[4] F. Gianviti, 'The Prevention and Resolution of International Financial Crises: A Perspective From The International Monetary Fund' in M. Giovanoli (ed) *International Monetary Law: Issues for the New Millennium* (Oxford: Oxford University Press, 2000) 97–109, 102–103.

[5] See Gianviti, n 4, where Gianviti cites a Fund report published in 1999 stating that the Fund had concluded that 'the criteria set out earlier for the case of sovereign arrears may be too restrictive and could lead to instances in which creditors—particularly bondholders—could exercise a *de facto* veto over Fund lending.'

premium on emerging market sovereign bonds dropping to their lowest level in the post-war period.

Another contributing factor to the low risk premium on emerging market sovereign bonds was that the contracts contained onerous financing and repayment terms that substantially limited the ability of sovereigns to share the costs of adjustment in a crisis with private sector creditors. This attracted the attention of the G10 industrial countries, who were concerned that such contracts might precipitate or exacerbate a sovereign debt or banking crisis. Indeed, there was a concern that allowing the parties freely to adopt contracts that contained financing and repayment terms imposed an undue burden of adjustment on sovereign debtors that could destabilize the financial system. This created an opportunity for intervention by the official sector to regulate the terms of sovereign bond contracts in order to achieve a more efficient risk allocation between the sovereign debtor and creditors.

The first G10 working group to address this issue analysed whether sovereign bond contracts should allow, or facilitate, in limited circumstances sovereign debt restructurings and what type of financing and payment terms the bond contracts should have to achieve a more balanced allocation of benefits and risks between the debtor and creditors. The G10 working group led by Jean-Jacques Rey, formerly of the Belgian National Bank, examined the Mexican sovereign debt crisis of 1994–1995 and concluded, in the Rey Report of 1996, that Mexican sovereign bond contracts had not adequately bailed-in private sector creditors during the crisis. The Rey Report proposed that all developing country and emerging market sovereign bond contracts should have the following features: collective representation of sovereign debt-holders to facilitate negotiations in a crisis to restructure sovereign debt; majority action clauses in sovereign bond contracts that would allow a super-majority of bond-holders for each tranche of debt to vote to alter the financing or repayment terms of the contract; and a formula for sharing amongst creditors the assets received from debtors when there has been a restructuring. The Asian financial crisis of 1997–1999 and the Russian sovereign default of 1998 led to another G10 working group report led by then Under Secretary of the US Treasury, Randal Quarles (the Quarles Report), which examined the weaknesses of sovereign bond contracts used by Asian countries and Russia and proposed model CACs to be used by all developing and emerging market countries. The design of model CACs would be based on market-based principles that would provide consistent negotiation procedures across jurisdictions that would allow bond-holders and sovereign debtors to bargain over the financing and payment terms in sovereign bond contracts, thereby leading to a more efficient burden-sharing over time. Sovereign bond contracts would follow a particular structure that would emphasize early dialogue, communication, and coordination between sovereign debtors and creditors when financing or repayment problems arise. If the debtor is able to reach agreement on new financing or repayment terms with a majority of creditors, they should be able to re-contract without obstruction by minority creditors. Further, the contract should not allow a recalcitrant creditor who is not a member of the creditor group that reached a restructuring agreement with the sovereign to enforce its rights under the contract in a way that would hamper or disrupt the restructuring agreement.

The importance of sovereign debt restructuring took on added significance in the Argentine sovereign debt crisis that began in December 2001 when the Argentine Government defaulted on most of its foreign currency denominated bonds. Argentine bonds did not have CACs or majority action clauses and instead contained unanimity clauses governed by New York law. Hold-out creditors were able to hamper the negotiations for a debt restructuring over a number of years and in some cases to disrupt preferential repayments to creditors who had agreed to a restructuring. Clearly, the sovereign bonds containing unanimity clauses governed by New York law were weak governance structures that did not allocate risk efficiently between the debtor and creditors. The International Monetary Fund eventually brokered an agreement between the Argentine Government and most of its bond-holders who tendered their original bonds for newly-issued Argentine bonds with a face value of about 38 per cent of the value of the original bonds and with a significantly lower interest rate. The Argentine crisis demonstrated major weaknesses in the governance structures of the traditional New York law bond contracts with unanimity clauses and the need to adopt contractual mechanisms to facilitate bargaining between the sovereign debtor and creditors and between the creditors themselves in order to have a more efficient sharing of risks between the parties.

Prior to the Argentine default in 2001, most sovereign bond contracts denominated in a foreign currency (usually a reserve currency) did not contain CACs, but rather contained so-called unanimity clauses that required a unanimous vote of all bondholders of a class of bonds to approve any change in the financing or payment terms of the bond contract. CACs—also known in English law as 'majority action clauses'—allow a supermajority of, for example, bond-holders holding a particular class of bond contracts to vote to restructure the financial or repayment terms of the bond.[6] The bond contract could provide, for instance, that 75 per cent of creditors—rather than 100 per cent—of a certain creditor class vote to restructure the financial and repayment terms (i.e. lower the interest rate or extend the maturity of the debt, respectively). The supermajority's decision would bind the minority bond-holders of the same class, thus preventing a small minority from delaying or otherwise disrupting a restructuring agreement, thereby making the restructuring process more predictable.[7]

The English law had traditionally used majority action clauses (a type of CAC) in its sovereign bond contracts. New York law, however, traditionally used the unanimity

[6] The financial terms of the contract would generally include the rate of interest (the coupon rate), the amount of the principal, and related financing terms, while the repayment terms would include the date of periodic payments and the means and place of payment, the loan's maturity date, and in some cases what amount of interest and principal would be included in each payment.

[7] CACs are in all sovereign bonds issued under English law and are increasingly being used under New York law sovereign bond contracts, which by tradition required unanimity or 100% of creditors of the same class to vote to restructure the financial or repayment terms of the bond contract.

clauses, requiring that all bond-holders of a particular class of bonds vote unanimously to change the financial or payment terms of the contract. This meant that a single bond-holder in that class of bond-holders could vote against a proposed restructuring of the financing or payment terms, thus thwarting a sovereign debt restructuring. Up until the Argentine sovereign default, most countries raising debt finance denominated in foreign currency did so with sovereign bond contracts governed by New York law and with unanimity clauses. The G10 formally proposed in 2002, however, that all sovereign bond contracts denominated in foreign currency should have CACs that allow a qualified majority of bond-holders to vote to restructure the financing or payment terms of the contracts.[8] This would be particularly helpful for emerging market sovereign debtors in market distress whose sovereign debt was mainly denominated in US dollars or other reserve currencies, and for whom it was almost impossible to persuade their foreign creditors to restructure the repayment or financing terms: A restructuring of the financing terms would involve, for instance, a reduction in the principal and interest owed, while changed repayment terms might involve a maturity extension of the bond. And so the promotion of CACs became part of international public policy to be used mainly by developing and emerging market countries whose sovereign debt was denominated in a foreign currency.

After the Argentine default, the IMF began to encourage all legal systems, even the US, to use CACs and by 2005 a great majority of the value of sovereign bonds issued under New York law by emerging market countries included CACs.[9] Moreover, the EU Council also adopted a common commitment to use CACs based on the G10 framework when the sovereign bond is governed by foreign law.[10] This has had a dramatic impact on the international law practice of negotiating and drafting sovereign bond contracts denominated in foreign currency, which has now become mostly based on the CAC structure. It is important to note, however, that the widespread use of CACs as a model contract provision supported by the G10 and IMF has largely applied only to sovereign debt that is denominated in a foreign currency—usually a reserve currency, such as the US dollar, the euro, or the Japanese yen.[11] In contrast, most euro area sovereigns issue

[8] The G10 reports, however, recommend CACs as a more efficient mechanism to share the costs of adjustment and more effectively bail-in private sector creditors.

[9] See IMF, 'Progress Report to the International Monetary and Financial Committee on Crisis Resolution' (12 April 2005); see also IMF, 'Progress Report to the International Monetary and Financial Committee on Crisis resolution' (28 September 2004). The IMF began to promote CACs in 2003 as international best practice, ibid. For a discussion of the dramatic increase in CAC use in developing countries, see H. J. Blommestein and J. Santiso, 'New Strategies for Emerging Domestic Sovereign Bond Markets in the Global Financial Landscape' (2007) 7(2) *Global Economy Journal* 19 (chart showing in 2005 that 97% of sovereign bond issuance by emerging countries had CACs).

[10] The EU Council adopted, in 2003 (through ECOFIN), a Common Commitment that 'the EU will use contractual provisions based on the framework developed by the G10 and where necessary in accordance with applicable law and adjusted to local legal practice, in their central government bonds *issued under a foreign jurisdiction and/or governed by foreign law* by the end of the year. Thereafter, EU Member States will no longer issue such bonds without CACs.' (emphasis added) ECOFIN President, April 2003.

[11] Other reserve currencies include the UK pound, Australian dollar, New Zealand dollar, Swiss franc and Hong Kong dollar.

sovereign bonds denominated in euros and the contracts do not contain CACs, but rather New York-style unanimity clauses. The euro area countries do not face foreign exchange risks on their sovereign bonds because their sovereign debt is denominated in euros. Consequently, they do not face the same type of risks that developing and emerging market countries do because their debt is largely denominated in foreign reserve currencies. These countries were encouraged to use CACs because they provided a more balanced allocation of risk between the sovereign debtor and the private sector creditors, and much of that risk was foreign exchange risk. The issue of foreign exchange risk has always been the main factor for a country in deciding whether it should use CACs for its sovereign debt issuance. But the euro area sovereign debt crisis has revealed other risks that threaten a country's fiscal sustainability unrelated to foreign exchange risk. These risks relate to sovereign credit risk and risks in the sovereign credit default swap market. The nature of the risks in the present eurozone fiscal crisis undermines the traditional view held by many that because there is no foreign exchange risk in a sovereign bond contract: a CAC is not necessary.[12]

The Greek sovereign debt crisis—which has spread to Ireland, Portugal, Italy, and Spain—demonstrates major weaknesses in euro area sovereign bond contracts and the need for enhanced governance reform of these contracts.[13] Most of the sovereign bonds issued by Greece and outstanding in 2010 (over 90 per cent) do not contain CACs. Before 2001, when Greece adopted the euro, most of Greece's sovereign bonds were denominated in US dollars, governed by New York law, and did not contain CACs. However, when Greece joined the eurozone, they began issuing euro-denominated debt governed by Greek law with unanimity clauses, not CACs. I would suggest that the absence of CACs has been one of the major difficulties in limiting Greece's ability to restructure its debts to a more sustainable level. This has also become the case with Portugal, Ireland, Italy, and Spain, all of whom have issued most of their sovereign bonds governed by local law in euros with unanimity clauses. In a recent report for the European Parliament, I argued that all euro area and EU sovereign bond contracts should contain CACs and that an EU sovereign debt agency should recommend best practice templates for sovereign bond contracts that cover, among other things, financing and repayment terms.[14] This would be achieved through the following steps.

First, sovereign debtors and investors should agree henceforth to incorporate CACs into sovereign bond contracts or sovereign loan contracts (i.e. bank loans) governed under the law of an EU state. Although investors and sovereigns are increasingly using CACs in their sovereign bond contracts following the Argentine default, significant differences in the structure of these contracts

[12] K. Alexander, Editorial, *Financial Times*, 15 July 2010 (arguing against the use of CACs in Euro area sovereign bonds).

[13] L. C. Buchheit, C. Lee, and G. Mitu Gulti. 'How to Restructure Greek Debt', 7 May 2010 (unpublished).

[14] K. Alexander, 'Market Impact of an Orderly Sovereign Debt Restructuring' (August 2010) European Parliament, Economic, and Monetary Affairs Committee Report (available at <http://wwwcfap.jbs.cam.ac.uk/publications/downloads/2010_alexander_market.pdf>).

still exist, thus increasing uncertainty regarding the renegotiation of repayment terms and how the overall restructuring process would operate. Sovereign bond contracts issued by EU states should have harmonised legal templates governing their overall structure, but would allow the parties to agree on some of the specific repayment terms.

Although a growing number of EU sovereign bond contracts contain CACs, the majority do not, which means that for most EU sovereign bond contracts the consent of 100% of the bond-holders of a particular class of bonds is necessary to change the repayment terms of the bond.[15]As a result, a small minority of bond-holders can prevent a restructuring that the majority believe to be in their best interests. Rather, EU legislation should require that all sovereign bond and loan contracts contain majority action clauses, but allowing the parties to agree on certain repayment terms, such as specifying the percentage of creditors holding a certain value of the debt (for example, 85 per cent, 75 per cent or 65 per cent) to approve a change in financing or payment terms. EU law should also require that sovereign bond or loan contracts contain a clause describing the process through which sovereign debtors and creditors negotiate if a restructuring event were to occur. This clause would specify how the creditors would be represented and by whom and on what date, or within what period of time, the debtor must provide financial and other information to the creditors' representative. The representative would be authorized to act on behalf of the creditors in the negotiations and have discretion to act based on the instructions of creditors with a specified percentage value of claims.[16]

Another important area concerns how the sovereign would initiate a restructuring. EU law could require that this could be provided in a clause describing what period of time—for example four weeks—for creditors to come together to obtain the relevant information regarding the sovereign's financial situation, choose a representative, and decide a timeline for the negotiation process. The notion of a 'cooling off' period or automatic stay on creditor action against non-sovereign corporate or individual debtors is already recognized in the insolvency laws of some countries, such as Chapter 11 of the US Bankruptcy Code.[17] The contract would be required to state when the 'cooling-off' period would begin, for example the date when the sovereign notifies its creditors that it wants to restructure its

[15] See E. B. Koch, *Challenges at the Bank for International Settlements: An Economist's (Re)view* (Basel: Bank for International Settlements, 2003) 56–60, stating (at xx) '[t]raditionally, CACs were included in sovereign bonds governed by English, Japanese and Luxembourgian law. Sovereign bonds issued under US, German, Italian and Swiss law did not include CACs', and thus required unanimous approval by bond-holders of a particular class of bonds to change repayment terms. Ibid., 60–65, providing data of the value of sovereign bond issuance with CACs.

[16] The specified percentage value of claims would be provided in the repayment terms of the contract. Moreover, the representative, and not individual creditors, would have the authority to initiate litigation for breach of the bond or loan covenants, but only with the approval of creditors with a specified value of claims.

[17] Although chap 11 of the US Bankruptcy Code does not apply to sovereign debt default or restructuring, chap 9 of the US Bankruptcy Code does provide insolvency proceedings and an automatic stay against creditor claims against a municipal or county government debtor while the sovereign debtor is formulating a repayment plan for judicial and creditor approval.

payments and/or the date that the creditors appoint their representative. The duration of the cooling-off period would be mandated by EU law at, say, 60 or 75 days. During this period, a temporary suspension or deferral of payments would be required and enforced by an EU court of law. EU law should mandate that the bond or loan contract should provide for the possibility of a suspension or deferral of payments and provide for damages or penalties for any creditor who violates the provision by seeking to enforce its claim without prior court approval.

Finally, the EU must have the institutional capacity to monitor the implementation of such debt contracts to ensure that vital data is communicated to creditors and debtors and that the parties negotiate terms and conditions with full access to relevant information. An EU sovereign debt agency could be created via regulation to exercise such a function and would have the authority to collect data and perform surveillance of sovereign debt markets and report market developments to the European Commission, Parliament, and market participants. The responsibilities of an EU sovereign debt agency could include overseeing EU Member State sovereign debt practices and providing data to the market regarding the risks that certain bond and loan contracts pose and to make recommendations and, if necessary, 'name and shame' states which appear to be developing unsustainable debt positions.

The agency could also exchange information with the European Central Bank, the European Supervisory Authorities, and the European Systemic Risk Board regarding financial stability issues in the sovereign debt markets. Moreover, it would clarify the process of how market participants could enforce their rights and obligations under the debt contracts in a court of law of an EU state, especially to ensure that any restructuring process is occurring according to contractual requirements.

Some economists might argue that this proposal is going to increase the cost of sovereign bond finance for EU states. Recent studies by economists, however, show empirically that the use of CACs does not increase the cost of sovereign debt issuance.[18] In fact, the data show that it is not more expensive for countries to use CACs, as opposed to the traditional New York law unanimity clauses.

The regulation of sovereign bind contracts through recommendations by the G10 and IMF shows that it is possible for policy-makers to improve the governance of private law contracts without resorting to onerous state intervention into the contractual process. The success of CACs in the emerging market country context demonstrates how regulating contractual governance by encouraging market participants to adopt different contract models can achieve socially optimal objectives without undermining the sanctity of private law contract rights. Moreover, the regulation of sovereign bond contracts through the use of CACs shows how regulating contract design can enhance allocative efficiency in sovereign debt markets and control some of the externalities that arise from moral hazard and excessive risk-taking.

[18] K. Kletzer, 'Sovereign Bond Restructuring: Collective Action Clauses and Official Crisis Intervention' (2003) 3 IMF Working Paper No. 134.

However, most EU countries and nearly all countries in the euro area have not addressed the need for sovereign bond contract reform. It is argued that the EU should strongly encourage that CACs are used in all sovereign bond contracts. CACs enhance the flow of information between debtor and creditors and facilitate negotiations and coordination to restructure debt when it becomes unsustainable and imposes a more optimal allocation of the risks between debtor and creditors and between creditors in sovereign debt finance.[19] EU legislation should harmonize the principles and guidelines that govern the operation of CACs, but parties should be permitted some freedom to decide certain CAC financing and repayment terms and some of the parameters of the restructuring process.

[19] See M. Chui and P. Gai, *Private Sector Involvement and International Financial Crises: An Analytical Perspective* (Oxford: Oxford University Press, 2005) 127–33.

Contract Governance, Disclosure, and Rule-setting between the Market and the Law

A View from Commercial and Company Law

*Klaus J. Hopt**

I write this Section as an expert on corporate governance of companies and banks[1] and not on contract governance—or, more specifically, 'Contract Governance and Political Dimensions,' as the title of this Chapter indicates. I would like to quickly raise two points that are discussed at length in my area of expertise, the corporate governance debate: transparency/disclosure and rule-setting between the market and the law.

1. What role do transparency and disclosure play in contract governance?

We can distinguish six stages of growing transparency and disclosure of contracts with consequences for contract governance.[2]

a. The Rule: Own responsibility of the parties for their contract terms without disclosure

The starting point, of course, is that contracts are private and quite often even outright secret. They are usually concluded between two persons or enterprises. In

* Professor and Director Emeritus of the Max Planck Institute for Foreign and International Private Law in Hamburg.

[1] Cf K. J. Hopt, 'Comparative Corporate Governance: The State of the Art and International Regulation' (2011) 59 *American Journal of Comparative Law* 1–73; K. J. Hopt, 'Corporate Governance of Banks and Other Financial Institutions After the Financial Crisis' (2013) 13(2) *Journal of Corporate Law Studies* 219–53.

[2] Academic contributions on transparency and disclosure are legion. S. Grundmann, W. Kerber, and S. Weatherill (eds) *Party Autonomy and the Role of Information in the Internal Market* (Berlin: Walter de Gruyter, 2001) and, most recently, R. Veil (ed) *European Capital Markets Law*, (Oxford: Hart Publishing, 2013) chap 4, 209–381, with an extensive bibliography at 209–10.

legal theory, the contracting parties are considered to make their own rules, and the contract then stands for the 'law of the parties'. This implies in principle the presumption that the contract balances the interests of both parties in a way that is fitting both of them (Schmidt-Rimpler has termed this *'Richtigkeitsgewähr'*).[3] If the contracting parties are experienced or if the matter is important, these private rules are negotiated in detail and finally set down in a more or less comprehensive document. Under the influence of Anglo-Saxon commercial contract and mergers and acquisitions practice, these documents tend to become very long and detailed. If the contracting parties are private persons, they may talk and convene on the key points of the contract only, the rest being left to the fallback rules contained in the law. But the relevant point here is that these contracts are not open and accessible to third parties or even the general public. The parties are responsible for their own contract governance. Disclosure does not come into play.

b. The case of the general business conditions

There are important exceptions where some disclosure takes place. The most frequent cases occur when the contracts are subject to the general business conditions of one or both contracting parties. These general business conditions are very common in Germany and some other countries, though, depending on the business sector, this is not the case in many other countries. For example, general banking conditions have long been established and used in the German banking sector, but not so in a number of other Western and Southern European countries.[4] The very fact that these conditions are used by the condition-setting, party implies some disclosure and opens the door to political and legal interference by consumer associations, the financial press, and finally the courts under the extensive general business condition law of Germany and the more rudimentary European Directive. In Germany, banking contract law is traditionally not a matter for the legislator; only more recently has the European Union stepped in, for example by a several directives in the field of money transfer and general payment law.[5] As to banking contracts, therefore, 'contract governance' was traditionally—and to a high degree still is—a matter for the banks and the courts. The relationship between the two is judicial as well as political, though the courts may not admit this. It can be more hostile, as it was in former times, or more cooperative, as it has become the case more recently.

In some cases, the general business conditions are not just set by one of the contracting parties, but by professional associations that are active in a certain business sector. This is the case in Germany, for example, for the general business

[3] W. Schmidt-Rimpler, *'Grundfragen der Erneuerung des Privatrechts'* (1941) 147 *Archiv für Civilistische Praxis* 130.

[4] K. J. Hopt, *'Der Vertrag zwischen der Bank und ihren Kunden'* in *Synthèses de droit bancaire et financier, Liber Amicorum André Bruyneel* (Bruxelles: Bruylant, 2008) 617.

[5] On bank contract law see K. Langenbucher, D. J. Bliesener, and G. Spindler (eds) *Bankrechts-Kommentar* (Munich: C. H. Beck, 2013).

conditions of the private banks and those of the savings associations.[6] For private persons it is difficult and often impossible to negotiate conditions that deviate from the general business conditions. Therefore, some sociologists consider general business conditions as quasi-legal rules.

The character of rules is even more evident if the general business conditions become the general standard of doing business in a certain sector—for example, the uniform contract conditions set up by the International Chamber of Commerce in Paris,[7] including the Incoterms (revision 2010), the Uniform Customs and Practice for Documentary Credits (revision 2007), the Uniform Rules for Collections (revision 1995), and the Rules of Arbitration of the International Court of Arbitration (version 2010). While the various business conditions of the International Chamber of Commerce are very transparent, are applicable only by the choice of the parties, and are often modified, the ISDA (International Swaps and Derivatives Association) Master Agreement of 2002[8] is the general standard of doing business in the field and is the rule in force in practice.

In certain cases, disclosure of the contract is used by the parties themselves for purposes outside the contract, namely for letting competitors know what kind of prices and/or conditions are convened between them to induce the competitors to follow. This is frequent in oligopoly situations unless national or international antitrust law steps in and prohibits this. Here disclosure is misused for other economically and politically detrimental purposes.

c. *Mandatory contracting at an open market place*

A third stage has been mentioned by Hugh Collins[9]. One way of regulating could be to force people to contract at an open market place. This is done, for example, by the stock exchange law of a number of countries.[10] The idea is to require the banks to conclude certain stock transactions only on the open market, i.e. the stock exchange, and thereby to get prices that reflect the supply and demand more openly and objectively.

This technique is discussed more generally and controversially as a means of better regulating the financial markets in the aftermath of the financial market crisis. By prescribing that the participants in certain markets have to act on an open floor—say, a stock exchange—or preventing them from contracting directly with the other party but requiring them to deal with a central contracting party,

[6] H.-J. Bunte, *AGB-Banken und Sonderbedingungen* (Munich: ,C. H. Beck, 3rd edn, 2011).

[7] For a short survey . K. J. Hopt, 'International Chamber of Commerce (ICC)' in J. Basedow, K. J. Hopt, and R. Zimmermann (eds) *The Max Planck Encyclopedia of European Private Law* (Oxford: Oxford University Press, 2012) Vol I, 958.

[8] ISDA 2002 Master Agreement with Schedule and Annex to the Definitions available in K. J. Hopt (ed) *Vertrags- und Formularbuch zum Handels-, Gesellschafts- und Bankrecht*, (Munich: C. H. Beck, 4th edn, 2013) 1909ff with short notes.

[9] See Chapter 12.

[10] Cf generally A. M. Fleckner and K. J. Hopt, 'Stock Exchange Law: Concept, History, Challenges' (2013) 7 *Virginia Law and Business Review* 514.

the legislators expect a certain governing effect. If the transaction is made openly on a regulated floor, it is not so easy for the parties to escape regulation; if there is a central counterparty, the counterparty risk is taken over by the central contracting party with the further consequence of possibly reducing systemic risk and stabilizing the financial system.

d. Voluntary commitments to make agreements public

Katharina Pistor[11] has mentioned a case in which parties may enter into a commitment to make agreements public. This might be considered the fourth stage. It makes a difference whether this is a commitment just by the private actors themselves—say, in order to show the public that the agreements are not discriminating or otherwise unfair—or whether governmental contractors are bound to make their commitments public, such as state-owned banks or industrial enterprises as a kind of netting between the private and public sectors. The policy behind the latter commitments then could be that the state acts as a standard-setter for contracts, not only for those in which the state is involved, but beyond. One special way to reach transparency can be found in the procurement law, which mandates that the state and other public bodies cannot freely choose their contract partner, but must make their offer public and start an auction process. This is the rule under European law designed to do away with national boundaries.

e. Codes of conduct

Codes of conduct may be considered a fifth stage. Codes of conduct set up a standard for the parties concerned and thereby achieve a certain expectation and transparency for the contracting partner and the general public.[12] Ideally this is in the interest of the very parties who set up these codes to create confidence and ultimately to do better business.

But this is not always the case with codes of conduct. Sometimes these codes are just a means to avoid legislation and to create expectations that are not well founded. In the early days of insider trading regulation in Germany, the industry and banks were confronted with ugly insider trading cases and a very critical financial press. So the idea of German insider trading guidelines was born. They were conceived to pacify the general public and to prevent the legislators from stepping in, but with the least cost possible, i.e. by providing for just the very minimum of regulation. The rules were not only merely voluntary; they were very opaque and without real sanctions. It is true that they provided for the possibility of a formal procedure, but transparency was lacking. It remained a closed shop. Worst of all, if the proceedings that were kept secret came to a point where an insider trading transaction was about to be found, the culprit could just withdraw

[11] See Chapter 13.

[12] K. J. Hopt, 'Private Rule-Making and Codes of Conduct' in Basedow, Hopt and Zimmermann, n 26, Vol II, 1348; Hopt, n 20, (2011) 59 *American Journal of Comparative Law*, 10ff.

its adherence to the code with the result that the proceeding had to be closed. The political consequence of this self-regulation failure was that the legislators finally stepped in—first the European legislators by way of an insider trading directive, and later the national legislators by national insider trading law.

In contrast, modern codes of behaviour make deliberate use of transparency and disclosure. They are voluntary in nature, but they are administered by the 'comply-or-disclose' mechanism. This means that the companies that agree in principal to follow the code commit themselves to either comply with the rules of the code or to disclose if they do not in a specific case. In the meantime, the mechanism has been developed further. Today it is international good practice for corporate governance codes to work with the 'comply-or-explain' principle. This is a good step forward. Deviation is possible, but it must be disclosed publicly and reasons must be given. Then the general public—i.e. the market—can judge for itself whether the reasons for the deviation are valid and whether the company is still so trustworthy that one may buy or hold its shares and conclude new contracts with it. Up to now there have been no concrete rules on what 'explaining' means. Some empirical studies show quite a wide range of 'explanation,' starting from saying nearly nothing or giving very short reasons to very detailed and well-founded explanations. A real 'culture of deviation' has been asked for by the former chairman of the German Corporate Governance Code Commission, but it is growing rather slowly. The European Commission has stepped in with a recommendation to make more detailed explanations.[13]

f. Legally enforced codes of conduct

The sixth range is reached when the codes, though still voluntary, are bolstered by legal provisions and even legal sanctions. Gunnar Folke Schuppert[14] called this phenomenon the 'hardening of soft law.' As to the German Corporate Governance Code, the stock corporation law now provides that the listed companies must comply or explain as a matter of law. If they do not, this may lead to legal sanctions. In recent cases, the federal court in Karlsruhe, the *Bundesgerichtshof*, decided that if a company does not disclose and explain that it did not follow certain rules of the code, the resolution of the general assembly to discharge the directors will be voidable. According to some opinions in legal academia, this could even lead to liability and damages suits for misrepresentation, though it is open who would be entitled to sue: the company, the shareholders, the investing public, or even individual investors who did or did not buy the shares. Still other authors maintain that a company that does not disclose that it did not follow certain

[13] Cf European Commission, Commission Recommendation of 9 April 2014 on the Quality of Corporate Governance Reporting ('Comply or Explain') OJEU L 109/43; See also European Company Law Experts, *Making Corporate Governance Codes More Effective, A Response to the European Commission's Action Plan of December 2012* (December 2013) (available at <http://www.ecle.eu> and at <http://papers.ssrn.com/sol3/papers.cfm?abstract_id=2366273>).

[14] See comment accompanying Chapter 13.

code provisions is violating the unfair competition law. By deceiving the investing public and/or the consumers, the company avoids the costs that the code-obeying competitors incurred by following the code. I will spare you the many legal niceties of the sanction mechanisms that are food for the lawyers.[15]

To conclude, transparency and disclosure of private contracts and of private behaviour in, and of, organizations can be used to reach socio-political and governing effects either by the parties themselves, by trade and industry, or by the national or European legislators. Today it is evident that legislators use private rule-making, and the technique of regulating by 'soft law' has been added to the regulatory toolset.

2. Multi-layered regulatory systems

Let me add a quick second remark concerning another main theme of this volume: the multi-layered regulatory system.[16] This remark is closely connected to the first one on disclosure. The various stages mentioned earlier for transparency and disclosure of contracts and their political nature and consequences can also be applied to the perspective of various forms of rules and regulation. This goes beyond the traditional German distinction between contract and legal rule.

a. Legal rules and contractual rules

At least in Germany, legal thinking is nearly exclusively concerned with the law, whether mandatory or fallback. There is a long-standing theory and methodology of law interpretation that is more or less followed by the practice and the courts. I say 'more or less' because in reality, at least in commercial practice, the German courts (unlike the English courts) prefer to use the teleological interpretation and the rule of good faith (for example, Treu and Glauben) which gives them a considerable and sometimes vast leeway of interpretation.

As to the other side—the contract—there is less legal sophistication, apart of course from a well-established practice and theory of interpretation of the contract. As mentioned before, in legal theory the rules of the contract are said to be 'the law of the parties,' but more recent concepts such as the 'incomplete contracts' of the law and economics movement have not yet been adopted by the legal mainstream. The wide field of making and negotiating contracts is also mostly left to practice. Legal academia and education often neglect to consider that whole fields of contracting are governed by industries, banks, and legal counsel that have developed very sophisticated contract forms and standard contracts that rarely

[15] Cf P. C. Leyens, comments on Section 161 of the German Stock Corporation Act in K. J. Hopt and H. Wiedemann (eds) *Großkommentar Aktiengesetz*, 38th issue (Berlin: Walter de Gruyter, 4th edn, 2012); K. J. Hopt, '*Der Deutsche Corporate Governance Kodex: Grundlagen und Praxisfragen*' in *Festschrift für Hoffmann-Becking* (Munich: C. H. Beck, 2013) 563.

[16] Cf H Fleischer, '*Corporate Governance in Europa als Mehrebenensystem*' in (2012) *Zeitschrift für Unternehmens- und Gesellschaftsrecht* 160.

come before the state courts. One of the best examples is the mergers and acquisition contract field, where the contract forms reflect Anglo-American mergers and acquisition practice to such a degree that even the terminology is English rather than German.[17] This method of contracting is the legal practice's reaction to achieve more complete contracts.

As far as making and negotiating contracts is concerned, the abstention of legal academia and legal methodology has its parallel in procedure and contract enforcement. In commercial matters, in particular in international commerce, the state courts have given up their role to the arbitral tribunals to a very considerable degree. Contract governance and contract enforcement is thereby left to the parties who choose the lawyers and arbitrators to form and enforce the contract. As a side effect, the resort to arbitral tribunal reduces transparency since most of the arbitrations end up in a compromize of the parties. If there is an arbitral award in exceptional cases, this award is very rarely made public since the parties do not allow exceptions from the arbitration secrecy. Whole areas of law thereby 'emigrate' from public oversight to private secrecy, with the consequence that contract governance is considerably reduced.

b. Between law and contract: soft law

The field between law and contract has traditionally been neglected by German jurisprudence. Yet the fact that is most interesting for our conference is that, more recently, these two have been complemented by soft law from above and from below.

(1) Soft law from above

To give you an example from my own research fields, soft law from above sometimes comes from the central bank. This is called 'moral suasion'.[18] The German Central Bank (the *Bundesbank* or *BuBa*) used this in the early days when there was not yet a transnational law of bank supervision. This was the only way to reach out to German bank subsidiaries in Luxembourg. Of course, the big problem with moral suasion is how to react on non-compliance. Usually this was done by soft retaliation: an implicit threat followed the merely moral suasion, with the risk of being treated unfavourably the next time. But this has many drawbacks. On the side of the addressees, there was no possibility of appeal and certainly no formal appeal procedure, while on the other side there was no reliable enforcement. Black sheep frequently got away with non-compliance. This is similar to soft law and mere recommendations, for example, by the European Commission and other international institutions such as the Basel Committee

[17] See the many mergers and acquisition forms in Hopt, n 27, 183ff.

[18] K. J. Hopt, 'Self-Regulation in Banking and Finance—Practice and Theory in Germany' in *La Déontologie bancaire et financière/The Ethical Standards in Banking & Finance*, Bruxelles: Bruylant, 1998) 53.

in international banking. The 2010 biannual meeting of the German Lawyers Association (*Deutscher Juristentag*) dealt with the financial crisis and its regulatory consequences.[19] On the panel were economists and academics/lawyers from the fields of both private law and public law. It was fascinating to see the difference between public lawyers on the one side talking about democracy and constitutional and fundamental rights, and the economists on the other side telling them that one cannot define a 'systemic crisis' *a priori* and that regulators need very broad notions and vast discretion. The 'private lawyers' were somewhere in between. This illustrates the fact that a common legal reaction to soft law has not yet been found.

Moral suasion and mere recommendations can also be further formalized by concluding public law contracts between the state agencies and the enterprises—a subject discussed extensively in this volume.

(2) Soft law from below

Soft law can also come from below, i.e., by way of self-regulation. There are, of course, many instances where self-regulation is really voluntary, either because the companies or merchants want to set up good standards of behaviour or contracting, or as a reaction to economic and societal pressure. For example, I remember that at an early stage, well before the German Corporate Governance Code was enacted, the Deutsche Bank published its own Deutsche Bank Code without any legal pressure. Instead, it was in reaction to the changes and criticisms levied toward 'Rhenisch capitalism' under which there was a (too) close relationship between the German industry (traditionally in iron and steel in the Rhine and Ruhr areas) and German banks.

But quite often self-regulation, while still from below and voluntary in form, is done under pressure from the law and the legislators. German examples are the former German Insider Trading Guidelines and the former voluntary German Takeover Code. I was involved in both, in the latter by serving on the voluntary Takeover Commission. Both codes consisted of self-regulation motivated by a fear of legislative intervention and an intention to avoid it. But this did not work, and they were replaced by formal law. I have also mentioned before the German law that bolsters the German Corporate Governance Code by a comply-or-explain mechanism. In the meantime, there are various instances in which the legislators go beyond this and actually legislate, either because they think that the Code Commission does not react quickly and stiffly enough, or, worse, because the politicians feel that they can earn political capital by taking up certain popular issues themselves, though under the premises and aims of the Code it would have been a matter for self-regulation. This is particularly true in the context of high pay to bankers and directors. It is obvious that this kind of reaction, which is

[19] *Deutscher Juristentag, 'Finanzmarktregulierung—Welche Regelungen empfehlen sich für den deutschen und europäischen Finanzsektor?'* in *Verhandlungen des 68. Deutschen Juristentags* (Berlin: C. H. Beck, 2010) vols II/1 and 2, Part P, Munich 2011.

premature and motivated solely by earning points in the next election, weakens self-regulation.[20] But after the financial crisis, self-regulation in the financial field and beyond has encountered a major crisis. Many expect the state to provide the best regulation without remembering the fate of the late Democratic German Republic and other historical facts. In my view this is wrong. In private law, the presumption must be for party autonomy and market forces, not for the state. But we shall see what the future brings.

[20] See, egs, K. J. Hopt, 'Comparative Corporate Governance: the State of the Art and International Regulation' in A. M. Fleckner and K. J. Hopt (eds) *Comparative Corporate Governance, A Functional and International Analysis* (Cambridge: Cambridge University Press, 2013) 3, 23 fn 74.

Index

agency 17, 90, 122, 356
agency costs 18, 218 et seq.
asset specificity 218, 222 et seqq, 266, 268

Bagehot, Walter 184 et seq., 208
best efforts 161, 224, 307, 316 et seq., 327, 331
braiding 156, 159 et seq., 167 et seq., 170, 173 et seq., 176
breach of Contract See contractual breach

care 277 et seq., 280–290, 295–300, 334 et seq., 365
central banks 113, 123, 184, 205, 216, 414, 421 et seq., 426 et seq., 431, 466
certification 352 et seq., 357–381
class actions 56, 122 et seq., 276–290, 292–300, 335–337
codes 213, 215 et seq., 338, 349, 385–387, 463 et seq.
collective action clauses 451
commercial law 302 et seq., 311, 327, 385, 406
consumers 10, 78, 108, 112 et seq., 136 et seq., 151, 258, 271, 277 et seq., 283 et seq., 293–300, 333–337, 345, 353, 364 et seq., 378 et seq., 389, 427, 465
contagion 4, 64, 100–104, 150 et seq., 196–201, 204–206, 413
contract governance See sub governance
contract interpretation 397, 402
contract theory 3, 5, 12, 157, 160, 257, 259, 440
contracting, formal and informal 155 et seq., 159 et seq., 162–167, 175, 208
contracting, mandatory 462
contracts 3, 6, 10–14, 16 et seq., 33 et seq., 41 et seq., 52–56, 77, 80, 84, 86, 110, 117 et seq., 121, 127 et seq., 130, 147 et seq., 156–161, 167–170, 178–181, 204–206, 218–221, 227, 235–239, 257–264, 266 et seq., 270, 275, 280, 301, 303–306, 310 et seq., 318–322, 327–329, 344 et seq., 349, 352–357, 368 et seq., 373 et seq., 384–386, 391–397, 407, 432, 438–440, 444, 447, 451–459, 461, 465 et seq.
contractual breach 309, 322, 339, 374
contractual governance See sub governance
contractual networks See networks of contracts
cooperation duties 139, 243, 249, 251 et seqq., 274, 358, 374, 413 et seq., 428 et seq.
corporate governance See sub governance
cultural market 69 et seq.
cure 23, 272, 304, 306, 309–311, 374, 453

disclosure 21, 117, 120, 125 et seq., 130 et seq., 138, 141–144, 151, 160, 186, 189 et seq., 195, 237, 460–462, 464 et seq.
duty to mitigate 374

efficiency 83, 149, 265, 279 et seq., 328, 330, 352, 359, 367, 370, 387, 390, 407, 409 et seq., 417, 424, 452, 459
emotional contagion 64
European Banking Coordinative Initiative (EBCI) 31, 419, 422–424, 426 et seq., 429 et seq.
European Central Bank (ECB) 190, 193, 201–204, 421, 459
European Financial Stability Facility (EFSF) 203
ex ante (analysis) 39 et seq., 90, 129, 131, 145, 157 et seq., 161, 164, 180, 258, 266, 276, 281, 301, 303, 307, 312, 320, 329, 335, 346, 418
ex-post (analysis) 18, 40, 90. 115, 124, 130 et seq., 136, 145, 157, 159, 161, 164, 180, 258, 266, 284, 295, 301 et seq., 307, 311 et seq., 315, 320, 329 et seq., 335, 346, 418

facial mimicry 64
fairness 18, 56, 243–247, 252, 255 et seq., 257 et seq., 262 et seq., 271–274, 333–335, 386
finance
  global 31, 413–418, 420 et seq., 425 et seq.
  international 415, 417
financial crisis 4, 12 et seq., 16, 19–21, 34, 56, 61, 82, 87, 98, 100, 113, 134, 148, 149, 151, 182 et seq., 193, 196, 198, 205, 207 et seq., 212, 215, 236, 238 et seq., 392, 409, 413 et seq., 417–420, 425, 430, 432, 444, 454, 467 et seq.
financial integration 425

Goldman Sachs 188 et seq.
good faith 169, 171 et seq, 173–177, 226, 232, 301, 307–311, 314, 320, 326 et seq., 331, 399, 465
governance
  contract 3–13, 19–25, 30, 34, 38 et seq., 40–44, 49, 51–56, 78–81, 83–85, 115, 120 et seq., 131 et seq., 134–138, 141, 143, 146, 148, 152, 238, 243, 257 et seq., 263 et seq., 265, 270 et seq., 410, 438 et seq., 444, 451, 460 et seq., 466, see also: contractual governance

governance (*cont.*):
  contractual 18, 31, 39, 77–80, 218, 220, 225, 227, 268 et seq., 344–346, 348, 352 et seq., 357 et seq., 370, 372 et seq.. 389, 403, 414, 420, 424, 429 et seq., 459, see also: contract governance
  corporate 3–5, 7–9, 11–14, 19–22, 24 et seq., 33, 84, 100, 111, 115, 117, 124, 142, 146, 148, 218–220, 225, 229, 233, 238, 271, 438 et seq., 444, 464, 467
  cooperative 429
  hierarchical 31, 43, 95, 98, 105, 359, 375, 391, 413 et seq., 427, 430
  inclusive 425 et seq.
  modes of contract 3, 84, 86, 131–135, 266, 269 et seq., 372, 413 et seq., 427, 430
  public 4, 7 et seq., 27, 30
Greece 183, 186–196, 198 et seq., 201–204, 457
group decision making 68 et seq.,

herd behavior 12, 61, 65, 67 et seq., 76, 89–91, 100, 102, 111–116, 121, 123–128, 130–135, 139, 141, 146 et seq., 149, 151 et seq., see also herding
herding 12 et seq., 41, 54–56, 61–63, 65, 67, 69, 71, 75 et seq., 81 et seq., 84, 87–92, 94–102, 110–114, 116, 120, 122–128, 131, 136, 138 et seq., 140–143, 145, 148–150, see also herd behavior
hierarchical structure 95, 98, 375
hold-up 17 et seq., 218, 222–227, 229, 233, 259, 311–314, 321, 324, 329, 331, 339 et seq.
homo oeconomicus 45, 49, 53, 245 et seq., 249, 258, 262 et seq.
homo reciprocans 245 et seq., 249, 252, 257, 262–264, 271
homo sociologicus 46 et seq., 49 et seq., 53
human resource policy 95

incentives 5, 12, 14, 21, 30, 34–36, 42, 90–96. 98, 101, 103, 110–112, 114, 116–120, 123 et seq., 126, 128, 130, 132, 138 et seq., 142–145, 149 et seq., 152, 158, 161 et seq., 167, 170, 178, 218 et seq., 221–226, 228 et seq., 231, 236, 243, 249, 252 et seq., 257, 260, 263, 267, 276–281, 291–300, 304, 307, 312–315, 318, 321, 329–332, 333 et seq., 337, 340, 348, 352, 378, 380, 408, 410, 425, 432, 435, 444, 452
innovation 16, 40, 48, 56, 61, 155–162, 164, 167–176, 178–181, 230, 234, 236 et seq., 413, 431 et seq., 445
insolvency 383, 391 et seq., 395–401, 403, 407, 409, 411, 442 et seq., 458
institutional factors 88, 95, 97–99
interdisciplinarity 3–5, 7, 12, 19, 35, 39 et seq., 44, 49, 54, 56, 61, 74 et seq., 78, 81, 84, 86, 272–274
international trade 308, 402
investment, relationship-specific 17 et seq., 23, 158–160, 178, 259, 267
ius cogens 385, 401, 403, 405, 442

lex mercatoria 28, 384–390, 392–394, 401–412, 441–445, 447
Liability 13, 110, 114 et seq., 119–121, 124, 126, 128 et seq., 133, 136, 151 et seq., 176, 179, 210, 219, 236, 278–280, 293–296, 298, 323–325, 336 et seq., 346, 365, 371, 374, 394, 452, 464
long-term contracts 4, 11, 17 et seq., 25, 33, 41, 55 et seq., 128, 130, 144, 218, 220–225, 258 et seq., 264, 267

Merton, Robert K. 184–186, 208
mirror neurons 64
modification 15, 311–314, 320–322, 337, 413
monitoring
  hierarchical 357, 359 et seq., 364–366, 372, 376
  peer 358–360, 362–364, 371 et seq., 376
moral hazard 18, 87, 100, 149, 164, 197, 218 et seq., 222, 224–227, 229, 230 et seq., 233, 280, 323, 440, 453, 459
motivation, intrinsic 56, 165, 180, 262, 276–279, 283, 288–291, 294 et seq., 297–300, 325
multi-level regulation 26

networks of contracts 3, 11, 13–16, 182, 234, 345, 348, 353, 355–357, 362 et seq., 366 et seq., 371 et seq., 375, 381, 438
networks, inter-firm 345, 352, 355, 380

opportunism 3, 17 et seq., 34, 157–160, 163 et seq., 168, 171, 249, 252, 263, 266 et seq., 274, 301–307, 310–316, 318–329, 331 et seq., 337–339, 351

performance, substantial 303–306, 328
private investors 113 et seq., 116–118, 120 et seq., 127, 131, 137, 139, 144
punishment, antisocial 254
pyramid games 108, 114, 130, 145

reciprocity, negative/positive 252 et seq., 256, 263
regulation
  theory 3, 5
  multi-layered 27 et seq., 463
  private 83, 85, 131, 133, 343, 346 et seq., 349, 357, 361, 370, 372, 374, 376, 379 et seq., 412, 437
  regulatory innovation 40, 431
repressed voice 87, 96
rule setting 5, 7, 19, 21, 41, 133, 458

sanctions 47, 65, 101, 103, 109, 119, 140, 150, 161 et seq., 164–167, 170 et seq., 173, 176 et seq., 244, 249, 251–255, 257, 261, 263 et seq., 270 et seq., 273–275, 301, 353, 357, 359–361, 365–368, 371 et seq., 375 et seq., 431 et seq., 448, 463–465
selfishness 245 et seq., 250 et seq., 262, 272
social receptiveness 54, 65, 71, 263
soft law 148, 385, 388 et seq., 393, 416 et seq., 441, 443, 447, 464–467
sovereign bond contracts 451–460
Sovereign Debt Agency 451, 457, 459
Sovereign Wealth Funds 419 et seq.
standards, private 346–351, 353, 358, 360 et seq., 372 et seq.
stress tests 203 et seq., 421
subprime crisis 110, 112–118, 120 et seq., 123 et seq., 127 et seq., 130 et seq., 136, 140–142, 145
supply chain 157, 343–355, 357–360, 363–365, 370 et seq., 373, 375–382
systemic risk 12, 80, 113, 118, 121, 130–132, 134–138, 140 et seq., 143, 145, 151 et seq., 200, 211, 384, 452, 463

tender, perfect 303–307, 328
third party impact 4, 7, 112 et seq., 115, 120 et seq., 128, 130, 132–141, 152
transaction costs 46, 51, 151, 234, 266, 354, 359, 378, 392 et seq., 410, 439, 452 et seq.
transnational law 379, 383 et seq., 394, 402, 405, 466
transparency 132–134, 333, 392 et seq., 395, 402, 410, 460, 463–466
Trichet, Jean-Claude 183, 196, 200–203

uncertainty 16 et seq., 31, 36, 45, 47 et seq., 52–55, 109, 112, 155–159, 161–164, 176, 178 et seq., 181, 223 et seq., 258, 266, 290, 320, 340, 381, 401, 414, 428–430, 458

wage policy 95, 98
wisdom of crowds 54, 67, 71, 148
Wittgenstein, Ludwig 185

The manufacturer's authorised representative in the EU for product
safety is Oxford University Press España S.A. of El Parque Empresarial
San Fernando de Henares, Avenida de Castilla, 2 - 28830 Madrid
(www.oup.es/en or product.safety@oup.com). OUP España S.A. also acts
as importer into Spain of products made by the manufacturer.
Printed and bound by CPI Group (UK) Ltd, Croydon, CR0 4YY
14/09/2026
02216304-0013